**PEARSON**

Ann Spurlock
*Director of Composition*

Daniel Austin • Shelly Sanders • Claire Sheperis
Abigail Voller

# MSU Reader
## Selections for
## EN 1113 - Comp II

Second Custom Edition for Mississippi State
University

Excerpts taken from:
*Literature and Society: An Introduction to
Fiction, Poetry, Drama, Nonfiction*, Fourth Edition
by Pamela J. Annas and Robert C. Rosen

*The Little, Brown Handbook*, Thirteenth Edition
by H. Ramsey Fowler and Jane E. Aaron

Cover Art: Courtesy of Megan Bean, MSU Photographer.

Excerpts taken from:

*Literature and Society: An Introduction to Fiction, Poetry, Drama, Nonfiction,*
Fourth Edition
by Pamela J. Annas and Robert C. Rosen
Copyright © 2007, 2000, 1994, 1990 by Pearson Education, Inc.
Published by Prentice Hall
Upper Saddle River, New Jersey 07458

*The Little, Brown Handbook*, Thirteenth Edition
by H. Ramsey Fowler and Jane E. Aaron
Copyright © 2016, 2012, and 2010 by Pearson Education, Inc.
330 Hudson Street, New York, NY 10013

Pearson Learning Solutions, 330 Hudson Street, New York, New York 10013
A Pearson Education Company
www.pearsoned.com

Printed in the United States of America

4    16


000200010272012029

CW/[[RE]]

ISBN 10: 1-323-31921-2
ISBN 13: 978-1-323-31921-5

# Copyright Acknowledgments

# Table of Contents

# Writing about Literature

## Reading and Writing about Literature

### By Sylvan Barnet

#### Chapter essentials

- Use the methods and evidence common in literary analysis (below).
- Understand your writing assignment (p. 8).
- Use the tools and language of literary analysis (p. 9).
- Use MLA style for citing sources and formatting papers (p. 10).
- Develop a thesis, gather evidence, and draft, revise, and edit your work (p. 10).
- Consider the distinctive approaches to writing about fiction, poetry, and drama (p. 14).

Visit MyWritingLab™ for more resources on reading and writing about literature.

---

Why read literature? Let's approach this question indirectly by asking why people *write* literature. A thousand years ago a Japanese writer, Lady Murasaki, offered an answer. Here is one of her characters talking about what motivates a writer:

> Again and again something in one's own life or in the life around one will seem so important that one cannot bear to let it pass into oblivion. There must never come a time, the writer feels, when people do not know about this.

When we read certain works—Murasaki's *The Tale of Genji* is one of them—we share this feeling; we are caught up in the writer's world, whether it is the Denmark of Shakespeare's *Hamlet* or the America of Toni Morrison's *Beloved*. We read literature because it gives us an experience that seems important, usually an experience that is both new and familiar. A common way of putting this is to say that reading broadens us and helps us understand our own experience.

### a) Using the Methods and Evidence of Literary Analysis

When we read nonliterary writings, it may be enough to get the gist of the argument; in fact, we may have to work through many words to find the heart of the matter—say, three claims on behalf of capital punishment. But when we read a story, a poem, or a play, we must pay extremely close attention to what might be called the feel of the words. For instance, the word *woods* in Robert Frost's

"Stopping by Woods on a Snowy Evening" has a rural, folksy quality that *forest* doesn't have, and many such small distinctions contribute to the poem's effect.

Literary authors are concerned with presenting human experience concretely, with *showing* rather than *telling*. Consider the following proverb and an unmemorable paraphrase of it.

> A rolling stone gathers no moss.
>
> If a rock is always moving around, vegetation won't have a chance to grow on it.

The familiar original offers a small but complete world: hard (stone) and soft (moss), inorganic and organic, at rest and in motion. The original is also shapely: each noun (*stone, moss*) has one syllable, and each word of motion (*rolling, gathers*) has two syllables, with the accent on the first of the two. Such relationships unify the proverb into a pleasing whole that stays in our minds.

## 1. Reading a Work of Literature

Reading literature critically involves interacting with a text. The techniques complement those for critically reading any text, so if you haven't read on such reading, you should do so. Responding critically is a matter not of making negative judgments but of analyzing the parts, interpreting their meanings, seeing how the parts relate, and evaluating significance or quality.

(CULTURE LANGUAGE) All readers benefit from hearing literature—particularly poetry—read out loud, but the experience can be especially helpful if standard English is not your first language or dialect. Listening reveals the pronunciation, tone, and rhythm of the words and can illuminate structure and themes. The Academy of American Poets, at *poets.org*, offers hundreds of poems read by their authors and by others.

### Previewing and Responding

You can preview a literary text somewhat as you can preview any other text. You may gauge the length of the text to determine whether you can read it in one sitting, and you may read a biographical note to learn about the author. In a literary text, however, you won't find aids such as section headings or summaries that can make previewing other texts especially informative. You have to dive into the words themselves.

*Do* write while reading. If you own the book you are reading, don't hesitate to underline or highlight passages that especially interest you for one reason or another. Don't hesitate to annotate the margins, indicating your pleasures, displeasures, and uncertainties with remarks such as *Nice detail* or *Do we need this long description?* or *Not believable*. If you don't own the book, make these notes on separate sheets or on your computer.

An effective way to interact with a text is to keep a **reading journal**. A journal is not a diary in which you record your doings; instead, it is a place to develop and store your reflections on what you read, such as an answer to a question you may have posed in the margin of the text. You could make an entry in the form of a letter to the author or from one character to another. In many literature courses, students collaborate to develop their understanding of a literary work. In such a case, you may want to use your journal to reflect on what other students have said—for instance, why your opinion differs so much from someone else's.

You can keep a reading journal in a notebook or on your computer. Some readers prefer a two-column format, with summaries, paraphrases, and quotations from the text on the left and with their own responses to these passages on the right. Or you may prefer a less structured format like that illustrated on pages 4–5.

## Reading a Sample Story

Here is a very short story by Kate Chopin (1851–1904). (The last name is pronounced in the French way, something like "show pan.") Following the story are a student's annotations and journal entry on the story.

### Kate Chopin
### The Story of an Hour

Knowing that Mrs. Mallard was afflicted with a heart trouble, great care was taken to break to her as gently as possible the news of her husband's death.

It was her sister Josephine who told her, in broken sentences, veiled hints that revealed in half concealing. Her husband's friend Richards was there, too, near her. It was he who had been in the newspaper office when intelligence of the railroad disaster was received, with Brently Mallard's name leading the list of "killed." He had only taken the time to assure himself of its truth by a second telegram, and had hastened to forestall any less careful, less tender friend in bearing the sad message.

She did not hear the story as many women have heard the same, with a paralyzed inability to accept its significance. She wept at once with sudden, wild abandonment, in her sister's arms. When the storm of grief had spent itself she went away to her room alone. She would have no one follow her.

There stood, facing the open window, a comfortable, roomy armchair. Into this she sank, pressed down by a physical exhaustion that haunted her body and seemed to reach into her soul.

She could see in the open square before her house the tops of trees that were all aquiver with the new spring life. The delicious breath of rain was in the air. In the street below a peddler was crying his wares. The notes of a distant song which some one was singing reached her faintly, and countless sparrows were twittering in the eaves.

There were patches of blue sky showing here and there through the clouds that had met and piled one above the other in the west facing her window.

She sat with her head thrown back upon the cushion of the chair quite motionless, except when a sob came up into her throat and shook her, as a child who has cried itself to sleep continues to sob in its dreams.

She was young, with a fair, calm face, whose lines bespoke repression and even a certain strength. But now there was a dull stare in her eyes, whose gaze was fixed away off yonder on one of those patches of blue sky. It was not a glance of reflection, but rather indicated a suspension of intelligent thought.

There was something coming to her and she was waiting for it, fearfully. What was it? She did not know; it was too subtle and elusive to name. But she felt it creeping out of the sky, reaching toward her through the sounds, the scents, the color that filled the air.

Now her bosom rose and fell tumultuously. She was beginning to recognize this thing that was approaching to possess her, and she was striving to beat it back with her will—as powerless as her two white slender hands would have been.

When she abandoned herself a little whispered word escaped her slightly parted lips. She said it over and over under her breath: "Free, free, free!" The vacant stare and the look of terror that had followed it went from her eyes. They stayed keen and bright. Her pulses beat fast, and the coursing blood warmed and relaxed every inch of her body.

She did not stop to ask if it were not a monstrous joy that held her. A clear and exalted perception enabled her to dismiss the suggestion as trivial.

She knew that she would weep again when she saw the kind, tender hands folded in death; the face that had never looked save with love upon her, fixed and gray and dead. But she saw beyond that bitter moment a long procession of years to come that would belong to her absolutely. And she opened and spread her arms out to them in welcome.

There would be no one to live for her during those coming years; she would live for herself. There would be no powerful will bending her in the blind persistence with which men and women believe they have a right to impose a private will upon a fellow creature. A kind intention or a cruel intention made the act seem no less a crime as she looked upon it in that brief moment of illumination.

And yet she had loved him—sometimes. Often she had not. What did it matter! What could love, the unsolved mystery, count for in face of this possession of self-assertion which she suddenly recognized as the strongest impulse of her being.

"Free! Body and soul free!" she kept whispering.

Josephine was kneeling before the closed door with her lips to the keyhole, imploring for admission. "Louise, open the door! I beg; open the door—you will make yourself ill. What are you doing, Louise? For heaven's sake open the door."

"Go away. I am not making myself ill." No; she was drinking in the very elixir of life through that open window.

Her fancy was running riot along those days ahead of her. Spring days, and summer days, and all sorts of days that would be her own. She breathed a quick prayer that life might be long. It was only yesterday she had thought with a shudder that life might be long.

She arose at length and opened the door to her sister's importunities. There was a feverish triumph in her eyes, and she carried herself unwittingly like a goddess of Victory. She clasped her sister's waist and together they descended the stairs. Richards stood waiting for them at the bottom.

Some one was opening the front door with a latchkey. It was Brently Mallard who entered, a little travel-stained, composedly carrying his gripsack and umbrella. He had been far from the scene of accident, and did not even know there had been one. He stood amazed at Josephine's piercing cry; at Richards' quick motion to screen him from the view of his wife.

But Richards was too late.

When the doctors came they said she had died of heart disease—of joy that kills.

### Following a Student's Work

In this chapter we'll follow the analysis and writing of a student, Janet Vong, to see one approach to Chopin's story. Vong first annotated the story while reading it. The opening five paragraphs, with her notes, appear below:

Knowing that Mrs. Mallard was afflicted with a <u>heart trouble</u>, great care was taken to break to her as gently as possible the news of her husband's death.

*"heart disease"*
*at end of story*

It was her sister Josephine who told her, in broken sentences, veiled hints that revealed in half concealing. Her husband's friend Richards was there, too, near her. It was he who had been in the newspaper office when intelligence of the railroad disaster was received, with Brently Mallard's name leading the list of "killed." He had only taken the time to assure himself of its truth by a second telegram, and had hastened to forestall any less careful, less tender friend in bearing the sad message. *Too hasty, it turns out*

*Would men have heard differently? Is au. sexist?* She did not hear the story as many women have heard the same, with a paralyzed inability to accept its significance. She wept at once with sudden, wild aban-donment, in her sister's arms. When the storm of grief had spent itself she went away to her room alone. She would have no one follow her. *old-fashioned style*

There stood, facing the open window, a comfortable, roomy armchair. Into this she sank, pressed down by a physical exhaustion that haunted her body and seemed to reach into her soul.

She could see in the open square before her house the tops of trees that were all aquiver with the new spring life. The delicious breath of rain was in the air. In the street below a peddler was crying his wares. The notes of a distant song which some one was singing reached her faintly, and countless sparrows were twittering in the eaves. *Notices spring: odd in a story of death*

Writing in her journal, Vong then posed questions about Chopin's story—critical points, curiosities about characters, possible implications:

Title nothing special. What might be a better title?
Could a woman who loved her husband be so heartless? *Is* she heartless? *Did* she love him?
What are (were) Louise's feelings about her husband?
Did she want too much? *What* did she want?
Could this story happen today? Feminist interpretation?
Sister (Josephine)—a busybody?
Tricky ending—but maybe it could be true.
"And yet she had loved him—sometimes. Often she had not." Why does one love someone "sometimes"?
Irony: plot has reversal. Are characters ironic too?

Vong's journal entry illustrates brainstorming—the discovery technique of listing ideas (or questions) however they occur, without editing. Another productive journal technique is focused freewriting—concentrating on a single issue (such as one of Vong's questions) and writing nonstop for a set amount of time, again without editing.

## 2. Analyzing a Work of Literature

Like any discipline, the study of literature involves particular frameworks of analysis—particular ways of seeing literary works that help determine what elements are identified and how they are interpreted. Literary frameworks include historical or cultural criticism, which considers the effect of the author's context on a work; feminist or gender criticism, which focuses on the representation of gender in a work; and reader-response criticism, which stresses the effect of a work on its readers.

## Questions for a literary analysis

See later boxes for specific questions on fiction (p. 15), and poetry (p. 16).

### Plot

**The relationships and patterns of events.** Even a poem has a plot, such as a change in mood from bitterness to resignation.

What actions happen?

What conflicts occur?

How do the events connect to each other and to the whole?

### Characters

**The people the author creates,** including the narrator of a story or the speaker of a poem.

Who are the principal people in the work?

How do they interact?

What do their actions, words, and thoughts reveal about their personalities and the personalities of others?

Do the characters stay the same, or do they change? Why?

### Point of view

**The perspective or attitude of the speaker in a poem or the voice who tells a story.** The point of view may be **first person** (a participant, using *I*) or **third person** (an outsider, using *he, she, it, they*). A first-person narrator may be a major or a minor character in the narrative and may be **reliable** or **unreliable** (unable to report events wholly or accurately). A third-person narrator may be **omniscient** (knows what goes on in all characters' minds), **limited** (knows what goes on in the mind of only one or two characters), or **objective** (knows only what is external to the characters).

Who is the narrator (or the speaker of a poem)?

How does the narrator's point of view affect the narrative?

### Tone

**The narrator's or speaker's attitude,** perceived through the words (for instance, joyful, bitter, or confident).

What tone (or tones) do you hear? If there is a change, how do you account for it?

Is there an ironic contrast between the narrator's tone (for instance, confidence) and what you take to be the author's attitude (for instance, pity for human overconfidence)?

### Imagery

**Word pictures or details involving the senses:** sight, sound, touch, smell, taste.

What images does the writer use? What senses do they draw on?

What patterns are evident in the images (for instance, religious or commercial images)?

What is the significance of the imagery?

### Symbolism

**Concrete things standing for larger and more abstract ideas.** For in-stance, the American flag may symbolize freedom, a tweeting bird may symbolize happiness, a dead flower may symbolize mortality.

What symbols does the author use? What do they seem to signify?

How does the symbolism relate to the other elements of the work, such as character or theme?

**Setting**
**The place where the action happens.**

What does the locale contribute to the work?

Are scene shifts significant?

**Form**
**The shape or structure of the work.**

What *is* the form? (For example, a story might divide sharply in the middle, moving from happiness to sorrow.)

What parts of the work does the form emphasize, and why?

**Themes**

**The main ideas**—conceptions of human experience suggested by the work as a whole. A theme is neither a plot (what happens) nor a subject (such as mourning or marriage). Rather it is what the author says with that plot about that subject.

Can you state each theme in a sentence? Avoid mentioning specific characters or actions; instead, write an observation applicable to humanity in general. For instance, you might state the following about Kate Chopin's "The Story of an Hour": *Happiness depends partly on freedom.*

Do certain words, passages of dialog or description, or situations seem to represent a theme most clearly?

How do the work's elements combine to develop each theme?

**Appeal**
**The degree to which the work pleases you.**

What do you especially like or dislike about the work?

Do you think your responses are unique, or would they be common to most readers? Why?

This chapter emphasizes so-called formalist criticism, which focuses on a literary work primarily as something to be understood in itself. This critical framework engages the reader immediately in the work of literature, without requiring extensive historical or cultural background, and it introduces the conventional elements of literature that all critical approaches discuss, even though they view the elements differently. The box on the next two pages lists these elements—plot, characters, setting, and so on—and offers questions about each one that can help you think constructively and imaginatively about what you read.

One significant attribute of a literary work is its meaning or themes, or what we can interpret to be its themes. Readers may well disagree over the persuasiveness of someone's argument, but they will rarely disagree over its meaning. With literature, however, disagreements over themes occur all the time because (as we have seen) literature *shows* rather than *tells*: it gives us concrete images of imagined human experiences, but it usually does not say how we ought to understand the images.

Further, readers bring to their reading not only different critical views, as noted earlier, but also different personal experiences. A woman who has recently lost her husband may interpret "The Story of an Hour" differently from most other readers. Or a story that bores a reader at age fifteen may deeply move him at twenty-five. The words on the page remain the same, but their meaning changes.

In writing about literature, we can offer only our *interpretation* of meaning rather than *the* meaning. Still, most people agree that there are limits to interpretation: it must be supported by evidence from the work that a reasonable reader will find at least plausible if not totally convincing. For instance, the student who says that in "The Story of an Hour" Mrs. Mallard does not die but merely falls into a deathlike trance goes beyond the permissible limits because the story offers no evidence for such an interpretation.

### 3.  Using Evidence in Writing About Literature

The evidence for a literary analysis always comes from at least one primary source (the work or works being discussed) and may come from secondary sources (critical and historical works). For example, if you were writing about Chopin's "The Story of an Hour," the primary material would be the story itself, and the secondary material (if you used it) might be critical studies of Chopin.

The bulk of your evidence in writing about literature will usually be quotations from the work, although you will occasionally summarize or paraphrase as well.

Your instructor will probably tell you if you are expected to consult secondary sources for an assignment. They can help you understand a writer's work, but your primary concern should always be the work itself, not what critics A, B, and C say about it. In general, then, quote or summarize secondary material sparingly. And always cite your sources.

### b)  Understanding Writing Assignments in Literature

Two common assignments in writing about literature are described and illustrated in this chapter:

- **A literary analysis (no secondary sources):** Give your ideas about a work of literature—your interpretation of its meaning, significance, or representations. Generally, a literary analysis centers on an arguable thesis statement that you support with evidence from the work. See pages 13–14 for literary analyses of fiction.

- **A literary research paper (with secondary sources):** Combine analysis of a literary work with research in secondary sources about the work. You might consider other scholars' interpretations of the work, biographical information about the author, or accounts of the context in which the author wrote the work. Generally, such a paper centers on an arguable thesis statement that you support with evidence from the text and from secondary sources, which must be cited. For example, you might respond to what scholars have written about a character in a play by Tennessee Williams. See pages 17–18 for examples of literary research papers.

In addition, a literature instructor may ask you to write papers in the following genres:

- **A personal response or reaction paper:** Give your thoughts and feelings about a work of literature. For example, you might compare a novel's description of a city with your experience of the same city.
- **A book review:** Give a summary of a book and a judgment about the book's value. In a review of a novel, for example, you might discuss whether the plot is interesting, the characters are believable, and the writing style is enjoyable. You might also compare the work to other works by the author.
- **A theater review:** Give your reactions to and opinions about a theatrical performance. You might summarize the plot of the play, describe the characters, identify the prominent themes, evaluate the other elements (writing, performances, direction, stage setting), and recommend whether others should see the performance.

## c) Using the Tools and Language of Literary Analysis

### 1. Writing Tools

The fundamental tool for writing about literature is reading critically. Asking analytical questions such as those on pages 6–7 can help you focus your ideas. In addition, keeping a reading journal can help you develop your thoughts. Keep careful, well-organized notes on any research materials. Finally, discuss the work with others who have read it. They may offer reactions and insights that will help you shape your own ideas.

### 2. Language Considerations

Use the present tense of verbs to describe both the action in a literary work (*Brently Mallard suddenly appears*) and the writing of an author (*Chopin briefly describes the view* or *In his essay he comments that . . .*). Use the past tense to describe events that actually occurred in the past (*Chopin was born in 1851*).

Some instructors discourage students from using the first-person *I* (as in *I felt sorry for the character*) in writing about literature. At least use *I* sparingly to avoid sounding egotistical. Rephrase sentences to avoid using *I* unnecessarily—for instance, *The character evokes the reader's sympathy.*

### d) Citing Sources and Formatting Papers in Writing About Literature

Unless your instructor specifies otherwise, use the documentation style of the Modern Language Association (MLA). In this style, citations in the text of the paper refer to a list of works cited at the end. Sample papers illustrating this style appear in this chapter.

Use MLA format for headings, margins, and other elements.

### e) Drafting and Revising a Literary Analysis

The process for writing a literary analysis is similar to that for any other kind of essay: once you've done the reading and thought about it, you need to focus your ideas, gather evidence, draft your paper, and revise it.

### 1. Conceiving a Thesis

After reading, rereading, and making notes, you will probably be able to formulate a tentative thesis statement—an assertion of your main point, your argument. Clear the air by glancing over your notes and by jotting down a few especially promising ideas—brief statements of what you think your key points may be and their main support. One approach is to seek patterns in the work, such as recurring words, phrases, images, events, symbols, or other elements. (Go back to the work, if necessary, to expand the patterns your notes reveal.) Such patterns can help you see themes both in the work itself and in your ideas about it.

Considering Kate Chopin's "The Story of an Hour," Janet Vong at first explored the idea that Mrs. Mallard, the main character, was unrealistic and thus unconvincing. (See Vong's journal entry on pp. 4–5.) But the more Vong examined the story and her notes, the more she was impressed by a pattern of ironies, or reversals, that helped to make Mrs. Mallard believable. In her journal Vong explored the idea that the many small reversals paved the way for Mrs. Mallard's own reversal from grief to joy:

> title? "Ironies in an Hour" (?) "An Hour of Irony" (?) "Kate Chopin's Irony" (?)
> thesis: irony at end is prepared for
> chief irony: Mrs. M. dies just as she is beginning to enjoy life
> smaller ironies:
>   1. "sad message" brings her joy
>   2. Richards is "too late" at end
>   3. Richards is too early at start
>   4. "joy that kills"
>   5. death brings joy and life

From these notes Vong developed her thesis statement:

> The irony of the ending is believable partly because it is consistent with earlier ironies in the story.

This thesis statement asserts a specific idea that can be developed and convincingly argued with evidence from Chopin's story. A good thesis statement will neither assert a fact (*Mrs. Mallard dies soon after hearing that her husband has died*) nor overgeneralize (*The story is an insult to women*).

## 2. Gathering Evidence

In writing about literature, you use mainly evidence gathered from the work itself: quotations and sometimes paraphrases and summaries that support your ideas about the work. You can see examples of quoting and paraphrasing in Janet Vong's final draft on pages 13–14. The box below offers guidelines for using quotations in literary analysis.

---

### Guidelines for using quotations in literary analysis

- Use quotations to support your assertions, not to pad the paper. Quote at length only when necessary to your argument.
- Specify how each quotation relates to your idea. Introduce the quotation—for example, At the outset Chopin conveys the sort of person Richards is: "..." Sometimes, comment after the quotation.
- Reproduce spelling, punctuation, capitalization, and all other features exactly as they appear in the source.
- Document your sources.

---

You may wonder how much you should summarize the plot of the work. A brief plot summary can be helpful to readers who are unfamiliar with the work. Sometimes plot elements place your ideas in the context of the work or remind readers where your quotations come from. Plot elements may even be used as evidence, as Vong uses the ironic ending of the Chopin story. But plot summary is not literary analysis, and summary alone is not sufficient evidence to support a thesis. Keep any plot summaries brief and to the point.

For a literary research paper, evidence will come from the work itself and from secondary sources such as scholarly works and critical appraisals. The thesis and principal ideas of the paper must still be your own, but you may supplement your reading of the work with the views of respected scholars or critics. Sometimes you may choose to build your own argument in part by disputing others' views. However you draw on secondary sources, remember that they must be clearly identified and documented, even when you use your own words.

**Note** You can find student essays on the Web that may lead you to other sources or may suggest ideas you hadn't considered. If you want to use another student's paper as a secondary source, you must evaluate it with special care because it will not have passed through a reviewing process, as an article in a scholarly journal does. You must also, of course, clearly identify and document the source: borrowing *any* other writer's ideas or words without credit is plagiarism.

### 3. Writing a Draft

Drafting your essay is your opportunity to develop your thesis or to discover it if you haven't already. The draft below was actually Janet Vong's second: she deleted some digressions from her first draft and added more evidence for her points. The numbers in parentheses refer to the pages from which she drew the quotations. Ask your instructor whether you should always give such citations, especially for a short poem or story like Chopin's.

#### Ironies in an Hour

After we know how the story turns out, if we reread it we find irony at the very start, as is true of many other stories. Mrs. Mallard's friends assume, mistakenly, that Mrs. Mallard is deeply in love with her husband, Brently Mallard. They take great care to tell her gently of his death. The friends mean well, and in fact they *do* well. They bring her an hour of life, an hour of freedom. They think their news is sad. Mrs. Mallard at first expresses grief when she hears the news, but soon she finds joy in it. So Richards's "sad message" (549), though sad in Richards's eyes, is in fact a happy message.

Among the ironic details is the statement that when Mallard enters the house, Richards tries to conceal him from Mrs. Mallard, but Richards is "too late" (551). This is ironic because earlier Richards has "hastened" (549) to bring his sad message; if he had been too late at the start, Brently Mallard would have arrived at home first, and Mrs. Mallard's life would not end an hour later but would simply go on as before. Yet another irony at the end of the story is the diagnosis of the doctors. The doctors say she died of "heart disease—of joy that kills" (551). In one sense the doctors are right: Mrs. Mallard has experienced a great joy. But of course the doctors totally misunderstand the joy that kills her.

The central irony resides not in the well-intentioned but ironic actions of Richards, or in the unconsciously ironic words of the doctors, but in her own life. She "sometimes" (550) loved her husband, but in a way she has been dead. Now, his apparent death brings her new life. This new life comes to her at the season of the year when "the tops of trees . . . were all aquiver with the new spring life" (550). But, ironically, her new life will last only an hour. She looks forward to "summer days" (550), but she will not see even the end of this spring day. Her years of marriage were ironic. They brought her a sort of living death instead of joy. Her new life is ironic, too. It grows out of her moment of grief for her supposedly dead husband, and her vision of a new life is cut short.

### 4. Revising and Editing

As in other writing, use at least two drafts to revise and edit, so that you can attend separately to the big structural issues and the smaller surface problems. The additional checklist below can help you with a literary analysis.

---

### Checklist for revising a literary analysis

- **Title:** Does the title of your essay give the title and author of the work you discuss and also an idea of your approach to the work?

- **Introduction:** Does the introductory paragraph name the author and the title so that readers know exactly what work you are discussing? (Avoid opening sentences such as "In this story. . . .") Does the introduction state and develop your thesis a bit so that readers know where they will be going?
- **Thesis:** Does the thesis state the interpretation you are arguing for?
- **Organization:** How effective is the organization? The essay should not dwindle or become anticlimactic; rather, it should build up.
- **Quotations:** What evidence does each quotation provide? Do quotations let readers hear the author's voice?
- **Analysis vs. summary:** Is the essay chiefly devoted to analysis, not to summary? Summarize the plot only briefly and only to further your own ideas. A summary is not an essay.
- **Verb tenses:** Have you used the present tense of verbs to describe both the author's work and the action in the work (for example, *Chopin shows* and *Mrs. Mallard dies*)?
- **Evaluation:** How well will readers understand your evaluation of the work and what it is based on? Give the reasons for your judgment of the work. It is not enough to express your likes or dislikes; readers need the support of specific evidence from the work.
- **Are all your sources documented in MLA style?**

Janet Vong's final draft follows, with annotations that highlight some of its features.

### *Literary analysis of fiction (no secondary sources)*

| | |
|---|---|
| Author's name and identification in MLA format | Janet Vong<br>Mr. Romano<br>English 102<br>20 February 2014 |
| Paper title incorporating author and title of analyzed work | |

**Ironies of Life in Kate Chopin's**
**"The Story of an Hour"**

| | |
|---|---|
| Introduction naming author/title | Kate Chopin's "The Story of an Hour"—which takes only a few minutes to read—has an ironic ending: Mrs. Mallard dies just when she is beginning |
| Thesis statement: student's interpretation | to live. On first reading, the ending seems almost too ironic for belief. On rereading the story, however, one sees that the ending is believable partly because it is consistent with other ironies in the story. |
| Detailing of story's ironies, using quotations and some summary to emphasize the reversals | Irony appears at the very start of the story. Because Mrs. Mallard's friends and her sister assume, mistakenly, that she is deeply in love with her husband, Brently Mallard, they take great care to tell her gently of his death. They mean well, and in fact they *do* well, bringing her an hour of life, an hour of joyous freedom, but it is ironic that they think their news is sad. True, Mrs. Mallard at first expresses grief when she hears the news, but soon (unknown to the others) she finds joy. So Richards's "sad message" (549), though sad in Richards's eyes, is in fact a happy message. |

Among the small but significant ironic details is the statement near the end of the story that when Mallard enters the house, Richards tries to conceal him from Mrs. Mallard, but Richards is "too late" (551). Almost at the start of the story, in the second paragraph, Richards has "hastened" (549) to bring his sad news. But if Richards had arrived too late at the start, Brently Mallard would have arrived at home first, and Mrs. Mallard's life would not end an hour later but would simply go on as before. Yet another irony at the end of the story is the diagnosis of the doctors. They say she died of "heart disease—of joy that kills" (551). In one sense they are right: Mrs. Mallard has for the last hour experienced a great joy. But of course the doctors totally misunderstand the joy that kills her. It is not joy at seeing her husband alive, but her realization that the great joy she experienced during the last hour is over.

> In-text citations in MLA style

All of these ironic details add richness to the story, but the central irony resides not in the well-intentioned but ironic actions of Richards, or in the unconsciously ironic words of the doctors, but in Mrs. Mallard's own life. She "sometimes" (550) loved her husband, but in a way she has been dead, a body subjected to her husband's will. Now, his apparent death brings her new life. Appropriately, this new life comes to her at the season of the year when "the tops of trees . . . were all aquiver with the new spring life" (550). But, ironically, her new life will last only an hour. She is "Free, free, free" (550)—but only until her husband walks through the doorway. She looks forward to "summer days" (550), but she will not see even the end of this spring day. If her years of marriage were ironic, bringing her a sort of living death instead of joy, her new life is ironic, too, not only because it grows out of her moment of grief for her supposedly dead husband, but also because her vision of "a long procession of years" (550) is cut short within an hour on a spring day.

[New page.]

Work Cited

Chopin, Kate. "The Story of an Hour." *Literature: An Introduction to Fiction, Poetry, and Drama.* Ed. X. J. Kennedy and Dana Gioia. 12th ed. New York: Longman, 2013. 549-51. Print.

> Work cited in MLA style

---

## The writing situation: Literary analysis (short story)

- **Subject:** Irony in "The Story of an Hour," by Kate Chopin; student's choice for an assignment in a literature course
- **Purpose:** To argue for an interpretation of a short story
- **Audience:** Classmates and instructor
- **Genre:** Literary analysis—writing that argues for an interpretation of a literary work, in this case a short story
- **Source:** Selection from an anthology (cited in MLA style); no secondary sources

---

### f) Writing About Fiction, Poetry, and Drama

A work of literature falls into a literary **genre**—fiction, poetry, or drama—depending on how it is structured. The different genres of literature require different approaches in writing.

---

### Questions for analyzing fiction

- **What happens in the story?** For yourself, summarize the plot (the gist of the happenings). Think about what your summary *leaves out*—what is in the story *besides* plot.
- **Is the story told in chronological order, or are there flashbacks or flashfor-wards?** On rereading, what foreshadowing (hints of what is to come) do you detect?
- **What conflicts does the work include?**
- **How does the writer develop characters?** Are the characters revealed by explicit comment or through action? With which character(s) do you sympathize? Are the characters plausible? What motivates them? What do minor characters contribute to the work?
- **Who tells the story?** Is the narrator a character, or does the narrator stand entirely outside the characters' world? What does the narrator's point of view contribute to the story's theme? (On narrative points of view, see p. 6.)
- **What is the setting?** What do the time and place of the action contribute to the work?
- **Are certain characters, settings, or actions symbolic?** Do they stand for some-thing in addition to themselves?
- **What are the themes?** That is, what does the work add up to? Do the themes reinforce your values, or do they challenge them?
- **Is the title informative?** Did its meaning change for you after you read the work?

---

## 1. Writing About Fiction

The "Questions for a literary analysis" on pages 6–7 will help you think about any work of literature, including a story or novel, and find a topic to write on. The following questions provide additional prompts for thinking about fic-tion. For an example of writing about fiction, see Janet Vong's essay begin-ning on the previous page.

## 2. Writing About Poetry

Two types of essays on poetry are especially common. One is an analysis of some aspect of the poem in relation to the whole—for instance, the changes in the speaker's tone or the functions of meter and rhyme. The second is an ex-plication, a line-by-line (sometimes almost word-by-word) reading that seeks to make explicit everything that is implicit in the poem. Thus an explication of the first line of Robert Frost's "Stopping by Woods on a Snowy Evening" (the line goes "Whose woods these are I think I know") might call attention to the tentativeness of the line ("I think I know") and to the fact that the words are not in the normal order ("I think I know whose woods these are"). These features might support the explanation that the poet is introducing—very quietly—a note of the *un*usual, in preparation for the experience that follows. Although one might conceivably explicate a long poem, the method is so detailed that in practice writers usually confine it to short poems or to short passages from long poems.

---

## Questions for analyzing poetry

- **What parts of the poem interest or puzzle you?** What words seem especially striking or unusual?
- **How can you describe the poem's speaker (sometimes called the persona or the voice)?** The speaker may be different from the author.
- **What tone or emotion do you detect**—for instance, anger, affection, sarcasm? Does the tone change during the poem?
- **What is the structure of the poem?** Are there stanzas (groups of lines separated by space)? If so, how does the thought relate to them?
- **What are the themes of the poem?** What is it about? Are the themes stated or implied?
- **What images do you find?** Look for evocations of sight, sound, taste, touch, or smell. Is there a surprising pattern of images—say, images of business in a poem about love? What does the poem suggest symbolically as well as literally? (Trust your responses. If you don't sense a symbolic overtone, move on. Don't hunt for symbols.)

---

The "Questions for a literary analysis" on pages 6–7 will help you think about any work of literature, including a poem, and find a topic to write on. The following questions provide additional ways to think about poetry.

### *Literary Research Paper on Poetry*

The sample paper beginning on the next page analyzes the short poem below by Agha Shahid Ali. The paper argues for a particular interpretation of the poem both by analyzing the poem and by drawing on secondary sources—that is, critical works *about* the poem. In the opening paragraph, for instance, the writer quotes a secondary source to establish how her interpretation differs from that of other readers. This quotation and the other uses of secondary sources are support for the writer's points, not padding.

**Note** In the paper, the in-text citations for Ali's poem give line numbers of the poem, whereas the citations for the secondary sources give page numbers of the sources.

#### *Agha Shahid Ali*

#### Postcard from Kashmir

Kashmir shrinks into my mailbox,
my home a neat four by six inches.
I always loved neatness. Now I hold
the half-inch Himalayas in my hand.

This is home. And this the closest                    5
I'll ever be to home. When I return,
the colors won't be so brilliant,
the Jhelum's waters so clean,
so ultramarine. My love
so overexposed.                                       10

And my memory will be a little
out of focus, in it
a giant negative, black
and white, still undeveloped.


Jessie Glenn
Professor Narracci
English 101
14 March 2014

Past and Future in
Agha Shahid Ali's "Postcard from Kashmir"

Most literary critics interpret Agha Shahid Ali's "Postcard from Kashmir" as a longing for a lost home, a poetic expression of the heartbreak of exile. For instance, Maimuna Dali Islam describes the speaker's futile effort "to capture his homeland" (262). However, such a reading of the poem seems too narrow. "Postcard from Kashmir" does evoke the experience of being displaced from a beloved home, but the speaker does not seem to feel an intense loss. Instead, he seems to reflect on his position of having more than one home.

> Introduction naming author/title and summarizing other interpretations

> Thesis statement: student's interpretation

Ali's brief poem consists of three stanzas and divides into two parts. In the first half, the speaker examines a postcard he has received from his former home of Kashmir (lines 1-6). In the second half, the speaker looks forward, imagining how Kashmir will look the next time he sees it and assuming that the place will be different from the idealized view of the postcard and his memory (6-14). The geography is significant. Kashmir has been in the news for many years as the focus of territorial conflict, often violent, among the bordering nations of India, Pakistan, and China. Many residents of the region have been killed, and many have left the region. One of the exiles was Ali: he moved to the United States in 1976 and lived here until his death in 2001, but he also regularly visited his family in Kashmir (Benvenuto 261, 263).

> Summary of poem

> Background information

> In-text citations in MLA style

---

**The writing situation: Literary research paper (poem)**

- **Subject:** The meaning of home in "Postcard from Kashmir," by Agha Shahid Ali; student's choice for an assignment in a first-year writing course emphasizing literature
- **Purpose:** To argue for an interpretation of a poem
- **Audience:** Classmates and instructor
- **Genre:** Literary research paper—writing that argues for an interpretation of a literary work, in this case a poem, in the context of others' interpretations and/or information
- **Sources:** Poem, published interview with the poet, and critics' interpretations of the poem (all cited in MLA style)

In the context of Kashmir, the literary theorist Jahan Ramazani concludes that the poem "dramatizes the . . . condition" of losing one's homeland to political turmoil (12). Yet several lines in the poem suggest that the speaker is not mourning a loss but musing about having a sense of home both in Kashmir and in the United States. This sense is evident in the opening stanza: "Kashmir shrinks into my mailbox, / my home a neat four by six inches" (1-2), with "my mailbox" conveying his current residence as home and "my home" referring to Kashmir. The dual sense of home is even more evident in the lines "This is home. And this is the closest / I'll ever be to home" (5-6). Although Maimuna Dali Islam assumes that "This" in these lines refers to the Kashmir pictured on the postcard (262), it could also or instead refer to the home attached to the mailbox.

The speaker also seems to perceive that his dual sense of home will continue into the future. The critics do not mention that the second half of the poem is written in the future tense. Beginning with "When I return" (6), the speaker makes it clear that he expects to find himself in Kashmir again, and he imagines how things will be, not how they were. Islam takes the image on the postcard as proof that "there is a place that can be captured in a snapshot" (263), but the speaker compares photography to memory, characterizing both as flawed and deceptive with terms such as "overexposed" (10) and "out of focus" (12). He acknowledges that the place won't be like the photograph: "the colors won't be so brilliant, / the Jhelum's waters so clean, / so ultramarine" (7-9). Kashmir still exists, but not as any photograph or memory has recorded it. And the speaker's relationship to his original home, his "love" (9), is changing with the place itself.

In "Postcard from Kashmir" the speaker reflects on home and displacement as he gazes into a representation of his past and considers the future. If the poem mourns a loss, as the critics suggest, it is a loss that has not happened yet, at least not completely. More convincingly, the poem captures a moment when the two homes and the past, present, and future all meet.

[New page.]

Works Cited

Ali, Agha Shahid. "Postcard from Kashmir." *The Half-Inch Himalayas*. Middletown: Wesleyan UP, 1987. 1. Print.

Benvenuto, Christine. "Agha Shahid Ali." *Massachusetts Review* 43.1 (2002): 261–73. Web. 7 Mar. 2014.

Islam, Maimuna Dali. "A Way in the World of an Asian American Existence: Agha Shahid Ali's Transimmigrant Spacing of North America and India and Kashmir." *Transnational Asian American Literature: Sites and Transits*. Ed. Shirley Lim et al. Philadelphia: Temple UP, 2006. 257–73. Print.

Ramazani, Jahan. *The Hybrid Muse: Postcolonial Poetry in English*. Chicago: U of Chicago P, 2001. Print.

Critic's interpretation

First point supporting thesis

Quotations from poem

Critic's interpretation

Second point supporting thesis

Quotation from secondary source

Conclusion restating critics' and student's interpretations

Works cited in MLA style

# CONFLICT

## FICTION

### DONALD BARTHELME

### *Report* (1968)

Our group is against the war. But the war goes on. I was sent to Cleveland to talk to the engineers. The engineers were meeting in Cleveland. I was supposed to persuade them not to do what they are going to do. I took United's 4:45 from LaGuardia arriving in Cleveland at 6:13. Cleveland is dark blue at that hour. I went directly to the motel, where the engineers were meeting. Hundreds of engineers attended the Cleveland meeting. I noticed many fractures among the engineers, bandages, traction. I noticed what appeared to be fracture of the carpal scaphoid in six examples. I notice numerous fractures of the humeral shaft, of the os calcis, of the pelvic girdle. I noticed a high incidence of clay-shoveller's fracture. I could not account for these fractures. The engineers were making calculations, taking measurements, sketching on the black board, drinking beer, throwing bread, buttonholing employers, hurling glasses into the fireplace. They were friendly.

They were friendly. They were full of love and information. The chief engineer wore shades. Patella in Monk's traction, clamshell fracture by the look of it. He was standing in a slum of beer bottles and microphone cable. "Have some of this chicken à la Isambard Kingdom Brunel[1] the Great Ingineer," he said. "And declare who you are and what we can do for you. What is your line, distinguished guest?"

"Software," I said. "In every sense. I am here representing a small group of interested parties. We are interested in your thing, which seems to be functioning in the midst of so much dysfunction, function is interesting. Other people's things don't seem to be working. The State Department's thing doesn't seem to be working. The U.N.'s thing doesn't seem to be working. The democratic left's thing doesn't seem to be working. Buddha's thing—"

"Ask us anything about our thing, which seems to be working," the chief engineer said. "We will open our hearts and heads to you, Software Man, because

---

[1]Nineteenth-century British engineer.

we want to be understood and loved by the great lay public, and have our marvels appreciated by that public, for which we daily unsung produce tons of new marvels each more life-enhancing than the last. Ask us anything. Do you want to know about evaporated thin-film metallurgy? Monolithic and hybrid integrated-circuit processes? The algebra of inequalities? Optimization theory? Complex high-speed micro-miniature closed and open loop systems? Fixed variable mathematical cost searches? Epitaxial deposition of semi-conductor materials? Gross interfaced space gropes? We also have specialists in the cuckooflower, the doctorfish, and the dumdum bullet as these relate to aspects of today's expanding technology, and they do in the damnedest ways."

I spoke to him then about the war. I said the same things people always say when they speak against the war. I said that the war was wrong. I said that large countries should not burn down small countries. I said that the government had made a series of errors. I said that these errors once small and forgivable were now immense and unforgivable. I said that the government was attempting to conceal its original errors under layers of new errors. I said that the government was sick with error, giddy with it. I said that ten thousand of our soldiers had already been killed in pursuit of the government's errors. I said that tens of thousands of the enemy's soldiers and civilians had been killed because of various errors, ours and theirs. I said that we are responsible for errors made in our name. I said that the government should not be allowed to make additional errors.

"Yes, yes," the chief engineer said, "there is doubtless much truth in what you say, but we can't possibly *lose* the war, can we? And stopping is losing, isn't it? The war regarded as a process, stopping regarded as an abort? We don't know *how* to lose a war. That skill is not among our skills. Our array smashes their array, that is what we know. That is the process. That is what is.

"But let's not have any more of this dispiriting downbeat counterproductive talk. I have a few new marvels here I'd like to discuss with you just briefly. A few new marvels that are just about ready to be gaped at by the admiring layman. Consider for instance the area of realtime online computer-controlled wish evaporation. Wish evaporation is going to be crucial in meeting the rising expectations of the world's peoples, which are as you know rising entirely too fast."

I noticed then distributed about the room a great many transverse fractures of the ulna. "The development of the pseudo-ruminant stomach for underdeveloped peoples," he went on, "is one of our interesting things you should be interested in. With the pseudo-ruminant stomach they can chew cuds, that is to say, eat grass. Blue is the most popular color worldwide and for that reason we are working with certain strains of your native Kentucky *Poa pratensis*, or bluegrass, as the staple input for the p/r stomach cycle, which would also give a shot in the arm to our balance-of-payments thing don't you know...." I noticed about me then a great number of metatarsal fractures in banjo splints. "The kangaroo initiative . . . eight hundred thousand harvested last year . . . highest percentage of edible protein of any herbivore yet studied . . ."

"Have new kangaroos been planted?"

The engineer looked at me.

"I intuit your hatred and jealousy of our thing," he said. "The ineffectual always hate our thing and speak of it as anti-human, which is not at all a meaningful way to speak of our thing. Nothing mechanical is alien to me," he said (amber spots making bursts of light in his shades), "because I am human, in a sense, and if I think it up, then 'it' is human too, whatever 'it' may be. Let me tell you, Software Man, we have been damned forbearing in the matter of this little war you declare yourself to be interested in. Function is the cry, and our thing is functioning like crazy. There are things we could do that we have not done. Steps we could take that we have not taken. These steps are, regarded in a certain light, the light of our enlightened self-interest, quite justifiable steps. We could, of course, get irritated. We could, of course, *lose patience.*

"We could, of course, release thousands upon thousands of self-powered crawling-along-the-ground lengths of titanium wire eighteen inches long with a diameter of .0005 centimetres (that is to say, invisible) which, scenting an enemy, climb up his trouser leg and wrap themselves around his neck. We have developed those. They are within our capabilities. We could, of course, release in the arena of the upper air our new improved pufferfish toxin which precipitates an identity crisis. No special technical problems there. That is almost laughably easy. We could, of course, place up to two million maggots in their rice within twenty-four hours. The maggots are ready, massed in secret staging areas in Alabama. We have hypodermic darts capable of piebalding the enemy's pigmentation. We have rots, blights, and rusts capable of attacking his alphabet. Those are dandies. We have a hut-shrinking chemical which penetrates the fibres of the bamboo, causing it, the hut, to strangle its occupants. This operates only after 10 P.M., when people are sleeping. Their mathematics are at the mercy of a suppurating surd we have invented. We have a family of fishes trained to attack their fishes. We have the deadly testicle-destroying telegram. The cable companies are coöperating. We have a green substance that, well, I'd rather not talk about. We have a secret word that, if pronounced, produces multiple fractures in all living things in an area the size of four football fields."

"That's why—"

"Yes. Some damned fool couldn't keep his mouth shut. The point is that the whole structure of enemy life is within our power to *rend, vitiate, devour,* and *crush.* But that's not the interesting thing."

"You recount these possibilities with uncommon relish."

"Yes I realize that there is too much relish here. But *you* must realize that these capabilities represent in and of themselves highly technical and complex and interesting problems and hurdles on which our boys have expended many thousands of hours of hard work and brilliance. And that the effects are often grossly exaggerated by irresponsible victims. And that the whole thing represents a fantastic series of triumphs for the multidisciplined problem-solving team concept."

"I appreciate that."

"We *could* unleash all this technology at once. You can imagine what would happen then. But that's not the interesting thing."

"What is the interesting thing?"

"The interesting thing is that we have a *moral sense*. It is on punched cards, perhaps the most advanced and sensitive moral sense the world has ever known."

"Because it is on punched cards?"

"It considers all considerations in endless and subtle detail," he said. "It even quibbles. With this great new moral tool, how can we go wrong? I confidently predict that, although we *could* employ all this splendid new weaponry I've been telling you about, *we're not going to do it.*"

"We're not going to do it?"

I took United's 5:44 from Cleveland arriving at Newark at 7:19. New Jersey is bright pink at that hour. Living things move about the surface of New Jersey at that hour molesting each other only in traditional ways. I made my report to the group. I stressed the friendliness of the engineers. I said, It's all right. I said, We have a moral sense. I said, *We're not going to do it.* They didn't believe me.

## Study and Discussion Questions

1. Describe the chief engineer's attitude toward the war, toward technology, toward social problems, and toward morality.
2. What do the chief engineer's discussions of "wish evaporation" and the "pseudo-ruminant stomach" suggest about how he views the people of poor nations?
3. What kind of person is Software Man? What does he represent? What effect does his talk with the chief engineer have on him?
4. Reread the long paragraph in which the chief engineer describes the new weapons available. How are we supposed to react? What is the effect of the matter-of-fact tone in which these bizarre horrors are described?
5. "Report" was first published during the Vietnam War. What in the story points to that war in particular?
6. Compare/contrast the attitude toward weapons technology in this story with actual attitudes toward weapons technology in the military and government today.

## Suggestions for Writing

1. Discuss a product of modern technology that you find frightening.
2. Speculate on how high-technology weaponry changes the nature of war.

## Critical Resources

1. Barthelme, Donald. *Not-Knowing: The Essays and Interviews of Donald Barthelme.* Ed. Kim Herzinger. New York: Random House, 1997.
2. Barthelme, Helen. *Donald Barthelme: The Genesis of a Cool Sound.* College Station, TX: Texas A&M University Press, 2001.
3. Roe, Barbara. *Donald Barthelme: A Study of the Short Fiction.* New York: Twayne Publishers, 1992.
4. Trachtenberg, Stanley. *Understanding Donald Barthelme.* Columbia: University of South Carolina Press, 1990.

❋ ❋ ❋

**AMBROSE BIERCE**

## *An Occurrence at Owl Creek Bridge* (1892)

### I

A man stood upon a railroad bridge in northern Alabama, looking down into the swift water twenty feet below. The man's hands were behind his back, the wrists bound with a cord. A rope closely encircled his neck. It was attached to a stout cross-timber above his head and the slack fell to the level of his knees. Some loose boards laid upon the sleepers supporting the metals of the railway supplied a footing for him and his executioners—two private soldiers of the Federal army, directed by a sergeant who in civil life may have been a deputy sheriff. At a short remove upon the same temporary platform was an officer in the uniform of his rank, armed. He was a captain. A sentinel at each end of the bridge stood with his rifle in the position known as "support," that is to say, vertical in front of the left shoulder, the hammer resting on the forearm thrown straight across the chest—a formal and unnatural position, enforcing an erect carriage of the body. It did not appear to be the duty of these two men to know what was occurring at the centre of the bridge; they merely blockaded the two ends of the foot planking that traversed it.

Beyond one of the sentinels nobody was in sight; the railroad ran straight away into a forest for a hundred yards, then, curving, was lost to view. Doubtless there was an outpost farther along. The other bank of the stream was open ground—a gentle acclivity topped with a stockade of vertical tree trunks, loopholed for rifles, with a single embrasure through which protruded the muzzle of a brass cannon commanding the bridge. Midway of the slope between bridge and fort were the spectators—a single company of infantry in line, at "parade rest," the butts of the rifles on the ground, the barrels inclining slightly backward against the right shoulder, the hands crossed upon the stock. A lieutenant stood at the right of the line, the point of his sword upon the ground, his left hand resting upon his right. Excepting the group of four at the centre of the bridge, not a man moved. The company faced the bridge, staring stonily, motionless. The sentinels, facing the banks of the stream, might have been statues to adorn the bridge. The captain stood with folded arms, silent, observing the work of his subordinates, but making no sign. Death is a dignitary who when he comes announced is to be received with formal manifestations of respect, even by those most familiar with him. In the code of military etiquette silence and fixity are forms of deference.

The man who was engaged in being hanged was apparently about thirty-five years of age. He was a civilian, if one might judge from his habit, which was that of a planter. His features were good—a straight nose, firm mouth, broad forehead, from which his long, dark hair was combed straight back, falling behind his ears to the collar of his well-fitting frock-coat. He wore a mustache and pointed beard, but no whiskers; his eyes were large and dark gray, and had a kindly expression which one would hardly have expected in one whose neck was in the hemp. Evidently this was no vulgar assassin. The liberal military code makes provision for hanging many kinds of persons, and gentlemen are not excluded.

The preparations being complete, the two private soldiers stepped aside and each drew away the plank upon which he had been standing. The sergeant turned to the captain, saluted and placed himself immediately behind that officer, who in turn moved apart one pace. These movements left the condemned man and the sergeant standing on the two ends of the same plank, which spanned three of the cross-ties of the bridge. The end upon which the civilian stood almost, but not quite, reached a fourth. This plank had been held in place by the weight of the captain; it was now held by that of the sergeant. At a signal from the former the latter would step aside, the plank would tilt and the condemned man go down between two ties. The arrangement commended itself to his judgment as simple and effective. His face had not been covered nor his eyes bandaged. He looked a moment at his "unsteadfast footing," then let his gaze wander to the swirling water of the stream racing madly beneath his feet. A piece of dancing driftwood caught his attention and his eyes followed it down the current. How slowly it appeared to move! What a sluggish stream!

He closed his eyes in order to fix his last thoughts upon his wife and children. The water, touched to gold by the early sun, the brooding mists under the banks at some distance down the stream, the fort, the soldiers, the piece of drift—all had distracted him. And now he became conscious of a new disturbance. Striking through the thought of his dear ones was a sound which he could neither ignore nor understand, a sharp, distinct, metallic percussion like the stroke of a blacksmith's hammer upon the anvil; it had the same ringing quality. He wondered what it was, and whether immeasurably distant or near by—it seemed both. Its recurrence was regular, but as slow as the tolling of a death knell. He awaited each stroke with impatience and—he knew not why—apprehension. The intervals of silence grew progressively longer; the delays became maddening. With their greater infrequency the sounds increased in strength and sharpness. They hurt his ear like the thrust of a knife; he feared he would shriek. What he heard was the ticking of his watch.

He unclosed his eyes and saw again the water below him. "If I could free my hands," he thought, "I might throw off the noose and spring into the stream. By diving I could evade the bullets and, swimming vigorously, reach the bank, take to the woods and get away home. My home, thank God, is as yet outside their lines; my wife and little ones are still beyond the invader's farthest advance."

As these thoughts, which have here to be set down in words, were flashed into the doomed man's brain rather than evolved from it, the captain nodded to the sergeant. The sergeant stepped aside.

## II

Peyton Farquhar was a well-to-do planter, of an old and highly respected Alabama family. Being a slave owner and like other slave owners a politician he was naturally an original secessionist and ardently devoted to the Southern cause. Circumstances of an imperious nature, which it is unnecessary to relate here, had prevented him from taking service with the gallant army that had fought the disastrous campaigns ending with the fall of Corinth, and he chafed under the inglorious restraint, longing for the release of his energies, the larger life of the soldier, the opportunity for distinction. That opportunity, he felt, would come, as it comes to all in war time. Meanwhile he did what he could. No service was too humble for him to perform in aid of the South, no adventure too perilous for him to undertake if consistent with the character of a civilian who was at heart a soldier, and who in good faith and without too much qualification assented to at least a part of the frankly villainous dictum that all is fair in love and war.

One evening while Farquhar and his wife were sitting on a rustic bench near the entrance to his grounds, a gray-clad soldier rode up to the gate and asked for a drink of water. Mrs. Farquhar was only too happy to serve him with her own white hands. While she was fetching the water her husband approached the dusty horseman and inquired eagerly for news from the front.

"The Yanks are repairing the railroads," said the man, "and are getting ready for another advance. They have reached the Owl Creek bridge, put it in order and built a stockade on the north bank. The commandant has issued an order, which is posted everywhere, declaring that any civilian caught interfering with the railroad, its bridges, tunnels or trains will be summarily hanged. I saw the order."

"How far is it to the Owl Creek bridge?" Farquhar asked.

"About thirty miles."

"Is there no force on this side the creek?"

"Only a picket post half a mile out, on the railroad, and a single sentinel at this end of the bridge."

"Suppose a man—a civilian and student of hanging—should elude the picket post and perhaps get the better of the sentinel," said Farquhar, smiling, "what could he accomplish?"

The soldier reflected. "I was there a month ago," he replied. "I observed that the flood of last winter had lodged a great quantity of driftwood against the wooden pier at this end of the bridge. It is now dry and would burn like tow."

The lady had now brought the water, which the soldier drank. He thanked her ceremoniously, bowed to her husband and rode away. An hour later, after nightfall, he repassed the plantation, going northward in the direction from which he had come. He was a Federal scout.

## III

As Peyton Farquhar fell straight downward through the bridge he lost consciousness and was as one already dead. From this state he was awakened—ages later, it seemed to him—by the pain of a sharp pressure upon his throat, followed by a sense of suffocation. Keen, poignant agonies seemed to shoot from his neck downward through every fibre of his body and limbs. These pains appeared to flash along well-defined lines of ramification and to beat with an inconceivably rapid periodicity. They seemed like streams of pulsating fire heating him to an intolerable temperature. As to his head, he was conscious of nothing but a feeling of fullness—of congestion. These sensations were unaccompanied by thought. The intellectual part of his nature was already effaced; he had power only to feel, and feeling was torment. He was conscious of motion. Encompassed in a luminous cloud, of which he was now merely the fiery heart, without material substance, he swung through unthinkable arcs of oscillation, like a vast pendulum. Then all at once, with terrible suddenness, the light about him shot upward with the noise of a loud plash; a frightful roaring was in his ears, and all was cold and dark. The power of thought was restored; he knew that the rope had broken and he had fallen into the stream. There was no additional strangulation; the noose about his neck was already suffocating him and kept the water from his lungs. To die of hanging at the bottom of a river!—the idea seemed to him ludicrous. He opened his eyes in the darkness and saw above him a gleam of light, but how distant, how inaccessible! He was still sinking, for the light became fainter and fainter until it was a mere glimmer. Then it began to grow and brighten, and he knew that he was rising toward the surface—knew it with reluctance, for he was now very comfortable. "To be hanged and drowned," he thought, "that is not so bad; but I do not wish to be shot. No; I will not be shot; that is not fair."

He was not conscious of an effort, but a sharp pain in his wrist apprised him that he was trying to free his hands. He gave the struggle his attention, as an idler might observe the feat of a juggler, without interest in the outcome. What splendid effort!—what magnificent, what superhuman strength! Ah, that was a fine endeavor! Bravo! The cord fell away; his arms parted and floated upward, the hands dimly seen on each side in the growing light. He watched them with a new interest as first one and then the other pounced upon the noose at his neck. They tore it away and thrust it fiercely aside, its undulations resembling those of a water-snake. "Put it back, put it back!" He thought he shouted these words to his hands, for the undoing of the noose had been succeeded by the direst pang that he had yet experienced. His neck ached horribly; his brain was on fire; his heart, which had been fluttering faintly, gave a great leap, trying to force itself out at his mouth. His whole body was racked and wrenched with an insupportable anguish! But his disobedient hands gave no heed to the command. They beat the water vigorously with quick, downward strokes, forcing him to the surface. He felt his head emerge; his eyes were blinded by the sunlight; his chest expanded convulsively, and with a supreme and crowning agony his lungs engulfed a great draught of air, which instantly he expelled in a shriek!

He was now in full possession of his physical senses. They were, indeed, preternaturally keen and alert. Something in the awful disturbance of his organic system had so exalted and refined them that they made record of things never before perceived. He felt the ripples upon his face and heard their separate sounds as they struck. He looked at the forest on the bank of the stream, saw the individual trees, the leaves and the veining of each leaf—saw the very insects upon them: the locusts, the brilliant-bodied flies, the gray spiders stretching their webs from twig to twig. He noted the prismatic colors in all the dewdrops upon a million blades of grass. The humming of the gnats that danced above the eddies of the stream, the beating of the dragon-flies' wings, the strokes of the water-spiders' legs, like oars which had lifted their boat—all these made audible music. A fish slid along beneath his eyes and he heard the rush of its body parting the water.

He had come to the surface facing down the stream; in a moment the visible world seemed to wheel slowly round, himself the pivotal point, and he saw the bridge, the fort, the soldiers upon the bridge, the captain, the sergeant, the two privates, his executioners. They were in silhouette against the blue sky. They shouted and gesticulated, pointing at him. The captain had drawn his pistol, but did not fire; the others were unarmed. Their movements were grotesque and horrible, their forms gigantic.

Suddenly he heard a sharp report and something struck the water smartly within a few inches of his head, spattering his face with spray. He heard a second report, and saw one of the sentinels with his rifle at his shoulder, a light cloud of blue smoke rising from the muzzle. The man in the water saw the eye of the man on the bridge gazing into his own through the sights of the rifle. He observed that it was a gray eye and remembered having read that gray eyes were keenest, and that all famous marksmen had them. Nevertheless, this one had missed.

A counter-swirl had caught Farquhar and turned him half round; he was again looking into the forest on the bank opposite the fort. The sound of a clear, high voice in a monotonous singsong now rang out behind him and came across the water with a distinctness that pierced and subdued all other sounds, even the beating of the ripples in his ears. Although no soldier, he had frequented camps enough to know the dread significance of that deliberate, drawling, aspirated chant; the lieutenant on shore was taking a part in the morning's work. How coldly and pitilessly—with what an even, calm intonation, presaging, and enforcing tranquility in the men—with what accurately measured intervals fell those cruel words:

"Attention, company! . . . Shoulder arms! . . . Ready! . . . Aim! . . . Fire!"

Farquhar dived—dived as deeply as he could. The water roared in his ears like the voice of Niagara, yet he heard the dulled thunder of the volley and, rising again toward the surface, met shining bits of metal, singularly flattened, oscillating slowly downward. Some of them touched him on the face and hands, then fell away, continuing their descent. One lodged between his collar and neck; it was uncomfortably warm and he snatched it out.

As he rose to the surface, gasping for breath, he saw that he had been a long time under water; he was perceptibly farther down stream—nearer to safety. The soldiers had almost finished reloading; the metal ramrods flashed all at once in the sunshine as they were drawn from the barrels, turned in the air, and thrust into their sockets. The two sentinels fired again, independently and ineffectually.

The hunted man saw all this over his shoulder; he was now swimming vigorously with the current. His brain was as energetic as his arms and legs; he thought with the rapidity of lightning.

"The officer," he reasoned, "will not make that martinet's error a second time. It is as easy to dodge a volley as a single shot. He has probably already given the command to fire at will. God help me, I cannot dodge them all!"

An appalling plash within two yards of him was followed by a loud, rushing sound, *diminuendo,* which seemed to travel back through the air to the fort and died in an explosion which stirred the very river to its deeps! A rising sheet of water curved over him, fell down upon him, blinded him, strangled him! The cannon had taken a hand in the game. As he shook his head free from the commotion of the smitten water he heard the deflected shot humming through the air ahead, and in an instant it was cracking and smashing the branches in the forest beyond.

"They will not do that again," he thought; "the next time they will use a charge of grape. I must keep my eye upon the gun; the smoke will apprise me—the report arrives too late; it lags behind the missile. That is a good gun."

Suddenly he felt himself whirled round and round—spinning like a top. The water, the banks, the forests, the now distant bridge, fort and men—all were commingled and blurred. Objects were represented by their colors only; circular horizontal streaks of color—that was all he saw. He had been caught in a vortex and was being whirled on with a velocity of advance and gyration that made him giddy and sick. In a few moments he was flung upon the gravel at the foot of the left bank of the stream—the southern bank—and behind a projecting point which concealed him from his enemies. The sudden arrest of his motion, the abrasion of one of his hands on the gravel, restored him, and he wept with delight. He dug his fingers into the sand, threw it over himself in handfuls and audibly blessed it. It looked like diamonds, rubies, emeralds; he could think of nothing beautiful which it did not resemble. The trees upon the bank were giant garden plants; he noted a definite order in their arrangement, inhaled the fragrance of their blooms. A strange, roseate light shone through the spaces among their trunks and the wind made in their branches the music of æolian harps. He had no wish to perfect his escape—was content to remain in that enchanting spot until retaken.

A whiz and rattle of grapeshot among the branches high above his head roused him from his dream. The baffled cannoneer had fired him a random farewell. He sprang to his feet, rushed up the sloping bank, and plunged into the forest.

All that day he traveled, laying his course by the rounding sun. The forest seemed interminable; nowhere did he discover a break in it, not even a wood-man's road. He had not known that he lived in so wild a region. There was something uncanny in the revelation.

By nightfall he was fatigued, footsore, famishing. The thought of his wife and children urged him on. At last he found a road which led him in what he knew to be the right direction. It was as wide and straight as a city street, yet it seemed untraveled. No fields bordered it, no dwelling anywhere. Not so much as the bark-ing of a dog suggested human habitation. The black bodies of the trees formed a straight wall on both sides, terminating on the horizon in a point, like a diagram in a lesson in perspective. Overhead, as he looked up through this rift in the wood, shone great golden stars looking unfamiliar and grouped in strange constellations. He was sure they were arranged in some order which had a secret and malign significance. The wood on either side was full of singular noises, among which— once, twice, and again—he distinctly heard whispers in an unknown tongue.

His neck was in pain and lifting his hand to it he found it horribly swollen. He knew that it had a circle of black where the rope had bruised it. His eyes felt con-gested; he could no longer close them. His tongue was swollen with thirst; he re-lieved its fever by thrusting it forward from between his teeth into the cold air. How softly the turf had carpeted the untraveled avenue—he could no longer feel the roadway beneath his feet!

Doubtless, despite his suffering, he had fallen asleep while walking, for now he sees another scene—perhaps he has merely recovered from a delirium. He stands at the gate of his own home. All is as he left it, and all bright and beauti-ful in the morning sunshine. He must have traveled the entire night. As he pushes open the gate and passes up the wide white walk, he sees a flutter of female gar-ments; his wife, looking fresh and cool and sweet, steps down from the veranda to meet him. At the bottom of the steps she stands waiting, with a smile of inef-fable joy, an attitude of matchless grace and dignity. Ah, how beautiful she is! He springs forward with extended arms. As he is about to clasp her he feels a stunning blow upon the back of the neck; a blinding white light blazes all about him with a sound like the shock of a cannon—then all is darkness and silence!

Peyton Farquhar was dead; his body, with a broken neck, swung gently from side to side beneath the timbers of the Owl Creek bridge.

### Study and Discussion Questions

1. How does Bierce work to make us think Farquhar's imagined escape is real? What hints are there along the way that it is in fact imaginary?
2. Trace Bierce's manipulation of point of view throughout the story. What does it accomplish? Why does Bierce narrate the events leading up to the hanging in a flashback in Part II rather than at the beginning of the story?
3. Characterize the way Bierce describes the hanging proceedings in the first two paragraphs. Compare it to the way he describes Farquhar's imaginary escape. What does this contrast in style suggest?

4. Why do you think Bierce, who himself volunteered to fight on the Union side in the Civil War, makes his hero a Southern planter, a slave owner, a supporter of the Confederates? How does this choice shape the kind of statement the story makes about war?

### Suggestions for Writing

1. One critic has argued that the story makes fun of "the orthodox war yarn in which the hero's death or survival is noble and significant." Interpret the story taking this statement as your thesis. (You might begin by reexamining the characterization of Farquhar in Part II.)
2. How would you go about making a film of this story? How would you handle the shifts in point of view, the flashback, and the imaginary nature of Farquhar's escape? (If you've seen and remember a film version, discuss how well you think it does the job.)

### Critical Resources

1. *An Occurrence at Owl Creek Bridge.* Director Brian James Egen. Performers Bradley M. Egen, Jody Chansuolme. Owl Creek Productions, 2003. For more information see <http://www.owlcreekproductions.com/>. This is most recent film adaptation. Robert Enrico's 1962 (28-minute) version is another notable interpretation of Bierce's story.
2. Blume, Donald. *Ambrose Bierce's Civilians and Soldiers in Context: A Critical Study.* Kent, OH: Kent State Press, 2004.
3. Evans, Robert, ed. *Ambrose Bierce's An Occurrence at Owl Creek Bridge: An Annotated Critical Edition.* West Cornwall CT: Locust Hill, 2003.
4. Gale, Robert. *An Ambrose Bierce Companion.* Westport, CI: Greenwood Press, 2001.
5. Stoicheff, Peter. "Something Uncanny: The Dream Structure in Ambrose Bierce's An Occurrence at Owl Creek Bridge." *Studies in Short Fiction* 30.3 (1993): 349–58.

## RAY BRADBURY

## *August 2026: There Will Come Soft Rains*                    (1950)

In the living room the voice-clock sang, *Tick-tock, seven o'clock, time to get up, time to get up, seven o'clock!* as if it were afraid that nobody would. The morning house lay empty. The clock ticked on, repeating and repeating its sounds into the emptiness. *Seven-nine, breakfast time, seven-nine!*

In the kitchen the breakfast stove gave a hissing sigh and ejected from its warm interior eight pieces of perfectly browned toast, eight eggs sunnyside up, sixteen slices of bacon, two coffees, and two cool glasses of milk.

"Today is August 4, 2026," said a second voice from the kitchen ceiling, "in the city of Allendale, California." It repeated the date three times for memory's sake. "Today is Mr. Featherstone's birthday. Today is the anniversary of Tilita's marriage. Insurance is payable, as are the water, gas, and light bills."

Somewhere in the walls, relays clicked, memory tapes glided under electric eyes.

*Eight-one, tick-tock, eight-one o'clock, off to school, off to work, run, run, eight-one!* But no doors slammed, no carpets took the soft tread of rubber heels. It was raining outside. The weather box on the front door sang quietly: "Rain, rain, go away; rubbers, raincoats for today . . ." And the rain tapped on the empty house, echoing.

Outside, the garage chimed and lifted its door to reveal the waiting car. After a long wait the door swung down again.

At eight-thirty the eggs were shriveled and the toast was like stone. An aluminum wedge scraped them into the sink, where hot water whirled them down a metal throat which digested and flushed them away to the distant sea. The dirty dishes were dropped into a hot washer and emerged twinkling dry.

*Nine-fifteen,* sang the clock, *time to clean.*

Out of warrens in the wall, tiny robot mice darted. The rooms were acrawl with the small cleaning animals, all rubber and metal. They thudded against chairs, whirling their mustached runners, kneading the rug nap, sucking gently at hidden dust. Then, like mysterious invaders, they popped into their burrows. Their pink electric eyes faded. The house was clean.

*Ten o'clock.* The sun came out from behind the rain. The house stood alone in a city of rubble and ashes. This was the one house left standing. At night the ruined city gave off a radioactive glow which could be seen for miles.

*Ten-fifteen.* The garden sprinklers whirled up in golden founts, filling the soft morning air with scatterings of brightness. The water pelted window-panes, running down the charred west side where the house had been burned evenly free of its white paint. The entire west face of the house was black, save for five places. Here the silhouette in paint of a man mowing a lawn. Here, as in a photograph, a woman bent to pick flowers. Still farther over, their images burned on wood in one titanic instant, a small boy, hands flung into the air; higher up, the image of a thrown ball, and opposite him a girl, hands raised to catch a ball which never came down.

The five spots of paint—the man, the woman, the children, the ball—remained. The rest was a thin charcoaled layer.

The gentle sprinkler rain filled the garden with falling light.

Until this day, how well the house had kept its peace. How carefully it had inquired, "Who goes there? What's the password?" and, getting no answer from lonely foxes and whining cats, it had shut up its windows and drawn shades in an old-maidenly preoccupation with self-protection which bordered on a mechanical paranoia.

It quivered at each sound, the house did. If a sparrow brushed a window, the shade snapped up. The bird, startled, flew off! No, not even a bird must touch the house!

The house was an altar with ten thousand attendants, big, small, servicing, attending, in choirs. But the gods had gone away, and the ritual of the religion continued senselessly, uselessly.

*Twelve noon.*

A dog whined, shivering, on the front porch.

The front door recognized the dog voice and opened. The dog, once huge and fleshy, but now gone to bone and covered with sores, moved in and through the house, tracking mud. Behind it whirred angry mice, angry at having to pick up mud, angry at inconvenience.

For not a leaf fragment blew under the door but what the wall panels flipped open and the copper scrap rats flashed swiftly out. The offending dust, hair, or paper, seized in miniature steel jaws, was raced back to the burrows. There, down tubes which fed into the cellar, it was dropped into the sighing vent of an incinerator which sat like evil Baal in a dark corner.

The dog ran upstairs, hysterically yelping to each door, at last realizing, as the house realized, that only silence was here.

It sniffed the air and scratched the kitchen door. Behind the door, the stove was making pancakes which filled the house with a rich baked odor and the scent of maple syrup.

The dog frothed at the mouth, lying at the door, sniffing, its eyes turned to fire. It ran wildly in circles, biting at its tail, spun in a frenzy, and died. It lay in the parlor for an hour.

*Two o'clock,* sang a voice.

Delicately sensing decay at last, the regiments of mice hummed out as softly as blown gray leaves in an electrical wind.

*Two-fifteen.*

The dog was gone.

In the cellar, the incinerator glowed suddenly and a whirl of sparks leaped up the chimney.

*Two thirty-five.*

Bridge tables sprouted from patio walls. Playing cards fluttered onto pads in a shower of pips. Martinis manifested on an oaken bench with egg-salad sandwiches. Music played.

But the tables were silent and the cards untouched.

At four o'clock the tables folded like great butterflies back through the paneled walls.

*Four-thirty.*

The nursery walls glowed.

Animals took shape: yellow giraffes, blue lions, pink antelopes, lilac panthers cavorting in crystal substance. The walls were glass. They looked out upon color and fantasy. Hidden films clocked through well-oiled sprockets, and the walls lived. The nursery floor was woven to resemble a crisp, cereal meadow. Over this ran aluminum roaches and iron crickets, and in the hot still air butterflies of delicate red tissue wavered among the sharp aroma of animal spoors! There was the sound like a great matted yellow hive of bees within a dark bellows, the lazy bumble of a purring lion. And there was the patter of okapi feet and the murmur of a fresh jungle rain, like other hoofs, falling upon the summer-starched grass. Now the walls dissolved into distances of parched weed, mile on mile, and warm endless sky. The animals drew away into thorn brakes and water holes.

It was the children's hour.

*Five o'clock.* The bath filled with clear hot water.

*Six, seven, eight o'clock.* The dinner dishes manipulated like magic tricks, and in the study a click. In the metal stand opposite the hearth where a fire now blazed up warmly, a cigar popped out, half an inch of soft gray ash on it, smoking, waiting.

*Nine o'clock.* The beds warmed their hidden circuits, for nights were cool here.

*Nine-five.* A voice spoke from the study ceiling:

"Mrs. McClellan, which poem would you like this evening?"

The house was silent.

The voice said at last, "Since you express no preference, I shall select a poem at random." Quiet music rose to back the voice. "Sara Teasdale.[1] As I recall, your favorite...."

"There will come soft rains and the smell of the ground,
And swallows circling with their shimmering sound;

And frogs in the pools singing at night,
And wild plum trees in tremulous white;

Robins will wear their feathery fire,
Whistling their whims on a low fence-wire;

And not one will know of the war, not one
Will care at last when it is done.

Not one would mind, neither bird nor tree,
If mankind perished utterly;

And Spring herself, when she woke at dawn
Would scarcely know that we were gone."

---

[1]American poet (1884–1933).

The fire burned on the stone hearth and the cigar fell away into a mound of quiet ash on its tray. The empty chairs faced each other between the silent walls, and the music played.

At ten o'clock the house began to die.

The wind blew. A falling tree bough crashed through the kitchen window. Cleaning solvent, bottled, shattered over the stove. The room was ablaze in an instant!

"Fire!" screamed a voice. The house lights flashed, water pumps shot water from the ceilings. But the solvent spread on the linoleum, licking, eating, under the kitchen door, while the voices took it up in chorus: "Fire, fire, fire!"

The house tried to save itself. Doors sprang tightly shut, but the windows were broken by the heat and the wind blew and sucked upon the fire.

The house gave ground as the fire in ten billion angry sparks moved with flaming ease from room to room and then up the stairs. While scurrying water rats squeaked from the walls, pistoled their water, and ran for more. And the wall sprays let down showers of mechanical rain.

But too late. Somewhere, sighing, a pump shrugged to a stop. The quenching rain ceased. The reserve water supply which had filled baths and washed dishes for many quiet days was gone.

The fire crackled up the stairs. It fed upon Picassos and Matisses in the upper halls, like delicacies, baking off the oily flesh, tenderly crisping the canvases into black shavings.

Now the fire lay in beds, stood in windows, changed the colors of drapes!

And then, reinforcements.

From attic trapdoors, blind robot faces peered down with faucet mouths gushing green chemical.

The fire backed off, as even an elephant must at the sight of a dead snake. Now there were twenty snakes whipping over the floor, killing the fire with a clear cold venom of green froth.

But the fire was clever. It had sent flame outside the house, up through the attic to the pumps there. An explosion! The attic brain which directed the pumps was shattered into bronze shrapnel on the beams.

The fire rushed back into every closet and felt of the clothes hung there.

The house shuddered, oak bone on bone, its bared skeleton cringing from the heat, its wire, its nerves revealed as if a surgeon had torn the skin off to let the red veins and capillaries quiver in the scalded air. Help, help! Fire! Run, run! Heat snapped mirrors like the first brittle winter ice. And the voices wailed Fire, fire, run, run, like a tragic nursery rhyme, a dozen voices, high, low, like children dying in a forest, alone, alone. And the voices fading as the wires popped their sheatings like hot chestnuts. One, two, three, four, five voices died.

In the nursery the jungle burned. Blue lions roared, purple giraffes bounded off. The panthers ran in circles, changing color, and ten million animals, running before the fire, vanished off toward a distant steaming river....

Ten more voices died. In the last instant under the fire avalanche, other choruses, oblivious, could be heard announcing the time, playing music, cutting the lawn by remote-control mower, or setting an umbrella frantically out and in the slamming and opening front door, a thousand things happening, like a clock shop when each clock strikes the hour insanely before or after the other, a scene of maniac confusion, yet unity; singing, screaming, a few last cleaning mice darting bravely out to carry the horrid ashes away! And one voice, with sublime disregard for the situation, read poetry aloud in the fiery study, until all the film spools burned, until all the wires withered and the circuits cracked.

The fire burst the house and let it slam flat down, puffing out skirts of spark and smoke.

In the kitchen, an instant before the rain of fire and timber, the stove could be seen making breakfasts at a psychopathic rate, ten dozen eggs, six loaves of toast, twenty dozen bacon strips, which, eaten by fire, started the stove working again, hysterically hissing!

The crash. The attic smashing into kitchen and parlor. The parlor into cellar, cellar into sub-cellar. Deep freeze, armchair, film tapes, circuits, beds, and all like skeletons thrown in a cluttered mound deep under.

Smoke and silence. A great quantity of smoke.

Dawn showed faintly in the east. Among the ruins, one wall stood alone. Within the wall, a last voice said, over and over again and again, even as the sun rose to shine upon the heaped rubble and steam:

"Today is August 5, 2026, today is August 5, 2026, today is. . . ."

### Study and Discussion Questions

1. Think about the Sara Teasdale poem that gives the story its title. How does it apply to the situation the story narrates?
2. Who is the main character of this story?
3. Summarize the story's plot. What does Bradbury use to move you from one event to the next?
4. Though there are no actual human beings in this story, list some of the traces or evidence of people.
5. What can this house do? What can't it do?
6. What is the mood or atmosphere of "August 2026: There Will Come Soft Rains"? What words and images create this mood?
7. Discuss the significance and the use of time in this story.

### Suggestions for Writing

1. This is a rare example of a story without any human beings in it. How is that absence necessary to the meaning of this story?
2. Compare/contrast this science fiction story with Pamela Zoline's "The Heat Death of the Universe" (Varieties of Protest).
3. Bradbury writes, "The house was an altar with ten thousand attendants, big, small, servicing, attending, in choirs. But the gods had gone away, and

the ritual of the religion continued senselessly, uselessly." Discuss this passage as a comment on our current relation to science and technology.

### Critical Resources

1. Aggelis, Steven. *Conversations with Ray Bradbury.* Jackson: University of Mississippi Press, 2004.
2. Eller, Jonathon and William Touponce, eds. *Ray Bradbury: The Life of Fiction.* Kent, OH.: Kent State Press, 2004.
3. Gallagher, Edward. "The Thematic Structure of The Martian Chronicles." *Ray Bradbury.* Joseph Olander, Ed. New York: Taplinger, 1980.
4. Reid, Robin. *Ray Bradbury: A Critical Companion.* Westport, CT: Greenwood Press, 2000.

❀ ❀ ❀

## LOUISE ERDRICH

## *The Red Convertible* (1984)

I was the first one to drive a convertible on my reservation. And of course it was red, a red Olds. I owned that car along with my brother Henry Junior. We owned it together until his boots filled with water on a windy night and he bought out my share. Now Henry owns the whole car, and his younger brother Lyman (that's myself), Lyman walks everywhere he goes.

How did I earn enough money to buy my share in the first place? My one talent was I could always make money. I had a touch for it, unusual in a Chippewa. From the first I was different that way, and everyone recognized it. I was the only kid they let in the American Legion Hall to shine shoes, for example, and one Christmas I sold spiritual bouquets for the mission door to door. The nuns let me keep a percentage. Once I started, it seemed the more money I made the easier the money came. Everyone encouraged it. When I was fifteen I got a job washing dishes at the Joliet Café, and that was where my first big break happened.

It wasn't long before I was promoted to bussing tables, and then the short-order cook quit and I was hired to take her place. No sooner than you know it I was managing the Joliet. The rest is history. I went on managing. I soon become part owner, and of course there was no stopping me then. It wasn't long before the whole thing was mine.

After I'd owned the Joliet for one year, it blew over in the worst tornado ever seen around here. The whole operation was smashed to bits. A total loss. The fryalator was up in a tree, the grill torn in half like it was paper. I was only sixteen. I had it all in my mother's name, and I lost it quick, but before I lost it I had every one of my relatives, and their relatives, to dinner, and I also bought that red Olds I mentioned, along with Henry.

The first time we saw it! I'll tell you when we first saw it. We had gotten a ride up to Winnipeg, and both of us had money. Don't ask me why, because we never mentioned a car or anything, we just had all our money. Mine was cash, a big bankroll from the Joliet's insurance. Henry had two checks—a week's extra pay for being laid off, and his regular check from the Jewel Bearing Plant.

We were walking down Portage anyway, seeing the sights, when we saw it. There it was, parked, large as life. Really as *if* it was alive. I thought of the word *repose,* because the car wasn't simply stopped, parked, or whatever. That car reposed, calm and gleaming, a FOR SALE sign in its left front window. Then, before we had thought it over at all, the car belonged to us and our pockets were empty. We had just enough money for gas back home.

We went places in that car, me and Henry. We took off driving all one whole summer. We started off toward the Little Knife River and Mandaree in Fort Berthold and then we found ourselves down in Wakpala somehow, and then suddenly we were over in Montana on the Rocky Boys, and yet the summer was not even half over. Some people hang on to details when they travel, but we didn't let them bother us and just lived our everyday lives here to there.

I do remember this one place with willows. I remember I laid under those trees and it was comfortable. So comfortable. The branches bent down all around me like a tent or a stable. And quiet, it was quiet, even though there was a powwow close enough so I could see it going on. The air was not too still, not too windy either. When the dust rises up and hangs in the air around the dancers like that, I feel good. Henry was asleep with his arms thrown wide. Later on, he woke up and we started driving again. We were somewhere in Montana, or maybe on the Blood Reserve—it could have been anywhere. Anyway it was where we met the girl.

All her hair was in buns around her ears, that's the first thing I noticed about her. She was posed alongside the road with her arm out, so we stopped. That girl was short, so short her lumber shirt looked comical on her, like a nightgown. She had jeans on and fancy moccasins and she carried a little suitcase.

"Hop on in," says Henry. So she climbs in between us.

"We'll take you home," I says. "Where do you live?"

"Chicken," she says.

"Where the hell's that?" I ask her.

"Alaska."

"Okay," says Henry, and we drive.

We got up there and never wanted to leave. The sun doesn't truly set there in summer, and the night is more a soft dusk. You might doze off, sometimes, but before you know it you're up again, like an animal in nature. You never feel like you have to sleep hard or put away the world. And things would grow up there. One day just dirt or moss, the next day flowers and long grass. The girl's name was Susy. Her family really took to us. They fed us and put us up. We had our own tent to live in by their house, and the kids would be in and out of there all day and night. They couldn't get over me and Henry being brothers, we looked so different. We told them we knew we had the same mother, anyway.

One night Susy came in to visit us. We sat around in the tent talking of this thing and that. The season was changing. It was getting darker by that time, and the cold was even getting just a little mean. I told her it was time for us to go. She stood up on a chair.

"You never seen my hair," Susy said.

That was true. She was standing on a chair, but still, when she unclipped her buns the hair reached all the way to the ground. Our eyes opened. You couldn't tell how much hair she had when it was rolled up so neatly. Then my brother Henry did something funny. He went up to the chair and said, "Jump on my shoulders." So she did that, and her hair reached down past his waist, and he started twirling, this way and that, so her hair was flung out from side to side.

"I always wondered what it was like to have long pretty hair," Henry says. Well we laughed. It was a funny sight, the way he did it. The next morning we got up and took leave of those people.

On to greener pastures, as they say. It was down through Spokane and across Idaho then Montana and very soon we were racing the weather right along under the Canadian border through Columbus, Des Lacs, and then we were in Bottineau County and soon home. We'd made most of the trip, that summer, without putting up the car hood at all. We got home just in time, it turned out, for the army to remember Henry had signed up to join it.

I don't wonder that the army was so glad to get my brother that they turned him into a Marine. He was built like a brick outhouse anyway. We liked to tease him that they really wanted him for his Indian nose. He had a nose big and sharp as a hatchet, like the nose on Red Tomahawk, the Indian who killed Sitting Bull, whose profile is on signs all along the North Dakota highways. Henry went off to training camp, came home once during Christmas, then the next thing you know we got an overseas letter from him. It was 1970, and he said he was stationed up in the northern hill country. Whereabouts I did not know. He wasn't such a hot letter writer, and only got off two before the enemy caught him. I could never keep it straight, which direction those good Vietnam soldiers were from.

I wrote him back several times, even though I didn't know if those letters would get through. I kept him informed all about the car. Most of the time I had it up on blocks in the yard or half taken apart, because that long trip did a hard job on it under the hood.

I always had good luck with numbers, and never worried about the draft myself. I never even had to think about what my number was. But Henry was never lucky in the same way as me. It was at least three years before Henry came home. By then I guess the whole war was solved in the government's mind, but for him it would keep on going. In those years I'd put his car into almost perfect shape. I always thought of it as his car while he was gone, even though when he left he said, "Now it's yours," and threw me his key.

"Thanks for the extra key," I'd said. "I'll put it up in your drawer just in case I need it." He laughed.

When he came home, though, Henry was very different, and I'll say this: the change was no good. You could hardly expect him to change for the better, I know. But he was quiet, so quiet, and never comfortable sitting still anywhere but always up and moving around. I thought back to times we'd sat still for whole afternoons, never moving a muscle, just shifting our weight along the ground, talking to whoever sat with us, watching things. He'd always had a joke, then, too, and now you couldn't get him to laugh, or when he did it was more the sound of a man choking, a sound that stopped up the throats of other people around him. They got to leaving him alone most of the time, and I didn't blame them. It was a fact: Henry was jumpy and mean.

I'd bought a color TV set for my mom and the rest of us while Henry was away. Money still came very easy. I was sorry I'd ever bought it though, because of Henry. I was also sorry I'd bought color, because with black-and-white the pictures seem older and farther away. But what are you going to do? He sat in front of it, watching it, and that was the only time he was completely still. But it was the kind of stillness that you see in a rabbit when it freezes and before it will bolt. He was not easy. He sat in his chair gripping the armrests with all his might, as if the chair itself was moving at a high speed and if he let go at all he would rocket forward and maybe crash right through the set.

Once I was in the room watching TV with Henry and I heard his teeth click at something. I looked over, and he'd bitten through his lip. Blood was going down his chin. I tell you right then I wanted to smash that tube to pieces. I went over to it but Henry must have known what I was up to. He rushed from his chair and shoved me out of the way, against the wall. I told myself he didn't know what he was doing.

My mom came in, turned the set off real quiet, and told us she had made something for supper. So we went and sat down. There was still blood going down Henry's chin, but he didn't notice it and no one said anything, even though every time he took a bite of his bread his blood fell onto it until he was eating his own blood mixed in with the food.

While Henry was not around we talked about what was going to happen to him. There were no Indian doctors on the reservation, and my mom was afraid of trusting Old Man Pillager because he courted her long ago and was jealous of her husbands. He might take revenge through her son. We were afraid that if we brought Henry to a regular hospital they would keep him.

"They don't fix them in those places," Mom said; "they just give them drugs."

"We wouldn't get him there in the first place," I agreed, "so let's just forget about it."

Then I thought about the car.

Henry had not even looked at the car since he'd gotten home, though like I said, it was in tip-top condition and ready to drive. I thought the car might bring the old Henry back somehow. So I bided my time and waited for my chance to interest him in the vehicle.

One night Henry was off somewhere. I took myself a hammer. I went out to that car and I did a number on its underside. Whacked it up. Bent the tail pipe double. Ripped the muffler loose. By the time I was done with the car it looked worse than any typical Indian car that has been driven all its life on reservation roads, which they always say are like government promises—full of holes. It just about hurt me, I'll tell you that! I threw dirt in the carburetor and I ripped all the electric tape off the seats. I made it look just as beat up as I could. Then I sat back and waited for Henry to find it.

Still, it took him over a month. That was all right, because it was just getting warm enough, not melting, but warm enough to work outside.

"Lyman," he says, walking in one day, "that red car looks like shit."

'Well it's old," I says. "You got to expect that."

"No way!" says Henry. "That car's a classic! But you went and ran the piss right out of it, Lyman, and you know it don't deserve that. I kept that car in A-one shape. You don't remember. You're too young. But when I left, that car was running like a watch. Now I don't even know if I can get it to start again, let alone get it anywhere near its old condition."

"Well you try," I said, like I was getting mad, "but I say it's a piece of junk."

Then I walked out before he could realize I knew he'd strung together more than six words at once.

After that I thought he'd freeze himself to death working on that car. He was out there all day, and at night he rigged up a little lamp, ran a cord out the window, and had himself some light to see by while he worked. He was better than he had been before, but that's still not saying much. It was easier for him to do the things the rest of us did. He ate more slowly and didn't jump up and down during the meal to get this or that or look out the window. I put my hand in the back of the TV set, I admit, and fiddled around with it good, so that it was almost impossible now to get a clear picture. He didn't look at it very often anyway. He was always out with that car or going off to get parts for it. By the time it was really melting outside, he had it fixed.

I had been feeling down in the dumps about Henry around this time. We had always been together before. Henry and Lyman. But he was such a loner now that I didn't know how to take it. So I jumped at the chance one day when Henry seemed friendly. It's not that he smiled or anything. He just said, "Let's take that old shitbox for a spin." Just the way he said it made me think he could be coming around.

We went out to the car. It was spring. The sun was shining very bright. My only sister, Bonita, who was just eleven years old, came out and made us stand together for a picture. Henry leaned his elbow on the red car's windshield, and he took his other arm and put it over my shoulder, very carefully, as though it was heavy for him to lift and he didn't want to bring the weight down all at once.

"Smile," Bonita said, and he did.

That picture. I never look at it anymore. A few months ago, I don't know why, I got his picture out and tacked it on the wall. I felt good about Henry at the time, close to him. I felt good having his picture on the wall, until one night when I was looking at television. I was a little drunk and stoned. I looked up at the wall and Henry was staring at me. I don't know what it was, but his smile had changed, or maybe it was gone. All I know is I couldn't stay in the same room with that picture. I was shaking. I got up, closed the door, and went into the kitchen. A little later my friend Ray came over and we both went back into that room. We put the picture in a brown bag, folded the bag over and over tightly, then put it way back in a closet.

I still see that picture now, as if it tugs at me, whenever I pass that closet door. The picture is very clear in my mind. It was so sunny that day Henry had to squint against the glare. Or maybe the camera Bonita held flashed like a mirror, blinding him, before she snapped the picture. My face is right out in the sun, big and round. But he might have drawn back, because the shadows on his face are deep as holes. There are two shadows curved like little hooks around the ends of his smile, as if to frame it and try to keep it there—that one, first smile that looked like it might have hurt his face. He has his field jacket on and the worn-in clothes he'd come back in and kept wearing ever since. After Bonita took the picture, she went into the house and we got into the car. There was a full cooler in the trunk. We started off, east, toward Pembina and the Red River because Henry said he wanted to see the high water.

The trip over there was beautiful. When everything starts changing, drying up, clearing off, you feel like your whole life is starting. Henry felt it, too. The top was down and the car hummed like a top. He'd really put it back in shape, even the tape on the seats was very carefully put down and glued back in layers. It's not that he smiled again or even joked, but his face looked to me as if it was clear, more peaceful. It looked as though he wasn't thinking of anything in particular except the bare fields and windbreaks and houses we were passing.

The river was high and full of winter trash when we got there. The sun was still out, but it was colder by the river. There were still little clumps of dirty snow here and there on the banks. The water hadn't gone over the banks yet, but it would, you could tell. It was just at its limit, hard swollen, glossy like an old gray scar. We made ourselves a fire, and we sat down and watched the current go. As I watched it I felt something squeezing inside me and tightening and trying to let go all at the same time. I knew I was not just feeling it myself; I knew I was feeling what Henry was going through at that moment. Except that I couldn't stand it, the closing and opening. I jumped to my feet. I took Henry by the shoulders and I started shaking him. "Wake up," I says, "wake up, wake up, wake up!" I didn't know what had come over me. I sat down beside him again.

His face was totally white and hard. Then it broke, like stones break all of a sudden when water boils up inside them.

"I know it," he says. "I know it. I can't help it. It's no use."

We start talking. He said he knew what I'd done with the car. It was obvious it had been whacked out of shape and not just neglected. He said he wanted to give the car to me for good now, it was no use. He said he'd fixed it just to give it back and I should take it.

"No way," I says, "I don't want it."

"That's okay," he says, "you take it."

"I don't want it, though," I says back to him, and then to emphasize, just to emphasize, you understand, I touch his shoulder. He slaps my hand off.

"Take that car," he says.

"No," I say, "make me," I say, and then he grabs my jacket and rips the arm loose. That jacket is a class act, suede with tags and zippers. I push Henry backwards, off the log. He jumps up and bowls me over. We go down in a clinch and come up swinging hard, for all we're worth, with our fists. He socks my jaw so hard I feel like it swings loose. Then I'm at his ribcage and land a good one under his chin so his head snaps back. He's dazzled. He looks at me and I look at him and then his eyes are full of tears and blood and at first I think he's crying. But no, he's laughing. "Ha! Ha!" he says. "Ha! Ha! Take good care of it."

"Okay," I says, "okay, no problem. Ha! Ha!"

I can't help it, and I start laughing, too. My face feels fat and strange, and after a while I get a beer from the cooler in the trunk, and when I hand it to Henry he takes his shirt and wipes my germs off. "Hoof-and-mouth disease," he says. For some reason this cracks me up, and so we're really laughing for a while, and then we drink all the rest of the beers one by one and throw them in the river and see how far, how fast, the current takes them before they fill up and sink.

"You want to go on back?" I ask after a while. "Maybe we could snag a couple nice Kashpaw girls."

He says nothing. But I can tell his mood is turning again.

"They're all crazy, the girls up here, every damn one of them."

"You're crazy too," I say, to jolly him up. "Crazy Lamartine boys!"

He looks as though he will take this wrong at first. His face twists, then clears, and he jumps up on his feet. "That's right!" he says. "Crazier 'n hell. Crazy Indians!"

I think it's the old Henry again. He throws off his jacket and starts swinging his legs out from the knees like a fancy dancer. He's down doing something between a grouse dance and a bunny hop, no kind of dance I ever saw before, but neither has anyone else on all this green growing earth. He's wild. He wants to pitch whoopee! He's up and at me and all over. All this time I'm laughing so hard, so hard my belly is getting tied up in a knot.

"Got to cool me off!" he shouts all of a sudden. Then he runs over to the river and jumps in.

There's boards and other things in the current. It's so high. No sound comes from the river after the splash he makes, so I run right over. I look around. It's getting dark. I see he's halfway across the water already, and I know he didn't swim there but the current took him. It's far. I hear his voice, though, very clearly across it.

"My boots are filling," he says.

He says this in a normal voice, like he just noticed and he doesn't know what to think of it. Then he's gone. A branch comes by. Another branch. And I go in.

By the time I get out of the river, off the snag I pulled myself onto, the sun is down. I walk back to the car, turn on the high beams, and drive it up the bank. I put it in first gear and then I take my foot off the clutch. I get out, close the door, and watch it plow softly into the water. The headlights reach in as they go down, searching, still lighted even after the water swirls over the back end. I wait. The wires short out. It is all finally dark. And then there is only the water, the sound of it going and running and going and running and running.

### Study and Discussion Questions

1. How does the tone of the story shift when Henry returns from Vietnam?
2. How has Henry changed now that he's back from Vietnam?
3. List the various ways that Erdrich gives us clues throughout "The Red Convertible" about how it will end.
4. What are the phases the car goes through? How do these stand for what Lyman and Henry are going through?
5. What does the description of Henry's picture tell us about Henry? About the narrator Lyman? Why is the picture incident placed where it is in the story?
6. Why do Henry and Lyman fight down by the river?
7. How does the first paragraph of the story manage to tell us exactly what the end of the story will be and yet not give that ending away?

### Suggestions for Writing

1. Discuss the image of the red convertible's "drowning." Why does Lyman send the car into the water? Why do you think the car's lights are left on?
2. Are there any ways in which Erdrich suggests that being Native Americans shapes Henry's and Lyman's experience?
3. Pick one incident in the story (e.g., the visit to long-haired Susy in Alaska, or Henry's watching TV and biting through his lip) and discuss why you think Erdrich included it.

### Critical Resources

1. Chavkin, Allan, ed. *The Chippewa Landscape of Louise Erdrich.* Tuscaloosa: University of Alabama Press, 1999.

2. Stookey, Lorena. *Louise Erdrich: A Critical Companion.* Westport, CT: Greenwood Press, 1999.
3. Wong, Hertha. *Louise Erdrich's Love Medicine: A Casebook.* New York: Oxford University Press, 2000.

❀ ❀ ❀

## GHASSAN KANAFANI

## *Letter from Gaza*                                                    (1956)

DEAR MUSTAFA,

I have now received your letter, in which you tell me that you've done everything necessary to enable me to stay with you in Sacramento. I've also received news that I have been accepted in the department of Civil Engineering in the University of California. I must thank you for everything, my friend. But it'll strike you as rather odd when I proclaim this news to you—and make no doubt about it, I feel no hesitation at all, in fact I am pretty well positive that I have never seen things so clearly as I do now. No, my friend, I have changed my mind. I won't follow you to "the land where there is greenery, water, and lovely faces," as you wrote. No, I'll stay here, and I won't ever leave.

I am really upset that our lives won't continue to follow the same course, Mustafa. For I can almost hear you reminding me of our vow to go on together, and of the way we used to shout: "We'll get rich!" But there's nothing I can do, my friend. Yes, I still remember the day when I stood in the hall of Cairo airport, pressing your hand and staring at the frenzied motor. At that moment everything was rotating in time with the ear-splitting motor, and you stood in front of me, your round face silent.

Your face hadn't changed from the way it used to be when you were growing up in the Shajiya quarter of Gaza, apart from those slight wrinkles. We grew up together, understanding each other completely, and we promised to go on together till the end. But ...

"There's a quarter of an hour left before the plane takes off. Don't look into space like that. Listen! You'll go to Kuwait next year, and you'll save enough from your salary to uproot you from Gaza and transplant you to California. We started off together and we must carry on. . . ."

At that moment I was watching your rapidly moving lips. That was always your manner of speaking, without commas or full stops. But in an obscure way I felt that you were not completely happy with your flight. You couldn't give three good reasons for it. I too suffered from this wrench, but the clearest thought was: why don't we abandon this Gaza and flee? Why don't we? Your situation had begun to improve, however. The Ministry of Education in Kuwait had given you a contract, though it hadn't given me one. In the trough of misery where I existed, you sent me small sums of money. You wanted me to consider them as loans, because you feared that I would feel slighted. You knew my family circumstances in and out; you knew that my meagre salary in the UN-RWA schools was inadequate to support my mother, my brother's widow, and her four children.

"Listen carefully. Write to me every day ... every hour ... every minute! The plane's just leaving. Farewell! Or rather, till we meet again!"

Your cold lips brushed my cheek, you turned your face away from me towards the plane, and when you looked at me again I could see your tears.

Later the Ministry of Education in Kuwait gave me a contract. There's no need to repeat to you how my life there went in detail. I always wrote to you about everything. My life there had a gluey, vacuous quality as though I were a small oyster, lost in oppressive loneliness, slowly struggling with a future as dark as the beginning of the night, caught in a rotten routine, a spewed-out combat with time. Everything was hot and sticky. There was a slipperiness to my whole life, it was all a hankering for the end of the month.

In the middle of the year, that year, the Jews bombarded the central district of Sabha and attacked Gaza, our Gaza, with bombs and flamethrowers. That event might have made some change in my routine, but there was nothing for me to take much notice of; I was going to leave this Gaza behind me and go to California where I would live for myself, my own self which had suffered so long. I hated Gaza and its inhabitants. Everything in the amputated town reminded me of failed pictures painted in gray by a sick man. Yes, I would send my mother and my brother's widow and her children a meagre sum to help them to live, but I would liberate myself from this last tie too, there in green California, far from the reek of defeat that for seven years had filled my nostrils. The sympathy that bound me to my brother's children, their mother, and mine would never be enough to justify my tragedy in taking this perpendicular dive. It mustn't drag me any farther down than it already had. I must flee!

You know these feelings, Mustafa, because you've really experienced them. What is this ill-defined tie we had with Gaza that blunted our enthusiasm for flight? Why didn't we analyze the matter in such a way as to give it a clear meaning? Why didn't we leave this defeat with its wounds behind us and move on to a brighter future that would give us deeper consolation! Why? We didn't exactly know.

When I went on holiday in June and assembled all my possessions, longing for the sweet departure, the start towards those little things which give life a nice, bright meaning, I found Gaza just as I had known it, closed like the introverted lining of a rusted snail-shell thrown up by the waves on the sticky, sandy shore by the slaughterhouse. This Gaza was more cramped than the mind of a sleeper in the throes of a fearful nightmare, with its narrow streets that had their peculiar smell, the smell of defeat and poverty, its houses with their bulging balconies ... this Gaza! But what are the obscure causes that draw a man to his family, his house, his memories, as a spring draws a small flock of mountain goats? I don't know. All I know is that I went to my mother in our house that morning. When I arrived my late brother's wife met me there and asked me, weeping, if I would do as her wounded daughter, Nadia, in Gaza hospital wished and visit her that evening. Do you know Nadia, my brother's beautiful thirteen-year-old daughter?

That evening I bought a pound of apples and set out for the hospital to visit Nadia. I knew that there was something about it that my mother and my sister-in-law were hiding from me, something that their tongues could not utter, something strange that I could not put my finger on. I loved Nadia from habit, the same habit that made me love all that generation which had been so brought up on defeat and displacement that it had come to think that a happy life was a kind of social deviation.

What happened at that moment? I don't know. I entered the white room very calm. Ill children have something of saintliness, and how much more so if the child is ill as a result of cruel, painful wounds. Nadia was lying on her bed, her back propped up on a big pillow over which her hair was spread like a thick pelt. There was a profound silence in her wide eyes and a tear always shining in the depths of her black pupils. Her face was calm and still but eloquent as the face of a tortured prophet might be. Nadia was still a child, but she seemed more than a child, much more, and older than a child, much older.

"Nadia!"

I've no idea whether I was the one who said it, or whether it was someone else behind me. But she raised her eyes to me and I felt them dissolve me like a piece of sugar that had fallen into a hot cup of tea. Together with her slight smile I heard her voice.

"Uncle! Have you just come from Kuwait?"

Her voice broke in her throat, and she raised herself with the help of her hands and stretched out her neck towards me. I patted her back and sat down near her.

"Nadia! I've brought you presents from Kuwait, lots of presents. I'll wait till you can leave your bed, completely well and healed, and you'll come to my house and I'll give them to you. I've bought you the red trousers you wrote and asked me for. Yes, I've bought them."

It was a lie, born of the tense situation, but as I uttered it I felt that I was speaking the truth for the first time. Nadia trembled as though she had had an electric shock, and lowered her head in a terrible silence. I felt her tears wetting the back of my hand.

"Say something, Nadia! Don't you want the red trousers?"

She lifted her gaze to me and made as if to speak, but then she stopped, gritted her teeth, and I heard her voice again, coming from far away.

"Uncle!"

She stretched out her hand, lifted the white coverlet with her fingers, and pointed to her leg, amputated from the top of the thigh.

My friend. . . . Never shall I forget Nadia's leg, amputated from the top of the thigh. No! Nor shall I forget the grief which had molded her face and merged into its traits forever. I went out of the hospital in Gaza that day, my hand clutched in silent derision on the two pounds I had brought with me to give Nadia. The blazing sun filled the streets with the color of blood. And Gaza was brand new, Mustafa! You and I never saw it like this. The stone piled up at the beginning of the Shajiya quarter where we lived had a meaning, and they seemed to have been put there for no other reason but to explain it. This Gaza in which we had lived and with whose good people we had spent seven years of defeat was something new. It seemed to me just a beginning. I don't know why I thought it was just a beginning. I imagined that the main street that I walked along on the way back home was only the beginning of a long, long road leading to Safad. Everything in this Gaza throbbed with sadness, which was not confined to weeping. It was a challenge; more than that, it was something like reclamation of the amputated leg!

I went out into the streets of Gaza, streets filled with blinding sunlight. They told me that Nadia had lost her leg when she threw herself on top of her little brothers and sisters to protect them from the bombs and flames that had fastened their claws into the house. Nadia could have saved herself, she could have run away, rescued her leg. But she didn't.

Why?

No, my friend, I won't come to Sacramento, and I've no regrets. No, and nor will I finish what we began together in childhood. This obscure feeling that you had as you left Gaza, this small feeling must grow into a giant deep within you. It must expand, you must seek it in order to find yourself, here among the ugly debris of defeat.

I won't come to you. But you, return to us! Come back, to learn from Nadia's leg, amputated from the top of the thigh, what life is and what existence is worth.

Come back, my friend! We are all waiting for you.


## Study and Discussion Questions

1. What metaphors and images does Kanafani use to describe Gaza? What do these suggest about Gaza and about the narrator?
2. Why does the narrator change his mind about emigrating to California? What did California mean to him and to Mustafa, and how does that meaning change for the narrator?
3. What kind of relationship do the narrator and Mustafa have? How does the language in the story describe this relationship?
4. Kanafani writes, "Ill children have something of saintliness." What role do children play in this story? How is the fate of children a part of the narrator's decision?
5. Why do you think Kanafani chose to tell this story in the form of a letter? What effect does this have on the reader? What does Kanafani gain by using the epistolary (letter) form? Does he lose anything?
6. "Letter from Gaza" was first published around 50 years ago. Does it, however, seem contemporary? And does that surprise you, as you consider the situation in the Middle East today? Discuss.

### Suggestions for Writing

1. Gaza has been a contested territory and the scene of long-standing tension and warfare. Research the history of Gaza, and write about how "Letter from Gaza" fits into and relates to the political and social events that have taken and are taking place there.
2. "Letter from Gaza" describes the conflict between leaving a difficult homeland in order to make a better life for yourself, or staying to try to make that country better for yourself and others. Do you know anyone personally who has had to make that kind of choice? Write about the different aspects of this conflict and the implications of the narrator's choice in this story.

### Critical Resources

1. Abdel-Malek, Kamel. "Living on Borderlines: War and Exile in Selected Works by Ghassan Kanafani, Fawaz Turki and Mahmud Darwish." *Israeli and Palestinian Identities in History and Literature.* Ed. David Jacobson. New York: St. Martin's, 1999.
2. Harlow, Barbara. *After Lives: Legacies of Revolutionary Writing.* London: Verso, 1996.
3. Kanafani, Ghassan. *Men in the Sun and Other Palestinian Stories.* Trans. Hilary Kilpatrick. London: Lynne Rienner Publishers, 1999.
4. Siddiq, Muhammad. *Man is a Cause: Political Consciousness and the Fiction of Ghassan Kanafani.* Seattle: University of Washington Press, 1984.

## KATHERINE MANSFIELD

## *The Fly* (1922)

"Y'are very snug in here," piped old Mr. Woodifield, and he peered out of the great, green-leather armchair by his friend the boss's desk as a baby peers out of its pram. His talk was over; it was time for him to be off. But he did not want to go. Since he had retired, since his...stroke, the wife and the girls kept him boxed up in the house every day of the week except Tuesday. On Tuesday he was dressed and brushed and allowed to cut back to the City for the day. Though what he did there the wife and girls couldn't imagine. Made a nuisance of himself to his friends, they supposed....Well, perhaps so. All the same, we cling to our last pleasures as the tree clings to its last leaves. So there sat old Woodifield, smoking a cigar and staring almost greedily at the boss, who rolled in his office chair, stout, rosy, five years older than he, and still going strong, still at the helm. It did one good to see him.

Wistfully, admiringly, the old voice added, "It's snug in here, upon my word!"

"Yes, it's comfortable enough," agreed the boss, and he flipped the *Financial Times* with a paper-knife. As a matter of fact he was proud of his room; he liked to have it admired, especially by old Woodifield. It gave him a feeling of deep, solid satisfaction to be planted there in the midst of it in full view of that frail old figure in the muffler.

"I've had it done up lately," he explained, as he had explained for the past — how many? — weeks. "New carpet," and he pointed to the bright red carpet with a pattern of large white rings. "New furniture," and he nodded towards the massive bookcase and the table with legs like twisted treacle. "Electric heating!" He waved almost exultantly towards the five transparent, pearly sausages glowing so softly in the tilted copper pan.

But he did not draw old Woodifield's attention to the photograph over the table of a grave-looking boy in uniform standing in one of those spectral photographers' parks with photographers' storm-clouds behind him. It was not new. It had been there for over six years.

"There was something I wanted to tell you," said old Woodifield, and his eyes grew dim remembering. "Now what was it? I had it in my mind when I started out this morning." His hands began to tremble, and patches of red showed above his beard.

Poor old chap, he's on his last pins, thought the boss. And, feeling kindly, he winked at the old man, and said jokingly, "I tell you what. I've got a little drop of something here that'll do you good before you go out into the cold again. It's beautiful stuff. It wouldn't hurt a child." He took a key off his watch-chain, unlocked a cupboard below his desk, and drew forth a dark, squat bottle. "That's the medicine," said he. "And the man from whom I got it told me on the strict Q.T. it came from the cellars at Windor Castle."

Old Woodifield's mouth fell open at the sight. He couldn't have looked more surprised if the boss had produced a rabbit.

"It's whisky, ain't it?" he piped feebly.

The boss turned the bottle and lovingly showed him the label. Whisky it was.

"D'you know," said he, peering up at the boss wonderingly, "they won't let me touch it at home." And he looked as though he was going to cry.

"Ah, that's where we know a bit more than the ladies," cried the boss, swooping across for two tumblers that stood on the table with the water-bottle, and pouring a generous finger into each. "Drink it down. It'll do you good. And don't put any water with it. It's sacrilege to tamper with stuff like this. Ah!" He tossed off his, pulled out his handkerchief, hastily wiped his moustaches, and cocked an eye at old Woodifield, who was rolling his in his chaps.

The old man swallowed, was silent a moment, and then said faintly, "It's nutty!"

But it warmed him; it crept into his chill old brain — he remembered.

"That was it," he said, heaving himself out of his chair. "I thought you'd like to know. The girls were in Belgium last week having a look at poor Reggie's grave, and they happened to come across your boy's. They're quite near each other, it seems."

Old Woodifield paused, but the boss made no reply. Only a quiver in his eyelids showed that he heard.

"The girls were delighted with the way the place is kept," piped the old voice. "Beautifully looked after. Couldn't be better if they were at home. You've not been across, have yer?"

"No, no!" For various reasons the boss had not been across.

"There's miles of it," quavered old Woodifield, "and it's all as neat as a garden. Flowers growing on all the graves. Nice broad paths." It was plain from his voice how much he liked a nice broad path.

The pause came again. Then the old man brightened wonderfully.

"D'you know what the hotel made the girls pay for a pot of jam?" he piped. "Ten francs! Robbery, I call it. It was a little pot, so Gertrude says, no bigger than a half-crown. And she hadn't taken more than a spoonful when they charged her ten francs. Gertrude brought the pot away with her to teach 'em a lesson. Quite right, too; it's trading on our feelings. They think because we're over there having a look round we're ready to pay anything. That's what it is." And he turned towards the door.

"Quite right, quite right!" cried the boss, though what was quite right he hadn't the least idea. He came round by his desk, followed the shuffling footsteps to the door, and saw the old fellow out. Woodifield was gone.

For a long moment the boss stayed, staring at nothing, while the grey-haired office messenger, watching him, dodged in and out of his cubby-hole like a dog that expects to be taken for a run. Then: "I'll see nobody for half an hour, Macey," said the boss. "Understand? Nobody at all."

"Very good, sir."

The door shut, the firm heavy steps recrossed the bright carpet, the fat body plumped down in the spring chair, and leaning forward, the boss covered his face with his hands. He wanted, he intended, he had arranged to weep....

It had been a terrible shock to him when old Woodifield sprang that remark upon him about the boy's grave. It was exactly as though the earth had opened and he had seen the boy lying there with Woodifield's girls staring down at him. For it was strange. Although over six years had passed away, the boss never thought of the boy except as lying unchanged, unblemished in his uniform, asleep for ever. "My son!" groaned the boss. But no tears came yet. In the past, in the first few months and even years after the boy's death, he had only to say those words to be overcome by such grief that nothing short of a violent fit of weeping could relieve him. Time, he had declared then, he had told everybody, could make no difference. Other men perhaps might recover, might live their loss down, but not he. How was it possible? His boy was an only son. Ever since his birth the boss had worked at building up this business for him; it had no other meaning if it was not for the boy. Life itself had come to have no other meaning. How on earth could he have slaved, denied himself, kept going all those years without the promise for ever before him of the boy's stepping into his shoes and carrying on where he left off?

And that promise had been so near being fulfilled. The boy had been in the office learning the ropes for a year before the war. Every morning they had started off together; they had come back by the same train. And what congratulations he had received as the boy's father! No wonder; he had taken to it marvellously. As to his popularity with the staff, every man jack of them down to old Macey couldn't make enough of the boy. And he wasn't the least spoilt. No, he was just his bright natural self, with the right word for everybody, with that boyish look and his habit of saying, "Simply splendid!"

But all that was over and done with as though it never had been. The day had come when Macey had handed him the telegram that brought the whole place crashing about his head. "Deeply regret to inform you..." And he had left the office a broken man, with his life in ruins.

Six years ago, six years....How quickly time passed! It might have happened yesterday. The boss took his hands from his face; he was puzzled. Something seemed to be wrong with him. He wasn't feeling as he wanted to feel. He decided to get up and have a look at the boy's photograph. But it wasn't a favourite photograph of his; the expression was unnatural. It was cold, even stern-looking. The boy had never looked like that.

At that moment the boss noticed that a fly had fallen into his broad inkpot, and was trying feebly but deperately to clamber out again. Help! help! said those struggling legs. But the sides of the inkpot were wet and slippery; it fell back again and began to swim. The boss took up a pen, picked the fly out of the ink, and shook it on to a piece of blotting-paper. For a fraction of a second it lay still on the dark patch that oozed round it. Then the front legs waved, took hold, and, pulling its small, sodden body up, it began the immense task of cleaning the ink from its wings. Over and under, over and under, went a leg along a wing, as the stone goes over and under the scythe. Then there was a pause, while the fly, seeming to stand on the tips of its toes, tried to expand first one wing and then the other. It succeeded at last, and, sitting down, it began, like a minute cat, to clean its face. Now one could imagine that the little front legs rubbed against each other lightly, joyfully. The horrible danger was over; it had escaped; 1t was ready for life again.

But just then the boss had an idea. He plunged his pen back into the ink, leaned his thick wrist on the blotting-paper, and as the fly tried its wings down came a great heavy blot. What would it make of that? What indeed! The little beggar seemed absolutely cowed, stunned, and afraid to move because of what would happen next. But then, as if painfully, it dragged itself forward. The front legs waved, caught hold, and, more slowly this time, the task began from the beginning.

He's a plucky little devil, thought the boss, and he felt a real admiration for the fly's courage. That was the way to tackle things; that was the right spirit.

Never say die; it was only a question of...But the fly had again finished its laborious task, and the boss had just time to refill his pen, to shake fair and square on the new-cleaned body yet another dark drop. What about it this time? A painful moment of suspense followed. But behold, the front legs were again waving; the boss felt a rush of relief. He leaned over the fly and said to it tenderly, "You artful little b..." And he actually had the brilliant notion of breathing on it to help the drying process. All the same, there was something timid and weak about its efforts now, and the boss decided that this time should be the last, as he dipped the pen deep into the inkpot.

It was. The last blot fell on the soaked blotting-paper, and the draggled fly lay in it and did not stir. The back legs were stuck to the body; the front legs were not to be seen.

"Come on," said the boss. "Look sharp!" And he stirred it with his pen — in vain. Nothing happened or was likely to happen. The fly was dead.

The boss lifted the corpse on the end of the paper-knife and flung it into the waste-paper basket. But such a grinding feeling of wretchedness seized him that he felt positively frightened. He started forward and pressed the bell for Macey.

"Bring me some fresh blotting-paper," he said sternly,"and look sharp about it." And while the old dog padded away he fell to wondering what it was he had been thinking about before. What was it? It was...He took out his handkerchief and passed it inside his collar. For the life of him he could not remember.

❋ ❋ ❋

## TIM O'BRIEN

## *The Man I Killed* (1990)

His jaw was in his throat, his upper lip and teeth were gone, his one eye was shut, his other eye was a star-shaped hole, his eyebrows were thin and arched like a woman's, his nose was undamaged, there was a slight tear at the lobe of one ear, his clean black hair was swept upward into a cowlick at the rear of the skull, his forehead was lightly freckled, his fingernails were clean, the skin at his left cheek was peeled back in three ragged strips, his right cheek was smooth and hairless, there was a butterfly on his chin, his neck was open to the spinal cord and the blood there was thick and shiny and it was this wound that had killed him. He lay face-up in the center of the trail, a slim, dead, almost dainty young man. He had bony legs, a narrow waist, long shapely fingers. His chest was sunken and poorly muscled—a scholar, maybe. His wrists were the wrists of a child. He wore a black shirt, black pajama pants, a gray ammunition belt, a gold ring on the third finger of his right hand. His rubber sandals had been blown off. One lay beside him, the other a few meters up the trail. He had been born, maybe, in 1946 in the village of My Khe near the central coastline of Quang Ngai Province,[1] where his parents farmed, and where his family had lived for several centuries, and where, during the time of the French, his father and two uncles and many neighbors had joined in the struggle for independence. He was not a Communist. He was a citizen and a soldier. In the village of My Khe, as in all of Quang Ngai, patriotic resistance had the force of tradition, which was partly the force of legend, and from his earliest boyhood the man I killed would have listened to stories about the heroic Trung sisters and Tran Hung Dao's famous rout of the Mongols and Le Loi's final victory against the Chinese at Tot Dong.[2] He would have been taught that to defend the land was a man's highest duty and highest privilege. He had accepted this. It was never open to question. Secretly, though, it also frightened him. He was not a fighter. His health was poor, his body small and frail. He liked books. He wanted someday to be a teacher of mathematics. At night, lying on his mat, he could not picture himself doing the brave things his father had done, or his uncles, or the heroes of the stories. He hoped in his heart that he would never be tested. He hoped the Americans would go away. Soon, he hoped. He kept hoping and hoping, always, even when he was asleep.

"Oh, man, you fuckin' trashed the fucker," Azar said. "You scrambled his sorry self, look at that, you *did*, you laid him out like Shredded fuckin' Wheat."

"Go away," Kiowa said.

"I'm just saying the truth. Like oatmeal."

"Go," Kiowa said.

"Okay, then, I take it back," Azar said. He started to move away, then stopped and said, "Rice Krispies, you know? On the dead test, this particular individual gets A-Plus."

Smiling at this, he shrugged and walked up the trail toward the village behind the trees.

Kiowa kneeled down.

"Just forget that crud," he said. He opened up his canteen and held it out for a while and then sighed and pulled it away. "No sweat, man. What else could you do?"

Later, Kiowa said, "I'm serious. Nothing *anybody* could do. Come on, stop staring."

The trail junction was shaded by a row of trees and tall brush. The slim young man lay with his legs in the shade. His jaw was in his throat. His one eye was shut and the other was a star-shaped hole.

Kiowa glanced at the body.

"All right, let me ask a question," he said. "You want to trade places with him? Turn it all upside down—you *want* that? I mean, be honest."

---

[1]Province in central South Vietnam.

[2]The Trung sisters led a Vietnamese rebellion against Chinese rule in A.D. 40; Tran Hung Dao repelled a Mongol attack in 1287; Le Loi defeated the Chinese in 1426.

The star-shaped hole was red and yellow. The yellow part seemed to be getting wider, spreading out at the center of the star. The upper lip and gum and teeth were gone. The man's head was cocked at a wrong angle, as if loose at the neck, and the neck was wet with blood.

"Think it over," Kiowa said.

Then later he said, "Tim, it's a *war.* The guy wasn't Heidi—he had a weapon, right? It's a tough thing, for sure, but you got to cut out that staring."

Then he said, "Maybe you better lie down a minute."

Then after a long empty time he said, "Take it slow. Just go wherever the spirit takes you."

The butterfly was making its way along the young man's forehead, which was spotted with small dark freckles. The nose was undamaged. The skin on the right cheek was smooth and fine-grained and hairless. Frail-looking, delicately boned, the young man would not have wanted to be a soldier and in his heart would have feared performing badly in battle. Even as a boy growing up in the village of My Khe, he had often worried about this. He imagined covering his head and lying in a deep hole and closing his eyes and not moving until the war was over. He had no stomach for violence. He loved mathematics. His eyebrows were thin and arched like a woman's, and at school the boys sometimes teased him about how pretty he was, the arched eyebrows and long shapely fingers, and on the playground they mimicked a woman's walk and made fun of his smooth skin and his love for mathematics. The young man could not make himself fight them. He often wanted to, but he was afraid, and this increased his shame. If he could not fight little boys, he thought, how could he ever become a soldier and fight the Americans with their airplanes and helicopters and bombs? It did not seem possible. In the presence of his father and uncles, he pretended to look forward to doing his patriotic duty, which was also a privilege, but at night he prayed with his mother that the war might end soon. Beyond anything else, he was afraid of disgracing himself, and therefore his family and village. But all he could do, he thought, was wait and pray and try not to grow up too fast.

"Listen to me," Kiowa said. "You feel terrible, I know that."

Then he said, "Okay, maybe I *don't* know."

Along the trail there were small blue flowers shaped like bells. The young man's head was wrenched sideways, not quite facing the flowers, and even in the shade a single blade of sunlight sparkled against the buckle of his ammunition belt. The left cheek was peeled back in three ragged strips. The wounds at his neck had not yet clotted, which made him seem animate even in death, the blood still spreading out across his shirt.

Kiowa shook his head.

There was some silence before he said, "Stop *staring.*"

The young man's fingernails were clean. There was a slight tear at the lobe of one ear, a sprinkling of blood on the forearm. He wore a gold ring on the third finger of his right hand. His chest was sunken and poorly muscled—a scholar, maybe. His life was now a constellation of possibilities. So, yes, maybe a scholar. And for years, despite his family's poverty, the man I killed would have been determined to continue his education in mathematics. The means for this were arranged, perhaps, through the village liberation cadres, and in 1964 the young man began attending classes at the university in Saigon, where he avoided politics and paid attention to the problems of calculus. He devoted himself to his studies. He spent his nights alone, wrote romantic poems in his journal, took pleasure in the grace and beauty of differential equations. The war, he knew, would finally take him, but for the time being he would not let himself think about it. He had stopped praying; instead, now, he waited. And as he waited, in his final year at the university, he fell in love with a classmate, a girl of seventeen, who one day told him that his wrists were like the wrists of a child, so small and delicate, and who admired his narrow waist and the cowlick that rose up like a bird's tail at the back of his head. She liked his quiet manner; she laughed at his freckles and bony legs. One evening, perhaps, they exchanged gold rings.

Now one eye was a star.

"You okay?" Kiowa said.

The body lay almost entirely in shade. There were gnats at the mouth, little flecks of pollen drifting above the nose. The butterfly was gone. The bleeding had stopped except for the neck wounds.

Kiowa picked up the rubber sandals, clapping off the dirt, then bent down to search the body. He found a pouch of rice, a comb, a fingernail clipper, a few soiled piasters, a snapshot of a young woman standing in front of a parked motorcycle. Kiowa placed these items in his rucksack along with the gray ammunition belt and rubber sandals.

Then he squatted down.

"I'll tell you the straight truth," he said. "The guy was dead the second he stepped on the trail. Understand me? We all had him zeroed. A good kill—weapon, ammunition, everything." Tiny beads of sweat glistened at Kiowa's forehead. His eyes moved from the sky to the dead man's body to the knuckles of his own hands. "So listen, you best pull your shit together. Can't just sit here all day."

Later he said, "Understand?"

Then he said, "Five minutes, Tim. Five more minutes and we're moving out."

The one eye did a funny twinkling trick, red to yellow. His head was wrenched sideways, as if loose at the neck, and the dead young man seemed to be staring at some distant object beyond the bell-shaped flowers along the trail. The blood at the neck had gone to a deep purplish black. Clean fingernails, clean hair—he had been a soldier for only a single day. After his years at the university, the man I killed returned with his new wife to the village of My Khe, where he enlisted as a common rifleman with the 48th Vietcong Battalion. He knew he would die quickly. He knew he would see a flash of light. He knew he would fall dead and wake up in the stories of his village and people.

Kiowa covered the body with a poncho.

"Hey, you're looking better," he said. "No doubt about it. All you needed was time—some mental R&R."

Then he said, "Man, I'm sorry."

Then later he said, "Why not talk about it?"

Then he said, "Come on, man, talk."

He was a slim, dead, almost dainty young man of about twenty. He lay with one leg bent beneath him, his jaw in his throat, his face neither expressive nor inexpressive. One eye was shut. The other was a star-shaped hole.

"Talk," Kiowa said.

### Study and Discussion Questions

1. Why do you think the narrator describes the dead man's body in such detail?
2. Why does the narrator persist in imagining the life of the man he killed?
3. What's the significance of the narrator's guess that the dead man was born in a place "where his family had lived for several centuries"?
4. Why do you think the narrator imagines that the man he killed was a fearful and reluctant soldier?
5. Why does the narrator assert that the dead man "was not a Communist"?
6. What role does Azar play in the story? What do his reactions add to the story's condemnation of war? And what is Kiowa's role?

### Suggestions for Writing

1. What can we infer about the narrator of "The Man I Killed"? Write a sketch of what you imagine him to be like.
2. In an effort to ease the narrator's guilt, Kiowa says: "Tim, it's a *war*. The guy wasn't Heidi—he had a weapon, right?" How might Tim reply? How might you?

### Critical Resources

1. Heberle, Mark. *A Trauma Artist: Tim O'Brien and the Fiction of Vietnam.* Iowa City: University of Iowa Press, 2001.
2. Heroz, Tobey. *Tim O'Brien.* New York: Twayne, 1997.
3. Kaplan Steven. *Understanding Tim O'Brien.* Columbia: University of South Carolina Press, 1995.
4. Robinson, Daniel. "Getting it Right: The Short Fiction of Tim O'Brien." *Critique: Studies in Contemporary Fiction* 40.3 (1999): 257–64.
5. Wharton, Lynn. "Journeying from Life to Literature: An Interview with American Novelist Tim O'Brien." *Interdisciplinary Studies: A Journal of Criticism and Theory* 1.2 (2000): 229–47.

❀ ❀ ❀

# TIM O'BRIEN

## *Sweetheart of the Song Tra Bong*                    (1990)

Vietnam was full of strange stories, some improbable, some well beyond that, but the stories that will last forever are those that swirl back and forth across the border between trivia and bedlam, the mad and the mundane. This one keeps returning to me. I heard it from Rat Kiley, who swore up and down to its truth, although in the end, I'll admit, that doesn't amount to much of a warranty. Among the men in Alpha Company, Rat had a reputation for exaggeration and overstatement, a compulsion to rev up the facts, and for most of us it was normal procedure to discount sixty or seventy percent of anything he had to say. If Rat told you, for example, that he'd slept with four girls one night, you could figure it was about a girl and a half. It wasn't a question of deceit. Just the opposite: he wanted to heat up the truth, to make it burn so hot that you would feel exactly what he felt. For Rat Kiley, I think, facts were formed by sensation, not the other way around, and when you listened to one of his stories, you'd find yourself performing rapid calculations in your head, subtracting superlatives, figuring the square root of an absolute and then multiplying by maybe.

Still, with this particular story, Rat never backed down. He claimed to have witnessed the incident with his own eyes, and I remember how upset he became one morning when Mitchell Sanders challenged him on its basic premise.

"It can't happen," Sanders said. "Nobody ships his honey over to Nam. It don't ring true. I mean, you just can't import your own personal poontang."

Rat shook his head. "I *saw* it, man. I was right there. This guy did it."

"His girlfriend?"

"Straight on. It's a fact." Rat's voice squeaked a little. He paused and looked at his hands. "Listen, the guy sends her the money. Flies her over. This cute blonde—just a kid, just barely out of high school—she shows up with a suitcase and one of those plastic cosmetic bags. Comes right out to the boonies. I swear to God, man, she's got on culottes. White culottes and this sexy pink sweater. There she *is*."

I remember Mitchell Sanders folding his arms. He looked over at me for a second, not quite grinning, not saying a word, but I could read the amusement in his eyes.

Rat saw it, too.

"No lie," he muttered. "Culottes."

When he first arrived in-country, before joining Alpha Company, Rat had been assigned to a small medical detachment up in the mountains west of Chu Lai, near the village of Tra Bong, where along with eight other enlisted men he ran an aid station that provided basic emergency and trauma care. Casualties were flown in by helicopter, stabilized, then shipped out to hospitals in Chu Lai or Danang. It was gory work, Rat said, but predictable. Amputations, mostly—legs and feet. The area was heavily mined, thick with Bouncing Betties and home-made booby traps. For a medic, though, it was ideal duty, and Rat counted him-self lucky. There was plenty of cold beer, three hot meals a day, a tin roof over his head. No humping at all. No officers, either. You could let your hair grow, he said, and you didn't have to polish your boots or snap off salutes or put up with the usual rear-echelon nonsense. The highest ranking NCO was an E-6 named Eddie Diamond, whose pleasures ran from dope to Darvon, and except for a rare field inspection there was no such thing as military discipline.

As Rat described it, the compound was situated at the top of a flat-crested hill along the northern outskirts of Tra Bong. At one end was a small dirt heli-pad; at the other end, in a rough semicircle, the mess hall and medical hootches overlooked a river called the Song Tra Bong. Surrounding the place were tan-gled rolls of concertina wire, with bunkers and reinforced firing positions at stag-gered intervals, and base security was provided by a mixed unit of RFs, PFs, and ARVN infantry. Which is to say virtually no security at all. As soldiers, the ARVNs were useless; the Ruff-and-Puffs were outright dangerous. And yet even with decent troops the place was clearly indefensible. To the north and west the country rose up in thick walls of wilderness, triple-canopied jungle, mountains un-folding into higher mountains, ravines and gorges and fast-moving rivers and wa-terfalls and exotic butterflies and steep cliffs and smoky little hamlets and great valleys of bamboo and elephant grass. Originally, in the early 1960s, the place had been set up as a Special Forces outpost, and when Rat Kiley arrived nearly a decade later, a squad of six Green Berets still used the compound as a base of operations. The Greenies were not social animals. Animals, Rat said, but far from social. They had their own hootch at the edge of the perimeter, fortified with sandbags and a metal fence, and except for the bare essentials they avoided con-tact with the medical detachment. Secretive and suspicious, loners by nature, the six Greenies would sometimes vanish for days at a time, or even weeks, then late in the night they would just as magically reappear, moving like shadows through the moonlight, filing in silently from the dense rain forest off to the west. Among the medics there were jokes about this, but no one asked questions.

While the outpost was isolated and vulnerable, Rat said, he always felt a cu-rious sense of safety there. Nothing much ever happened. The place was never mortared, never taken under fire, and the war seemed to be somewhere far away. On occasion, when casualties came in, there were quick spurts of activity, but oth-erwise the days flowed by without incident, a smooth and peaceful time. Most mornings were spent on the volleyball court. In the heat of mid-day the men would head for the shade, lazing away the long afternoons, and after sundown there were movies and card games and sometimes all-night drinking sessions.

It was during one of those late nights that Eddie Diamond first brought up the tantalizing possibility. It was an offhand comment. A joke, really. What they should do, Eddie said, was pool some bucks and bring in a few mama-sans from Saigon, spice things up, and after a moment one of the men laughed and said, "Our own little EM club," and somebody else said, "Hey, yeah, we pay our fuckin' dues, don't we?" It was nothing serious. Just passing time, playing with the possibilities, and so for a while they tossed the idea around, how you could actually get away with it, no officers or anything, nobody to clamp down, then they dropped the subject and moved on to cars and baseball.

Later in the night, though, a young medic named Mark Fossie kept coming back to the subject.

"Look, if you think about it," he said, "it's not that crazy. You could actually do it."

"Do what?" Rat said.

"You know. Bring in a girl. I mean, what's the problem?"

Rat shrugged. "Nothing. A war."

"Well, see, that's the thing," Mark Fossie said. "No war *here*. You could really do it. A pair of solid brass balls, that's all you'd need."

There was some laughter, and Eddie Diamond told him he'd best strap down his dick, but Fossie just frowned and looked at the ceiling for a while and then went off to write a letter.

Six weeks later his girlfriend showed up.

The way Rat told it, she came in by helicopter along with the daily resupply shipment out of Chu Lai. A tall, big-boned blonde. At best, Rat said, she was seventeen years old, fresh out of Cleveland Heights Senior High. She had long white legs and blue eyes and a complexion like strawberry ice cream. Very friendly, too.

At the helipad that morning, Mark Fossie grinned and put his arm around her and said, "Guys, this is Mary Anne."

The girl seemed tired and somewhat lost, but she smiled.

There was a heavy silence. Eddie Diamond, the ranking NCO, made a small motion with his hand, and some of the others murmured a word or two, then they watched Mark Fossie pick up her suitcase and lead her by the arm down to the hootches. For a long while the men were quiet.

"That fucker," somebody finally said.

At evening chow Mark Fossie explained how he'd set it up. It was expensive, he admitted, and the logistics were complicated, but it wasn't like going to the moon. Cleveland to Los Angeles, LA to Bangkok, Bangkok to Saigon. She'd hopped a C-130 up to Chu Lai and stayed overnight at the USO and the next morning hooked a ride west with the resupply chopper.

"A cinch," Fossie said, and gazed down at his pretty girlfriend. "Thing is, you just got to *want* it enough."

Mary Anne Bell and Mark Fossie had been sweethearts since grammar school. From the sixth grade on they had known for a fact that someday they would be married, and live in a fine gingerbread house near Lake Erie, and have three healthy yellow-haired children, and grow old together, and no doubt die in each other's arms and be buried in the same walnut casket. That was the plan. They were very much in love, full of dreams, and in the ordinary flow of their lives the whole scenario might well have come true.

On the first night they set up house in one of the bunkers along the perimeter, near the Special Forces hootch, and over the next two weeks they stuck together like a pair of high school steadies. It was almost disgusting, Rat said, the way they mooned over each other. Always holding hands, always laughing over some private joke. All they needed, he said, were a couple of matching sweaters. But among the medics there was some envy. It was Vietnam, after all, and Mary Anne Bell was an attractive girl. Too wide in the shoulders, maybe, but she had terrific legs, a bubbly personality, a happy smile. The men genuinely liked her. Out on the volleyball court she wore cut-off blue jeans and a black swimsuit top, which the guys appreciated, and in the evenings she liked to dance to music from Rat's portable tape deck. There was a novelty to it; she was good for morale. At times she gave off a kind of come-get-me energy, coy and flirtatious, but apparently it never bothered Mark Fossie. In fact he seemed to enjoy it, just grinning at her, because he was so much in love, and because it was the sort of show that a girl will sometimes put on for her boyfriend's entertainment and education.

Though she was young, Rat said, Mary Anne Bell was no timid child. She was curious about things. During her first days in-country she liked to roam around the compound asking questions: What exactly was a trip flare? How did a Claymore work? What was behind those scary green mountains to the west? Then she'd squint and listen quietly while somebody filled her in. She had a good quick mind. She paid attention. Often, especially during the hot afternoons, she would spend time with the ARVNs out along the perimeter, picking up little phrases of Vietnamese, learning how to cook rice over a can of Sterno, how to eat with her hands. The guys sometimes liked to kid her about it—our own little native, they'd say—but Mary Anne would just smile and stick out her tongue. "I'm here," she'd say, "I might as well learn something."

The war intrigued her. The land, too, and the mystery. At the beginning of her second week she began pestering Mark Fossie to take her down to the village at the foot of the hill. In a quiet voice, very patiently, he tried to tell her that it was a bad idea, way too dangerous, but Mary Anne kept after him. She wanted to get a feel for how people lived, what the smells and customs were. It did not impress her that the VC owned the place.

"Listen, it can't be that bad," she said. "They're human beings, aren't they? Like everybody else?"

Fossie nodded. He loved her.

And so in the morning Rat Kiley and two other medics tagged along as security while Mark and Mary Anne strolled through the ville like a pair of tourists. If the girl was nervous, she didn't show it. She seemed comfortable and entirely at home; the hostile atmosphere did not seem to register. All morning Mary Anne chattered away about how quaint the place was, how she loved the thatched roofs and naked children, the wonderful simplicity of village life. A strange thing to watch, Rat said. This seventeen-year-old doll in her goddamn culottes, perky and fresh-faced, like a cheerleader visiting the opposing team's locker room. Her pretty blue eyes seemed to glow. She couldn't get enough of it. On their way back up to the compound she stopped for a swim in the Song Tra Bong, stripping down to her underwear, showing off her legs while Fossie tried to explain to her about things like ambushes and snipers and the stopping power of an AK-47.

The guys, though, were impressed.

"A real tiger," said Eddie Diamond. "D-cup guts, trainer-bra brains."

"She'll learn," somebody said.

Eddie Diamond gave a solemn nod. "There's the scary part. I promise you, this girl will most definitely learn."

In parts, at least, it was a funny story, and yet to hear Rat Kiley tell it you'd almost think it was intended as straight tragedy. He never smiled. Not even at the crazy stuff. There was always a dark, far-off look in his eyes, a kind of sadness, as if he were troubled by something sliding beneath the story's surface. Whenever we laughed, I remember, he'd sigh and wait it out, but the one thing he could not tolerate was disbelief. He'd get edgy if someone questioned one of the details. "She *wasn't* dumb," he'd snap. "I never said that. Young, that's all I said. Like you and me. A *girl*, that's the only difference, and I'll tell you something: it didn't amount to jack. I mean, when we first got here—all of us—we were real young and innocent, full of romantic bullshit, but we learned pretty damn quick. And so did Mary Anne."

Rat would peer down at his hands, silent and thoughtful. After a moment his voice would flatten out.

"You don't believe it?" he'd say. "Fine with me. But you don't know human nature. You don't know Nam."

Then he'd tell us to listen up.

A good sharp mind, Rat said. True, she could be silly sometimes, but she picked up on things fast. At the end of the second week, when four casualties came in, Mary Anne wasn't afraid to get her hands bloody. At times, in fact, she seemed fascinated by it. Not the gore so much, but the adrenaline buzz that went with the job, that quick hot rush in your veins when the choppers settled down and you had to do things fast and right. No time for sorting through options, no thinking at all; you just stuck your hands in and started plugging up holes. She was quiet and steady. She didn't back off from the ugly cases. Over the next day or two, as more casualties trickled in, she learned how to clip an artery and pump up a plastic splint and shoot in morphine. In times of action her face took on a sudden new composure, almost serene, the fuzzy blue eyes narrowing into a tight, intelligent focus. Mark Fossie would grin at this. He was proud, yes, but also amazed. A different person, it seemed, and he wasn't sure what to make of it.

Other things, too. The way she quickly fell into the habits of the bush. No cosmetics, no fingernail filing. She stopped wearing jewelry, cut her hair short and wrapped it in a dark green bandanna. Hygiene became a matter of small consequence. In her second week Eddie Diamond taught her how to disassemble an M-16, how the various parts worked, and from there it was a natural progression to learning how to use the weapon. For hours at a time she plunked away at C-ration cans, a bit unsure of herself, but as it turned out she had a real knack for it. There was a new confidence in her voice, a new authority in the way she carried herself. In many ways she remained naive and immature, still a kid, but Cleveland Heights now seemed very far away.

Once or twice, gently, Mark Fossie suggested that it might be time to think about heading home, but Mary Anne laughed and told him to forget it. "Everything I want," she said, "is right here."

She stroked his arm, and then kissed him.

On one level things remained the same between them. They slept together. They held hands and made plans for after the war. But now there was a new imprecision in the way Mary Anne expressed her thoughts on certain subjects. Not necessarily three kids, she'd say. Not necessarily a house on Lake Erie. "Naturally we'll still get married," she'd tell him, "but it doesn't have to be right away. Maybe travel first. Maybe live together. Just test it out, you know?"

Mark Fossie would nod at this, even smile and agree, but it made him uncomfortable. He couldn't pin it down. Her body seemed foreign somehow—too stiff in places, too firm where the softness used to be. The bubbliness was gone. The nervous giggling, too. When she laughed now, which was rare, it was only when something struck her as truly funny. Her voice seemed to reorganize itself at a lower pitch. In the evenings, while the men played cards, she would sometimes fall into long elastic silences, her eyes fixed on the dark, her arms folded, her foot tapping out a coded message against the floor. When Fossie asked about it one evening, Mary Anne looked at him for a long moment and then shrugged. "It's nothing," she said. "Really nothing. To tell the truth, I've never been happier in my whole life. Never."

Twice, though, she came in late at night. Very late. And then finally she did not come in at all.

Rat Kiley heard about it from Fossie himself. Before dawn one morning, the kid shook him awake. He was in bad shape. His voice seemed hollow and stuffed up, nasal-sounding, as if he had a bad cold. He held a flashlight in his hand, clicking it on and off.

"Mary Anne," he whispered, "I can't *find* her."

Rat sat up and rubbed his face. Even in the dim light it was clear that the boy was in trouble. There were dark smudges under his eyes, the frayed edges of somebody who hadn't slept in a while.

"Gone," Fossie said. "Rat, listen, she's sleeping with somebody. Last night, she didn't even... I don't know what to *do*."

Abruptly then, Fossie seemed to collapse. He squatted down, rocking on his heels, still clutching the flashlight. Just a boy—eighteen years old. Tall and blond. A gifted athlete. A nice kid, too, polite and good-hearted, although for the moment none of it seemed to be serving him well.

He kept clicking the flashlight on and off.

"All right, start at the start," Rat said. "Nice and slow. Sleeping with who?"

"I don't know who. Eddie Diamond."

"Eddie?"

"Has to be. The guy's always there, always hanging on her."

Rat shook his head. "Man, I don't know. Can't say it strikes a right note, not with Eddie."

"Yes, but he's—"

"Easy does it," Rat said. He reached out and tapped the boy's shoulder. "Why not just check some bunks? We got nine guys. You and me, that's two, so there's seven possibles. Do a quick body count."

Fossie hesitated. "But I can't... If she's there, I mean, if she's with somebody—"

"Oh, Christ."

Rat pushed himself up. He took the flashlight, muttered something, and moved down to the far end of the hootch. For privacy, the men had rigged up curtained walls around their cots, small makeshift bedrooms, and in the dark Rat went quickly from room to room, using the flashlight to pluck out the faces. Eddie Diamond slept a hard deep sleep—the others, too. To be sure, though, Rat checked once more, very carefully, then he reported back to Fossie.

"All accounted for. No extras."

"Eddie?"

"Darvon dreams." Rat switched off the flashlight and tried to think it out. "Maybe she just—I don't know—maybe she camped out tonight. Under the stars or something. You search the compound?"

"Sure I did."

"Well, come on," Rat said. "One more time."

Outside, a soft violet light was spreading out across the eastern hillsides. Two or three ARVN soldiers had built their breakfast fires, but the place was mostly quiet and unmoving. They tried the helipad first, then the mess hall and supply hootches, then they walked the entire six hundred meters of perimeter.

"Okay," Rat finally said. "We got a problem."

When he first told the story, Rat stopped there and looked at Mitchell Sanders for a time.

"So what's your vote? Where was she?"

"The Greenies," Sanders said.

"Yeah?"

Sanders smiled. "No other option. That stuff about the Special Forces—how they used the place as a base of operations, how they'd glide in and out—all that had to be there for a *reason*. That's how stories work, man."

Rat thought about it, then shrugged.

"All right, sure, the Greenies. But it's not what Fossie thought. She wasn't sleeping with any of them. At least not exactly. I mean, in a way she was sleeping with *all* of them, more or less, except it wasn't sex or anything. They was just lying together, so to speak, Mary Anne and these six grungy weirded-out Green Berets."

"Lying down?" Sanders said.

"You got it."

"Lying down how?"

Rat smiled. "Ambush. All night long, man, Mary Anne's out on fuckin' *ambush*."

Just after sunrise, Rat said, she came trooping in through the wire, tired-looking but cheerful as she dropped her gear and gave Mark Fossie a brisk hug. The six Green Berets did not speak. One of them nodded at her, and the others gave Fossie a long stare, then they filed off to their hootch at the edge of the compound.

"Please," she said. "Not a word."

Fossie took a half step forward and hesitated. It was as though he had trouble recognizing her. She wore a bush hat and filthy green fatigues; she carried the standard M-16 automatic assault rifle; her face was black with charcoal.

Mary Anne handed him the weapon. "I'm exhausted," she said. "We'll talk later."

She glanced over at the Special Forces area, then turned and walked quickly across the compound toward her own bunker. Fossie stood still for a few seconds. A little dazed, it seemed. After a moment, though, he set his jaw and whispered something and went after her with a hard, fast stride.

"Not later!" he yelled. "Now!"

What happened between them, Rat said, nobody ever knew for sure. But in the mess hall that evening it was clear that an accommodation had been reached. Or more likely, he said, it was a case of setting down some new rules. Mary Anne's hair was freshly shampooed. She wore a white blouse, a navy blue skirt, a pair of plain black flats. Over dinner she kept her eyes down, poking at her food, subdued to the point of silence. Eddie Diamond and some of the others tried to nudge her into talking about the ambush—What was the feeling out there? What exactly did she see and hear?—but the questions seemed to give her trouble. Nervously, she'd look across the table at Fossie. She'd wait a moment, as if to receive some sort of clearance, then she'd bow her head and mumble out a vague word or two. There were no real answers.

Mark Fossie, too, had little to say.

"Nobody's business," he told Rat that night. Then he offered a brief smile. "One thing for sure, though, there won't be any more ambushes. No more late nights."

"You laid down the law?"

"Compromise," Fossie said. "I'll put it this way—we're officially engaged."

Rat nodded cautiously.

"Well hey, she'll make a sweet bride," he said. "Combat ready."

Over the next several days there was a strained, tightly wound quality to the way they treated each other, a rigid correctness that was enforced by repetitive acts of will-power. To look at them from a distance, Rat said, you would think they were the happiest two people on the planet. They spent the long afternoons sunbathing together, stretched out side by side on top of their bunker, or playing backgammon in the shade of a giant palm tree, or just sitting quietly. A model of togetherness, it seemed. And yet at close range their faces showed the tension. Too polite, too thoughtful. Mark Fossie tried hard to keep up a self-assured pose, as if nothing had ever come between them, or even could, but there was a fragility to it, something tentative and false. If Mary Anne happened to move a few steps away from him, even briefly, he'd tighten up and force himself not to watch her. But then a moment later he'd be watching.

In the presence of others, at least, they kept on their masks. Over meals they talked about plans for a huge wedding in Cleveland Heights—a two-day bash, lots of flowers. And yet even then their smiles seemed too intense. They were too quick with their banter; they held hands as if afraid to let go.

It had to end, and eventually it did.

Near the end of the third week Fossie began making arrangements to send her home. At first, Rat said, Mary Anne seemed to accept it, but then after a day or two she fell into a restless gloom, sitting off by herself at the edge of the perimeter. She would not speak. Shoulders hunched, her blue eyes opaque, she seemed to disappear inside herself. A couple of times Fossie approached her and tried to talk it out, but Mary Anne just stared out at the dark green mountains to the west. The wilderness seemed to draw her in. A haunted look, Rat said—partly terror, partly rapture. It was as if she had come up on the edge of something, as if she were caught in that no-man's-land between Cleveland Heights and deep jungle. Seventeen years old. Just a child, blond and innocent, but then weren't they all?

The next morning she was gone. The six Greenies were gone, too.

In a way, Rat said, poor Fossie expected it, or something like it, but that did not help much with the pain. The kid couldn't function. The grief took him by the throat and squeezed and would not let go.

"Lost," he kept whispering.

It was nearly three weeks before she returned. But in a sense she never returned. Not entirely, not all of her.

By chance, Rat said, he was awake to see it. A damp misty night, he couldn't sleep, so he'd gone outside for a quick smoke. He was just standing there, he said, watching the moon, and then off to the west a column of silhouettes appeared as if by magic at the edge of the jungle. At first he didn't recognize her—a small, soft shadow among six other shadows. There was no sound. No real substance either. The seven silhouettes seemed to float across the surface of the earth, like spirits, vaporous and unreal. As he watched, Rat said, it made him think of some weird opium dream. The silhouettes moved without moving. Silently, one by one, they came up the hill, passed through the wire, and drifted in a loose file across the compound. It was then, Rat said, that he picked out Mary Anne's face. Her eyes seemed to shine in the dark—not blue, though, but a bright glowing jungle green. She did not pause at Fossie's bunker. She cradled her weapon and moved swiftly to the Special Forces hootch and followed the others inside.

Briefly, a light came on, and someone laughed, then the place went dark again.

Whenever he told the story, Rat had a tendency to stop now and then, interrupting the flow, inserting little clarifications or bits of analysis and personal opinion. It was a bad habit, Mitchell Sanders said, because all that matters is the raw material, the stuff itself, and you can't clutter it up with your own half-baked commentary. That just breaks the spell. It destroys the magic. What you have to do, Sanders said, is trust your own story. Get the hell out of the way and let it tell itself.

But Rat Kiley couldn't help it. He wanted to bracket the full range of meaning.

"I know it sounds far-out," he'd tell us, "but it's not like *impossible* or anything. We all heard plenty of wackier stories. Some guy comes back from the bush, tells you he saw the Virgin Mary out there, she was riding a goddamn goose or something. Everybody buys it. Everybody smiles and asks how fast was they going, did she have spurs on. Well, it's not like that. This Mary Anne wasn't no virgin but at least she was real. I saw it. When she came in through the wire that night, I was right there, I saw those eyes of hers, I saw how she wasn't even the same person no more. What's so impossible about that? She was a girl, that's all. I mean, if it was a guy, everybody'd say, Hey, no big deal, he got caught up in the Nam shit, he got seduced by the Greenies. See what I mean? You got these blinders on about women. How gentle and peaceful they are. All that crap about how if we had a pussy for president there wouldn't be no more wars. Pure garbage. You got to get rid of that sexist attitude."

Rat would go on like that until Mitchell Sanders couldn't tolerate it any longer. It offended his inner ear.

"The story," Sanders would say. "The whole tone, man, you're wrecking it."

"Tone?"

"The *sound*. You need to get a consistent sound, like slow or fast, funny or sad. All these digressions, they just screw up your story's *sound*. Stick to what happened."

Frowning, Rat would close his eyes.

"Tone?" he'd say. "I didn't know it was all that complicated. The girl joined the zoo. One more animal—end of story."

"Yeah, fine. But tell it right."

At daybreak the next morning, when Mark Fossie heard she was back, he stationed himself outside the fenced-off Special Forces area. All morning he waited for her, and all afternoon. Around dusk Rat brought him something to eat.

"She has to come out," Fossie said. "Sooner or later, she has to."

"Or else what?" Rat said.

"I go get her. I bring her out."

Rat shook his head. "Your decision. I was you, though, no way I'd mess around with any Greenie types, not for nothing."

"It's Mary Anne in there."

"Sure, I know that. All the same, I'd knock real extra super polite."

Even with the cooling night air Fossie's face was slick with sweat. He looked sick. His eyes were bloodshot; his skin had a whitish, almost colorless cast. For a few minutes Rat waited with him, quietly watching the hootch, then he patted the kid's shoulder and left him alone.

It was after midnight when Rat and Eddie Diamond went out to check on him. The night had gone cold and steamy, a low fog sliding down from the mountains, and somewhere out in the dark they heard music playing. Not loud but not soft either. It had a chaotic, almost unmusical sound, without rhythm or form or progression, like the noise of nature. A synthesizer, it seemed, or maybe an electric organ. In the background, just audible, a woman's voice was half singing, half chanting, but the lyrics seemed to be in a foreign tongue.

They found Fossie squatting near the gate in front of the Special Forces area. Head bowed, he was swaying to the music, his face wet and shiny. As Eddie bent down beside him, the kid looked up with dull eyes, ashen and powdery, not quite in register.

"Hear that?" he whispered. "You *hear?* It's Mary Anne."

Eddie Diamond took his arm. "Let's get you inside. Somebody's radio, that's all it is. Move it now."

"Mary Anne. Just listen."

"Sure, but—"

"Listen!"

Fossie suddenly pulled away, twisting sideways, and fell back against the gate. He lay there with his eyes closed. The music—the noise, whatever it was—came from the hootch beyond the fence. The place was dark except for a small glowing window, which stood partly open, the panes dancing in bright reds and yellows as though the glass were on fire. The chanting seemed louder now. Fiercer, too, and higher pitched.

Fossie pushed himself up. He wavered for a moment then forced the gate open.

"That voice," he said. "Mary Anne."

Rat took a step forward, reaching out for him, but Fossie was already moving fast toward the hootch. He stumbled once, caught himself, and hit the door hard with both arms. There was a noise—a short screeching sound, like a cat—and the door swung in and Fossie was framed there for an instant, his arms stretched out, then he slipped inside. After a moment Rat and Eddie followed quietly. Just inside the door they found Fossie bent down on one knee. He wasn't moving.

Across the room a dozen candles were burning on the floor near the open window. The place seemed to echo with a weird deep-wilderness sound—tribal music—bamboo flutes and drums and chimes. But what hit you first, Rat said, was the smell. Two kinds of smells. There was a topmost scent of joss sticks and incense, like the fumes of some exotic smokehouse, but beneath the smoke lay a deeper and much more powerful stench. Impossible to describe, Rat said. It paralyzed your lungs. Thick and numbing, like an animal's den, a mix of blood and scorched hair and excrement and the sweet-sour odor of moldering flesh—the stink of the kill. But that wasn't all. On a post at the rear of the hootch was the decayed head of a large black leopard; strips of yellow-brown skin dangled from the overhead rafters. And bones. Stacks of bones—all kinds. To one side, propped up against a wall, stood a poster in neat black lettering: ASSEMBLE YOUR OWN GOOK!! FREE SAMPLE KIT!! The images came in a swirl, Rat said, and there was no way you could process it all. Off in the gloom a few dim figures lounged in hammocks, or on cots, but none of them moved or spoke. The background music came from a tape deck near the circle of candles, but the high voice was Mary Anne's.

After a second Mark Fossie made a soft moaning sound. He started to get up but then stiffened.

"Mary Anne?" he said.

Quietly then, she stepped out of the shadows. At least for a moment she seemed to be the same pretty young girl who had arrived a few weeks earlier.

She was barefoot. She wore her pink sweater and a white blouse and a simple cotton skirt.

For a long while the girl gazed down at Fossie, almost blankly, and in the candlelight her face had the composure of someone perfectly at peace with herself. It took a few seconds, Rat said, to appreciate the full change. In part it was her eyes: utterly flat and indifferent. There was no emotion in her stare, no sense of the person behind it. But the grotesque part, he said, was her jewelry. At the girl's throat was a necklace of human tongues. Elongated and narrow, like pieces of blackened leather, the tongues were threaded along a length of copper wire, one overlapping the next, the tips curled upward as if caught in a final shrill syllable.

Briefly, it seemed, the girl smiled at Mark Fossie.

"There's no sense talking," she said. "I know what you think, but it's not... it's not *bad*."

"Bad?" Fossie murmured.

"It's not."

In the shadows there was laughter.

One of the Greenies sat up and lighted a cigar. The others lay silent.

"You're in a place," Mary Anne said softly, "where you don't belong."

She moved her hand in a gesture that encompassed not just the hootch but everything around it, the entire war, the mountains, the mean little villages, the trails and trees and rivers and deep misted-over valleys.

"You just don't *know*," she said. "You hide in this little fortress, behind wire and sandbags, and you don't know what it's all about. Sometimes I want to *eat* this place. Vietnam. I want to swallow the whole country—the dirt, the death— I just want to eat it and have it there inside me. That's how I feel. It's like... this appetite. I get scared sometimes—lots of times—but it's not *bad*. You know? I feel close to myself. When I'm out there at night, I feel close to my own body, I can feel my blood moving, my skin and my fingernails, everything, it's like I'm full of electricity and I'm glowing in the dark—I'm on fire almost—I'm burning away into nothing—but it doesn't matter because I know exactly who I am. You can't feel like that anywhere else."

All this was said softly, as if to herself, her voice slow and impassive. She was not trying to persuade. For a few moments she looked at Mark Fossie, who seemed to shrink away, then she turned and moved back into the gloom.

There was nothing to be done.

Rat took Fossie's arm, helped him up, and led him outside. In the darkness there was that weird tribal music, which seemed to come from the earth itself, from the deep rain forest, and a woman's voice rising up in a language beyond translation.

Mark Fossie stood rigid.

"Do something," he whispered. "I can't just let her go like that."

Rat listened for a time, then shook his head.

"Man, you must be deaf. She's already gone."

Rat Kiley stopped there, almost in midsentence, which drove Mitchell Sanders crazy.

"What next?" he said.

"Next?"

"The girl. What happened to her?"

Rat made a small, tired motion with his shoulders. "Hard to tell for sure. Maybe three, four days later I got orders to report here to Alpha Company. Jumped the first chopper out, that's the last I ever seen of the place. Mary Anne, too."

Mitchell Sanders stared at him.

"You can't do that."

"Do what?"

"Jesus Christ, it's against the *rules*," Sanders said. "Against human *nature*. This elaborate story, you can't say, Hey, by the way, I don't know the *ending*. I mean, you got certain obligations."

Rat gave a quick smile. "Patience, man. Up to now, everything I told you is from personal experience, the exact truth, but there's a few other things I heard secondhand. Thirdhand, actually. From here on it gets to be… I don't know what the word is."

"Speculation."

"Yeah, right." Rat looked off to the west, scanning the mountains, as if expecting something to appear on one of the high ridgelines. After a second he shrugged. "Anyhow, maybe two months later I ran into Eddie Diamond over in Bangkok—I was on R&R, just this fluke thing—and he told me some stuff I can't vouch for with my own eyes. Even Eddie didn't really see it. He heard it from one of the Greenies, so you got to take this with a whole shakerful of salt."

Once more, Rat searched the mountains, then he sat back and closed his eyes.

"You know," he said abruptly, "I loved her."

"Say again?"

"A lot. We all did, I guess. The way she looked, Mary Anne made you think about those girls back home, how clean and innocent they all are, how they'll never understand any of this, not in a billion years. Try to tell them about it, they'll just stare at you with those big round candy eyes. They won't understand zip. It's like trying to tell somebody what chocolate tastes like."

Mitchell Sanders nodded. "Or shit."

"There it is, you got to taste it, and that's the thing with Mary Anne. She was *there*. She was up to her eyeballs in it. After the war, man, I promise you, you won't find nobody like her."

Suddenly, Rat pushed up to his feet, moved a few steps away from us, then stopped and stood with his back turned. He was an emotional guy.

"Got hooked, I guess," he said. "I loved her. So when I heard from Eddie about what happened, it almost made me… Like you say, it's pure speculation."

"Go on," Mitchell Sanders said. "Finish up."

What happened to her, Rat said, was what happened to all of them. You come over clean and you get dirty and then afterward it's never the same. A question of degree. Some make it intact, some don't make it at all. For Mary Anne Bell, it seemed, Vietnam had the effect of a powerful drug: that mix of unnamed terror and unnamed pleasure that comes as the needle slips in and you know you're risking something. The endorphins start to flow, and the adrenaline, and you hold your breath and creep quietly through the moonlit nightscapes; you become intimate with danger; you're in touch with the far side of yourself, as though it's another hemisphere, and you want to string it out and go wherever the trip takes you and be host to all the possibilities inside yourself. Not *bad*, she'd said. Vietnam made her glow in the dark. She wanted more, she wanted to penetrate deeper into the mystery of herself, and after a time the wanting became needing, which turned then to craving.

According to Eddie Diamond, who heard it from one of the Greenies, she took a greedy pleasure in night patrols. She was good at it; she had the moves. All camouflaged up, her face smooth and vacant, she seemed to flow like water through the dark, like oil, without sound or center. She went barefoot. She stopped carrying a weapon. There were times, apparently, when she took crazy, death-wish chances—things that even the Greenies balked at. It was as if she were taunting some wild creature out in the bush, or in her head, inviting it to show itself, a curious game of hide-and-go-seek that was played out in the dense terrain of a nightmare. She was lost inside herself. On occasion, when they were taken under fire, Mary Anne would stand quietly and watch the tracer rounds snap by, a little smile at her lips, intent on some private transaction with the war. Other times she would simply vanish altogether—for hours, for days.

And then one morning, all alone, Mary Anne walked off into the mountains and did not come back.

No body was ever found. No equipment, no clothing. For all he knew, Rat said, the girl was still alive. Maybe up in one of the high mountain villes, maybe with the Montagnard tribes. But that was guesswork.

There was an inquiry, of course, and a week-long air search, and for a time the Tra Bong compound went crazy with MP and CID types. In the end, however, nothing came of it. It was a war and the war went on. Mark Fossie was busted to PFC, shipped back to a hospital in the States, and two months later received a medical discharge. Mary Anne Bell joined the missing.

But the story did not end there. If you believed the Greenies, Rat said, Mary Anne was still somewhere out there in the dark. Odd movements, odd shapes. Late at night, when the Greenies were out on ambush, the whole rain forest seemed to stare in at them—a watched feeling—and a couple of times they almost saw her sliding through the shadows. Not quite, but almost. She had crossed to the other side. She was part of the land. She was wearing her culottes, her pink sweater, and a necklace of human tongues. She was dangerous. She was ready for the kill.

# POETRY

## JULIA ALVAREZ

### *How I Learned to Sweep* (1996)

My mother never taught me sweeping.
One afternoon she found me watching
t.v. She eyed the dusty floor
boldly, and put a broom before
me, and said she'd like to be able                                   5
to eat her dinner off that table,
and nodded at my feet, then left.
I knew right off what she expected
and went at it. I stepped and swept;
the t.v. blared the news; I kept                                    10
my mind on what I had to do,
until in minutes, I was through.
Her floor was immaculate
as a just-washed dinner plate.
I waited for her to return                                         15
and turned to watch the President,
live from the White House, talk of war:
in the Far East our soldiers were
landing in their helicopters
into jungles their propellers                                      20
swept like weeds seen underwater
while perplexing shots were fired
from those beautiful green gardens
into which these dragonflies
filled with little men descended.                                  25
I got up and swept again
as they fell out of the sky.
I swept all the harder when
I watched a dozen of them die—
as if their dust fell through the screen                           30
upon the floor I had just cleaned.
She came back and turned the dial;
the screen went dark. *That's beautiful*,
she said, and ran her clean hand through
my hair, and on, over the window-                                  35

sill, coffee table, rocker, desk,
and held it up—I held my breath—
That's beautiful, she said, impressed,
she hadn't found a speck of death.

## MARGARET ATWOOD

### *At first I was given centuries*                    (1971)

At first I was given centuries
to wait in caves, in leather
tents, knowing you would never come back

Then it speeded up: only
several years between                                    5
the day you jangled off
into the mountains, and the day (it was
spring again) I rose from the embroidery
frame at the messenger's entrance.

That happened twice, or was it
10
more; and there was once, not so
long ago, you failed,
and came back in a wheelchair
with a moustache and a sunburn
and were insufferable.                                   15

Time before last though, I remember
I had a good eight months between
running alongside the train, skirts hitched, handing
you violets in at the window
and opening the letter; I watched                        20
your snapshot fade for twenty years.

And last time (I drove to the airport
still dressed in my factory
overalls, the wrench
I had forgotten sticking out of the back                 25
pocket; there you were,

zippered and helmeted, it was zero
hour, you said Be
Brave) it was at least three weeks before
I got the telegram and could start regretting.                          30

But recently, the bad evenings
there are only seconds
between the warning on the radio and the
explosion; my hands
don't reach you                                                         35

and on quieter nights
you jump up from
your chair without even touching your dinner
and I can scarcely kiss you goodbye
before you run out into the street and they shoot                       40

## Study and Discussion Questions

1. Who is speaking; who is the "I" of the poem? Who is the "you" of the poem?
2. In what ways does the speaker change and in what ways remain the same?
3. Describe the progression of situations from stanza to stanza.
4. Discuss how time is used in this poem.
4. Who are "they" in the last line?
5. Why do you think there is no period at the end of the poem?
6. Discuss the gender roles described in the poem.

## Suggestions for Writing

1. Can you identify any particular wars the speaker has lived through? What are the clues?
2. What is the mood of the poem? What feelings does it evoke as you read it?
3. Compare/contrast "At first I was given centuries" to another Margaret Atwood poem about war, "The Loneliness of the Miliary Historian," on the issues of both war and gender.

## Critical Resources

1. Cooke, Natalie. *Margaret Atwood: A Biography.* Toronto: ECW Press, 1998.
2. Nischik, Reingard, ed. *Margaret Atwood: Works and Impact.* Rochester, NY: Camden House, 2000.
3. Wilson, Sharon, ed. *Margaret Atwood's Textual Assassinations: Recent Poetry and Fiction.* Columbus: Ohio State University Press, 2003.
4. York, Lorraine, ed. *Various Atwoods: Essays on the Later Poems, Short Fiction and Novels.* Toronto: Anansi, 1995.

❀ ❀ ❀

## EMILY DICKINSON

### *Success is counted sweetest*                    (1890)

Success is counted sweetest
By those who ne'er succeed.
To comprehend a nectar
Requires sorest need.

Not one of all the purple Host                        5
Who took the Flag today
Can tell the definition
So clear of victory

As he defeated – dying –
On whose forbidden ear                               10
The distant strains of triumph
Burst agonized and clear!

❋ ❋ ❋

## YUSEF KOMUNYAKAA

### *Facing It*                                      (1988)

My black face fades,
hiding inside the black granite.
I said I wouldn't,
dammit: No tears.
I'm stone. I'm flesh.                                 5
My clouded reflection eyes me
like a bird of prey, the profile of night
slanted against morning. I turn
this way—the stone lets me go.
I turn that way—I'm inside                            10
the Vietnam Veterans Memorial
again, depending on the light
to make a difference.
I go down the 58,022 names,

half-expecting to find                                                15
my own in letters like smoke.
I touch the name Andrew Johnson;
I see the booby trap's white flash.
Names shimmer on a woman's blouse
but when she walks away                                               20
the names stay on the wall.
Brushstrokes flash, a red bird's
wings cutting across my stare.
The sky. A plane in the sky.
A white vet's image floats                                            25
closer to me, then his pale eyes
look through mine. I'm a window.
He's lost his right arm
inside the stone. In the black mirror
a woman's trying to erase names:                                      30
No, she's brushing a boy's hair.

❀ ❀ ❀

## RICHARD LOVELACE

### *To Lucasta, Going to the Wars*                              (1649)

Tell me not, sweet, I am unkind
That from the nunnery
Of thy chaste breast and quiet mind,
To war and arms I fly.

True, a new mistress now I chase,                                     5
The first foe in the field;
And with a stronger faith embrace
A sword, a horse, a shield.

Yet this inconstancy is such
As you too shall adore;                                               10
I could not love thee, dear, so much,
Loved I not honor more.

**WILFRED OWEN**

## *Anthem for Doomed Youth* (1917)

What passing-bells for these who die as cattle?
　　— Only the monstrous anger of the guns.
　　Only the stuttering rifles' rapid rattle
Can patter out their hasty orisons.
No mockeries now for them; no prayers nor bells;　　　　5
　　Nor any voice of mourning save the choirs,—
The shrill, demented choirs of wailing shells;
　　And bugles calling for them from sad shires.

What candles may be held to speed them all?
　　Not in the hands of boys, but in their eyes　　　　10
Shall shine the holy glimmers of goodbyes.
　　The pallor of girls' brows shall be their pall;
Their flowers the tenderness of patient minds,
And each slow dusk a drawing-down of blinds.

**WILFRED OWEN**

## *Arms and the Boy* (1931)

Let the boy try along this bayonet-blade
How cold steel is, and keen with hunger of blood;
Blue with all malice, like a madman's flash;
And thinly drawn with famishing for flesh.

Lend him to stroke these blind, blunt bullet-leads,　　　　5
Which long to nuzzle in the hearts of lads,
Or give him cartridges of fine zinc teeth
Sharp with the sharpness of grief and death.

For his teeth seem for laughing round an apple.
There lurk no claws behind his fingers supple;　　　　10
And God will grow no talons at his heels,
Nor antlers through the thickness of his curls.

**WILFRED OWEN**

## *Dulce Et Decorum Est*[1]  (1920)


Bent double, like old beggars under sacks,
Knock-kneed, coughing like hags, we cursed through sludge,
Till on the haunting flares we turned our backs
And towards our distant rest began to trudge.
Men marched asleep. Many had lost their boots 5
But limped on, blood-shod. All went lame; all blind;
Drunk with fatigue; deaf even to the hoots
Of tired, outstripped Five-Nines[2] that dropped behind.

Gas! Gas! Quick boys!—An ecstasy of fumbling,
Fitting the clumsy helmets just in time; 10
But someone still was yelling out and stumbling
And flound'ring like a man in fire or lime ...
Dim, through the misty panes and thick green light,
As under a green sea, I saw him drowning.

In all my dreams, before my helpless sight, 15
He plunges at me, guttering, choking, drowning.

If in some smothering dreams you too could pace
Behind the wagon that we flung him in,
And watch the white eyes writhing in his face,
His hanging face, like a devil's sick of sin; 20
If you could hear, at every jolt, the blood
Come gargling from the froth-corrupted lungs,
Obscene as cancer, bitter as the cud
Of vile, incurable sores on innocent tongues,—
My friend, you would not tell with such high zest 25
To children ardent for some desperate glory,
The old Lie: Dulce et decorum est
Pro patria mori.

---

[1]See the last two lines for full quotation from Horace: "It is sweet and proper to die for one's country."
[2]Gas shells.

## Study and Discussion Questions

1.  Who is speaking in the poem? Where is he? What does he list in the first stanza about the conditions of himself and the other soldiers?
2.  In terms of the "plot" of this poem, what happens, suddenly, in the second stanza?
3.  Where is the speaker of the poem in the third, two-line, stanza?
4.  Note the change in verb tense in the final stanza. How is this prepared for in the previous couplet?
5.  To whom is the poem addressed? How does Owens involve the reader before the poem is done? And why does he want to do so?
6.  Look at the images: What are the soldiers in general and the dying soldier in particular compared to?
7.  Do some research on World War I weapons and modes of warfare. How does Owen's use of metaphor and simile capture the experience?

## Suggestions for Writing

1.  Which image in the poem strikes you most forcefully? Why?
2.  Write your own critique (or defense) of the quote from Horace.
3.  Compare World War I warfare and weapons with contemporary warfare and weapons.
4.  Write a contemporary poem on the actual experience of battle. What is your theme? Choose the words and the images to convey that theme and mood.

## Critical Resources

1.  Fussell, Paul. *The Great War and Modern Memory.* London: Oxford University Press, 1975.
2.  Hibberd, Dominic. *Wilfred Owen: A New Biography.* Chicago: Ivan R. Dee, 2003.
3.  Hipp, Daniel. "By Degrees Regain[ing] Cool Peaceful Air in Wonder: Wilfred Owen's War Poetry as Psychological Therapy." *Journal of the Midwest Modern Language Association* 35.1 (2002) 25–49.
4.  Purkis, John. *A Preface to Wilfred Owen.* London: Longman, 1999.

❀ ❀ ❀

# ADRIENNE RICH

## *The School Among the Ruins* (2004)

Beirut. Baghdad. Sarajevo. Bethlehem. Kabul. Not of course here.

### 1.

Teaching the first lesson and the last
—great falling light of summer will you last
longer than schooltime?

When children flow
in columns at the doors                                    5
BOYS GIRLS and the busy teachers

open or close high windows
with hooked poles drawing darkgreen shades

closets unlocked, locked
questions unasked, asked, when                            10

love of the fresh impeccable
sharp-pencilled yes
order without cruelty

a street on earth neither heaven nor hell
busy with commerce and worship                           15
young teachers walking to school

fresh bread and early-open foodstalls

### 2.

When the offensive rocks the sky when nightglare
misconstrues day and night when lived-in

rooms from the upper city                                20
tumble cratering lower streets

cornices of olden ornament human debris
when fear vacuums out the streets

When the whole town flinches
blood on the undersole thickening to glass                    25

Whoever crosses hunched knees bent a contested zone
knows why she does this suicidal thing

School's now in session day and night
children sleep
in the classrooms teachers rolled close                       30

**3.**

How the good teacher loved
his school the students
the lunchroom with fresh sandwiches

lemonade and milk
the classroom glass cages                                     35
of moss and turtles
teaching responsibility

A morning breaks without bread or fresh-poured milk
parents or lesson-plans
diarrhea first question of the day                            40
children shivering it's September
Second question: where is my mother?

**4.**

One: I don't know where your mother
is Two: I don't know
why they are trying to hurt us                                45
Three: or the latitude and longitude
of their hatred Four: I don't know if we
hate them as much I think there's more toilet paper
in the supply closet I'm going to break it open

Today this is your lesson:                                    50
write as clearly as you can
your name home street and number
down on this page
No you can't go home yet
but you aren't lost                                           55
this is our school

I'm not sure what we'll eat
we'll look for healthy roots and greens
searching for water though the pipes are broken

**5.**

There's a young cat sticking                               60
her head through window bars
she's hungry like us
but can feed on mice
her bronze erupting fur
speaks of a life already wild                              65

her golden eyes
don't give quarter She'll teach us Let's call her
Sister
when we get milk we'll give her some

**6.**

I've told you, let's try to sleep in this funny camp       70
All night pitiless pilotless things go shrieking
above us to somewhere

Don't let your faces turn to stone
Don't stop asking me why
Let's pay attention to our cat she needs us                75

Maybe tomorrow the bakers can fix their ovens

**7.**

"We sang them to naps told stories made
shadow-animals with our hands

washed human debris off boots and coats
sat learning by heart the names                            80
some were too young to write
some had forgotten how"

## Study and Discussion Questions

1. What function does the preface to the poem—"Beruit. Baghdad. Sarajevo. Bethlehem. Kabul. Not of course here."—serve?
2. There are seven sections to "The School Among the Ruins." What purpose does each section have? How does each section develop the overall image of the school among the ruins? As well as an image, is there a story being told here? What is it?
3. List at least four things that have changed for the students and teachers now that the school is in a war zone.
4. Discuss the images and the importance of food in the poem.
5. Discuss the appearance of the cat in section 5. How does the teacher turn this into a lesson? How is this lesson a measure of their changed circumstances?
6. In section 6 the teacher says to the students: "Don't let your faces turn to stone/ Don't stop asking me why." Discuss.
7. Section seven is in quotation marks. Who is speaking here and to whom? Identify the point of view in each of the seven sections of "The School Among the Ruins."
8. "The School Among the Ruins" gives us a vivid image of the situation of children in a time of war. Why do you think Adrienne Rich set this poem in a school instead of, say, in a refugee camp or some other location?

## Suggestions for Writing

1. Do some research on the situation of children in a contemporary war zone. Unfortunately, you have quite a few to choose from.
2. Write a short poem or vivid prose piece from the point of view of one of the boys or girls in Rich's "The School Among the Ruins."

## Critical Resources

1. *Adrienne Rich*. The Lannen Foundation, 1992 (60 minutes). For more information go to <http://www.lannan.org>. This is one film of several on Adrienne Rich's work.
2. Birkle, Carmen. *Women's Stories of the Looking Glass: Autobiographical Reflections and Self-Representations in the Poetry of Sylvia Plath, Adrienne Rich, and Audre Lorde.* Munich, Germany: Fink, 1996.
3. Charlesworth, Barbara and Albert Gelpi, eds. *Adrienne Rich's Poetry and Prose: Poems, Prose, Reviews and Criticism.* New York: Norton, 1993.
4. Rich, Adrienne. *Arts of the Possible: Essays and Conversations.* New York: Norton, 2001.
5. Sielke, Sabine. *Fashioning the Female Subject: The Intertextual Networking of Dickinson, Moore, and Rich.* Ann Arbor: University of Michigan Press, 1997.

❀ ❀ ❀

**BRUCE WEIGL**

## *Song of Napalm* (1988)

*for my wife*

After the storm, after the rain stopped pounding,
we stood in the doorway watching horses
walk off lazily across the pasture's hill.
We stared through the black screen,
our vision altered by the distance                                    5
so I thought I saw a mist
kicked up around their hooves when they faded
like cut-out horses
away from us.
The grass was never more blue in that light, more              10
scarlet; beyond the pasture
trees scraped their voices into the wind, branches
crisscrossed the sky like barbed wire
but you said they were only branches.

Okay. The storm stopped pounding.                              15
I am trying to say this straight: for once
I was sane enough to pause and breathe
outside my wild plans and after the hard rain
I turned my back on the old curses. I believed
they swung finally away from me ...                            20

But still the branches are wire
and thunder is the pounding mortar,
still I close my eyes and see the girl
running from her village, napalm
stuck to her dress like jelly,                                 25
her hands reaching for the no one
who waits in waves of heat before her.

So I can keep on living,
so I can stay here beside you,
I try to imagine she runs down the road and wings              30
beat inside her until she rises
above the stinking jungle and her pain
eases, and your pain, and mine.
But the lie swings back again.
The lie works only as long as it takes to speak                35

and the girl runs only as far
as the napalm allows

until her burning tendons and crackling
muscles draw her up
into that final position                                    40
burning bodies so perfectly assume. Nothing
can change that, she is burned behind my eyes
and not your good love and not the rain-swept air
and not the jungle-green
pasture unfolding before us can deny it.                    45

# IDENTITY

## FICTION

**SHERMAN ALEXIE**

### *Jesus Christ's Half-Brother Is Alive and Well on the Spokane Indian Reservation* (1993)

#### 1966

Rosemary MorningDove gave birth to a boy today and seeing as how it was nearly Christmas and she kept telling everyone she was still a virgin even though Frank Many Horses said it was his we all just figured it was an accident. Anyhow she gave birth to him but he came out all blue and they couldn't get him to breathe for a long time but he finally did and Rosemary MorningDove named him ———— which is unpronounceable in Indian and English but it means: *He Who Crawls Silently Through the Grass with a Small Bow and One Bad Arrow Hunting for Enough Deer to Feed the Whole Tribe.*

We just call him James.

#### 1967

Frank Many Horses and Lester FallsApart and I were drinking beers in the Breakaway Bar playing pool and talking stories when we heard the sirens. Indians get all excited when we hear sirens because it means fires and it means they need firefighters to put out the fires and it means we get to be firefighters and it means we get paid to be firefighters. Hell somebody always starts a fire down at the Indian burial grounds and it was about time for the Thirteenth Annual All-Indian Burial Grounds Fire so Frank and Lester and I ran down to the fire station expecting to get hired but we see smoke coming from Commodity Village where all the really poor Indians live so we run down there instead and it was Rosemary MorningDove's house that was on fire. Indians got buckets of water but this fire was way too big and we could hear a baby crying and Frank Many

Horses gets all excited even though it's Lillian Many's baby right next to us. But Frank knows James is in the house so he goes running in before any of us can stop him and pretty soon I see Frank leaning out the upstairs window holding James and they're both a little on fire and Frank throws James out the window and I'm running my ass over to catch him before he hits the ground making like a high school football hero again but I miss him just barely slipping through my fingers and James hits the ground hard and I pick him up right away and slap the flames out with my hands all the while expecting James to be dead but he's just looking at me almost normal except the top of his head looks all dented in like a beer can.

He wasn't crying.

## 1967

I went down to the reservation hospital to see how James and Frank and Rosemary were doing and I got drunk just before I went so I wouldn't be scared of all the white walls and the sound of arms and legs getting sawed off down in the basement. But I heard the screams anyway and they were Indian screams and those can travel forever like all around the world and sometimes from a hundred years ago so I close my ears and hide my eyes and just look down at the clean clean floors. Oh Jesus I'm so drunk I want to pray but I don't and before I can change my mind about coming here Moses MorningDove pulls me aside to tell me Frank and Rosemary have died and since I saved James's life I should be the one who raises him. Moses says it's Indian tradition but somehow since Moses is going on about two hundred years old and still drinking and screwing like he was twenty I figure he's just trying to get out of his grandfatherly duties. I don't really want any of it and I'm sick and the hospital is making me sicker and my heart is shaking and confused like when the nurse wakes you up in the middle of the night to give you a sleeping pill but I know James will end up some Indian kid at a welfare house making baskets and wearing itchy clothes and I'm only twenty myself but I take one look at James all lumpy and potato looking and I look in the mirror and see myself holding him and I take him home.

Tonight the mirror will forgive my face.

## 1967

All dark tonight and James couldn't sleep and just kept looking at the ceiling so I walk on down to the football field carrying James so we can both watch the stars looking down at the reservation. I put James down on the fifty-yard line and I run and run across the frozen grass wishing there was snow enough to make a trail and let the world know I was there in the morning. Thinking I could spell out my name or James's name or every name I could think of until I stepped on every piece of snow on the field like it was every piece of the world or at least every piece of this reservation that has so many pieces it might just be the world. I want to walk circles around James getting closer and closer to him in a new dance and a better kind of healing which could make James talk and walk before he learns to cry. But he's not crying and he's not walking and he's not talking and I see him sometimes like an old man passed out in the back of a reservation van with shit in his pants and a battered watch in his pocket that always shows the same damn time. So I pick James up from the cold and the grass that waits for spring and the sun to change its world but I can only walk home through the cold with another future on my back and James's future tucked in my pocket like an empty wallet or a newspaper that feeds the fire and never gets read.

Sometimes all of this is home.

## 1968

The world changing the world changing the world. I don't watch the TV anymore since it exploded and left a hole in the wall. The woodpile don't dream of me no more. It sits there by the ax and they talk about the cold that waits in corners and surprises you on a warm almost spring day. Today I stood at the window for hours and then I took the basketball from inside the wood stove and shot baskets at the hoop nailed to a pine tree in the yard. I shot and shot until the cold meant I was protected because my skin was too warm to feel any of it. I shot and shot until my fingertips bled and my feet ached and my hair stuck to the skin of my bare back. James waited by the porch with his hands in the dirt and his feet stuck into leather shoes I found in the dump under a washing machine. I can't believe the details I am forced to remember with each day that James comes closer to talking. I change his clothes and his dirty pants and I wash his face and the crevices of his little body until he shines like a new check.

This is my religion.

## 1968

Seems like the cold would never go away and winter would be like the bottom of my feet but then it is gone in one night and in its place comes the sun so large and laughable. James sitting up in his chair so young and he won't talk and the doctors at the Indian clinic say it's way too early for him to be talking anyhow but I see in his eyes something and I see in his eyes a voice and I see in his eyes a whole new set of words. It ain't Indian or English and it ain't cash register and it ain't traffic light or speed bump and it ain't window or door. Late one day James and I watch the sun fly across the sky like a basketball on fire until it falls down completely and lands in Benjamin Lake with a splash and shakes the ground and even wakes up Lester Falls-Apart who thought it was his father come back to slap his face again.

Summer coming like a car from down the highway.

## 1968

James must know how to cry because he hasn't cried yet and I know he's wait-ing for that one moment to cry like it was five hundred years of tears. He ain't walked anywhere and there are no blisters on his soles but there are dreams worn clean into his rib cage and it shakes and shakes with each breath and I see he's trying to talk when he grabs at the air behind his head or stares up at the sky so hard. All of this temperature rising hot and I set James down in the shade by the basketball court and I play and I play until the sweat of my body makes it rain everywhere on the reservation. I play and I play until the music of my shoes against pavement sounds like every drum. Then I'm home alone and I watch the cockroaches live their complicated lives.

I hold James with one arm and my basketball with the other arm and I hold everything else inside my whole body.

## 1969

I take James to the Indian clinic because he ain't crying yet and because all he does sometimes is stare and stare and sometimes he'll wrap his arms around the stray dogs and let them carry him around the yard. He's strong enough to hold his body off the ground but he ain't strong enough to lift his tongue from the bottom of his mouth to use the words for love or anger or hunger or good morning. Maybe he's only a few years old but he's got eyes that are ancient and old and dark like a castle or a lake where the turtles go to die and sometimes even to live. Maybe he's going to howl out the words when I least expect it or want it and he'll yell out a cuss word in church or a prayer in the middle of a grocery store. Today I moved through town and walked and walked past the peo-ple who hadn't seen me in so long maybe for months and they asked questions about me and James and no one bothered to knock on the door and look for the answers. It's just me and James walking and walking except he's on my back and his eyes are looking past the people who are looking past us for the coyote of our soul and the wolverine of our heart and the crazy crazy man that touches every Indian who spends too much time alone. I stand in the Trading Post touch-ing the canned goods and hoping for a vision of all the miles until Seymour comes in with a twenty-dollar bill and buys a couple cases of beer and we drink and drink all night long. James gets handed from woman to woman and from man to man and a few children hold this child of mine who doesn't cry or rec-ognize the human being in his own body. All the drunks happy to see me drunk again and back from the wagon and I fell off that wagon and broke my ass and dreams and I wake up the next morning in a field watching a cow watch me. With piss in my pants I make the long walk home past the HUD houses and aban-doned cars and past the powwow grounds and the Assembly of God where the sinless sing like they could forgive us all. I get home and James is there with Suzy Song feeding him and rocking him like a boat or a three-legged chair.

I say no and I take James away and put him in his crib and I move into Suzy's arms and let her rock and rock me away from my stomach and thin skin.


**1969**


Long days and nights mean the sky looks the same all the time and James has no words yet but he dreams and kicks in his sleep and sometimes kicks his body against my body as he sleeps in my arms. Nobody dreams all the time because it would hurt too much but James keeps dreaming and sleeping through a summer rainstorm and heat lightning reaching down a hand and then a fist to tear a tree in half and then to tear my eyes in half with the light. We had venison for dinner. We ate deer and its wild taste shook me up and down my spine. James spit his mouthful out on the floor and the dogs came to finish it up and I ate and ate and the dogs ate and ate what they could find and the deer grew in my stomach. The deer grew horns and hooves and skin and eyes that pushed at my rib cage and I ate and ate until I could not feel anything but my stomach expanding and stretched full.

All my life the days I remember most with every detail sharp and clear are the days when my stomach was full.


**1969**


We played our first basketball game of the season tonight in the community center and I had Suzy Song watch James while I played and all of us warriors roaring against the air and the nets and the clock that didn't work and our memories and our dreams and the twentieth-century horses we called our legs. We played some Nez Percé team and they ran like they were still running from the cavalry and they were kicking the shit out of us again when I suddenly steal the ball from their half-white point guard and drive all the way to the bucket. I jump in the air planning to dunk it when the half-white point guard runs under me knocking my ass to the floor and when I land I hear a crunch and my leg bends in half the wrong way. They take me to the reservation hospital and later on they tell me my leg has exploded and I can't play ball for a long time or maybe forever and when Suzy comes by with James and they ask me if this is my wife and son and I tell them yes and James still doesn't make a noise and so they ask me how old he is. I tell them he's almost four years old and they say his physical development is slow but that's normal for an Indian child. Anyhow I have to have an operation and all but since I don't have the money or the strength or the memory and it's not covered by Indian Health I just get up and walk home almost crying because my leg and life hurt so bad. Suzy stays with me that night and in the dark she touches my knee and asks me how much it hurts and I tell her it hurts more than I can talk about so she kisses all my scars and she huddles up close to me and she's warm and she talks into my ear close. She isn't always asking questions and sometimes she has the answers. In the morning I wake up before her and I hobble into the kitchen and make some coffee and fix a couple of bowls of cornflakes and we sit in bed eating together while James lies still in his crib watching the ceiling so Suzy and I watch the ceiling too.

The ordinary can be like medicine.

## 1970

Early snow this year and James and I sit at home by the stove because I can't walk anywhere with my bad knee and since it is snowing so hard outside nobody could drive out to get us but I know somebody must be thinking about us because if they weren't we'd just disappear just like those Indians who used to climb the pueblos. Those Indians disappeared with food still cooking in the pot and air waiting to be breathed and they turned into birds or dust or the blue of the sky or the yellow of the sun.

There they were and suddenly they were forgotten for just a second and for just a second nobody thought about them and then they were gone.

## 1970

I took James down to the reservation hospital again because he was almost five years old and still hadn't bothered to talk yet or crawl or cry or even move when I put him on the floor and once I even dropped him and his head was bleeding and he didn't make a sound. They looked him over and said there was nothing wrong with him and that he's just a little slow developing and that's what the doctors always say and they've been saying that about Indians for five hundred years. Jesus I say don't you know that James wants to dance and to sing and to pound a drum so hard it hurts your ears and he ain't ever going to drop an eagle feather and he's always going to be respectful to elders at least the Indian elders and he's going to change the world. He's going to dynamite Mount Rushmore or hijack a plane and make it land on the reservation highway. He's going to be a father and a mother and a son and a daughter and a dog that will pull you from a raging river.

He'll make gold out of commodity cheese.

## 1970

Happy birthday James and I'm in the Breakaway Bar drinking too many beers when the Vietnam war comes on television. The white people always want to fight someone and they always get the dark-skinned people to do the fighting. All I know about this war is what Seymour told me when he came back from his tour of duty over there and he said all the gooks he killed looked like us and

Seymour said every single gook he killed looked exactly like someone he knew on the reservation. Anyhow I go to a Christmas party over at Jana Wind's house and leave James with my auntie so I could get really drunk and not have to worry about coming home for a few days or maybe for the rest of my life. We all get really drunk and Jana's old man Ray challenges me to a game of one-on-one since he says I'm for shit now and was never any good anyway but I tell him I can't since my knee is screwed up and besides there's two feet of snow on the ground and where are we going to play anyhow? Ray says I'm chickenshit so I tell him come on and we drive over to the high school to the outside court and there's two feet of snow on the court and we can't play but Ray smiles and pulls out a bottle of kerosene and pours it all over the court and lights it up and pretty soon the snow is all melted down along with most of Lester FallsApart's pants since he was standing too close to the court when Ray lit the fire. Anyhow the court is clear and Ray and I go at it and my knee only hurts a little and everyone was cheering us on and I can't remember who won since I was too drunk and so was everyone else. Later I hear how Ray and Joseph got arrested for beating some white guy half to death and I say that Ray and Joseph are just kids but Suzy says nobody on the reservation is ever a kid and that we're all born grown up anyway. I look at James and I think maybe Suzy is wrong about Indian kids being born adults and that maybe James was born this way and wants to stay this way like a baby because he doesn't want to grow up and see and do everything we all do?

There are all kinds of wars.

## 1971

So much time alone with a bottle of one kind or another and James and I remember nothing except the last drink and a drunk Indian is like the thinker statue except nobody puts a drunk Indian in a special place in front of a library. For most Indians the only special place in front of a library might be a heating grate or a piece of sun-warmed cement but that's an old joke and I used to sleep with my books in piles all over my bed and sometimes they were the only thing keeping me warm and always the only thing keeping me alive.

Books and beer are the best and worst defense.

## 1971

Jesse WildShoe died last night and today was the funeral and usually there's a wake but none of us had the patience or energy to mourn for days so we buried Jesse right away and dug the hole deep because Jesse could fancydance like God had touched his feet. Anyhow we dug the hole all day and since the ground was still a little frozen we kept doing the kerosene trick and melting the ice and frost and when we threw a match into the bottom of the grave it looked like I suppose hell must look and it was scary. There we were ten little Indians making a hell on earth for a fancydancer who already had enough of that shit and probably wouldn't want to have any more of it and I kept wondering if maybe we should just take his body high up in the mountains and bury him in the snow that never goes away. Maybe we just sort of freeze him so he doesn't have to feel anything anymore and especially not some crazy ideas of heaven or hell. I don't know anything about religion and I don't confess my sins to anybody except the walls and the wood stove and James who forgives everything like a rock. He ain't talking or crying at all and sometimes I shake him a little too hard or yell at him or leave him in his crib for hours all alone but he never makes a sound. One night I get so drunk I leave him at somebody's house and forget all about him and can you blame me? The tribal police drag me into the cell for abandonment and I'm asking them who they're going to arrest for abandoning me but the world is spinning and turning back on itself like a snake eating its own tail. Like a snake my TV dinner rises from the table the next day and snaps at my eyes and wrists and I ask the tribal cop how long I've been drunk and he tells me for most of a year and I don't remember any of it. I've got the DT's so bad and the walls are Nazis making lampshades out of my skin and the toilet is a white man in a white hood riding me down on horseback and the floor is a skinny man who wants to teach me a trick he's learned to do with a knife and my shoes squeal and kick and pull me down into the dead pig pit of my imagination. Oh Jesus I wake up on the bottom of that mass grave with the bones of generations of slaughter and I crawl and dig my way up through layers and years of the lunch special. I dig for hours through the skin and eyes and the fresh blood soon enough and pull myself through the eye of a sow and pluck the maggots from my hair and I want to scream but I don't want to open my mouth and taste and taste and taste.

Like the heroin addict said I just want to be pure.

## 1971

Been in A.A. for a month because that was the only way to keep James with me and my auntie and Suzy Song both moved into the house with me to make sure I don't drink and to help take care of James. They show the same old movies in A.A. and it's always the same white guy who almost destroys his life and his wife and his children and his job but finally realizes the alcohol is killing him and he quits overnight and spends the rest of the movie and the rest of his whole life at a picnic with his family and friends and boss all laughing and saying we didn't even recognize you back then Bob and we're glad to have you back Daddy and we'll hire you back at twice the salary you old dog you. Yesterday I get this postcard from Pine Ridge and my cousin says all the Indians there are gone and do I know where they went? I write back and tell him to look in the A.A. meeting and then I ask him if there are more birds with eyes that look like his and I ask him if the sky is more blue and the sun more yellow because those are the colors we all become when we die. I tell him to search his dreams for a man dressed in red with a red tie and red shoes and a hawk head. I tell him that man is fear and will eat you like a sandwich and will eat you like an ice cream cone and will never be full and he'll come for you in your dreams like he was a bad movie. I tell him to turn his television toward the wall and to study the walls for imperfections and those could be his mother and father and the stain on the ceiling could be his sisters and maybe the warped floorboard squeaking and squeaking is his grandfather talking stories.

Maybe they're all hiding on a ship in a bottle.


**1972**


Been sober so long it's like a dream but I feel better somehow and Auntie was so proud of me she took James and me into the city for James's checkup and James still wasn't talking but Auntie and James and I ate a great lunch at Woolworth's before we headed back to the reservation. I got to drive and Auntie's uranium money Cadillac is a hell of a car and it was raining a little and hot so there were rainbows rainbows rainbows and the pine trees looked like wise men with wet beards or at least I thought they did. That's how I do this life sometimes by making the ordinary just like magic and just like a card trick and just like a mirror and just like the disappearing. Every Indian learns how to be a magician and learns how to misdirect attention and the dark hand is always quicker than the white eye and no matter how close you get to my heart you will never find out my secrets and I'll never tell you and I'll never show you the same trick twice.

I'm traveling heavy with illusions.


**1972**


Every day I'm trying not to drink and I pray but I don't know who I'm praying to and if it's the basketball gathering ash on the shelf or the blank walls crushing me into the house or the television that only picks up public channels. I've seen only painters and fishermen and I think they're both the same kind of men who made a different choice one time in their lives. The fisherman held a rod in his hand and said yes and the painter held a brush in his hand and said yes and sometimes I hold a beer in my hand and say yes. At those moments I want to drink so bad that it aches and I cry which is a strange noise in our house because James refuses tears and he refuses words but sometimes he holds a hand up above his head like he's reaching for something. Yesterday I neatly trip over Lester FallsApart lying drunk as a skunk in front of the Trading Post and I pick him up and he staggers and trembles and falls back down. Lester I say you got to stand up on your own and I pick him up and he falls down again.

Only a saint would have tried to pick him up the third time.

## 1972

The streetlight outside my house shines on tonight and I'm watching it like it could give me vision. James ain't talked ever and he looks at that streetlight like it was a word and maybe like it was a verb. James wanted to streetlight me and make me bright and beautiful so all the moths and bats would circle me like I was the center of the world and held secrets. Like Joy said that everything but humans keeps secrets. Today I get my mail and there's a light bill and a postcard from an old love from Seattle who asks me if I still love her like I used to and would I come to visit?

I send her my light bill and tell her I don't ever want to see her again.

## 1973

James talked today but I had my back turned and I couldn't be sure it was real. He said potato like any good Indian would because that's all we eat. But maybe he said I love you because that's what I wanted him to say or maybe he said geology or mathematics or college basketball. I pick him up and ask him again and again what did you say? He just smiles and I take him to the clinic and the doctors say it's about time but are you sure you didn't imagine his voice? I said James's voice sounded like a beautiful glass falling off the shelf and landing safely on a thick shag carpet.

The doctor said I had a very good imagination.

## 1973

I'm shooting hoops again with the younger Indian boys and even some Indian girls who never miss a shot. They call me old man and elder and give me a little bit of respect like not running too fast or hard and even letting me shoot a few more than I should. It's been a long time since I played but the old feelings and old moves are there in my heart and in my fingers. I see these Indian kids and I know that basketball was invented by an Indian long before that Naismith guy ever thought about it. When I play I don't feel like drinking so I wish I could play twenty-four hours a day seven days a week and then I wouldn't wake up shaking and quaking and needing just one more beer before I stop for good. James knows it too and he sits on the sideline clapping when my team scores and clapping when the other team scores too. He's got a good heart. He always talks whenever I'm not in the room or I'm not looking at him but never when anybody else might hear so they all think I'm crazy. I am crazy. He says things like I can't believe. He says $E = MC^2$ and that's why all my cousins drink themselves to death. He says the earth is an oval marble that nobody can win. He says the sky is not blue and the grass is not green.

He says everything is a matter of perception.

## 1973

Christmas and James gets his presents and he gives me the best present of all when he talks right at me. He says so many things and the only thing that matters is that he says he and I don't have the right to die for each other and that we should be living for each other instead. He says the world hurts. He says the first thing he wanted after he was born was a shot of whiskey. He says all that and more. He tells me to get a job and to grow my braids. He says I better learn how to shoot left-handed if I'm going to keep playing basketball. He says to open a fireworks stand.

Every day now there are little explosions all over the reservation.

## 1974

Today is the World's Fair in Spokane and James and I drive to Spokane with a few cousins of mine. All the countries have exhibitions like art from Japan and pottery from Mexico and mean-looking people talking about Germany. In one little corner there's a statue of an Indian who's supposed to be some chief or another. I press a little button and the statue talks and moves its arms over and over in the same motion. The statue tells the crowd we have to take care of the earth because it is our mother. I know that and James says he knows more. He says the earth is our grandmother and that technology has become our mother and that they both hate each other. James tells the crowd that the river just a few yards from where we stand is all we ever need to believe in. One white woman asks me how old James is and I tell her he's seven and she tells me that he's so smart for an Indian boy. James hears this and tells the white woman that she's pretty smart for an old white woman. I know this is how it will all begin and how the rest of my life will be. I know when I am old and sick and ready to die that James will wash my body and take care of my wastes. He'll carry me from HUD house to sweathouse and he will clean my wounds. And he will talk and teach me something new every day.

But all that is so far ahead.

### Study and Discussion Questions

1. Discuss the title of Alexie's story. (*Note:* Jesus did have a brother or cousin named James.) What possibilities for redemption exist in the story?

2. Consider the child's two names.
3. How does Alexie's narrator become a (single) parent? How does this change his life? How does he change in response? Note several examples of the narrator's development throughout the story.
4. What do we learn about life on the Reservation from this story? List at least five points, citing evidence from the text.
5. Discuss the structure of the story. Why do you think Alexie chose to narrate the story in short, date-headed sections? Why the pattern of the substantial paragraph followed by a short one-sentence paragraph? Do you find this an effective way of telling this particular story?
6. Choose a few *images* (literal or figurative) that particularly strike you and discuss each. What does each image evoke for you? How and why are they effective?
7. Alexie said in a 1996 talk, (November 9, 1996, University of Massachusetts/Boston) "The most revolutionary thing I can do is raise a kid that loves him or her self." Discuss Alexie's statement in relation to this story.
8. How is Alexie's narrator as a parent? List positive and negative qualities, citing examples for each.
9. If it takes a village to raise a child, how is the Spokane Indian community as parenting support for the narrator?
10. Discuss both the religious (in the sense of allusions to the story of Christ) and the spiritual (e.g., the circumstances of the adoption, James's "strangeness," the language Alexie uses) implications of "Jesus Christ's Half-Brother Is Alive and Well on the Spokane Indian Reservation."
11. Does James finally talk? Give evidence from the story to support your opinion.
12. As it happens, 1966, the year the story of James begins, is also the year Sherman Alexie was born. How might this biographical fact add to your interpretation of the story?

**Suggestions for Writing**

1. Do some reading and research on life on Indian reservations in the United States. Then discuss this story along with the three Sherman Alexie poems "Futures," "The Reservation Cab Driver," and "The Powwow at the End of the World".
2. In the Bible (the King James translation, if possible), read the Epistle of James in the New Testament. Also read Acts XV, where James makes an important speech to the Apostles. How do some of the issues and themes connected with the Biblical James resonate with the story of James and his adoptive father in Alexie's story?
3. Consider Alexie's choice to structure his story in short titled sections. Compare/contrast to Pamela Zoline's use of an analogous form in her story "The Heat Death of the Universe" (Varieties of Protest). How are their purposes different, and how does this structure support each?
4. Exercise in form/technique: Try writing a short story in numbered or labeled sections.
5. See *Smoke Signals,* a film based on Sherman Alexie's short stories, and write a paper on film adaptation—how the film uses material and themes

from this short story. You might want to read the other stories in Alexie's 1993 collection, *The Lone Ranger and Tonto Fistfight in Heaven.*

### Critical Resources

1. City Lore and Poets House. *People's Poetry Gathering.* April 18, 2005. <http://www.peoplespoetry.org/pg_clips_audvid.html>.
2. Fraser, Joelle. "An Interview with Sherman Alexie." *Iowa Review.* (2000): 59–70.
3. *shermanalexie.com.* 18 April 2005. <http://www.shermanalexie.com>.
4. Spencer, Russ. "What It Means to Be Sherman Alexie." *Book Magazine.com.* 18 April 2005. <http://www.bookmagazine.com/archive/issue11/alexie.shtml>.

## JAMES BALDWIN

## *Sonny's Blues*                                                   (1957)

I read about it in the paper, in the subway, on my way to work. I read it, and I couldn't believe it, and I read it again. Then perhaps I just stared at it, at the newsprint spelling out his name, spelling out the story. I stared at it in the swinging lights of the subway car, and in the faces and bodies of the people, and in my own face, trapped in the darkness which roared outside.

It was not to be believed and I kept telling myself that, as I walked from the subway station to the high school. And at the same time I couldn't doubt it. I was scared, scared for Sonny. He became real to me again. A great block of ice got settled in my belly and kept melting there slowly all day long, while I taught my classes algebra. It was a special kind of ice. It kept melting, sending trickles of ice water all up and down my veins, but it never got less. Sometimes it hardened and seemed to expand until I felt my guts were going to come spilling out or that I was going to choke or scream. This would always be at a moment when I was remembering some specific thing Sonny had once said or done.

When he was about as old as the boys in my classes his face had been bright and open, there was a lot of copper in it; and he'd had wonderfully direct brown eyes, and great gentleness and privacy. I wondered what he looked like now. He had been picked up, the evening before, in a raid on an apartment downtown, for peddling and using heroin.

I couldn't believe it: but what I mean by that is that I couldn't find any room for it anywhere inside me. I had kept it outside me for a long time. I hadn't wanted to know. I had had suspicions, but I didn't name them, I kept putting them away. I told myself that Sonny was wild, but he wasn't crazy. And he'd always been a good boy, he hadn't ever turned hard or evil or disrespectful, the way kids can, so quick, so quick, especially in Harlem. I didn't want to believe that I'd ever see my brother going down, coming to nothing, all that light in his face gone out, in the condition I'd already seen so many others. Yet it had happened and here I was, talking about algebra to a lot of boys who might, every one of them for all I knew, be popping off needles every time they went to the head. Maybe it did more for them than algebra could.

I was sure that the first time Sonny had ever had horse, he couldn't have been much older than these boys were now. These boys, now, were living as we'd been living then, they were growing up with a rush and their heads bumped abruptly against the low ceiling of their actual possibilities. They were filled with rage. All they really knew were two darknesses, the darkness of their lives, which was now closing in on them, and the darkness of the movies, which had blinded them to that other darkness, and in which they now, vindictively, dreamed, at once more together than they were at any other time, and more alone.

When the last bell rang, the last class ended, I let out my breath. It seemed I'd been holding it for all that time. My clothes were wet—I may have looked as though I'd been sitting in a steam bath, all dressed up, all afternoon. I sat alone in the classroom a long time. I listened to the boys outside, downstairs, shouting and cursing and laughing. Their laughter struck me for perhaps the first time. It was not the joyous laughter which—God knows why—one associates with children. It was mocking and insular, its intent was to denigrate. It was disenchanted, and in this, also, lay the authority of their curses. Perhaps I was listening to them because I was thinking about my brother and in them I heard my brother. And myself.

One boy was whistling a tune, at once very complicated and very simple, it seemed to be pouring out of him as though he were a bird, and it sounded very cool and moving through all that harsh, bright air, only just holding its own through all those other sounds.

I stood up and walked over to the window and looked down into the courtyard. It was the beginning of the spring and the sap was rising in the boys. A teacher passed through them every now and again, quickly, as though he or she couldn't wait to get out of that courtyard, to get those boys out of their sight and off their minds. I started collecting my stuff. I thought I'd better get home and talk to Isabel.

The courtyard was almost deserted by the time I got downstairs. I saw this boy standing in the shadow of a doorway, looking just like Sonny. I almost called his name. Then I saw that it wasn't Sonny, but somebody we used to know, a boy from around our block. He'd been Sonny's friend. He'd never been mine, having been too young for me, and, anyway, I'd never liked him. And now, even though he was a grown-up man, he still hung around that block, still spent hours on the street corners, was always high and raggy. I used to run into him from time to time and he'd often work around to asking me for a quarter or fifty cents. He always had some real good excuse, too, and I always gave it to him, I don't know why.

But now, abruptly, I hated him. I couldn't stand the way he looked at me, partly like a dog, partly like a cunning child. I wanted to ask him what the hell he was doing in the school courtyard.

He sort of shuffled over to me, and he said, "I see you got the papers. So you already know about it."

"You mean about Sonny? Yes, I already know about it. How come they didn't get you?"

He grinned. It made him repulsive and it also brought to mind what he'd looked like as a kid. "I wasn't there. I stay away from them people."

"Good for you." I offered him a cigarette and I watched him through the smoke. "You come all the way down here just to tell me about Sonny?"

"That's right." He was sort of shaking his head and his eyes looked strange, as though they were about to cross. The bright sun deadened his damp dark brown skin and it made his eyes look yellow and showed up the dirt in his kinked hair. He smelled funky. I moved a little away from him and I said, "Well, thanks. But I already know about it and I got to get home."

"I'll walk you a little ways," he said. We started walking. There were a couple of kids still loitering in the courtyard and one of them said goodnight to me and looked strangely at the boy beside me.

"What're you going to do?" he asked me. "I mean, about Sonny?"

"Look. I haven't seen Sonny for over a year, I'm not sure I'm going to do anything. Anyway, what the hell *can* I do?"

"That's right," he said quickly, "ain't nothing you can do. Can't much help old Sonny no more, I guess."

It was what I was thinking and so it seemed to me he had no right to say it.

"I'm surprised at Sonny, though," he went on—he had a funny way of talking, he looked straight ahead as though he were talking to himself—"I thought Sonny was a smart boy, I thought he was too smart to get hung."

"I guess he thought so too," I said sharply, "and that's how he got hung. And how about you? You're pretty goddamn smart, I bet."

Then he looked directly at me, just for a minute. "I ain't smart," he said. "If I was smart, I'd have reached for a pistol a long time ago."

"Look. Don't tell *me* your sad story, if it was up to me, I'd give you one." Then I felt guilty—guilty, probably, for never having supposed that the poor bastard *had* a story of his own, much less a sad one, and I asked, quickly, "What's going to happen to him now?"

He didn't answer this. He was off by himself some place. "Funny thing," he said, and from his tone we might have been discussing the quickest way to get to Brooklyn, "when I saw the papers this morning, the first thing I asked myself was if I had anything to do with it. I felt sort of responsible."

I began to listen more carefully. The subway station was on the corner, just before us, and I stopped. He stopped, too. We were in front of a bar and he ducked slightly, peering in, but whoever he was looking for didn't seem to be there. The juke box was blasting away with something black and bouncy and I half watched the barmaid as she danced her way from the juke box to her place behind the bar. And I watched her face as she laughingly responded to something someone said to her, still keeping time to the music. When she smiled one saw the little girl, one sensed the doomed, still-struggling woman beneath the battered face of the semiwhore.

"I never *give* Sonny nothing," the boy said finally, "but a long time ago I come to school high and Sonny asked me how it felt." He paused, I couldn't bear to watch him, I watched the barmaid, and I listened to the music which seemed to be causing the pavement to shake. "I told him it felt great." The music stopped, the barmaid paused and watched the juke box until the music began again. "It did."

All this was carrying me some place I didn't want to go. I certainly didn't want to know how it felt. It filled everything, the people, the houses, the music, the dark, quicksilver barmaid, with menace; and this menace was their reality.

"What's going to happen to him now?" I asked again.

"They'll send him away some place and they'll try to cure him." He shook his head. "Maybe he'll even think he's kicked the habit. Then they'll let him loose"— he gestured, throwing his cigarette into the gutter. "That's all."

"What do you mean, that's *all?*"

But I knew what he meant.

"I *mean*, that's *all.*" He turned his head and looked at me, pulling down the corners of his mouth. "Don't you know what I mean?" he asked, softly.

"How the hell *would* I know what you mean?" I almost whispered it, I don't know why.

"That's right," he said to the air, "how would *he* know what I mean?" He turned toward me again, patient and calm, and yet I somehow felt him shaking, shaking as though he were going to fall apart. I felt that ice in my guts again, the dread I'd felt all afternoon; and again I watched the barmaid, moving about the bar, washing glasses, and singing. "Listen. They'll let him out and then it'll just start all over again. That's what I mean."

"You mean—they'll let him out. And then he'll just start working his way back in again. You mean he'll never kick the habit. Is that what you mean?"

"That's right," he said, cheerfully. "*You* see what I mean."

"Tell me," I said at last, "why does he want to die? He must want to die, he's killing himself, why does he want to die?"

He looked at me in surprise. He licked his lips. "He don't want to die. He wants to live. Don't nobody want to die, ever."

Then I wanted to ask him—too many things. He could not have answered, or if he had, I could not have borne the answers. I started walking. "Well, I guess it's none of my business."

"It's going to be rough on old Sonny," he said. We reached the subway station. "This is your station?" he asked. I nodded. I took one step down. "Damn!" he said, suddenly. I looked up at him. He grinned again. "Damn it if I didn't leave all my money home. You ain't got a dollar on you, have you? Just for a couple of days, is all."

All at once something inside gave and threatened to come pouring out of me. I didn't hate him any more. I felt that in another moment I'd start crying like a child.

"Sure," I said. "Don't sweat." I looked in my wallet and didn't have a dollar, I only had a five. "Here," I said. "That hold you?"

He didn't look at it—he didn't want to look at it. A terrible, closed look came over his face, as though he were keeping the number on the bill a secret from him and me. "Thanks," he said, and now he was dying to see me go. "Don't worry about Sonny. Maybe I'll write him or something."

"Sure," I said. "You do that. So long."

"Be seeing you," he said. I went on down the steps.

And I didn't write Sonny or send him anything for a long time. When I finally did, it was just after my little girl died, he wrote me back a letter which made me feel like a bastard.

Here's what he said:

Dear brother,

You don't know how much I needed to hear from you. I wanted to write you many a time but I dug how much I must have hurt you and so I didn't write. But now I feel like a man who's been trying to climb up out of some deep, real deep and funky hole and just saw the sun up there, outside. I got to get outside.

I can't tell you much about how I got here. I mean I don't know how to tell you. I guess I was afraid of something or I was trying to escape from something and you know I have never been very strong in the head (smile). I'm glad Mama and Daddy are dead and can't see what's happened to their son and I swear if I'd known what I was doing I would never have hurt you so, you and a lot of other fine people who were nice to me and who believed in me.

I don't want you to think it had anything to do with me being a musician. It's more than that. Or maybe less than that. I can't get anything straight in my head down here and I try not to think about what's going to happen to me when I get outside again. Sometime I think I'm going to flip and *never* get outside and some-time I think I'll come straight back. I tell you one thing, though, I'd rather blow my brains out than go through this again. But that's what they all say, so they tell me. If I tell you when I'm coming to New York and if you could meet me, I sure would appreciate it. Give my love to Isabel and the kids and I was sure sorry to hear about little Gracie. I wish I could be like Mama and say the Lord's will be done, but I don't know it seems to me that trouble is the one thing that never does get stopped and I don't know what good it does to blame it on the Lord. But maybe it does some good if you believe it.

Your brother,
Sonny

Then I kept in constant touch with him and I sent him whatever I could and I went to meet him when he came back to New York. When I saw him many things I thought I had forgotten came flooding back to me. This was because I had begun, finally, to wonder about Sonny, about the life that Sonny lived inside. This life, whatever it was, had made him older and thinner and it had deepened the distant stillness in which he had always moved. He looked very unlike my baby brother. Yet, when he smiled, when we shook hands, the baby brother I'd never known looked out from the depths of his private life, like an animal waiting to be coaxed into the light.

"How you been keeping?" he asked me.

"All right. And you?"

"Just fine." He was smiling all over his face. "It's good to see you again."

"It's good to see you."

The seven years' difference in our ages lay between us like a chasm: I wondered if these years would ever operate between us as a bridge. I was remembering, and it made it hard to catch my breath, that I had been there when he was born; and I had heard the first words he had ever spoken. When he started to walk, he walked from our mother straight to me. I caught him just before he fell when he took the first steps he ever took in this world.

"How's Isabel?"

"Just fine. She's dying to see you."

"And the boys?"

"They're fine, too. They're anxious to see their uncle."

"Oh, come on. You know they don't remember me."

"Are you kidding? Of course they remember you."

He grinned again. We got into a taxi. We had a lot to say to each other, far too much to know how to begin.

As the taxi began to move, I asked, "You still want to go to India?"

He laughed. "You still remember that. Hell, no. This place is Indian enough for me."

"It used to belong to them," I said.

And he laughed again. "They damn sure knew what they were doing when they got rid of it."

Years ago, when he was around fourteen, he'd been all hipped on the idea of going to India. He read books about people sitting on rocks, naked, in all kinds of weather, but mostly bad, naturally, and walking barefoot through hot coals and arriving at wisdom. I used to say that it sounded to me as though they were getting away from wisdom as fast as they could. I think he sort of looked down on me for that.

"Do you mind," he asked, "if we have the driver drive alongside the park? On the west side—I haven't seen the city in so long."

"Of course not," I said. I was afraid that I might sound as though I were humoring him, but I hoped he wouldn't take it that way.

So we drove along, between the green of the park and the stony, lifeless elegance of hotels and apartment buildings, toward the vivid, killing streets of our childhood. These streets hadn't changed, though housing projects jutted up out of them now like rocks in the middle of a boiling sea. Most of the houses in which we had grown up had vanished, as had the stores from which we had stolen, the basements in which we had first tried sex, the rooftops from which we had hurled tin cans and bricks. But houses exactly like the houses of our past yet dominated the landscape, boys exactly like the boys we once had been found themselves smothering in these houses, came down into the streets for light and air and found themselves encircled by disaster. Some escaped the trap, most didn't. Those who got out always left something of themselves behind, as some animals amputate a leg and leave it in the trap. It might be said, perhaps, that I had escaped, after all, I was a school teacher; or that Sonny had, he hadn't lived in Harlem for years. Yet, as the cab moved uptown through streets which seemed, with a rush, to darken with dark people, and as I covertly studied Sonny's face, it came to me that what we both were seeking through our separate cab windows was that part of ourselves which had been left behind. It's always at the hour of trouble and confrontation that the missing member aches.

We hit 110th Street and started rolling up Lenox Avenue. And I'd known this avenue all my life, but it seemed to me again, as it had seemed on the day I'd first heard about Sonny's trouble, filled with a hidden menace which was its very breath of life.

"We almost there," said Sonny.

"Almost." We were both too nervous to say anything more.

We live in a housing project. It hasn't been up long. A few days after it was up it seemed uninhabitably new, now, of course, it's already rundown. It looks like a parody of the good, clean, faceless life—God knows the people who live in it do their best to make it a parody. The beat-looking grass lying around isn't enough to make their lives green, the hedges will never hold out the streets, and they know it. The big windows fool no one, they aren't big enough to make space out of no space. They don't bother with the windows, they watch the TV screen instead. The playground is most popular with the children who don't play at jacks, or skip rope, or roller skate, or swing, and they can be found in it after dark. We moved in partly because it's not too far from where I teach, and partly for the kids; but it's really just like the houses in which Sonny and I grew up. The same things happen, they'll have the same things to remember. The moment Sonny and I started into the house I had the feeling that I was simply bringing him back into the danger he had almost died trying to escape.

Sonny has never been talkative. So I don't know why I was sure he'd be dying to talk to me when supper was over the first night. Everything went fine, the oldest boy remembered him, and the youngest boy liked him, and Sonny had remembered to bring something for each of them; and Isabel, who is really much nicer than I am, more open and giving, had gone to a lot of trouble about dinner and was genuinely glad to see him. And she's always been able to tease Sonny in a way that I haven't. It was nice to see her face so vivid again and to hear her laugh and watch her make Sonny laugh. She wasn't, or, anyway, she didn't seem to be, at all uneasy or embarrassed. She chatted as though there were no subject which had to be avoided and she got Sonny past his first, faint stiffness. And thank God she was there, for I was filled with that icy dread again. Everything I did seemed awkward to me, and everything I said sounded freighted with hidden meaning. I was trying to remember everything I'd heard about dope addiction and I couldn't help watching Sonny for signs. I wasn't doing it out of malice. I was trying to find out something about my brother. I was dying to hear him tell me he was safe.

"Safe!" my father grunted, whenever Mama suggested trying to move to a neighborhood which might be safer for children. "Safe, hell! Ain't no place safe for kids, nor nobody."

He always went on like this, but he wasn't, ever, really as bad as he sounded, not even on weekends, when he got drunk. As a matter of fact, he was always on the lookout for "something a little better," but he died before he found it. He died suddenly, during a drunken weekend in the middle of the war, when Sonny was fifteen. He and Sonny hadn't ever got on too well. And this was partly because Sonny was the apple of his father's eye. It was because he loved Sonny so much and was frightened for him, that he was always fighting with him. It doesn't do any good to fight with Sonny. Sonny just moves back, inside himself, where he can't be reached. But the principal reason that they never hit it off is that they were so much alike. Daddy was big and rough and loud-talking, just the opposite of Sonny, but they both had—that same privacy.

Mama tried to tell me something about this, just after Daddy died. I was home on leave from the army.

This was the last time I ever saw my mother alive. Just the same, this picture gets all mixed up in my mind with pictures I had of her when she was younger. The way I always see her is the way she used to be on a Sunday afternoon, say, when the old folks were talking after the big Sunday dinner. I always see her wearing pale blue. She'd be sitting on the sofa. And my father would be sitting in the easy chair, not far from her. And the living room would be full of church folks and relatives. There they sit, in chairs all around the living room, and the night is creeping up outside, but nobody knows it yet. You can see the darkness growing against the windowpanes and you hear the street noises every now and again, or maybe the jangling beat of a tambourine from one of the churches close by, but it's real quiet in the room. For a moment nobody's talking, but every face looks darkening, like the sky outside. And my mother rocks a little from the waist, and my father's eyes are closed. Everyone is looking at something a child can't see. For a minute they've forgotten the children. Maybe a kid is lying on the rug, half asleep. Maybe somebody's got a kid in his lap and is absentmindedly stroking the kid's head. Maybe there's a kid, quiet and big-eyed, curled up in a big chair in the corner. The silence, the darkness coming, and the darkness in the faces frightens the child obscurely. He hopes that the hand which strokes his forehead will never stop—will never die. He hopes that there will never come a time when the old folks won't be sitting around the living room, talking about where they've come from, and what they've seen, and what's happened to them and their kinfolk.

But something deep and watchful in the child knows that this is bound to end, is already ending. In a moment someone will get up and turn on the light. Then the old folks will remember the children and they won't talk any more that day. And when the light fills the room, the child is filled with darkness. He knows that every time this happens he's moved just a little closer to that darkness outside. The darkness outside is what the old folks have been talking about. It's what they've come from. It's what they endure. The child knows that they won't talk any more because if he knows too much about what's happened to *them,* he'll know too much too soon, about what's going to happen to *him.*

The last time I talked to my mother, I remember I was restless. I wanted to get out and see Isabel. We weren't married then and we had a lot to straighten out between us.

There Mama sat, in black, by the window. She was humming an old church song, *Lord, you brought me from a long ways off.* Sonny was out somewhere. Mama kept watching the streets.

"I don't know," she said, "if I'll ever see you again, after you go off from here. But I hope you'll remember the things I tried to teach you."

"Don't talk like that," I said, and smiled. "You'll be here a long time yet."

She smiled, too, but she said nothing. She was quiet for a long time. And I said, "Mama, don't you worry about nothing. I'll be writing all the time, and you be getting the checks. . . ."

"I want to talk to you about your brother," she said, suddenly. "If anything happens to me he ain't going to have nobody to look out for him."

"Mama," I said, "ain't nothing going to happen to you *or* Sonny. Sonny's all right. He's a good boy and he's got good sense."

"It ain't a question of his being a good boy," Mama said, "nor of his having good sense. It ain't only the bad ones, nor yet the dumb ones that gets sucked under." She stopped, looking at me. "Your Daddy once had a brother," she said, and she smiled in a way that made me feel she was in pain. "You didn't never know that, did you?"

"No," I said, "I never knew that," and I watched her face.

"Oh, yes," she said, "your Daddy had a brother." She looked out of the window again. "I know you never saw your Daddy cry. But *I* did—many a time, through all these years."

I asked her, "What happened to his brother? How come nobody's ever talked about him?"

This was the first time I ever saw my mother look old.

"His brother got killed," she said, "when he was just a little younger than you are now. I knew him. He was a fine boy. He was maybe a little full of the devil, but he didn't mean nobody no harm."

Then she stopped and the room was silent, exactly as it had sometimes been on those Sunday afternoons. Mama kept looking out into the streets.

"He used to have a job in the mill," she said, "and, like all young folks, he just liked to perform on Saturday nights. Saturday nights, him and your father would drift around to different places, go to dances and things like that, or just sit around with people they knew, and your father's brother would sing, he had a fine voice, and play along with himself on his guitar. Well, this particular Saturday night, him and your father was coming home from some place, and they were both a little drunk and there was a moon that night, it was bright like day. Your father's brother was feeling kind of good, and he was whistling to himself, and he had his guitar slung over his shoulder. They was coming down a hill and beneath them was a road that turned off from the highway. Well, your father's brother, being always kind of frisky, decided to run down this hill, and he did, with that guitar banging and clanging behind him, and he ran across the road, and he was making water behind a tree. And your father was sort of amused at him and he was still coming down the hill, kind of slow. Then he heard a car motor and that same minute his brother stepped from behind the tree, into the road, in the moonlight. And he started to cross the road. And your father started to run down the hill, he says he don't know why. This car was full of white men. They was all drunk, and when they seen your father's brother they let out a great whoop and holler and they aimed the car straight at him. They was having fun, they just wanted to scare him, the way they do sometimes, you know. But they was drunk. And I guess the boy, being drunk, too, and scared, kind of lost his head. By the time he jumped it was too late. Your father says he heard his brother scream when the car rolled over him, and he heard the wood of that guitar when it give, and he heard them strings go flying, and he heard them white men shouting, and the car kept on a-going and it ain't stopped till this day. And, time your father got down the hill, his brother weren't nothing but blood and pulp."

Tears were gleaming on my mother's face. There wasn't anything I could say.

"He never mentioned it," she said, "because I never let him mention it before you children. Your Daddy was like a crazy man that night and for many a night thereafter. He says he never in his life seen anything as dark as that road after the lights of that car had gone away. Weren't nothing, weren't nobody on that road, just your Daddy and his brother and that busted guitar. Oh, yes. Your Daddy never did really get right again. Till the day he died he weren't sure but that every white man he saw was the man that killed his brother."

She stopped and took out her handkerchief and dried her eyes and looked at me.

"I ain't telling you all this," she said, "to make you scared or bitter or to make you hate nobody. I'm telling you this because you got a brother. And the world ain't changed."

I guess I didn't want to believe this. I guess she saw this in my face. She turned away from me, toward the window again, searching those streets.

"But I praise my Redeemer," she said at last, "that He called your Daddy home before me. I ain't saying it to throw no flowers at myself, but, I declare, it keeps me from feeling too cast down to know I helped your father get safely through this world. Your father always acted like he was the roughest, strongest man on earth. And everybody took him to be like that. But if he hadn't had *me* there—to see his tears!"

She was crying again. Still, I couldn't move. I said, "Lord, Lord, Mama, I didn't know it was like that."

"Oh, honey," she said, "there's a lot that you don't know. But you are going to find it out." She stood up from the window and came over to me. "You got to hold on to your brother," she said, "and don't let him fall, no matter what it looks like is happening to him and no matter how evil you gets with him. You going to be evil with him many a time. But don't you forget what I told you, you hear?"

"I won't forget," I said. "Don't you worry, I won't forget. I won't let nothing happen to Sonny."

My mother smiled as though she were amused at something she saw in my face. Then, "You may not be able to stop nothing from happening. But you got to let him know you's *there.*"

Two days later I was married, and then I was gone. And I had a lot of things on my mind and I pretty well forgot my promise to Mama until I got shipped home on a special furlough for her funeral.

And, after the funeral, with just Sonny and me alone in the empty kitchen, I tried to find out something about him.

"What do you want to do?" I asked him.

"I'm going to be a musician," he said.

For he had graduated, in the time I had been away, from dancing to the juke box to finding out who was playing what, and what they were doing with it, and he had bought himself a set of drums.

"You mean, you want to be a drummer?" I somehow had the feeling that being a drummer might be all right for other people but not for my brother Sonny.

"I don't think," he said, looking at me very gravely, "that I'll ever be a good drummer. But I think I can play a piano."

I frowned. I'd never played the role of the older brother quite so seriously before, had scarcely ever, in fact, *asked* Sonny a damn thing. I sensed myself in the presence of something I didn't really know how to handle, didn't understand. So I made my frown a little deeper as I asked: "What kind of musician do you want to be?"

He grinned, "How many kinds do you think there are?"

"Be *serious,*" I said.

He laughed, throwing his head back, and then looked at me. "I *am* serious."

"Well, then, for Christ's sake, stop kidding around and answer a serious question. I mean, do you want to be a concert pianist, you want to play classical music and all that, or—or what?" Long before I finished he was laughing again. "For Christ's *sake,* Sonny!"

He sobered, but with difficulty. "I'm sorry, But you sound so—*scared!*" and he was off again.

"Well, you may think it's funny now, baby, but's not going to be so funny when you have to make your living at it, let me tell you *that.*" I was furious because I knew he was laughing at me and I didn't know why.

"No," he said, very sober now, and afraid, perhaps, that he'd hurt me, "I don't want to be a classical pianist. That isn't what interests me. I mean"—he paused, looking hard at me, as though his eyes would help me to understand, and then gestured helplessly, as though perhaps his hand would help—"I mean, I'll have a lot of studying to do, and I'll have to study *everything,* but, I mean, I want to play *with*—jazz musicians." He stopped. "I want to play jazz," he said.

Well, the word had never before sounded as heavy, as real, as it sounded that afternoon in Sonny's mouth. I just looked at him and I was probably frowning a real frown by this time. I simply couldn't see why on earth he'd want to spend his time hanging around nightclubs, clowning around on bandstands, while people pushed each other around a dance floor. It seemed—beneath him, somehow. I had never thought about it before, had never been forced to, but I suppose I had always put jazz musicians in a class with what Daddy called "good-time people."

"Are you *serious?*"

"Hell, *yes,* I'm serious."

He looked more helpless than ever, and annoyed, and deeply hurt.

I suggested, helpfully: "You mean—like Louis Armstrong?"

His face closed as though I'd struck him. "No. I'm not talking about none of that old-time, down home crap."

"Well, look, Sonny, I'm sorry, don't get mad. I just don't altogether get it, that's all. Name somebody—you know, a jazz musician you admire."

"Bird."

"Who?"

"Bird! Charlie Parker! Don't they teach you nothing in the goddamn army?"

I lit a cigarette. I was surprised and then a little amused to discover that I was trembling. "I've been out of touch," I said. "You'll have to be patient with me. Now. Who's this Parker character?"

"He's just one of the greatest jazz musicians alive," said Sonny, sullenly, his hands in his pockets, his back to me. "Maybe *the* greatest," he added, bitterly, "that's probably why *you* never heard of him."

"All right," I said, "I'm ignorant. I'm sorry. I'll go out and buy all the cat's records right away, all right?"

"It don't," said Sonny, with dignity, "make any difference to me. I don't care what you listen to. Don't do me no favors."

I was beginning to realize that I'd never seen him so upset before. With another part of my mind I was thinking that this would probably turn out to be one of those things kids go through and that I shouldn't make it seem important by pushing it too hard. Still, I didn't think it would do any harm to ask: "Doesn't all this take a lot of time? Can you make a living at it?"

He turned back to me and half leaned, half sat, on the kitchen table. "Everything takes time," he said, "and—well, yes, sure, I can make a living at it. But what I don't seem to be able to make you understand is that it's the only thing I want to do."

"Well, Sonny," I said, gently, "you know people can't always do exactly what they *want* to do—"

"*No,* I don't know that," said Sonny, surprising me. "I think people *ought* to do what they want to do, what else are they alive for?"

"You getting to be a big boy," I said desperately, "it's time you started thinking about your future."

"I'm thinking about my future," said Sonny, grimly. "I think about it all the time."

I gave up. I decided, if he didn't change his mind, that we could always talk about it later. "In the meantime," I said, "you got to finish school." We had already decided that he'd have to move in with Isabel and her folks. I knew this wasn't the ideal arrangement because Isabel's folks are inclined to be dicty[1] and they hadn't especially wanted Isabel to marry me. But I didn't know what else to do. "And we have to get you fixed up at Isabel's."

There was a long silence. He moved from the kitchen table to the window. "That's a terrible idea. You know it yourself."

"Do you have a *better* idea?"

He just walked up and down the kitchen for a minute. He was as tall as I was. He had started to shave. I suddenly had the feeling that I didn't know him at all.

He stopped at the kitchen table and picked up my cigarettes. Looking at me with a kind of mocking, amused defiance, he put one between his lips. "You mind?"

"You smoking already?"

He lit the cigarette and nodded, watching me through the smoke. "I just wanted to see if I'd have the courage to smoke in front of you." He grinned and blew a great cloud of smoke to the ceiling. "It was easy." He looked at my face. "Come on, now. I bet you was smoking at my age, tell the truth."

I didn't say anything but the truth was on my face, and he laughed. But now there was something very strained in his laugh. "Sure. And I bet that ain't all you was doing."

He was frightening me a little. "Cut the crap," I said. "We already decided that you was going to go and live at Isabel's. Now what's got into you all of a sudden?"

"*You* decided it," he pointed out. "*I* didn't decide nothing." He stopped in front of me, leaning against the stove, arms loosely folded. "Look, brother. I don't want to stay in Harlem no more, I really don't." He was very earnest. He looked at me, then over toward the kitchen window. There was something in his eyes I'd never seen before, some thoughtfulness, some worry all his own. He rubbed the muscle of one arm. "It's time I was getting out of here."

"Where do you want to *go,* Sonny?"

"I want to join the army. Or the navy, I don't care. If I say I'm old enough, they'll believe me."

Then I got mad. It was because I was so scared. "You must be crazy. You goddamn fool, what the hell do you want to go and join the *army* for?"

---

[1]Having upper-class pretensions.

"I just told you. To get out of Harlem."

"Sonny, you haven't even finished *school*. And if you really want to be a musician, how do you expect to study if you're in the *army?*"

He looked at me, trapped, and in anguish. "There's ways. I might be able to work out some kind of deal. Anyway, I'll have the G.I. Bill when I come out."

"*If* you come out." We stared at each other. "Sonny, please. Be reasonable. I know the setup is far from perfect. But we got to do the best we can."

"I ain't learning nothing in school," he said. "Even when I go." He turned away from me and opened the window and threw his cigarette out into the narrow alley. I watched his back. "At least, I ain't learning nothing you'd want me to learn." He slammed the window so hard I thought the glass would fly out, and turned back to me. "And I'm sick of the stink of these garbage cans!"

"Sonny," I said, "I know how you feel. But if you don't finish school now, you're going to be sorry later that you didn't." I grabbed him by the shoulders. "And you only got another year. It ain't so bad. And I'll come back and I swear I'll help you do *whatever* you want to do. Just try to put up with it till I come back. Will you please do that? For me?"

He didn't answer and he wouldn't look at me.

"Sonny. You hear me?"

He pulled away. "I hear you. But you never hear anything *I* say."

I didn't know what to say to that. He looked out of the window and then back at me. "OK," he said, and sighed. "I'll try."

Then I said, trying to cheer him up a little, "They got a piano at Isabel's. You can practice on it."

And as a matter of fact, it did cheer him up for a minute. "That's right," he said to himself. "I forgot that." His face relaxed a little. But the worry, the thoughtfulness, played on it still, the way shadows play on a face which is staring into the fire.

But I thought I'd never hear the end of that piano. At first, Isabel would write me, saying how nice it was that Sonny was so serious about his music and how, as soon as he came in from school, or wherever he had been when he was supposed to be at school, he went straight to that piano and stayed there until suppertime. And, after supper, he went back to that piano and stayed there until everybody went to bed. He was at the piano all day Saturday and all day Sunday. Then he bought a record player and started playing records. He'd play one record over and over again, all day long sometimes, and he'd improvise along with it on the piano. Or he'd play one section of the record, one chord, one change, one progression, then he'd do it on the piano. Then back to the record. Then back to the piano.

Well, I really don't know how they stood it. Isabel finally confessed that it wasn't like living with a person at all, it was like living with sound. And the sound didn't make any sense to her, didn't make any sense to any of them—naturally. They began, in a way, to be afflicted by this presence that was living in their home. It was as though Sonny were some sort of god, or monster. He moved in an atmosphere which wasn't like theirs at all. They fed him and he ate, he washed himself, he walked in and out of their door; he certainly wasn't nasty or unpleasant or rude, Sonny isn't any of those things; but it was as though he were all wrapped up in some cloud, some fire, some vision all his own; and there wasn't any way to reach him.

At the same time, he wasn't really a man yet, he was still a child, and they had to watch out for him in all kinds of ways. They certainly couldn't throw him out. Neither did they dare to make a great scene about that piano because even they dimly sensed, as I sensed, from so many thousands of miles away, that Sonny was at that piano playing for his life.

But he hadn't been going to school. One day a letter came from the school board and Isabel's mother got it—there had, apparently, been other letters but Sonny had torn them up. This day, when Sonny came in, Isabel's mother showed him the letter and asked where he'd been spending his time. And she finally got it out of him that he'd been down in Greenwich Village, with musicians and other characters, in a white girl's apartment. And this scared her and she started to scream at him and what came up, once she began—though she denies it to this day—was what sacrifices they were making to give Sonny a decent home and how little he appreciated it.

Sonny didn't play the piano that day. By evening, Isabel's mother had calmed down but then there was the old man to deal with, and Isabel herself. Isabel says she did her best to be calm but she broke down and started crying. She says she just watched Sonny's face. She could tell, by watching him, what was happening with him. And what was happening was that they penetrated his cloud, they had reached him. Even if their fingers had been a thousand times more gentle than human fingers ever are, he could hardly help feeling that they had stripped him naked and were spitting on that nakedness. For he also had to see that his presence, that music, which was life or death to him, had been torture for them and that they had endured it, not at all for his sake, but only for mine. And Sonny couldn't take that. He can take it a little better today than he could then but he's still not very good at it and, frankly, I don't know anybody who is.

The silence of the next few days must have been louder than the sound of all the music ever played since time began. One morning, before she went to work, Isabel was in his room for something and she suddenly realized that all of his records were gone. And she knew for certain that he was gone. And he was. He went as far as the navy would carry him. He finally sent me a postcard from some place in Greece and that was the first I knew that Sonny was still alive. I didn't see him any more until we were both back in New York and the war had long been over.

He was a man by then, of course, but I wasn't willing to see it. He came by the house from time to time, but we fought almost every time we met. I didn't like the way he carried himself, loose and dreamlike all the time, and I didn't like his friends, and his music seemed to be merely an excuse for the life he led. It sounded just that weird and disordered.

Then we had a fight, a pretty awful fight, and I didn't see him for months. By and by I looked him up, where he was living, in a furnished room in the Village, and I tried to make it up. But there were lots of other people in the room and Sonny just lay on his bed, and he wouldn't come downstairs with me, and he treated these other people as though they were his family and I weren't. So I got mad and then he got mad, and then I told him that he might just as well be dead as live the way he was living. Then he stood up and he told me not to worry about him any more in life, that he *was* dead as far as I was concerned. Then he pushed me to the door and the other people looked on as though nothing were happening, and he slammed the door behind me. I stood in the hallway, staring at the door. I heard somebody laugh in the room and then the tears came to my eyes. I started down the steps, whistling to keep from crying. I kept whistling to myself, *You going to need me, baby, one of these cold, rainy days.*

I read about Sonny's trouble in the spring. Little Grace died in the fall. She was a beautiful little girl. But she only lived a little over two years. She died of polio and she suffered. She had a slight fever for a couple of days, but it didn't seem like anything and we just kept her in bed. And we would certainly have called the doctor, but the fever dropped, she seemed to be all right. So we thought it had just been a cold. Then, one day, she was up, playing, Isabel was in the kitchen fixing lunch for the two boys when they'd come in from school, and she heard Grace fall down in the living room. When you have a lot of children you don't always start running when one of them falls, unless they start screaming or something. And, this time, Grace was quiet. Yet, Isabel says that when she heard that *thump* and then that silence, something happened in her to make her afraid. And she ran to the living room and there was little Grace on the floor, all twisted up, and the reason she hadn't screamed was that she couldn't get her breath. And when she did scream, it was the worst sound, Isabel says, that she'd ever heard in all her life, and she still hears it sometimes in her dreams. Isabel will sometimes wake me up with a low, moaning, strangled sound and I have to be quick to awaken her and hold her to me and where Isabel is weeping against me seems a mortal wound.

I think I may have written Sonny the very day that little Grace was buried. I was sitting in the living room in the dark, by myself, and I suddenly thought of Sonny. My trouble made his real.

One Saturday afternoon, when Sonny had been living with us, or, anyway, been in our house, for nearly two weeks, I found myself wandering aimlessly about the living room, drinking from a can of beer, and trying to work up the courage to search Sonny's room. He was out, he was usually out whenever I was home, and Isabel had taken the children to see their grandparents. Suddenly I was standing still in front of the living room window, watching Seventh Avenue. The idea of searching Sonny's room made me still. I scarcely dared to admit to myself what I'd be searching for. I didn't know what I'd do if I found it. Or if I didn't.

On the sidewalk across from me, near the entrance to a barbecue joint, some people were holding an old-fashioned revival meeting. The barbecue cook, wearing a dirty white apron, his conked[2] hair reddish and metallic in the pale sun, and a cigarette between his lips, stood in the doorway, watching them. Kids and older people paused in their errands and stood there, along with some older men and a couple of very tough-looking women who watched everything that happened on the avenue, as though they owned it, or were maybe owned by it. Well, they were watching this, too. The revival was being carried on by three sisters in black, and a brother. All they had were their voices and their Bibles and a tambourine. The brother was testifying and while he testified two of the sisters stood together, seeming to say, amen, and the third sister walked around with the tambourine outstretched and a couple of people dropped coins into it. Then the brother's testimony ended and the sister who had been taking up the collection dumped the coins into her palm and transferred them to the pocket of her long black robe. Then she raised both hands, striking the tambourine against the air, and then against one hand, and she started to sing. And the two other sisters and the brother joined in.

It was strange, suddenly, to watch, though I had been seeing these street meetings all my life. So, of course, had everybody else down there. Yet, they paused and watched and listened and I stood still at the window. "*Tis the old ship of Zion,*" they sang, and the sister with the tambourine kept a steady, jangling beat, "*it has rescued many a thousand!*" Not a soul under the sound of their voices was hearing this song for the first time, not one of them had been rescued. Nor had they seen much in the way of rescue work being done around them. Neither did they especially believe in the holiness of the three sisters and the brother, they knew too much about them, knew where they lived, and how. The woman with the tambourine, whose voice dominated the air, whose face was bright with joy, was divided by very little from the woman who stood watching her, a cigarette between her heavy, chapped lips, her hair a cuckoo's nest, her face scarred and swollen from many beatings, and her black eyes glittering like coal. Perhaps they both knew this, which was why, when, as rarely, they addressed each other, they addressed each other as Sister. As the singing filled the air the watching, listening faces underwent a change, the eyes focusing on something within; the music seemed to soothe a poison out of them; and time seemed, nearly, to fall away from the sullen, belligerent, battered faces, as though they were fleeing back to their first condition, while dreaming of their last. The barbecue cook half shook his head and smiled, and dropped his cigarette and disappeared into his joint. A man fumbled in his pockets for change and stood holding it in his hand impatiently, as though he had just remembered a pressing appointment further up the avenue. He looked furious. Then I saw Sonny, standing on the edge of the crowd. He was carrying a wide, flat notebook with a green cover, and it made him look, from where I was standing, almost like a schoolboy. The coppery sun brought out the copper in his skin, he was very faintly smiling, standing very still. Then the singing stopped, the tambourine turned into a collection plate again. The furious

---

[2]Straightened.

man dropped in his coins and vanished, so did a couple of the women, and Sonny dropped some change in the plate, looking directly at the woman with a little smile. He started across the avenue, toward the house. He has a slow, loping walk, something like the way Harlem hipsters walk, only he's imposed on this his own half-beat. I had never really noticed it before.

I stayed at the window, both relieved and apprehensive. As Sonny disappeared from my sight, they began singing again. And they were still singing when his key turned in the lock.

"Hey," he said.

"Hey, yourself. You want some beer?"

"No. Well, maybe." But he came up to the window and stood beside me, looking out. "What a warm voice," he said.

They were singing *If I could only hear my mother pray again!*

"Yes," I said, "and she can sure beat that tambourine."

"But what a terrible song," he said, and laughed. He dropped his notebook on the sofa and disappeared into the kitchen. "Where's Isabel and the kids?"

"I think they went to see their grandparents. You hungry?"

"No." He came back into the living room with his can of beer. "You want to come some place with me tonight?"

I sensed, I don't know how, that I couldn't possibly say no. "Sure. Where?"

He sat down on the sofa and picked up his notebook and started leafing through it. "I'm going to sit in with some fellows in a joint in the Village."

"You mean, you're going to play, tonight?"

"That's right." He took a swallow of his beer and moved back to the window. He gave me a sidelong look. "If you can stand it."

"I'll try," I said.

He smiled to himself and we both watched as the meeting across the way broke up. The three sisters and the brother, heads bowed, were singing *God be with you till we meet again.* The faces around them were very quiet. Then the song ended. The small crowd dispersed. We watched the three women and the lone man walk slowly up the avenue.

"When she was singing before," said Sonny, abruptly, "her voice reminded me for a minute of what heroin feels like sometimes—when it's in your veins. It makes you feel sort of warm and cool at the same time. And distant. And—and sure." He sipped his beer, very deliberately not looking at me. I watched his face. "It makes you feel—in control. Sometimes you've got to have that feeling."

"Do you?" I sat down slowly in the easy chair.

"Sometimes." He went to the sofa and picked up his notebook again. "Some people do."

"In order," I asked, "to play?" And my voice was very ugly, full of contempt and anger.

"Well"—he looked at me with great, troubled eyes, as though, in fact, he hoped his eyes would tell me things he could never otherwise say—"they *think* so. And *if* they think so—!"

"And what do *you* think?" I asked.

He sat on the sofa and put his can of beer on the floor. "I don't know," he said, and I couldn't be sure if he were answering my question or pursuing his thoughts. His face didn't tell me. "It's not so much to *play*. It's to *stand* it, to be able to make it at all. On any level." He frowned and smiled: "In order to keep from shaking to pieces."

"But these friends of yours," I said, "they seem to shake themselves to pieces pretty goddamn fast."

"Maybe." He played with the notebook. And something told me that I should curb my tongue, that Sonny was doing his best to talk, that I should listen. "But of course you only know the ones that've gone to pieces. Some don't—or at least they haven't *yet* and that's just about all *any* of us can say." He paused. "And then there are some who just live, really, in hell, and they know it and they see what's happening and they go right on. I don't know." He sighed, dropped the notebook, folded his arms. "Some guys, you can tell from the way they play, they on something *all* the time. And you can see that, well, it makes something real for them. But of course," he picked up his beer from the floor and sipped it and put the can down again, "they *want* to, too, you've got to see that. Even some of them that say they don't—*some,* not all."

"And what about you?" I asked—I couldn't help it. "What about you? Do *you* want to?"

He stood up and walked to the window and remained silent for a long time. Then he sighed. "Me," he said. Then: "While I was downstairs before, on my way here, listening to that woman sing, it struck me all of a sudden how much suffering she must have had to go through—to sing like that. It's *repulsive* to think you have to suffer that much."

I said: "But there's no way not to suffer—is there, Sonny?"

"I believe not," he said and smiled, "but that's never stopped anyone from trying." He looked at me. "Has it?" I realized, with this mocking look, that there stood between us, forever, beyond the power of time or forgiveness, the fact that I had held silence—so long!—when he had needed human speech to help him. He turned back to the window. "No, there's no way not to suffer. But you try all kinds of ways to keep from drowning in it, to keep on top of it, and to make it seem—well, like *you*. Like you did something, all right, and now you're suffering for it. You know?" I said nothing. "Well you know," he said, impatiently, "why *do* people suffer? Maybe it's better to do something to give it a reason, *any* reason."

"But we just agreed," I said, "that there's no way not to suffer. Isn't it better, then, just to—take it?"

"But nobody just takes it," Sonny cried, "that's what I'm telling you! *Everybody* tries not to. You're just hung up on the *way* some people try—it's not *your* way!"

The hair on my face began to itch, my face felt wet. "That's not true," I said, "that's not true. I don't give a damn what other people do, I don't even care how they suffer. I just care how *you* suffer." And he looked at me. "Please believe me," I said, "I don't want to see you—die—trying not to suffer."

"I won't," he said, flatly, "die trying not to suffer. At least, not any faster than anybody else."

"But there's no need," I said, trying to laugh, "is there? in killing yourself."

I wanted to say more, but I couldn't. I wanted to talk about will power and how life could be—well, beautiful. I wanted to say that it was all within; but was it? or, rather, wasn't that exactly the trouble? And I wanted to promise that I would never fail him again. But it would all have sounded—empty words and lies.

So I made the promise to myself and prayed that I would keep it.

"It's terrible sometimes, inside," he said, "that's what's the trouble. You walk these streets, black and funky and cold, and there's not really a living ass to talk to, and there's nothing shaking, and there's no way of getting it out—that storm inside. You can't talk it and you can't make love with it, and when you finally try to get with it and play it, you realize *nobody's* listening. So *you've* got to listen. You got to find a way to listen."

And then he walked away from the window and sat on the sofa again, as though all the wind had suddenly been knocked out of him. "Sometimes you'll do *anything* to play, even cut your mother's throat." He laughed and looked at me. "Or your brother's." Then he sobered. "Or your own." Then: "Don't worry. I'm all right now and I think I'll *be* all right. But I can't forget—where I've been. I don't mean just the physical place I've been, I mean where I've *been*. And *what* I've been."

"What have you been, Sonny?" I asked.

He smiled—but sat sideways on the sofa, his elbow resting on the back, his fingers playing with his mouth and chin, not looking at me. "I've been something I didn't recognize, didn't know I could be. Didn't know anybody could be." He stopped, looking inward, looking helplessly young, looking old. "I'm not talking about it now because I feel *guilty* or anything like that—maybe it would be better if I did, I don't know. Anyway, I can't really talk about it. Not to you, not to anybody," and now he turned and faced me. "Sometimes, you know, and it was actually when I was most *out* of the world, I felt that I was in it, that I was *with* it, really, and I could play or I didn't really have to *play,* it just came out of me, it was there. And I don't know how I played, thinking about it now, but I know I did awful things, those times, sometimes, to people. Or it wasn't that I *did* anything to them—it was that they weren't real." He picked up the beer can; it was empty; he rolled it between his palms: "And other times—well, I needed a fix, I needed to find a place to lean, I needed to clear a space to *listen*—and I couldn't find it, and I—went crazy, I did terrible things to *me,* I was terrible *for* me." He began pressing the beer can between his hands, I watched the metal begin to give. It glittered, as he played with it, like a knife, and I was afraid he would cut himself, but I said nothing. "Oh well. I can never tell you. I was all by myself at the bottom of something, stinking and sweating and crying and shaking, and I smelled it, you know? *my* stink, and I thought I'd die if I couldn't get away from it and yet, all the same, I knew that everything I was doing was just locking me in with it. And I didn't know," he paused, still flattening the beer can, "I didn't know, I still *don't* know, something kept telling me that maybe it was good to smell your own stink, but I didn't think that *that* was what I'd been trying to do—and—who can stand it?" and he abruptly dropped the ruined beer can, looking at me with a small, still smile, and then rose, walking to the window as though it were the lodestone rock. I watched his face, he watched the avenue. "I couldn't tell you when Mama died—but the reason I wanted to leave Harlem so bad was to get away from drugs. And then, when I ran away, that's what I was running from—really. When I came back, nothing had changed, *I* hadn't changed, I was just—older." And he stopped, drumming with his fingers on the windowpane. The sun had vanished, soon darkness would fall. I watched his face. "It can come again," he said, almost as though speaking to himself. Then he turned to me. "It can come again," he repeated. "I just want you to know that."

"All right," I said, at last. "So it can come again, All right."

He smiled, but the smile was sorrowful. "I had to try to tell you," he said.

"Yes," I said. "I understand that."

"You're my brother," he said, looking straight at me, and not smiling at all.

"Yes," I repeated, "yes. I understand that."

He turned back to the window, looking out. "All that hatred down there," he said, "all that hatred and misery and love. It's a wonder it doesn't blow the avenue apart."

We went to the only nightclub on a short, dark street, downtown. We squeezed through the narrow, chattering, jampacked bar to the entrance of the big room, where the bandstand was. And we stood there for a moment, for the lights were very dim in this room and we couldn't see. Then, "Hello, boy," said a voice and an enormous black man, much older than Sonny or myself, erupted out of all that atmospheric lighting and put an arm around Sonny's shoulder. "I been sitting right here," he said, "waiting for you."

He had a big voice, too, and heads in the darkness turned toward us.

Sonny grinned and pulled a little away, and said, "Creole, this is my brother. I told you about him."

Creole shook my hand. "I'm glad to meet you, son," he said, and it was clear that he was glad to meet me *there,* for Sonny's sake. And he smiled, "You got a real musician in *your* family," and he took his arm from Sonny's shoulder and slapped him, lightly, affectionately, with the back of his hand.

"Well. Now I've heard it all," said a voice behind us. This was another musician, and a friend of Sonny's, a coal-black, cheerful-looking man, built close to the ground. He immediately began confiding to me, at the top of his lungs, the most terrible things about Sonny, his teeth gleaming like a lighthouse and his laugh coming up out of him like the beginning of an earthquake. And it turned out that everyone at the bar knew Sonny, or almost everyone; some were musicians, working there, or nearby, or not working, some were simply hangers-on, and some were there to hear Sonny play. I was introduced to all of them and they were all very polite to me. Yet, it was clear that, for them, I was only Sonny's brother. Here, I was in Sonny's world. Or, rather: his kingdom. Here, it was not even a question that his veins bore royal blood.

They were going to play soon and Creole installed me, by myself, at a table in a dark corner. Then I watched them, Creole, and the little black man, and Sonny, and the others, while they horsed around, standing just below the bandstand. The light from the bandstand spilled just a little short of them and, watching them laughing and gesturing and moving about, I had the feeling that they, nevertheless, were being most careful not to step into that circle of light too suddenly: that if they moved into the light too suddenly, without thinking, they would perish in flame. Then, while I watched, one of them, the small, black man, moved into the light and crossed the bandstand and started fooling around with his drums. Then—being funny and being, also, extremely ceremonious—Creole took Sonny by the arm and led him to the piano. A woman's voice called Sonny's name and a few hands started clapping. And Sonny, also being funny and being ceremonious, and so touched, I think, that he could have cried, but neither hiding it nor showing it, riding it like a man, grinned, and put both hands to his heart and bowed from the waist.

Creole then went to the bass fiddle and a lean, very bright-skinned brown man jumped up on the bandstand and picked up his horn. So there they were, and the atmosphere on the bandstand and in the room began to change and tighten. Someone stepped up to the microphone and announced them. Then there were all kinds of murmurs. Some people at the bar shushed others. The waitress ran around, frantically getting in the last orders, guys and chicks got closer to each other, and the lights on the bandstand, on the quartet, turned to a kind of indigo. Then they all looked different there. Creole looked about him for the last time, as though he were making certain that all his chickens were in the coop, and then he—jumped and struck the fiddle. And there they were.

All I know about music is that not many people ever really hear it. And even then, on the rare occasions when something opens within, and the music enters, what we mainly hear, or hear corroborated, are personal, private, vanishing evocations. But the man who creates the music is hearing something else, is dealing with the roar rising from the void and imposing order on it as it hits the air. What is evoked in him, then, is of another order, more terrible because it has no words, and triumphant, too, for that same reason. And his triumph, when he triumphs, is ours. I just watched Sonny's face. His face was troubled, he was working hard, but he wasn't with it. And I had the feeling that, in a way, everyone on the bandstand was waiting for him, both waiting for him and pushing him along. But as I began to watch Creole, I realized that it was Creole who held them all back. He had them on a short rein. Up there, keeping the beat with his whole body, wailing on the fiddle, with his eyes half closed, he was listening to everything, but he was listening to Sonny. He was having a dialogue with Sonny. He wanted Sonny to leave the shoreline and strike out for the deep water. He was Sonny's witness that deep water and drowning were not the same thing—he had been there, and he knew. And he wanted Sonny to know. He was waiting for Sonny to do the things on the keys which would let Creole know that Sonny was in the water.

And, while Creole listened, Sonny moved, deep within, exactly like someone in torment. I had never before thought of how awful the relationship must be between the musician and his instrument. He has to fill it, this instrument, with the breath of life, his own. He has to make it do what he wants it to do. And a piano is just a piano. It's made out of so much wood and wires and little hammers and big ones, and ivory. While there's only so much you can do with it, the only way to find this out is to try; to try and make it do everything.

And Sonny hadn't been near a piano for over a year. And he wasn't on much better terms with his life, not the life that stretched before him now. He and the piano stammered, started one way, got scared, stopped; started another way, panicked, marked time, started again; then seemed to have found a direction, panicked again, got stuck. And the face I saw on Sonny I'd never seen before. Everything had been burned out of it, and, at the same time, things usually hidden were being burned in, by the fire and fury of the battle which was occurring in him up there.

Yet, watching Creole's face as they neared the end of the first set, I had the feeling that something had happened, something I hadn't heard. Then they finished, there was scattered applause, and then, without an instant's warning, Creole started into something else, it was almost sardonic, it was *Am I Blue*. And, as though he commanded, Sonny began to play. Something began to happen. And Creole let out the reins. The dry, low, black man said something awful on the drums, Creole answered, and the drums talked back. Then the horn insisted, sweet and high, slightly detached perhaps, and Creole listened, commenting now and then, dry, and driving, beautiful and calm and old. Then they all came together again, and Sonny was part of the family again. I could tell this from his face. He seemed to have found, right there beneath his fingers, a damn brand-new piano. It seemed that he couldn't get over it. Then, for awhile, just being happy with Sonny, they seemed to be agreeing with him that brand-new pianos certainly were a gas.

Then Creole stepped forward to remind them that what they were playing was the blues. He hit something in all of them, he hit something in me, myself, and the music tightened and deepened, apprehension began to beat the air. Creole began to tell us what the blues were all about. They were not about anything very new. He and his boys up there were keeping it new, at the risk of ruin, destruction, madness, and death, in order to find new ways to make us listen. For, while the tale of how we suffer, and how we are delighted, and how we may triumph is never new, it always must be heard. There isn't any other tale to tell, it's the only light we've got in all this darkness.

And this tale, according to that face, that body, those strong hands on those strings, has another aspect in every country, and a new depth in every generation. Listen, Creole seemed to be saying, listen. Now these are Sonny's blues. He made the little black man on the drums know it, and the bright, brown man on the horn. Creole wasn't trying any longer to get Sonny in the water. He was wishing him Godspeed. Then he stepped back, very slowly, filling the air with the immense suggestion that Sonny speak for himself.

Then they all gathered around Sonny and Sonny played. Every now and again one of them seemed to say, amen. Sonny's fingers filled the air with life, his life.

But that life contained so many others. And Sonny went all the way back, he really began with the spare, flat statement of the opening phrase of the song. Then he began to make it his. It was very beautiful because it wasn't hurried and it was no longer a lament. I seemed to hear with what burning he had made it his, with what burning we had yet to make it ours, how we could cease lamenting. Freedom lurked around us and I understood, at last, that he could help us to be free if we would listen, that he would never be free until we did. Yet, there was no battle in his face now. I heard what he had gone through, and would continue to go through until he came to rest in earth. He had made it his: that long line, of which we knew only Mama and Daddy. And he was giving it back, as everything must be given back, so that, passing through death, it can live forever. I saw my mother's face again, and felt, for the first time, how the stones of the road she had walked on must have bruised her feet. I saw the moonlit road where my father's brother died. And it brought something else back to me, and carried me past it, I saw my little girl again and felt Isabel's tears again, and I felt my own tears begin to rise. And I was yet aware that this was only a moment, that the world waited outside, as hungry as a tiger, and that trouble stretched above us, longer than the sky.

Then it was over. Creole and Sonny let out their breath, both soaking wet, and grinning. There was a lot of applause and some of it was real. In the dark, the girl came by and I asked her to take drinks to the bandstand. There was a long pause, while they talked up there in the indigo light and after awhile I saw the girl put a Scotch and milk on top of the piano for Sonny. He didn't seem to notice it, but just before they started playing again, he sipped from it and looked toward me, and nodded. Then he put it back on top of the piano. For me, then, as they began to play again, it glowed and shook above my brother's head like the very cup of trembling.

### Study and Discussion Questions

1. In what ways are Sonny and his brother different? How, for example, do their relationships to the Harlem community differ? What might account for these differences?
2. Why does Baldwin begin the story with the narrator reading about Sonny in the newspaper? Why does the narrator have so little interest in his brother at first? What is he afraid of? Why does he feel guilty?
3. How were the narrator and Sonny able to grow up together and yet remain such strangers?
4. What experiences bring the narrator closer to Sonny and help him understand his brother better?
5. Why does Sonny use heroin? Why does his music mean so much to him? Why the blues?
6. What has the narrator learned by the end of the story?
7. Events in the story are narrated out of chronological order. What is the effect of the story's structure?

### Suggestions for Writing

1. What do you think Sonny's future might be? Write a brief narrative of the next five or ten years.
2. Listen to some instrumental music and try to put into words what is going on in it, in the way Baldwin does at the end of the story.
3. Imagine that, at the end of Sonny's performance, the narrator were, for some reason, swept off to another country, never to see or talk to his brother again. Write the letter he might have written, telling Sonny how he now feels about him.

### Critical Resources

1. Lemming, David. *James Baldwin: A Biography.* New York: Alfred Knopf, 1994.
2. Reid, Robert. "The Powers of Darkness in 'Sonny's Blues.'" *CLA Journal* 43.4 (2000): 443–453.
3. Standley, Fred and Nancy Burt, eds. *Critical Essays on James Baldwin.* Boston: Hall, 1988.
4. Standley, Fred and Louis Pratt, eds. *Conversations with James Baldwin.* Jackson: UP of Mississippi, 1989.

## RAYMOND CARVER

## *A Small, Good Thing*                                    (1983)

Saturday afternoon she drove to the bakery in the shopping center. After looking through a loose-leaf binder with photographs of cakes taped onto the pages, she ordered chocolate, the child's favorite. The cake she chose was decorated with a spaceship and launching pad under a sprinkling of white stars, and a planet made of red frosting at the other end. His name, SCOTTY, would be in green letters beneath the planet. The baker, who was an older man with a thick neck, listened without saying anything when she told him the child would be eight years old next Monday. The baker wore a white apron that looked like a smock. Straps cut under his arms, went around in back and then to the front again, where they were secured under his heavy waist. He wiped his hands on his apron as he listened to her. He kept his eyes down on the photographs and let her talk. He let her take her time. He'd just come to work and he'd be there all night, baking, and he was in no real hurry.

She gave the baker her name, Ann Weiss, and her telephone number. The cake would be ready on Monday morning, just out of the oven, in plenty of time for the child's party that afternoon. The baker was not jolly. There were no pleasantries between them, just the minimum exchange of words, the necessary information. He made her feel uncomfortable, and she didn't like that. While he was bent over the counter with the pencil in his hand, she studied his coarse features and wondered if he'd ever done anything else with his life besides be a baker. She was a mother and thirty-three years old, and it seemed to her that everyone, especially someone the baker's age-a man old enough to be her father-must have children who'd gone through this special time of cakes and birthday parties. There must be that between them, she thought. But he was abrupt with her-not rude, just abrupt. She gave up trying to make friends with him. She looked into the back of the bakery and could see a long, heavy wooden table with aluminum pie pans stacked at one end; and beside the table a metal container filled with empty racks. There was an enormous oven. A radio was playing country-western music.

The baker finished printing the information on the special order card and closed up the binder. He looked at her and said, "Monday morning." She thanked him and drove home.

On Monday morning, the birthday boy was walking to school with another boy. They were passing a bag of potato chips back and forth and the birthday boy was trying to find out what his friend intended to give him for his birthday that afternoon. Without looking, the birthday boy stepped off the curb at an intersection and was immediately knocked down by a car. He fell on his side with his head in the gutter and his legs out in the road. His eyes were closed, but his legs moved back and forth as if he were trying to climb over something. His friend dropped the potato chips and started to cry. The car had gone a hundred feet or so and stopped in the middle of the road. The man in the driver's seat looked back over his shoulder. He waited until the boy got unsteadily to his feet. The boy wobbled a little. He looked dazed, but okay. The driver put the car into gear and drove away.

The birthday boy didn't cry, but he didn't have anything to say about anything either. He wouldn't answer when his friend asked him what it felt like to be hit by a car. He walked home, and his friend went on to school. But after the birthday boy was inside his house and was telling his mother about it-she sitting beside him on the sofa, holding his hands in her lap, saying, "Scotty, honey, are you sure you feel all right, baby?" thinking she would call the doctor anyway-he suddenly lay back on the sofa, closed his eyes, and went limp When she couldn't wake him up, she hurried to the telephone and called her husband at work. Howard told her to remain calm, remain calm, and then he called an ambulance for the child and left for the hospital himself.

Of course, the birthday party was canceled. The child was in the hospital with a mild concussion and suffering from shock. There'd been vomiting, and his lungs had taken in fluid which needed pumping out that afternoon. Now he simply seemed to be in a very deep sleep-but no coma, Dr. Francis had emphasized, no coma, when he saw the alarm in the parents' eyes. At eleven o'clock that night, when the boy seemed to be resting comfortably enough after the many X-rays and the lab work, and it was just a matter of his waking up and coming around, Howard left the hospital. He and Ann had been at the hospital with the child since that afternoon, and he was going home for a short while to bathe and change clothes. "I'll be back in an hour," he said. She nodded. "It's fine," she said. "I'll be right here." He kissed her on the forehead, and they touched hands. She sat in the chair beside the bed and looked at the child. She was waiting for him to wake up and be all right. Then she could begin to relax.

Howard drove home from the hospital. He took the wet, dark streets very fast, then caught himself and slowed down. Until now, his life had gone smoothly and to his satisfaction-college, marriage, another year of college for the advanced degree in business, a junior partnership in an investment firm. Fatherhood. He was happy and, so far, lucky-he knew that. His parents were still living, his brothers and his sister were established, his friends from college had gone out to take their places in the world. So far, he had kept away from any real harm, from those forces he knew existed and that could cripple or bring down a man if the luck went bad, if things suddenly turned. He pulled into the driveway and parked. His left leg began to tremble. He sat in the car for a minute and tried to deal with the present situation in a rational manner. Scotty had been hit by a car and was in the hospital, but he was going to be all right. Howard closed his eyes and ran his hand over his face. He got out of the car and went up to the front door. The dog was barking inside the house. The telephone rang and rang while he unlocked the door and fumbled for the light switch. He shouldn't have left the hospital, he shouldn't have. "Goddamn it!" he said. He picked up the receiver and said, "I just walked in the door!"

"There's a cake here that wasn't picked up," the voice on the other end of the line said.

"What are you saying?" Howard asked.

"A cake," the voice said. "A sixteen-dollar cake."

Howard held the receiver against his ear, trying to understand. "I don't know anything about a cake," he said. "Jesus, what are you talking about?"

"Don't hand me that," the voice said.

Howard hung up the telephone. He went into the kitchen and poured himself some whiskey. He called the hospital. But the child's condition remained the same; he was still sleeping and nothing had changed there. While water poured into the tub, Howard lathered his face and shaved. He'd just stretched out in the tub and closed his eyes when the telephone rang again. He hauled himself out, grabbed a towel, and hurried through the house, saying, "Stupid, stupid," for having left the hospital. But when he picked up the receiver and shouted, "Hello!" there was no sound at the other end of the line. Then the caller hung up.

He arrived back at the hospital a little after midnight. Ann still sat in the chair beside the bed. She looked up at Howard, and then she looked back at the child. The child's eyes stayed closed, the head was still wrapped in bandages. His breathing was quiet and regular. From an apparatus over the bed hung a bottle of glucose with a tube running from the bottle to the boy's arm.

"How is he?" Howard said. "What's all this?" waving at the glucose and the tube.

"Dr. Francis's orders," she said. "He needs nourishment. He needs to keep up his strength. Why doesn't he wake up, Howard? I don't understand, if he's all right."

Howard put his hand against the back of her head. He ran his fingers through her hair. "He's going to be all right. He'll wake up in a little while. Dr. Francis knows what's what."

After a time, he said, "Maybe you should go home and get some rest. I'll stay here. Just don't put up with this creep who keeps calling. Hang up right away."

"Who's calling?" she asked.

"I don't know who, just somebody with nothing better to do than call up people. You go on now. She shook her head. "No," she said, "I'm fine."

"Really," he said. "Go home for a while, and then come back and spell me in the morning. It'll be all right. What did Dr. Francis say? He said Scotty's going to be all right. We don't have to worry. He's just sleeping now, that's all."

A nurse pushed the door open. She nodded at them as she went to the bedside. She took the left arm out from under the covers and put her fingers on the wrist, found the pulse, then consulted her watch. In a little while, she put the arm back under the covers and moved to the foot of the bed, where she wrote something on a clipboard attached to the bed.

"How is he?" Ann said. Howard's hand was a weight on her shoulder. She was aware of the pressure from his fingers.

"He's stable," the nurse said. Then she said, "Doctor will be in again shortly. Doctor's back in the hospital. He's making rounds right now."

"I was saying maybe she'd want to go home and get a little rest," Howard said. "After the doctor comes," he said.

"She could do that," the nurse said. "I think you should both feel free to do that, if you wish." The nurse was a big Scandinavian woman with blond hair. There was the trace of an accent in her speech.

"We'll see what the doctor says," Ann said. "I want to talk to the doctor. I don't think he should keep sleeping like this. I don't think that's a good sign." She brought her hand up to her eyes and let her head come forward a little. Howard's grip tightened on her shoulder, and then his hand moved up to her neck, where his fingers began to knead the muscles there.

"Dr. Francis will be here in a few minutes," the nurse said. Then she left the room.

Howard gazed at his son for a time, the small chest quietly rising and falling under the covers. For the first time since the terrible minutes after Ann's telephone call to him at his office, he felt a genuine fear starting in his limbs. He began shaking his head. Scotty was fine, but instead of sleeping at home in his own bed, he was in a hospital bed with bandages around his head and a tube in his arm. But this help was what he needed right now.

Dr. Francis came in and shook hands with Howard, though they'd just seen each other a few hours before. Ann got up from the chair. "Doctor?"

"Ann," he said and nodded. "Let's just first see how he's doing," the doctor said. He moved to the side of the bed and took the boy's pulse. He peeled back one eyelid and then the other. Howard and Ann stood beside the doctor and watched. Then the doctor turned back the covers and listened to the boy's heart and lungs with his stethoscope. He pressed his fingers here and there on the abdomen. When he was finished, he went to the end of the bed and studied the chart. He noted the time, scribbled something on the chart, and then looked at Howard and Ann.

"Doctor, how is he?" Howard said. "What's the matter with him exactly?"

"Why doesn't he wake up?" Ann said.

The doctor was a handsome, big-shouldered man with a tanned face. He wore a three-piece blue suit, a striped tie, and ivory cuff links. His gray hair was combed along the sides of his head, and he looked as if he had just come from a concert. "He's all right," the doctor said. "Nothing to shout about, he could be better, I think. But he's all right. Still, I wish he'd wake up. He should wake up pretty soon." The doctor looked at the boy again. "We'll know some more in a couple of hours, after the results of a few more tests are in. But he's all right, believe me, except for the hairline fracture of the skull. He does have that."

"Oh, no," Ann said.

"And a bit of a concussion, as I said before. Of course, you know he's in shock," the doctor said. "Sometimes you see this in shock cases. This sleeping."

"But he's out of any real danger?" Howard said. "You said before he's not in a coma. You wouldn't call this a coma, then-would you, doctor?" Howard waited. He looked at the doctor.

"No, I don't want to call it a coma," the doctor said and glanced over at the boy once more. 'He's just in a very deep sleep. It's a restorative measure the body is taking on its own. He's out of any real danger, I'd say that for certain, yes. But we'll know more when he wakes up and the other tests are in," the doctor said.

"It's a coma," Ann said. "Of sorts."

"It's not a coma yet, not exactly," the doctor said. "I wouldn't want to call it coma. Not yet, anyway. He's suffered shock. In shock cases, this kind of reaction is common enough; it's a temporary reaction to bodily trauma. Coma. Well, coma is a deep, prolonged unconsciousness, something that could go on for days, or weeks even. Scotty's not in that area, not as far as we can tell. I'm certain his condition will show improvement by morning. I'm betting that it will. We'll know more when he wakes up, which shouldn't be long now. Of course, you may do as you like, stay here or go home for a time. But by all means feel free to leave the hospital for a while if you want. This is not easy, I know." The doctor gazed at the boy again, watching him, and then he turned to Ann and said, "You try not to worry, little mother. Believe me, we re doing all that can be done. It's just a question of a little more time now." He nodded at her, shook hands with Howard again, and then he left the room.

Ann put her hand over the child's forehead. "At least he doesn't have a fever," she said. Then she said, "My God, he feels so cold, though. Howard? Is he supposed to feel like this? Feel his head."

Howard touched the child's temples. His own breathing had slowed. "I think he's supposed to feel this way right now," he said. "He's in shock, remember? That's what the doctor said. The doctor was just in here. He would have said something if Scotty wasn't okay."

Ann stood there a while longer, working her lip with her teeth. Then she moved over to her chair and sat down.

Howard sat in the chair next to her chair. They looked at each other. He wanted to say something else and reassure her, but he was afraid, too. He took her hand and put it in his lap, and this made him feel better, her hand being there. He picked up her hand and squeezed it. Then he just held her hand. They sat like that for a while, watching the boy and not talking. From time to time, he squeezed her hand. Finally, she took her hand away.

"I've been praying," she said.

He nodded.

She said, "I almost thought I'd forgotten how, but it came back to me. All I had to do was close my eyes and say, 'Please God, help us-help Scotty,' and then the rest was easy. The words were right there. Maybe if you prayed, too," she said to him.

"I've already prayed," he said. "I prayed this afternoon-yesterday afternoon, I mean-after you called, while I was driving to the hospital. I've been praying," he said.

"That's good," she said. For the first time, she felt they were together in it, this trouble. She realized with a start that, until now, it had only been happening to her and to Scotty. She hadn't let Howard into it, though he was there and needed all along. She felt glad to be his wife.

The same nurse came in and took the boy's pulse again and checked the flow from the bottle hanging above the bed.

In an hour, another doctor came in. He said his name was Parsons, from Radiology. He had a bushy moustache. He was wearing loafers, a western shirt, and a pair of jeans.

"We're going to take him downstairs for more pictures," he told them. "We need to do some more pictures, and we want to do a scan."

"What's that?" Ann said. "A scan?" She stood between this new doctor and the bed. "I thought you'd already taken all your X-rays.'"

"I'm afraid we need some more, he said. "Nothing to be alarmed about. We just need some more pictures, and we want to do a brain scan on him."

"My God," Ann said.

"It's perfectly normal procedure in cases like this," this new doctor said. "We just need to find out for sure why he isn't back awake yet. It's normal medical procedure, and nothing to be alarmed about. We'll be taking him down in a few minutes," this doctor said.

In a little while, two orderlies came into the room with a gurney. They were black-haired, dark-complexioned men in white uniforms, and they said a few words to each other in a foreign tongue as they unhooked the boy from the tube and moved him from his bed to the gurney. Then they wheeled him from the room.

Howard and Ann got on the same elevator. Ann gazed at the child. She closed her eyes as the elevator began its descent. The orderlies stood at either end of the gurney without saying anything, though once one of the men made a comment to the other in their own language, and the other man nodded slowly in response.

Later that morning, just as the sun was beginning to lighten the windows in the waiting room outside the X-ray department, they brought the boy out and moved him back up to his room. Howard and Ann rode up on the elevator with him once more, and once more they took up their places beside the bed.

They waited all day, but still the boy did not wake up. Occasionally, one of them would leave the room to go downstairs to the cafeteria to drink coffee and then, as if suddenly remembering and feeling guilty, get up from the table and hurry back to the room. Dr. Francis came again that afternoon and examined the boy once more and then left after telling them he was coming along and could wake up at any minute now. Nurses, different nurses from the night before, came in from time to time. Then a young woman from the lab knocked and entered the room. She wore white slacks and a white blouse and carried a little tray of things which she put on the stand beside the bed. Without a word to them, she took blood from the boy's arm. Howard closed his eyes as the woman found the right place on the boy's arm and pushed the needle in.

"I don't understand this," Ann said to the woman.

"Doctor's orders," the young woman said. "I do what I'm told. They say draw that one, I draw. What's wrong with him, anyway?" she said. "He's a sweetie."

"He was hit by a car," Howard said. "A hit-and-run."

The young woman shook her head and looked again at the boy. Then she took her tray and left the room.

"Why won't he wake up?" Ann said. "Howard? I want some answers from these people." Howard didn't say anything. He sat down again in the chair and crossed one leg over the other. He rubbed his face. He looked at his son and then he settled back in the chair, closed his eyes, and went to sleep.

Ann walked to the window and looked out at the parking lot. It was night, and cars were driving into and out of the parking lot with their lights on. She stood at the window with her hands gripping the sill, and knew in her heart that they were into something now, something hard. She was afraid, and her teeth began to chatter until she tightened her jaws. She saw a big car stop in front of the hospital and someone, a woman in a long coat, get into the car. She wished she were that woman and somebody, anybody, was driving her away from here to somewhere else, a place where she would find Scotty waiting for her when she stepped out of the car, ready to say Mom and let her gather him in her arms.

In a little while, Howard woke up. He looked at the boy again. Then he got up from the chair, stretched, and went over to stand beside her at the window. They both stared out at the parking lot. They didn't say anything. But they seemed to feel each other's insides now, as though the worry had made them transparent in a perfectly natural way.

The door opened and Dr. Francis came in. He was wearing a different suit and tie this time. His gray hair was combed along the sides of his head, and he looked as if he had just shaved. He went straight to the bed and examined the boy. "He ought to have come around by now. There's just no good reason for this," he said. "But I can tell you we're all convinced he's out of any danger. We'll just feel better when he wakes up. There's no reason, absolutely none, why he shouldn't come around. Very soon. Oh, he'll have himself a dilly of a headache when he does, you can count on that. But all of his signs are fine. They're as normal as can be."

"It is a coma, then?" Ann said.

The doctor rubbed his smooth cheek. "We'll call it that for the time being, until he wakes up. But you must be worn out. This is hard. I know this is hard. Feel free to go out for a bite," he said. "It would do you good. I'll put a nurse in here while you're gone if you'll feel better about going. Go and have yourselves something to eat."

"I couldn't eat anything," Ann said.

"Do what you need to do, of course," the doctor said. "Anyway, I wanted to tell you that all the signs are good, the tests are negative, nothing showed up at all, and just as soon as he wakes up he'll be over the hill."

"Thank you, doctor," Howard said. He shook hands with the doctor again. The doctor patted Howard's shoulder and went out.

"I suppose one of us should go home and check on things," Howard said. "Slug needs to be fed, for one thing."

"Call one of the neighbors," Ann said. "Call the Morgans. Anyone will feed a dog if you ask them to."

"All right," Howard said. After a while, he said, "Honey, why don't you do it? Why don't you go home and check on things, and then come back? It'll do you good. I'll be right here with him. Seriously," he said. "We need to keep up our strength on this. We'll want to be here for a while even after he wakes up.

"Why don't you go?" she said. "Feed Slug. Feed your-self."

"I already went," he said. "I was gone for exactly an hour and fifteen minutes. You go home for an hour and freshen up. Then come back."

She tried to think about it, but she was too tired. She closed her eyes and tried to think it again. After a time, she said, "Maybe I will go home for a few minutes. Maybe if I'm not just sitting right here watching him every second, he'll wake up and be all right. You know? Maybe he'll wake up if I'm not here. I'll go home and take a bath and put on clean clothes. I'll feed Slug. Then I'll come back."

"I'll be right here," he said. "You go on home, honey. I'll keep an eye on things here." His eyes were bloodshot and small, as if he'd been drinking for a long time. His clothes were rumpled. His beard had come out again. She touched his face, and then she took her hand back. She understood he wanted to be by himself for a while, not have to talk or share his worry for a time. She picked her purse up from the nightstand, and he helped her into her coat.

"I won't be gone long," she said.

"Just sit and rest for a little while when you get home," he said. "Eat some-thing. Take a bath. After you get out of the bath, just sit for a while and rest. It'll do you a world of good, you'll see. Then come back," he said. "Let's try not to worry. You heard what Dr. Francis said."

She stood in her coat for a minute trying to recall the doctor's exact words, looking for any nuances, any hint of something behind his words other than what he had said. She tried to remember if his expression had changed any when he bent over to examine the child. She remember the way his features had composed themselves as he rolled back the child's eyelids and then listened to his breathing.

She went to the door, where she turned and looked back. She looked at the child, and then she looked at the father. Howard nodded. She stepped out of the room and pulled the door closed behind her.

She went past the nurses' station and down to the end of the corridor, looking for the elevator. At the end of the corridor, she turned to her right and entered a little waiting room where a Negro family sat in wicker chairs. There was a middle-aged man in a khaki shirt and pants, a baseball cap pushed back on his head. A large woman wearing a housedress and slippers was slumped in one of the chairs. A teenaged girl in jeans, hair done in dozens of little braids, lay stretched out in one of the chairs smoking a cigarette, her legs crossed at the ankles. The family swung their eyes to Ann as she entered the room. The little table was littered with hamburger wrappers and Styrofoam cups.

"Franklin," the large woman said as she roused herself. "Is it about Franklin?" Her eyes widened. "Tell me now, lady," the woman said. "Is it about Franklin?" She was trying to rise from her chair, but the man had closed his hand over her arm.

"Here, here," he said. "Evelyn."

"I'm sorry," Ann said. "I'm looking for the elevator. My son is in the hospital, and now I can't find the elevator."

"Elevator is down that way, turn left," the man said as he aimed a finger.

The girl drew on her cigarette and stared at Ann. Her eyes were narrowed to slits, and her broad lips parted slowly as she let the smoke escape. The Negro woman let her head fall on her shoulder and looked away from Ann, no longer interested.

"My son was hit by a car," Ann said to the man. She seemed to need to explain herself. "He has a concussion and a little skull fracture, but he's going to be all right. He's in shock now, but it might be some kind of coma, too. That's what really worries us, the coma part. I'm going out for a little while, but my husband is with him. Maybe he'll wake up while I'm gone.

"That's too bad," the man said and shifted in the chair. He shook his head. He looked down at the table, and then he looked back at Ann. She was still standing there. He said, "Our Franklin, he's on the operating table. Somebody cut him. Tried to kill him. There was a fight where he was at. At this party. They say he was just standing and watching. Not bothering nobody. But that don't mean nothing these days. Now he's on the operating table. We're just hoping and praying, that's all we can do now." He gazed at her steadily.

Ann looked at the girl again, who was still watching her, and at the older woman, who kept her head down, but whose eyes were now closed. Ann saw the lips moving silently, making words. She had an urge to ask what those words were. She wanted to talk more with these people who were in the same kind of waiting she was in. She was afraid, and they were afraid. They had that in common. She would have liked to have said something else about the accident, told them more about Scotty, that it had happened on the day of his birthday, Monday, and that he was still unconscious. Yet she didn't know how to begin. She stood looking at them without saying anything more.

She went down the corridor the man had indicated and found the elevator. She waited a minute in front of the closed doors, still wondering if she was doing the right thing. Then she put out her finger and touched the button.

She pulled into the driveway and cut the engine. She closed her eyes and leaned her head against the wheel for a minute. She listened to the ticking sounds the engine made as it began to cool. Then she got out of the car. She could hear the dog barking inside the house. She went to the front door, which was unlocked. She went inside and turned on lights and put on a kettle of water for tea. She opened some dog food and fed Slug on the back porch. The dog ate in hungry little smacks. It kept running into the kitchen to see that she was going to stay. As she sat down on the sofa with her tea, the telephone rang.

"Yes!" she said as she answered. "Hello!"

"Mrs. Weiss," a man's voice said. It was five o'clock in the morning, and she thought she could hear machinery or equipment of some kind in the background.

"Yes, yes! What is it?" she said. "This is Mrs. Weiss. This is she. What is it, please?" She listened to whatever it was in the background. "Is it Scotty, for Christ's sake?"

"Scotty," the man's voice said. "It's about Scotty, yes. It has to do with Scotty, that problem. Have you forgotten about Scotty?" the man said. Then he hung up.

She dialed the hospital's number and asked for the third floor. She demanded information about her son from the nurse who answered the telephone. Then she asked to speak to her husband. It was, she said, an emergency.

She waited, turning the telephone cord in her fingers. She closed her eyes and felt sick at her stomach. She would have to make herself eat. Slug came in from the back porch and lay down near her feet. He wagged his tail. She pulled at his ear while he licked her fingers. Howard was on the line.

"Somebody just called here," she said. She twisted the telephone cord. "He said it was about Scotty," she cried.

"Scotty's fine," Howard told her. "I mean, he's still sleeping. There's been no change. The nurse has been in twice since you've been gone. A nurse or else a doctor. He's all right."

"This man called. He said it was about Scotty," she told him.

"Honey, you rest for a little while, you need the rest. It must be that same caller I had. Just forget it. Come back down here after you've rested. Then we'll have breakfast or something."

"Breakfast," she said. "I don't want any breakfast."

"You know what I mean," he said. "Juice, something. I don't know. I don't know anything, Ann. Jesus, I'm not hungry, either. Ann, it's hard to talk now. I'm standing here at the desk. Dr. Francis is coming again at eight o'clock this morning. He's going to have something to tell us then, something more definite. That's what one of the nurses said. She didn't know any more than that. Ann? Honey, maybe we'll know something more then. At eight o'clock. Come back here before eight. Meanwhile, I'm right here and Scotty's all right. He's still the same," he added.

"I was drinking a cup of tea," she said, "when the telephone rang. They said it was about Scotty. There was a noise in the background. Was there a noise in the background on that call you had, Howard?"

"I don't remember," he said. "Maybe the driver of the car, maybe he's a psychopath and found out about Scotty somehow. But I'm here with him. Just rest like you were going to do. Take a bath and come back by seven or so, and we'll talk to the doctor together when he gets here. It's going to be all right, honey. I'm here, and there are doctors and nurses around. They say his condition is stable."

"I'm scared to death," she said.

She ran water, undressed, and got into the tub. She washed and dried quickly, not taking the time to wash her hair. She put on clean underwear, wool slacks, and a sweater. She went into the living room, where the dog looked up at her and let its tail thump once against the floor. It was just starting to get light outside when she went out to the car.

She drove into the parking lot of the hospital and found a space close to the front door. She felt she was in some obscure way responsible for what had happened to the child. She let her thoughts move to the Negro family. She remembered the name Franklin and the table that was covered with hamburger papers, and the teenaged girl staring at her as she drew on her cigarette. "Don't have children," she told the girl's image as she entered the front door of the hospital. "For God's sake, don't."

She took the elevator up to the third floor with two nurses who were just going on duty. It was Wednesday morning, a few minutes before seven. There was a page for a Dr. Madison as the elevator doors slid open on the third floor. She got off behind the nurses, who turned in the other direction and continued the conversation she had interrupted when she'd gotten into the elevator. She walked down the corridor to the little alcove where the Negro family had been waiting. They were gone now, but the chairs were scattered in such a way that it looked as if people had just jumped up from them the minute before. The tabletop was cluttered with the same cups and papers, the ashtray was filled with cigarette butts.

She stopped at the nurses' station. A nurse was standing behind the counter, brushing her hair and yawning.

"There was a Negro boy in surgery last night," Ann said. "Franklin was his name. His family was in the waiting room. I'd like to inquire about his condition."

A nurse who was sitting at a desk behind the counter looked up from a chart in front of her. The telephone buzzed and she picked up the receiver, but she kept her eyes on Ann.

"He passed away," said the nurse at the counter. The nurse held the hairbrush and kept looking at her. "Are you a friend of the family or what?"

"I met the family last night," Ann said. "My own son is in the hospital. I guess he's in shock. We don't know for sure what's wrong. I lust wondered about Franklin, that's all. Thank you." She moved down the corridor. Elevator doors the same color as the walls slid open and a gaunt, bald man in white pants and white canvas shoes pulled a heavy cart off the elevator. She hadn't noticed these doors last night. The man wheeled the cart out into the corridor and stopped in front of the room nearest the elevator and consulted a clipboard. Then he reached down and slid a tray out of the cart. He rapped lightly on the door and entered the room. She could smell the unpleasant odors of warm food as she passed the cart. She hurried on without looking at any of the nurses and pushed open the door to the child's room.

Howard was standing at the window with his hands behind his back. He turned around as she came in.

"How is he?" she said. She went over to the bed. She dropped her purse on the floor beside the nightstand. It seemed to her she had been gone a long time. She touched the child's face. "Howard?"

"Dr. Francis was here a little while ago," Howard said. She looked at him closely and thought his shoulders were bunched a little.

"I thought he wasn't coming until eight o'clock this morning," she said quickly.

"There was another doctor with him. A neurologist."

"A neurologist," she said.

Howard nodded. His shoulders were bunching, she could see that. "What'd they say, Howard? For Christ's sake, what'd they say? What is it?"

"They said they're going to take him down and run more tests on him, Ann. They think they're going to operate, honey. Honey, they are going to operate. They can't figure out why he won't wake up. It's more than just shock or concussion, they know that much now. It's in his skull, the fracture, it has something, something to do with that, they think. So they're going to operate. I tried to call you, but I guess you'd already left the house."

"Oh, God," she said. 'Oh, please, Howard, please," she said, taking his arms.

"Look!' " Howard said. "Scotty! Look, Ann!" He turned her toward the bed.

The boy had opened his eyes, then closed them. He opened them again now. The eyes stared straight ahead for a minute, then moved slowly in his head until they rested on Howard and Ann, then traveled away again.

"Scotty," his mother said, moving to the bed.

"Hey, Scott," his father said. "Hey, son."

They leaned over the bed. Howard took the child's hand in his hands and began to pat and squeeze the hand. Ann bent over the boy and kissed his forehead again and again. She put her hands on either side of his face. "Scotty, honey, it's Mommy and Daddy," she said. "Scotty?"

The boy looked at them, but without any sign of recognition. Then his mouth opened, his eyes scrunched closed, and he howled until he had no more air in his lungs. His face seemed to relax and soften then. His lips parted as his last breath was puffed through his throat and exhaled gently through the clenched teeth.

The doctors called it a hidden Occlusion and said it was a one-in-a-million circumstance. Maybe if it could have been detected somehow and surgery undertaken immediately, they could have saved him. But more than likely not. In any case, what would they have been looking for? Nothing had shown up in the tests or in the X-rays.

Dr. Francis was shaken. "I can't tell you how badly I feel. I'm so very sorry, I can't tell you," he said as he led them into the doctors' lounge. There was a doctor sitting in a chair with his legs hooked over the back of another chair, watching an early-morning TV show. He was wearing a green delivery room outfit, loose green pants and green blouse, and a green cap that covered his hair. He looked at Howard and Ann and then looked at Dr. Francis. He got to his feet and turned off the set and went out of the room. Dr. Francis guided Ann to the sofa, sat down beside her, and began to talk in a low, consoling voice. At one point, he leaned over and embraced her. She could feel his chest rising and falling evenly against her shoulder. She kept her eyes open and let him hold her. Howard went into the bathroom, but he left the door open. After a violent fit of weeping, he ran water and washed his face. Then he came out and sat down at the little table that held a telephone. He looked at the telephone as though deciding what to do first. He made some calls. After a time, Dr. Francis used the telephone.

"Is there anything else I can do for the moment?" he asked them.

Howard shook his head. Ann stared at Dr. Francis as if unable to comprehend his words.

The doctor walked them to the hospital's front door. People were entering and leaving the hospital. It was eleven o'clock in the morning. Ann was aware of how slowly, almost reluctantly, she moved her feet. It seemed to her that Dr. Francis was making them leave when she felt they should stay, when it would be more the right thing to do to stay. She gazed out into the parking lot and then turned around and looked back at the front of the hospital. She began shaking her head. "No, no," she said. "I can't leave him here, no." She heard herself say that and thought how unfair it was that the only words that came out were the sort of words used on TV shows where people were stunned by violent or sudden deaths. She wanted her words to be her own. "No," she said, and for some reason the memory of the Negro woman's head lolling on the woman's shoulder came to her. "No," she said again.

"I'll be talking to you later in the day," the doctor was saying to Howard. "There are still some things that have to be done, things that have to be cleared up to our satisfaction. Some things that need explaining."

"An autopsy," Howard said.

Dr. Francis nodded.

"I understand," Howard said. Then he said, "Oh, Jesus. No, I don't understand, doctor. I can't, I can't. I just can't."

Dr. Francis put his arm around Howard's shoulders. "I'm sorry. God, how I'm sorry." He let go of Howard's shoulders and held out his hand. Howard looked at the hand, and then he took it. Dr. Francis put his arms around Ann once more. He seemed full of some goodness she didn't understand. She let her head rest on his shoulder, but her eyes stayed open. She kept looking at the hospital. As they drove out of the parking lot, she looked back at the hospital.

At home, she sat on the sofa with her hands in her coat pockets. Howard closed the door to the child's room. He got the coffee-maker going and then he found an empty box. He had thought to pick up some of the child's things that were scattered around the living room. But instead he sat down beside her on the sofa, pushed the box to one side, and leaned forward, arms between his knees. He began to weep. She pulled his head over into her lap and patted his shoulder. "He's gone," she said. She kept patting his shoulder. Over his sobs, she could hear the coffee-maker hissing in the kitchen. "There, there," she said tenderly. "Howard, he's gone. He's gone and now we'll have to get used to that. To being alone."

In a little while, Howard got up and began moving aimlessly around the room with the box, not putting anything into it, but collecting some things together on the floor at one end of the sofa. She continued to sit with her hands in her coat pockets. Howard put the box down and brought coffee into the living room. Later, Ann made calls to relatives. After each call had been placed and the party had answered, Ann would blurt out a few words and cry for a minute. Then she would quietly explain, in a measured voice, what had happened and tell them about arrangements. Howard took the box out to the garage, where he saw the child's bicycle. He dropped the box and sat down on the pavement beside the bicycle. He took hold of the bicycle awkwardly so that it leaned against his chest. He held it, the rubber pedal sticking into his chest. He gave the wheel a turn.

Ann hung up the telephone after talking to her sister. She was looking up another number when the telephone rang. She picked it up on the first ring.

"Hello," she said, and she heard something in the background, a humming noise. "Hello!" she said. "For God's sake," she said. "Who is this? What is it you want?"

"Your Scotty, I got him ready for you," the man's voice said. "Did you forget him?"

"You evil bastard!" she shouted into the receiver. "How can you do this, you evil son of a bitch?"

"Scotty," the man said. "Have you forgotten about Scotty?" Then the man hung up on her.

Howard heard the shouting and came in to find her with her head on her arms over the table, weeping. He picked up the receiver and listened to the dial tone.

Much later, just before midnight, after they had dealt with many things, the telephone rang again.

"You answer it," she said. "Howard, it's him, I know." They were sitting at the kitchen table with coffee in front of them. Howard had a small glass of whiskey beside his cup. He answered on the third ring.

"Hello," he said. "Who is this? Hello! Hello!" The line went dead. "He hung up," Howard said. "Whoever it was."

"It was him," she said. "That bastard. I'd like to kill him," she said. "I'd like to shoot him and watch him kick," she said.

"Ann, my God," he said.

"Could you hear anything?" she said. "In the background? A noise, machinery, something humming?"

"Nothing, really. Nothing like that," he said. "There wasn't much time. I think there was some radio music. Yes, there was a radio going, that's all I could tell. I don't know what in God's name is going on," he said.

She shook her head. "If I could, could get my hands on him." It came to her then. She knew who it was. Scotty, the cake, the telephone number. She pushed the chair away from the table and got up. "Drive me down to the shopping center," she said. "Howard."

"What are you saying?"

"The shopping center. I know who it is who's calling. I know who it is. It's the baker, the son-of-a-bitching baker, Howard. I had him bake a cake for Scotty's birthday. That's who's calling. That's who has the number and keeps calling us. To harass us about that cake. The baker, that bastard."

They drove down to the shopping center. The sky was clear and stars were out. It was cold, and they ran the heater in the car. They parked in front of the bakery. All of the shops and stores were closed, but there were cars at the far end of the lot in front of the movie theater. The bakery windows were dark, but when they looked through the glass they could see a light in the back room and, now and then, a big man in an apron moving in and out of the white, even light. Through the glass, she could see the display cases and some little tables with chairs. She tried the door. She rapped on the glass. But if the baker heard them, he gave no sign. He didn't look in their direction.

They drove around behind the bakery and parked. They got out of the car. There was a lighted window too high up for them to see inside. A sign near the back door said THE PANTRY BAKERY, SPECIAL ORDERS. She could hear faintly a radio playing inside and something creak-an oven door as it was pulled down? She knocked on the door and waited. Then she knocked again, louder. The radio was turned down and there was a scraping sound now, the distinct sound of something, a drawer, being pulled open and then closed.

Someone unlocked the door and opened it. The baker stood in the light and peered out at them. "I'm closed for business," he said. "What do you want at this hour? It's midnight. Are you drunk or something?"

She stepped into the light that fell through the open door. He blinked his heavy eyelids as he recognized her. "It's you, he said.

"It's me," she said. "Scotty's mother. This is Scotty's father. We'd like to come in."

The baker said, "I'm busy now. I have work to do."

She had stepped inside the doorway anyway. Howard came in behind her. The baker moved back. "It smells like a bakery in here. Doesn't it smell like a bakery in here, Howard?"

"What do you want?" the baker said. "Maybe you want your cake? That's it, you decided you want your cake. You ordered a cake, didn't you?"

"You're pretty smart for a baker," she said. "Howard, this is the man who's been calling us." She clenched her fists. She stared at him fiercely. There was a deep burning inside her, an anger that made her feel larger than herself, larger than either of these men.

"Just a minute here," the baker said. "You want to pick up your three-day-old cake? That it? I don't want to argue with you, lady. There it sits over there, getting stale. I'll give it to you for half of what I quoted you. No. You want it? You can have it. It's no good to me, no good to anyone now. It cost me time and money to make that cake. If you want it, okay, if you don't, that's okay, too. I have to get back to work." He looked at them and rolled his tongue behind his teeth.

"More cakes," she said. She knew she was in control of it, of what was increasing in her. She was calm.

"Lady, I work sixteen hours a day in this place to earn a living," the baker said. He wiped his hands on his apron. "I work night and day in here, trying to make ends meet." A look crossed Ann's face that made the baker move back and say, "No trouble, now." He reached to the counter and picked up a rolling pin with his right hand and began to tap it against the palm of his other hand. "You want the cake or not? I have to get back to work. Bakers work at night," he said again. His eyes were small, mean-looking, she thought, nearly lost in the bristly flesh around his cheeks. His neck was thick with fat.

"I know bakers work at night," Ann said. "They make phone calls at night, too. You bastard," she said.

The baker continued to tap the rolling pin against his hand. He glanced at Howard. "Careful, careful," he said to Howard.

"My son's dead," she said with a cold, even finality. "He was hit by a car Monday morning. We've been waiting with him until he died. But, of course, you couldn't be expected to know that, could you? Bakers can't know everything-can they, Mr. Baker? But he's dead. He's dead, you bastard!" Just as suddenly as it had welled in her, the anger dwindled, gave way to something else, a dizzy feeling of nausea. She leaned against the wooden table that was sprinkled with flour, put her hands over her face, and began to cry, her shoulders rocking back and forth. "It isn't fair," she said. "It isn't, isn't fair."

Howard put his hand at the small of her back and looked at the baker. "Shame on you," Howard said to him. "Shame."

The baker put the rolling pin back on the counter. He undid his apron and threw it on the counter. He looked at them, and then he shook his head slowly. He pulled a chair out from under the card table that held papers and receipts, an adding machine, and a telephone directory. "Please sit down," he said. "Let me get you a chair," he said to Howard. "Sit down now, please." The baker went into the front of the shop and returned with two little wrought-iron chairs. "Please sit down, you people."

Ann wiped her eyes and looked at the baker. "I wanted to kill you," she said. "I wanted you dead."

The baker had cleared a space for them at the table. He shoved the adding machine to one side, along with the stacks of notepaper and receipts. He pushed the telephone directory onto the floor, where it landed with a thud. Howard and Ann sat down and pulled their chairs up to the table. The baker sat down, too.

"Let me say how sorry I am," the baker said, putting his elbows on the table. "God alone knows how sorry. Listen to me. I'm just a baker. I don't claim to be anything else. Maybe once, maybe years ago, I was a different kind of human being. I've forgotten, I don't know for sure. But I'm not any longer, if I ever was. Now I'm just a baker. That don't excuse my doing what I did, I know. But I'm deeply sorry. I'm sorry for your son, and sorry for my part in this," the baker said. He spread his hands out on the table and turned them over to reveal his palms. "I don't have any children myself, so I can only imagine what you must be feeling. All I can say to you now is that I'm sorry. Forgive me, if you can," the baker said. "I'm not an evil man, I don't think. Not evil, like you said on the phone. You got to understand what it comes down to is I don't know how to act anymore, it would seem. Please," the man said, "let me ask you if you can find it in your hearts to forgive me?"

It was warm inside the bakery. Howard stood up from the table and took off his coat. He helped Ann from her coat. The baker looked at them for a minute and then nodded and got up from the table. He went to the oven and turned off some switches. He found cups and poured coffee from an electric coffee-maker. He put a carton of cream on the table, and a bowl of sugar.

"You probably need to eat something," the baker said. "I hope you'll eat some of my hot rolls. You have to eat and keep going. Eating is a small, good thing in a time like this," he said.

He served them warm cinnamon rolls just out of the oven, the icing still runny. He put butter on the table and knives to spread the butter. Then the baker sat down at the table with them. He waited. He waited until they each took a roll from the platter and began to eat. "It's good to eat something," he said, watching them. "There's more. Eat up. Eat all you want. There's all the rolls in the world in here."

They ate rolls and drank coffee. Ann was suddenly hungry, and the rolls were warm and sweet. She ate three of them, which pleased the baker. Then he began to talk. They listened carefully. Although they were tired and in anguish, they listened to what the baker had to say. They nodded when the baker began to speak of loneliness, and of the sense of doubt and limitation that had come to him in his middle years. He told them what it was like to be childless all these years. To repeat the days with the ovens endlessly full and endlessly empty. The party food, the celebrations he'd worked over. Icing knuckle-deep. The tiny wedding couples stuck into cakes. Hundreds of them, no, thousands by now. Birthdays. Just imagine all those candles burning. He had a necessary trade. He was a baker. He was glad he wasn't a florist. It was better to be feeding people. This was a better smell anytime than flowers.

"Smell this," the baker said, breaking open a dark loaf. "It's a heavy bread, but rich." They smelled it, then he had them taste it. It had the taste of molasses and coarse grains. They listened to him. They ate what they could. They swallowed the dark bread. It was like daylight under the fluorescent trays of light. They talked on into the early morning, the high, pale cast of light in the windows, and they did not think of leaving.

1983

❀ ❀ ❀

## NATHANIEL HAWTHORNE

## *Young Goodman Brown* (1846)

Young Goodman[1] Brown came forth at sunset into the street at Salem village; but put his head back, after crossing the threshold, to exchange a parting kiss with his young wife. And Faith, as the wife was aptly named, thrust her own pretty head into the street, letting the wind play with the pink ribbons of her cap while she called to Goodman Brown.

"Dearest heart," whispered she, softly and rather sadly, when her lips were close to his ear, "prithee put off your journey until sunrise and sleep in your own bed to-night. A lone woman is troubled with such dreams and such thoughts that she's afeard of herself sometimes. Pray tarry with me this night, dear husband, of all nights in the year."

"My love and my Faith," replied young Goodman Brown, "of all nights in the year, this one night must I tarry away from thee. My journey, as thou callest it, forth and back again, must needs be done 'twixt now and sunrise. What, my sweet, pretty wife, dost thou doubt me already, and we but three months married?"

"Then God bless you!" said Faith, with the pink ribbons; "and may you find all well when you come back."

"Amen!" cried Goodman Brown. "Say thy prayers, dear Faith, and go to bed at dusk, and no harm will come to thee."

---

[1]Goodman and Goody (used later) were respectful terms of address for men and women not of the upper classes.

So they parted; and the young man pursued his way until, being about to turn the corner by the meeting-house, he looked back and saw the head of Faith still peeping after him with a melancholy air, in spite of her pink ribbons.

"Poor little Faith!" thought he, for his heart smote him. "What a wretch am I to leave her on such an errand! She talks of dreams, too. Methought as she spoke there was trouble in her face, as if a dream had warned her what work is to be done to-night. But no, no; 'twould kill her to think it. Well, she's a blessed angel on earth; and after this one night I'll cling to her skirts and follow her to heaven."

With this excellent resolve for the future, Goodman Brown felt himself justified in making more haste on his present evil purpose. He had taken a dreary road, darkened by all the gloomiest trees of the forest, which barely stood aside to let the narrow path creep through, and closed immediately behind. It was all as lonely as could be; and there is this peculiarity in such a solitude, that the traveller knows not who may be concealed by the innumerable trunks and the thick boughs overhead; so that with lonely footsteps he may yet be passing through an unseen multitude.

"There may be a devilish Indian behind every tree," said Goodman Brown to himself; and he glanced fearfully behind him as he added, "What if the devil himself should be at my very elbow!"

His head being turned back, he passed a crook of the road, and, looking forward again, beheld the figure of a man, in grave and decent attire, seated at the foot of an old tree. He arose at Goodman Brown's approach and walked onward side by side with him.

"You are late, Goodman Brown," said he. "The clock of the Old South was striking as I came through Boston, and that is full fifteen minutes agone."

"Faith kept me back a while," replied the young man, with a tremor in his voice, caused by the sudden appearance of his companion, though not wholly unexpected.

It was now deep dusk in the forest, and deepest in that part of it where these two were journeying. As nearly as could be discerned, the second traveller was about fifty years old, apparently in the same rank of life as Goodman Brown, and bearing a considerable resemblance to him, though perhaps more in expression than features. Still they might have been taken for father and son. And yet, though the elder person was as simply clad as the younger, and as simple in manner too, he had an indescribable air of one who knew the world, and who would not have felt abashed at the governor's dinner table or in King William's court, were it possible that his affairs should call him thither. But the only thing about him that could be fixed upon as remarkable was his staff, which bore the likeness of a great black snake, so curiously wrought that it might almost be seen to twist and wriggle itself like a living serpent. This, of course, must have been an ocular deception, assisted by the uncertain light.

"Come, Goodman Brown," cried his fellow-traveller, "this is a dull pace for the beginning of a journey. Take my staff, if you are so soon weary."

"Friend," said the other, exchanging his slow pace for a full stop, "having kept covenant by meeting thee here, it is my purpose now to return whence I came. I have scruples touching the matter thou wot'st of."

"Sayest thou so?" replied he of the serpent, smiling apart. "Let us walk on, nevertheless, reasoning as we go; and if I convince thee not thou shalt turn back. We are but a little way in the forest yet."

"Too far! too far!" exclaimed the goodman, unconsciously resuming his walk. "My father never went into the woods on such an errand, nor his father before him. We have been a race of honest men and good Christians since the days of the martyrs; and shall I be the first of the name of Brown that ever took this path and kept"—

"Such company, thou wouldst say," observed the elder person, interpreting his pause. "Well said, Goodman Brown! I have been as well acquainted with your family as with ever a one among the Puritans; and that's no trifle to say. I helped your grandfather, the constable, when he lashed the Quaker woman so smartly through the streets of Salem; and it was I that brought your father a pitch-pine knot, kindled at my own hearth, to set fire to an Indian village, in King Philip's war.[2] They were my good friends, both; and many a pleasant walk have we had along this path, and returned merrily after midnight. I would fain be friends with you for their sake."

"If it be as thou sayest," replied Goodman Brown, "I marvel they never spoke of these matters; or, verily, I marvel not, seeing that the least rumor of the sort would have driven them from New England. We are a people of prayer, and good works to boot, and abide no such wickedness."

"Wickedness or not," said the traveller with the twisted staff, "I have a very general acquaintance here in New England. The deacons of many a church have drunk the communion wine with me; the selectmen of divers towns make me their chairman; and a majority of the Great and General Court are firm supporters of my interest. The governor and I, too—But these are state secrets."

"Can this be so?" cried Goodman Brown, with a stare of amazement at his undisturbed companion. "Howbeit, I have nothing to do with the governor and council; they have their own ways, and are no rule for a simple husbandman like me. But, were I to go on with thee, how should I meet the eye of that good old man, our minister, at Salem village? Oh, his voice would make me tremble both Sabbath day and lecture day."

Thus far the elder traveller had listened with due gravity; but now burst into a fit of irrepressible mirth, shaking himself so violently that his snake-like staff actually seemed to wriggle in sympathy.

"Ha! ha! ha!" shouted he again and again; then composing himself, "Well, go on, Goodman Brown, go on; but, prithee, don't kill me with laughing."

"Well, then, to end the matter at once," said Goodman Brown, considerably nettled, "there is my wife, Faith. It would break her dear little heart; and I'd rather break my own."

---

[2]War between Indians and New England colonists, 1675–1676.

"Nay, if that be the case," answered the other, "e'en go thy ways, Goodman Brown. I would not for twenty old women like the one hobbling before us that Faith should come to any harm."

As he spoke he pointed his staff at a female figure on the path, in whom Goodman Brown recognized a very pious and exemplary dame, who had taught him his catechism in youth, and was still his moral and spiritual adviser, jointly with the minister and Deacon Gookin.

"A marvel, truly, that Goody Cloyse should be so far in the wilderness at nightfall," said he. "But with your leave, friend, I shall take a cut through the woods until we have left this Christian woman behind. Being a stranger to you she might ask whom I was consorting with and whither I was going."

"Be it so," said his fellow-traveller. "Betake you the woods, and let me keep the path."

Accordingly the young man turned aside, but took care to watch his companion, who advanced softly along the road until he had come within a staff's length of the old dame. She, meanwhile, was making the best of her way, with singular speed for so aged a woman, and mumbling some indistinct words—a prayer, doubtless—as she went. The traveller put forth his staff and touched her withered neck with what seemed the serpent's tail.

"The devil!" screamed the pious old lady.

"Then Goody Cloyse knows her old friend?" observed the traveller, confronting her and leaning on his writhing stick.

"Ah, forsooth, and is it your worship indeed?" cried the good dame. "Yea, truly is it, and in the very image of my old gossip, Goodman Brown, the grandfather of the silly fellow that now is. But—would your worship believe it?—my broomstick hath strangely disappeared, stolen, as I suspect, by that unhanged witch, Goody Cory, and that, too, when I was all anointed with the juice of smallage, and cinquefoil, and wolf's bane"—

"Mingled with fine wheat and the fat of a new-born babe," said the shape of old Goodman Brown.

"Ah, your worship knows the recipe," cried the old lady, cackling aloud. "So, as I was saying, being all ready for the meeting, and no horse to ride on, I made up my mind to foot it; for they tell me there is a nice young man to be taken into communion to-night. But now your good worship will lend me your arm, and we shall be there in a twinkling."

"That can hardly be," answered her friend. "I may not spare you my arm, Goody Cloyse; but here is my staff, if you will."

So saying, he threw it down at her feet, where, perhaps, it assumed life, being one of the rods which its owner had formerly lent to the Egyptian magi. Of this fact, however, Goodman Brown could not take cognizance. He had cast up his eyes in astonishment, and, looking down again, beheld neither Goody Cloyse nor the serpentine staff, but this fellow-traveller alone, who waited for him as calmly as if nothing had happened.

"That old woman taught me my catechism," said the young man; and there was a world of meaning in this simple comment.

They continued to walk onward, while the elder traveller exhorted his companion to make good speed and persevere in the path, discoursing so aptly that his arguments seemed rather to spring up in the bosom of his auditor than to be suggested by himself. As they went, he plucked a branch of maple to serve for a walking stick, and began to strip it of the twigs and little boughs, which were wet with evening dew. The moment his fingers touched them they became strangely withered and dried up as with a week's sunshine. Thus the pair proceeded, at a good free pace, until suddenly, in a gloomy hollow of the road, Goodman Brown sat himself down on the stump of a tree and refused to go any farther.

"Friend," said he, stubbornly, "my mind is made up. Not another step will I budge on this errand. What if a wretched old woman do choose to go to the devil when I thought she was going to heaven: is that any reason why I should quit my dear Faith and go after her?"

"You will think better of this by and by," said his acquaintance, composedly. "Sit here and rest yourself a while; and when you feel like moving again, there is my staff to help you along."

Without more words, he threw his companion the maple stick, and was as speedily out of sight as if he had vanished into the deepening gloom. The young man sat a few moments by the roadside, applauding himself greatly, and thinking with how clear a conscience he should meet the minister in his morning walk, nor shrink from the eye of good old Deacon Gookin. And what calm sleep would be his that very night, which was to have been spent so wickedly, but so purely and sweetly now, in the arms of Faith! Amidst these pleasant and praiseworthy meditations, Goodman Brown heard the tramp of horses along the road, and deemed it advisable to conceal himself within the verge of the forest, conscious of the guilty purpose that had brought him thither, though now so happily turned from it.

On came the hoof tramps and the voices of the riders, two grave old voices, conversing soberly as they drew near. These mingled sounds appeared to pass along the road, within a few yards of the young man's hiding-place; but, owing doubtless to the depth of the gloom at that particular spot, neither the travellers nor their steeds were visible. Though their figures brushed the small boughs by the wayside, it could not be seen that they intercepted, even for a moment, the faint gleam from the strip of bright sky athwart which they must have passed. Goodman Brown alternately crouched and stood on tiptoe, pulling aside the branches and thrusting forth his head as far as he durst without discerning so much as a shadow. It vexed him the more, because he could have sworn, were such a thing possible, that he recognized the voices of the minister and Deacon Gookin, jogging along quietly, as they were wont to do, when bound to some ordination or ecclesiastical council. While yet within hearing, one of the riders stopped to pluck a switch.

"Of the two, reverend sir," said the voice like the deacon's, "I had rather miss an ordination dinner than to-night's meeting. They tell me that some of our community are to be here from Falmouth and beyond, and others from Connecticut and Rhode Island, besides several of the Indian powwows, who, after their fashion, know almost as much deviltry as the best of us. Moreover, there is a goodly young woman to be taken into communion."

"Mighty well, Deacon Gookin!" replied the solemn old tones of the minister. "Spur up, or we shall be late. Nothing can be done, you know, until I get on the ground."

The hoofs clattered again; and the voices, talking so strangely in the empty air, passed on through the forest, where no church had ever been gathered or solitary Christian prayed. Wither, then, could these holy men be journeying so deep into the heathen wilderness? Young Goodman Brown caught hold of a tree for support, being ready to sink down on the ground, faint and overburdened with the heavy sickness of his heart. He looked up to the sky, doubting whether there really was a heaven above him. Yet there was the blue arch, and the stars brightening in it.

"With heaven above and Faith below, I will yet stand firm against the devil!" cried Goodman Brown.

While he still gazed upward into the deep arch of the firmament and had lifted his hands to pray, a cloud, though no wind was stirring, hurried across the zenith and hid the brightening stars. The blue sky was still visible, except directly overhead, where this black mass of cloud was sweeping swiftly northward. Aloft in the air, as if from the depths of the cloud, came a confused and doubtful sound of voices. Once the listener fancied that he could distinguish the accents of towns-people of his own, men and women, both pious and ungodly, many of whom he had met at the communion table, and had seen others rioting at the tavern. The next moment, so indistinct were the sounds, he doubted whether he had heard aught but the murmur of the old forest, whispering without a wind. Then came a stronger swell of those familiar tones, heard daily in the sunshine at Salem village, but never until now from a cloud of night. There was one voice, of a young woman, uttering lamentations, yet with an uncertain sorrow, and entreating for some favor, which, perhaps, it would grieve her to obtain; and all the unseen multitude, both saints and sinners, seemed to encourage her onward.

"Faith!" shouted Goodman Brown, in a voice of agony and desperation; and the echoes of the forest mocked him, crying, "Faith! Faith!" as if bewildered wretches were seeking her all through the wilderness.

The cry of grief, rage, and terror was yet piercing the night, when the unhappy husband held his breath for a response. There was a scream, drowned immediately in a louder murmur of voices, fading into far-off laughter, as the dark cloud swept away, leaving the clear and silent sky above Goodman Brown. But something fluttered lightly down through the air and caught on the branch of a tree. The young man seized it, and beheld a pink ribbon.

"My Faith is gone!" cried he, after one stupefied moment. "There is no good on earth; and sin is but a name. Come, devil; for to thee is this world given."

And, maddened with despair, so that he laughed loud and long, did Goodman Brown grasp his staff and set forth again, at such a rate that he seemed to fly along the forest path rather than to walk or run. The road grew wilder and

drearier and more faintly traced, and vanished at length, leaving him in the heart
of the dark wilderness, still rushing onward with the instinct that guides mortal
man to evil. The whole forest was peopled with frightful sounds—the creaking
of the trees, the howling of wild beasts, and the yell of Indians; while sometimes
the wind tolled like a distant church bell, and sometimes gave a broad roar
around the traveller, as if all Nature were laughing him to scorn. But he was himself the chief horror of the scene, and shrank not from its other horrors.

"Ha! ha! ha!" roared Goodman Brown when the wind laughed at him. "Let
us hear which will laugh loudest. Think not to frighten me with your deviltry.
Come witch, come wizard, come Indian powwow, come devil himself, and here
comes Goodman Brown. You may as well fear him as he fear you."

In truth, all through the haunted forest there could be nothing more frightful
than the figure of Goodman Brown. On he flew among the black Pines, bran-
dishing his staff with frenzied gestures, now giving vent to an inspiration of horrid blasphemy, and now shouting forth such laughter as set all the echoes of the
forest laughing like demons around him. The fiend in his own shape is less
hideous than when he rages in the breast of man. Thus sped the demoniac on his
course, until, quivering among the trees, he saw a red light before him, as when
the felled trunks and branches of a clearing have been set on fire, and throw up
their lurid blaze against the sky, at the hour of midnight. He paused, in a lull of
the tempest that had driven him onward, and heard the swell of what seemed a
hymn, rolling solemnly from a distance with the weight of many voices. He knew
the tune; it was a familiar one in the choir of the village meeting-house. The verse
died heavily away, and was lengthened by a chorus, not of human voices, but of
all the sounds of the benighted wilderness pealing in awful harmony together.
Goodman Brown cried out, and his cry was lost to his own ear by its unison with
the cry of the desert.

In the interval of silence he stole forward until the light glared full upon his
eyes. At one extremity of an open space, hemmed in by the dark wall of the forest, arose a rock, bearing some rude, natural resemblance either to an altar or a
pulpit, and surrounded by four blazing pines, their tops aflame, their stems untouched, like candles at an evening meeting. The mass of foliage that had overgrown the summit of the rock was all on fire, blazing high into the night and
fitfully illuminating the whole field. Each pendent twig and leafy festoon was in
a blaze. As the red light arose and fell, a numerous congregation alternately
shone forth, then disappeared in shadow, and again grew, as it were, out of the
darkness, peopling the heart of the solitary woods at once.

"A grave and dark-clad company," quoth Goodman Brown.

In truth they were such. Among them, quivering to and fro between gloom
and splendor, appeared faces that would be seen next day at the council board
of the province, and others which, Sabbath after Sabbath, looked devoutly heavenward, and benignantly over the crowded pews, from the holiest pulpits in the
land. Some affirm that the lady of the governor was there. At least there were
high dames well known to her, and wives of honored husbands, and widows, a
great multitude, and ancient maidens, all of excellent repute, and fair young girls,

who trembled lest their mothers should espy them. Either the sudden gleams of light flashing over the obscure field bedazzled Goodman Brown, or he recognized a score of the church members of Salem village famous for their especial sanctity. Good old Deacon Gookin had arrived, and waited at the skirts of that venerable saint, his revered pastor. But, irreverently consorting with these grave, reputable, and pious people, these elders of the church, these chaste dames and dewy virgins, there were men of dissolute lives and women of spotted fame, wretches given over to all mean and filthy vice, and suspected even of horrid crimes. It was strange to see that the good shrank not from the wicked, nor were the sinners abashed by the saints. Scattered also among their pale-faced enemies were the Indian priests, or powwows, who had often scared their native forest with more hideous incantations than any known to English witchcraft.

"But where is Faith?" thought Goodman Brown; and as hope came into his heart, he trembled.

Another verse of the hymn arose, a slow and mournful strain, such as the pious love, but joined to words which expressed all that our nature can conceive of sin, and darkly hinted at far more. Unfathomable to mere mortals is the lore of fiends. Verse after verse was sung; and still the chorus of the desert swelled between like the deepest tone of a mighty organ; and with the final peal of that dreadful anthem there came a sound, as if the roaring wind, the rushing streams, the howling beasts, and every other voice of the unconcerted wilderness were mingling and according with the voice of guilty man in homage to the prince of all. The four blazing pines threw up a loftier flame, and obscurely discovered shapes and visages of horror on the smoke wreaths above the impious assembly. At the same moment the fire on the rock shot redly forth and formed a glowing arch above its base, where now appeared a figure. With reverence be it spoken, the figure bore no slight similitude, both in garb and manner, to some grave divine of the New England churches.

"Bring forth the converts!" cried a voice that echoed through the field and rolled into the forest.

At the word, Goodman Brown stepped forth from the shadow of the trees and approached the congregation, with whom he felt a loathful brotherhood by the sympathy of all that was wicked in his heart. He could have well-nigh sworn that the shape of his own dead father beckoned him to advance, looking downward from a smoke wreath, while a woman, with dim features of despair, threw out her hand to warn him back. Was it his mother? But he had no power to retreat one step, nor to resist, even in thought, when the minister and good old Deacon Gookin seized his arms and led him to the blazing rock. Thither came also the slender form of a veiled female, led between Goody Cloyse, that pious teacher of the catechism, and Martha Carrier, who had received the devil's promise to be queen of hell. A rampant hag was she. And there stood the proselytes beneath the canopy of fire.

"Welcome, my children," said the dark figure, "to the communion of your race. Ye have found thus young your nature and your destiny. My children, look behind you!"

They turned; and flashing forth, as it were, in a sheet of flame, the fiend worshippers were seen; the smile of welcome gleamed darkly on every visage.

"There," resumed the sable form, "are all whom ye have reverenced from youth. Ye deemed them holier than yourselves, and shrank from your own sin, contrasting it with their lives of righteousness and prayerful aspirations heavenward. Yet here are they all in my worshipping assembly. This night it shall be granted you to know their secret deeds: how hoary-bearded elders of the church have whispered wanton words to the young maids of their households; how many a woman, eager for widows' weeds, has given her husband a drink at bedtime and let him sleep his last sleep in her bosom; how beardless youths have made haste to inherit their fathers' wealth; and how fair damsels—blush not, sweet ones—have dug little graves in the garden, and bidden me, the sole guest, to an infant's funeral. By the sympathy of your human hearts for sin ye shall scent out all the places—whether in church, bed-chamber, street, field, or forest—where crime has been committed, and shall exult to behold the whole earth one stain of guilt, one mighty blood spot. Far more than this. It shall be yours to penetrate, in every bosom, the deep mystery of sin, the fountain of all wicked arts, and which inexhaustibly supplies more evil impulses than human power—than my power at its utmost—can make manifest in deeds. And now, my children, look upon each other."

They did so; and, by the blaze of the hell-kindled torches, the wretched man beheld his Faith, and the wife her husband, trembling before that unhallowed altar.

"Lo, there ye stand, my children," said the figure, in a deep and solemn tone, almost sad with its despairing awfulness, as if his once angelic nature could yet mourn for our miserable race. "Depending upon one another's hearts, ye had still hoped that virtue were not all a dream. Now are ye undeceived. Evil is the nature of mankind. Evil must be your only happiness. Welcome again, my children, to the communion of your race."

"Welcome," repeated the fiend worshippers, in one cry of despair and triumph.

And there they stood, the only pair, as it seemed, who were yet hesitating on the verge of wickedness in this dark world. A basin was hollowed, naturally, in the rock. Did it contain water, reddened by the lurid light? or was it blood? or, perchance, a liquid flame? Herein did the shape of evil dip his hand and prepare to lay the mark of baptism upon their foreheads, that they might be partakers of the mystery of sin, more conscious of the secret guilt of others, both in deed and thought, than they could now be of their own. The husband cast one look at his pale wife, and Faith at him. What polluted wretches would the next glance show them to each other, shuddering alike at what they disclosed and what they saw.

"Faith! Faith!" cried the husband, "look up to heaven, and resist the wicked one."

Whether Faith obeyed he knew not. Hardly had he spoken when he found himself amid calm night and solitude, listening to a roar of the wind which died heavily away through the forest. He staggered against the rock, and felt it chill and damp; while a hanging twig, that had been all on fire, besprinkled his cheek with the coldest dew.

The next morning young Goodman Brown came slowly into the street of Salem village, staring around him like a bewildered man. The good old minister was taking a walk along the graveyard to get an appetite for breakfast and meditate his sermon, and bestowed a blessing, as he passed, on Goodman Brown. He shrank from the venerable saint as if to avoid an anathema. Old Deacon Gookin was at domestic worship, and the holy words of his prayer were heard through the open window. "What God doth the wizard pray to?" quoth Goodman Brown. Goody Cloyse, that excellent old Christian, stood in the early sunshine at her own lattice, catechizing a little girl who had brought her a pint of morning's milk. Goodman Brown snatched away the child as from the grasp of the fiend himself. Turning the corner by the meeting-house, he spied the head of Faith, with the pink ribbons, gazing anxiously forth, and bursting into such joy at sight of him that she skipped along the street and almost kissed her husband before the whole village. But Goodman Brown looked sternly and sadly into her face, and passed on without a greeting.

Had Goodman Brown fallen asleep in the forest and only dreamed a wild dream of a witch-meeting?

Be it so if you will; but, alas! it was a dream of evil omen for young Goodman Brown. A stern, a sad, a darkly meditative, a distrustful, if not a desperate man did he become from the night of that fearful dream. On the Sabbath day, when the congregation were singing a holy psalm, he could not listen because an anthem of sin rushed loudly upon his ear and drowned all the blessed strain. When the minister spoke from the pulpit with power and fervid eloquence, and, with his hand on the open Bible, of the sacred truths of our religion, and of saint-like lives and triumphant deaths, and of future bliss or misery unutterable, then did Goodman Brown turn pale, dreading lest the roof should thunder down upon the gray blasphemer and his hearers. Often, awaking suddenly at midnight, he shrank from the bosom of Faith; and at morning or eventide, when the family knelt down at prayer, he scowled and muttered to himself, and gazed sternly at his wife, and turned away. And when he had lived long, and was borne to his grave a hoary corpse, followed by Faith, an aged woman, and children and grandchildren, a goodly procession, besides neighbors not a few, they carved no hopeful verse upon his tombstone, for his dying hour was gloom.

## Study and Discussion Questions

1. Think about the names of the characters. What is the significance of these names?
2. Who is the person young Goodman Brown meets in the forest? Why does Hawthorne mention that the two resemble each other?
3. What is young Goodman Brown's errand this night? Why doesn't he tell his wife what it is?
4. What are the travelling companion's means of persuasion?
5. What finally causes Goodman Brown to go on with his journey?

6. Who is at the meeting in the woods? In what ways does that community differ from the one Goodman Brown (a) comes from and (b) expected to find there?
7. What does this story suggest is the "real" nature of human beings?

### Suggestions for Writing

1. Write about a time you discovered something (or thought you discovered something) that caused a major shift in the way you saw the world.
2. How would the story and your response to it have been changed if Hawthorne had left out the suggestion that all this might have been a dream?

### Critical Resources

1. Berkove, Lawrence. "'Reasoning as We Go': The Flawed Logic of Young Goodman Brown." *Nathaniel Hawthorne Review* 24.1 (1998): 46–52.
2. Frank, Albert von. *Critical Essays on Hawthorne's Short Stories.* Boston: G. K. Hall, 1991.
3. Keil, James. "Hawthorne's 'Young Goodman Brown': Early 19th Century and Puritan Constructions of Gender." *New England Quarterly* 69.1 (1996): 33–55.
4. Reynolds, Larry. *A Historical Guide to Nathaniel Hawthorne.* Oxford: Oxford UP, 2001.

## JAMAICA KINCAID

## *Girl*                                                                (1983)

Wash the white clothes on Monday and put them on the stone heap; wash the color clothes on Tuesday and put them on the clothesline to dry; don't walk bare-head in the hot sun; cook pumpkin fritters in very hot sweet oil; soak your little cloths right after you take them off; when buying cotton to make yourself a nice blouse, be sure that it doesn't have gum on it, because that way it won't hold up well after a wash; soak salt fish overnight before you cook it; is it true that you sing benna[1] in Sunday school?; always eat your food in such a way that it won't turn someone else's stomach; on Sundays try to walk like a lady and not like the slut you are so bent on becoming; don't sing benna in Sunday school; you mustn't speak to wharf-rat boys, not even to give directions; don't eat fruits on the street—flies will follow you; *but I don't sing benna on Sundays at all and never in Sunday school;* this is how to sew on a button; this is how to make a button-

---

[1]Calypso or rock and roll.

hole for the button you have just sewed on; this is how to hem a dress when you see the hem coming down and so to prevent yourself from looking like the slut I know you are so bent on becoming; this is how you iron your father's khaki shirt so that it doesn't have a crease; this is how you iron your father's khaki pants so that they don't have a crease; this is how you grow okra—far from the house, because okra tree harbors red ants; when you are growing dasheen, make sure it gets plenty of water or else it makes your throat itch when you are eating it; this is how you sweep a corner; this is how you sweep a whole house; this is how you sweep a yard; this is how you smile to someone you don't like too much; this is how you smile to someone you don't like at all; this is how to smile to someone you like completely; this is how you set a table for tea; this is how you set a table for dinner; this is how you set a table for dinner with an important guest; this is how you set a table for lunch; this is how you set a table for breakfast, this is how to behave in the presence of men who don't know you very well, and this way they won't recognize immediately the slut I have warned you against becoming; be sure to wash every day, even if it is with your own spit; don't squat down to play marbles—you are not a boy, you know; don't pick people's flowers—you might catch something; don't throw stones at blackbirds, because it might not be a blackbird at all; this is how to make a bread pudding; this is how to make doukona; this is how to make pepper pot; this is how to make a good medicine for a cold; this is how to make a good medicine to throw away a child before it even becomes a child; this is how to catch a fish; this is how to throw back a fish you don't like, and that way something bad won't fall on you; this is how to bully a man; this is how a man bullies you; this is how to love a man, and if this doesn't work there are other ways, and if they don't work don't feel too bad about giving up; this is how to spit up in the air if you feel like it, and this is how to move quick so that it doesn't fall on you; this is how to make ends meet; always squeeze bread to make sure it's fresh; *but what if the baker won't let me feel the bread?;* you mean to say that after all you are really going to be the kind of woman who the baker won't let near the bread?

### Study and Discussion Questions

1. Who is speaking? To whom? How old do you think the girl being addressed is?
2. Categorize and characterize the advice given.
3. What seems to be the speaker's main concern? What evidence is there that she has it in mind even when she's not talking about it directly?
4. Analyze the impact of the narrator's stringing so many words of advice together. What else makes the story funny?

### Suggestions for Writing

1. What would the girl grow up to be like if the followed all the advice given? Discuss the story as a comment on women's roles in society.

2. Choose someone—a parent, older sibling, employer, teacher—who gives
   too much advice and write a short piece modeled on "Girl."

### Critical Resources

1. Ferguson, Moira. *Jamaica Kincaid: Where the Land Meets the Body.* Char-
   lottesville, VA: U of Virginia P, 1994.
2. Paravisini, Moira. *Jamaica Kincaid: A Critical Companion.* Westport, CT:
   Greenwood, 1999.
3. Vorda, Allan. "An Interview with Jamaica Kincaid." *Mississippi Review* 20
   1.2 (1991): 7–26.

❀ ❀ ❀

# TONI MORRISON

FROM *The Bluest Eye*                                                    (1970)

It had begun with Christmas and the gift of dolls. The big, the special, the loving gift was always a big, blue-eyed Baby Doll. From the clucking sounds of
adults I knew that the doll represented what they thought was my fondest wish.
I was bemused with the thing itself, and the way it looked. What was I supposed
to do with it? Pretend I was its mother? I had no interest in babies or the concept of motherhood. I was interested only in humans my own age and size, and
could not generate any enthusiasm at the prospect of being a mother. Motherhood was old age, and other remote possibilities. I learned quickly, however, what
I was expected to do with the doll: rock it, fabricate storied situations around it,
even sleep with it. Picture books were full of little girls sleeping with their dolls.
Raggedy Ann dolls usually, but they were out of the question. I was physically
revolted by and secretly frightened of those round moronic eyes, the pancake
face, and orangeworms hair.
   The other dolls, which were supposed to bring me great pleasure, succeeded
in doing quite the opposite. When I took it to bed, its hard unyielding limbs re-
sisted my flesh—the tapered fingertips on those dimpled hands scratched. If, in
sleep, I turned, the bone-cold head collided with my own. It was a most uncomfortable, patently aggressive sleeping companion. To hold it was no more re-
warding. The starched gauze or lace on the cotton dress irritated any embrace. I
had only one desire: to dismember it. To see of what it was made, to discover the
dearness, to find the beauty, the desirability that had escaped me, but apparently
only me. Adults, older girls, shops, magazines, newspapers, window signs—all the
world had agreed that a blue-eyed, yellow-haired, pink-skinned doll was what
every girl child treasured. "Here," they said, "this is beautiful, and if you are on

this day 'worthy' you may have it." I fingered the face, wondering at the single-stroke eyebrows; picked at the pearly teeth stuck like two piano keys between red bowline lips. Traced the turned-up nose, poked the glassy blue eyeballs, twisted the yellow hair. I could not love it. But I could examine it to see what it was that all the world said was lovable. Break off the tiny fingers, bend the flat feet, loosen the hair, twist the head around, and the thing made one sound—a sound they said was the sweet and plaintive cry "Mama," but which sounded to me like the bleat of a dying lamb, or, more precisely, our icebox door opening on rusty hinges in July. Remove the cold and stupid eyeball, it would bleat still, "Ahhhhhh," take off the head, shake out the sawdust, crack the back against the brass bed rail, it would bleat still. The gauze back would split, and I could see the disk with six holes, the secret of the sound. A mere metal roundness.

Grown people frowned and fussed: "You-don't-know-how-to-take-care-of-nothing. I-never-had-a-baby-doll-in-my-whole-life-and-used-to-cry-my-eyes-out-for-them. Now-you-got-one-a-beautiful-one-and-you-tear-it-up-what's-the-matter-with-you?"

How strong was their outrage. Tears threatened to erase the aloofness of their authority. The emotion of years of unfulfilled longing preened in their voices. I did not know why I destroyed those dolls. But I did know that nobody ever asked me what I wanted for Christmas. Had any adult with the power to fulfill my desires taken me seriously and asked me what I wanted, they would have known that I did not want to have anything to own, or to possess any object. I wanted rather to feel something on Christmas day. The real question would have been, "Dear Claudia, what experience would you like on Christmas?" I could have spoken up, "I want to sit on the low stool in Big Mama's kitchen with my lap full of lilacs and listen to Big Papa play his violin for me alone." The lowness of the stool made for my body, the security and warmth of Big Mama's kitchen, the smell of the lilacs, the sound of the music, and, since it would be good to have all of my senses engaged, the taste of a peach, perhaps, afterward.

Instead I tasted and smelled the acridness of tin plates and cups designed for tea parties that bored me. Instead I looked with loathing on new dresses that required a hateful bath in a galvanized zinc tub before wearing. Slipping around on the zinc, no time to play or soak, for the water chilled too fast, no time to enjoy one's naked-ness, only time to make curtains of soapy water careen down between the legs. Then the scratchy towels and the dreadful and humiliating absence of dirt. The irritable, unimaginative cleanliness. Gone the ink marks from legs and face, all my creations and accumulations of the day gone, and replaced by goose pimples.

I destroyed white baby dolls.

But the dismembering of dolls was not the true horror. The truly horrifying thing was the transference of the same impulses to little white girls. The indifference with which I could have axed them was shaken only by my desire to do so. To discover what eluded me: the secret of the magic they weaved on others. What made people look at them and say, "Awwwww," but not for me? The eye slide of black women as they approached them on the street, and the possessive gentleness of their touch as they handled them.

If I pinched them, their eyes—unlike the crazed glint of the baby doll's eyes—would fold in pain, and their cry would not be the sound of an icebox door, but a fascinating cry of pain. When I learned how repulsive this disinterested violence was, that it was repulsive because it was disinterested, my shame floundered about for refuge. The best hiding place was love. Thus the conversion from pristine sadism to fabricated hatred, to fraudulent love. It was a small step to Shirley Temple. I learned much later to worship her, just as I learned to delight in cleanliness, knowing, even as I learned, that the change was adjustment without improvement.

### Study and Discussion Questions

1. Why do adults give dolls to little girls?
2. Why does Claudia hate Shirley Temple?
3. What's wrong with the Christmas baby doll Claudia is given?
4. What would Claudia really like for Christmas?
5. How does Claudia's description of the doll undermine its purported beauty? What words and images does Morrison use?
6. What does the paragraph about taking a bath have to do with the subject of baby dolls?
7. Claudia says she transferred her destructive impulses toward dolls "to little white girls." How do you think this happens? Is she justified in feeling this way?
8. Why is love the best hiding place for shame?

### Suggestions for Writing

1. Select one of the substantial paragraphs in this excerpt and analyze Morrison's imagery, her language, and how she makes a small unified episode out of the paragraph.
2. Were you given a Christmas or birthday present you hated when you were a child? Write a letter to the giver saying how and why you hated the present.
3. Make an argument for or against giving children toys that socialize them into gender-specific roles as adults. You might pick a particular toy to use as an example.
4. What is "adjustment without improvement" in the context of this piece of writing? What do you think Morrison is saying about how children are socialized—and particularly about how black children are socialized into a white world?

### Critical Resources

1. *Beloved.* Dir. Johnathan Demme. Perf. Oprah Winfrey, Danny Glover. Touchstone Pictures, 1998.

2. Gates, Henry Louis and K. Appiah, eds. *Toni Morrison: Critical Perspectives Past and Present.* New York: Amistad, 1993.
3. Gutherie, Danille. *Conversations with Toni Morrison.* Jackson: U of Mississippi P, 1994.
4. Middleton, David. *Toni Morrison's Fiction: Contemporary Criticism.* New York: Garland, 2000.

❀ ❀ ❀

## ALICE MUNRO

## *An Ounce of Cure*                                     (1968)

My parents didn't drink. They weren't rabid about it, and in fact I remember that when I signed the pledge in grade seven, with the rest of that superbly if impermanently indoctrinated class, my mother said, "It's just nonsense and fanaticism, children of that age." My father would drink a beer on a hot day, but my mother did not join him, and—whether accidentally or symbolically—this drink was always consumed *outside* the house. Most of the people we knew were the same way, in the small town where we lived. I ought not to say that it was this which got me into difficulties, because the difficulties I got into were a faithful expression of my own incommodious nature—the same nature that caused my mother to look at me, on any occasion which traditionally calls for feelings of pride and maternal accomplishment (my departure for my first formal dance, I mean, or my hellbent preparations for a descent on college) with an expression of brooding and fascinated despair, as if she could not possibly expect, did not ask, that it should go with me as it did with other girls; the dreamed-of spoils of daughters—orchids, nice boys, diamond rings—would be borne home in due course by the daughters of her friends, but not by me; all she could do was hope for a lesser rather than a greater disaster—an elopement, say, with a boy who could never earn his living, rather than an abduction into the White Slave trade.

But ignorance, my mother said, ignorance, or innocence if you like, is not always such a fine thing as people think and I am not sure it may not be dangerous for a girl like you; then she emphasized her point, as she had a habit of doing, with some quotation which had an innocent promposity and odour of mothballs. I didn't even wince at it, knowing full well how it must have worked wonders with Mr. Berryman.

The evening I baby-sat for the Berrymans must have been in April. I had been in love all year, or at least since the first week in September, when a boy named Martin Collingwood had given me a surprised, appreciative, and rather ominously complacent smile in the school assembly. I never knew what surprised him; I was not looking like anybody but me; I had an old blouse on and my home-permanent had turned out badly. A few weeks after that he took me out for the first time, and kissed me on the dark side of the porch—also, I ought to say, on the mouth; I am sure it was the first time anybody had ever kissed me effectively, and I know that I did not wash my face that night or the next morning, in order to keep the imprint of those kisses intact. (I showed the most painful banality in the conduct of this whole affair, as you will see.) Two months, and a few amatory stages later, he dropped me. He had fallen for the girl who played opposite him in the Christmas production of *Pride and Prejudice*.

I said I was not going to have anything to do with that play, and I got another girl to work on Makeup in my place, but of course I went to it after all, and sat down in front with my girl friend Joyce, who pressed my hand when I was overcome with pain and delight at the sight of Mr. Darcy in white breeches, silk waistcoat, and sideburns. It was surely seeing Martin as Darcy that did for me; every girl is in love with Darcy anyway, and the part gave Martin an arrogance and male splendour in my eyes which made it impossible to remember that he was simply a high-school senior, passably good-looking and of medium intelligence (and with a reputation slightly tainted, at that, by such preferences as the Drama Club and the Cadet *Band*) who happened to be the first boy, the first really presentable boy, to take an interest in me. In the last act they gave him a chance to embrace Elizabeth (Mary Bishop, with a sallow complexion and no figure, but big vivacious eyes) and during this realistic encounter I dug my nails bitterly into Joyce's sympathetic palm.

That night was the beginning of months of real, if more or less self-inflicted, misery for me. Why is it a temptation to refer to this sort of thing lightly, with irony, with amazement even, at finding oneself involved with such preposterous emotions in the unaccountable past? That is what we are apt to do, speaking of love; with adolescent love, of course, it's practically obligatory; you would think we sat around, dull afternoons, amusing ourselves with these tidbit recollections of pain. But it really doesn't make me feel very gay—worse still, it doesn't really surprise me—to remember all the stupid, sad, half-ashamed things I did, that people in love always do. I hung around the places where he might be seen, and then pretended not to see him; I made absurdly roundabout approaches, in conversation, to the bitter pleasure of casually mentioning his name. I daydreamed endlessly; in fact if you want to put it mathematically, I spent perhaps ten times as many hours thinking about Martin Collingwood—yes, pining and weeping for him—as I ever spent with him; the idea of him dominated my mind relentlessly and, after a while, against my will. For if at first I had dramatized my feelings, the time came when I would have been glad to escape them; my well-worn daydreams had become depressing and not even temporarily consoling. As I worked my math problems I would torture myself, quite mechanically and helplessly, with an exact recollection of Martin kissing my throat. I had an exact recollection of *everything*. One night I had an impulse to swallow all the aspirins in the bathroom cabinet, but stopped after I had taken six.

My mother noticed that something was wrong and got me some iron pills. She said, "Are you sure everything is going all right at school?" *School!* When I told her that Martin and I had broken up all she said was, "Well so much the better for that. I never saw a boy so stuck on himself." "Martin has enough conceit to sink a battleship," I said morosely and went upstairs and cried.

The night I went to the Berrymans was a Saturday night. I baby-sat for them quite often on Saturday nights because they liked to drive over to Baileyville, a much bigger, livelier town about twenty miles away, and perhaps have supper and go to a show. They had been living in our town only two or three years—Mr. Berryman had been brought in as plant manager of the new door-factory—and they remained, I suppose by choice, on the fringes of its society; most of their friends were youngish couples like themselves, born in other places, who lived in new ranch-style houses on a hill outside town where we used to go tobogganing. This Saturday night they had two other couples in for drinks before they all drove over to Baileyville for the opening of a new supper-club; they were all rather festive. I sat in the kitchen and pretended to do Latin. Last night had been the Spring Dance at the High School. I had not gone, since the only boy who had asked me was Millerd Crompton, who asked so many girls that he was suspected of working his way through the whole class alphabetically. But the dance was held in the Armouries, which was only half a block away from our house; I had been able to see the boys in dark suits, the girls in long pale formals under their coats, passing gravely under the street-lights, stepping around the last patches of snow. I could even hear the music and I have not forgotten to this day that they played "Ballerina," and—oh, song of my aching heart—"Slow Boat to China." Joyce had phoned me up this morning and told me in her hushed way (we might have been discussing an incurable disease I had) that yes, M.C. *had* been there with M.B., and she had on a formal that must have been made out of somebody's old lace tablecloth, it just *hung*.

When the Berrymans and their friends had gone I went into the living room and read a magazine. I was mortally depressed. The big softly lit room, with its green and leaf-brown colours, made an uncluttered setting for the development of the emotions, such as you would get on a stage. At home the life of the emotions went on all right, but it always seemed to get buried under the piles of mending to be done, the ironing, the children's jigsaw puzzles and rock collections. It was the sort of house where people were always colliding with one another on the stairs and listening to hockey games and Superman on the radio.

I got up and found the Berrymans' "Danse Macabre" and put it on the record player and turned out the living-room lights. The curtains were only partly drawn. A street light shone obliquely on the windowpane, making a rectangle of thin dusty gold, in which the shadows of bare branches moved, caught in the huge sweet winds of spring. It was a mild black night when the last snow was melting. A year ago all this—the music, the wind and darkness, the shadows of the branches—would have given me tremendous happiness; when they did not do so now, but only called up tediously familiar, somehow humiliatingly personal thoughts, I gave up my soul for dead and walked into the kitchen and decided to get drunk.

No, it was not like that. I walked into the kitchen to look for a coke or something in the refrigerator, and there on the front of the counter were three tall beautiful bottles, all about half full of gold. But even after I had looked at them and lifted them to feel their weight I had not decided to get drunk; I had decided to have a drink.

Now here is where my ignorance, my disastrous innocence, comes in. It is true that I had seen the Berrymans and their friends drinking their highballs as casually as I would drink a coke, but I did not apply this attitude to myself. No; I thought of hard liquor as something to be taken in extremities, and relied upon for extravagant results, one way or another. My approach could not have been less casual if I had been the Little Mermaid drinking the witch's crystal potion. Gravely, with a glance at my set face in the black window above the sink, I poured a little whisky from each of the bottles (I think now there were two brands of rye and an expensive Scotch) until I had my glass full. For I had never in my life seen anyone pour a drink and I had no idea that people frequently diluted their liquor with water, soda, et cetera, and I had seen that the glasses the Berrymans' guests were holding when I came through the living room were nearly full.

I drank it off as quickly as possible. I set the glass down and stood looking at my face in the window, half expecting to see it altered. My throat was burning, but I felt nothing else. It was very disappointing, when I had worked myself up to it. But I was not going to let it go at that. I poured another full glass, then filled each of the bottles with water to approximately the level I had seen when I came in. I drank the second glass only a little more slowly than the first. I put the empty glass down on the counter with care, perhaps feeling in my head a rustle of things to come, and went and sat down on a chair in the living room. I reached up and turned on a floor lamp beside the chair, and the room jumped on me.

When I say that I was expecting extravagant results I do not mean that I was expecting this. I had thought of some sweeping emotional change, an upsurge of gaiety and irresponsibility, a feeling of lawlessness and escape, accompanied by a little dizziness and perhaps a tendency to giggle out loud. I did not have in mind the ceiling spinning like a great plate somebody had thrown at me, nor the pale green blobs of the chairs swelling, converging, disintegrating, playing with me a game full of enormous senseless inanimate malice. My head sank back; I closed my eyes. And at once opened them, opened them wide, threw myself out of the chair and down the hall and reached—thank God, thank God!—the Berrymans' bathroom, where I was sick everywhere, everywhere, and dropped like a stone.

From this point on I have no continuous picture of what happened; my memories of the next hour or two are split into vivid and improbable segments, with nothing but murk and uncertainty between. I do remember lying on the bathroom floor looking sideways at the little six-sided white tiles, which lay together in such an admirable and logical pattern, seeing them with the brief broken gratitude and sanity of one who has just been torn to pieces with vomiting. Then I remember sitting on the stool in front of the hall phone, asking weakly for Joyce's number. Joyce was not home. I was told by her mother (a rather rattlebrained woman, who didn't seem to notice a thing the matter—for which I felt weakly, mechanically grateful) that she was at Kay Stringer's house. I didn't know Kay's number so I just asked the operator; I felt I couldn't risk looking down at the telephone book.

Kay Stringer was not a friend of mine but a new friend of Joyce's. She had a vague reputation for wildness and a long switch of hair, very oddly, though naturally, coloured—from soap-yellow to caramel-brown. She knew a lot of boys more exciting than Martin Collingwood, boys who had quit school or been imported into town to play on the hockey team. She and Joyce rode around in these boys' cars, and sometimes went with them—having lied of course to their mothers—to the Gay-la dance hall on the highway north of town.

I got Joyce on the phone. She was very keyed-up, as she always was with boys around, and she hardly seemed to hear what I was saying.

"Oh, I can't tonight," she said. "Some kids are here. We're going to play cards. You know Bill Kline? He's here. Ross Armour—"

"I'm *sick*," I said trying to speak distinctly; it came out an inhuman croak. "I'm *drunk*. Joyce!" Then I fell off the stool and the receiver dropped out of my hand and banged for a while dismally against the wall.

I had not told Joyce where I was, so after thinking about it for a moment she phoned my mother, and using the elaborate and unnecessary subterfuge that young girls delight in, she found out. She and Kay and the boys—there were three of them—told some story about where they were going to Kay's mother, and got into the car and drove out. They found me still lying on the broadloom carpet in the hall; I had been sick again, and this time I had not made it to the bathroom.

It turned out that Kay Stringer, who arrived on this scene only by accident, was exactly the person I needed. She loved a crisis, particularly one like this, which had a shady and scandalous aspect and which must be kept secret from the adult world. She became excited, aggressive, efficient; that energy which was termed wildness was simply the overflow of a great female instinct to manage, comfort and control. I could hear her voice coming at me from all directions, telling me not to worry, telling Joyce to find the biggest coffeepot they had and make it full of coffee (*strong* coffee, she said), telling the boys to pick me up and carry me to the sofa. Later, in the fog beyond my reach, she was calling for a scrub-brush.

Then I was lying on the sofa, covered with some kind of crocheted throw they had found in the bedroom. I didn't want to lift my head. The house was full of the smell of coffee. Joyce came in, looking very pale; she said that the Berryman kids had wakened up but she had given them a cookie and told them to go back to bed, it was all right; she hadn't let them out of their room and she didn't believe they'd remember. She said that she and Kay had cleaned up the bathroom and the hall though she was afraid there was still a spot on the rug. The coffee was ready. I didn't understand anything very well. The boys had turned on the radio and were going through the Berrymans' record collection; they had it out on the floor. I felt there was something odd about this but I could not think what it was.

Kay brought me a huge breakfast mug full of coffee.

"I don't know if I can," I said. "Thanks."

"Sit up," she said briskly, as if dealing with drunks was an everyday business for her, I had no need to feel myself important. (I met, and recognized, that tone of voice years later, in the maternity ward.) "Now drink," she said. I drank, and at the same time realized that I was wearing only my slip. Joyce and Kay had taken off my blouse and skirt. They had brushed off the skirt and washed out the blouse, since it was nylon; it was hanging in the bathroom. I pulled the throw up under my arms and Kay laughed. She got everybody coffee. Joyce brought in the coffeepot and on Kay's instructions she kept filling my cup whenever I drank from it. Somebody said to me with interest. "You must have really wanted to tie one on."

"No," I said rather sulkily, obediently drinking my coffee. "I only had two drinks."

Kay laughed, "Well it certainly gets to you, I'll say that. What time do you expect *they*'ll be back?" she said.

"Late, After one I think."

"You should be all right by that time. Have some more coffee."

Kay and one of the boys began dancing to the radio. Kay danced very sexily, but her face had the gently superior and indulgent, rather cold look it had when she was lifting me up to drink the coffee. The boy was whispering to her and she was smiling, shaking her head. Joyce said she was hungry, and she went out to the kitchen to see what there was—potato chips or crackers, or something like that, that you could eat without making too noticeable a dint. Bill Kline came over and sat on the sofa beside me and patted my legs through the crocheted throw. He didn't say anything to me, just patted my legs and looked at me with what seemed to me a very stupid, half-sick, absurd and alarming expression. I felt very uncomfortable; I wondered how it had ever got around that Bill Kline was so good looking, with an expression like that. I moved my legs nervously and he gave me a look of contempt, not ceasing to pat me. Then I scrambled off the sofa, pulling the throw around me, with the idea of going to the bathroom to see if my blouse was dry. I lurched a little when I started to walk, and for some reason—probably to show Bill Kline that he had not panicked me—I immediately exaggerated this, and calling out, "Watch me walk a straight line!" I lurched and stumbled, to the accompaniment of everyone's laughter, towards the hall. I was standing in the archway between the hall and the living room when the knob of the front door turned with a small matter-of-fact click and everything became silent behind me except the radio of course and the crocheted throw inspired by some delicate malice of its own slithered down around my feet and there—oh, delicious moment in a well-organized farce!—there stood the Berrymans,

Mr. and Mrs., with expressions on their faces as appropriate to the occasion as any old-fashioned director of farces could wish. They must have been preparing those expressions, of course; they could not have produced them in the first moment of shock; with the noise we were making, they had no doubt heard us as soon as they got out of the car; for the same reason, we had not heard them. I don't think I ever knew what brought them home so early—a headache, an argument—and I was not really in a position to ask.

Mr. Berryman drove me home. I don't remember how I got into that car, or how I found my clothes and put them on, or what kind of a good-night, if any, I said to Mrs. Berryman. I don't remember what happened to my friends, though I imagine they gathered up their coats and fled, covering up the ignominy of their departure with a mechanical roar of defiance. I remember Joyce with a box of crackers in her hand, saying that I had become terribly sick from eating—I think she said *sauerkraut*—for supper, and that I had called them for help. (When I asked her later what they made of this she said, "It wasn't any use. You *reeked.*") I remember also her saying, "Oh, no, Mr. Berryman I beg of you, my mother is a terribly nervous person I don't know what the shock might do to her. I will go down on my knees to you if you like but *you must not phone my mother.*" I have no picture of her down on her knees—and she would have done it in a minute—so it seems this threat was not carried out.

Mr. Berryman said to me, "Well I guess you know your behaviour tonight is a pretty serious thing." He made it sound as if I might be charged with criminal negligence or something worse. "It would be very wrong of me to overlook it," he said. I suppose that besides being angry and disgusted with *me*, he was worried about taking me home in this condition to my strait-laced parents, who could always say I got the liquor in his house. Plenty of Temperance people would think that enough to hold him responsible, and the town was full of Temperance people. Good relations with the town were very important to him from a business point of view.

"I have an idea it wasn't the first time," he said. "If it was the first time, would a girl be smart enough to fill three bottles up with water? No. Well in this case, she *was* smart enough, but not smart enough to know I could spot it. What do you say to that?" I opened my mouth to answer and although I was feeling quite sober the only sound that came out was a loud, desolate-sounding giggle. He stopped in front of our house. "Light's on," he said. "Now go in and tell your parents the straight truth. And if you don't, remember I will." He did not mention paying me for my baby-sitting services of the evening and the subject did not occur to me either.

I went into the house and tried to go straight upstairs but my mother called to me. She came into the front hall, where I had not turned on the light, and she must have smelled me at once for she ran forward with a cry of pure amazement, as if she had seen somebody falling, and caught me by the shoulders as I did indeed fall down against the bannister, overwhelmed by my fantastic lucklessness, and I told her everything from the start, not omitting even the name of Martin Collingwood and my flirtation with the aspirin bottle, which was a mistake.

On Monday morning my mother took the bus over to Baileyville and found the liquor store and bought a bottle of Scotch whisky. Then she had to wait for a bus back, and she met some people she knew and she was not quite able to hide the bottle in her bag; she was furious with herself for not bringing a proper shopping-bag. As soon as she got back she walked out to the Berrymans'; she had not even had lunch. Mr. Berryman had not gone back to the factory. My mother went in and had a talk with both of them and made an excellent impression and then Mr. Berryman drove her home. She talked to them in the forthright and unemotional way she had, which was always agreeably surprising to people prepared to deal with a mother, and she told them that although I seemed to do well enough at school I was extremely backward—or perhaps eccentric—in my emotional development. I imagine that this analysis of my behaviour was especially effective with Mrs. Berryman, a great reader of Child Guidance books. Relations between them warmed to the point where my mother brought up a specific instance of my difficulties, and disarmingly related the whole story of Martin Collingwood.

Within a few days it was all over town and the school that I had tried to commit suicide over Martin Collingwood. But it was already all over school and the town that the Berrymans had come home on Saturday night to find me drunk, staggering, wearing nothing but my slip, in a room with three boys, one of whom was Bill Kline. My mother had said that I was to pay for the bottle she had taken the Berrymans out of my baby-sitting earnings, but my clients melted away like the last April snow, and it would not be paid for yet if newcomers to town had not moved in across the street in July, and needed a baby sitter before they talked to any of their neighbours.

My mother also said that it had been a great mistake to let me go out with boys and that I would not be going out again until well after my sixteenth birthday, if then. This did not prove to be a concrete hardship at all, because it was at least that long before anybody asked me. If you think that news of the Berrymans adventure would put me in demand for whatever gambols and orgies were going on in and around that town, you could not be more mistaken. The extraordinary publicity which attended my first debauch may have made me seemed marked for a special kind of ill luck, like the girl whose illegitimate baby turns out to be triplets: nobody wants to have anything to do with her. At any rate I had at the same time one of the most silent telephones and positively the most sinful reputation in the whole High School. I had to put up with this until the next fall, when a fat blonde girl in Grade Ten ran away with a married man and was picked up two months later, living in sin—though not with the same man— in the city of Sault Ste. Marie. Then everybody forgot about me.

But there was a positive, a splendidly unexpected, result of this affair: I got completely over Martin Collingwood. It was not only that he at once said, publicly, that he had always thought I was a nut; where he was concerned I had no pride, and my tender fancy could have found a way around that, a month, a week, before. What was it that brought me back into the world again? It was the terrible and fascinating reality of my disaster; it was *the way things happened*. Not that I enjoyed it; I was a self-conscious girl and I suffered a good deal from all this exposure. But the development of events on that Saturday night—that fascinated me; I felt that I had had a glimpse of the shameless, marvellous, shattering absurdity with which the plots of life, though not of fiction, are improvised. I could not take my eyes off it.

And of course Martin Collingwood wrote his Senior Matric that June, and went away to the city to take a course at a school for Morticians, as I think it is called, and when he came back he went into his uncle's undertaking business. We lived in the same town and we would hear most things that happened to each other but I do not think we met face to face or saw one another, except at a distance, for years. I went to a shower for the girl he married, but then everybody went to everybody else's showers. No, I do not think I really saw him again until I came home after I had been married several years, to attend a relative's funeral. Then I saw him; not quite Mr. Darcy but still very nice-looking in those black clothes. And I saw him looking over at me with an expression as close to a reminiscent smile as the occasion would permit, and I knew that he had been surprised by a memory either of my devotion or my little buried catastrophe. I gave him a gentle uncomprehending look in return. I am a grown-up woman now; let him unbury his own catastrophes.

## LEWIS NORDAN

## *The All-Girl Football Team* (1986)

Dressing in drag was not new to me. I had never worn a dress myself, but my father had.

My father was all man. His maleness defined him to me. Evenings, when he came home from work, I loved to hug him and to feel the rasp of a day's growth of beard against my face and neck. I loved to smell him, a fragrance of wool and leather and whiskey and shoepolish and aftershave.

Drag was not a frequent thing, only twice a year. Halloween, of course. Kids in costume would come to our house and ring the bell and Father would answer it in women's clothes. "Trick or treat, Gilbert," the children would say, and my father would try to guess who was behind each mask. He would drop candy into the plastic pumpkins or paper sacks and send the children on to the next house.

The other time was the Womanless Wedding. It was an annual affair, a minstrel show in rouge instead of blackface. The Rotary and the Lions—all the solid male citizens of Arrow Catcher, Mississippi—would put on a raucous play in

drag and donate the money to charity. One year Mr. Rant got drunk and fell off
the stage in a floor-length gown.

My father loved the Womanless Wedding. He took a different part each year:
bride, mother of the bride, flower girl, maid of honor, whatever was available.
He shaved his legs and Naired his chest and bleached the hair on his arms and
plucked his eyebrows and rouged his lips and mascaraed his lashes and he was
ready. He owned wigs. With a pedicure and a close shave, my father was a pretty
good looking woman for his age.

So dressing in drag was not new.

In my junior year of high school, my class got the idea of putting on an
all-girl football game. We were raising money for some worthwhile project or
other—a new scoreboard for the gym, I think. The idea was for the junior and
senior girls to put on uniforms and helmets and to play football against each
other. The school principal agreed to let us use the stadium. We would charge
admission and sell hot dogs and Cokes at the concession stand.

It seemed like a good idea.

The idea seemed even better when I first saw the girls in uniform. They were
beautiful. Hulda Raby had long legs and boyish hips and large breasts, and when
she was dressed in our school colors and was wearing pads and cleats and a rubber mouthpiece, I thought no one on earth had ever had such a good idea as the
all-girl football team.

The girls were enthusiastic. They found a senior boy who agreed to coach
them, Tony Pirelli, whose father owned the Arrow Cafe.

Positions were tried out for and assigned. Plays were drawn up and
mimeographed and passed out to the players and carried around in notebooks
and memorized. A wide-hipped girl named Tootie Nell Hightower learned to
snap the ball, and Nadine Johnson learned to take the snap from center.

I stood on the sidelines and watched Nadine hunker into position behind the
center's upturned rear-end and put her hands into position. *Green forty-two . . .*
My heart jumped out of my chest.

Pads began to clash, helmets to clatter. Nadine was a natural at quarterback
and could throw the bomb. Ednita Gillespie could get open. I saw these girls
through new eyes. I feared them and I loved them.

The days passed. No one except the players was allowed inside the locker
room, of course, not even Tony Pirelli, the kid who coached them. But each day
after practice I hung outside in the parking lot and imagined them in there. I saw
them unlace their cleats and fling them into a corner. I saw them strip dirty tape
from their ankles and remove the Tuff-skin with alcohol. I smelled the pungency
of their skin. I watched them walk through the locker room wearing only their
shoulderpads, nothing else, the padding stained with sweat. I watched them soap
up in the shower and play grabass and snap each other with towels. I saw them
stand under the shower and let the water pour into their upturned faces and I
watched one or another of them relax her bladder and allow the urine to run
down her leg and swirl away in the drain.

Never before in the history of the whole wide world had anyone ever had such a good idea as the all-girl football team.

I wanted to be near the girls. I hung around the parking lot to watch them. At first a few other boys did the same, and we punched each other's arms and made jokes, but my interest outlasted theirs and soon I was the only boy in the parking lot.

My favorite part of the day was when the girls came out of the locker rooms after practice, after their showers.

Nadine Johnson came out, the quarterback. She had short hair and it was still wet and slicked back like a man's. Hulda Raby had blonde hair that hung down to her hips. One day she stepped out of the gym into the late afternoon sun and bent over and allowed her wet hair to hang down over her face, almost to the ground. She toweled it roughly with a white locker room towel and then flung her hair back over her head so that it hung down her back again. She dropped the towel behind her, arrogant, and she seemed to know that someone would pick it up for her. It was my joy to rush across the lot and place the towel into a bin of soiled linens.

Hulda Raby did not notice me, of course. My reward was to be close to the locker room door when the others came out.

Tootie Nell Hightower, the center—I could not look at her without seeing her bent over the ball, its leather nap gripped in her certain hands. Lynn Koontz—I heard the beauty of her name for the first time. It was a football player's name. You could play tight end for the Steelers with a name like Lynn Koontz. The twins, Exie Lee and Nora Lee Prestridge. The Sewell girls, Marty and Ruby. Ednita Gillespie, the wide receiver. I heard Nadine say to her, "Nita, honey, you got a great pair of hands."

I envied them their womanhood.

I watched them on the practice field each day after school. Tony Pirelli, their coach, seemed to me the luckiest boy in the world.

I insinuated myself into their midst. I volunteered to act as a flunky for the team. I helped line the field. I asked parents to act as referees and scorekeepers, and I made sure everyone had clean socks. I carried equipment and water bottles and the first aid kit. I saddlesoaped footballs and replaced broken elastic. I dealt with the high school principal, who was worried about the light bill, since the game was to be held at night.

It was springtime and the Mississippi Delta was Eden to me. I saw it as I had never seen it before, the whippoorwills and coons and owls and little bobwhites. Mornings the pecan trees outside my window were heavy with dew and smelled like big wet flowers.

In my dreams I listened to the music of *green forty-two hut hut hut* . . . It floated on the air like a fragrance of wisteria. I knew why men married, as my father had, and were true to the same woman over a lifetime. I thought of my father's mortality.

I went into my father's room and found his revolver and broke it open and poured its cartridges onto the chenille bedspread. I thought of my own mortal-

ity. I understood for the first time the difficulty of ever knowing who I am.
I longed to be held as a lover by a woman in a football suit.

The all-girl football team idea got out of hand. It became elaborate.

Somebody suggested that we should have boy cheerleaders, dressed up in
girls' cheerleading costumes. It would be hilarious, everybody said. What fun.
Somebody else thought it would be just great if we made it homecoming as well.
You know, with a homecoming court. Everyone agreed, Sure! Oh boy! It would
be like the Womanless Wedding, only better. We'll hold the ceremony at halftime. We'll crown a homecoming queen!

I didn't like the idea. I said, "I'm against it. It's a silly idea. I vote no."

Everybody else said, "It'll be hilarious. Let's do it, sure it's great."

I wanted to say, Are you insane? We have discovered what makes women
beautiful. The girl-children who were our classmates three weeks ago are now
women—they are constellations! Do you want a constellation walking in a parade with some goon in a dress?

Instead I said, "No way. I'm not doing it. I've got to line the field. I've got to
pump up the balls. Count me out, brother."

I did it anyway. I was elected cheerleader. That's small-town high school for
you. It was a big joke. I didn't want to do it, so everybody voted on me.
No try-outs, nothing. One day I get the news and a box with a cheerleader
costume in it. I said, "Forget it."

Everybody said, "Be a sport."

Right up until the night of the big game I still wasn't going to do it. I
wasn't even going to the game. Why should I? Nobody was taking the game seriously—nobody but me and the girls who were knocking their heads together.

Maybe this will explain it: One day after practice I saw Ednita Gillespie get
into her father's pickup alone. She yanked open the door and, as she did, she
put her fingers to one side of her nose and blew snot into the gravel driveway
of the schoolhouse parking lot. The door banged shut behind her and she
drove away.

Do you understand what I mean? It was not Ednita I loved. Not Tootie Nell
or Lynn Koontz or Nadine Johnson. It was Woman. I had never known her before. She was a presence as essential and dangerous as geology. Somehow she
held the magic that could make me whole and give me life.

That's why I wasn't going to the all-girl football game.

I said all this to my father in his room at the back of our house. In this room
I could say anything. I could smell my father's whole life in this room, the guns
in the closet, the feathers of birds he had killed, the blood of mammals, the mut-
ton that greased the line of his fly-casting equipment.

I said, "It would take a fool. To dress up like a girl, when there are women—
women, Daddy, not girls—dressed in pads and cleats."

What do you suppose my father said to me? Can you guess? Do you think he
said, "Don't be silly, it's a school project. I want you to participate." Do you think
he said, "It's up to you, of course, but I just want to tell you, you're going to be
missing out on a whole lot of fun."

My father was a housepainter. He went to sixth grade and no further. He said, "I will dress you in a skirt and a sweater and nice underwear and you will feel beautiful."

I said, "Uh . . ."

He said, "You have never felt beautiful."

I said, "Well. . ."

It was near dark. The fall air had turned cold. In two hours the all-girl football game would begin. My mother was still at work.

Father drew my bath and put almond oil into the water and swished the water back and forth with his hand until it foamed up. He hung a green silk bathrobe on a hook on the bathroom door. He set out bathpowder and a powder puff he had bought new for me. He showed me how to shave my legs and underarms. It didn't matter that no one else would be able to see.

When I was clean and sweet-smelling, I came into his room wearing the robe. He gave me the clothes I would dress in.

I said, "Dad, is this queer?"

He did not answer.

I took the box with the uniform in it, and a small bag with new underwear.

I slipped into the lacy underpants, and then into the pantyhose.

I let him show me how to hook the bra, which he did not stuff with Kleenex. He gave me tiny false breasts, cups made of foam rubber, with perfect nipples on the ends. When I slipped on my sweater with the big AC on the front, you could see my nipples showing through.

I put on a half-slip and the skirt. He showed me how to apply my makeup. I could choose any wig I wanted. He spritzed me with Windsong.

I did not feel beautiful. I felt like a fool. I looked at myself in the mirror and saw that I looked like a fool as well. I stood like a boy, I walked like a boy, I scratched myself like a boy. I had a dumb boy-look on my face. My hands were boy-hands. My dick, for no good reason, was stiff and aching.

The masculine smells of my father's room-the rubber raingear and gun oil and fish scales stuck to his tacklebox—reached me through my false femininity and mocked me.

My father said, "How do you feel?"

I said, "Like a fucking fool."

I said, "I've got a hard on."

He said, "Do you know any cheers? Can you do one cheer for me before you go?"

I said, "I don't think so, Dad."

He said, "Well, I'll have my eyes on you the whole game. I'll be watching you from the stadium."

I said, "I wish there was a Book of Life, with all the right answers in the back."

He said, "Do 'Satisfied.' Just once, before you go. 'Satisfied' is my favorite cheer."

There was something about that football field: the brilliant natural carpet of green grass, the incredible lights, the strong straight lines of chalkdust, the serviceable steel bleachers filled with cheering people and the little Arrow Catcher High School marching band in uniform—there was something in all that scene that told me who I was. I did not feel beautiful, as my father had predicted. I was the same person I had always been, and yet the bass drum, with its flaking bow-and-arrow design and the words ARROW CATCHER, MISSISSIPPI, printed in faded letters around the perimeter of the drumhead, told me that the worst things about myself were not my enemies and that the Womanless Wedding held meaning for my father that I might never understand and did not need to understand.

I had come to the game late. The referees in their striped suits had already taken the field. The opposing teams, in black and gold uniforms, had finished warm-up calisthenics. Steel whistles sounded and drew the players from their final huddle and prayers.

The captains walked like warriors to the middle of the field. They watched the toss of the coin.

I watched it also, from the sidelines. The coin went up and up. It seemed suspended in the air beneath those blazing lights, above the green table of Delta land. The coin seemed forged of pure silver and big as a discus. It turned over and over, as if in slow motion. It hung for a century.

I jumped up and down in my wool skirt and saddle oxfords. I was a cheerleader at the center of the universe. I waved my pom-poms and clapped my hands and kicked my heels up behind me. I tossed my hair and fluttered my lashes without knowing I knew how to do these things. The coin that I was watching was a message of hope and goodness throughout the land.

It was a land I loved, this fine ellipse in a crook of the Yazoo River—its alligators and mallards and beaver dams, its rice paddies and soybeans and catfish farms.

Suddenly I knew that my father was right, that I did feel beautiful, except that now beauty had a different meaning for me. It meant that I was who I was, the core of me, the perfect center, and that the world was who it was and that those two facts were unchangeable. Grief had no sting, the future was not a thing to fear, all things were possible and personal and pure.

I watched the opening kickoff. It was a short grounder that scooted between the legs of the front line of girls in uniform.

By the time someone in the backfield picked it up, my small breasts had become a part of me, not rubber but flesh. My cock, beneath the lacy underpants, was what it had always been, this odd hard unpredictable equipment I had been born with, and yet it was also a moist opening into the hidden fragrance of another self that was me as well. My arms were woman-arms, my feet woman-feet, my voice, my lips, my fingers. I stood on the sweet sad brink of womanhood, and somehow I shared this newness with my father.

The game had begun, and I was the cheeriest cheerleader on the sidelines. One team scored a touchdown. Hulda Raby sustained a serious knee injury. Nadine threw the bomb to Ednita but had it intercepted. The band played the fight song, and we went through all the cheers.

My father and mother were in the bleachers, far up, and I could see the pride in their faces. I was a wonderful cheerleader, and they knew that I was.

We did "Satisfied," and in my heart I dedicated the cheer to my father.

*I went to the principal*, we cheerleaders called out, with our hands on our hips, sashaying as we pretended to walk haughtily into the principal's office.

*Satisfied*, came the refrain back from the cheering section, including my father and mother.

*And the principal said*, we called out, shaking our finger, as if the principal were giving us a stern talking-to.

And again the loud refrain, *Satisfied*.

*That we couldn't lose...*

*Satisfied...*

*With the stuff we use...*

*Satisfied...*

*You take-a one step back...* Here we put our hands behind our backs and jumped one step backward, cute and coy, as if we were obeying the principal's stern order.

*Satisfied...*

*You take-a two steps up...* Here we put on a look of mock surprise, as if we just could not understand what the principal was getting at with all his complicated instructions, but we put our hands on our hips and took two cute steps forward anyway.

The principal's final line is: *And then you strut your stuff, And then you strut your stuff, And then you strut your stuff.* Which we did, by wagging our sexy hips and prankishly twirling our index fingers in the air.

*Sat-isss-fied!*

The Mississippi Delta air was the Garden of Eden, filled with innocence and ripe apples. The blue of the skies shone through the darkness of the night and through the glare of the stadium lights. I smelled fig trees and a fragrance of weevil poison and sweet fishy water from the swamp.

The game went on. The huddles and the time-outs, the sweat and the bloody noses and the fourth-down punts.

And then halftime. I had literally forgotten all about halftime.

My whole world exploded into ceremony and beautiful ritual. The band was on the field in full uniform. The goalposts, were wrapped in black and gold crepe paper, and streamers were blowing in the autumn breeze. Boys with shaven legs strutted past the bleachers wearing majorette costumes. They carried bright banners on long poles. The band marched in formation, and then it formed a huge heart in the center of the field. It played "Let Me Call You Sweetheart," and I felt tears of joy and the fullness of nature well up in me. I knew that the world was a place of safety and hope and that my father was a great man. I knew that I was a beautiful woman and that because of this I had a chance of growing up to be as fine a man as my father. *Let me call you sweetheart I'm in love with you, Let me hear you whisper that you love me too*, I loved the girls in uniform; I would always love them. They were lined up under the home-team goalposts with the maids of the homecoming court. *Keep the lovelight burning in your eyes so true . . .*

Nadine Johnson was the captain. She led the beautiful slow processional of players and maids toward the center of the field. The band played. There was a sweetness of Mowdown in the air from the rice paddies nearby.

I knew the meaning of love. I thought of my father, the way he had looked on the day of his wedding, the first of his weddings that I was old enough to attend. He had been the bride and had worn a high-bodice floor-length gown, antique white, with a train and veil. He carried a nosegay at his waist. When the minister asked whether any person here present could show just cause why this couple should not be joined in holy matrimony, a drunken pharmacist named H. L. Berryman, wearing a print dress and heels, jumped up out of the audience and fired a pistol in the air. My father fell into a swoon.

It was all part of the show, of course—and although I knew it was only a play and that my father was only an actor in it, I wanted to leap from my seat in the audience and make known to all the world that he was my father and that without him my own life was without meaning.

On the football field Nadine Johnson turned to a tiny boy child, three or four years old, who was a part of the homecoming ceremonies. He was wearing a ruffled dress with stiff petticoats and was standing beside Nadine with a satin pillow in his hands. There was a silvery crown on the pillow. The homecoming court was assembled around them, arms hooked in arms, smiles bright.

Nadine took the crown from the pillow, as flashbulbs went off.

A boy named Jeep Bennett was standing beside Nadine. He was wearing a yellow evening gown and had only three fingers on one hand. He had been in a hunting accident the year before and this year had been elected homecoming queen.

Nadine placed the crown on his proud head, and the flashbulbs went off again. The bleachers roared with applause and cheers and approval. Nadine kissed Jeep, and Jeep was demure and embarrassed.

I had wanted—dreamed!—of this moment, dreaded it in a way, because I had believed I would envy Jeep this perfection, this public kiss of a woman in a football suit, which I had believed for three weeks was the completion of love and sex and holy need.

And yet now that it was here, it was oddly meaningless to me. There was no jealousy in my heart, no lust for Nadine in all her sweaty beauty.

And yet there was lust in my heart, sweet romance. My breath caught in my throat, my tiny breasts rose and my nipples hardened. (Seemed to harden, I swear!)

I looked down the line of suited-up women and their male maids. Tootie Nell, wide-hipped and solid; Hulda, with a damaged knee; Lynn Koontz, her magical name. I looked at the drag-dressed boys who clung violet-like to the certain arms of these beautiful women.

And yes there was lust and even love in my heart, but not for the women in black-and-gold. The person I loved was wearing a business suit with a back-pleat in the skirt, so that when he walked you could see a triangle of his gray satin slip and the back of his beautiful knee. Tony Pirelli, the kid who coached the team, was an Italian boy with dark skin and dark eyes and a nut-brown wig that caressed his shoulders. He wore a soft gray silk blouse with ruffled sleeves and, at his throat, a ruffled ascot. His shoes were patent leather slingback pumps with two-inch heels, and the girls had given him a corsage, which he wore on his breast.

I hated my thoughts and my feelings. I was certain my father could read them all the way to the top of the bleachers.

I had never seen anyone so beautiful as Tony Pirelli. He never smiled, and now his sadness called out to me, it made me want to hold him and protect him from all harm, to kiss his lips and neck, to close his brown eyes with my kisses, to hold his small breasts in my hands and to have him touch my own breasts.

I believed I was a lesbian. What else could I call myself? I felt like a fool for not having noticed before. I was a fool for having strutted my stuff during the cheers, for having loved the Mississippi Delta and the sentimental songs played by the band.

I didn't see the rest of the game. The band played and the crepe paper rattled and the banners whipped and the crowds cheered, and I ran away from the sidelines and through the gate and away from the football field and the school grounds.

This happened in the autumn I was sixteen years old. Now I am forty-five years old, and all of it seems too fantastic to be true. Maybe my memory has exaggerated the facts, somehow.

I remember what happened afterward very accurately, though.

I ran through the little town of Arrow Catcher, Mississippi, toward my parents' home. I don't know what I wanted there, the safety of my father's room, I think, the fishing rods and reels with names like Shakespeare and Garcia, the suits of camouflage and the rubber hip-waders. I was still wearing my cheerleader costume and my makeup and false breasts and even the wig.

And then something happened, by magic I suppose, that stopped me. The Southern sky seemed to fill with light—no, not light, but with something like light, with meaning, I want to say.

I stood in the street where I had stopped and I listened to the distant brass of the Arrow Catcher High School marching band. It sounded like the blare of circus horns. I took deep breaths and exhaled them into the frosty air.

I took from my skirt pocket the lace handkerchief my father had put there for me, and I dabbed at my eyes, careful not to smear the mascara more than it was already smeared.

I began walking back toward the football field. I was not a woman. I did not feel like a woman. I was not in love with a boy. I was a boy in costume for one night of the year, and I was my father's child and the child of this strange southern geography. I was beautiful, and also wise and sad and somehow doomed with joy.

The gymnasium was decorated in black and gold. There was a table with a big crystal punch bowl, and other tables with ironed white tablecloths and trays of sandwiches and cookies. Around the walls of the gym our parents had placed potted plants and baskets of flowers. The girls had changed to their party dresses, the boys had put on the trousers and sport jackets our parents had brought for us. We were proper boys and girls, and our costumes were stuffed into bags in the locker rooms where we changed.

A phonograph blared out the music we loved.

I danced close to Nadine Johnson and imagined, as I felt her cool cheek against mine, that I could see the future. I imagined I would marry—not Nadine but some woman like Nadine, some beautiful woman, faceless for now—and that together we would have sons and that we would love them and teach them to be gentle and to love the music we were dancing to and to wear dresses and that, in doing this, we would somehow never grow old and that love would last forever.

### Study and Discussion Questions

1. What might dressing in drag symbolize for the narrator throughout the story? Apply the same question to the girls dressed in football gear and the narrator's father.
2. What is the transformation the girls have gone through and why is the narrator so obsessed with their transformation?
3. Make a list of different actions performed by the girls and the narrator throughout the story. Which actions are traditionally classified as masculine and which actions are classified as feminine?
4. This story is set in the Mississippi Delta. How does the setting influence the reading of the story, and how does it influence the narrator's questions concerning his sexual identity?
5. Considering the narrator's struggle with conventional gender roles, can a man be beautiful?

### Suggestions for Writing

1. Though the narrator obsesses over the girls' transformation throughout much of the story, he undergoes a transformation of his own. Describe his transformation and development throughout the story.
2. The narrator says that dressing in drag holds special significance for his father. Considering what the narrator tells us about the father and his actions, write a short essay or paragraph discussing the impact of this knowledge on the narrator.
3. Starting with the narrator's arrival at the football game, reread the football game scene and the halftime pageantry. Explain what the coin toss and cheering teach the narrator about himself.
4. Compare this story with another work that questions gender roles, such as "Boys at the Rodeo."

**JOYCE CAROL OATES**

## *Where Are You Going, Where Have You Been?*     (1966)

Her name was Connie. She was fifteen and she had a quick, nervous giggling habit of craning her neck to glance into mirrors or checking other people's faces to make sure her own was all right. Her mother, who noticed everything and knew everything and who hadn't much reason any longer to look at her own face, always scolded Connie about it. "Stop gawking at yourself. Who are you? You think you're so pretty?" she would say. Connie would raise her eyebrows at these familiar old complaints and look right through her mother, into a shadowy vision of herself as she was right at that moment: she knew she was pretty and that was everything. Her mother had been pretty once too, if you could believe those old snapshots in the album, but now her looks were gone and that was why she was always after Connie.

"Why don't you keep your room clean like your sister? How've you got your hair fixed—what the hell stinks? Hair spray? You don't see your sister using that junk."

Her sister June was twenty-four and still lived at home. She was a secretary in the high school Connie attended, and if that wasn't bad enough—with her in the same building—she was so plain and chunky and steady that Connie had to hear her praised all the time by her mother and her mother's sisters. June did this, June did that, she saved money and helped clean the house and cooked and Connie couldn't do a thing, her mind was all filled with trashy daydreams. Their father was away at work most of the time and when he came home he wanted supper and he read the newspaper at supper and after supper he went to bed. He didn't bother talking much to them, but around his bent head Connie's mother kept picking at her until Connie wished her mother was dead and she herself was dead and it was all over. "She makes me want to throw up sometimes," she complained to her friends. She had a high, breathless, amused voice that made everything she said sound a little forced, whether it was sincere or not.

There was one good thing: June went places with girl friends of hers, girls who were just as plain and steady as she, and so when Connie wanted to do that her mother had no objections. The father of Connie's best girl friend drove the girls the three miles to town and left them at a shopping plaza so they could walk through the stores or go to a movie, and when he came to pick them up again at eleven he never bothered to ask what they had done.

They must have been familiar sights, walking around the shopping plaza in their shorts and flat ballerina slippers that always scuffed the sidewalk, with charm bracelets jingling on their thin wrists; they would lean together to whisper and laugh secretly if someone passed who amused or interested them. Connie had long dark blond hair that drew anyone's eye to it, and she wore part of it pulled up on her head and puffed out and the rest of it she let fall down her back. She wore a pull-over jersey blouse that looked one way when she was at home and another way when she was away from home. Everything about her had two sides to it, one for home and one for anywhere that was not home: her walk, which could be childlike and bobbing, or languid enough to make anyone think she was hearing music in her head; her mouth, which was pale and smirking most of the time, but bright and pink on these evenings out; her laugh, which was cynical and drawling at home—"Ha, ha, very funny,"—but highpitched and nervous anywhere else, like the jingling of the charms on her bracelet.

Sometimes they did go shopping or to a movie, but sometimes they went across the highway, ducking fast across the busy road, to a drive-in restaurant where older kids hung out. The restaurant was shaped like a big bottle, though squatter than a real bottle, and on its cap was a revolving figure of a grinning boy holding a hamburger aloft. One night in midsummer they ran across, breathless with daring, and right away someone leaned out a car window and invited them over, but it was just a boy from high school they didn't like. It made them feel good to be able to ignore him. They went up through the maze of parked and cruising cars to the bright-lit, fly-infested restaurant, their faces pleased and expectant as if they were entering a sacred building that loomed up out of the night to give them what haven and blessing they yearned for. They sat at the counter and crossed their legs at the ankles, their thin shoulders rigid with excitement, and listened to the music that made everything so good: the music was always in the background, like music at a church service; it was something to depend upon.

A boy named Eddie came in to talk with them. He sat backwards on his stool, turning himself jerkily around in semicircles and then stopping and turning back again, and after a while he asked Connie if she would like something to eat. She said she would and so she tapped her friend's arm on her way out—her friend pulled her face up into a brave, droll look—and Connie said she would meet her at eleven, across the way. "I just hate to leave her like that," Connie said earnestly, but the boy said that she wouldn't be alone for long. So they went out to his car, and on the way Connie couldn't help but let her eyes wander over the windshields and faces all around her, her face gleaming with a joy that had nothing to do with Eddie or even this place; it might have been the music. She drew her shoulders up and sucked in her breath with the pure pleasure of being alive, and just at that moment she happened to glance at a face just a few feet from hers. It was a boy with shaggy black hair, in a convertible jalopy painted gold. He started at her and then his lips widened into a grin. Connie slit her eyes at him and turned away, but she couldn't help glancing back and there he was, still watching her. He wagged a finger and laughed and said, "Gonna get you, baby," and Connie turned away again without Eddie noticing anything.

She spent three hours with him, at the restaurant where they ate hamburgers and drank Cokes in wax cups that were always sweating, and then down an alley a mile or so away, and when he left her off at five to eleven only the movie house was still open at the plaza. Her girl friend was there, talking with a boy.

When Connie came up, the two girls smiled at each other and Connie said, "How was the movie?" and the girl said, 'You should know." They rode off with the girl's father, sleepy and pleased, and Connie couldn't help but look back at the darkened shopping plaza with its big empty parking lot and its signs that were faded and ghostly now, and over at the drive-in restaurant where cars were still circling tirelessly. She couldn't hear the music at this distance.

Next morning June asked her how the movie was and Connie said, "So-so."

She and that girl and occasionally another girl went out several times a week, and the rest of the time Connie spent around the house—it was summer vacation—getting in her mothers way and thinking, dreaming about the boys she met. But all the boys fell back and dissolved into a single face that was not even a face but an idea, a feeling, mixed up with the urgent insistent pounding of the music and the humid night air of July. Connie's mother kept dragging her back to the daylight by finding things for her to do or saying suddenly, 'What's this about the Pettinger girl?"

And Connie would say nervously, "Oh, her. That dope." She always drew thick clear lines between herself and such girls, and her mother was simple and kind enough to believe it. Her mother was so simple, Connie thought, that it was maybe cruel to fool her so much. Her mother went scuffling around the house in old bedroom slippers and complained over the telephone to one sister about the other, then the other called up and the two of them complained about the third one. If June's name was mentioned her mother's tone was approving, and if Connie's name was mentioned it was disapproving. This did not really mean she disliked Connie, and actually Connie thought that her mother preferred her to June just because she was prettier, but the two of them kept up a pretense of exasperation, a sense that they were tugging and struggling over something of little value to either of them. Sometimes, over coffee, they were almost friends, but something would come up—some vexation that was like a fly buzzing suddenly around their heads—and their faces went hard with contempt.

One Sunday Connie got up at eleven—none of them bothered with church— and washed her hair so that it could dry all day long in the sun. Her parents and sister were going to a barbecue at an aunt's house and Connie said no, she wasn't interested, rolling her eyes to let her mother know just what she thought of it. "Stay home alone then," her mother said sharply. Connie sat out back in a lawn chair and watched them drive away, her father quiet and bald, hunched around so that he could back the car out, her mother with a look that was still angry and not at all softened through the windshield, and in the back seat poor old June, all dressed up as if she didn't know what a barbecue was, with all the running yelling kids and the flies. Connie sat with her eyes closed in the sun, dreaming and dazed with the warmth about her as if this were a kind of love, the caresses of love, and her mind slipped over onto thoughts of the boy she had been with the night before and how nice he had been, how sweet it always was, not the way someone like June would suppose but sweet, gentle, the way it was in movies and promised in songs; and when she opened her eyes she hardly knew where she was, the back yard ran off into weeds and a fence-like line of trees and behind it the sky was perfectly blue and still. The asbestos ranch house that was now three years old startled her—it looked small. She shook her head as if to get awake.

It was too hot. She went inside the house and turned on the radio to drown out the quiet. She sat on the edge of her bed, barefoot, and listened for an hour and a half to a program called XYZ Sunday Jamboree, record after record of hard, fast, shrieking songs she sang along with, interspersed by exclamations from "Bobby King": "An' look here, you girls at Napoleon's—Son and Charley want you to pay real close attention to this song coming up!"

And Connie paid close attention herself, bathed in a glow of slow-pulsed joy that seemed to rise mysteriously out of the music itself and lay languidly about the airless little room, breathed in and breathed out with each gentle rise and fall of her chest.

After a while she heard a car coming up the drive. She sat up at once, startled, because it couldn't be her father so soon. The gravel kept crunching all the way in from the road—the driveway was long—and Connie ran to the window. It was a car she didn't know. It was an open jalopy, painted a bright gold that caught the sunlight opaquely. Her heart began to pound and her fingers snatched at her hair, checking it, and she whispered, "Christ. Christ," wondering how bad she looked. The car came to a stop at the side door and the horn sounded four short taps, as if this were a signal Connie knew.

She went into the kitchen and approached the door slowly, then hung out the screen door, her bare toes curling down off the step. There were two boys in the car and now she recognized the driver: he had shaggy, shabby black hair that looked crazy as a wig and he was grinning at her.

"I ain't late, am I?" he said.

"Who the hell do you think you are?" Connie said.

"Toldja I'd be out, didn't I?"

"I don't even know who you are."

She spoke sullenly, careful to show no interest or pleasure, and he spoke in a fast, bright monotone. Connie looked past him to the other boy, taking her time. He had fair brown hair, with a lock that fell onto his forehead. His sideburns gave him a fierce, embarrassed look, but so far he hadn't even bothered to glance at her. Both boys wore sunglasses. The driver's glasses were metallic and mirrored everything in miniature.

"You wanta come for a ride?" he said.

Connie smirked and let her hair fall loose over one shoulder.

"Don'tcha like my car? New paint job," he said. "Hey."

"What?"

"You're cute."

She pretended to fidget, chasing flies away from the door.

"Don'tcha believe me, or what?" he said.

"Look, I don't even know who you are," Connie said in disgust.

"Hey, Ellie's got a radio, see. Mine broke down." He lifted his friend's arm and showed her the little transistor radio the boy was holding, and now Connie began to hear the music. It was the same program that was playing inside the house.

"Bobby King?" she said.

"I listen to him all the time. I think he's great."

"He's kind of great," Connie said reluctantly.

"Listen, that guy's *great*. He knows where the action is."

Connie blushed a little, because the glasses made it impossible for her to see just what this boy was looking at. She couldn't decide if she liked him or if he was just a jerk, and so she dawdled in the doorway and wouldn't come down or go back inside. She said, "What's all that stuff painted on your car?"

"Can'tcha read it?" He opened the door very carefully, as if he were afraid it might fall off. He slid out just as carefully, planting his feet firmly on the ground, the tiny metallic world in his glasses slowing down like gelatine hardening, and in the midst of it Connie's bright green blouse. "This here is my name, to begin with, he said. ARNOLD FRIEND was written in tarlike black letters on the side, with a drawing of a round, grinning face that reminded Connie of a pumpkin, except it wore sunglasses. "I wanta introduce myself, I'm Arnold Friend and that's my real name and I'm gonna be your friend, honey, and inside the car's Ellie Oscar, he's kinda shy." Ellie brought his transistor radio up to his shoulder and balanced it there. "Now, these numbers are a secret code, honey," Arnold Friend explained. He read off the numbers 33, 19, 17 and raised his eyebrows at her to see what she thought of that, but she didn't think much of it. The left rear fender had been smashed and around it was written, on the gleaming gold background: DONE BY CRAZY WOMAN DRIVER. Connie had to laugh at that. Arnold Friend was pleased at her laughter and looked up at her. "Around the other side's a lot more—you wanta come and see them?"

"No."

"Why not?"

"Why should I?"

"Don'tcha wanta see what's on the car? Don'tcha wanta go for a ride?"

"I don't know."

"Why not?"

"I got things to do."

"Like what?"

"Things."

He laughed as if she had said something funny. He slapped his thighs. He was standing in a strange way, leaning back against the car as if he were balancing himself. He wasn't tall, only an inch or so taller than she would be if she came down to him. Connie liked the way he was dressed, which was the way all of them dressed: tight faded jeans stuffed into black, scuffed boots, a belt that pulled his waist in and showed how lean he was, and a white pull-over shirt that was a little soiled and showed the hard small muscles of his arms and shoulders. He looked as if he probably did hard work, lifting and carrying things. Even his neck looked muscular. And his face was a familiar face, somehow: the jaw and chin and cheeks slightly darkened because he hadn't shaved for a day or two, and the nose long and hawk-like, sniffing as if she were a treat he was going to gobble up and it was all a joke.

"Connie, you ain't telling the truth. This is your day set aside for a ride with me and you know it," he said, still laughing. The way he straightened and recovered from his fit of laughing showed that it had been all fake.

"How do you know what my name is?" she said suspiciously.

"It's Connie."

"Maybe and maybe not."

"I know my Connie," he said, wagging his finger. Now she remembered him even better, back at the restaurant, and her cheeks warmed at the thought of how she had sucked in her breath just at the moment she passed him—how she must have looked to him. And he had remembered her. "Ellie and I come out here especially for you," he said. "Ellie can sit in back. How about it?"

"Where?"

"Where what?"

"Where're we going?"

He looked at her. He took off the sunglasses and she saw how pale the skin around his eyes was, like holes that were not in shadow but instead in light. His eyes were like chips of broken glass that catch the light in an amiable way. He smiled. It was as if the idea of going for a ride somewhere, to someplace, was a new idea to him.

"Just for a ride, Connie sweetheart."

"I never said my name was Connie," she said.

"But I know what it is. I know your name and all about you, lots of things," Arnold Friend said. He had not moved yet but stood still leaning back against the side of his jalopy. "I took a special interest in you, such a pretty girl, and found out all about you—like I know your parents and sister are gone somewheres and I know where and how long they're going to be gone, and I know who you were with last night, and your best girl friend's name is Betty. Right?"

He spoke in a simple lilting voice, exactly as if he were reciting the words to a song. His smile assured her that everything was fine. In the car Ellie turned up the volume on his radio and did not bother to look around at them.

"Ellie can sit in the back seat," Arnold Friend said. He indicated his friend with a casual jerk of his chin, as if Ellie did not count and she should not bother with him.

"How'd you find out all that stuff?" Connie said.

"Listen: Betty Schultz and Tony Fitch and Jimmy Pettinger and Nancy Pettinger," he said in a chant. "Raymond Stanley and Bob Hutter—"

"Do you know all those kids?"

"I know everybody."

"Look, you're kidding. You're not from around here."

"Sure."

"But—how come we never saw you before?"

"Sure you saw me before," he said. He looked down at his boots, as if he were a little offended. "You just don't remember."

"I guess I'd remember you," Connie said.

"Yeah?" He looked up at this, beaming. He was pleased. He began to mark time with the music from Ellie's radio, tapping his fists lightly together. Connie looked away from his smile to the car, which was painted so bright it almost hurt her eyes to look at it. She looked at that name, ARNOLD FRIEND. And up at the front fender was an expression that was familiar—MAN THE FLYING SAUCERS. It was an expression kids had used the year before but didn't use this year. She looked at it for a while as if the words meant something to her that she did not yet know.

"What're you thinking about? Huh?" Arnold Friend demanded. "Not worried about your hair blowing around in the car, are you?"

"No."

"Think I maybe can't drive good?"

"How do I know?"

"You're a hard girl to handle. How come?" he said. "Don't you know I'm your friend? Didn't you see me put my sign in the air when you walked by?"

"What sign?"

"My sign." And he drew an X in the air, leaning out toward her. They were maybe ten feet apart. After his hand fell back to his side the X was still in the air, almost visible. Connie let the screen door close and stood perfectly still inside it, listening to the music from her radio and the boy's blend together. She stared at Arnold Friend. He stood there so stiffly relaxed, pretending to be relaxed, with one hand idly on the door handle as if he were keeping himself up that way and had no intention of ever moving again. She recognized most things about him, the tight jeans that showed his thighs and buttocks and the greasy leather boots and the tight shirt, and even that slippery friendly smile of his, that sleepy dreamy smile that all the boys used to get across ideas they didn't want to put into words. She recognized all this and also the singsong way he talked, slightly mocking, kidding, but serious and a little melancholy, and she recognized the way he tapped one fist against the other in homage to the perpetual music behind him. But all these things did not come together.

She said suddenly, "Hey, how old are you?"

His smiled faded. She could see then that he wasn't a kid, he was much older—thirty, maybe more. At this knowledge her heart began to pound faster.

"That's a crazy thing to ask. Can'tcha see I'm your own age?"

"Like hell you are."

"Or maybe a couple years older. I'm eighteen."

"Eighteen?" she said doubtfully.

He grinned to reassure her and lines appeared at the corners of his mouth. His teeth were big and white. He grinned so broadly his eyes became slits and she saw how thick the lashes were, thick and black as if painted with a black tarlike material. Then, abruptly, he seemed to become embarrassed and looked over his shoulder at Ellie. "*Him*, he's crazy," he said. "Ain't he a riot? He's a nut, a real character." Ellie was still listening to the music. His sunglasses told nothing about what he was thinking. He wore a bright orange shirt unbuttoned halfway to show his chest, which was a pale, bluish chest and not muscular like Arnold Friend's. His shirt collar was turned up all around and the very tips of the collar pointed out past his chin as if they were protecting him. He was pressing the transistor radio up against his ear and sat there in a kind of daze, right in the sun.

"He's kinda strange," Connie said.

"Hey, she says you're kinda strange! Kinda strange!" Arnold Friend cried. He pounded on the car to get Ellie's attention. Ellie turned for the first time and Connie saw with shock that he wasn't a kid either—he had a fair, hairless face, cheeks reddened slightly as if the veins grew too close to the surface of his skin, the face of a forty-year-old baby. Connie felt a wave of dizziness rise in her at this sight and she stared at him as if waiting for something to change the shock of the moment, make it all right again. Ellie's lips kept shaping words, mumbling along with the words blasting in his ear.

"Maybe you two better go away," Connie said faintly.

"What? How come?" Arnold Friend cried. "We come out here to take you for a ride. It's Sunday." He had the voice of the man on the radio now. It was the same voice, Connie thought. "Don'tcha know it's Sunday all day? And honey, no matter who you were with last night, today you're with Arnold Friend and don't you forget it! Maybe you better step out here," he said, and this last was in a different voice. It was a little flatter, as if the heat was finally getting to him.

"No. I got things to do."

"Hey."

"You two better leave."

"We ain't leaving until you come with us."

"Like hell I am—"

"Connie, don't fool around with me. I mean—I mean, don't fool *around*," he said, shaking his head. He laughed incredulously. He placed his sunglasses on top of his head, carefully, as if he were indeed wearing a wig, and brought the stems down behind his ears. Connie stared at him, another wave of dizziness and fear rising in her so that for a moment he wasn't even in focus but was just a blur standing there against his gold car, and she had the idea that he had driven up the driveway all right but had come from nowhere before that and belonged nowhere and that everything about him and even about the music that was so familiar to her was only half real.

"If my father comes and sees you—"

"He ain't coming. He's at a barbecue."

"How do you know that?"

"Aunt Tillie's. Right now they're uh—they're drinking. Sitting around," he said vaguely, squinting as if he were staring all the way to town and over to Aunt Tille's back yard. Then the vision seemed to get clear and he nodded energetically. "Yeah. Sitting around. There's your sister in a blue dress, huh? And high heels, the poor sad bitch—nothing like you, sweetheart! And your mother's helping some fat woman with the corn, they're cleaning the corn—husking the corn—"

"What fat woman?" Connie cried.

"How do I know what fat woman, I don't know every goddamn fat woman in the world!" Arnold Friend laughed.

"Oh, that's Mrs. Hornsby... Who invited her?" Connie said. She felt a little lightheaded. Her breath was coming quickly.

"She's too fat. I don't like them fat. I like them the way you are, honey," he said, smiling sleepily at her. They stared at each other for a while through the screen door. He said softly, "Now, what you're going to do is this: you're going to come out that door. You re going to sit up front with me and Ellie's going to sit in the back, the hell with Ellie, right? This isn't Ellie's date. You're my date. I'm your lover, honey."

"What? You're crazy—"

"Yes, I'm your lover. You don't know what that is but you will," he said. "I know that too. I know all about you. But look: it's real nice and you couldn't ask for nobody better than me, or more polite. I always keep my word. I'll tell you how it is, I'm always nice at first, the first time. I'll hold you so tight you won't think you have to try to get away or pretend anything because you'll know you can't. And I'll come inside you where it's all secret and you'll give in to me and you'll love me"

"Shut up! You're crazy!" Connie said. She backed away from the door. She put her hands up against her ears as if she'd heard something terrible, something not meant for her. "People don't talk like that, you're crazy," she muttered. Her heart was almost too big now for her chest and its pumping made sweat break out all over her. She looked out to see Arnold Friend pause and then take a step toward the porch, lurching. He almost fell. But, like a clever drunken man, he managed to catch his balance. He wobbled in his high boots and grabbed hold of one of the porch posts.

"Honey?" he said. "You still listening?"

"Get the hell out of here!"

"Be nice, honey. Listen."

"I'm going to call the police—"

He wobbled again and out of the side of his mouth came a fast spat curse, an aside not meant for her to hear. But even this "Christ!" sounded forced. Then he began to smile again. She watched this smile come, awkward as if he were smiling from inside a mask. His whole face was a mask, she thought wildly, tanned down to his throat but then running out as if he had plastered makeup on his face but had forgotten about his throat.

"Honey—? Listen, here's how it is. I always tell the truth and I promise you this: I ain't coming in that house after you."

"You better not! I'm going to call the police if you—if you don't—"

"Honey," he said, talking right through her voice, "honey, I'm not coming in there but you are coming out here. You know why?"

She was panting. The kitchen looked like a place she had never seen before, some room she had run inside but that wasn't good enough, wasn't going to help her. The kitchen window had never had a curtain, after three years, and there were dishes in the sink for her to do—probably—and if you ran your hand across the table you'd probably feel something sticky there.

"You listening, honey? Hey?" "—going to call the police—"

"Soon as you touch the phone I don't need to keep my promise and can come inside. You won't want that."

She rushed forward and tried to lock the door. Her fingers were shaking. "But why lock it," Arnold Friend said gently, talking right into her face. "It's just a screen door. It's just nothing." One of his boots was at a strange angle, as if his foot wasn't in it. It pointed out to the left, bent at the ankle. "I mean, anybody can break through a screen door and glass and wood and iron or anything else if he needs to, anybody at all, and specially Arnold Friend. If the place got lit up with a fire, honey, you'd come runnin' out into my arms, right into my arms an' safe at home—like you knew I was your lover and'd stopped fooling around. I don't mind a nice shy girl but I don't like no fooling around." Part of those words were spoken with a slight rhythmic lilt, and Connie somehow recognized them—the echo of a song from last year, about a girl rushing into her boy friend's arms and coming home again—

Connie stood barefoot on the linoleum floor, staring at him. "What do you want?" she whispered.

"I want you," he said.

"What?"

"Seen you that night and thought, that's the one, yes sir. I never needed to look anymore."

"But my father's coming back. He's coming to get me. I had to wash my hair first—" She spoke in a dry, rapid voice, hardly raising it for him to hear.

"No, your daddy is not coming and yes, you had to wash your hair and you washed it for me. It's nice and shining and all for me. I thank you sweetheart," he said with a mock bow, but again he almost lost his balance. He had to bend and adjust his boots. Evidently his feet did not go all the way down; the boots must have been stuffed with something so that he would seem taller. Connie stared out at him and behind him at Ellie in the car, who seemed to be looking off toward Connie's right, into nothing. This Ellie said, pulling the words out of the air one after another as if he were just discovering them, "You want me to pull out the phone?"

"Shut your mouth and keep it shut," Arnold Friend said, his face red from bending over or maybe from embarrassment because Connie had seen his boots. "This ain't none of your business."

"What—what are you doing? What do you want?" Connie said. "If I call the police they'll get you, they'll arrest you—"

"Promise was not to come in unless you touch that phone, and I'll keep that promise," he said. He resumed his erect position and tried to force his shoulders back. He sounded like a hero in a movie, declaring something important. But he spoke too loudly and it was as if he were speaking to someone behind Connie. "I ain't made plans for coming in that house where I don't belong but just for you to come out to me, the way you should. Don't you know who I am?"

"You're crazy," she whispered. She backed away from the door but did not want to go into another part of the house, as if this would give him permission to come through the door. "What do you... you're crazy, you..."

"Huh? What're you saying, honey?"

Her eyes darted everywhere in the kitchen. She could not remember what it was, this room.

"This is how it is, honey: you come out and we'll drive away, have a nice ride. But if you don't come out we're gonna wait till you people come home and then they're all going to get it."

"You want that telephone pulled out?" Ellie said. He held the radio away from his ear and grimaced, as if without the radio the air was too much for him.

"I toldja shut up, Ellie," Arnold Friend said, "you're deaf, get a hearing aid, right? Fix yourself up. This little girl's no trouble and's gonna be nice to me, so Ellie keep to yourself, this ain't your date right? Don't hem in on me, don't hog, don't crush, don't bird dog, don't trail me," he said in a rapid, meaningless voice, as if he were running through all the expressions he'd learned but was no longer sure which of them was in style, then rushing on to new ones, making them up with his eyes closed. "Don't crawl under my fence, don't squeeze in my chipmonk hole, don't sniff my glue, suck my popsicle, keep your own greasy fingers on yourself!" He shaded his eyes and peered in at Connie, who was backed against the kitchen table. "Don't mind him, honey, he's just a creep. He's a dope. Right? I'm the boy for you, and like I said, you come out here nice like a lady and give me your hand, and nobody else gets hurt, I mean, your nice old bald-headed daddy and your mummy and your sister in her high heels. Because listen: why bring them in this?"

"Leave me alone," Connie whispered.

"Hey, you know that old woman down the road, the one with the chickens and stuff—you know her?"

"She's dead!"

"Dead? What? You know her?" Arnold Friend said.

"She's dead—"

"Don't you like her?"

"She's dead—she's—she isn't here any more—"

"But don't you like her, I mean, you got something against her? Some grudge or something?" Then his voice dipped as if he were conscious of a rudeness. He touched the sunglasses perched up on top of his head as if to make sure they were still there. "Now, you be a good girl."

"What are you going to do?"

"Just two things, or maybe three," Arnold Friend said. "But I promise it won't last long and you'll like me the way you get to like people you're close to. You will. It's all over for you here, so come on out. You don't want your people in any trouble, do you?"

She turned and bumped against a chair or something, hurting her leg, but she ran into the back room and picked up the telephone. Something roared in her ear, a tiny roaring, and she was so sick with fear that she could do nothing but listen to it—the telephone was clammy and very heavy and her fingers groped down to the dial but were too weak to touch it. She began to scream into the phone, into the roaring. She cried out, she cried for her mother, she felt her breath start jerking back and forth in her lungs as if it were something Arnold Friend was stabbing her with again and again with no tenderness. A noisy sorrowful wailing rose all about her and she was locked inside it the way she was locked inside this house.

After a while she could hear again. She was sitting on the floor with her wet back against the wall.

Arnold Friend was saying from the door, "That's a good girl. Put the phone back."

She kicked the phone away from her.

"No, honey. Pick it up. Put it back right."

She picked it up and put it back. The dial tone stopped.

"That's good girl. Now, you come outside."

She was hollow with what had been fear but what was now just an emptiness. All that screaming had blasted it out of her. She sat, one leg cramped under her, and deep inside her brain was something like a pinpoint of light that kept going and would not let her relax. She thought, I'm not going to see my mother again. She thought, I'm not going to sleep in my bed again. Her bright green blouse was all wet.

Arnold Friend said, in a gentle-loud voice that was like a stage voice, "The place where you came from ain't there any more, and where you had in mind to go is cancelled out. This place you are now—inside your daddy's house—is nothing but a cardboard box I can knock down any time. You know that and always did know it. You hear me?"

She thought, I have got to think. I have got to know what to do.

"We'll go out to a nice field, out in the country here where it smells so nice and it's sunny," Arnold Friend said. "I'll have my arms tight around you so you won't need to try to get away and I'll show you what love is like, what it does. The hell with this house! It looks solid all right," he said. He ran a fingernail down the screen and the noise did not make Connie shiver, as it would have the day before. "Now, put your hand on your heart, honey. Feel that? That feels solid too but we know better. Be nice to me, be sweet like you can because what else is there for a girl like you but to be sweet and pretty and give in?—and get away before her people come back?"

She felt her pounding heart. Her hand seemed to enclose it. She thought for the first time in her life that it was nothing that was hers, that belonged to her, but just a pounding, living thing inside this body that wasn't really hers either.

"You don't want them to get hurt," Arnold Friend went on. "Now, get up, honey. Get up all by yourself."

She stood.

"Now, turn this way. That's right. Come over here to me.—Ellie, put that away, didn't I tell you? You dope. You miserable creepy dope," Arnold Friend said. His words were not angry but only part of an incantation. The incantation was kindly. "Now come out through the kitchen to me, honey, and let's see a smile, try it, you re a brave, sweet little girl and now they're eating corn and hot dogs cooked to bursting over an outdoor fire, and they don't know one thing about you and never did and honey, you're better than them because not a one of them would have done this for you."

Connie felt the linoleum under her feet; it was cool. She brushed her hair back out of her eyes. Arnold Friend let go of the post tentatively and opened his arms for her, his elbows pointing in toward each other and his wrists limp, to show that this was an embarrassed embrace and a little mocking, he didn't want to make her self-conscious.

She put out her hand against the screen. She watched herself push the door slowly open as if she were back safe somewhere in the other doorway, watching this body and this head of long hair moving out into the sunlight where Arnold Friend waited.

"My sweet little blue-eyed girl," he said in a half-sung sigh that had nothing to do with her brown eyes but was taken up just the same by the vast sunlit reaches of the land behind him and on all sides of him—so much land that Connie had never seen before and did not recognize except to know that she was going to it.

❋ ❋ ❋

## EDGAR ALLAN POE

## *The Pit and the Pendulum*                                    (1842)

> Impia tortorum longas hic turba furores
> Sanguinis innocui, non satiata, aluit.
> Sospite nunc patria, fracto nunc funeris antro,
> Mors ubi dira fuit vita salusque patent.

[*Quatrain composed for the gates of a market to be erected upon the site of the Jacobin Club House at Paris.*]

I WAS sick—sick unto death with that long agony; and when they at length unbound me, and I was permitted to sit, I felt that my senses were leaving me. The sentence—the dread sentence of death—was the last of distinct accentuation which reached my ears. After that, the sound of the inquisitorial voices seemed merged in one dreamy indeterminate hum. It conveyed to my soul the idea of *revolution*—perhaps from its association in fancy with the burr of a mill-wheel. This only for a brief period, for presently I heard no more. Yet, for a while,

I saw—but with how terrible an exaggeration! I saw the lips of the black-robed judges. They appeared to me white—whiter than the sheet upon which I trace these words—and thin even to grotesqueness; thin with the intensity of their expression of firmness—of immovable resolution—of stern contempt of human torture. I saw that the decrees of what to me was Fate were still issuing from those lips. I saw them writhe with a deadly locution. I saw them fashion the syllables of my name; and i shuddered because no sound succeeded. I saw, too, for a few moments of delirious horror, the soft and nearly imperceptible waving of the sable draperies which enwrapped the walls of the apartment. And then my vision fell upon the seven tall candles upon the table. At first they wore the aspect of charity, and seemed white slender angels who would save me; but then, all at once, there came a most deadly nausea over my spirit, and I felt every fibre in my frame thrill as if I had touched the wire of a galvanic battery, while the angel forms became meaningless spectres, with heads of flame, and I saw that from them there would be no help. And then there stole into my fancy, like a rich musical note, the thought of what sweet rest there must be in the grave. The thought came gently and stealthily, and it seemed long before it attained full appreciation; but just as my spirit came at length properly to feel and entertain it, the figures of the judges vanished, as if magically, from before me; the tall candles sank into nothingness; their flames went out utterly; the blackness of darkness supervened; all sensations appeared swallowed up in a mad rushing descent as of the soul into Hades. Then silence, and stillness, and night were the universe.

I had swooned; but still will not say that all of consciousness was lost. What of it there remained I will not attempt to define, or even to describe; yet all was not lost. In the deepest slumber—no! In delirium—no! In a swoon—no! In death—no! even in the grave all *is not* lost. Else there is no immortality for man. Arousing from the most profound of slumbers, we break the gossamer web of *some* dream. Yet in a second afterward (so frail may that web have been) we remember not that we have dreamed. In the return to life from the swoon there are two stages: first, that of the sense of mental or spiritual; secondly, that of the sense of physical, existence. It seems probable that if, upon reaching the second stage, we could recall the impressions of the first, we should find these impressions eloquent in memories of the gulf beyond. And that gulf is—what? How at least shall we distinguish its shadows from those of the tomb? But if the impressions of what I have termed the first stage are not, at will, recalled, yet, after long interval, do they not come unbidden, while we marvel whence they come? He who has never swooned, is not he who finds strange palaces and wildly familiar faces in coals that glow; is not he who beholds floating in mid-air the sad visions that the many may not view; is not he who ponders over the perfume of some novel flower; is not he whose brain grows bewildered with the meaning of some musical cadence which has never before arrested his attention.

Amid frequent and thoughtful endeavors to remember, amid earnest struggles to regather some token of the state of seeming nothingness into which my soul had lapsed, there have been moments when I have dreamed of success; there have been brief, very brief periods when I have conjured up remembrances which the lucid reason of a later epoch assures me could have had reference only to that condition of seeming unconsciousness. These shadows of memory tell, indistinctly, of tall figures that lifted and bore me in silence down—down—still down—till a hideous dizziness oppressed me at the mere idea of the interminableness of the descent. They tell also of a vague horror at my heart, on account of that heart's unnatural stillness. Then comes a sense of sudden motionlessness throughout all things; as if those who bore me (a ghastly train!) had outrun, in their descent, the limits of the limitless, and paused from the wearisomeness of their toil. After this I call to mind flatness and dampness; and then all is *madness*—the madness of a memory which busies itself among forbidden things.

Very suddenly there came back to my soul motion and sound—the tumultuous motion of the heart, and, in my ears, the sound of its beating. Then a pause in which all is blank. Then again sound, and motion, and touch—a tingling sensation pervading my frame. Then the mere consciousness of existence, without thought—a condition which lasted long. Then, very suddenly, *thought*, and shuddering terror, and earnest endeavor to comprehend my true state. Then a strong desire to lapse into insensibility. Then a rushing revival of soul and a successful effort to move. And now a full memory of the trial, of the judges, of the sable draperies, of the sentence, of the sickness, of the swoon. Then entire forgetfulness of all that followed; of all that a later day and much earnestness of endeavor have enabled me vaguely to recall.

So far, I had not opened my eyes. I felt that I lay upon my back, unbound. I reached out my hand, and it fell heavily upon something damp and hard. There I suffered it to remain for many minutes, while I strove to imagine where and *what* I could be. I longed, yet dared not, to employ my vision. I dreaded the first glance at objects around me. It was not that I feared to look upon things horrible, but that I grew aghast lest there should be *nothing* to see. At length, with a wild desperation at heart, I quickly unclosed my eyes. My worst thoughts, then, were confirmed. The blackness of eternal night encompassed me. I struggled for breath. The intensity of the darkness seemed to oppress and stifle me. The atmosphere was intolerably close. I still lay quietly, and made effort to exercise my reason. I brought to mind the inquisitorial proceedings, and attempted from that point to deduce my real condition. The sentence had passed; and it appeared to me that a very long interval of time had since elapsed. Yet not for a moment did I suppose myself actually dead. Such a supposition, notwithstanding what we read in fiction, is altogether inconsistent with real existence;—but where and in what state was I? The condemned to death, I knew, perished usually at the *autos-da-fé*, and one of these had been held on the very night of the day of my trial. Had I been remanded to my dungeon, to await the next sacrifice, which would not take place for many months? This I at once saw could not be. Victims had been in immediate demand. Moreover, my dungeon, as well as all the condemned cells at Toledo, had stone floors, and light was not altogether excluded.

A fearful idea now suddenly drove the blood in torrents upon my heart, and for a brief period I once more relapsed into insensibility. Upon recovering, I at once started to my feet, trembling convulsively in every fibre. I thrust my arms wildly above and around me in all directions. I felt nothing; yet dreaded to move a step, lest I should be impeded by the walls of a *tomb*. Perspiration burst from every pore, and stood in cold big beads upon my forehead. The agony of suspense grew at length intolerable, and I cautiously moved forward, with my arms extended, and my eyes straining from their sockets in the hope of catching some faint ray of light. I proceeded for many paces; but still all was blackness and vacancy. I breathed more freely. It seemed evident that mine was not, at least, the most hideous of fates.

And now, as I still continued to step cautiously onward, there came thronging upon my recollection a thousand vague rumors of the horrors of Toledo. Of the dungeons there had been strange things narrated—fables I had always deemed them—but yet strange, and too ghastly to repeat, save in a whisper. Was I left to perish of starvation in this subterranean world of darkness; or what fate, perhaps even more fearful, awaited me? That the result would be death, and a death of more than customary bitterness, I knew too well the character of my judges to doubt. The mode and the hour were all that occupied or distracted me.

My outstretched hands at length encountered some solid obstruction. It was a wall, seemingly of stone masonry—very smooth, slimy, and cold. I followed it up; stepping with all the careful distrust with which certain antique narratives had inspired me. This process, however, afforded me no means of ascertaining the dimensions of my dungeon, as I might make its circuit and return to the point whence I set out without being aware of the fact, so perfectly uniform seemed the wall. I therefore sought the knife which had been in my pocket when led into the inquisitorial chamber; but it was gone; my clothes had been exchanged for a wrapper of coarse serge. I had thought of forcing the blade in some minute crevice of the masonry, so as to identify my point of departure. The difficulty, nevertheless, was but trivial; although, in the disorder of my fancy, it seemed at first insuperable. I tore a part of the hem from the robe and placed the fragment at full length, and at right angles to the wall. In groping my way around the prison, I could not fail to encounter this rag upon completing the circuit. So, at least, I thought; but I had not counted upon the extent of the dungeon, or upon my own weakness. The ground was moist and slippery. I staggered onward for some time, when I stumbled and fell. My excessive fatigue induced me to remain prostrate; and sleep soon overtook me as I lay.

Upon awaking, and stretching forth an arm, I found beside me a loaf and a pitcher with water. I was too much exhausted to reflect upon this circumstance, but ate and drank with avidity. Shortly afterward, I resumed my tour around the prison, and with much toil, came at last upon the fragment of the serge. Up to the period when I fell, I had counted fifty-two paces, and, upon resuming my walk, I had counted forty-eight more—when I arrived at the rag. There were in all, then, a hundred paces; and, admitting two paces to the yard, I presumed the dungeon to be fifty yards in circuit. I had met, however, with many angles in the wall, and thus I could form no guess at the shape of the vault, for vault I could not help supposing it to be.

I had little object—certainly no hope—in these researches; but a vague curiosity prompted me to continue them. Quitting the wall, I resolved to cross the
area of the enclosure. At first, I proceeded with extreme caution, for the floor,
although seemingly of solid material, was treacherous with slime. At length, however, I took courage, and did not hesitate to step firmly—endeavoring to cross
in as direct a line as possible. I had advanced some ten or twelve paces in this
manner, when the remnant of the torn hem of my robe became entangled between my legs. I stepped on it, and fell violently on my face.

In the confusion attending my fall, I did not immediately apprehend a somewhat startling circumstance, which yet, in a few seconds afterward, and while I
still lay prostrate, arrested my attention. It was this: my chin rested upon the floor
of the prison, but my lips, and the upper portion of my head, although seemingly
at a less elevation than the chin, touched nothing. At the same time, my forehead seemed bathed in a clammy vapor, and the peculiar smell of decayed fungus arose to my nostrils. I put forward my arm, and shuddered to find that I had
fallen at the very brink of a circular pit, whose extent, of course, I had no means
of ascertaining at the moment. Groping about the masonry just below the margin, I succeeded in dislodging a small fragment, and let it fall into the abyss. For
many seconds I hearkened to its reverberations as it dashed against the sides of
the chasm in its descent; at length, there was a sullen plunge into water, succeeded by loud echoes. At the same moment, there came a sound resembling
the quick opening and as rapid closing of a door overhead, while a faint gleam
of light flashed suddenly through the gloom, and as suddenly faded away.

I saw clearly the doom which had been prepared for me, and congratulated
myself upon the timely accident by which I had escaped. Another step before
my fall, and the world had seen me no more. And the death just avoided was of
that very character which I had regarded as fabulous and frivolous in the tales
respecting the Inquisition. To the victims of its tyranny, there was the choice of
death with its direst physical agonies, or death with its most hideous moral horrors. I had been reserved for the latter. By long suffering my nerves had been un-
strung, until I trembled at the sound of my own voice, and had become in every
respect a fitting subject for the species of torture which awaited me.

Shaking in every limb, I groped my way back to the wall—resolving there to
perish rather than risk the terrors of the wells, of which my imagination now pictured many in various positions about the dungeon. In other conditions of mind,
I might have had courage to end my misery at once, by a plunge into one of these
abysses; but now I was the veriest of cowards. Neither could I forget what I had
read of these pits—that the *sudden* extinction of life formed no part of their most
horrible plan.

Agitation of spirit kept me awake for many long hours, but at length I again
slumbered. Upon arousing, I found by my side, as before, a loaf and a pitcher of
water. A burning thirst consumed me, and I emptied the vessel at a draught. It
must have been drugged—for scarcely had I drunk, before I became irresistibly
drowsy. A deep sleep fell upon me—a sleep like that of death. How long it lasted,
of course I know not; but when, once again, I unclosed my eyes, the objects

around me were visible. By a wild, sulphurous lustre, the origin of which I could not at first determine, I was enabled to see the extent and aspect of the prison.

In its size I had been greatly mistaken. The whole circuit of its walls did not exceed twenty-five yards. For some minutes this fact occasioned me a world of vain trouble; vain indeed—for what could be of less importance, under the terrible circumstances which environed me, than the mere dimensions of my dungeon? But my soul took a wild interest in trifles, and I busied myself in endeavors to account for the error I had committed in my measurement. The truth at length flashed upon me. In my first attempt at exploration I had counted fifty-two paces, up to the period when I fell: I must then have been within a pace or two of the fragment of serge; in fact, I had nearly performed the circuit of the vault. I then slept and, upon awaking, I must have returned upon my steps—thus supposing the circuit nearly double what it actually was. My confusion of mind prevented me from observing that I began my tour with the wall to the left, and ended it with the wall to the right.

I had been deceived, too, in respect to the shape of the enclosure. In feeling my way I had found many angles, and thus deduced an idea of great irregularity; so potent is the effect of total darkness upon one arousing from lethargy or sleep! The angles were simply those of a few slight depressions, or niches, at odd intervals. The general shape of the prison was square. What I had taken for masonry seemed now to be iron, or some other metal, in huge plates, whose sutures or joints occasioned the depression. The entire surface of this metallic enclosure was rudely daubed in all the hideous and repulsive devices to which the charnel superstition of the monks has given rise. The figures of fiends in aspects of menace, with skeleton forms, and other more really fearful images, overspread and disfigured the walls. I observed that the outlines of these monstrosities were sufficiently distinct, but that the colors seemed faded and blurred, as if from the effects of a damp atmosphere. I now noticed the floor, too, which was of stone. In the centre yawned the circular pit from whose jaws I had escaped; but it was the only one in the dungeon.

All this I saw indistinctly and by much effort—for my personal condition had been greatly changed during slumber. I now lay upon my back, and at full length, on a species of low framework of wood. To this I was securely bound by a long strap resembling a surcingle. It passed in many convolutions about my limbs and body, leaving at liberty only my head, and my left arm to such an extent, that I could, by dint of much exertion, supply myself with food from an earthen dish which lay by my side on the floor. I saw, to my horror, that the pitcher had been removed. I say to my horror—for I was consumed with intolerable thirst. This thirst it appeared to be the design of my persecutors to stimulate—for the food in the dish was meat pungently seasoned.

Looking upward, I surveyed the ceiling of my prison. It was some thirty or forty feet overhead, and constructed much as the side walls. In one of its panels a very singular figure riveted my whole attention. It was the painted figure of Time as he is commonly represented, save that, in lieu of a scythe, he held what, at a casual glance, I supposed to be the pictured image of a huge pendulum, such as we see on antique clocks. There was something, however, in the appearance of this machine which caused me to regard it more attentively. While I gazed directly upward at it (for its position was immediately over my own) I fancied that I saw it in motion. In an instant afterward the fancy was confirmed. Its sweep was brief, and of course slow. I watched it for some minutes somewhat in fear, but more in wonder. Wearied at length with observing its dull movement, I turned my eyes upon the other objects in the cell.

A slight noise attracted my notice, and looking to the floor, I saw several enormous rats traversing it. They had issued from the well which lay just within view to my right. Even then, while I gazed, they came up in troops, hurriedly, with ravenous eyes, allured by the scent of the meat. From this it required much effort and attention to scare them away.

It might have been half an hour, perhaps even an hour (for I could take but imperfect note of time), before I again cast my eyes upward. What I then saw confounded and amazed me. The sweep of the pendulum had increased in extent by nearly a yard. As a natural consequence its velocity was also much greater. But what mainly disturbed me was the idea that it had perceptibly *descended*. I now observed—with what horror it is needless to say—that its nether extremity was formed of a crescent of glittering steel, about a foot in length from horn to horn; the horns upward, and the under edge evidently as keen as that of a razor. Like a razor also, it seemed massy and heavy, tapering from the edge into a solid and broad structure above. It was appended to a weighty rod of brass, and the whole *hissed* as it swung through the air.

I could no longer doubt the doom prepared for me by monkish ingenuity in torture. My cognizance of the pit had become known to the inquisitorial agents—*the pit*, whose horrors had been destined for so bold a recusant as myself—*the pit*, typical of hell and regarded by rumor as the Ultima Thule of all their punishments. The plunge into this pit I had avoided by the merest of accidents, and I knew that surprise, or entrapment into torment, formed an important portion of all the grotesquerie of these dungeon deaths. Having failed to fall, it was no part of the demon plan to hurl me into the abyss, and thus (there being no alternative) a different and a milder destruction awaited me. Milder! I half smiled in my agony as I thought of such application of such a term.

What boots it to tell of the long, long hours of horror more than mortal, during which I counted the rushing oscillations of the steel! Inch by inch—line by line—with a descent only appreciable at intervals that seemed ages—down and still down it came! Days passed—it might have been that many days passed—ere it swept so closely over me as to fan me with its acrid breath. The odor of the sharp steel forced itself into my nostrils. I prayed—I wearied heaven with my prayer for its more speedy descent. I grew frantically mad, and struggled to force myself upward against the sweep of the fearful scimitar. And then I fell suddenly calm, and lay smiling at the glittering death, as a child at some rare bauble.

There was another interval of utter insensibility; it was brief; for, upon again lapsing into life, there had been no perceptible descent in the pendulum. But it might have been long—for I knew there were demons who took note of my swoon, and who could have arrested the vibration at pleasure. Upon my recovery, too, I felt very—oh! inexpressibly—sick and weak, as if through long inanition. Even amid the agonies of that period, the human nature craved food. With painful effort I outstretched my left arm as far as my bonds permitted, and took possession of the small remnant which had been spared me by the rats. As I put a portion of it within my lips, there rushed to my mind a half-formed thought of joy—of hope. Yet what business had *I* with hope? It was, as I say, a half-formed thought—man has many such, which are never completed. I felt that it was of joy—of hope; but I felt also that it had perished in its formation. In vain I struggled to perfect—to regain it. Long suffering had nearly annihilated all my ordinary powers of mind. I was an imbecile—an idiot.

The vibration of the pendulum was at right angles to my length. I saw that the crescent was designed to cross the region of the heart. It would fray the serge of my robe—it would return and repeat its operations—again—and again. Notwithstanding its terrifically wide sweep (some thirty feet or more), and the hissing vigor of its descent, sufficient to sunder these very walls of iron, still the fraying of my robe would be all that, for several minutes, it would accomplish. And at this thought I paused. I dared not go further than this reflection. I dwelt upon it with a pertinacity of attention—as if, in so dwelling, I could arrest *here* the descent of the steel. I forced myself to ponder upon the sound of the crescent as it should pass across the garment—upon the peculiar thrilling sensation which the friction of cloth produces on the nerves. I pondered upon all this frivolity until my teeth were on edge.

Down—steadily down it crept. I took a frenzied pleasure in contrasting its downward with its lateral velocity. To the right—to the left—far and wide—with the shriek of a damned spirit! to my heart, with the stealthy pace of the tiger! I alternately laughed and howled, as the one or the other idea grew predominant.

Down—certainly, relentlessly down! It vibrated within three inches of my bosom! I struggled violently—furiously—to free my left arm. This was free only from the elbow to the hand. I could reach the latter, from the platter beside me, to my mouth, with great effort, but no farther. Could I have broken the fastenings above the elbow, I would have seized and attempted to arrest the pendulum. I might as well have attempted to arrest an avalanche!

Down—still unceasingly—still inevitably down! I gasped and struggled at each vibration. I shrunk convulsively at its every sweep. My eyes followed its outward or upward whirls with the eagerness of the most unmeaning despair; they closed themselves spasmodically at the descent, although death would have been a relief, oh, how unspeakable! Still I quivered in every nerve to think how slight a sinking of the machinery would precipitate that keen, glistening axe upon my bosom. It was *hope* that prompted the nerve to quiver—the frame to shrink. It was *hope*—the hope that triumphs on the rack—that whispers to the death-condemned even in the dungeons of the Inquisition.

I saw that some ten or twelve vibrations would bring the steel in actual contact with my robe—and with this observation there suddenly came over my spirit all the keen, collected calmness of despair. For the first time during many hours—or perhaps days—I *thought*. It now occurred to me, that the bandage, or surcingle, which enveloped me, was *unique*. I was tied by no separate cord. The first stroke of the razor-like crescent athwart any portion of the band would so detach it that it might be unwound from my person by means of my left hand. But how fearful, in that case, the proximity of the steel! The result of the slightest struggle, how deadly! Was it likely, moreover, that the minions of the torturer had not foreseen and provided for this possibility? Was it probable that the bandage crossed my bosom in the track of the pendulum? Dreading to find my faint and, as it seemed, my last hope frustrated, I so far elevated my head as to obtain a distinct view of my breast. The surcingle enveloped my limbs and body close in all directions—*save in the path of the destroying crescent.*

Scarcely had I dropped my head back into its original position, when there flashed upon my mind what I cannot better describe than as the unformed half of that idea of deliverance to which I have previously alluded, and of which a moiety only floated indeterminately through my brain when I raised food to my burning lips. The whole thought was now present—feeble, scarcely sane, scarcely definite,—but still entire. I proceeded at once, with the nervous energy of despair, to attempt its execution.

For many hours the immediate vicinity of the low framework upon which I lay had been literally swarming with rats. They were wild, bold, ravenous—their red eyes glaring upon me as if they waited but for motionlessness on my part to make me their prey. "To what food," I thought, "have they been accustomed in the well?"

They had devoured, in spite of all my efforts to prevent them, all but a small remnant of the contents of the dish. I had fallen into an habitual see-saw or wave of the hand about the platter; and, at length, the unconscious uniformity of the movement deprived it of effect. In their voracity, the vermin frequently fastened their sharp fangs in my fingers. With the particles of the oily and spicy viand which now remained, I thoroughly rubbed the bandage wherever I could reach it; then, raising my hand from the floor, I lay breathlessly still.

At first, the ravenous animals were startled and terrified at the change—at the cessation of movement. They shrank alarmedly back; many sought the well. But this was only for a moment. I had not counted in vain upon their voracity. Observing that I remained without motion, one or two of the boldest leaped upon the framework, and smelt at the surcingle. This seemed the signal for a general rush. Forth from the well they hurried in fresh troops. They clung to the wood—they overran it, and leaped in hundreds upon my person. The measured movement of the pendulum disturbed them not at all. Avoiding its strokes they busied themselves with the anointed bandage. They pressed—they swarmed upon me in ever accumulating heaps. They writhed upon my throat; their cold lips sought my own; I was half stifled by their thronging pressure; disgust, for which the world has no name, swelled my bosom, and chilled, with a heavy clamminess, my heart. Yet one minute, and I felt that the struggle would be over. Plainly I perceived the loosening of the bandage. I knew that in more than one place it must be already severed. With a more than human resolution I lay *still*.

Nor had I erred in my calculations—nor had I endured in vain. I at length felt that I was *free*. The surcingle hung in ribands from my body. But the stroke of the pendulum already pressed upon my bosom. It had divided the serge of the robe. It had cut through the linen beneath. Twice again it swung, and a sharp sense of pain shot through every nerve. But the moment of escape had arrived. At a wave of my hand my deliverers hurried tumultuously away. With a steady movement—cautious, sidelong, shrinking, and slow—I slid from the embrace of the bandage and beyond the reach of the scimitar. For the moment, at least, *I was free*.

Free!—and in the grasp of the Inquisition! I had scarcely stepped from my wooden bed of horror upon the stone floor of the prison, when the motion of the hellish machine ceased, and I beheld it drawn up, by some invisible force, through the ceiling. This was a lesson which I took desperately to heart. My every motion was undoubtedly watched. Free!—I had but escaped death in one form of agony, to be delivered unto worse than death in some other. With that thought I rolled my eyes nervously around on the barriers of iron that hemmed me in. Something unusual—some change which, at first, I could not appreciate distinctly—it was obvious, had taken place in the apartment. For many minutes of a dreamy and trembling abstraction, I busied myself in vain, unconnected conjecture. During this period, I became aware, for the first time, of the origin of the sulphurous light which illumined the cell. It proceeded from a fissure, about half an inch in width, extending entirely around the prison at the base of the walls, which thus appeared, and were completely separated from the floor. I endeavored, but of course in vain, to look through the aperture.

As I arose from the attempt, the mystery of the alteration in the chamber broke at once upon my understanding. I have observed that, although the outlines of the figures upon the walls were sufficiently distinct, yet the colors seemed blurred and indefinite. These colors had now assumed, and were momentarily assuming, a startling and most intense brilliancy, that gave to the spectral and fiendish portraitures an aspect that might have thrilled even firmer nerves than my own. Demon eyes, of a wild and ghastly vivacity, glared upon me in a thousand directions, where none had been visible before, and gleamed with the lurid lustre of a fire that I could not force my imagination to regard as unreal.

*Unreal!*—Even while I breathed there came to my nostrils the breath of the vapor of heated iron! A suffocating odor pervaded the prison! A deeper glow settled each moment in the eyes that glared at my agonies! A richer tint of crimson diffused itself over the pictured horrors of blood. I panted! I gasped for breath! There could be no doubt of the design of my tormentors—oh! most unrelenting! oh! most demoniac of men! I shrank from the glowing metal to the centre of the cell. Amid the thought of the fiery destruction that impended, the idea of the coolness of the well came over my soul like balm. I rushed to its deadly brink. I threw my straining vision below. The glare from the enkindled roof illumined its inmost recesses. Yet, for a wild moment, did my spirit refuse to comprehend the meaning of what I saw. At length it forced—it wrestled its way into my soul—it burned itself in upon my shuddering reason. Oh! for a voice to speak!—oh! horror!—oh! any horror but this! With a shriek, I rushed from the margin, and buried my face in my hands—weeping bitterly.

The heat rapidly increased, and once again I looked up, shuddering as with a fit of the ague. There had been a second change in the cell—and now the change was obviously in the *form*. As before, it was in vain that I at first endeavored to appreciate or understand what was taking place. But not long was I left in doubt. The Inquisitorial vengeance had been hurried by my two-fold escape, and there was to be no more dallying with the King of Terrors. The room had been square. I saw that two of its iron angles were now acute—two, consequently, obtuse. The fearful difference quickly increased with a low rumbling or moaning sound. In an instant the apartment had shifted its form into that of a lozenge. But the alteration stopped not here—I neither hoped nor desired it to stop. I could have clasped the red walls to my bosom as a garment of eternal peace. "Death," I said, "any death but that of the pit!" Fool! might I not have known that *into the pit* it was the object of the burning iron to urge me? Could I resist its glow? or if even that, could I withstand its pressure? And now, flatter and flatter grew the lozenge, with a rapidity that left me no time for contemplation. Its centre, and of course its greatest width, came just over the yawning gulf. I shrank back—but the closing walls pressed me resistlessly onward. At length for my seared and writhing body there was no longer an inch of foothold on the firm floor of the prison. I struggled no more, but the agony of my soul found vent in one loud, long, and final scream of despair. I felt that I tottered upon the brink—I averted my eyes—

There was a discordant hum of human voices! There was a loud blast as of many trumpets! There was a harsh grating as of a thousand thunders! The fiery walls rushed back! An outstretched arm caught my own as I fell, fainting, into the abyss. It was that of General Lasalle. The French army had entered Toledo. The Inquisition was in the hands of its enemies.

## ALICE WALKER

## *The Flowers* (1973)

It seemed to Myop as she skipped lightly from hen house to pigpen to smokehouse that the days had never been as beautiful as these. The air held a keenness that made her nose twitch. The harvesting of the corn and cotton, peanuts and squash, made each day a golden surprise that caused excited little tremors to run up her jaws.

Myop carried a short, knobby stick. She struck out at random at chickens she liked, and worked out the beat of a song on the fence around the pigpen.

She felt light and good in the warm sun. She was ten, and nothing existed for her but her song, the stick clutched in her dark brown hand, and the tat-de-ta-ta-ta of accompaniment,

Turning her back on the rusty boards of her family's sharecropper cabin, Myop walked along the fence till it ran into the stream made by the spring. Around the spring, where the family got drinking water, silver ferns and wildflowers grew. Along the shallow banks pigs rooted. Myop watched the tiny white bubbles disrupt the thin black scale of soil and the water that silently rose and slid away down the stream.

She had explored the woods behind the house many times. Often, in late autumn, her mother took her to gather nuts among the fallen leaves. Today she made her own path, bouncing this way and that way, vaguely keeping an eye out for snakes. She found, in addition to various common but pretty ferns and leaves, an armful of strange blue flowers with velvety ridges and a sweet suds bush full of the brown, fragrant buds.

By twelve o'clock, her arms laden with sprigs of her findings, she was a mile or more from home. She had often been as far before, but the strangeness of the land made it not as pleasant as her usual haunts. It seemed gloomy in the little cove in which she found herself. The air was damp, the silence close and deep.

Myop began to circle back to the house, back to the peacefulness of the morning. It was then she stepped smack into his eyes. Her heel became lodged in the broken ridge between brow and nose, and she reached down quickly, unafraid, to free herself. It was only when she saw his naked grin that she gave a little yelp of surprise.

He had been a tall man. From feet to neck covered a long space. His head lay beside him. When she pushed back the leaves and layers of earth and debris Myop saw that he'd had large white teeth, all of them cracked or broken, long fingers, and very big bones. All his clothes had rotted away except some threads of blue denim from his overalls. The buckles of the overall had turned green.

Myop gazed around the spot with interest. Very near where she'd stepped into the head was a wild pink rose. As she picked it to add to her bundle she noticed a raised mound, a ring, around the rose's root. It was the rotted remains of a noose, a bit of shredding plowline, now blending benignly into the soil. Around an overhanging limb of a great spreading oak clung another piece. Frayed, rotted, bleached, and frazzled—barely there—but spinning restlessly in the breeze. Myop laid down her flowers.

And the summer was over.

❀ ❀ ❀

# Poetry

**WILLIAM BLAKE**

## *The Chimney Sweeper[1]*                                    (1789)

When my mother died I was very young,
And my father sold me while yet my tongue,
Could scarcely cry weep weep weep weep.
So your chimneys I sweep & in soot I sleep.

Theres little Tom Dacre, who cried when his head                5
That curl'd like a lambs back, was shav'd, so I said.
Hush Tom never mind it, for when your head's bare,
You know that the soot cannot spoil your white hair.

And so he was quiet, & that very night,
As Tom was a sleeping he had such a sight,                      10
That thousands of sweepers Dick, Joe Ned & Jack
Were all of them lock'd up in coffins of black

And by came an Angel who had a bright key,
And he open'd the coffins & set them all free.
Then down a green plain leaping laughing they run              15
And wash in a river and shine in the Sun.

Then naked & white, all their bags left behind,
They rise upon clouds, and sport in the wind.
And the Angel told Tom if he'd be a good boy,
He'd have God for his father & never want joy.                 20

And so Tom awoke and we rose in the dark
And got with our bags & our brushes to work.
Tho' the morning was cold, Tom was happy & warm,
So if all do their duty, they need not fear harm.

---

[1]Small boys had to go through the city crying out "Chimneys swept," but also cried because they were forced to do dirty and dangerous work because they were small enough to go up (or down) chimneys.

---

First published in *Songs of Innocence* in 1789.

### Study and Discussion Questions

1. Who is the speaker of the poem? What experience is he describing?
2. What is significant about the speaker's repetition of the word " 'weep!" in line 3?
3. Discuss the function of imagery in the poem. More specifically, consider how images of light and darkness highlight the speaker's perception of self and his job.
4. In line 24, the speaker concludes, "So if all do their duty they need not fear harm." How does he reach this conclusion? Additionally, do the speaker's final words generate hopefulness or desperation? Explain your answer.
5. Tom Dacre's hair is compared to "a lamb's back" in line 6. Discuss the symbolism of this line and relate this symbol to the function of Tom's dream.


## *The Chimney Sweeper*                                        (1794)

A little black thing among the snow:
Crying weep, weep, in notes of woe!
Where are thy father & mother! say!
They are both gone up to the church to pray.

Because I was happy upon the heath,
And smil'd among the winters snow:
They clothed me in the clothes of death,
And taught me to sing the notes of woe.

And because I am happy, & dance & sing,
They think they have done me no injury:
And are gone to praise God & his Priest & King
Who make up a heaven of our misery.


### Study and Discussion Questions

1. Who is the speaker of the poem? Explain the difference between this speaker and the speaker from the *Songs of Innocence* poem. Why is the shift in speakers important?
2. The poem begins, "A little black thing among the snow." What is the significance of this juxtaposition of light and darkness?
3. Explain the meaning of the final two lines in which the speaker notes that his parents "are gone to praise God and His priest and king, / Who made up a heaven of our misery." How is this paradoxical statement used to emphasize the thematic elements of the poem?
4. Is the tone in this poem different from the tone in *Songs of Innocence?* Use evidence from the poem to support your answer.

First published in *Songs of Experience* in 1794.

5. How does the poet conceptualize the church in this poem? Is this conception ironic? Why or why not?
6. Focusing on "The Chimney Sweeper" poems from Blake's *Songs of Innocence and Songs of Experience*, discuss how each poem complicates and modifies a reading of the other.

## T. S. ELIOT

## *The Love Song of J. Alfred Prufrock*     (1917)

*S'io credesse che mia risposta fosse*
*A persona che mai tornasse al mondo,*
*Questa fiamma staria senza piu scosse.*
*Ma perciocche giammai di questo fondo*
*Non torno vivo alcun, s'i'odo il vero,*
*Senza tema d'infamia ti rispondo.[1]*

Let us go then, you and I,
When the evening is spread out against the sky
Like a patient etherised upon a table;
Let us go, through certain half-deserted streets,
The muttering retreats                                                  5
Of restless nights in one-night cheap hotels
And sawdust restaurants with oyster-shells:
Streets that follow like a tedious argument
Of insidious intent
To lead you to an overwhelming question ...                            10
Oh, do not ask, "What is it?"
Let us go and make our visit.
In the room the women come and go
Talking of Michelangelo.
The yellow fog that rubs its back upon the window-panes,               15
The yellow smoke that rubs its muzzle on the window-panes
Licked its tongue into the corners of the evening,
Lingered upon the pools that stand in drains,
Let fall upon its back the soot that falls from chimneys,
Slipped by the terrace, made a sudden leap,                            20
And seeing that it was a soft October night,
Curled once about the house, and fell asleep.

---

[1]From Dante's *Inferno*, spoken to Dante by Guido da Montelfeltro, who is wrapped in flame: "If I thought that my reply were to someone who could ever return to the world, this flame would shake no more. But since no one has ever returned alive from this place, if what I hear is true, without fear of infamy I answer you."

And indeed there will be time
For the yellow smoke that slides along the street,
Rubbing its back upon the window-panes;                              25
There will be time, there will be time
To prepare a face to meet the faces that you meet;
There will be time to murder and create,
And time for all the works and days of hands
That lift and drop a question on your plate;                         30
Time for you and time for me,
And time yet for a hundred indecisions,
And for a hundred visions and revisions,
Before the taking of a toast and tea.

In the room the women come and go                                    35
Talking of Michelangelo.

And indeed there will be time
To wonder, "Do I dare?" and, "Do I dare?"
Time to turn back and descend the stair,
With a bald spot in the middle of my hair—                          40
[They will say: "How his hair is growing thin!"]
My morning coat, my collar mounting firmly to the chin,
My necktie rich and modest, but asserted by a simple pin—
[They will say: "But how his arms and legs are thin!"]
Do I dare                                                            45
Disturb the universe?
In a minute there is time
For decisions and revisions which a minute will reverse.

For I have known them all already, known them all:—
Have known the evenings, mornings, afternoons,                       50
I have measured out my life with coffee spoons;
I know the voices dying with a dying fall
Beneath the music from a farther room.
    So how should I presume?
And I have known the eyes already, known them all—                  55
The eyes that fix you in a formulated phrase,
And when I am formulated, sprawling on a pin,
When I am pinned and wriggling on the wall,
Then how should I begin
To spit out all the butt-ends of my days and ways?                  60
    And how should I presume?
And I have known the arms already, known them all—
Arms that are braceleted and white and bare
[But in the lamplight, downed with light brown hair!]
Is it perfume from a dress                                           65

That makes me so digress?
Arms that lie along a table, or wrap about a shawl.
     And should I then presume?
     And how should I begin?

                         . . . . .

Shall I say, I have gone at dusk through narrow streets                    70
And watched the smoke that rises from the pipes
Of lonely men in shirt-sleeves, leaning out of windows? . . .

I should have been a pair of ragged claws
Scuttling across the floors of silent seas.


                         . . . . .


And the afternoon, the evening, sleeps so peacefully!                     75
Smoothed by long fingers,
Asleep . . . tired . . . or it malingers,
Stretched on the floor, here beside you and me.
Should I, after tea and cakes and ices,
Have the strength to force the moment to its crisis?                      80
But though I have wept and fasted, wept and prayed,
Though I have seen my head [grown slightly bald] brought in upon a platter,
I am no prophet—and here's no great matter;
I have seen the moment of my greatness flicker,                          85
And I have seen the eternal Footman hold my coat, and snicker,
And in short, I was afraid.

And would it have been worth it, after all,
After the cups, the marmalade, the tea,
Among the porcelain, among some talk of you and me,                      90
Would it have been worth while,
To have bitten off the matter with a smile,
To have squeezed the universe into a ball
To roll it toward some overwhelming question,
To say: "I am Lazarus, come from the dead,                               95
Come back to tell you all, I shall tell you all"—
If one, settling a pillow by her head,
     Should say: "That is not what I meant at all.
     That is not it, at all."

And would it have been worth it, after all,                             100
Would it have been worth while,
After the sunsets and the dooryards and the sprinkled streets,
After the novels, after the teacups, after the skirts that trail along the floor—

And this, and so much more?—                                          105
It is impossible to say just what I mean!
But as if a magic lantern threw the nerves in patterns on a screen:
Would it have been worth while
If one, settling a pillow or throwing off a shawl,
And turning toward the window, should say:                            110
    "That is not it at all,
    That is not what I meant, at all."

· · · · ·

No! I am not Prince Hamlet, nor was meant to be;
Am an attendant lord, one that will do
To swell a progress, start a scene or two,                            115
Advise the prince; no doubt, an easy tool,
Deferential, glad to be of use,
Politic, cautious, and meticulous;
Full of high sentence, but a bit obtuse;
At times, indeed, almost ridiculous—                                  120
Almost, at times, the Fool.

I grow old . . . I grow old . . .
I shall wear the bottoms of my trousers rolled.

Shall I part my hair behind? Do I dare to eat a peach?
I shall wear white flannel trousers, and walk upon the beach.          125
I have heard the mermaids singing, each to each.

I do not think that they will sing to me.

I have seen them riding seaward on the waves
Combing the white hair of the waves blown back
When the wind blows the water white and black.                        130
We have lingered in the chambers of the sea
By sea-girls wreathed with seaweed red and brown
Till human voices wake us, and we drown.

## Study and Discussion Questions

1. Who are the "you and I" in line 1? What are they doing?
2. How does what Prufrock comments on in the first 69 lines reveal his
   state of mind? What different emotions do you see him feeling throughout the poem?
3. Characterize Prufrock. What is his self-image? What are his fears?
4. What kind of world does Prufrock live in? Describe the setting(s) of
   Prufrock's journey.
5. Prufrock is concerned with the past and future. He says, "For I have known
   them all already," and, though he says he is no prophet, he does look into

the future and speculate about what will happen to him. How do what Prufrock sees in the past and fears in the future affect his present behavior?
6. Is this poem about love?
7. How does the allusion to Dante's *Inferno* help in understanding the poem? The allusion to John the Baptist? to Lazarus? to Hamlet?
8. How does Eliot use repetition in the poem? Note slight changes in some of the repeated phrases.

### Suggestions for Writing

1. List every question Prufrock asks in the poem. Do they have anything in common?
2. Choose one image from the poem and explain what it adds to your knowledge of Prufrock.
3. What advice would you give Prufrock?

### Critical Resources

1. Eliot, T. S. "Tradition and the Individual Talent (1919)." *Contemporary Literary Criticism: Literary and Cultural Studies.* Eds. Robert Con Davis and Ronald Schleifer. New York: Longman, 1998.
2. Hayman, Bruch. "How Old Is Prufrock? Does He Want To Get Married?" *College Language Association Journal* 38.1 (1994): 59–68.
3. Jain, Manju. *A Critical Reading of the Selected Poetry of TS Eliot.* New York: Oxford UP, 2001.
4. Sharpe, Tony. *TS Eliot: A Literary Life.* New York: St. Martin's, 1992.

❀ ❀ ❀

## ROBERT FRANCIS

## *Catch* (1950)

Two boys uncoached are tossing a poem together,
Overhand, underhand, backhand, sleight of hand, everyhand,
Teasing with attitudes, latitudes, interludes, altitudes,
High, make him fly off the ground for it, low, make him stoop,
Make him scoop it up, make him as-almost-as possible miss it,      5
Fast, let him sting from it, now, now fool him slowly,
Anything, everything tricky, risky, nonchalant,
Anything under the sun to outwit the prosy,
Over the tree and the long sweet cadence down,
Over his head, make him scramble to pick up the meaning,      10
And now, like a posy, a pretty one plump in his hands.

❀ ❀ ❀

**ROBERT FRANCIS**

## *The Pitcher* (1960)

His art is eccentricity, his aim
How not to hit the mark he seems to aim at,

His passion how to avoid the obvious,
His technique how to vary the avoidance.

The others throw to be comprehended. He      5
Throws to be a moment misunderstood.

Yet not too much. Not errant, arrant, wild,
But every seeming aberration willed.

Not to, yet still, still to communicate
Making the batter understand too late.      10

❀ ❀ ❀

**ROBERT FROST**

## *Mending Wall* (1914)

Something there is that doesn't love a wall,
That sends the frozen-ground-swell under it,
And spills the upper boulders in the sun;
And makes gaps even two can pass abreast.
The work of hunters is another thing:      5
I have come after them and made repair
Where they have left not one stone on a stone,
But they would have the rabbit out of hiding,
To please the yelping dogs. The gaps I mean,
No one has seen them made or heard them made,      10
But at spring mending-time we find them there.
I let my neighbour know beyond the hill;
And on a day we meet to walk the line
And set the wall between us once again.
We keep the wall between us as we go.      15
To each the boulders that have fallen to each.
And some are loaves and some so nearly balls
We have to use a spell to make them balance:

"Stay where you are until our backs are turned!"
We wear our fingers rough with handling them.                          20
Oh, just another kind of out-door game,
One on a side. It comes to little more:
There where it is we do not need the wall:
He is all pine and I am apple orchard.
My apple trees will never get across                                   25
And eat the cones under his pines, I tell him.
He only says, "Good fences make good neighbours."
Spring is the mischief in me, and I wonder
If I could put a notion in his head:
"*Why* do they make good neighbours? Isn't it                          30
Where there are cows? But here there are no cows.
Before I built a wall I'd ask to know
What I was walling in or walling out,
And to whom I was like to give offence.
Something there is that doesn't love a wall,                           35
That wants it down." I could say "Elves" to him,
But it's not elves exactly, and I'd rather
He said it for himself. I see him there
Bringing a stone grasped firmly by the top
In each hand, like an old-stone savage armed.                          40
He moves in darkness as it seems to me,
Not of woods only and the shade of trees.
He will not go behind his father's saying,
And he likes having thought of it so well
He says again, "Good fences make good neighbours."                     45

**ROBERT FROST**

## *The Road Not Taken*                                               (1915)

Two roads diverged in a yellow wood,
And sorry I could not travel both
And be one traveler, long I stood
And looked down one as far as I could
To where it bent in the undergrowth;                                   5

First appeared in the *Atlantic Monthly*, August 1915. First collected in *Mountain Interval* in 1916.

Then took the other, as just as fair,
And having perhaps the better claim,
Because it was grassy and wanted wear;
Though as for that the passing there
Had worn them really about the same,                           10

And both that morning equally lay
In leaves no step had trodden black.
Oh, I kept the first for another day!
Yet knowing how way leads on to way,
I doubted if I should ever come back.                           15

I shall be telling this with a sigh
Somewhere ages and ages hence:
Two roads diverged in a wood, and I—
I took the one less traveled by,
And that has made all the difference.                           20

## Study and Discussion Questions

1. What is implicit in the poem's title?
2. After a first reading, and based on what many have been taught, what is the most obvious interpretation of this poem?
3. After closely rereading, is the meaning of this poem as obvious as it may have initially seemed? What could be an alternative interpretation of the poem?
4. How do the phrases "just as fair," "both that morning equally lay," and "I shall be telling this with a sigh" reveal more about the choice the speaker makes? How do these phrases further the tone of the poem?
5. What does the last line of the poem mean?

## Suggestions for Writing

1. Many readers interpret this as a poem about individuality and making choices in life; however, Frost suggests that this poem is "tricky" and is merely a jest toward his friend Edward Thomas who was oftentimes indecisive about which path to take during their walks in the woods. Using a current issue or event, discuss what can happen when a person's initial intentions or situation is misinterpreted.
2. Think about this poem using the more commonly suggested theme of the *inescapable necessity to make a choice.* Using this theme, discuss the greater implications these inescapable choices can impose on society. Possible contexts for consideration are religion, politics, education, and humanitarian aid.
3. Discuss how Lyon's title "Neither Road Taken" initially complicates the idea of choice illustrated in Frost's title "The Road Not Taken." How do the poems' situations complement one another?

**BRIGIT PEGEEN KELLY**

## *The Leaving* (1988)

My father said I could not do it,
but all night I picked the peaches.
The orchard was still, the canals ran steadily.
I was a girl then, my chest its own walled garden.
How many ladders to gather an orchard?                        5
I had only one and a long patience with lit hands
and the looking of the stars which moved right through me
the way the water moved through the canals with a voice
that seemed to speak of this moonless gathering
and those who had gathered before me.                        10
I put the peaches in the pond's cold water,
all night up the ladder and down, all night my hands
twisting fruit as if I were entering a thousand doors,
all night my back a straight road to the sky.
And then out of its own goodness, out                        15
of the far fields of the stars, the morning came,
and inside me was the stillness a bell possesses
just after it has been rung, before the metal
begins to long again for the clapper's stroke.
The light came over the orchard.                             20
The canals were silver and then were not.
and the pond was—I could see as I laid
the last peach in the water—full of fish and eyes.

**GALWAY KINNELL**

## *Saint Francis and the Sow* (1980)

The bud
stands for all things,
even for those things that don't flower,
for everything flowers, from within, of self-blessing;
though sometimes it is necessary                             5
to reteach a thing its loveliness,

to put a hand on its brow
of the flower
and retell it in words and in touch
it is lovely                                                    10
until it flowers again from within, of self-blessing;
as Saint Francis
put his hand on the creased forehead
of the sow, and told her in words and in touch
blessings of earth on the sow, and the sow                      15
began remembering all down her thick length,
from the earthen snout all the way
through the fodder and slops to the spiritual curl of the tail,
from the hard spininess spiked out from the spine
down through the great broken heart                             20
to the sheer blue milken dreaminess spurting and shuddering
from the fourteen teats into the fourteen mouths sucking and blowing
        beneath them:
the long, perfect loveliness of sow.

# CHRISTINA ROSSETTI

## *Goblin Market*                 composed in 1859, published in 1862

MORNING and evening
Maids heard the goblins cry:
"Come buy our orchard fruits,
Come buy, come buy:
Apples and quinces,                                             5
Lemons and oranges,
Plump unpecked cherries-
Melons and raspberries,
Bloom-down-cheeked peaches,
Swart-headed mulberries,                                        10
Wild free-born cranberries,
Crab-apples, dewberries,
Pine-apples, blackberries,
Apricots, strawberries—
All ripe together                                              15
In summer weather—

Morns that pass by,
Fair eves that fly;
Come buy, come buy;
Our grapes fresh from the vine,                              20
Pomegranates full and fine,
Dates and sharp bullaces,
Rare pears and greengages,
Damsons and bilberries,
Taste them and try:                                         25
Currants and gooseberries,
Bright-fire-like barberries,
Figs to fill your mouth,
Citrons from the South,
Sweet to tongue and sound to eye,                           30
Come buy, come buy."

Evening by evening
Among the brookside rushes,
Laura bowed her head to hear,
Lizzie veiled her blushes:                                  35
Crouching close together
In the cooling weather,
With clasping arms and cautioning lips,
With tingling cheeks and finger-tips.
"Lie close," Laura said,                                    40
Pricking up her golden head:
We must not look at goblin men,
We must not buy their fruits:
Who knows upon what soil they fed
Their hungry thirsty roots?"                                45
"Come buy," call the goblins
Hobbling down the glen.
"O! cried Lizzie, Laura, Laura,
You should not peep at goblin men."
Lizzie covered up her eyes                                  50
Covered close lest they should look;
Laura reared her glossy head,
And whispered like the restless brook:
"Look, Lizzie, look, Lizzie,
Down the glen tramp little men.                             55
One hauls a basket,
One bears a plate,
One lugs a golden dish
Of many pounds' weight.
How fair the vine must grow                                 60

Whose grapes are so luscious;
How warm the wind must blow
Through those fruit bushes."
"No," said Lizzie, "no, no, no;
Their offers should not charm us,                            65
Their evil gifts would harm us."
She thrust a dimpled finger
In each ear, shut eyes and ran:
Curious Laura chose to linger
Wondering at each merchant man.                              70
One had a cat's face,
One whisked a tail,
One tramped at a rat's pace,
One crawled like a snail,
One like a wombat prowled obtuse and furry,                 75
One like a ratel tumbled hurry-scurry.
Lizzie heard a voice like voice of doves
Cooing all together:
They sounded kind and full of loves
In the pleasant weather.                                    80

Laura stretched her gleaming neck
Like a rush-imbedded swan,
Like a lily from the beck,
Like a moonlit poplar branch,
Like a vessel at the launch                                 85
When its last restraint is gone.

Backwards up the mossy glen
Turned and trooped the goblin men,
With their shrill repeated cry,
"Come buy, come buy."                                       90
When they reached where Laura was
They stood stock still upon the moss,
Leering at each other,
Brother with queer brother;
Signalling each other,                                      95
Brother with sly brother.
One set his basket down,
One reared his plate;
One began to weave a crown
Of tendrils, leaves, and rough nuts brown                  100
(Men sell not such in any town);
One heaved the golden weight
Of dish and fruit to offer her:

"Come buy, come buy," was still their cry.
Laura stared but did not stir, 105
Longed but had no money:
The whisk-tailed merchant bade her taste
In tones as smooth as honey,
The cat-faced purr'd,
The rat-paced spoke a word 110
Of welcome, and the snail-paced even was heard;
One parrot-voiced and jolly
Cried "Pretty Goblin" still for "Pretty Polly";
One whistled like a bird.

But sweet-tooth Laura spoke in haste: 115
"Good folk, I have no coin;
To take were to purloin:
I have no copper in my purse,
I have no silver either,
And all my gold is on the furze 120
That shakes in windy weather
Above the rusty heather."
"You have much gold upon your head,"
They answered altogether:
"Buy from us with a golden curl." 125
She clipped a precious golden lock,
She dropped a tear more rare than pearl,
Then sucked their fruit globes fair or red:
Sweeter than honey from the rock,
Stronger than man-rejoicing wine, 130
Clearer than water flowed that juice;
She never tasted such before,
How should it cloy with length of use?
She sucked and sucked and sucked the more
Fruits which that unknown orchard bore, 135
She sucked until her lips were sore;
Then flung the emptied rinds away,
But gathered up one kernel stone,
And knew not was it night or day
As she turned home alone. 140

Lizzie met her at the gate
Full of wise upbraidings:
"Dear, you should not stay so late,
Twilight is not good for maidens;
Should not loiter in the glen 145
In the haunts of goblin men.

Do you not remember Jeanie,
How she met them in the moonlight,
Took their gifts both choice and many,
Ate their fruits and wore their flowers                                    150
Plucked from bowers
Where summer ripens at all hours?
But ever in the moonlight
She pined and pined away;
Sought them by night and day,                                              155
Found them no more, but dwindled and grew gray;
Then fell with the first snow,
While to this day no grass will grow
Where she lies low:
I planted daisies there a year ago                                         160
That never blow.
You should not loiter so."
"Nay hush," said Laura.
"Nay hush, my sister:
I ate and ate my fill,                                                     165
Yet my mouth waters still;
To-morrow night I will
Buy more," and kissed her.
"Have done with sorrow;
I'll bring you plums to-morrow                                             170
Fresh on their mother twigs,
Cherries worth getting;
You cannot think what figs
My teeth have met in,
What melons, icy-cold                                                      175
Piled on a dish of gold
Too huge for me to hold,
What peaches with a velvet nap,
Pellucid grapes without one seed:
Odorous indeed must be the mead                                            180
Whereon they grow, and pure the wave they drink,
With lilies at the brink,
And sugar-sweet their sap."

Golden head by golden head,
Like two pigeons in one nest                                               185
Folded in each other's wings,
They lay down, in their curtained bed:
Like two blossoms on one stem,
Like two flakes of new-fallen snow,
Like two wands of ivory                                                    190

Tipped with gold for awful kings.
Moon and stars beamed in at them,
Wind sang to them lullaby,
Lumbering owls forbore to fly,
Not a bat flapped to and fro                                    195
Round their rest:
Cheek to cheek and breast to breast
Locked together in one nest.

Early in the morning
When the first cock crowed his warning,                         200
Neat like bees, as sweet and busy,
Laura rose with Lizzie:
Fetched in honey, milked the cows,
Aired and set to rights the house,
Kneaded cakes of whitest wheat,                                 205
Cakes for dainty mouths to eat,
Next churned butter, whipped up cream,
Fed their poultry, sat and sewed;
Talked as modest maidens should
Lizzie with an open heart,                                      210
Laura in an absent dream,
One content, one sick in part;
One warbling for the mere bright day's delight,
One longing for the night.

At length slow evening came—                                    215
They went with pitchers to the reedy brook;
Lizzie most placid in her look,
Laura most like a leaping flame.
They drew the gurgling water from its deep
Lizzie plucked purple and rich golden flags,                    220
Then turning homeward said: "The sunset flushes
Those furthest loftiest crags;
Come, Laura, not another maiden lags,
No wilful squirrel wags,
The beasts and birds are fast asleep."                          225
But Laura loitered still among the rushes
And said the bank was steep.

And said the hour was early still,
The dew not fallen, the wind not chill:
Listening ever, but not catching                                230
The customary cry,
"Come buy, come buy,"

With its iterated jingle
Of sugar-baited words:
Not for all her watching                                        235
Once discerning even one goblin
Racing, whisking, tumbling, hobbling;
Let alone the herds
That used to tramp along the glen,
In groups or single,                                            240
Of brisk fruit-merchant men.

Till Lizzie urged, "O Laura, come,
I hear the fruit-call, but I dare not look:
You should not loiter longer at this brook:
Come with me home.                                              245
The stars rise, the moon bends her arc,
Each glow-worm winks her spark,
Let us get home before the night grows dark;
For clouds may gather even
Though this is summer weather,                                  250
Put out the lights and drench us through;
Then if we lost our way what should we do?"

Laura turned cold as stone
To find her sister heard that cry alone,
That goblin cry,                                                255
"Come buy our fruits, come buy."
Must she then buy no more such dainty fruit?
Must she no more such succous pasture find,
Gone deaf and blind?
Her tree of life drooped from the root:                        260
She said not one word in her heart's sore ache;
But peering thro' the dimness, naught discerning,
Trudged home, her pitcher dripping all the way;
So crept to bed, and lay
Silent 'til Lizzie slept;                                       265
Then sat up in a passionate yearning,
And gnashed her teeth for balked desire, and wept
As if her heart would break.

Day after day, night after night,
Laura kept watch in vain,                                       270
In sullen silence of exceeding pain.
She never caught again the goblin cry:
"Come buy, come buy,"
She never spied the goblin men

Hawking their fruits along the glen: 275
But when the noon waxed bright
Her hair grew thin and gray;
She dwindled, as the fair full moon doth turn
To swift decay, and burn
Her fire away. 280

One day remembering her kernel-stone
She set it by a wall that faced the south;
Dewed it with tears, hoped for a root,
Watched for a waxing shoot,
But there came none; 285
It never saw the sun,
It never felt the trickling moisture run:
While with sunk eyes and faded mouth
She dreamed of melons, as a traveller sees
False waves in desert drouth 290
With shade of leaf-crowned trees,
And burns the thirstier in the sandful breeze.

She no more swept the house,
Tended the fowls or cows,
Fetched honey, kneaded cakes of wheat, 295
Brought water from the brook:
But sat down listless in the chimney-nook
And would not eat.

Tender Lizzie could not bear
To watch her sister's cankerous care, 300
Yet not to share.
She night and morning
Caught the goblins' cry:
"Come buy our orchard fruits,
Come buy, come buy." 305
Beside the brook, along the glen
She heard the tramp of goblin men,
The voice and stir
Poor Laura could not hear;
Longed to buy fruit to comfort her, 310
But feared to pay too dear,

She thought of Jeanie in her grave,
Who should have been a bride;
But who for joys brides hope to have

Fell sick and died                                                            315
In her gay prime,
In earliest winter-time,
With the first glazing rime,
With the first snow-fall of crisp winter-time.

Till Laura, dwindling,                                                        320
Seemed knocking at Death's door:
Then Lizzie weighed no more
Better and worse,
But put a silver penny in her purse,
Kissed Laura, crossed the heath with clumps of furze                          325
At twilight, halted by the brook,
And for the first time in her life
Began to listen and look.

Laughed every goblin
When they spied her peeping:                                                   330
Came towards her hobbling,
Flying, running, leaping,
Puffing and blowing,
Chuckling, clapping, crowing,
Clucking and gobbling,                                                         335
Mopping and mowing,
Full of airs and graces,
Pulling wry faces,
Demure grimaces,
Cat-like and rat-like,                                                         340
Ratel and wombat-like,
Snail-paced in a hurry,
Parrot-voiced and whistler,
Helter-skelter, hurry-skurry,
Chattering like magpies,                                                       345
Fluttering like pigeons,
Gliding like fishes, —
Hugged her and kissed her;
Squeezed and caressed her;
Stretched up their dishes,                                                     350
Panniers and plates:
"Look at our apples
Russet and dun,
Bob at our cherries
Bite at our peaches,                                                          355
Citrons and dates,
Grapes for the asking,

Pears red with basking  
Out in the sun,  
Plums on their twigs;                                         360  
Pluck them and suck them,  
Pomegranates, figs."  

"Good folk," said Lizzie,  
Mindful of Jeanie,  
"Give me much and many"; —                                   365  
Held out her apron,  
Tossed them her penny.  
"Nay, take a seat with us,  
Honor and eat with us,"  
They answered grinning;                                       370  
"Our feast is but beginning.  
Night yet is early,  
Warm and dew-pearly,  
Wakeful and starry:  
Such fruits as these                                         375  
No man can carry;  
Half their bloom would fly,  
Half their dew would dry,  
Half their flavor would pass by.  
Sit down and feast with us,                                   380  
Be welcome guest with us,  
Cheer you and rest with us."  
"Thank you," said Lizzie; "but one waits  
At home alone for me:  
So, without further parleying,                               385  
If you will not sell me any  
Of your fruits though much and many,  
Give me back my silver penny  
I tossed you for a fee."  
They began to scratch their pates,                           390  
No longer wagging, purring,  
But visibly demurring,  
Grunting and snarling.  
One called her proud,  
Cross-grained, uncivil;                                      395  
Their tones waxed loud,  
Their looks were evil.  
Lashing their tails  
They trod and hustled her,  
Elbowed and jostled her,                                     400  
Clawed with their nails,

Barking, mewing, hissing, mocking,
Tore her gown and soiled her stocking,
Twitched her hair out by the roots,
Stamped upon her tender feet,        405
Held her hands and squeezed their fruits
Against her mouth to make her eat.

White and golden Lizzie stood,
Like a lily in a flood,
Like a rock of blue-veined stone       410
Lashed by tides obstreperously, —
Like a beacon left alone
In a hoary roaring sea,
Sending up a golden fire, —
Like a fruit-crowned orange-tree       415
White with blossoms honey-sweet
Sore beset by wasp and bee, —
Like a royal virgin town
Topped with gilded dome and spire
Close beleaguered by a fleet        420
Mad to tear her standard down.

One may lead a horse to water,
Twenty cannot make him drink.
Though the goblins cuffed and caught her,
Coaxed and fought her,        425
Bullied and besought her,
Scratched her, pinched her black as ink,
Kicked and knocked her,
Mauled and mocked her,
Lizzie uttered not a word;        430
Would not open lip from lip
Lest they should cram a mouthful in;
But laughed in heart to feel the drip
Of juice that syruped all her face,
And lodged in dimples of her chin,      435
And streaked her neck which quaked like curd.
At last the evil people,
Worn out by her resistance,
Flung back her penny, kicked their fruit
Along whichever road they took,      440
Not leaving root or stone or shoot.
Some writhed into the ground,
Some dived into the brook

With ring and ripple.
Some scudded on the gale without a sound,                    445
Some vanished in the distance.

In a smart, ache, tingle,
Lizzie went her way;
Knew not was it night or day;
Sprang up the bank, tore through the furze,                  450
Threaded copse and dingle,
And heard her penny jingle
Bouncing in her purse, —
Its bounce was music to her ear.
She ran and ran                                               455
As if she feared some goblin man
Dogged her with gibe or curse
Or something worse:
But not one goblin skurried after,
Nor was she pricked by fear;                                 460
The kind heart made her windy-paced
That urged her home quite out of breath with haste
And inward laughter.

She cried "Laura," up the garden,
"Did you miss me?                                            465
Come and kiss me.
Never mind my bruises,
Hug me, kiss me, suck my juices
Squeezed from goblin fruits for you,
Goblin pulp and goblin dew.                                 470
Eat me, drink me, love me;
Laura, make much of me:
For your sake I have braved the glen
And had to do with goblin merchant men."

Laura started from her chair,                               475
Flung her arms up in the air,
Clutched her hair:
"Lizzie, Lizzie, have you tasted
For my sake the fruit forbidden?
Must your light like mine be hidden,                        480
Your young life like mine be wasted,
Undone in mine undoing,
And ruined in my ruin;
Thirsty, cankered, goblin-ridden?"

She clung about her sister,                                            485
Kissed and kissed and kissed her:
Tears once again
Refreshed her shrunken eyes,
Dropping like rain
After long sultry drouth;                                              490
Shaking with aguish fear, and pain,
She kissed and kissed her with a hungry mouth.

Her lips began to scorch,
That juice was wormwood to her tongue,
She loathed the feast:                                                 495
Writhing as one possessed she leaped and sung,
Rent all her robe, and wrung
Her hands in lamentable haste,
And beat her breast.
Her locks streamed like the torch                                     500
Borne by a racer at full speed,
Or like the mane of horses in their flight,
Or like an eagle when she stems the light
Straight toward the sun,
Or like a caged thing freed,                                          505
Or like a flying flag when armies run.

Swift fire spread through her veins, knocked at her heart,
Met the fire smouldering there
And overbore its lesser flame,
She gorged on bitterness without a name:                              510
Ah! fool, to choose such part
Of soul-consuming care!
Sense failed in the mortal strife:
Like the watch-tower of a town
Which an earthquake shatters down,                                    515
Like a lightning-stricken mast,
Like a wind-uprooted tree
Spun about,
Like a foam-topped water-spout
Cast down headlong in the sea,                                        520
She fell at last;
Pleasure past and anguish past,
Is it death or is it life?

Life out of death.
That night long Lizzie watched by her,                                525

Counted her pulse's flagging stir,
Felt for her breath,
Held water to her lips, and cooled her face
With tears and fanning leaves:
But when the first birds chirped about their eaves,                    530
And early reapers plodded to the place
Of golden sheaves,
And dew-wet grass
Bowed in the morning winds so brisk to pass,
And new buds with new day                                              535
Opened of cup-like lilies on the stream,
Laura awoke as from a dream,
Laughed in the innocent old way,
Hugged Lizzie but not twice or thrice;
Her gleaming locks showed not one thread of gray,                      540
Her breath was sweet as May,
And light danced in her eyes.

Days, weeks, months, years
Afterwards, when both were wives
With children of their own;                                            545
Their mother-hearts beset with fears,
Their lives bound up in tender lives;
Laura would call the little ones
And tell them of her early prime,
Those pleasant days long gone                                          550
Of not-returning time:
Would talk about the haunted glen,
The wicked, quaint fruit-merchant men,
Their fruits like honey to the throat,
But poison in the blood;                                               555
(Men sell not such in any town;)
Would tell them how her sister stood
In deadly peril to do her good,
And win the fiery antidote:
Then joining hands to little hands                                     560
Would bid them cling together,
"For there is no friend like a sister,
In calm or stormy weather,
To cheer one on the tedious way,
To fetch one if one goes astray,
To lift one if one totters down,                                       565
To strengthen whilst one stands."

**Study and Discussion Questions:**

1. What is the effect of Rossetti's consistent use of animal imagery throughout the poem?
2. Why do you think Rossetti uses fruit to bring about Laura's downfall?
3. Both Laura and Lizzie make some sort of personal sacrifice to the goblin
   men. What is the significance of these sacrifices, and how does this relate
   to the poem's theme?
4. What is the effect of the poem's irregular meter and rhyme scheme?
5. Rossetti makes her intended message clear in the final lines of the poem,
   but how specifically do the events in the poem relate this message?
6. Why does Rossetti include the mention of the character Jeanie in the
   poem, and why is this character important?

**Suggestions for Writing**

1. "Goblin Market" focuses on the idea of the "fallen woman." Discuss Rossetti's approach to this concept, and explain whether or not modern society still holds similar beliefs.
2. To some degree, "Goblin Market" reads much like a fable or folktale, as
   it contains many fantasy elements and conveys a moral at the end.
   Compare and contrast the poem with other popular fables or folktales, addressing both narrative elements and moral lessons.

# WILLIAM SHAKESPEARE

## *That time of year thou mayst in me behold*                    (1609)

### LXXIII

That time of year thou mayst in me behold
When yellow leaves, or none, or few, do hang
Upon those boughs which shake against the cold,
Bare ruined choirs where late the sweet birds sang:
In me thou see'st the twilight of such day                                    5
As after sunset fadeth in the west,
Which by and by black night doth take away,
Death's second self that seals up all in rest:
In me thou see'st the glowing of such fire

That on the ashes of his youth doth lie                                    10
As the death-bed whereon it must expire,
Consumed with that which it was nourished by:
   This thou perceivest, which makes thy love more strong
   To love that well which thou must leave ere long.

### Study and Discussion Questions

1. Who is speaking, and to whom? What are the relative ages of the two?
2. Explain line 12.
3. Explain in detail each of the three metaphors for growing old. How are they similar and how do they differ? What is the meaning of the order in which they appear?
4. How confident does the speaker seem in the assertion the final couplet makes?

### Suggestions for Writing

1. Write a prose paragraph or two describing the speaker's attitude toward growing older.
2. What other metaphors might one use to describe aging? What are the associations and implications of each?

### Critical Resources

1. Booth, Stephen. *Shakespeare's Sonnets: Edited with Analytical Commentary.* New Haven: Yale UP, 2001.
2. Tetsumaro, Hiyashi. *Shakespeare's Sonnets: A Record of 20th Century Criticism.* Metchuen, NJ: Scarecrow, 1972.
3. Vendler, Helen. *The Art of Shakespeare's Sonnets.* Cambridge, MA: Belknap Press of Harvard UP, 1997.

## JOHN UPDIKE

## *Ex-Basketball Player*                                    (1957)

Pearl Avenue runs past the high-school lot,
Bends with the trolley tracks, and stops, cut off
Before it has a chance to go two blocks,
At Colonel McComsky Plaza. Berth's Garage
Is on the corner facing west, and there,                                    5
Most days, you'll find Flick Webb, who helps Berth out

Flick stands tall among the idiot pumps—
Five on a side, the old bubble-head style,
Their rubber elbows hanging loose and low
One's nostrils are two S's, and his eyes                              10
An E and O. And one is squat, without
A head at all—more of a football type.

Once Flick played for the high-school team, the Wizards.
He was good: in fact, the best. In '46
He bucketed three hundred ninety points,                              15
A county record still. The ball loved Flick.
I saw him rack up thirty-eight or forty
In one home game. His hands were like wild birds.

He never learned a trade, he just sells gas,
Checks oil, and changes flats. Once in a while,                       20
As a gag, he dribbles an inner tube,
But most of us remember anyway.
His hands are fine and nervous on the lug wrench.
It makes no difference to the lug wrench, though.

Off work, he hangs around Mae's luncheonette                          25
Grease-gray and kind of coiled, he plays pinball,
Smokes those thin cigars, nurses lemon phosphates.
Flick seldom says a word to Mae, just nods
Beyond her face toward bright applauding tiers
Of Necco Wafers, Nibs, and JuJu Beads.                                30

### Study and Discussion Questions

1. What are the various indications that Flick is diminished in the present?
2. What is the significance of the first four lines?
3. Analyze the imagery of the second stanza.
4. What is the meaning of the last line of the fourth stanza?

### Suggestions for Writing

1. Is Flick unhappy now?
2. Describe someone you knew in high school whom you think is or soon
   will be somehow less than he or she then was. Is social class a factor?

❀ ❀ ❀

# ROBERT WALLACE

## *The Double Play* (1965)

In his sea-lit
distance, the pitcher winding
like a clock about to chime comes down with

the ball, hit
sharply, under the artificial 5
bank of lights, bounds like a vanishing string

over the green
to the shortstop magically
scoops to his right whirling above his invisible

shadows 10
in the dust redirects
its flight to the running poised second baseman

pirouettes
leaping, above the slide, to throw
from mid-air, across the colored tightened interval, 15

to the leaning-
out first baseman ends the dance
drawing it disappearing into his long brown glove

stretches. What
is too swift for deception 20
is final, lost, among the loosened figures

jogging off the field
(the pitcher walks), casual
in the space where the poem has happened.

## WALT WHITMAN

### *a child said, What is the grass?*

FROM *Leaves of Grass*                                    (1855)

A child said *What is the grass?* fetching it to me with full hands;
How could I answer the child? I do not know what it is any more than he.

I guess it must be the flag of my disposition, out of hopeful green stuff woven.

Or I guess it is the handkerchief of the Lord,
A scented gift and remembrancer designedly dropt,                    5
Bearing the owner's name someway in the corners, that we may see and
         remark, and say *Whose?*

Or I guess the grass is itself a child, the produced babe of the vegetation.

Or I guess it is a uniform hieroglyphic,
And it means, Sprouting alike in broad zones and narrow zones,
Growing among black folks as among white,                           10

Kanuck, Tuckahoe, Congressman. Cuff[1] I give them the same, I receive
         them the same.
And now it seems to me the beautiful uncut hair of graves.

Tenderly will I use you curling grass,
It may be you transpire from the breasts of young men,
It may be if I had known them I would have loved them,              15
It may be you are from old people, or from offspring taken soon out of their
         mothers' laps,
And here you are the mothers' laps

This grass is very dark to be from the white heads of old mothers,
Darker than the colorless beards of old men,
Dark to come from under the faint red roofs of mouths              20

O I perceive after all so many uttering tongues,
And I perceive they do not come from the roofs of mouths for nothing.
I wish I could translate the hints about the dead young men and women,
And the hints about old men and mothers, and the offspring taken soon out of
         their laps.

---

[1]Kanuck, a French Canadian; Tuckahoe, someone from Virginia; Cuff, a black person

What do you think has become of the young and old men? 25
And what do you think has become of the women and children?

They are alive and well somewhere,
The smallest sprout shows there is really no death,
And if ever there was it led forward life, and does not wait at the end to arrest it,
And ceas'd the moment life appear'd. 30

All goes onward and outward, nothing collapses,
And to die is different from what any one supposed, and luckier.

# WILLIAM CARLOS WILLIAMS

## *To a Poor Old Woman* (1935)

munching a plum on
the street a paper bag
of them in her hand

They taste good to her
They taste good 5
to her. They taste
good to her

You can see it by
the way she gives herself
to the one half 10
sucked out in her hand

Comforted
a solace of ripe plums
seeming to fill the air
They taste good to her 15

### Study and Discussion Questions

1. Discuss the sounds in and the sound of the poem. List the repeated consonant sounds (consonance). What effect do these sounds have?
2. In stanza two the same sentence is used three times. Why? How is the sentence changed by breaking the lines in different places?

3. If this four-stanza poem were a four-paragraph essay, what would be the main point of each paragraph? How does Williams gradually develop our understanding of the experience he is describing?
4. Is the first stanza really only three lines?
5. Discuss the dynamic tension between the title "To a Poor Old Woman" and the experience the poem presents. What images does the title conjure up for you? What images and sensations does the poem actually present? Is there any irony here and, if so, who is it directed at?
6. Why do you think Williams titles his poem "To A Poor Old Woman" rather than "A Poor Old Woman"?

## Suggestion for Writing

1. Characterize someone through **images** of his or her relation to a particular food. This could end up as a poem in lines or as a short vivid prose piece. It could be serious, funny, or in any mood you choose.

## Critical Resources

1. Deese, Helen and Steven Gould Axelrod, eds. *Critical Essays on William Carlos Williams.* New York: G. K. Hall, 1995.
2. Larson, Kelli. *Guide to the Poetry of William Carlos Williams.* London: Prentice Hall, 1995.
3. Wagner, Linda Welshimer, ed. *Interviews With William Carlos Williams: "Speaking Straight Ahead."* New York: New Directions, 1976.
4. Williams, William Carlos. *I Wanted to Write a Poem: The Autobiography of The Works of A Poet.* Boston: Beacon, 1968.

# Relationships

## Fiction

**RAYMOND CARVER**

### *Popular Mechanics* (1981)

Early that day the weather turned and the snow was melting into dirty water. Streaks of it ran down from the little shoulder-high window that faced the
backyard. Cars slushed by on the street outside, where it was getting dark. But
it was getting dark on the inside too.

He was in the bedroom pushing clothes into a suitcase when she came to the
door.

I'm glad you're leaving! I'm glad you're leaving! she said. Do you hear?

He kept on putting his things into the suitcase.

Son of a bitch! I'm so glad you're leaving! She began to cry. You can't even
look me in the face, can you?

Then she noticed the baby's picture on the bed and picked it up.

He looked at her and she wiped her eyes and stared at him before turning
and going back to the living room.

Bring that back, he said.

Just get your things and get out, she said.

He did not answer. He fastened the suitcase, put on his coat, looked around
the bedroom before turning off the light. Then he went out to the living room.

She stood in the doorway of the little kitchen, holding the baby.

I want the baby, he said.

Are you crazy?

No, but I want the baby. I'll get someone to come for his things.

You're not touching this baby, she said. The baby had begun to cry and she
uncovered the blanket from around his head.

Oh, oh, she said, looking at the baby.

He moved toward her.

For God's sake! she said. She took a step back into the kitchen.

I want the baby.

Get out of here!

She turned and tried to hold the baby over in a corner behind the stove.

But he came up. He reached across the stove and tightened his hands on the baby.

Let go of him, he said.

Get away, get away! she cried.

The baby was red-faced and screaming. In the scuffle they knocked down a flowerpot that hung behind the stove. He crowded her into the wall then, trying to break her grip. He held onto the baby and pushed with all his weight.

Let go of him, he said.

Don't, she said. You're hurting the baby, she said.

I'm not hurting the baby, he said.

The kitchen window gave no light. In the near dark he worked on her fisted fingers with one hand and with the other hand he gripped the screaming baby up under an arm near the shoulder.

She felt her fingers being forced open. She felt the baby going from her.

No! she screamed just as her hands came loose.

She would have it, this baby. She grabbed for the baby's other arm. She caught the baby around the wrist and leaned back.

But he would not let go. He felt the baby slipping out of his hands and he pulled back very hard.

In this manner, the issue was decided.

❀ ❀ ❀

## RAYMOND CARVER

## *What We Talk About When We Talk About Love*          [1981]

My friend Mel McGinnis was talking. Mel McGinnis is a cardiologist, and sometimes that gives him the right.

The four of us were sitting around his kitchen table drinking gin. Sunlight filled the kitchen from the big windows behind the sink. There were Mel and me and his second wife, Teresa—Terri, we called her—and my wife, Laura. We lived in Albuquerque then. But we were all from somewhere else.

There was an ice bucket on the table. The gin and the tonic water kept going around, and we somehow got on the subject of love. Mel thought real love was nothing less than spiritual love. He said he'd spent five years of his life in a seminary before quitting to go to medical school. He said he still looked back on those years in the seminary as the most important years in his life.

Terri said the man she lived with before she lived with Mel loved her so much he tried to kill her. Then Terri said, "He beat me up one night. He dragged me around the living room by my ankles. He kept saying, "I love you, I love you, you bitch." He went on dragging me around the living room by my ankles. My head kept knocking on things." Terri looked around the room. "What do you do with love like that?"

She was a bone-thin woman with a pretty face, dark eyes, and brown hair that hung down her back. She liked necklaces made of turquoise, and long pendant earrings.

"My God, don't be silly. That's not love, and you know it," Mel said. "I don't know what you'd call it, but I sure know you wouldn't call it love."

"Say what you want to, but I know what it was," Terri said. "It may sound crazy to you, but it's true just the same. People are different, Mel. Sure, sometimes he may have aced crazy. Okay. But he loved me. In his own way maybe, but he loved me. There was love there, Mel. Don't say there wasn't."

Mel let out his breathe. He held his glass and turned to Laura and me. "The man threatened to kill me," Mel said. He finished his drink and went for the gin bottle. "Terri's a romantic. Terri's of the kick-me-so-I'll-know-you-love-me-school. Terri, hon, don't look that way." Mel reached across the table and touched Terri's cheeks with his fingers. He grinned at her.

"Now he wants to make up," Terri said.

"Make up what?" Mel said. "What is there to make up? I know what I know. That's all."

"How'd we get started on this subject anyway?" Terri said. She raised her glass and drank from it. "Mel always has love on his mind," she said. "Don't you, honey?" She smiled and I thought that was he last of it.

"I just wouldn't call Ed's behavior love. That's all I'm saying, honey," Mel said. "What about you guys?" Mel said to Laura and me. "Does that sound like love to you?"

"I'm the wrong person to ask," I said. "I didn't even know the man. I heard his name mentioned in passing. I wouldn't know. You'd have to know the particulars. But I think what you're saying is that love is an absolute."

Mel said, "The kind of love I'm talking about is. The kind of love I'm talking about, you don't try and kill people."

Laura said, "I don't know anything about Ed, or about the situation. But who can judge anyone else's situation?"

I touched the back of Laura's hand. She gave me a quick smile. I picked up Laura's hand. It was warm, the nails polished, perfectly manicured. I encircled the broad wrist with my fingers, and I held her

"When I left, he drank rat poison," Terri said. She clasped her arms with her hands. "They took him to the hospital in Santa Fe. That's where we lived then, about ten miles out. They saved his life. But his gums went crazy from it. I mean they pulled away his teeth. After that, his teeth stood out like fangs. My God," Terri said. She waited a minute, then let go of her arms and picked up her glass.

"What people won't do!" Laura said.

"He's out of the action now," Mel said. "He's dead."

Mel handed me the saucer of limes. I took a section, squeezed it over my drink, and stirred the ice cubes with my fingers.

"It gets worse," Terri said. "He shot himself in the mouth. But he bungles that too. Poor Ed," she said. Terri shook her head.

"Poor Ed nothing," Mel said. "He was dangerous."

Mel was forty-five years old. He was tall and rangy with curly soft hair. His face and arms were brown from the tennis he played.  When he was sober, his gestures, all his movements, were precise, very careful.

"He did love me though, Mel. Grant me that," Terri said. "That's all I'm asking. He didn't love me the way you love me. I'm not saying that. But he loved me. You can grant me that, can't you?"

"What do you mean, he bungled it?" I said.

Laura leaned forward with her glass. She put her elbows on the table and her glass with both hands. She glanced from Mel to Terri and waited with a look of bewilderment on her face, as if amazed such things happened to people you were friendly with.

"How'd he bungle it when he killed himself?" I asked.

"I'll tell you what happened," Mel said. "He took his twenty-two pistol he'd bought to threaten Terri and me with. Oh, I'm serious, the man was always threatening. You should have seen the way we lived in those days. Like fugitives. I even bought a gun myself. Can you believe it? A guy like me? But I did. I bought a gun for self-defense and carried it in my glove compartment. Sometimes I'd have to leave the apartment in the middle of the night. To go to the hospital, you know? Terri and I weren't married then, and my first wife had the house and kids, the dog, everything, and Terri and I were living in this apartment here. Sometimes, as I say, I'd get a call in the middle of the night and have to go to the hospital at two or three in the morning. It'd be dark out there in the parking lot, and I'd break into a sweat before I could even get to my car. I never knew if he was going to come out of the shrubbery or from behind a car and start shooting. I mean, the man was crazy. He was capable of wiring a bomb, anything. He used to call my service at all hours and say he needed to talk to the doctor, and when I'd return the call, he'd say, 'Son of a bitch, your days are numbered.' Little things like that. It was scary, I'm telling you."

"I still feel sorry for him," Terri said.

"It sounds like a nightmare," Laura said. "But what exactly happened after he shot himself?"

Laura is a legal secretary. We'd met in a professional capacity. Before we knew it, it was a courtship. She's thirty-five, three years younger than I am. In addition to being in love, we like each other and enjoy each other's company. She's easy to be with.

"What happened?" Laura asked.

Mel said, "He shot himself in the mouth in his room. Someone heard the shot and told the manager. They came in with a passkey, saw what had happened, and called an ambulance. I happened to be there when they brought him in, alive but past recall. The man lived for three days. His head swelled up to twice the size of a normal head. I'd never seen anything like it, and I hope I never do again. Terri wanted to go in and sit with him when she found out about it. We had a fight over it. I didn't think she should see him like that. I didn't think she should see him, and I still don't."

"Who won the fight?" Laura said.

"I was in the room with him when he died," Terri said. "He never came up out of it. But I sat with him. He didn't have anyone else."

"He was dangerous," Mel said. "If you call that love, you can have it."

"It was love," Terri said. "Sure, it's abnormal in most people's eyes. But he was willing to die for it. He did die for it."

"I sure as hell wouldn't call it love," Mel said. "I mean, no one knows what he did it for. I've seen a lot of suicides, and I couldn't say anybody knew what they did it for."

Mel put his hands behind his neck and tilted his chair back. "I'm not interested in that kind of love," he said. "If that's love, you can have."

Terri said, "We were afraid. Mel even made a will out and wrote to his brother in California who used to be a Green Beret. Mel told him who to look for if something happened to him." Terri drank from her glass. "But Mel's right—we lived like fugitives. We were afraid. Mel was, weren't you, honey? I even called the police at one point, but they were no help. They said they couldn't do anything until Ed actually did something. Isn't that a laugh?" Terri said.

She poured the last of the gin into her glass and waggled the bottle. Mel rose from the table and went to the cupboard. He took down another bottle.

"Well, Nick and I know what love is," Laura said. "For us, I mean." Laura bumped my knee with her knee. "You're supposed to say something now," Laura said, and turned her smile on me.

For an answer, I took Laura's hand and raised it to my lips. I made a big production out of kissing her hand. Everyone was amused.

"We're lucky," I said.

"You guys," Terri said. "Stop that now. You're making me sick. You're still on the honeymoon, for God's sake. You're still gaga, for crying out loud. Just wait. How long have you been together now? How long has it been? A year? Longer than a year?"

"Going on a year and a half," Laura said, flushed and smiling.

"Oh, now," Terri said. "Wait awhile."

She held her drink and gazed at Laura.

"I'm only kidding," Terri said.

Mel opened the gin and went around the table with the bottle.

"Here, you guys," he said. "Let's have a toast. I want to propose a toast. A toast to love. To true love," Mel said.

Outside in the backyard, one of the dogs began to bark. The leaves of the aspen that leaned against the window ticked against the glass. The afternoon sun was like a presence in the room, the spacious light of ease and generosity. We could have been anywhere, somewhere enchanted. We raised our glasses again and grinned at each other like children who agreed on something forbidden.

"I'll tell you what real love is," Mel said. "I mean, I'll give you a good example. And then you can draw your own conclusions." He poured more gin into his glass. He added an ice cube and a sliver of lime. We waited and sipped our drinks. Laura and I touched knees again. I put a hand on her warm thigh and left it there.

"What do any of us really know about love?" Mel said. "It seems to me we're just beginners at love. We say we love each other and we do, I don't doubt it. I love Terri and Teri loves me, and you guys love each other and we do, I don't doubt it. You know the kind of love I'm talking about now. Physical love, that impulse that drives you to someone special, as well as love of the other person's being, his or her essence, as it were. Carnal love and, well, call it sentimental love, the day-to-day caring about the other person. But sometimes I have a hard time accounting for the fact that I must have loved my first wife too. But I did, I know I did. So I suppose I am like Terri in that regard. Terri and Ed." He thought about it and then he went on. "There was a time that I thought I loved my first wife more than life itself. But now I hate her guts. I do. How do you explain that? What happened to that love? What happened to it is what I'd like to know. I wish someone could tell me. Then there's Ed. Okay, we're back to Ed. He loves Terri so much he tries to kill her and he winds up killing himself." Mel stopped talking and swallowed from his glass. "You guys have been together eighteen months and you love each other. It shows all over you. You glow with it. But you both loved other people before you met each other. You've both been married before, just like us. And you probably loved other people before that too, even. Terri and I have been together for five years, been married for four. And the terrible thing is, the terrible thing is, but the good thing too, the saving grace, you might say, is that if something happened to one of us–excuse me for saying this–but if something happened to one of us tomorrow, I think the other one, the other person, would grieve for awhile, you know, but then the surviving party would go out and love again, have someone else soon enough. All this, all this love we're talking about, it would just be a memory. Maybe not even a memory. Am I wrong? Am I way off base?? Because I want you to set me straight if you think I'm wrong. I want to know. I mean, I don't know anything, and I'm the first one to admit it."

"Mel, for God's sake," Terri said. She reached out and took hold of his wrist. "Are you getting drunk?? Honey? Are you drunk?"

"Honey, I'm just talking," Mel said. "All right. I don't have to be drunk to say what I think. I mean, we're all just talking, right?" Mel said. He fixed his eyes on her.

"Sweetie, I'm not criticizing," Terri said. She picked up her glass.

"I'm not on call today," Mel said. "Let me remind you of that. I'm not on call."

"Mel, we love you," Laura said.

Mel looked at Laura. He looked at her as if he could not place her, as if she was not the woman she was. "Love you too, Laura," Mel said. "And you, Nick, love you too. You know something?" Mel said. "You guys are our pals." He picked up his glass.

Mel said, "I was going to tell you about something. I mean, I was going to prove a point. You see, this happened a few months ago, but it's still going on right now, and it ought to make us feel ashamed when we talk like we know what we're talking about when we talk about love."

"Come on now," Terri. "Don't talk like you're drunk if you're not drunk."

"Just shut up for once in your life," Mel said very quietly. "Will you do me a favor and do that for a minute? So as I was saying, there's this old couple who had this car wreck out on the interstate. A kid hit them and they were all torn to shit and no one was giving them much chance to pull through."

Terri looked at us and then back at Mel. She seemed anxious, but maybe that's too strong of a word.   Mel was handing the bottle around the table.

"I was on call that night," Mel said. "It was May or maybe it was June. Terri and I had just sat down to dinner when the hospital had called. There'd been this thing out on the Interstate. Drunk kid, teenager, plowed his dad's pickup into this camper with this old couple in it. They were up in their mid-seventies, that couple. The kid–eighteen, nineteen, something–he was DOA. Taken the steering wheel through the sternum. The old couple, they were alive, you understand. I mean, just barely. But they had everything. Multiple fractures, internal injuries, hemorrhaging, contusions, lacerations, the works, and the each of them had them-selves concussions. They were in a bad way, believe me. And, of course, their age was two strikes against them. I'd say she was worse off than he was. Ruptured spleen along with everything else. Both kneecaps broken. But they'd been wear-ing their seatbelts and, God knows, that's what saved them for the time being."

"Folks, this is an advertisement for the National Security Council," Terri said. "This is your spokesman, Dr. Melivin R. McGinnis, talking." Terri laughed. "Mel," she said, "sometimes you're just too much. But I love you, hon," she said.

"Honey, I love you," Mel said.

He leaned across the table. Terri met him halfway. They kissed.

"Terri's right," Mel said as he settled himself. "Get those seatbelts on. But se-riously, they were in some shape, those oldsters. By the time I got down there, the kid was dead, as I said. He was off in a corner, laid out on a gurney. I took one look at the couple and told the ER nurse to get me a neurologist and an or-thopedic man and a couple of surgeons down there right away."

He drank from his glass. "I'll try to keep this short," he said. "So we took the both of them up to the OR and worked like fuck on them for most of the night. They had these incredible reserves, those two. You see that once in awhile. So we did everything that could be done, and toward the morning we're giving them a fifty-fifty chance, maybe less than that for her. So here they are, still alive the next morning. So, okay, we move them into the ICU, which is where they both kept plugging away at it for two weeks, hitting it better and better on all the scopes. So we transfer them out to their own room." Mel stopped talking. "Here," he said, "let's drink this cheapo gin the hell up. Then we're going to dinner, right?

Terri and I know a new place. That's where we'll go, to this new place we know about. But we're not going until we finish this cut-rate losy gin."

Terri said, "We haven't actually eaten there yet. But it looks good. From the outside, you know."

"I like food," Mel said. "If I had to do it all over again, I'd be chef, you know? Right, Terri?" Mel said. He laughed. He fingered the ice in the glass. "Terri knows," he said. "Terri can tell you. But let me say this. If I could come back again in a different life, a different time, and all, you know what? I'd like to come back as a knight. You were pretty safe wearing all that armor. It was all right being a knight until gunpowder and muskets and pistols came along."

"Mel, would you like to ride a horse and carry a lance," Terri said.

"Carry a woman's scarf with you everywhere," Laura said.

"Or just a woman," Mel said.

"Shame on you," Laura said.

Terri said, "Suppose you came back as a serf. The serfs didn't have it so good in those days."

"The serfs never had it good," Mel said. "But I guess even the knights were vessels to someone. Isn't that the way it worked. But then everyone is always a vessel to someone. Isn't that right? Terri? But what I liked about knights, besides their ladies, was that they had that suit of armor, you know, and they couldn't get hurt very easy. No cars in those days, you know. No drunk teenagers to tear into your ass."

"Vassals," Terri said.

"What?" Mel said.

"Vassals," Terri said. "They were called vassals, not vessels."

"Vassals, vessels," Mel said, "what the fuck's the difference? You knew what I meant anyway. All right," Mel said. "So I'm not educated. I learned my stuff. I'm a heart surgeon, sure. But I'm just a mechanic. I go in and I fuck around and I fix things. Shit," Mel said.

"Modesty doesn't become you," Terri said.

"He's just a humble sawbones," I said. "But sometimes they suffocated in all that armor, Mel. They'd even have heart attacks if it got too hot and they were too tired and worn out. I read somewhere that they'd fall off their horses and not be able to get up because they were too tired to stand with all that armor on them. They got trampled by their own horses sometimes."

"That's terrible," Mel said. "That's a terrible think, Nicky. I guess they'd just lay there and wait until somebody came along and made a shish kebob out of them."

"Some other vessel," Terri said.

"That's right," Mel said. "Some vassal would come along and spear the bastard in the name of love. Or whatever the fuck it was they fought over in those days."

"Same things we fight over these days," Terri said.

Laura said, "Nothing's changed."

The color was still high in Laura's cheeks. Her eyes were bright. She brought her glass to her lips. Mel poured himself another drink. He looked at the label closely as if studying a long row of numbers. Then he slowly put the bottle down on the table and slowly reached for the tonic water.

"What about the old couple?" Laura said. "You didn't finish the story you started.

Laura was having a hard time lighting her cigarette. Her matches kept going out.

The sunshine inside the room was different now, changing, getting thinner. But the leaves outside the window were still shimmering, and I stared at the pattern they made on the panes and on the Formica counter. They weren't the same patterns, of course.

"What about the old couple?" I said.

"Older but wiser," Terri said.

Mel stared at her.

Terri said, "Go on with your story, hon. I was only kidding. Then what happened??"

"Terri, sometimes," Mel said.

"Please, Mel," Terri said. "Don't always be so serious, sweetie. Can't you take a joke?"

"Where's the joke?" Mel said.

He held his glass and gazed steadily at his wife.

"What happened?" Laura said.

Mel fastened his eyes on Laura. He said, "Laura, if I didn't have Terri and if I didn't love her so much, and if Nick wasn't my best friend, I'd fall in love with you, I'd carry you off, honey," he said.

"Tell your story," Terri said. "Then we'll go to that new place, okay?"

"Okay," Mel said. "Where was I?" he said. He stared at the table and then he began again.

"I dropped in to see each of them every day, sometimes twice a day if I was up doing other calls anyway. Casts and bandages, head to foot, the both of them. You know, you've seen it in the movies. Little eye-holes and nose-holes and mouth-holes. And she had to have her legs slung up on top of it. Well, the husband was very depressed for the longest while. Not about the accident, though. I mean, the accident was one thing, but it wasn't everything. I'd get up to his mouth hole, you know, and he'd say no, it wasn't the accident exactly but it was because he couldn't see her through his eye-holes. He said that was what was making him feel so bad. Can you imagine? The man's heart was breaking because he couldn't turn his goddamn head and *see* his goddamn wife."

Mel looked around the table and shook his head at what he was going to say.

"I mean, it was killing the old fart just because he couldn't *look* at the fucking woman."

We all looked at Mel.

"Do you see what I'm saying?"

Maybe we were a little drunk by then. I know it was hard keeping things in focus. The light was draining out of the room, going back through the window where it had come from. Yet nobody made a move to get up from the table to turn on the overhead light."

"Listen," Mel said. "Let's finish this fucking gin. There's enough left here for one shooter all around. Then let's go eat. Let's go to the new place."

"He's depressed," Terri said. "Mel, why don't you take a pill?"

Mel shook his head. "I've taken everything there is."

"We all need a pill now and then," I said.

"Some people are born needing them," Terri said.

She was using her finger to rub at something on the table. Then she stopped rubbing.

"I think I want to call my kids," Mel said. "Is that all right with everybody? I'll call my kids."

Terri said, "What if Marjorie answers the phone? You guys, you've heard us on the subject of Marjorie? Honey, you know you don't want to talk to Marjorie. It'll make you feel even worse."

"I don't want to talk to Marjorie." Mel said. "But I want to talk to my kids."

"There isn't a day goes by that Mel doesn't say he wishes she'd get married again. Or else die," Terri said. "For one thing," Terri said, "she's bankrupting us. Mel says it's just to spite him that she won't get married again. She has a boyfriend who lives with her and the kids, so Mel is supporting the boyfriend too."

"She's allergic to bees," Mel said. "If I'm not praying she'll get married again, I'm praying she'll get herself stung to death by a swarm of fucking bees."

"Shame on you," Laura said.

"Bzzzzzz," Mel said, turning his fingers into bees and buzzing them at Terri's throat. Then he let his hands drop all the way to his sides. "She's vicious," Mel said. "Sometimes I think I'll go up there dressed like a beekeeper. You know, that hat that's like a helmet with the plate that comes down over your face, the big gloves, and the padded coat? I'll knock on the door and let loose a hive of bees in the house. But first I'd make sure the kids were out, of course."

He crossed one leg over the other. It seemed to take him a lot of time to do it. Then he put both feet on the floor and leaned forward, elbows on the table, his chin cupped in his hands. "Maybe I won't call the kids, after all. Maybe it isn't such a hot idea. Maybe we'll just go eat. How does that sound?"

"Sounds fine to me," I said. "Eat or not eat. Or keep drinking. I could head right on out into the sunset."

"What does that mean, honey?" Laura said.

"It just means what I said," I said. "It means I could just keep going. That's all it means."

"I could eat something myself," Laura said. "I don't think I've ever been so hungry in my life. Is there something to nibble on?"

"I'll put out some cheese and crackers," Terri said.

But Terri just sat there. She did not get up to get anything.

Mel turned his glass over. He spilled it out on the table.

"Gin's gone." Mel said.

Terri said, "Now what?"

I could hear my heart beating. I could hear everyone's heart. I could hear the human noise we sat there making, not one of us moving, not even when the room went dark.

❀ ❀ ❀

## KATE CHOPIN

## *Désirée's Baby* (1893)

As the day was pleasant, Madame Valmondé drove over to L'Abri to see Désirée and the baby.

It made her laugh to think of Désirée with a baby. Why, it seemed but yesterday that Désirée was little more than a baby herself; when Monsieur in riding through the gateway of Valmondé had found her lying asleep in the shadow of the big stone pillar.

The little one awoke in his arms and began to cry for "Dada." That was as much as she could do or say. Some people thought she might have strayed there of her own accord, for she was of the toddling age. The prevailing belief was that she had been purposely left by a party of Texans, whose canvas-covered wagon, late in the day, had crossed the ferry that Coton Maïs kept, just below the plantation. In time Madame Valmondé abandoned every speculation but the one that Désirée had been sent to her by a beneficent Providence to be the child of her affection, seeing that she was without child of the flesh. For the girl grew to be beautiful and gentle, affectionate and sincere,—the idol of Valmondé.

It was no wonder, when she stood one day against the stone pillar in whose shadow she had lain asleep, eighteen years before, that Armand Aubigny riding by and seeing her there, had fallen in love with her. That was the way all the Aubignys fell in love, as if struck by a pistol shot. The wonder was that he had not loved her before; for he had known her since his father brought him home from Paris, a boy of eight, after his mother died there. The passion that awoke in him that day, when he saw her at the gate, swept along like an avalanche, or like a prairie fire, or like anything that drives headlong over all obstacles.

Monsieur Valmondé grew practical and wanted things well considered: that is, the girl's obscure origin. Armand looked into her eyes and did not care. He was reminded that she was nameless. What did it matter about a name when he could give her one of the oldest and proudest in Louisiana? He ordered the *corbeille* from Paris, and contained himself with what patience he could until it arrived; then they were married.

Madame Valmondé had not seen Désirée and the baby for four weeks. When she reached L'Abri she shuddered at the first sight of it, as she always did. It was a sad looking place, which for many years had not known the gentle presence of a mistress, old Monsieur Aubigny having married and burried his wife in France, and she having loved her own land too well ever to leave it. The roof came down steep and black like a cowl, reaching out beyond the wide galleries that encircled the yellow stuccoed house. Big, solemn oaks grew close to it, and their thick-leaved, far-reaching branches shadowed it like a pall. Young Aubigny's rule was a strict one, too, and under it his negroes had forgotten how to be gay, as they had been during the old master's easy-going and indulgent lifetime.

The young mother was recovering slowly, and lay full length, in her soft white muslins and laces, upon a couch. The baby was beside her, upon her arm, where he had fallen asleep, at her breast. The yellow nurse woman sat beside a window fanning herself.

Madame Valmondé bent her portly figure over Désirée and kissed her, holding her an instant tenderly in her arms. Then she turned to the child.

"This is not the baby!" she exclaimed, in startled tones. French was the language spoken at Valmondé in those days.

"I knew you would be astonished," laughed Désirée, "at the way he has grown. The little *cochon de lait!* Look at his legs, mamma, and his hands and finger-nails,—real finger-nails. Zandrine had to cut them this morning Is n't it true, Zandrine?"

The woman bowed her turbaned head majestically, "Mais si, Madame."

"And the way he cries," went on Désirée, "is deafening. Armand heard him the other day as far away as La Blanche's cabin."

Madame Valmondé had never removed her eyes from the child. She lifted it and walked with it over to the window that was lightest. She scanned the baby narrowly, then looked as searchingly at Zandrine, whose face was turned to gaze across the fields.

"Yes, the child has grown, has changed;" said Madame Valmondé, slowly, as she replaced it beside its mother. "What does Armand say?"

Désirée's face became suffused with a glow that was happiness itself.

"Oh, Armand is the proudest father in the parish, I believe, chiefly because it is a boy, to bear his name; though he says not,—that he would have loved a girl as well. But I know it is n't true I know he says that to please me. And mamma," she added, drawing Madame Valmondé's head down to her, and speaking in a whisper, "he has n't punished one of them—not one of them—since baby is born. Even Négrillon, who pretended to have burnt his leg that he might rest from work—he only laughed, and said Négrillon was a great scamp. Oh, mamma, I'm so happy; it frightens me."

What Désirée said was true. Marriage, and later the birth of his son had softened Armand Aubigny's imperious and exacting nature greatly. This was what made the gentle Désirée so happy, for she loved him desperately. When he frowned she trembled, but loved him. When he smiled, she asked no greater blessing of God. But Armand's dark, handsome face had not often been disfigured by frowns since the day he fell in love with her.

When the baby was about three months old, Désirée awoke one day to the conviction that there was something in the air menacing her peace. It was at first too subtle to grasp. It had only been a disquieting suggestion; an air of mystery among the blacks; unexpected visits from far-off neighbors who could hardly account for their coming. Then a strange, an awful change in her husband's manner, which she dared not ask him to explain. When he spoke to her, it was with averted eyes, from which the old love-light seemed to have gone out. He absented himself from home; and when there, avoided her presence and that of her child, without excuse. And the very spirit of Satan seemed suddenly to take hold of him in his dealings with the slaves. Désirée was miserable enough to die.

She sat in her room, one hot afternoon, in her *peignoir*, listlessly drawing through her fingers the strands of her long, silky brown hair that hung about her shoulders. The baby, half naked, lay asleep upon her own great mahogany bed, that was like a sumptuous throne, with its satin-lined half-canopy. One of La Blanche's little quadroon boys—half naked too—stood fanning the child slowly with a fan of peacock feathers. Désirée's eyes had been fixed absently and sadly upon the baby, while she was striving to penetrate the threatening mist that she felt closing about her. She looked from her child to the boy who stood beside him, and back again; over and over. "Ah!" It was a cry that she could not help; which she was not conscious of having uttered. The blood turned like ice in her veins, and a clammy moisture gathered upon her face.

She tried to speak to the little quadroon boy; but no sound would come, at first. When he heard his name uttered, he looked up, and his mistress was pointing to the door. He laid aside the great, soft fan, and obediently stole away, over the polished floor, on his bare tiptoes.

She stayed motionless, with gaze riveted upon her child, and her face the picture of fright. Presently her husband entered the room, and without noticing her, went to a table and began to search among some papers which covered it.

"Armand," she called to him, in a voice which must have stabbed him, if he was human. But he did not notice. "Armand," she said again Then she rose and tottered towards him. "Armand," she panted once more, clutching his arm, "look at our child. What does it mean? Tell me."

He coldly but gently loosened her fingers from about his arm and thrust the hand away from him. "Tell me what it means!" she cried despairingly.

"It means," he answered lightly, "that the child is not white; it means that you are not white."

A quick conception of all that this accusation meant for her nerved her with unwonted courage to deny it. "It is a lie; it is not true, I am white! Look at my hair, it is brown; and my eyes are gray, Armand, you know they are gray. And my skin is fair," seizing his wrist. "Look at my hand; whiter than yours, Armand," she laughed hysterically.

"As white as La Blanche's," he returned cruelly; and went away leaving her alone with their child.

When she could hold a pen in her hand, she sent a despairing letter to Madame Valmondé.

"My mother, they tell me I am not white. Armand has told me I am not white. For God's sake tell them it is not true. You must know it is not true. I shall die. I must die. I cannot be so unhappy, and live."

The answer that came was as brief:

"My own Désirée: Come home to Valmondé; back to your mother who loves you. Come with your child."

When the letter reached Désirée she went with it to her husband's study, and laid it open upon the desk before which he sat. She was like a stone image: silent, white, motionless after she placed it there.

In silence he ran his cold eyes over the written words. He said nothing. "Shall I go, Armand?" she asked in tones sharp with agonized suspense.

"Yes, go."

"Do you want me to go?"

"Yes, I want you to go."

He thought Almighty God had dealt cruelly and unjustly with him; and felt, somehow, that he was paying Him back in kind when he stabbed thus into his wife's soul. Moreover he no longer loved her, because of the unconscious injury she had brought upon his home and his name.

She turned away like one stunned by a blow, and walked slowly towards the door, hoping he would call her back.

"Good-by, Armand," she moaned.

He did not answer her. That was his last blow at fate.

Désirée went in search of her child. Zandrine was pacing the sombre gallery with it. She took the little one from the nurse's arms with no word of explanation, and descending the steps, walked away, under the live-oak branches.

It was an October afternoon; the sun was just sinking. Out in the still fields the negroes were picking cotton.

Desiree had not changed the thin white garment nor the slippers which she wore. Her hair was uncovered and the sun's rays brought a golden gleam from its brown meshes. She did not take the broad, beaten road which led to the far-off plantation of Valmondé. She walked across a deserted field, where the stubble bruised her tender feet, so delicately shod, and tore her thin gown to shreds.

She disappeared among the reeds and willows that grew thick along the banks of the deep, sluggish bayou; and she did not come back again.

Some weeks later there was a curious scene enacted at L'Abri. In the centre of the smoothly swept back yard was a great bonfire. Armand Aubigny sat in the wide hallway that commanded a view of the spectacle; and it was he who dealt out to a half dozen negroes the material which kept this fire ablaze.

A graceful cradle of willow, with all its dainty furbishings, was laid upon the pyre, which had already been fed with the richness of a priceless *layette*. Then there were silk gowns, and velvet and satin ones added to these; laces, too, and embroideries; bonnets and gloves; for the *corbeille* had been of rare quality.

The last thing to go was a tiny bundle of letters; innocent little scribblings that Désirée had sent to him during the days of their espousal. There was the remnant of one back in the drawer from which he took them. But it was not Désirée's; it was part of an old letter from his mother to his father. He read it. She was thanking God for the blessing of her husband's love:—

"But, above all," she wrote, "night and day, I thank the good God for having so arranged our lives that our dear Armand will never know that his mother, who adores him, belongs to the race that is cursed with the brand of slavery."

❀ ❀ ❀

## KATE CHOPIN

## *The Story of an Hour*                                     (1894)

Knowing that Mrs. Mallard was afflicted with a heart trouble, great care was taken to break to her as gently as possible the news of her husband's death.

It was her sister Josephine who told her, in broken sentences, veiled hints that revealed in half concealing. Her husband's friend Richards was there, too, near her. It was he who had been in the newspaper office when intelligence of the railroad disaster was received, with Brently Mallard's name leading the list of "killed." He had only taken the time to assure himself of its truth by a second telegram, and had hastened to forestall any less careful, less tender friend in bearing the sad message.

She did not hear the story as many women have heard the same, with a paralyzed inability to accept its significance. She wept at once, with sudden, wild abandonment, in her sister's arms. When the storm of grief had spent itself she went away to her room alone. She would have no one follow her.

There stood, facing the open window, a comfortable, roomy armchair. Into this she sank, pressed down by a physical exhaustion that haunted her body and seemed to reach into her soul.

She could see in the open square before her house the tops of trees that were all aquiver with the new spring life. The delicious breath of rain was in the air.

In the street below a peddler was crying his wares. The notes of a distant song which some one was singing reached her faintly, and countless sparrows were twittering in the eaves.

There were patches of blue sky showing here and there through the clouds that had met and piled above the other in the west facing her window.

She sat with her head thrown back upon the cushion of the chair quite motionless, except when a sob came up into her throat and shook her, as a child who has cried itself to sleep continues to sob in its dreams.

She was young, with a fair, calm face, whose lines bespoke repression and even a certain strength. But now there was a dull stare in her eyes, whose gaze was fixed away off yonder on one of those patches of blue sky. It was not a glance of reflection, but rather indicated a suspension of intelligent thought.

There was something coming to her and she was waiting for it, fearfully. What was it? She did not know; it was too subtle and elusive to name. But she felt it, creeping out of the sky, reaching toward her through the sounds, the scents, the color that filled the air.

Now her bosom rose and fell tumultuously. She was beginning to recognize this thing that was approaching to possess her, and she was striving to beat it back with her will—as powerless as her two white slender hands would have been.

When she abandoned herself a little whispered word escaped her slightly parted lips. She said it over and over under her breath: "Free, free, free!" The vacant stare and the look of terror that had followed it went from her eyes. They stayed keen and bright. Her pulses beat fast, and the coursing blood warmed and relaxed every inch of her body.

She did not stop to ask if it were not a monstrous joy that held her. A clear and exalted perception enabled her to dismiss the suggestion as trivial.

She knew that she would weep again when she saw the kind, tender hands folded in death; the face that had never looked save with love upon her, fixed and gray and dead. But she saw beyond that bitter moment a long procession of years to come that would belong to her absolutely. And she opened and spread her arms out to them in welcome.

There would be no one to live for during those coming years; she would live for herself. There would be no powerful will bending her in that blind persistence with which men and women believe they have a right to impose a private will upon a fellow-creature. A kind intention or a cruel intention made the act seem no less a crime as she looked upon it in that brief moment of illumination.

And yet she had loved him—sometimes. Often she had not. What did it matter! What could love, the unsolved mystery, count for in face of this possession of self-assertion which she suddenly recognized as the strongest impulse of her being!

"Free! Body and soul free!" she kept whispering.

Josephine was kneeling before the closed door with her lips to the keyhole, imploring for admission. "Louise, open the door! I beg; open the door—you will make yourself ill. What are you doing, Lousie? For heaven's sake open the door."

"Go away. I am not making myself ill." No; she was drinking in a very elixir of life through that open window.

Her fancy was running riot along those days ahead of her. Spring days, and summer days, and all sorts of days that would be her own. She breathed a quick prayer that life might be long. It was only yesterday she had thought with a shudder that life might be long.

She arose at length and opened the door to her sister's importunities. There was a feverish triumph in her eyes, and she carried herself unwittingly like a goddess of Victory. She clasped her sister's waist, and together they descended the stairs. Richards stood waiting for them at the bottom.

Some one was opening the front door with a latchkey. It was Brently Mallard who entered, a little travel-stained, composedly carrying his grip-sack and umbrella. He had been far from the scene of accident, and did not even know there had been one. He stood amazed at Josephine's piercing cry; at Richards' quick motion to screen him from the view of his wife.

But Richards was too late.

When the doctors came they said she had died of heart disease—of joy that kills.

## Study and Discussion Questions

1. Does Louise Mallard love her husband?
2. Why is it important that Louise goes to her room alone immediately after she hears the news of her husband's death?
3. Look at paragraphs 4, 5, and 6. How do the language, tone, and imagery in this section begin to prepare us (and Louise) for Louise's shift in feeling?
4. When Louise begins to recognize "the thing that was approaching to possess her," why does she initially try to will it out of existence? Also, think about that quote. Why do you think she describes the new feeling in this way?
5. What kind of life does Louise envision as a widow, as a woman who "would live for herself"?
6. Though the point of view in this story is that of a woman, is Chopin blaming men for what is wrong with marriage?

## Suggestions for Writing

1. Discuss the narrator's attitude toward the institution of marriage.
2. Irony refers to the recognition of a reality different from appearance. How is the situation of "The Story of an Hour" ironic in several ways?
3. What, if anything, has changed about marriage in the hundred years since this story was written? If you think much has changed, how would you rewrite the story for a contemporary audience?

**Critical Resources**

1. Beer, Janet. *Kate Chopin, Edith Wharton, and Charlotte Perkins Gilman: Studies in Short Fiction.* New York: St. Martin's, 1997.
2. Berkove, Lawrence. "Fatal Self-Assertion in Kate Chopin's The Story of An Hour." *Literary Realism* 32.2 (2000): 152–58.
3. *Five Stories of an Hour.* Director Paul Kafno et al. Princeton: Films for the Humanities and Sciences, 1999. 26 minutes. For more information go to <http://www.films.com/id/3992>.
4. Petry, Alice, ed. *Critical Essays on Kate Chopin.* New York: G. K. Hall, 1996.
5. Toth, Emily. *Unveiling Kate Chopin.* Jackson: UP of Mississippi, 1999.

# CRISTINA GARCÍA

## *Inés in the Kitchen*                                          (1996)

Inés Maidique is twelve weeks pregnant and nauseous. Her back hurts, her breasts are swollen, and her feet no longer fit into her dressy shoes. Although she is barely showing, she walks around in sneakers to ease the soreness that has settled in every corner of her body. The eleven pounds she's gained feel like fifty.

When her husband returns home he'll expect her trussed up in a silk dress and pearls and wearing make-up and high heels. It's Friday and Richard likes for her to make a fuss over him at the end of the week. He'll be home in two hours so Inés busies herself preparing their dinner—a poached loin of lamb with mint chutney, cumin rice, ratatouille, and spiced bananas for dessert.

Richard will question her closely about what she's eaten that day. Inés will avoid telling him about the fudge cookies she devoured that morning in the supermarket parking lot. She hadn't wanted to eat the whole box, but bringing it home was unthinkable. Richard scoured the kitchen cabinets for what he called "illegal foods" and she was in no mood for his usual harangue.

With a long length of string Inés ties together the eye of loin and tenderloin at one inch intervals, leaving enough string at the ends to suspend the meat from the handles of the kettle. She slits the lamb in several places and inserts slivers of garlic. Then she sets about preparing the stock, skimming the froth as it simmers. Inés thinks about the initial excitement she'd felt when the blood test came back positive. She always knew, or thought she knew, she wanted a child, but now she is less certain.

The mint leaves give off a tart scent that clears her head with each pulse of the food processor. She adds fresh coriander, minced garlic, ginger root, honey, and a little lemon until the chutney congeals. Then she whisks it together with plain yogurt in a stainless steel bowl. Inés remembers the abortion she'd had the month before her college graduation. She was twenty-one and, like now, twelve weeks pregnant. The baby's father was Cuban, like her, a hematology resident at the hospital where Inés was finishing her practicum. Manolo Espada was not opposed to having the baby, only against getting married. This was unacceptable to Inés. After the abortion, she bled for five days and cramped so hard she passed out. Inés spent the summer working a double shift at an emergency room in Yonkers. Her child would have been eight years old by now. Inés thinks of this often.

Shortly before she was to marry Richard, Inés tracked down her old lover to San Francisco, where he'd been doing AIDS research with an eminent name in the field. Over the phone, Manolo told her he was leaving for Africa the following month on a two-year grant from the Department of Health. Inés abruptly forgot everything she had planned to say. Even if she'd wanted him again, it was too late. She'd already sent out her wedding invitations and Richard had put a down payment on the colonial house across from the riding stables. Manolo was going to Africa. It would have never worked out.

Ratatouille is one of Inés's favorite dishes. It's easy to prepare and she cooks big batches of it at a time then freezes it. The red peppers give the ratatouille a slightly sweetish taste. Inés heats the olive oil in a skillet then tosses in the garlic and chopped onion. She adds the cubed egg-plants and stirs in the remaining ingredients one at a time. On another burner she prepares the rice with chicken broth, cuminseed, and fresh parsley. If she times it right, dinner will be ready just as Richard walks through the door.

Her husband doesn't know about Inés's abortion, and only superficially about Manolo Espada. It is better this way. Richard doesn't like it when Inés's attention is diverted from him in any significant way. How, she wonders, will he get used to having a baby around? Richard was the only boy in a family of older sisters, and accustomed to getting his way. His father died when Richard was eight and his three sisters had worked as secretaries to put him through medical school. Richard had been the great hope of the Roth family. When he told them he was marrying a Catholic, his mother and sisters were devastated. Janice, the oldest, told him point-blank that Inés would ruin his life. Perhaps, Inés thinks, his sister was right.

Inés strains the stock through a fine sieve into an enormous ceramic bowl, discarding the bones and scraps. She pours the liquid back into the kettle and turns on the burner to moderately high. Carefully, she lowers the lamb into the stock without letting it touch the sides or the bottom of the kettle, then she ties the string to the handles, and sets the timer for twelve minutes.

Other things concern Inés. She's heard about men running off when their wives become pregnant and she's afraid that Richard, who places such a premium on her looks, will be repelled by her bloating body. As it is, Inés feels that Richard scrutinizes her for nascent imperfections. He abhors cellulite and varicose veins, the corporal trademarks of his mother and sisters, and so Inés works hard to stay fit. She swims, plays tennis, takes aerobics classes, and works out twice a week on the Nautilus machines at her gym. Her major weakness is a fondness for sweets. Inés loves chocolate, but Richard glares at her in restaurants if she so much as asks to see the dessert menu. To him a lack of self-discipline on such small matters is indicative of more serious character flaws.

What of her husband's good qualities? Richard takes her to the Bahamas every winter, although he spends most of the time scuba-diving, a sport which Inés does not share. And he is intelligent and well-informed and she believes he is faithful. Also, he isn't a tightwad like so many of her friends' husbands, watching every penny, and he doesn't hang out with the boys or play poker or anything like that. Richard is an adequate lover, too, although he lacks imagination. He likes what he likes, which does not include many of the things that Inés likes. Once, in bed, she asked Richard to pretend he was Henry Kissinger. The request offended him deeply. If Richard rejected so harmless a game, what would he say to the darker, more elaborate rituals she'd engaged in with Manolo?

The loin of lamb is medium rare, just the way Richard likes it. Inés lets it cool off on the cutting board for a few minutes before slicing it diagonally into thick, juicy slabs. She sets the table with their wedding linen and china and wedges two white candles into squat crystal holders. Inés thinks back on the five years she worked as a nurse. She was good at what she did and was sought after for the most important cardiology cases. More than one surgeon had jokingly proposed to her after she'd made a life-saving suggestion in the operating room. But like most men, they assumed she was unavailable. Someone so pretty, so self-contained, they thought, must already be spoken for.

When Richard first started working at the hospital, Inés felt drawn to him. There was something about his manner, about his nervous energy that appealed to her. It certainly wasn't his looks. Richard was skinny and tall with fleecy colorless hair, not at all like the mesomorphic Manolo whose skin seemed more of a pelt. For three months she and Richard worked side by side on coronary bypasses, ventricular aneurysm resections, mitral valve replacements. Their manner was always cordial and efficient, with none of the macabre bantering one often hears in operating rooms. One day, Richard looked up at her from a triple bypass and said, "Marry me, Inés." And so she did.

When Inés was a child, her father had predicted wistfully that she would never marry, while her mother seemed to gear her for little else. Inés remembers the beauty pageants she was forced to enter from an early age, the banana curls that hung from her skull like so many sausages. She'd won the "Little Miss Latin New York" pageant in 1964, when she was seven years old. Her mother still considers this to be Inés's greatest achievement. Inés had sung and played the piano to "Putting on the Ritz," which she'd translated to Spanish herself. Gerardo complained to his wife about sharing Inés with an auditorium full of leering strangers, but Haydée would not budge. "This is better than a dowry, Gerardo." But Gerardo preferred to have his daughter, dolled up in her starched Sunday dress and ruffled anklets, all to himself.

Gerardo expected Inés to drop everything to play the piano for him, and for many years she complied. This became more and more difficult as she got older.

Her parents separated and her father would call at all hours on the private phone line he'd installed in Inés's bedroom, pleading with her to come play the white baby grand he had rented just for her. Sometimes he would stroke her hair or tickle her spine as she played, tease her about her tiny new breasts or affectionately pat her behind. Inés remembers how the air seemed different during those times, charged and hard to swallow. Now her father is dead. And what, she asks herself, does she really know about him?

Inés turns off all the burners and pours herself a glass of whole milk. She is doing all the right things to keep the life inside her thriving. But she accomplishes this without anticipation, only a sense of obligation. Sometimes she has a terrible urge to pour herself a glass of rum, although she hates the taste, and she knows what it would do to the baby, or to burn holes in the creamy calfskin upholstery of her husband's sports car. Other times, mostly in the early afternoons, she feels like setting fire to the damask curtains that keep their living room in a perpetual dusk. She dreams about blowing up her herb garden with its fragrant basil leaves, then stealing a thoroughbred from the stable across the street and riding it as fast as she can.

Inés finishes the last of her milk. She rinses the glass and leans against the kitchen sink. There is a jingling of keys at the front door. Richard is home.

## Study and Discussion Questions

1.  What do we suspect about Inés's state of mind from the title and the opening sentence of the story?
2.  List four or five significant *facts* we learn about Inés during the course of the story.
3.  Who are the men in Inés's life that we hear about? Characterize her relation with each one.
4.  How and why does being pregnant become a crisis point for Inés?
5.  Garcia intersperses Inés's musings with vivid detailed paragraphs on what she is cooking for dinner. Why? What is the function of these paragraphs in the story? What effect do they have on the reader?
6.  How does Inés feel about her pregnancy? Locate and discuss three passages in the story that may bear on her attitude toward being pregnant.
7.  Discuss Inés's fantasies of escape in the second to last paragraph.
8.  How might ethnicity be a factor in this story? Locate passages where Inés's Cuban identity (or her husband's Anglo identity) is explicitly or implicitly part of the story's tension.
9.  Does Inés develop and change, however subtly, as the story progresses? Has she come to some realization by the end of the story?

## Suggestions for Writing

1.  Is Inés feeling trapped in her life? What evidence do you have either way? What do you think she will do next?
2.  Write a postscript to "Inés in the Kitchen" set sometime later—you choose the time.

3. Write a couple of paragraphs from Richard's point of view.
4. Why and how do you think pregnancy is an important transitional event, perhaps even a rite of passage, in the lives of women? If you haven't been pregnant or had children yourself, talk to a few women who have gone through that experience and discuss with them any ponderings about or crises of identity they had during their pregnancy or any significant realizations they came to.
5. Is there a comparably significant "rite of passage" event in the lives of men? (This rite of passage doesn't have to be biological.) Discuss its components and compare to pregnancy as a rite of passage.

### Critical Resources

1. Arujo, Nara. "I Came All the Way from Cuba So I Could Speak Like This? Cuban and Cuban- American Literatures in the US." *Comparing Postcolonial Literatures: Dislocations.* Ed. Ashok Bery. New York: Macmillan, St. Martin's, 2000.
2. Gomez-Vega, Ibis. "The Journey Home: Defining Identity in Cristina Garcia's *Dreaming in Cuban." Voices: A Journal of Chicana/Latina Studies* 1.2 (1997): 71–100.
3. López, Iraida H. "'. . . And There Is Only My Imagination Where Our History Should Be': An Interview with Cristina García." *Bridges to Cuba/Puentes a Cuba.* Ed. Ruth Behar. Ann Arbor: U of Michigan P, 1995. 102–114.

❀ ❀ ❀


## DAGOBERTO GILB


## *Love in L.A.*                                                    (1993)


Jake slouched in a clot of near motionless traffic, in the peculiar gray of concrete, smog, and early morning beneath the overpass of the Hollywood Freeway on Alvarado Street. He didn't really mind because he knew how much worse it could be trying to make a left onto the onramp. He certainly didn't do that every day of his life, and he'd assure anyone who'd ask that he never would either. A steady occupation had its advantages and he couldn't deny thinking about that too. He needed an FM radio in something better than this '58 Buick he drove. It would have crushed velvet interior with electric controls for the L.A. summer, a nice warm heater and defroster for the winter drives at the beach, a cruise control for those longer trips, mellow speakers front and rear of course, windows that hum closed, snuffing out that nasty exterior noise of freeways. The fact was that he'd probably have to change his whole style. Exotic colognes, plush, dark nightclubs, maitais and daiquiris, necklaced ladies in satin gowns, misty and sexy like in a tequila ad. Jake could imagine lots of possibilities when he let himself, but none that ended up with him pressed onto a stalled freeway.

Jake was thinking about this freedom of his so much that when he glimpsed its green light he just went ahead and stared bye bye to the steadily employed. When he turned his head the same direction his windshield faced, it was maybe one second too late. He pounced the brake pedal and steered the front wheels away from the tiny brakelights but the smack was unavoidable. Just one second sooner and it would only have been close. One second more and he'd be crawling up the Toyota's trunk. As it was, it seemed like only a harmless smack, much less solid than the one against his back bumper.

Jake considered driving past the Toyota but was afraid the traffic ahead would make it too difficult. As he pulled up against the curb a few carlengths ahead, it occurred to him that the traffic might have helped him get away too. He slammed the car door twice to make sure it was closed fully and to give himself another second more, then toured front and rear of his Buick for damage on or near the bumpers. Not an impressionable scratch even in the chrome. He perked up. Though the car's beauty was secondary to its ability to start and move, the body and paint were clean except for a few minor dings. This stood out as one of his few clearcut accomplishments over the years.

Before he spoke to the driver of the Toyota, whose looks he could see might present him with an added complication, he signaled to the driver of the car that hit him, still in his car and stopped behind the Toyota, and waved his hands and shook his head to let the man know there was no problem as far as he was concerned. The driver waved back and started his engine.

"It didn't even scratch my paint," Jake told her in that way of his. "So how you doin? Any damage to the car? I'm kinda hoping so, just so it takes a little more time and we can talk some. Or else you can give me your phone number now and I won't have to lay my regular b.s. on you to get it later."

He took her smile as a good sign and relaxed. He inhaled her scent like it was clean air and straightened out his less than new but not unhip clothes.

"You've got Florida plates. You look like you must be Cuban."

"My parents are from Venezuela."

"My name's Jake." He held out his hand.

"Mariana."

They shook hands like she'd never done it before in her life.

"I really am sorry about hitting you like that." He sounded genuine. He fondled the wide dimple near the cracked taillight. "It's amazing how easy it is to put a dent in these new cars. They're so soft they might replace waterbeds soon." Jake was confused about how to proceed with this. So much seemed so unlikely, but there was always possibility. "So maybe we should go out to breakfast somewhere and talk it over."

"I don't eat breakfast."

"Some coffee then."

"Thanks, but I really can't."

"You're not married, are you? Not that that would matter that much to me. I'm an openminded kinda guy."

She was smiling. "I have to get to work."

"That sounds boring."

"I better get your driver's license," she said.

Jake nodded, disappointed. "One little problem," he said. "I didn't bring it. I just forgot it this morning. I'm a musician," he exaggerated greatly, "and, well, I dunno, I left my wallet in the pants I was wearing last night. If you have some paper and a pen I'll give you my address and all that."

He followed her to the glove compartment side of her car.

"What if we don't report it to the insurance companies? I'll just get it fixed for you."

"I don't think my dad would let me do that."

"Your dad? It's not your car?"

"He bought it for me. And I live at home."

"Right." She was slipping away from him. He went back around to the back of her new Toyota and looked over the damage again. There was the trunk lid, the bumper, a rear panel, a taillight.

"You do have insurance?" she asked, suspicious, as she came around the back of the car.

"Oh yeah," he lied.

"I guess you better write the name of that down too."

He made up a last name and address and wrote down the name of an insurance company an old girlfriend once belonged to. He considered giving a real phone number but went against that idea and made one up.

"I act too," he lied to enhance the effect more. "Been in a couple of movies." She smiled like a fan.

"So how about your phone number?" He was rebounding maturely.

She gave it to him.

"Mariana, you are beautiful," he said in his most sincere voice.

"Call me," she said timidly.

Jake beamed. "We'll see you, Mariana," he said holding out his hand. Her hand felt so warm and soft he felt like he'd been kissed.

Back in his car he took a moment or two to feel both proud and sad about his performance. Then he watched the rear view mirror as Mariana pulled up behind him. She was writing down the license plate numbers on his Buick, ones that he'd taken off a junk because the ones that belonged to his had expired so long ago. He turned the ignition key and revved the big engine and clicked into drive. His sense of freedom swelled as he drove into the now moving street traffic, though he couldn't stop the thought about that FM stereo radio and crushed velvet interior and the new car smell that would even make it better.

❀ ❀ ❀

# CHARLOTTE PERKINS GILMAN

## *The Yellow Wallpaper* (1892)

It is very seldom that mere ordinary people like John and myself secure ancestral halls for the summer.

A colonial mansion, a hereditary estate, I would say a haunted house and reach the height of romantic felicity—but that would be asking too much of fate!

Still I will proudly declare that there is something queer about it.

Else, why should it be let so cheaply? And why have stood so long untenanted?

John laughs at me, of course, but one expects that.

John is practical in the extreme. He has no patience with faith, an intense horror of superstition, and he scoffs openly at any talk of things not to be felt and seen and put down in figures.

John is a physician, and *perhaps*—(I would not say it to a living soul, of course, but this is dead paper and a great relief to my mind)—*perhaps* that is one reason I do not get well faster.

You see, he does not believe I am sick! And what can one do?

If a physician of high standing, and one's own husband, assures friends and relatives that there is really nothing the matter with one but temporary nervous depression—a slight hysterical tendency—what is one to do?

My brother is also a physician, and also of high standing, and he says the same thing.

So I take phosphates or phosphites—whichever it is—and tonics, and air and exercise, and journeys, and am absolutely forbidden to "work" until I am well again.

Personally, I disagree with their ideas.

Personally, I believe that congenial work, with excitement and change, would do me good.

But what is one to do?

I did write for a while in spite of them; but it *does* exhaust me a good deal—having to be so sly about it, or else meet with heavy opposition.

I sometimes fancy that in my condition, if I had less opposition and more society and stimulus—but John says the very worst thing I can do is to think about my condition, and I confess it always makes me feel bad.

So I will let it alone and talk about the house.

The most beautiful place! It is quite alone, standing well back from the road, quite three miles from the village. It makes me think of English places that you read about, for there are hedges and walls and gates that lock, and lots of separate little houses for the gardeners and people.

There is a *delicious* garden! I never saw such a garden—large and shady, full of box-bordered paths, and lined with long grape-covered arbors with seats under them.

There were greenhouses, but they are all broken now.

There was some legal trouble, I believe, something about the heirs and co-heirs; anyhow, the place has been empty for years.

That spoils my ghostliness, I am afraid, but I don't care—there is something strange about the house—I can feel it.

I even said so to John one moonlight evening, but he said what I felt was a draught, and shut the window.

I get unreasonably angry with John sometimes. I'm sure I never used to be so sensitive. I think it is due to this nervous condition.

But John says if I feel so I shall neglect proper self-control; so I take pains to control myself—before him, at least, and that makes me very tired.

I don't like our room a bit. I wanted one downstairs that opened onto the piazza and had roses all over the window, and such pretty old-fashioned chintz hangings! But John would not hear of it.

He said there was only one window and not room for two beds, and no near room for him if he took another.

He is very careful and loving, and hardly lets me stir without special direction.

I have a schedule prescription for each hour in the day; he takes all care from me, and so I feel basely ungrateful not to value it more.

He said he came here solely on my account, that I was to have perfect rest and all the air I could get. "Your exercise depends on your strength, my dear," said he, "and your food somewhat on your appetite; but air you can absorb all the time." So we took the nursery at the top of the house.

It is a big, airy room, the whole floor nearly, with windows that look all ways, and air and sunshine galore. It was nursery first, and then playroom and gymnasium, I should judge, for the windows are barred for little children, and there are rings and things in the walls.

The paint and paper look as if a boys' school had used it. It is stripped off—the paper—in great patches all around the head of my bed, about as far as I can reach, and in a great place on the other side of the room low down. I never saw a worse paper in my life. One of those sprawling, flamboyant patterns committing every artistic sin.

It is dull enough to confuse the eye in following, pronounced enough constantly to irritate and provoke study, and when you follow the lame uncertain curves for a little distance they suddenly commit suicide—plunge off at outrageous angles, destroy themselves in unheard-of contradictions.

The color is repellent, almost revolting: a smouldering unclean yellow, strangely faded by the slow-turning sunlight. It is a dull yet lurid orange in some places, a sickly sulphur tint in others.

No wonder the children hated it! I should hate it myself if I had to live in this room long.

There comes John, and I must put this away—he hates to have me write a word.

We have been here two weeks, and I haven't felt like writing before, since that first day.

I am sitting by the window now, up in this atrocious nursery, and there is nothing to hinder my writing as much as I please, save lack of strength.

John is away all day, and even some nights when his cases are serious.

I am glad my case is not serious!

But these nervous troubles are dreadfully depressing.

John does not know how much I really suffer. He knows there is no reason to suffer, and that satisfies him.

Of course it is only nervousness. It does weigh on me so not to do my duty in any way!

I meant to be such a help to John, such a real rest and comfort, and here I am a comparative burden already!

Nobody would believe what an effort it is to do what little I am able—to dress and entertain, and order things.

It is fortunate Mary is so good with the baby. Such a dear baby!

And yet I *cannot* be with him, it makes me so nervous.

I suppose John never was nervous in his life. He laughs at me so about this wallpaper!

At first he meant to repaper the room, but afterward he said that I was letting it get the better of me, and that nothing was worse for a nervous patient than to give way to such fancies.

He said that after the wallpaper was changed it would be the heavy bedstead, and then the barred windows, and then that gate at the head of the stairs, and so on.

"You know the place is doing you good," he said, "and really, dear, I don't care to renovate the house just for a three months' rental."

"Then do let us go downstairs," I said. "There are such pretty rooms there."

Then he took me in his arms and called me a blessed little goose, and said he would go down cellar, if I wished, and have it whitewashed into the bargain.

But he is right enough about the beds and windows and things.

It is as airy and comfortable a room as anyone need wish, and, of course, I would not be so silly as to make him uncomfortable just for a whim.

I'm really getting quite fond of the big room, all but that horrid paper.

Out of one window I can see the garden—those mysterious deep-shaded arbors, the riotous old-fashioned flowers, and bushes and gnarly trees.

Out of another I get a lovely view of the bay and a little private wharf belonging to the estate. There is a beautiful shaded lane that runs down there from the house. I always fancy I see people walking in these numerous paths and arbors, but John has cautioned me not to give way to fancy in the least. He says that with my imaginative power and habit of story-making, a nervous weakness like mine is sure to lead to all manner of excited fancies, and that I ought to use my will and good sense to check the tendency. So I try.

I think sometimes that if I were only well enough to write a little it would relieve the press of ideas and rest me.

But I find I get pretty tired when I try.

It is so discouraging not to have any advice and companionship about my work. When I get really well, John says we will ask Cousin Henry and Julia down for a long visit; but he says he would as soon put fireworks in my pillow-case as to let me have those stimulating people about now.

I wish I could get well faster.

But I must not think about that. This paper looks to me as if it *knew* what a vicious influence it had!

There is a recurrent spot where the pattern lolls like a broken neck and two bulbous eyes stare at you upside down.

I get positively angry with the impertinence of it and the everlastingness. Up and down and sideways they crawl, and those absurd unblinking eyes are everywhere. There is one place where two breadths didn't match, and the eyes go all up and down the line, one a little higher than the other.

I never saw so much expression in an inanimate thing before, and we all know how much expression they have! I used to lie awake as a child and get more entertainment and terror out of blank walls and plain furniture than most children could find in a toy-store.

I remember what a kindly wink the knobs of our big old bureau used to have, and there was one chair that always seemed like a strong friend.

I used to feel that if any of the other things looked too fierce I could always hop into that chair and be safe.

The furniture in this room is no worse than inharmonious, however, for we had to bring it all from downstairs. I suppose when this was used as a playroom they had to take the nursery things out, and no wonder! I never saw such ravages as the children have made here.

The wallpaper, as I said before, is torn off in spots, and it sticketh closer than a brother—they must have had perseverance as well as hatred.

Then the floor is scratched and gouged and splintered, the plaster itself is dug out here and there, and this great heavy bed, which is all we found in the room, looks as if it had been through the wars.

But I don't mind it a bit—only the paper.

There comes John's sister. Such a dear girl as she is, and so careful of me! I must not let her find me writing.

She is a perfect and enthusiastic housekeeper, and hopes for no better profession. I verily believe she thinks it is the writing which made me sick!

But I can write when she is out, and see her a long way off from these windows.

There is one that commands the road, a lovely shaded winding road, and one that just looks off over the country. A lovely country, too, full of great elms and velvet meadows.

This wallpaper has a kind of sub-pattern in a different shade, a particularly irritating one, for you can only see it in certain lights, and not clearly then.

But in the places where it isn't faded and where the sun is just so—I can see a strange, provoking, formless sort of figure that seems to skulk about behind that silly and conspicuous front design.

There's sister on the stairs!

Well, the Fourth of July is over! The people are all gone, and I am tired out. John thought it might do me good to see a little company, so we just had Mother and Nellie and the children down for a week.

Of course I didn't do a thing. Jennie sees to everything now.

But it tired me all the same.

John says if I don't pick up faster he shall send me to Weir Mitchell[1] in the fall.

But I don't want to go there at all. I had a friend who was in his hands once, and she says he is just like John and my brother, only more so!

Besides, it is such an undertaking to go so far.

I don't feel as if it was worthwhile to turn my hand over for anything, and I'm getting dreadfully fretful and querulous.

I cry at nothing, and cry most of the time.

Of course I don't when John is here, or anybody else, but when I am alone.

And I am alone a good deal just now. John is kept in town very often by serious cases, and Jennie is good and lets me alone when I want her to.

So I walk a little in the garden or down that lovely lane, sit on the porch under the roses, and lie down up here a good deal.

I'm getting really fond of the room in spite of the wallpaper. Perhaps *because* of the wallpaper.

It dwells in my mind so!

I lie here on this great immovable bed—it is nailed down, I believe—and follow that pattern about by the hour. It is as good as gymnastics, I assure you. I start, we'll say, at the bottom, down in the corner over there where it has not been touched, and I determine for the thousandth time that I *will* follow that pointless pattern to some sort of a conclusion.

I know a little of the principle of design, and I know this thing was not arranged on any laws of radiation, or alternation, or repetition, or symmetry, or anything else that I ever heard of.

It is repeated, of course, by the breadths, but not otherwise.

Looked at in one way, each breadth stands alone; the bloated curves and flourishes—a kind of "debased Romanesque" with delirium tremens—go waddling up and down in isolated columns of fatuity.

But, on the other hand, they connect diagonally, and the sprawling outlines run off in great slanting waves of optic horror, like a lot of wallowing sea-weeds in full chase.

The whole thing goes horizontally, too, at least it seems so, and I exhaust myself trying to distinguish the order of its going in that direction.

They have used a horizontal breadth for a frieze, and that adds wonderfully to the confusion.

There is one end of the room where it is almost intact, and there, when the crosslights fade and the low sun shines directly upon it, I can almost fancy radi-

---

[1] American neurologist (1829–1914) who treated Gilman.

ation after all—the interminable grotesque seems to form around a common center and rush off in headlong plunges of equal distraction.

It makes me tired to follow it. I will take a nap, I guess.

I don't know why I should write this.

I don't want to.

I don't feel able.

And I know John would think it absurd. But I *must* say what I feel and think in some way—it is such a relief!

But the effort is getting to be greater than the relief.

Half the time now I am awfully lazy, and lie down ever so much. John says I mustn't lose my strength, and has me take cod liver oil and lots of tonics and things, to say nothing of ale and wine and rare meat.

Dear John! He loves me very dearly, and hates to have me sick. I tried to have a real earnest reasonable talk with him the other day, and tell him how I wish he would let me go and make a visit to Cousin Henry and Julia.

But he said I wasn't able to go, nor able to stand it after I got there; and I did not make out a very good case for myself, for I was crying before I had finished.

It is getting to be a great effort for me to think straight. Just this nervous weakness, I suppose.

And dear John gathered me up in his arms, and just carried me upstairs and laid me on the bed, and sat by me and read to me till it tired my head.

He said I was his darling and his comfort and all he had, and that I must take care of myself for his sake, and keep well.

He says no one but myself can help me out of it, that I must use my will and self-control and not let any silly fancies run away with me.

There's one comfort—the baby is well and happy, and does not have to occupy this nursery with the horrid wallpaper.

If we had not used it, that blessed child would have! What a fortunate escape! Why, I wouldn't have a child of mine, an impressionable little thing, live in such a room for worlds.

I never thought of it before, but it is lucky that John kept me here after all; I can stand it so much easier than a baby, you see.

Of course I never mention it to them any more—I am too wise—but I keep watch for it all the same.

There are things in that wallpaper that nobody knows about but me, or ever will.

Behind that outside pattern the dim shapes get clearer every day.

It is always the same shape, only very numerous.

And it is like a woman stooping down and creeping about behind that pattern. I don't like it a bit. I wonder—I begin to think—I wish John would take me away from here!

It is so hard to talk with John about my case, because he is so wise, and because he loves me so.

But I tried it last night.

It was moonlight. The moon shines in all around just as the sun does.

I hate to see it sometimes, it creeps so slowly, and always comes in by one window or another.

John was asleep and I hated to waken him, so I kept still and watched the moonlight on that undulating wallpaper till I felt creepy.

The faint figure behind seemed to shake the pattern, just as if she wanted to get out.

I got up softly and went to feel and see if the paper *did* move, and when I came back John was awake.

"What is it, little girl?" he said. "Don't go walking about like that—you'll get cold."

I thought it was a good time to talk, so I told him that I really was not gaining here, and that I wished he would take me away.

"Why, darling!" said he. "Our lease will be up in three weeks, and I can't see how to leave before.

"The repairs are not done at home, and I cannot possibly leave town just now. Of course, if you were in any danger, I could and would, but you really are better, dear, whether you can see it or not. I am a doctor, dear, and I know. You are gaining flesh and color, your appetite is better, I feel really much easier about you."

"I don't weigh a bit more," said I, "nor as much; and my appetite may be better in the evening when you are here but it is worse in the morning when you are away!"

"Bless her little heart!" said he with a big hug. "She shall be as sick as she pleases! But now let's improve the shining hours by going to sleep, and talk about it in the morning!"

"And you won't go away?" I asked gloomily.

"Why, how can I, dear? It is only three weeks more and then we'll take a nice little trip of a few days while Jennie is getting the house ready. Really, dear, you are better!"

"Better in body perhaps—" I began, and stopped short, for he sat up straight and looked at me with such a stern, reproachful look that I could not say another word.

"My darling," said he, "I beg of you, for my sake and for our child's sake, as well as for your own, that you will never for one instant let that idea enter your mind! There is nothing so dangerous, so fascinating, to a temperament like yours. It is a false and foolish fancy. Can you not trust me as a physician when I tell you so?"

So of course I said no more on that score, and we went to sleep before long. He thought I was asleep first, but I wasn't, and lay there for hours trying to decide whether that front pattern and the back pattern really did move together or separately.

On a pattern like this, by daylight, there is a lack of sequence, a defiance of law, that is a constant irritant to a normal mind.

The color is hideous enough, and unreliable enough, and infuriating enough, but the pattern is torturing.

You think you have mastered it, but just as you get well under way in following, it turns a back-somersault and there you are. It slaps you in the face, knocks you down, and tramples upon you. It is like a bad dream.

The outside pattern is a florid arabesque, reminding one of a fungus. If you can imagine a toadstool in joints, an interminable string of toadstools, budding and sprouting in endless convolutions—why, that is something like it.

That is, sometimes!

There is one marked peculiarity about this paper, a thing nobody seems to notice but myself, and that is that it changes as the light changes.

When the sun shoots in through the east window—I always watch for that first long, straight ray—it changes so quickly that I never can quite believe it.

That is why I watch it always.

By moonlight—the moon shines in all night when there is a moon—I wouldn't know it was the same paper.

At night in any kind of light, in twilight, candlelight, lamplight, and worst of all by moonlight, it becomes bars! The outside pattern, I mean, and the woman behind it is as plain as can be.

I didn't realize for a long time what the thing was that showed behind, that dim sub-pattern, but now I am quite sure it is a woman.

By daylight she is subdued, quiet. I fancy it is the pattern that keeps her so still. It is so puzzling. It keeps me quiet by the hour.

I lie down ever so much now. John says it is good for me, and to sleep all I can.

Indeed he started the habit by making me lie down for an hour after each meal.

It is a very bad habit, I am convinced, for you see, I don't sleep.

And that cultivates deceit, for I don't tell them I'm awake—oh, no!

The fact is I am getting a little afraid of John.

He seems very queer sometimes, and even Jennie has an inexplicable look.

It strikes me occasionally, just as a scientific hypothesis, that perhaps it is the paper!

I have watched John when he did not know I was looking, and come into the room suddenly on the most innocent excuses, and I've caught him several times *looking at the paper!* And Jennie too. I caught Jennie with her hand on it once.

She didn't know I was in the room, and when I asked her in a quiet, a very quiet voice, with the most restrained manner possible, what she was doing with the paper, she turned around as if she had been caught stealing, and looked quite angry—asked me why I should frighten her so!

Then she said that the paper stained everything it touched, that she had found yellow smooches on all my clothes and John's and she wished we would be more careful!

Did not that sound innocent? But I know she was studying that pattern, and I am determined that nobody shall find it out but myself.

Life is very much more exciting now than it used to be. You see, I have something more to expect, to look forward to, to watch. I really do eat better, and am more quiet than I was.

John is so pleased to see me improve! He laughed a little the other day, and said I seemed to be flourishing in spite of my wallpaper.

I turned it off with a laugh. I had no intention of telling him it was *because* of the wallpaper—he would make fun of me. He might even want to take me away.

I don't want to leave now until I have found it out. There is a week more, and I think that will be enough.

I'm feeling so much better!

I don't sleep much at night, for it is so interesting to watch developments; but I sleep a good deal during the daytime.

In the daytime it is tiresome and perplexing.

There are always new shoots on the fungus, and new shades of yellow all over it. I cannot keep count of them, though I have tried conscientiously.

It is the strangest yellow, that wallpaper! It makes me think of all the yellow things I ever saw—not beautiful ones like buttercups, but old, foul, bad yellow things.

But there is something else about that paper—the smell! I noticed it the moment we came into the room, but with so much air and sun it was not bad. Now we have had a week of fog and rain, and whether the windows are open or not, the smell is here.

It creeps all over the house.

I find it hovering in the dining-room, skulking in the parlor, hiding in the hall, lying in wait for me on the stairs.

It gets into my hair.

Even when I go to ride, if I turn my head suddenly and surprise it—there is that smell!

Such a peculiar odor, too! I have spent hours in trying to analyze it, to find what it smelled like.

It is not bad—at first—and very gentle, but quite the subtlest, most enduring odor I ever met.

In this damp weather it is awful. I wake up in the night and find it hanging over me.

It used to disturb me at first. I thought seriously of burning the house—to reach the smell.

But now I am used to it. The only thing I can think of that it is like is the *color* of the paper! A yellow smell.

There is a very funny mark on this wall, low down, near the mopboard. A streak that runs round the room. It goes behind every piece of furniture, except the bed, a long, straight, even *smooch,* as if it had been rubbed over and over.

I wonder how it was done and who did it, and what they did it for. Round and round and round—round and round and round—it makes me dizzy!

I really have discovered something at last.

Through watching so much at night, when it changes so, I have finally found out.

The front pattern *does* move—and no wonder! The woman behind shakes it!

Sometimes I think there are a great many women behind, and sometimes only one, and she crawls around fast, and her crawling shakes it all over.

Then in the very bright spots she keeps still, and in the very shady spots she just takes hold of the bars and shakes them hard.

And she is all the time trying to climb through. But nobody could climb through that pattern—it strangles so; I think that is why it has so many heads.

They get through, and then the pattern strangles them off and turns them upside down, and makes their eyes white!

If those heads were covered or taken off it would not be half so bad.

I think that woman gets out in the daytime!

And I'll tell you why—privately—I've seen her!

I can see her out of every one of my windows!

It is the same woman, I know, for she is always creeping, and most women do not creep by daylight.

I see her in that long shaded lane, creeping up and down. I see her in those dark grape arbors, creeping all around the garden.

I see her on that long road under the trees, creeping along, and when a carriage comes she hides under the blackberry vines.

I don't blame her a bit. It must be very humiliating to be caught creeping by daylight!

I always lock the door when I creep by daylight. I can't do it at night, for I know John would suspect something at once.

And John is so queer now that I don't want to irritate him. I wish he would take another room! Besides, I don't want anybody to get that woman out at night but myself.

I often wonder if I could see her out of all the windows at once.

But, turn as fast as I can, I can only see out of one at one time.

And though I always see her, she *may* be able to creep faster than I can turn! I have watched her sometimes away off in the open country, creeping as fast as a cloud shadow in a wind.

If only that top pattern could be gotten off from the under one! I mean to try it, little by little.

I have found out another funny thing, but I shan't tell it this time! It does not do to trust people too much.

There are only two more days to get this paper off, and I believe John is beginning to notice. I don't like the look in his eyes.

And I heard him ask Jennie a lot of professional questions about me. She had a very good report to give.

She said I slept a good deal in the daytime.

John knows I don't sleep very well at night, for all I'm so quiet!

He asked me all sorts of questions, too, and pretended to be very loving and kind. As if I couldn't see through him!

Still, I don't wonder he acts so, sleeping under this paper for three months.

It only interests me, but I feel sure John and Jennie are affected by it. Hurrah! This is the last day, but it is enough. John is to stay in town over night, and won't be out until this evening.

Jennie wanted to sleep with me—the sly thing; but I told her I should undoubtedly rest better for a night all alone.

That was clever, for really I wasn't alone a bit! As soon as it was moonlight and that poor thing began to crawl and shake the pattern, I got up and ran to help her.

I pulled and she shook. I shook and she pulled, and before morning we had peeled off yards of that paper.

A strip about as high as my head and half around the room.

And then when the sun came and that awful pattern began to laugh at me, I declared I would finish it today!

We go away tomorrow, and they are moving all my furniture down again to leave things as they were before.

Jennie looked at the wall in amazement, but I told her merrily that I did it out of pure spite at the vicious thing.

She laughed and said she wouldn't mind doing it herself, but I must not get tired.

How she betrayed herself that time!

But I am here, and no person touches this paper but Me—not *alive!*

She tried to get me out of the room—it was too patent! But I said it was so quiet and empty and clean now that I believed I would lie down again and sleep all I could, and not to wake me even for dinner—I would call when I woke.

So now she is gone, and the servants are gone, and the things are gone, and there is nothing left but that great bedstead nailed down, with the canvas mattress we found on it.

We shall sleep downstairs tonight, and take the boat home tomorrow.

I quite enjoy the room, now it is bare again.

How those children did tear about here!

This bedstead is fairly gnawed!

But I must get to work.

I have locked the door and thrown the key down into the front path.

I don't want to go out, and I don't want to have anybody come in, till John comes.

I want to astonish him.

I've got a rope up here that even Jennie did not find. If that woman does get out, and tries to get away, I can tie her!

But I forgot I could not reach far without anything to stand on!

This bed will *not* move!

I tried to lift and push it until I was lame, and then I got so angry I bit off a little piece at one corner—but it hurt my teeth.

Then I peeled off all the paper I could reach standing on the floor. It sticks horribly and the pattern just enjoys it! All those strangled heads and bulbous eyes and waddling fungus growths just shriek with derision!

I am getting angry enough to do something desperate. To jump out of the window would be admirable exercise, but the bars are too strong even to try.

Besides I wouldn't do it. Of course not. I know well enough that a step like that is improper and might be misconstrued.

I don't like to *look* out of the windows even—there are so many of those creeping women, and they creep so fast.

I wonder if they all come out of that wallpaper as I did?

But I am securely fastened now by my well-hidden rope—you don't get *me* out in the road there!

I suppose I shall have to get back behind the pattern when it comes night, and that is hard!

It is so pleasant to be out in this great room and creep around as I please!

I don't want to go outside. I won't, even if Jennie asks me to.

For outside you have to creep on the ground, and everything is green instead of yellow.

But here I can creep smoothly on the floor, and my shoulder just fits in that long smooch around the wall, so I cannot lose my way.

Why, there's John at the door!

It is no use, young man, you can't open it!

How he does call and pound!

Now he's crying to Jennie for an axe.

It would be a shame to break down that beautiful door!

"John, dear!" said I in the gentlest voice. "The key is down by the front steps, under a plantain leaf!"

That silenced him for a few moments.

Then he said, very quietly indeed, "Open the door, my darling!"

"I can't," said I. "The key is down by the front door under a plantain leaf!" And then I said it again, several times, very gently and slowly, and said it so often that he had to go and see, and he got it of course, and came in. He stopped short by the door.

"What is the matter?" he cried. "For God's sake, what are you doing!"

I kept on creeping just the same, but I looked at him over my shoulder.

"I've got out at last," said I, "in spite of you and Jane. And I've pulled off most of the paper, so you can't put me back!"

Now why should that man have fainted? But he did, and right across my path by the wall, so that I had to creep over him every time!

### Study and Discussion Questions

1. What do the narrator and the woman in the wallpaper have in common?
2. Is the narrator right to be suspicious of her husband or is her suspicion simply a manifestation of her nervous ailment?
3. Why is the narrator so tired?
4. What kind of person does John want his wife to be? How does he try to maneuver her into being that?
5. What is the significance of the fact that the narrator's room was originally a nursery?
6. "There comes John, and I must put this away—he hates to have me write a word." Why doesn't John want her to write? Why does she disagree with him?
7. How does the way the narrator sees and feels about the yellow wallpaper change during the story?

**Suggestions for Writing**

1. Who is John? List the words that describe him. Write a brief character sketch.
2. Gilman wrote this story in 1890 as a warning about a treatment for nervous depression fashionable then. Gilman herself was told to "live as domestic a life as possible," to "have but two hours' intellectual life a day" and "never to touch pen, brush, or pencil again." Discuss the way in which the treatment which is supposed to cure the narrator worsens her condition, and speculate about the reasons.
3. What is wrong with this marriage?

**Critical Resources**

1. Dock, Julie, ed. *"The Yellow Wallpaper" and the History of Its Publication and Reception: A Critical Edition and Casebook.* University Park: U of Pennsylvania P, 1998.
2. Golden, Catherine, ed. *The Captive Imagination: A Casebook on The Yellow Wallpaper.* New York: Feminist Press at City University, 1992.
3. Karpinsky, Joanne, ed. *Critical Essays on Charlotte Perkins Gilman.* Toronto: G.K. Hall, 1992.

❋ ❋ ❋

**JUDY GRAHN**

## *Boys at the Rodeo* (1978)

A lot of people have spent time on some women's farm this summer of 1972 and one day six of us decide to go to the rodeo. We are all mature and mostly in our early thirties. We wear levis and shirts and short hair. Susan has shaved her head.

The man at the gate, who looks like a cousin of the sheriff, is certain we are trying to get in for free. It must have been something in the way we are walking. He stares into Susan's face. "I know you're at least fourteen," he says. He slaps her shoulder, in that comradely way men have with each other. That's when we know he thinks we are boys.

"You're over thirteen," he says to Wendy.

"You're over thirteen," he says to me. He examines each of us closely, and sees only that we have been outdoors, are muscled, and look him directly in the eye. Since we are too short to be men, we must be boys. Everyone else at the rodeo are girls.

We decide to play it straight, so to speak. We make up boys' names for each other. Since Wendy has missed the episode with Susan at the gate, I slap her on the shoulder to demonstrate. "This is what he did." Slam. She never missed a step. It didn't feel bad to me at all. We laugh uneasily. We have achieved the status of fourteen year old boys, what a disguise for travelling through the world. I split into two pieces for the rest of the evening, and have never decided if it is worse to be 31 years old and called a boy or to be 31 years old and called a girl.

Irregardless, we are starved so we decide to eat, and here we have the status of boys for real. It seems to us that all the men and all the women attached to the men and most of the children are eating steak dinner plates; and we are the only women not attached to men. We eat hot dogs, which cost one tenth as much. A man who has taken a woman to the rodeo on this particular day has to have at least $12.00 to spend. So he has charge of all of her money and some of our money too, for we average $3.00 apiece and have taken each other to the rodeo.

Hot dogs in hand we escort ourselves to the wooden stands, and first is the standing up ceremony. We are pledging allegiance for the way of life—the competition, the supposed masculinity and pretty girls. I stand up, cursing, pretending I'm in some other country. One which has not been rediscovered. The loudspeaker plays Anchors Aweigh, that's what I like about rodeos, always something unexpected. At the last one I attended in another state the men on horses threw candy and nuts to the kids, chipping their teeth and breaking their noses. Who is it, I wonder, that has put these guys in charge. Even quiet mothers raged over that episode.

Now it is time for the rodeo queen contest, and a display of four very young women on horses. They are judged for queen 30% on their horse*man*ship and 70% on the number of queen tickets which people bought on their behalf to 'elect' them. Talk about stuffed ballot boxes. I notice the winner as usual is the one on the registered thoroughbred whose daddy owns tracts and tracts of something—lumber, minerals, animals. His family name is all over the county.

The last loser sits well on a scrubby little pony and lives with her aunt and uncle. I pick her for the dyke even though it is speculation without clues. I can't help it, it's a pleasant habit. I wish I could give her a ribbon. Not for being a dyke, but for sitting on her horse well. For believing there ever was a contest, for not being the daughter of anyone who owns thousands of acres of anything.

Now the loudspeaker announces the girls' barrel races, which is the only grown women's event. It goes first because it is not really a part of the rodeo, but more like a mildly athletic variation of a parade by women to introduce the real thing. Like us boys in the stand, the girls are simply bearing witness to someone else's act.

The voice is booming that barrel racing is a new, modern event, that these young women are the wives and daughters of cowboys, and barrel racing is a way for them to participate in their own right. How generous of these northern cowboys to have resurrected barrel racing for women and to have forgotten the hard roping and riding which women always used to do in rodeos when I was younger. Even though I was a town child, I heard thrilling rumors of the all-women's rodeo in Texas, including that the finest brahma bull rider in all of Texas was a forty year old woman who weighed a hundred pounds.

Indeed, my first lover's first lover was a big heavy woman who was normally slow as a cold python, but she was just hell when she got up on a horse. She could rope and tie a calf faster than any cowboy within 500 miles of Sweetwater, Texas. That's what the West Texas dykes said, and they never lied about anything as important to them as calf roping, or the differences between women and men. And what about that news story I had heard recently on the radio, about a bull rider who was eight months pregnant? The newsman just had apoplectic fits over her, but not me. I was proud of her. She makes me think of all of us who have had our insides so overly protected from jarring we cannot possibly get through childbirth without an anesthetic.

While I have been grumbling these thoughts to myself, three barrels have been set up in a big triangle on the field, and the women one by one have raced their horses around each one and back to start. The trick is to turn your horse as sharply as possible without overthrowing the barrel.

After this moderate display, the main bulk of the rodeo begins, with calf roping, bronco riding, bull riding. It's a very male show during which the men demonstrate their various abilities at immobilizing, cornering, maneuvering and conquering cattle of every age.

A rodeo is an interminable number of roped and tied calves, ridden and unridden broncoes. The repetition is broken by a few antics from the agile, necessary clown. His long legs nearly envelope the little jackass he is riding for the satire of it.

After a number of hours they produce an event I have never seen before—goat tying. This is for the girls eleven and twelve. They use one goat for fourteen participants. The goat is supposed to be held in place on a rope by a large man on horseback. Each girl rushes out in a long run half way across the field, grabs the animal, knocks it down, ties its legs together. Sometimes the man lets his horse drift so the goat pulls six or eight feet away from her, something no one would allow to happen in a male event. Many of the girls take over a full minute just to do their tying, and the fact that only one goat has been used makes everybody say, 'poor goat, poor goat,' and start laughing. This has become the real comedy event of the evening, and the purpose clearly is to show how badly girls do in the rodeo.

Only one has broken through this purpose to the other side. One small girl is not disheartened by the years of bad training, the ridiculous crossfield run, the laughing superior man on his horse, *or* the shape-shifting goat. She downs it in a beautiful flying tackle. This makes me whisper, as usual, 'that's the dyke,' but for the rest of it we watch the girls look ludicrous, awkward, outclassed and totally dominated by the large handsome man on horse. In the stands we six boys drink beer in disgust, groan and hug our breasts, hold our heads and twist our faces at each other in embarrassment.

As the calf roping starts up again, we decide to use our disguises to walk around the grounds. Making our way around to the cowboy side of the arena, we pass the intricate mazes of rail where the stock is stored, to the chutes where they are loading the bull riders onto the bulls.

I wish to report that although we pass by dozens of men, and although we have pressed against wild horses and have climbed on rails overlooking thousands of pounds of angry animal flesh, though we touch ropes and halters, we are never once warned away, never told that this is not the proper place for us, that we had better get back for our own good, are not safe, etc., none of the dozens of warnings and threats we would have gotten if we had been recognized as thirty one year old girls instead of fourteen year old boys. It is a most interesting way to wander around the world for the day.

We examine everything closely. The brahma bulls are in the chutes, ready to be released into the ring. They are bulky, kindly looking creatures with rolling eyes; they resemble overgrown pigs. One of us whispers, "Aren't those the same kind of cattle that walk around all over the streets in India and never hurt anybody?"

Here in the chutes made exactly their size, they are converted into wild antagonistic beasts by means of a nasty belt around their loins, squeezed tight to mash their most tender testicles just before they are released into the ring. This torture is supplemented by a jolt of electricity from an electric cattle prod to make sure they come out bucking. So much for the rodeo as a great drama between man and nature.

A pale, nervous cowboy sits on the bull's back with one hand in a glove hooked under a strap around the bull's midsection. He gains points by using his spurs during the ride. He has to remain on top until the timing buzzer buzzes a few seconds after he and the bull plunge out of the gate. I had always considered it the most exciting event.

Around the fence sit many eager young men watching, helping, and getting in the way. We are easily accepted among them. How depressing this can be.

Out in the arena a dismounted cowboy reaches over and slaps his horse fiercely on the mouth because it has turned its head the wrong way.

I squat down peering through the rails where I see the neat, tight-fitting pants of two young men standing provocatively chest to chest.

"Don't you think Henry's a queer," one says with contempt.

"Hell, I *know* he's a queer," the other says. They hold an informal spitting contest for the punctuation. Meantime their eyes have brightened and their fronts are moving toward each other in their clean, smooth shirts. I realize they are flirting with each other, using Henry to bring up the dangerous subject of themselves. I am remembering all the gay cowboys I ever knew. This is one of the things I like about cowboys. They don't wear those beautiful pearl button shirts and tight levis for nothing.

As the events inside the arena subside, we walk down to a roped off pavillion where there is a dance. The band consists of one portly, bouncing enthusiastic man of middle age who is singing with great spirit into the microphone. The rest of the band are three grim, lean young men over fourteen. The drummer drums angrily, while jerking his head behind himself as though searching the air for someone who is already two hours late and had seriously promised to take him away from here. The two guitar players are sleepwalking from the feet up with their eyes so glassy you could read by them.

A redhaired man appears, surrounded by redhaired children who ask, "Are you drunk, Daddy?"

"No, I am not drunk," Daddy says.

"Can we have some money?"

"No," Daddy says, "I am not drunk enough to give you any money."

During a break in the music the redhaired man asks the bandleader where he got his band.

"Where did I get this band?" the bandleader puffs up, "I raised this band myself. These are all my sons—I raised this band myself." The redhaired man is so very impressed he is nearly bowing and kissing the hand of the bandleader, as they repeat this conversation two or three times. "This is *my* band," the bandleader says, and the two guitar players exchange grim and glassy looks.

Next the bandleader has announced "Okie From Muskogee," a song intended to portray the white country morality of cowboys. The crowd does not respond but he sings enthusiastically anyway. Two of his more alert sons drag themselves to the microphone to wail that they don't smoke marijuana in Muskogee—as those hippies down in San Francisco do, and they certainly don't. From the look of it they shoot hard drugs and pop pills.

In the middle of the song a very drunk thirteen year old boy has staggered up to Wendy, pounding her on the shoulder and exclaiming, "Can you dig it, brother?" Later she tells me she has never been called brother before, and she likes it. Her first real identification as one of the brothers, in the brotherhood of man.

We boys begin to walk back to our truck, past a cowboy vomiting on his own pretty boots, past another lying completely under a car. Near our truck, a young man has calf-roped a young woman. She shrieks for him to stop, hopping weakly along behind him. This is the first bid for public attention I have seen from any woman here since the barrel race. I understand that this little scene is a re-enactment of the true meaning of the rodeo, and of the conquest of the west. And oh how much I do not want to be her; I do not want to be the conquest of the west.

I am remembering how the clown always seems to be tall and riding on an ass, that must be a way of poking fun at the small and usually dark people who tried to raise sheep or goats or were sod farmers and rode burros instead of tall handsome blond horses, and who were driven under by the beef raisers. And so today we went to a display of cattle handling instead of a sheep shearing or a goat milking contest—or to go into even older ghost territory, a corn dance, or acorn gathering. . . .

As we reach the truck, the tall man passes with the rodeo queen, who must surely be his niece, or something. All this non-contest, if it is for anyone, must certainly be for him. As a boy, I look at him. He is his own spitting image, of what is manly and white and masterly, so tall in his high heels, so *well horsed*. His manner portrays his theory of life as the survival of the fittest against wild beasts, and all the mythical rest of us who are too female or dark, not straight, or much too native to the earth to now be trusted as more than witnesses, flags, cheerleaders and unwilling stock.

As he passes, we step out of the way and I am glad we are in our disguise. I hate to step out of his way as a full grown woman, one who hasn't enough class status to warrant his thinly polite chivalry. He has knocked me off the sidewalk of too many towns, too often.

Yet somewhere in me I know I have always wanted to be manly, what I mean is having that expression of courage, control, coordination, ability I associate with men. To *provide*.

But here I am in this truck, not a man at all, a fourteen year old boy only. Tomorrow is my thirty second birthday. We six snuggle together in the bed of this rickety truck which is our world for the time being. We are headed back to the bold and shakey adventures of our all-women's farm, our all-women's households and companies, our expanding minds, ambitions and bodies, we who are neither male nor female at this moment in the pageant world, who are not the rancher's wife, mother earth, Virgin Mary or the rodeo queen—we who are really the one who took her self seriously, who once took an all out dive at the goat believing that the odds were square and that she was truly in the contest.

And now that we know it is not a contest, just a play—we have run off with the goat ourselves to try another way of life.

Because I certainly do not want to be a 32 year old girl, or calf either, and I certainly also do always remember Gertrude Stein's[1] beautiful dykely voice saying, what is the use of being a boy if you grow up to be a man.


### Study and Discussion Questions

1. Why does the man at the gate decide the women are boys?
2. What kind of freedom does being seen as 14-year-old boys give to these women in their thirties?
3. By providing a narrator who is an outsider to the scene, Grahn is able to penetrate the mystique of the rodeo. Discuss how this works in the section on the brahma bull riding.
4. Is Grahn only talking about the rodeo in this story or are there larger implications?
5. Why does the narrator award the word *dyke* to one of the losers of the queen contest and to the one girl who takes the goat-tying event seriously?
6. What is the tone of "Boys at the Rodeo"?


### Suggestions for Writing

1. What does Grahn suggest about the rodeo as a male ritual?

---

[1]American writer (1874–1946).

2. If these six women had been seen as "girls," what would their day at the rodeo have been like?
3. Discuss the depiction of the goat-tying event as an example of social criticism.

### Critical Resources

1. Felstiner, John. "Judy Grahn." *Women Writers of the West Coast: Speaking of Their Lives and Careers.* Ed. Marilyn Yalom. Santa Barbara, CA: Capra, 1983. 92–102
2. *Stolen Moments.* (documentary) Director Margaret Wescott. Appearing: Judy Grahn, Audre Lorde, Joan Nestle. 1997. 90 minutes.
3. Whitehead, Kim. *The Feminist Poetry Movement.* Jackson: UP of Mississippi, 1996.

## ERNEST HEMINGWAY

## *Hills Like White Elephants*                                          (1927)

The hills across the valley of the Ebro were long and white. On this side there was no shade and no trees and the station was between two lines of rails in the sun. Close against the side of the station there was the warm shadow of the building and a curtain, made of strings of bamboo beads, hung across the open door into the bar, to keep out flies. The American and the girl with him sat at a table in the shade, outside the building. It was very hot and the express from Barcelona would come in forty minutes. It stopped at this junction for two minutes and went on to Madrid.

"What should we drink?" the girl asked. She had taken off her hat and put it on the table.

"It's pretty hot," the man said.

"Let's drink beer."

"*Dos cervezas,*" the man said into the curtain.

"Big ones?" a woman asked from the doorway.

"Yes. Two big ones."

The woman brought two glasses of beer and two felt pads. She put the felt pads and the beer glasses on the table and looked at the man and the girl. The girl was looking off at the line of hills. They were white in the sun and the country was brown and dry.

"They look like white elephants," she said.

"I've never seen one," the man drank his beer.

"No, you wouldn't have."

"I might have," the man said. "Just because you say I wouldn't have doesn't prove anything."

The girl looked at the bead curtain. "They've painted something on it," she said. "What does it say?"

"Anis del Toro. It's a drink."

"Could we try it?"

The man called "Listen" through the curtain. The woman came out from the bar.

"Four reales."

"We want two Anis del Toro."

"With water?"

"Do you want it with water?"

"I don't know," the girl said. "Is it good with water?"

"It's all right."

"You want them with water?" asked the woman.

"Yes, with water."

"It tastes like licorice," the girl said and put the glass down.

"That's the way with everything."

"Yes," said the girl. "Everything tastes of licorice. Especially all the things you've waited so long for, like absinthe."

"Oh, cut it out."

"You started it," the girl said. "I was being amused. I was having a fine time."

"Well, let's try and have a fine time."

"All right. I was trying. I said the mountains looked like white elephants. Wasn't that bright?"

"That was bright."

"I wanted to try this new drink. That's all we do, isn't it—look at things and try new drinks?"

"I guess so."

The girl looked across at the hills.

"They're lovely hills," she said. "They don't really look like white elephants. I just meant the coloring of their skin through the trees."

"Should we have another drink?"

"All right."

The warm wind blew the bead curtain against the table.

"The beer's nice and cool," the man said.

"It's lovely," the girl said.

"It's really an awfully simple operation, Jig," the man said. "It's not really an operation at all."

The girl looked at the ground the table legs rested on.

"I know you wouldn't mind it, Jig. It's really not anything. It's just to let the air in."

The girl did not say anything.

"I'll go with you and I'll stay with you all the time. They just let the air in and then it's all perfectly natural."

"Then what will we do afterward?"

"We'll be fine afterward. Just like we were before."

"What makes you think so?"

"That's the only thing that bothers us. It's the only thing that's made us unhappy."

The girl looked at the bead curtain, put her hand out and took hold of two of the strings of beads.

"And you think then we'll be all right and be happy."

"I know we will. You don't have to be afraid. I've known lots of people that have done it."

"So have I," said the girl. "And afterward they were all so happy."

"Well," the man said, "if you don't want to you don't have to. I wouldn't have you do it if you don't want to. But I know it's perfectly simple."

"And you really want to?"

"I think it's the best thing to do. But I don't want you to do it if you don't really want to."

"And if I do it you'll be happy and things will be like they were and you'll love me?"

"I love you now. You know I love you."

"I know. But if I do it, then it will be nice again if I say things are like white elephants, and you'll like it?"

"I'll love it. I love it now but I just can't think about it. You know how I get when I worry."

"If I do it you won't ever worry?"

"I won't worry about that because it's perfectly simple."

"Then I'll do it. Because I don't care about me."

"What do you mean?"

"I don't care about me."

"Well, I care about you."

"Oh, yes. But I don't care about me. And I'll do it and then everything will be fine."

"I don't want you to do it if you feel that way."

The girl stood up and walked to the end of the station. Across, on the other side, were fields of grain and trees along the banks of the Ebro. Far away, beyond the river, were mountains. The shadow of a cloud moved across the field of grain and she saw the river through the trees.

"And we could have all this," she said. "And we could have everything and every day we make it more impossible."

"What did you say?"

"I said we could have everything."

"We can have everything."

"No, we can't."

"We can have the whole world."

"No, we can't."

"We can go everywhere."

"No, we can't. It isn't ours any more."

"It's ours."

"No, it isn't. And once they take it away, you never get it back."

"But they haven't taken it away."

"We'll wait and see."

"Come on back in the shade," he said. "You mustn't feel that way."

"I don't feel any way," the girl said. "I just know things."

"I don't want you to do anything that you don't want to do—"

"Nor that isn't good for me," she said. "I know. Could we have another beer?"

"All right. But you've got to realize—"

"I realize," the girl said. "Can't we maybe stop talking?"

They sat down at the table and the girl looked across at the hills on the dry side of the valley and the man looked at her and at the table.

"You've got to realize," he said, "that I don't want you to do it if you don't want to. I'm perfectly willing to go through with it if it means anything to you."

"Doesn't it mean anything to you? We could get along."

"Of course it does. But I don't want anybody but you. I don't want any one else. And I know it's perfectly simple."

"Yes, you know it's perfectly simple."

"It's all right for you to say that, but I do know it."

"Would you do something for me now?"

"I'd do anything for you."

"Would you please please please please please please please stop talking?"

He did not say anything but looked at the bags against the wall of the station. There were labels on them from all the hotels where they had spent nights.

"But I don't want you to," he said, "I don't care anything about it."

"I'll scream," the girl said.

The woman came out through the curtains with two glasses of beer and put them down on the damp felt pads. "The train comes in five minutes," she said.

"What did she say?" asked the girl.

"That the train is coming in five minutes."

The girl smiled brightly at the woman, to thank her.

"I'd better take the bags over to the other side of the station," the man said. She smiled at him.

"All right. Then come back and we'll finish the beer."

He picked up the two heavy bags and carried them around the station to the other tracks. He looked up the tracks but could not see the train. Coming back, he walked through the barroom, where people waiting for the train were drinking. He drank an Anis at the bar and looked at the people. They were all waiting reasonably for the train. He went out through the bead curtain. She was sitting at the table and smiled at him.

"Do you feel better?" he asked.

"I feel fine," she said. "There's nothing wrong with me. I feel fine."

## Study and Discussion Questions

1. What is this couple arguing about? What clues let you know? Why do you think Hemingway doesn't allow his characters to say directly what they are talking about?
2. What is the balance of power between the man and the woman in this story? How does Hemingway construct this balance of power? What factors are involved in the situation? What factors are involved in Hemingway's stylistic choices, including how the two characters are referred to?
3. What effects do the descriptions of the setting have in the midst of this couple's argument?
4. Why this particular title—"Hills Like White Elephants"? What does that mean to you? How does it fit the story?
5. The "girl" says: "That's all we do, isn't it—look at things and try new drinks?" Describe the life they seem to be leading. When do you think this story is set?
6. What is the man's argument? What does he want? Is he conflicted? How is he trying to get his way?
7. What is the woman's argument, or defense? What does she want—Is it possible that she wants more than one thing?
8. How does the lack of attribution in the dialogue affect the story and the way you perceive the characters?

## Suggestions for Writing:

1. Write about communication and miscommunication between men and women, or between couples, from your own experience. How is communication and miscommunication happening in "Hills Like White Elephants"?
2. Jump to six months later and write a scene between the two characters in this story.

## Critical Resources

1. Benson, Jackson, ed. *New Critical Approaches to the Short Stories of Ernest Hemingway.* Durham, NC: Duke UP, 1990.
2. Broer, Lawerence and Gloria Holland, eds. *Hemingway and Women: Female Critics and Female Voices.* Tuscaloosa: U of Alabama P, 2002.
3. Brucolli, Matthew. *Conversations with Ernest Hemingway.* Jackson: U of Mississippi P, 1986.
4. Lynn, Kenneth. *Hemingway.* Cambridge: Harvard UP, 1995.
5. Tyler, Lisa. *Student Companion to Ernest Hemingway.* Westport: Greenwood, 2001.

❀ ❀ ❀

**BRENDAN MATHEWS**

## *My Last Attempt to Explain to You What Happened with the Lion Tamer*                                    (2010)

HE WASN'T EVEN a good lion tamer, not before you showed up. He had always looked the part, with his whip and his chair and his spangled pants, but honestly, watching him in the cage with those lions was like watching a man stagger blindfolded across a four-lane highway. One night in Glens Falls, the chair slipped from his hand, and the cats swatted it around the cage like a chew toy. In Council Bluffs, a claw snapped his patent leather bandolier like an old shoestring. And in Granite City, a lion caught the whip between its jaws and yanked him around the ring like a fish on a line. It was a minor miracle every time he stepped out of the cage—bruised and bleeding, but still intact. He didn't seem to care that the clapping was never the thunderous peal you'd expect when a man emerges from a cage full of beasts, and he didn't care that it petered out before half a minute was up. He'd just stand there with his arms raised, like some avatar of victory, and he'd beam that ivory smile and shake his blond mane. You'd think the lions had just elected him King of the Serengeti.

Looking at the scars and the shredded outfits with their missing sequins and webs of crooked stitching, I'd wonder why the guy was doing this to himself. You told me once that his father was a lion tamer, and that these things run in the family. I don't know. My old man was no clown, but maybe that skips a generation.

The first time I saw you. I was alone behind the big top, adjusting the mix in the confetti buckets. Most of the others were still in bed, nursing hangovers or aching limbs, asking themselves for the ten thousandth time what it was going to take to get moving today. Me, I was up early because no one else would be.

Right away I knew you were no first-of-May, no circus rookie. Five-foot-nothing, barefoot in a leotard, you strutted like you owned not just the big top but the fairgrounds it stood on, like the rest of us better get your say-so before we turned a single somersault.

"You the new girl on the flying trapeze?" I said, although I knew without asking: you smelled like chalk dust and hairspray.

"You the old clown?" you said, eyeing my tattered plaid pants and my flop-collared shirt, my white face and painted-on smile. I danced a little jig, letting my head loll from side to side, and ended with a pratfall—straight down on my keister.

"The one and only." Immediately I wished I hadn't said that.

Still, you smiled. It wasn't a toothy, whole-face-blooming-into-a-laugh sort of smile, but it was a smile. Then without another word you made tracks for the big top.

That confetti wasn't going to mix itself, but how could I take my eyes off you, with your legs like cables of braided silk? It wasn't just that you were beautiful;

there are a lot of pretty ladies in the circus, tattooed and otherwise. It was that strut. I followed you into the tent, and by the time my eyes adjusted to the light filtering through the canvas you were already halfway up the ladder to the high wire. Whoa-ho, I said to myself, a double threat: the tightrope and the trapeze. The wire and the swing.

The roustabouts had started to hoist the net into place, cursing at the lines and jabbering about this broad who shows up out of nowhere and puts them to work right in the middle of a union-mandated coffee break. They were ornery that morning, still grousing about the case of Jonah's luck they'd had with the blow-off in Sandusky—the skies had opened, the canvas became cement-heavy, and the fists of soaked rope that gripped the tent pegs couldn't be pulled apart. Two days later they were still looking for someone to piss on, and a greenhorn tumbler was just the ticket.

"Hey down there," you said, your voice knifing through the morning haze. "I don't want the net!"

They kept hoisting the lines, because it's one thing to perform without a net, but no one practices without one—unless you want your first mistake to be your last. So this time you shouted, "Gentlemen!" and that stopped them in their tracks, because no one ever called them gentlemen. "I said no net!"

The net flopped to the floor, kicking up a fog of sawdust. One of them called you a crazy bitch, but I swear the words were tinged with respect, and even a little awe.

You were at the top of the ladder, and although you could have stepped lightly onto the tightrope, testing its thickness and tension, you raised your arms above your head and cartwheeled to the middle of the wire. I heard one of the razorbacks gasp. Another mumbled something that might have been a curse but could have been a prayer.

And me? My heart burst like a child's balloon. Right then and there I knew I loved you.

I made it a habit to run into you on the midway whenever I scrounged for breakfast. There was always plenty of lukewarm coffee in the pie car, but tracking down a meal that didn't come with a side of day-old funnel cakes was a challenge.

In those early days I wasn't shy about giving advice: watch out for the sword swallowers and the fire eaters, I told you, because they're only interested in one thing. And steer clear of the midget couple, Tom and Tina Thumb. They had each cheated—him with the fat lady, her with the dog-faced boy—but they were as perfectly matched as salt and pepper shakers, and neither could call it quits. But here's something I don't remember, though I've squeezed my brain like a soggy dishrag: Did you ever ask me about him? Did I ever volunteer anything that made you think, why not?

You didn't say much about yourself, and what little you told me didn't add up. Once you said you had been born into the circus, and another time that you'd run away and joined up when you were a little girl. You said your parents were your first audience, and then later that they had never seen you perform. But the one thing you didn't waver on was this: you had never worked with a net.

"It wouldn't count," you said one morning as we set up our breakfast on the counter of the ringtoss booth: bananas looted from dozing monkeys, apples left out for the Arabian stallions, honey from the trailer of the freak show's Bee Man. "It just wouldn't, if you knew you could fall and get right back up like nothing had happened."

"What if you're trying something new?" I said. "You know, in practice." You smirked. "You either know what you're doing, or you don't."

I tried to tell you I knew exactly what you were talking about—that we were like two sides of the same coin, even if it was engraved on one side with some mythic diva and on the flipside with the dull, muddy squiggle of a horse's ass. Still, I knew that when I went out there every night, the only options were mass murder or a public hanging. Either I killed, or I bombed. I don't think you got it, though—then or ever—because in your eyes you were risking the long fall from the top of the tent, and I was just another groundling hoofing it around the center ring. Come to think of it, I don't think you ever really appreciated what the rest of us did. We were just the scenery: the human cannonballs with their nightly blowups; the elephant riders preening like royalty while their pachyderms did the heavy lifting; and the clowns, sweating and grinding for every laugh, our stomachs in knots for fear that this might be the night when nobody laughs and we stand out there naked, wilting under the glare of a thousand cut-the-crap stares. Or maybe that's just me.

Looking back, I don't know what I was expecting—okay, I do, but I was smart enough to understand that it wasn't going to happen without a bop on the head, a bad case of amnesia, and a tropical island where no one could remind you who you really were.

Then came that first night: your big debut.

I should have known something was up when the lion tamer strode out of the cage in better shape than usual. No stitches required. The applause from the local gillies wasn't exactly hearty, but it seemed a little more genuine. Then, as the lights cut out on him, a single spot lasered the ringmaster, who directed the crowd's attention to the uppermost reaches of the tent, where you were frozen in place, the trapeze in your hands. "Ladies and gentlemen! I present to you the aerialist, who dances on the high wire and works magic on the trapeze. The flying girl, the acrobat of the air. Thrill to her breathtaking feats! Gape in amazement as she flirts with death, because folks—hold on to your hats—there's nothing between her and the ground but the force of gravity! That's right; she does it all without a net!" I'd swear the sides of the tent snapped like a ship's sail as the crowd, in one big gasp, sucked the oxygen out of the big top.

You soared. Head over heels—once, twice, a third time—a hundred feet above the floor. There wasn't a sound among the yokels who packed the bleachers, their necks craned upward, their eyes following the klieg lights. Every time your body snapped open like a switchblade, your sequined leotard burst into a thousand tiny flashbulbs. When you came out of a rotation, arms extended, there wasn't a single heart beating. You twirled and floated, riding on the fear and wonder of the crowd, and when you finally came to rest on the platform, they absolutely exploded.

The applause lasted for hours, or so it seemed, but eventually the audience grew peckish for some new treat. While their eyes were drawn to a family of Chinese acrobats, I waited near the bottom of the ladder to congratulate you—and if the opportunity arose, to pour my heart into your hands. I counted down the dwindling number of rungs (yes, the view was exquisite, and from the tips of my size-twenty-four shoes to the top of my busted stovepipe hat I wanted you), but before your feet touched the floor, the lion tamer had you in his arms. He crushed you up against his chest—I'll admit it, the guy was ripped—and you buried your hands in his thick pile of hair. Then you kissed him.

You had never mentioned this over breakfast.

It was after that kiss that I started performing that new bit, the takeoff on the lion tamer's act, where I used Scottie terriers with tutus around their necks for lions. I'd fill my back pockets with kibble so the terriers would chase me in circles trying to tear the seat out of my pants, and by the end my clothes would be shredded, my tiny chair broken to pieces, and I'd have two or three dogs hanging onto my padded rear. I didn't know how the lion tamer would take it—just a joke, right, all in good fun—but after I saw him in a clinch with you, I didn't care.

That's not true. I cared. I wanted the clamor of the crowd to drown him: all the laughs they held back when he was in the cage would come pouring out when they saw me. Not just because the bit was funny but because everyone would see I was goofing on him. But it was just for laughs. Honestly. That's all I wanted.

The dog-tamer act was a big hit, but the joke was on me. I planned to go on with it right after the lion tamer finished. Bing-bang. Agony, then ecstatic laughter. The problem was, he was great that night; everything a lion tamer is supposed to be. Forceful. Authoritative. Daring. For once he lived up to the words of the ring-master's nightly, and heretofore ironic, introduction: the Man with the Indomitable Will. He cracked his whip and thrust the chair, and I couldn't tell who was more surprised, me or the lions. He shouted commands, and the beasts obeyed. Nothing too technically difficult—jumping through hoops, getting the lions to sit up on their hind legs—but he pulled it off without a hitch. He even finished by prying open one animal's mouth and sticking that big blond head of his between the cat's jaws. I thought for sure the lion was going to snatch his head like a grape from a vine, but the big cat didn't even twitch. If a lion can think, I know exactly what was on its mind: Who *is* this guy? I kept asking myself the same question.

He finished to robust applause. I wouldn't say *thunderous,* but the crowd was impressed. And then it was my turn—me with crisscross sequined bandoliers, modeled on his costume, drooping into my baggy pants. The Scotties did their part, and the audience laughed in all the right places. Laughed a lot, actually. It was a great bit, but it had none of its intended punch. It was supposed to be two parts funny, mixed with one part catharsis, spiked with a shot of derision. A satire. Or a parody—one or the other. What do I know? I'm no clown-college clown, but that's what I was aiming for. But now that he had his act together, I was the only one worth laughing at. Which is my job—I'm the one they're supposed to be laughing at—but still.

After a week of asserting his newfound mastery of all things vicious and feline, the lion tamer became unbearable. When he was one misstep away from being lion chow, it was easy to work up some sympathy for him—or it would have been, if I wasn't congenitally deficient in the sympathy department. But now? It was bad enough that he was in the spotlight, in the center ring, and that he had you in his life; now he seemed to think he deserved it. Maybe I was the only one who noticed, but he was acting like he, with his buffed arms and bushy mane, was the only one who belonged under the big top.

Here I go again, yakking like a sideshow barker, but I have to wonder: This high-and-mighty King of the Jungle routine didn't bother you? I've tried to convince myself that you couldn't help it, because let me tell you, some women are just drawn to lion tamers. It must be the smell of the lions—some pheromone that women can't resist. I don't know if he told you this, but even when he wasn't impressing *anyone* with his ability to Bend the Lions to His Indomitable Will, he was still getting laid like a sailor on leave. He used to talk about it all the time, and he had this way of making it sound like it was such a chore, telling me how women expect a lot from a lion tamer. In the sack, he meant. They would growl at him and curl their fingers into claws and bare their teeth. More than once a woman asked him to use his whip or to prod her with an overturned chair. And the ones who brought the lion tamer back to their apartments always wanted to see his scars. They wanted to hear the stories behind each mark and kiss the ropy flesh and say, *There now; all better.*

"You clowns have it easy," he once said. "All you have to do is make them laugh."

I swear, I almost popped him one, right in the kisser. And not with a cream pie.

Do you remember the time you told me he needed a better moniker? It was late one afternoon, as we packed for the trek to the next town. We'd had a good run through Kalamazoo, Crown Point, and the Quad Cities, but it was time to move on. You said he needed a name that looked good on a poster—an all-caps, red-letter name.

I was wrapping up bottles of seltzer, stacking pie plates, stowing the balloon-animal balloons. "How about 'The Preposterous?'" I said.

You cracked a smile—yes, you did—before you said, "I was thinking 'The Great,' or 'The Magnificent,' but those seem—"

"Incongruous?" I said.

"No," you said, the smile blooming into something larger. "Too common. Everyone thinks they're great or amazing or magnificent. It needs to be"—and here you paused—"more awesome." You cocked your head, perhaps considering a thesaurus full of possibilities. "Hey, what about that?"

"The Awful?" I said. "Sure. It's kinda catchy. It suits him."

"For someone who calls himself a clown, you're not as funny as you think," you said (trust me, I have this committed to memory). And here's the kicker: that smile hadn't faded. Can't you see what this meant to me? A smile. A chuckle. A stifled laugh. To me, these have all the come-hither power of a wink, a pout, a gaze that lasts a second too long.

And what about the time you told me he needed a new costume? "Maybe something with animal prints," you said. The image of the lion tamer in leopard-spotted jodhpurs flared into my mind: ridiculous and horrifying at once. A getup like that could put my dog-tamer bit out of business, another case of life over-taking art.

"Now that," I said, "would be awesome."

You let loose with a big laugh, and I should have been in my glory. Score one for me, and a goose egg for the lion tamer. But I was beginning to see that he had been right all along: getting a laugh was the easy part.

The funny thing was, you were burning up mental energy on how best to describe his greatness when all along you were the only thing awesome about that circus. Take it from me, who was nothing more than a tiny red-nosed planet in far-flung orbit—you were the star, and you knew it. You had to. After that first night, crowds packed the stands in town after town, waiting for your act. You did things in the upper reaches of the big top that were impossible even in a dream. Some people looked up and thought: Brave. Magical. Intoxicating. You were liv-ing a life they were too timid to even contemplate. Others saw you use the trapeze like a catapult and the tightrope like a dance floor, and then they looked at the empty space where the net was supposed to be, and they thought: Naïve. Foolish. Shameless. But they watched, just as spellbound as the others, waiting—and, I have to wonder, hoping—for you to get what you deserved. Depending who you asked, you either loved life more than the rest of us, or you craved death and spent every night auditioning a new crowd of witnesses.

Maybe that second group, the nasty naysayers, saw something that I didn't see then but do now: all that time you were up there, you weren't flying—you were falling. You dressed it up, with the flipping and the spinning and the soaring, but from the second you let go of that trapeze, you were plummeting to the unfor-giving floor.

And maybe that's why none of your catchers lasted more than a week. They were close enough to see what was what. And you sure didn't make it easy on them. In every trapeze act that I've ever seen, the tumblers take turns: one night you've got your legs wrapped tight around the trapeze as you wait to catch your partner; the next you're the one counting on your partner to be there when you come out of a tuck and stick out your hands. But you were the only one who flew, and the weight of it—night after night without a net—got to be too much for them. It never seemed to bother you; if anything, it inspired you. Like I've said, you soared—or appeared to, which was good enough for everyone under the big top. But the guys waiting to reel you in—guys whose names we never both-ered to learn—were worn out, used up, exhausted. And while they always caught you, they could only do it for so long. The poor, lucky saps.

Was it these small moments—packing for the next town, shooting the breeze, watching you tumble—that pushed me to say what I said? Of course it was, but it was bigger than just that. It was the whole way we lived—in trailers and tents like tinkers, like refugees, like some kind of traveling circus. The romantically inclined probably think we're one big carefree troupe, laughing and drinking and dancing the mazurka, but romance here is as rare as an honest answer. There are no harlequin tents, no barrel-roofed Gypsy wagons. Our trailers are frosted with rust. Our pitted windows spill fluorescent light onto the hard-packed fairgrounds and black-topped lots. The tents are drafty, or else stifling. From inside come shouts or sobs, or the rare soft words that only fill our hearts with envy at another's happiness or hasty climax. The only advantage of our portable habitations is our ability to cluster and recluster them, depending on the latest feuds or fondnesses, the couplings and the coming-aparts.

This is a roundabout way of saying that one night I heard noises from his trailer—thumps, bangs, the echoes of exertion—and I thought, Here we go again. Another night torturing myself with images of you and him: your teeth bared, your back arched in feline submission, your throat emitting a low rumble. (Please tell me, if nothing else, that you weren't one of those women.) But before I could stuff my fingers in my ears it became clear that you were griping, not groaning. After weeks when I swore I could hear every whispered moment, I strained and stretched but couldn't make out a word. What filtered through the tin-can walls were the smoky remnants of anger and frustration.

I confess I went to bed happy. I think that's the name for what I was feeling; I've never been good with names. I only knew I hadn't felt it in a long time, and it made me giddy to lie there in my sheets and imagine I might have stirred something up by putting in my time and playing games with big red-letter names. I had stalked around the edges of the thing I most wanted to say, and look what happened. A rift, a breach; perhaps a doorway was opening that I could walk through. And while I was in the business of wishful thinking, I put in a request that I would have one clean shot at the bop on the head, the island, and all the rest.

Then there was that night, in that town. I don't remember where—let's just say it was somewhere in the Heartland; we spent a lot of time in the Heartland. We were walking the midway, and you were telling me how hard things were for him, with the big cats lunging and the crowd hungry for excitement. But your heart wasn't in it. You were telling me this because you always told me this.

"He's nice," you said. "He is." You stopped near the booth where the swami read palms. "He told me his father was a lion tamer, and his mother was a lion tamer's assistant. So what choice did he have?"

"I don't know," I said. "Traveling salesman? Electrical engineer? Auto-parts dealer?"

"If only it were that easy," you said. "We'd all be traveling salesmen, right?"

I felt boldness, never one of my strong suits, rising inside me, buoyed by the memory of that happiness I'd felt in the darkness of my trailer. "No, we wouldn't," I said. "You'd still be you, and I'd still be me—but he could be someone else entirely."

Your eyes had a dreamy, faraway look to them. If he were someone else entirely, would you have been more interested in him, or less? If you were someone else entirely, could that person see herself with me? If I were someone else— but that's enough of that. All of these things were spinning through my noggin, but what was I supposed to do with them? Or with you? There were no straight answers. No firm pronouncements. No signs, no portents. I was ready to burst.

That was when the words popped out of me: "Why do you do this?" I meant everything—the trapeze, the wire, the lion tamer, the time you spent with me, the empty space where the net should be. I left it up to you to decide how much of the question you wanted to bite off.

"I guess I like it," you said, which cleared up nothing.

"You guess?"

"I must, right? Why else would I do it?" Whether you were asking a question or defending yourself, I wasn't sure. All I knew was that your eyes were on me, and the temperature out there on the midway had skyrocketed. Had it ever been so hot under the spotlights, in the tent in midsummer with the thousands sweating in their seats and the trampled straw and pissed-on sawdust rising, rising, rising through my head? Better men than me would have had an answer for you, or at least something to say. I had nothing. You were staring right at me, but your eyes were fixed on some secret spot inside you. If that door had been left open, it seemed to me that the wind was pushing it shut.

"Say something funny," you said, your eyes like jewels in the lamplight.

"I love you" tumbled out of me, the words pushing their way into the open like clowns from a car.

"That's not funny," you said, and your eyes snapped shut like I had slapped you.

And you were right. It wasn't funny—it was hilarious. Coming from me, it was absolutely ridiculous.

As time crawled from one second to the next, your head ticked from side to side in a slow-motion no, and I could feel the pressure of all the things I'd left unsaid mounting in my head. If I had been a cartoon, steam would have shot from my ears. I would have blown my stack, complete with a red whistle and smoldering dome. But I am what I am, and I did what clowns do. I started turning my arm faster and faster, as if cranking some giant flywheel, and when I couldn't go any faster I ratcheted my fist up and bopped myself smack on top of the head. It's a standard sight gag—anyone who's been to the circus has seen it a million times—that ends with a woozy roll of the eyes, a loll of the tongue, and after a second's delay, a gimpy-kneed collapse. But I left all of that out. I wasn't going for the gag. I wanted so badly to believe my arm had become a sledgehammer that could drive my body deep into the ground, deeper than the pegs that keep the big top tight, deep enough to get away from you and the truth of what I'd said, and the truth of what you felt.

This is how what happened happened: I heard you behind the cotton candy stand, and I honestly thought you were talking to me. I didn't so much hear your voice as I detected a fluttering in the atmosphere. It was a whisper, an intake of breath, nothing more. I heard it again, then again, growing louder as I drew near.

There were hay bales piled in the gap between the booth and the outer wall of the big top, and as I poked my head over the top of one, my nose rising like a poster-paint sun, I saw it all. It wasn't me you were talking to, and it wasn't the lion tamer. It wasn't me straddling you, and it wasn't the corrugated expanse of my back concealing everything but your sculpted legs and taped feet.

Ladies and gentlemen, in the center ring I give you the strong man, the human steam engine! Watch as he twists bars of solid iron like saltwater taffy! Thrill to the display of brute force as he juggles bank safes like baseballs! Nothing is beyond his power, and nothing can crush his forged steel frame!

My knees buckled, and in that moment of ecstasy (yours, of course) and agony (mine, as always), I swear I heard you laugh: a tinkling sound like a bag full of broken glass, like some candy-faced kid pounding the twinkly end of a piano.

As I staggered away, the water-squirting daisy in my lapel started gushing, and my shoes flapped against the flattened earth. That laughter followed me, echoing, louder than any tent full of yokels in any town I'd ever played. It broke over me like a tidal wave, and that's when I stumbled out onto the midway and ran right into him.

I want to make this part clear. I didn't go looking for him. I didn't have a tale to tell. I tripped; I fell; I looked up. And there he was.

He looked golden. Since his act had taken off, he had acquired a deeply bronze tan—a sheen, even—that only made him look more like the lord of some grassland kingdom. He glanced down, and before he said a word he shook that mane of his. I wouldn't have been surprised if he had roared at me. But instead he asked a simple question: Did I know where you were? I was practically deaf from the laughter ringing in my head, and there he was, looking so polished, so confident, so unshakeable. So without getting up, without dusting off my pants, without saying a word, I pointed one white-gloved hand down the path that led to the hay bales behind the cotton candy booth.

I would have explained all of this, if you had let me, but all I knew was what I heard around the midway: you were spending all of your time up on the wire, the lion tamer was holed up with his big cats, and the strong man had already been seen testing his mettle with the bearded lady. The lion tamer claimed he was putting the finishing touches on a brand-new act, something no one had ever seen before. In the meantime he was still doing the old routine, but he was slipping. And here's the part that really got me: it wasn't any fun to watch. Before, he had been oblivious, like a dopey kid trying to jam a fork into an electrical outlet. You had to admire his moxie, even if you knew he was in for a shock. Now he was just plain angry, whipping the cats through their paces. After watching this for two nights and a matinee, I put the dog-tamer bit on hiatus. He wasn't bad enough for it to be funny the way I had wanted, and he wasn't good enough for it to be funny the way the ringmaster wanted. We figured we'd muddle through with something else until his new act was ready, and then we'd bring back the Scotties. The crowd loved those Scotties.

Then, the grand finale. The night the lion tamer was going to unveil his new act, and the night I would debut a bigger and better dog-tamer bit. I wanted to hold off until I knew which way things were going to break with the lion tamer, but the ringmaster insisted. He could tell how tense things had been around the big top, and he believed that one good show could clear it all up.

From the first minutes after the come-in, as the rubes lined up and handed over their ducats, there was a buzz in the air, right up until the moment that the lights went down and the big top was bathed in black. When the spotlights came back up, the lion tamer was in the center ring, surrounded by his big cats. Only it wasn't just his big cats. It was a pride of them. He must have had a dozen lions in there. Torches guttered at every corner of the cage, and an entire row of flaming hoops was fanned out across the middle. The lions looked skittish, distracted by the spotlights, angered by all that fire, nipping at each other, and feeling decidedly unbent by the until recently Indomitable Will of the lion tamer. Who just looked awful. Like he hadn't slept in days, hadn't showered, hadn't been near a blow dryer. Even at his worst, he had always had his vanity to keep him afloat.

I don't know what he had planned. It's a safe bet that he wanted to run the entire line of cats through that fiery tunnel, just to prove it could be done—to prove that he could do it—and it might have really been something to see. When he waded in among the lions, the crowd went church-quiet. Then he started shouting, urging the lions in one direction or another, and when they didn't respond he went to the whip. He waved it over his head like a pompom, and the lions seemed happy to ignore him until he jerked it back in one quick motion and the tip of the whip bit into the haunches of the biggest cat in that cage.

The lion's yellowed eyes narrowed, and if something that big can pounce, then that's exactly what it did. No growling, no swatting, no warning. It pushed off with its meaty legs, and before the lion tamer could raise his little chair it was on top of him. Once he was on the ground, the other lions moved in.

The lights went out in the center ring—too late, I'm sure, to spare the ladies and gentlemen and children of all ages the firelit sight that would linger long after we left town. And that's when the lights came on over me and the dogs, because that's how it works in the circus. When something goes wrong, you send in the clowns. So the lights came on, and we snapped to life, the dogs with their tutu manes, and me in my spangled bandoliers and my pockets full of kibble.

The crowd was distracted for a second or two—I am the shiny penny on the sidewalk, the light bulb that flares before it dies—but when they caught on to the gist of the act, they turned on me as surely as the big cats had turned on the lion tamer. Garbage rained down on me, and I swear it wasn't until the first wadded-up bag of popcorn hit me in my big ugly mug that I realized how the dogtamer bit must have looked. But what was I supposed to do? Pick up the Scotties and juggle them? That's the act we had ready to go. That's all I had.

I froze out there, and the second I stopped moving the Scotties dug their teeth into the seat of my pants with all their little terrier jaws could give. This indignity, not thirty feet from what was left of the lion tamer, sent the crowd into a cascade of boos—booing like I had never heard before. Thunderous. And while the crowd pelted me with paper cups and half-eaten hot dogs, I looked up into the big top and saw you on the platform, sparkling vaguely in the shadows. You had seen it all; you would understand that I was only doing my job. I tried to use my own will, which no one had ever described as indomitable, to draw your eyes off the darkened cage and over to me. I wanted you to see how I had been swept up in all of this, and to give me one sequined smile, one dewy look from those kohl-black eyes. There I was, the focus of the crowd's anger and disgust, but not for one second did I blame you for any of it: not for choosing the lion tamer, or burying your fingernails in the strong man's beefy back, or even for my own predicament—the dogs, the boos, my ass. I could have laid this at your petite, rope-burned feet, but I didn't—I couldn't—because only mess and misery connected me to you.

You could have looked at me, and all of this would have been clear. Instead, you stood on that shaky cocktail table of a platform, feeling gravity's pull. Below, the horror of the lion cage, the fury of the crowd, and one clownish heart calling out for a moment's tender notice. Which of these caused you to do what you did? Which one of us—the strong and weak, brave and cowardly, funny and foolish—steeled you for that first step? No lights lit your way, but you walked onto that wire like it could take you out of the big top and away from all of us.

❁ ❁ ❁

## OCTAVIO PAZ

### *My Life with the Wave*                                                    (1927)

When I left that sea, a wave moved ahead of the others. She was tall and light. In spite of the shouts of the others who grabbed her by her floating clothes, she clutched my arm and went off with me leaping. I didn't want to say anything to her, because it hurt me to shame her in front of her friends. Besides, the furious stares of the elders paralyzed me. When we got to town, I explained to her that it was impossible, that life in the city was not what she had been able to imagine with the ingenuity of a wave that had never left the sea. She watched me gravely: "No, your decision is made. You can't go back." I tried sweetness, hardness, irony. She cried, screamed, hugged, threatened. I had to apologize.

The next day my troubles began. How could we get on the train without being seen by the conductor, the passengers, the police? Certainly the rules say nothing in respect to the transport of waves on the railroad, but this same reserve was an indication of the severity with which our act would be judged. After much thought I arrived at the station an hour before departure, took my seat, and, when no one was looking, emptied the water tank for the passengers; then, carefully, poured in my friend.

The first incident came about when the children of a nearby couple declared their noisy thirst. I stopped them and promised them refreshments and lemonade. They were at the point of accepting when another thirsty passenger approached. I was about to invite her also, but the stare of her companion stopped me. The lady took a paper cup, approached the tank, and turned the faucet. Her cup was barely half full when I leaped between the woman and my friend. She looked at me astonished. While I apologized, one of the children turned the faucet again. I closed it violently. The lady brought the cup to her lips:

"Agh, this water is salty."

The boy echoed her. Various passengers rose. The husband called the conductor:

"This man put salt in the water."

The conductor called the Inspector:

"So you put substances in the water?"

The Inspector in turn called the police:

"So you poisoned the water?"

The police in turn called the Captain:

"So you're the poisoner?"

The Captain called three agents. The agents took me to an empty car, amid the stares and whispers of the passengers. At the next station they took me off and pushed and dragged me to the jail. For days no one spoke to me, except during the long interrogations. When I explained my story no one believed me, not even the jailer, who shook his head, saying: "The case is grave, truly grave. You didn't want to poison the children?" One day they brought me before the Magistrate.

"Your case is difficult," he repeated. "I will assign you to the Penal Judge."

A year passed. Finally they judged me. As there were no victims, my sentence was light. After a short time, my day of liberty arrived.

The Chief of the Prison called me in:

"Well, now you're free. You were lucky. Lucky there were no victims. But don't do it again, because the next time won't be so short…"

And he stared at me with the same grave stare with which everyone watched me.

The same afternoon I took the train and after hours of uncomfortable traveling arrived in Mexico City. I took a cab home. At the door of my apartment I heard laughter and singing. I felt a pain in my chest, like the smack of a wave of surprise when surprise smacks us across the chest: my friend was there, singing and laughing as always.

"How did you get back?"

"Simple: in the train. Someone, after making sure that I was only salt water, poured me in the engine. It was a rough trip: soon I was a white plume of vapor, soon I fell in a fine rain on the machine. I thinned out a lot. I lost many drops."

Her presence changed my life. The house of dark corridors and dusty furniture was filled with air, with sun, with sounds and green and blue reflections, a numerous and happy populace of reverberations and echoes. How many waves is one wave, and how it can make a beach or a rock or jetty out of a wall, a chest, a forehead that it crowns with foam! Even the abandoned corners, the abject corners of du st and debris were touched by her light hands. Everything began to laugh and everywhere shined with teeth. The sun entered the old rooms with pleasure and stayed in my house for hours, abandoning the other houses, the district, the city, the country. And some nights, very late, the scandalized stars watched it sneak from my house.

Love was a game, a perpetual creation. All was beach, sand, a bed of sheets that were always fresh. If I embraced her, she swelled with pride, incredibly tall, like the liquid stalk of a poplar; and soon that thinness flowered into a fountain of white feathers, into a plume of smiles that fell over my head and back and covered me with whiteness. Or she stretched out in front of me, infinite as the horizon, until I too became horizon and silence. Full and sinuous, it enveloped me like music or some giant lips. Her presence was a going and coming of caresses, of murmurs, of kisses. Entered in her waters, I was drenched to the socks and in a wink of an eye I found myself up above, at the height of vertigo, mysteriously suspended, to fall like a stone and feel myself gently deposited on the dryness, like a feather. Nothing is comparable to sleeping in those waters, to wake pounded by a thousand happy light lashes, by a thousand assaults that withdrew laughing.

But never did I reach the center of her being. Never did I touch the nakedness of pain and of death. Perhaps it does not exist in waves, that secret site that renders a woman vulnerable and mortal, that electric button where all interlocks, twitches, and straightens out to then swoon. Her sensibility, like that of women, spread in ripples, only they weren't concentric ripples, but rather excentric, spreading each time farther, until they touched other galaxies. To love her was to extend to remote contacts, to vibrate with far-off stars we never suspected. But her center… no, she had no center, just an emptiness as in a whirlwind, that sucked me in and smothered me.

Stretched out side by side, we exchanged confidences, whispers, smiles. Curled up, she fell on my chest and there unfolded like a vegetation of murmurs. She sang in my ear, a little snail. She became humble and transparent, clutching my feet like a small animal, calm water. She was so clear I could read all of her thoughts. Certain nights her skin was covered with phosphorescence and to embrace her was to embrace a piece of night tattooed with fire. But she also became black and bitter. At unexpected hours she roared, moaned, twisted. Her groans woke the neighbors. Upon hearing her, the sea wind would scratch at the door of the house or rave in a loud voice on the roof. Cloudy days irritated her;

she broke furniture, said bad words, covered me with insults and green and gray foam. She spit, cried, swore, prophesied. Subject to the moon, to the stars, to the influence of the light of other worlds, she changed her moods and appearance in a way that I thought fantastic, but it was as fatal as the tide.

She began to miss solitude. The house was full of snails and conches, of small sailboats that in her fury she had shipwrecked (together with the others, laden with images, that each night left my forehead and sank in her ferocious or pleasant whirlwinds). How many little treasures were lost in that time! But my boats and the silent song of the snails was not enough. I had to install in the house a colony of fish. I confess that it was not without jealousy that I watched them swimming in my friend, caressing her breasts, sleeping between her legs, adorning her hair with light flashes of color.

Among all those fish there were a few particularly repulsive and ferocious ones, little tigers from the aquarium, with large fixed eyes and jagged and blood-thirsty mouths. I don't know by what aberration my friend delighted in playing with them, shamelessly showing them a preference whose significance I preferred to ignore. She passed long hours confined with those horrible creatures. One day I couldn't stand it any more; I threw open the door and launched after them. Agile and ghostly they escaped my hands while she laughed and pounded me until I fell. I thought I was drowning. And when I was at the point of death, and purple, she deposited me on the bank and began to kiss me, saying I don't know what things. I felt very weak, fatigued and humiliated. And at the same time her voluptuousness made me close my eyes, because her voice was sweet and she spoke to me of the delicious death of the drowned. When I recovered, I began to fear and hate her.

I had neglected my affairs. Now I began to visit friends and renew old and dear relations. I met an old girlfriend. Making her swear to keep my secret, I told her of my life with the wave. Nothing moves women so much as the possibility of saving a man. My redeemer employed all of her arts, but what could a woman, master of a limited number of souls and bodies, do in front of my friend who was always changing—and always identical to herself in her incessant metamorphoses.

Winter came. The sky turned gray. Fog fell on the city. Frozen drizzle rained. My friend cried every night. During the day she isolated herself, quiet and sinister, stuttering a single syllable, like an old woman who grumbles in a corner. She became cold; to sleep with her was to shiver all night and to feel freeze, little by little, the blood, the bones, the thoughts. She turned deep, impenetrable, restless. I left frequently and my absences were each time more prolonged. She, in her corner, howled loudly. With teeth like steel and a corrosive tongue she gnawed the walls, crumbled them. She passed the nights in mourning, reproaching me. She had nightmares, deliriums of the sun, of warm beaches. She dreamt of the pole and of changing into a great block of ice, sailing beneath black skies in nights long as months. She insulted me. She cursed and laughed; filled the house with guffaws and phantoms. She called up the monsters of the depths, blind ones, quick ones, blunt. Charged with electricity, she carbonized all she touched; full of acid, she dissolved whatever she brushed against. Her sweet embraces became knotty cords that strangled me. And her body, greenish and elastic, was an implacable whip that lashed, lashed, lashed. I fled. The horrible fish laughed with ferocious smiles.

There in the mountains, among the tall pines and precipices, I breathed the cold thin air like a thought of liberty. At the end of a month I returned. I had decided. It had been so cold that over the marble of the chimney, next to the extinct fire, I found a statue of ice. I was unmoved by her weary beauty. I put her in a big canvas sack and went out to the streets with the sleeper on my shoulders. In a restaurant in the outskirts I sold her to a waiter friend who immediately began to chop her into little pieces, which he carefully deposited in the buckets where bottles are chilled.

### Explorations of the Text

1.  What merger of the real and the fantastic propels this story? Why does the narrator compare the sea and an elusive lover?
2.  How is the wave like a woman? like a man's fantasy of a woman?
3.  Explore the incident of the water fountain. Why is the water "salty"? What does the narrator's imprisonment suggest?
4.  Once he returns home, how does her presence at first change his life? What stage of love is depicted?
5.  What are the implications of these statements: "But never did I reach the center of her being," and "She had no center, just an emptiness as in a whirlwind, that sucked me in and smothered me"?
6.  Why does the narrator have to install a colony of fish? Why does she prefer the "little tigers... with large fixed eyes and jagged and bloodthirsty mouths"?
7.  Explore the sign of the "drowning" episode. Why does he begin "to fear and hate her"?
8.  What is the outcome of their relationship? Explore the symbolic dimension of the wave's association with ice.
9.  What visions of romantic love, of sexuality, and of relationships does the story present?
10. Why does Paz depict human love through an affair with a wave instead of an affair with a real lover? What is the impact of this metaphor? Is it effective?

❀ ❀ ❀

# RON RASH

## *The Ascent* (2010)

Jared had never been this far before, over Sawmill Ridge and across a creek glazed with ice, then past the triangular metal sign that said GREAT SMOKY MOUNTAINS NATIONAL PARK. If it had still been snowing and his tracks were being covered up, he'd have turned back. People had gotten lost in this park. Children wandered off from family picnics, hikers strayed off trails. Sometimes it took days to find them. But today the sun was out, the sky deep and blue. No more snow would fall, so it would be easy to retrace his tracks. Jared heard a helicopter hovering somewhere to the west, which meant that after a week they still hadn't found the airplane. They'd been searching all the way from Bryson City to the Tennessee line, or so he'd heard at school.

The land slanted downward and the sound of the helicopter disappeared. In the steepest places, Jared leaned sideways and held on to trees to keep from slipping. As he made his way into the denser woods, he wasn't thinking of the lost airplane or if he would get the mountain bike he'd asked for as his Christmas present. Not thinking about his parents either, though they were the main reason he was spending his first day of Christmas vacation out here—better to be outside on a cold day than in the house where everything, the rickety chairs and sagging couch, the gaps where the TV and microwave had been, felt sad.

He thought instead of Lyndee Starnes, the girl who sat in front of him in fifth-grade homeroom. Jared pretended she was walking beside him and he was showing her the tracks in the snow, telling her which markings were squirrel and which rabbit and which deer. Pointing out a bear's tracks too and Lyndee telling him she was afraid of bears and Jared saying he'd protect her.

Jared stopped walking. He hadn't seen any human tracks, but he looked behind him to be sure no one was around. He took out the pocketknife and raised it, making believe that the pocketknife was a hunting knife and that Lyndee was beside him. If a bear comes, I'll take care of you, he said out loud. Jared imagined Lyndee reaching out and taking his free arm. He kept the knife out as he walked up another ridge, one whose name he didn't know. Lyndee still grasped his arm as they walked up the ridge. Lyndee told him how sorry she was that at school she'd said his clothes smelled bad.

At the ridge top, Jared pretended a bear suddenly raised up, baring its teeth and growling. He slashed at the bear with the knife and the bear ran away. Jared held the knife before him as he descended the ridge. Sometimes they'll come back, he said aloud.

He was halfway down the ridge when the knife blade caught the midday sun and the steel flashed. Another flash came from below, as if it was answering. At first Jared saw only a glimmer of metal in the dull green of rhododendron, but as he came nearer he saw more, a crumpled silver propeller and white tailfin and part of a shattered wing.

For a few moments Jared thought about turning around, but then told himself that someone who'd just fought a bear shouldn't be afraid to get close to a crashed airplane. He made his way down the ridge, snapping rhododendron branches to clear a path. When he finally made it to the plane, he couldn't see much because snow and ice covered the windows. He turned the passenger-side door's outside handle, but the door didn't budge until Jared wedged in the pocketknife's blade. The door made a sucking sound as it opened.

A woman was in the passenger seat, her body bent forward like a horseshoe. Long brown hair fell over her face. The hair had frozen and looked as if it would snap off like icicles. She wore blue jeans and a yellow sweater. Her left arm was flung out before her and on one finger was a ring. The man across from her leaned toward the pilot window, his head cocked against the glass. Bloodstains reddened the window and his face was not covered like the woman's. There was a seat in the back, empty. Jared placed the knife in his pocket and climbed into the back seat and closed the passenger door. Because it's so cold, that's why they don't smell much, he thought.

For a while he sat and listened to how quiet and still the world was. He couldn't hear the helicopter or even the chatter of a gray squirrel or caw of a crow. Here between the ridges not even the sound of the wind. Jared tried not to move or breathe hard, to make it even quieter, quiet as the man and woman up front. The plane was snug and cozy. After a while he heard something, just the slightest sound, coming from the man's side. Jared listened harder, then knew what it was. He leaned forward between the front seats. The man's right forearm rested against a knee. Jared pulled back the man's shirtsleeve and saw the watch. He checked the time, almost four o'clock. He'd been sitting in the back seat two hours, though it seemed only a few minutes. The light that would let him follow the tracks back home would be gone soon.

As he got out of the back seat, Jared saw the woman's ring. Even in the cabin's muted light, it shone. He took the ring off the woman's finger and placed it in his jeans pocket. He closed the passenger door and followed his boot prints back the way he came. Jared tried to step into his earlier tracks, pretending that he needed to confuse a wolf following him.

It took longer than he'd thought, the sun almost down when he crossed the park boundary. As he came down the last ridge, Jared saw that the blue pickup was parked in the yard, the lights on in the front room. He remembered it was Saturday and his father had gotten his paycheck. When Jared opened the door, the small red glass pipe was on the coffee table, an empty baggie beside it. His father kneeled before the fireplace, meticulously arranging and rearranging kindling around an oak log. A dozen crushed beer cans lay amid the kindling, balanced on the log itself three red and white fishing bobbers. His mother sat on the couch, her eyes glazed, as she told Jared's father how to arrange the cans. In her lap lay a roll of tinfoil she was cutting into foot-long strips.

"Look what we're making," she said, smiling at Jared. "It's going to be our Christmas tree."

When he didn't speak, his mother's smile quivered.

"Don't you like it, honey?"

His mother got up, strips of tinfoil in her left hand. She knelt beside his father and carefully draped them on the oak log and kindling.

Jared walked into the kitchen and took the milk from the refrigerator. He washed a bowl and spoon left in the sink and poured some cereal. After he ate, Jared went into his bedroom and closed the door. He sat on his bed and took the ring from his pocket and set it in his palm. He held the ring under the lamp's bulb and swayed his hand slowly back and forth so the stone's different colors flashed and merged. He'd give it to Lyndee when they were on the playground, on the first sunny day after Christmas vacation, so she could see how pretty the ring's colors were. Once he gave it to her, Lyndee would finally like him, and it would be for real.

Jared didn't hear his father until the door swung open.

"Your mother wants you to help light the tree."

The ring fell onto the wooden floor. Jared picked it up and closed his hand.

"What's that?" his father asked.

"Nothing," Jared said. "Just something I found in the woods."

"Let me see."

Jared opened his hand. His father stepped closer and took the ring. He pressed the ring with his thumb and finger.

"That's surely a fake diamond, but the ring looks to be real gold."

His father tapped it against the bedpost as if the sound could confirm its authenticity. His father called his mother and she came into the room.

"Look what Jared found," he said, and handed her the ring. "It's gold."

His mother set the ring in her palm, held it out before her so they all three could see it.

"Where'd you find it, honey?"

"In the woods," Jared said.

"I didn't know you could find rings in the woods," his mother said dreamily. "But isn't it wonderful that you can."

"That diamond can't be real, can it?" his father asked.

His mother stepped close to the lamp. She cupped her hand and slowly rocked it back and forth, watching the different colors flash inside the stone.

"It might be," his mother said.

"Can I have it back?" Jared asked.

"Not until we find out if it's real, son," his father said.

His father took the ring from his mother's palm and placed it in his pants pocket. Then he went into the other bedroom and got his coat.

"I'm going down to town and find out if it's real or not."

"But you're not going to sell it," Jared said.

"I'm just going to have a jeweler look at it," his father said, already putting on his coat. "We need to know what it's worth, don't we? We might have to insure it. You and your momma go ahead and light our Christmas tree. I'll be back in just a few minutes."

"It's not a Christmas tree," Jared said.

"Sure it is, son," his father replied. "It's just one that's chopped up, is all."

He wanted to stay awake until his father returned, so he helped his mother spread the last strips of tinfoil on the wood. His mother struck a match and told him it was time to light the tree. The kindling caught and the foil and cans withered and blackened. The fishing bobbers melted. His mother kept adding kindling to the fire, telling Jared if he watched closely he'd see angel wings folding and unfolding inside the flames. Angels come down the chimney sometimes, just like Santa Claus, she told him. Midnight came and his father still wasn't back. Jared went to his room. I'll lay down just for a few minutes, he told himself, but when he opened his eyes it was light outside.

As soon as he came into the front room, Jared could tell his parents hadn't been to bed. The fire was still going, kindling piled around the hearth. His mother sat where she'd been last night, wearing the same clothes. She was tearing pages out of a magazine one at a time, using scissors to make ragged stars she stuck on the walls with tape. His father sat beside her, watching intently.

The glass pipe lay on the coffee table beside four baggies, two with powder still in them. There'd never been more than one before.

His father grinned at him.

"I got you some of that cereal you like," he said, and pointed to a box with a green leprechaun on its front.

"Where's the ring?" Jared asked.

"The sheriff took it," his father said. "When I showed it to the jeweler, he said the sheriff had been in there just yesterday. A woman had reported it missing. I knew you'd be disappointed, that's why I bought you that cereal. Got something else for you too."

His father nodded toward the front door where a mountain bike was propped against the wall. Jared walked over to it. He could tell it wasn't new, some of the blue paint chipped away and one of the rubber handle grips missing, but the tires didn't sag and the handlebars were straight.

"It didn't seem right for you to have to wait till Christmas to have it," his father said. "Too bad there's snow on the ground, but it'll soon enough melt and you'll be able to ride it."

Jared's mother looked up.

"Wasn't that nice of your daddy," she said, her eyes bright and gleaming. Go ahead and eat your cereal, son. A growing boy needs his breakfast."

Jared ate as his parents sat in the front room passing the pipe back and forth. He looked out the window and saw the sky held nothing but blue, not even a few white clouds. He wanted to go back to the plane, but as soon as he laid his bowl in the sink his father announced that the three of them were going to go find a real Christmas tree.

"The best Christmas tree ever," his mother told Jared.

They put on their coats and walked up the ridge, his father carrying a rusty saw. Near the ridge top, they found Fraser firs and white pines.

"Which one do you like best?" his father asked.

Jared looked over the trees, then picked a Fraser fir no taller than himself.

"You don't want a bigger one?" his father asked.

When Jared shook his head no, his father knelt before the tree. The saw's teeth were dull but his father finally broke the bark and worked the saw through. They dragged the tree down the ridge and propped it in the corner by the fireplace. His parents smoked the pipe again and then his father went out to the shed and got a hammer and nails and two boards. While his father built the make-shift tree stand, Jared's mother cut more stars from a magazine.

"I think I'll go outside a while," Jared said.

"But you can't," his mother replied. "You've got to help me tape the stars to the tree."

By the time they'd finished, the sun was falling behind Sawmill Ridge. I'll go tomorrow, he told himself.

On Monday morning the baggies were empty and his parents were sick. His mother sat on the couch wrapped in a quilt, shivering. She hadn't bathed since Friday and her hair was stringy and greasy. His father looked little better, his blue eyes receding deep into his skull, his lips chapped and bleeding.

"Your momma, she's sick," his father said.

Jared watched his mother all morning. After a while she lit the pipe and sucked deeply for what residue might remain. His father crossed his arms, rubbing his biceps as he looked around the room, as if expecting to see something he'd not seen moments earlier. The fire had gone out, the cold causing his mother to shake more violently.

"You got to go see Wesley," she told Jared's father.

"We got no money left," he answered.

Jared watched them, waiting for the sweep of his father's eyes to stop beside the front door where the mountain bike was. But his father's eyes went past it without the slightest pause. The kerosene heater in the kitchen was on, but its heat hardly radiated into the front room.

His mother looked up at Jared.

"Can you fix us a fire, honey?"

He went out to the back porch and gathered an armload of kindling, then placed a thick oak log on the andirons as well. Beneath it he wedged newspaper left over from the star cutting. He lit the newspaper and watched the fire slowly take hold, then watched the flames a while longer before turning to his parents.

"You can take the bike to town and sell it," he said.

"No, son," his mother said. "That's your Christmas present."

"We'll be all right," his father said. "Your momma and me just did too much partying yesterday is all."

But as the morning passed, they got no better. At noon Jared went to his room and got his coat.

"Where you going, honey?" his mother asked as he walked toward the door.

"To get more firewood."

Jared walked into the shed but did not gather wood. Instead, he took a length of dusty rope off the shed's back wall and wrapped it around his waist and then knotted it. He left the shed and followed his own tracks west into the park. The snow had become harder, and it crunched beneath his boots. The sky was gray, darker clouds farther west. More snow would soon come, maybe by afternoon. Jared told Lyndee it was too dangerous for her to go with him. He was on a rescue mission in Alaska, the rope tied around him dragging a sled filled with food and medicine. The footprints weren't his but of the people he'd been sent to find.

When he got to the airplane, Jared pretended to unpack the supplies and give the man and woman something to eat and drink. He told them they were too hurt to walk back with him and he'd have to go and get more help. Jared took the watch off the man's wrist. He set it in his palm, face upward. I've got to take your compass, he told the man. A blizzard's coming, and I may need it.

Jared slipped the watch into his pocket. He got out of the plane and walked back up the ridge. The clouds were hard and granite-looking now, and the first flurries were falling. Jared pulled out the watch every few minutes, pointed the hour hand east as he followed his tracks back to the house.

The truck was still out front, and through the window Jared saw the mountain bike. He could see his parents as well, huddled together on the couch. For a few moments Jared simply stared through the window at them.

When he went inside, the fire was out and the room was cold enough to see his breath. His mother looked up anxiously from the couch.

"You shouldn't go off that long without telling us where you're going, honey."

Jared lifted the watch from his pocket.

"Here," he said, and gave it to his father.

His father studied it a few moments, then broke into a wide grin.

"This watch is a Rolex," his father said.

"Thank you, Jared," his mother said, looking as if she might cry. "How much can we get for it?"

"I bet a couple of hundred at least," his father answered.

His father clamped the watch onto his wrist and got up. Jared's mother rose as well.

"I'm going with you. I need something quick as I can get it." She turned to Jared. "You stay here, honey. We'll be back in just a little while. We'll bring you back a hamburger and a Co-Cola, some more of that cereal too."

Jared watched as they drove down the road. When the truck had vanished, he sat down on the couch and rested a few minutes. He hadn't taken his coat off. He checked to make sure the fire was out and then went to his room and emptied his backpack of schoolbooks. He went out to the shed and picked up a wrench and a hammer and placed them in the backpack. The flurries were thicker now, already beginning to fill in his tracks. He crossed over Sawmill Ridge, the tools clanking in his backpack. More weight to carry, he thought, but at least he wouldn't have to carry them back.

When he got to the plane, he didn't open the door, not at first. Instead, he took the tools from the backpack and laid them before him. He studied the plane's crushed nose and propeller, the broken right wing. The wrench was best to tighten the propeller, he decided. He'd straighten out the wing with the hammer.

As he switched tools and moved around the plane, the snow fell harder. Jared looked behind him and on up the ridge and saw his footprints were growing fainter. He chipped the snow and ice off the windshields with the hammer's claw. Finished, he said, and dropped the hammer on the ground. He opened the passenger door and got in.

"I fixed it so it'll fly now," he told the man.

He sat in the back seat and waited. The work and walk had warmed him but he quickly grew cold. He watched the snow cover the plane's front window with a darkening whiteness. After a while he began to shiver but after a longer while he was no longer cold. Jared looked out the side window and saw the whiteness was not only in front of him but below. He knew then that they had taken off and risen so high that they were enveloped inside a cloud, but still he looked down, waiting for the clouds to clear so he might look for the blue pickup, making its way through the snow, toward the place they were all headed.

# POETRY

## ELIZABETH BISHOP

### *One Art* (1976)

The art of losing isn't hard to master;
so many things seem filled with the intent
to be lost that their loss is no disaster.

Lose something every day. Accept the fluster
of lost door keys, the hour badly spent. 5
The art of losing isn't hard to master.

Then practice losing farther, losing faster:
places, and names, and where it was you meant
to travel. None of these will bring disaster.

I lost my mother's watch. And look! my last, or 10
next-to-last, of three loved houses went.
The art of losing isn't hard to master.

I lost two cities, lovely ones. And, vaster,
some realms I owned, two rivers, a continent.
I miss them, but it wasn't a disaster. 15

—Even losing you (the joking voice, a gesture
I love) I shan't have lied. It's evident
the art of losing's not too hard to master
though it may look like (*Write* it!) like disaster.

### Study and Discussion Questions

1. Bishop's "One Art" is a type of poem called a villanelle. Figure out the
   rhyme scheme of the poem, labeling the first rhyme "A" and marking
   those throughout the poem and the second rhyme "B" and marking those
   throughout the poem. Note that the rhymes do not have to be exact.

2. The first line—"The art of losing isn't hard to master"—becomes a refrain, repeated throughout the poem. Does the line change its meaning or carry a different emotional resonance as the poem goes on? Discuss.
3. There is a second and partial refrain in the poem, built on the lines that end with the word *disaster.* How do the two refrains together create a tension in the poem?
3. What are the "things" lost in this poem? How do the losses change as the poem develops?
4. What does the speaker of the poem keep telling herself she feels or should be feeling about these losses?
5. How would you describe the tone of "One Art"? Does it change in the course of the poem?
6. "It's evident" in the last stanza of "One Art" that the poet has been working up to mentioning a very serious loss. What is it? How might a) writing about such a loss, and b) using a very strict form in which to do so, be of help in such a situation?

### Suggestion for Writing

1. If you were to write a poem (not necessarily a villanelle) titled "One Art," what would your poem be about? What is the "one art" *you* would write about? Give it a try.

### Critical Resources

1. "Elizabeth Bishop." *The Academy of American Poets.* 22 April 2005 <http://www.poets.org/index.cfm>.
2. Miller, Brett Candlish. *Elizabeth Bishop: Life and The Memory of It.* Berkeley: U of California P, 1993 (includes a section on the drafts of "One Art").
3. McCabe, Susan. *Elizabeth Bishop: Her Poetics of Loss.* University Park: Penn State UP, 1994.
4. Schwartz, Lloyd and Sybil Estess, eds. *Elizabeth Bishop and Her Art.* Ann Arbor: U of Michigan P, 1983.

✲ ✲ ✲

# OLGA BROUMAS

## *Cinderella*                                    (1977)

> *. . . the joy that isn't shared*
> *I heard, dies young.*
> > Anne Sexton, 1928–1974

Apart from my sisters, estranged
from my mother, I am a woman alone
in a house of men
who secretly
call themselves princes, alone                                    5
with me usually, under cover of dark. I am the one allowed in

to the royal chambers, whose small foot conveniently
fills the slipper of glass. The woman writer, the lady
umpire, the madam chairman, anyone's wife.
I know what I know.                                                10
And I once was glad

of the chance to use it, even alone
in a strange castle, doing overtime on my own, cracking
the royal code. The princes spoke
in their fathers' language, were eager to praise me               15
my nimble tongue. I am a woman in a state of siege, alone

as one piece of laundry, strung on a windy clothesline a
mile long. A woman co-opted by promises: the lure
of a job, the ruse of a choice, a woman forced
to bear witness, falsely                                          20
against my kind, as each
other sister was judged inadequate, bitchy, incompetent,
jealous, too thin, too fat. I know what I know.
What sweet bread I make

for myself in this prosperous house                               25
is dirty, what good soup I boil turns
in my mouth to mud. Give
me my ashes. A cold stove, a cinder-block pillow, wet
canvas shoes in my sisters', my sisters' hut. Or I swear

I'll die young                                                    30
like those favored before me, hand-picked each one
for her joyful heart.

### Study and Discussion Questions

1. What price has the speaker of the poem had to pay for success?
2. List specific images of loneliness in the poem.
3. What is the speaker's relation to other women? What is her relation to men?

### Suggestion for Writing

1. How has Broumas rewritten the Cinderella fairy tale for modern readers? What changes has she made in the story? (Remember, there is more than one version of the fairy tale.) How do the changes serve her purpose?

### Critical Resources

1. Carruthers, Mary. "The Re-Vision of the Muse: Adrienne Rich, Audre Lorde, Judy Grahn, Olga Broumas." *Hudson Review* 36.2 (1983): 293–322.
2. Hammond, Karla. "An Interview with Olga Broumas." *Northwest Review* 18.3 (1980): 33–44.
3. Horton, Diane. " 'Scarlet Liturgies': The Poetry of Olga Broumas." *North Dakota Quarterly* 55.4 (1987): 322–47.
4. Prins, Yopie. *Dwelling In Possibility: Women Poets and Critics On Poetry.* Ithaca, NY: Cornell UP, 1997.

## ROBERT BROWNING

## *My Last Duchess* (1842)

*Ferrara*[1]

That's my last Duchess painted on the wall,
Looking as if she were alive. I call
That piece a wonder, now; Frà Pandolf's hands
Worked busily a day, and there she stands.
Will't please you sit and look at her? I said          5
"Frà Pandolf" by design, for never read
Strangers like you that pictured countenance,
The depth and passion of its earnest glance,
But to myself they turned (since none puts by
The curtain I have drawn for you, but I)          10
And seemed as they would ask me, if they durst,

---

[1]Ferrara, a city in northern Italy, is the scene.

How such a glance came there; so, not the first
Are you to turn and ask thus. Sir, 't was not
Her husband's presence only, called that spot
Of joy into the Duchess' cheek; perhaps          15
Frà Pandolf chanced to say, "Her mantle laps
Over my lady's wrist too much," or "Paint
Must never hope to reproduce the faint
Half-flush that dies along her throat." Such stuff
Was courtesy, she thought, and cause enough          20
For calling up that spot of joy. She had
A heart—how shall I say?—too soon made glad,
Too easily impressed; she liked whate'er
She looked on, and her looks went everywhere.
Sir, 't was all one! My favor at her breast,          25
The dropping of the daylight in the West,
The bough of cherries some officious fool
Broke in the orchard for her, the white mule
She rode with round the terrace—all and each
Would draw from her alike the approving speech,          30
Or blush, at least. She thanked men,—good! but thanked
Somehow—I know not how—as if she ranked
My gift of a nine-hundred-years-old name
With anybody's gift. Who'd stoop to blame
This sort of trifling? Even had you skill          35
In speech—which I have not—to make your will
Quite clear to such an one, and say "Just this
Or that in you disgusts me; here you miss,
Or there exceed the mark"—and if she let
Herself be lessoned so, nor plainly set          40
Her wits to yours, forsooth, and made excuse—
E'en then would be some stooping; and I choose
Never to stoop. Oh, sir, she smiled, no doubt,
Whene'er I passed her; but who passed without
Much the same smile? This grew; I gave commands;          45
Then all smiles stopped together. There she stands
As ifalive. Will't please you rise? We'll meet
The company below, then. I repeat,
The Count your master's known munificence
Is ample warrant that no just pretense          50
Of mine for dowry will be disallowed;

First published in *Dramatic Lyrics* 1842 and retitled as printed in the 1849 *Dramatic Romances and Lyrics.*

Though his fair daughter's self, as I avowed
At starting, is my object. Nay, we'll go
Together down, sir. Notice Neptune, though,
Taming a sea-horse, thought a rarity,                    55
Which Claus of Innsbruck cast in bronze for me!

### Study and Discussion Questions

1. What does the Duke reveal about his personality throughout the poem?
2. How does the Duke present his former Duchess? Is his description reliable? Why or why not?
3. Browning's poem is an example of an "ekphrasis," which is a piece of literature that discusses a visual work of art. What is the significance of Browning's use of this literary device?
4. What is the effect of the prevalent use of enjambment in this poem?
5. To whom is the Duke speaking and why?
6. What is the significance of the statue of Neptune mentioned in the final lines?

### Suggestions for Writing

1. Write a response to this poem from the point of view of the Duchess giving an account of the events the Duke describes as well as a description of the Duke himself.
2. Browning's poem deals squarely with the issue of power struggles between men and women in romantic relationships. Pinpoint some of these instances of conflict present in the poem and discuss whether modern day couples experience such conflicts.

## BRUCE COHEN

## *An Honest Man's Profile for Internet Dating*    (2010)

I like to call my women Cookie or Doll, but never That Dame. I expect them comfortable with self-service, able to pump high octane in an evening gown while sipping a ginormous Blue Raspberry Slushie. I like my chicks to be twins at least, or triplets, interchangeable. I like my girls talking on their cells while speeding over the limit, the radio cranked up, doughnut crumbs multiplying in their laps. A gentlemen, I could lick the crumbs off but only if they want me to. I like my ladies okay with pouring hydrogen peroxide and warm olive oil in my ear to loosen the caked in wax. I like women who say words like *ditto* to amplify a retort, or *back at cha'* to definitively end an argument that's going no where. I like my date to order her steak rare-blue with a double martini, three olives, no sides. I appreciate a gal who knows the difference between lay and lie but keeps it to herself, confident enough to pick up hitchhikers, order a beer and a bump at a dive that smells like sour urine and sawdust, who is way too good at pool and has no qualms about asking for a fist full of quarters and shaking her moneymaker over to the juke box. *Do you like Tony Bennett,* she coos? I like my broads tough yet still able to take a damp cloth to the baby puke on my shoulder before I'm out the door to work! I like the kind of woman who stares in the mirror and sees someone else, who tries on her friends' dresses and perfume when they're not home, who riffles through medicine cabinets at business socials, who doesn't carry a pocketbook when solo. I like my ladies with southern polysyllabic names and I abuse every single syllable, slowly. I like my dreamboat sweating on the treadmill, singing to herself. I'm not old fashioned but I like my women to be cheery and well groomed in high heels when I come home, my dinner on the table, wisps of steam rising, linen napkins, the children already bathed, read to, spanked, threatened, who refer to their breasts as "my girls". I like my ball and chain working two jobs and funneling the cash into my pockets while I nap. I like women who are accustomed to talking to a dead sister, not related by blood. I like a babe who says *especially yes* without any pre-thought. I especially enjoy careful thinkers. I like how my other half turns the ignition key after the motor is already running and when it makes that horrible noise says, *what's that horrible noise?* I like women who recognize it cannot be this way, who take charge then back off. I like a lady to take my elbow when we're walking on an icy sidewalk. Across the street, other women are bobbling fatherless babies and holding blank picket signs; their mouths are sewn shut; they're wearing secret dark contact lenses. When I meet women in gothic lipstick or Little Bo-Peep dresses entire continents break off from their lips and their mode of escape appears to be as poetic stowaways on cargo liners. I like it when they cry and when I ask what's wrong they say it's nothing, mascara running. I like my baby on time, waiting for me; I like my baby to show up when I don't expect her, sometimes. I like my women to be paper cookie cutter cutouts, and the rare one, in flesh, who doesn't know she's so, so beautiful.

❋ ❋ ❋

# JOHN DONNE

## *The Flea*           (1633)

Mark but this flea, and mark in this,
How little that which thou deny'st me is;
It sucked me first, and now sucks thee,
And in this flea, our two bloods mingled be;
Thou know'st that this cannot be said          5
A sin, or shame, or loss of maidenhead,
    Yet this enjoys before it woo,
    And pampered swells with one blood made of two,
    And this, alas, is more than we would do.

Oh stay, three lives in one flea spare,         10
Where we almost, yea more than married are.
This flea is you and I, and this
Our marriage bed, and marriage temple is;
Though parents grudge, and you, we are met,
And cloistered in these living walls of jet.        15
    Though use make you apt to kill me,
    Let not to this, self murder added be,
    And sacrilege, three sins in killing three.

Cruel and sudden, hast thou since
Purpled thy nail, in blood of innocence?        20
Wherein could this flea guilty be,
Except in that drop which it sucked from thee?
Yet thou triumph'st, and say'st that thou
Find'st not thyself, nor me the weaker now;
    'Tis true, then learn how false, fears be;      25
    Just so much honour, when thou yield'st to me,
    Will waste, as this flea's death took life from thee.

### Study and Discussion Questions

1. To whom is the poem addressed?
2. "The Flea" is an example of a *conceit,* an ingenious metaphor. What does the speaker of the poem mean when he says: "This flea is you and I, and this/ Our marriage bed, and marriage temple is"?
3. What literally is happening in this poem?
4. What is the tone of the poem?

### Suggestions for Writing

1. Write a description of how you imagine the setting and characters in this poem.
2. What is happening in each stanza of "The Flea"? That is, what are the stages of the speaker's argument?
3. Write an answer to the speaker of the poem from the point of view of the person to whom the poem is addressed.

### Critical Resources

1. Carey, John, ed. *John Donne.* Oxford, England: Oxford UP, 1990.
2. Manfred, Malzahn. "The Flea, the Sun and the Critic: A Communicational Approach to John Donne's Poetry." *Symbolism: An International Annual of Critical Aesthetics* 3 (2003): 53–70.
3. Marotti, Arthur, ed. *Critical Essays on John Donne.* New York: G. K. Hall, 1994.
4. Perrine, Laurence. "Explicating Donne: 'The Apparition' and 'The Flea.'" *College Literature* 17 (1990): 1–20.

## ROBERT HAYDEN

## *Those Winter Sundays*            (1962)


Sundays too my father got up early
and put his clothes on in the blueblack cold,
then with cracked hands that ached
from labor in the weekday weather made
banked fires blaze. No one ever thanked him.       5

I'd wake and hear the cold splintering, breaking.
When the rooms were warm, he'd call,
and slowly I would rise and dress,
fearing the chronic angers of that house,

Speaking indifferently to him,            10
who had driven out the cold
and polished my good shoes as well.
What did I know, what did I know
of love's austere and lonely offices?

## Study and Discussion Questions

1. Is the contrast in the poem between coldness and warmth only physical?
2. What is the significance of "and polished my good shoes as well"?
3. What, besides simply growing up, seems to have happened to change the speaker's attitude toward his father?
4. What does the last word of the poem mean? Why does Hayden use that word? Explain the last two lines.

### Suggestion for Writing

1. Given the subject of the poem, how does Hayden avoid sentimentality?

### Critical Resources

1. Fetrow, Fred. *Robert Hayden.* Boston: Twayne, 1984.
2. Goldstein, Laurence and Robert Chrisman, eds. *Robert Hayden: Essays of the Poetry.* Ann Arbor: U of Michigan P, 2001.
3. Hatcher, John. *From the Auroral Darkness: The Life and Poetry of Robert Hayden.* Oxford: George Ronald, 1984.
4. Williams, Pontheolla. *Robert Hayden: A Critical Analysis of His Poetry.* Urbana: U of Illinois P, 1987.

# ANDREW MARVELL

## *To His Coy Mistress*                                               (1681)

 Had we but world enough, and time,
This coyness, Lady, were no crime.
We would sit down, and think which way
To walk, and pass our long love's day.
Thou by the Indian Ganges' side           5
Shouldst rubies find; I by the tide
Of Humber would complain. I would
Love you ten years before the Flood,
And you should, if you please, refuse
Till the Conversion of the Jews.           10
My vegetable[1] love should grow
Vaster than empires and more slow;
An hundred years should go to praise

---

[1]Growing on its own.

Thine eyes, and on thy forehead gaze;
Two hundred to adore each breast,                                         15
But thirty thousand to the rest;
An age at least to every part,
And the last age should show your heart.
For, Lady, you deserve this state,
Nor would I love at lower rate.                                          20
    But at my back I always hear
Time's wingèd chariot hurrying near;
And yonder all before us lie
Deserts of vast eternity.
Thy beauty shall no more be found,                                       25
Nor, in thy marble vault, shall sound
My echoing song; then worms shall try
That long-preserved virginity,
And your quaint honour turn to dust,
And into ashes all my lust:                                              30
The grave's a fine and private place,
But none, I think, do there embrace.
    Now therefore, while the youthful hue
Sits on thy skin like morning dew,
And while thy willing soul transpires                                    35
At every pore with instant fires,
Now let us sport us while we may,
And now, like amorous birds of prey,
Rather at once our time devour
Than languish in his slow chapt[2] power.                                40
Let us roll all our strength and all
Our sweetness up into one ball,
And tear our pleasures with rough strife
Thorough[3] the iron gates of life;
Thus, though we cannot make our sun                                      45
Stand still, yet we will make him run.

_____
[2]Slow-jawed.
[3]Through.

**PETER MEINKE**

## *Advice to My Son*                                (1976)

The trick is, to live your days
as if each one may be your last
(for they go fast, and young men lose their lives
in strange and unimaginable ways)
but at the same time, plan long range                5
(for they go slow; if you survive
the shattered windshield and the bursting shell
you will arrive
at our approximation here below
of heaven or hell).                                  10

To be specific, between the peony and the rose
plant squash and spinach, turnips and tomatoes;
beauty is nectar
and nectar, in a desert, saves–
but the stomach craves stronger sustaenance          15
than the honied vine.
Therefore, marry a pretty girl
after seeing her mother;
Show your soul to one man,
work with another;                                   20
and always serve bread with your wine.
But son, always serve wine.

**EDNA ST. VINCENT MILLAY**

## *An Ancient Gesture*                              (1954)

I thought, as I wiped my eyes on the corner of my apron:
Penelope did this too.
And more than once: you can't keep weaving all day
And undoing it all through the night;
Your arms get tired, and the back of your neck gets tight    5
And along towards morning, when you think it will never be light,
And your husband has been gone, and you don't know where, for years,
Suddenly you burst into tears;
There is simply nothing else to do.

And I thought, as I wiped my eyes on the corner of my apron:     10
This is an ancient gesture, authentic, antique,
In the very best tradition, classic, Greek;
Ulysses did this too.
But only as a gesture,—a gesture which implied
To the assembled throng that he was much too moved to speak.     15
He learned it from Penelope . . .
Penelope,[1] who really cried.

## Study and Discussion Questions

1. What are the two senses of the word *gesture* which emerge in the poem? Note the references to *gesture.* Look up the word in an unabridged dictionary.
2. Compare/contrast the characters of Penelope and of Ulysses (Odysseus) as they are presented in Millay's poem.
3. Who is the third character in the poem? What does it appear her situation is? How does she feel about it?
4. Trace the rhyme scheme of this poem using the method where each subsequent letter in the alphabet identifies a new rhyme.
5. Look at the first line of each stanza. Why do you think Millay did this? What effect does it have?

## Suggestion for Writing

1. Write a paragraph exploring the tone of "An Ancient Gesture." How does the speaker of the poem feel about her own situation and how does this develop through the poem? Why do you think she chose to foreground the story of Penelope while only implying her own? What emotion are you feeling by the end of "An Ancient Gesture" and how might that be connected to choices of word and structure the poet made?

## Critical Resources

1. Freedman, Diane, ed. *Millay at 100: A Critical Reappraisal.* Carbondale: Southern Illinois UP, 1995.
2. Michaildou, Artemis. "Edna St. Vincent Millay and Anne Sexton: The Disruption of Domestic Bliss." *Journal of American Studies* 38.1 (2004): 67–88.
3. Milford, Nancy. *Savage Beauty: The Life of Edna St. Vincent Millay.* New York: Random House, 2001.
4. Miller, Nina. *Making Love Modern: The Intimate Public Worlds of New York Literary Women.* New York: Oxford UP, 1999.

---

[1]Penelope: Wife of Odysseus (Ulysses) in Homer's *Odyssey,* who waited years for her husband, thought dead, to return from the Trojan War. She promised to marry one of her numerous suitors when she had finished her weaving, but each night she unwove what she had done that day.

# THEODORE ROETHKE

## *Dolor* (1948)

I have known the inexorable sadness of pencils,
Neat in their boxes, dolor of pad and paper-weight,
All the misery of manila folders and mucilage,
Desolation in immaculate public places,
Lonely reception room, lavatory, switchboard, 5
The unalterable pathos of basin and pitcher,
Ritual of multigraph, paper-clip, comma,
Endless duplication of lives and objects.
And I have seen dust from the walls of institutions,
Finer than flour, alive, more dangerous than silica, 10
Sift, almost invisible, through long afternoons of tedium,
Dropping a fine film on nails and delicate eyebrows,
Glazing the pale hair, the duplicate grey standard faces.

### Study and Discussion Questions

1. Look up *dolor* in the dictionary. How does the poem convey the various aspects of the definition of that word? (And of course, look up any other word you don't know all the meanings of.)
2. What does Roethke suggest is the effect of office work on office workers?
3. What specific kinds of office work does Roethke have in mind? It can be said that the boss also works in an office. Do you think Roethke's poem refers to that person?
4. Many of the words in "Dolor," like the title itself, are abstract rather than concrete. List some of those words. How does the extensive use of abstractions add to the effect of the poem?
5. What has power and life in this poem? What is powerless and lifeless? How does Roethke achieve this transformation?

### Suggestion for Writing

1. Gather the materials to write a comparable poem about some kind of work you have done. What objects would you select? What are their qualities? What is the relation between the workers and those objects? What kind of mood would you want to convey? What would you title your poem?

### Critical Resources

1. Allan, Seager. *The Glass House: The Life of Theodore Roethke.* Introduction by Donald Hall. Ann Arbor: University of Michigan Press, 1991.

2. Bogen, Don. *Theodore Roethke and the Writing Process.* Athens: Ohio University Press, 1991.
3. Kalaidjian, Walter. *Understanding Theodore Roethke.* Columbia: University of South Carolina Press 1987.
4. Malkoff, Karl. *Theodore Roethke: An Introduction to the Poetry.* New York: Columbia University Press, 1971.

❀ ❀ ❀

## THEODORE ROETHKE

### *My Papa's Waltz*                               (1948)

The whiskey on your breath
Could make a small boy dizzy;
But I hung on like death:
Such waltzing was not easy.

We romped until the pans                           5
Slid from the kitchen shelf;
My mother's countenance
Could not unfrown itself.

The hand that held my wrist
Was battered on one knuckle;                       10
At every step you missed
My right ear scraped a buckle.

You beat time on my head
With a palm caked hard by dirt,
Then waltzed me off to bed                          15
Still clinging to your shirt.

❀ ❀ ❀

## WILLIAM SHAKESPEARE

### *My mistress' eyes are nothing like the sun*      (1609)

My mistress' eyes are nothing like the sun;
Coral is far more red than her lips' red;
If snow be white, why then her breasts are dun;
If hairs be wires, black wires grow on her head.
I have seen roses damasked, red and white,      5
But no such roses see I in her cheeks;
And in some perfumes is there more delight
Than in the breath that from my mistress reeks.
I love to hear her speak, yet well I know
That music hath a far more pleasing sound;      10
I grant I never saw a goddess go;
My mistress when she walks treads on the ground.
     And yet, by heaven, I think my love as rare
     As any she belied with false compare.

❀ ❀ ❀

## KARL SHAPIRO

### *Buick*      (1953)

As a sloop with a sweep of immaculate wing on her delicate spine
And a keel as steel as a root that holds in the sea as she leans,
Leaning and laughing, my warm-hearted beauty, you ride, you ride,
You tack on the curves with parabola speed and a kiss of goodbye,
Like a thoroughbred sloop, my new high-spirited spirit, my kiss.      5

As my foot suggests that you leap in the air with your hips of a girl,
My finger that praises your wheel and announces your voices of song,
Flouncing your skirts, you blueness of joy, you flirt of politeness,
You leap, you intelligence, essence of wheelness with silvery nose,
And your platinum clocks of excitement stir like the hairs of a fern.      10

But how alien you are from the booming belts of your birth and the smoke
Where you turned on the stinging lathes of Detroit and Lansing at night

And shrieked at the torch in your secret parts and the amorous tests,
But now with your eyes that enter the future of roads you forget;
You are all instinct with your phosphorous glow and your streaking hair.          15

And now when we stop it is not as the bird from the shell that I leave
Or the leathery pilot who steps from his bird with a sneer of delight,
And not as the ignorant beast do you squat and watch me depart,
But with exquisite breathing you smile, with satisfaction of love,
And I touch you again as you tick in the silence and settle in sleep.              20

### Study and Discussion Questions

1.  Who is speaking in the poem? Why can you assume the speaker is male? What else can you say about him?
2.  Go through the poem and list the ways in which the speaker compares his car to a woman. The poem is ostensibly about the speaker's feelings for his car. But what does it suggest about how he perceives women?
3.  How do sound and rhythm in the first stanza help convey the speaker's experience as he drives? How and why is the first line of the third stanza different from what comes before? What new emotion does the third stanza reveal?
4.  What is the function of the negative comparisons ("it is not as . . .") in the last stanza? How is the speaker feeling at the end of the poem?
5.  What is the poet's attitude toward the speaker, towards the *persona* he has created? How can you tell?

### Suggestions for Writing

1.  To what extent is "Buick" an accurate portrayal of male feelings rather than just a parody of them?
2.  Why are cars in our culture usually seen as female? What other kinds of objects or machines are viewed in gendered terms? Why are they so often seen as female?
3.  Which line or phrase from the poem stands out most in your mind? Try to explain why.
4.  Try writing a poem or prose passage in which the speaker dramatizes his or her intense emotional relationship with an object other than an automobile. Think carefully before ascribing a gender to this object.

### Critical Resources

1.  Phillips, Robert. "Poetry, Prosody and Meta-Poetics: Karl Shapiro's Self-Reflexive Poetry." *Poetics in the Poem: Critical Essays on American Self-Reflexive Poetry.* Dorothy Baker, ed. New York: Peter Lang, 1997.
2.  Phillips, Robert. *The Madness of Art: Interview with Poets and Writers.* Syracuse, NY: Syracuse UP, 2003.

3. Shapiro, Karl. *Poet: An Autobiography In Three Parts.* Chapel Hill, NC: Algonquin, 1988.
4. Walker, Sue. *Seriously Meeting Karl Sharpiro.* Mobile, AL: Negative Capability, 1993.

# PATRICIA SMITH

## *Undertaker*                                                               (1993)

*For Floyd Williams*

When a bullet enters the brain, the head explodes.
I can think of no softer warning for the mothers
who sit doubled before my desk,
knotting their smooth brown hands,
and begging, fix my boy, fix my boy.                                          5
*Here's his high school picture.*
And the smirking, mildly mustachioed player
in the crinkled snapshot
looks nothing like the plastic bag of boy
stored and dated in the cold room downstairs.                                 10
In the picture, he is cocky and chiseled,
clutching the world by the balls. I know the look.
Now he is flaps of cheek,
slivers of jawbone, a surprised eye,
assorted teeth, bloody tufts of napped hair.                                  15
The building blocks of my business.
So I swallow hard, turn the photo face down
and talk numbers instead. The high price
of miracles startles the still-young woman,
but she is prepared. I know that she has sold                                 20
everything she owns, that cousins and uncles
have emptied their empty bank accounts,
that she dreams of her baby
in tuxedoed satin, flawless in an open casket,
a cross or blood red rose tacked to his fingers,                              25
his halo set at a cocky angle.
I write a figure on a piece of paper

and push it across to her
while her chest heaves with hoping.
She stares at the number, pulls in                                    30
a slow weepy breath: *"Jesus."*

But Jesus isn't on this payroll. I work alone
until the dim insistence of morning,
bent over my grisly puzzle pieces, gluing,
stitching, creating a chin with a brushstroke.                        35
I plop glass eyes into rigid sockets,
then carve eyelids from a forearm, an inner thigh.
I plump shattered skulls, and paint the skin
to suggest warmth, an impending breath.
I reach into collapsed cavities to rescue                             40
a tongue, an ear. Lips are never easy to recreate.

And I try not to remember the stories,
the tales the mothers must bring me
to ease their own hearts. *Oh, they cry,*
*my Ronnie, my Willie, my Michael, my Chico.*                        45
It was self-defense. He was on his way home,
a dark car slowed down, they must have thought
he was someone else. He stepped between
two warring gang members at a party.
Really, he was trying to get off the streets,                        50
trying to pull away from the crowd.
He was just trying to help a friend.
He was in the wrong place at the wrong time.
*Fix my boy; he was a good boy. Make him the way he was.*

But I have explored the jagged gaps                                   55
in the boy's body, smoothed the angry edges
of bulletholes. I have touched him in places
no mother knows, and I have birthed
his new face. I know he believed himself
invincible, that he most likely hissed                               60
"Fuck you, man" before the bullets lifted him
off his feet. I try not to imagine
his swagger, his lizard-lidded gaze,
his young mother screaming into the phone.

She says she will find the money, and I know                          65
this is the truth that fuels her, forces her
to place one foot in front of the other.
Suddenly, I want to take her down
to the chilly room, open the bag

and shake its terrible bounty onto the                              70
gleaming steel table. I want her to see him,
to touch him, to press her lips to the flap of cheek.
The woman needs to wither, finally, and move on.

We both jump as the phone rattles in its hook.
I pray it's my wife, a bill collector, a wrong number.          75
But the wide, questioning silence on the other end
is too familiar. Another mother needing a miracle.
Another homeboy coming home.


## Study and Discussion Questions

1. How is "Undertaker" a *dramatic* poem (look up the definition of dramatic poetry in "How Poetry Works"), both (a) technically and (b) emotionally?
2. How many "characters" are there in this poem? Who are they? What do we know about each one?
3. How does money come into the story this poem presents? Discuss "the high price of miracles."
4. What does the mother want? What does the undertaker want? Discuss the dramatic tension between the two characters.
5. Look up the word *irony* in an unabridged dictionary and in a dictionary of literary terms. Then discuss at least three ironies in Smith's poem.
6. The speaker of this poem is the undertaker himself. What do we see him doing in the poem? How does he feel about his job? What is the speaker's *tone?*


## Suggestions for Writing

1. Imagine this dramatic poem being performed. How would you stage "Undertaker"?
2. Write a paragraph discussing what you think Smith means by the undertaker's last line: "Another homeboy coming home."
3. What figures from myth, fiction, history, and/or popular culture does the undertaker remind you of? How do these associations add to the poem's resonance?


## Critical Resources

1. Glazner, Gary, ed. *Poetry Slam: The Competitive Art of Performance Poetry.* San Francisco: Manic D Press, 2000.
2. Holman, Bob. "Patricia Smith, Journalism and Poetry: Shall We Meditate on Truth." *Modern American Poetry Online.* Department of English, University of Illinois at Urbana-Champaign. 18 April 2005. <http://www.english.uiuc.edu/maps/poets/s_z/p_smith/about.htm>.

3. Schmid, Julie. "What's Going On: Poetics, Performance and Patricia's Smith's "Close to Death." *Modern American Poetry Online.* Department of English, University of Illinois at Urbana-Champaign. 18 April 2005. <http://www.english.uiuc.edu/maps/poets/s_z/p_smith/about.htm>.

4. *Slamnation.* Dir. Paul Devlin. Documentary. 90 minutes, 1996. For more information go to <http://www.slamnation.com>.

❀ ❀ ❀

# ALFRED, LORD TENNYSON

## *The Lady of Shalott* (1832)

### Part I

On either side the river lie
Long fields of barley and of rye,
That clothe the wold and meet the sky;
And thro' the field the road runs by
      To many-tower'd Camelot;                              5
And up and down the people go,
Gazing where the lilies blow
Round an island there below,
      The island of Shalott.

Willows whiten, aspens quiver,                                      10
Little breezes dusk and shiver
Thro' the wave that runs for ever
By the island in the river
      Flowing down to Camelot.
Four gray walls, and four gray towers,                             15
Overlook a space of flowers,
And the silent isle imbowers
      The Lady of Shalott.

By the margin, willow-veil'd
Slide the heavy barges trail'd                                      20
By slow horses; and unhail'd
The shallop flitteth silken-sail'd
      Skimming down to Camelot:

But who hath seen her wave her hand?
Or at the casement seen her stand?                              25
Or is she known in all the land,
   The Lady of Shalott?

Only reapers, reaping early
In among the bearded barley,
Hear a song that echoes cheerly                                 30
From the river winding clearly,
   Down to tower'd Camelot:
And by the moon the reaper weary,
Piling sheaves in uplands airy,
Listening, whispers "'Tis the fairy                            35
   Lady of Shalott."


**Part II**


There she weaves by night and day
A magic web with colours gay.
She has heard a whisper say,
A curse is on her if she stay                                   40
   To look down to Camelot.
She knows not what the curse may be,
And so she weaveth steadily,
And little other care hath she,
   The Lady of Shalott.                          45

And moving thro' a mirror clear
That hangs before her all the year,
Shadows of the world appear.
There she sees the highway near
   Winding down to Camelot:                      50
There the river eddy whirls,
And there the surly village-churls,
And the red cloaks of market girls,
   Pass onward from Shalott.
Sometimes a troop of damsels glad,                             55
An abbot on an ambling pad,
Sometimes a curly shepherd-lad,
Or long-hair'd page in crimson clad,
   Goes by to tower'd Camelot;

And sometimes thro' the mirror blue                    60
The knights come riding two and two:
She hath no loyal knight and true,
        The Lady of Shalott.

But in her web she still delights
To weave the mirror's magic sights,                    65
For often thro' the silent nights
A funeral, with plumes and lights
        And music, went to Camelot:
Or when the moon was overhead,
Came two young lovers lately wed;                       70
"I am half-sick of shadows," said
        The Lady of Shalott.


## Part III

A bow-shot from her bower-eaves,
He rode between the barley-sheaves,
The sun came dazzling thro' the leaves,                 75
And flamed upon the brazen greaves
        Of bold Sir Lancelot.
A redcross knight for ever kneel'd
To a lady in his shield,
That sparkled on the yellow field,                     80
        Beside remote Shalott.

The gemmy bridle glitter'd free,
Like to some branch of stars we see
Hung in the golden Galaxy.
The bridle-bells rang merrily                           85
        As he rode down to Camelot:
And from his blazon'd baldric slung
A mighty silver bugle hung,
And as he rode his armour rung,
        Beside remote Shalott.                          90

All in the blue unclouded weather
Thick-jewell'd shone the saddle-leather,
The helmet and the helmet-feather
Burn'd like one burning flame together,
        As he rode down to Camelot.                     95

As often thro' the purple night,
Below the starry clusters bright,
Some bearded meteor, trailing light,
  Moves over still Shalott.

His broad clear brow in sunlight glow'd;      100
On burnish'd hooves his war-horse trode;
From underneath his helmet flow'd
His coal-black curls as on he rode,
  As he rode down to Camelot.
From the bank and from the river      105
He flash'd into the crystal mirror,
"Tirra lirra," by the river
  Sang Sir Lancelot.

She left the web, she left the loom,
She made three paces thro' the room,     110
She saw the water-lily bloom,
She saw the helmet and the plume,
  She look'd down to Camelot.
Out flew the web and floated wide;
The mirror crack'd from side to side;     115
"The curse is come upon me," cried
  The Lady of Shalott.

**Part IV**

In the stormy east-wind straining,
The pale-yellow woods were waning,
The broad stream in his banks complaining,   120
Heavily the low sky raining
  Over tower'd Camelot;
Down she came and found a boat
Beneath a willow left afloat,
And round about the prow she wrote    125
  The Lady of Shalott.

And down the river's dim expanse—
Like some bold seër in a trance,
Seeing all his own mischance—
With a glassy countenance      130
  Did she look to Camelot.
And at the closing of the day
She loosed the chain, and down she lay;

The broad stream bore her far away,
    The Lady of Shalott.                                      135

Lying, robed in snowy white
That loosely flew to left and right—
The leaves upon her falling light—
Thro' the noises of the night
    She floated down to Camelot:                              140
And as the boat-head wound along
The willowy hills and fields among,
They heard her singing her last song,
    The Lady of Shalott.

Heard a carol, mournful, holy,                                        145
Chanted loudly, chanted lowly,
Till her blood was frozen slowly,
And her eyes were darken'd wholly,
    Turn'd to tower'd Camelot;
For ere she reach'd upon the tide                                     150
The first house by the water-side,
Singing in her song she died,
    The Lady of Shalott.

Under tower and balcony,
By garden-wall and gallery,                                           155
A gleaming shape she floated by,
A corse between the houses high,
    Silent into Camelot.
Out upon the wharfs they came,
Knight and burgher, lord and dame,                                    160
And round the prow they read her name,
    The Lady of Shalott.

Who is this? and what is here?
And in the lighted palace near
Died the sound of royal cheer;                                        165
And they cross'd themselves for fear,
    All the knights at Camelot:
But Lancelot mused a little space;
He said, "She has a lovely face;
God in his mercy lend her grace,                                      170
    The Lady of Shalott."

### Study and Discussion Questions

1. How does Tennyson's use of the ballad format affect the poem?
2. What is significant about the detailed descriptions of the activity beyond the Lady's tower room?
3. What role does Lancelot play in this poem?
4. How are the Lady's mirror and her weaving symbolic?
5. What exactly is the Lady's curse, and what do you think Tennyson is metaphorically trying to convey with it?
6. Why do you think Tennyson incorporates so much sound imagery throughout the poem, and what is its effect?

### Suggestions for Writing

1. "The Lady of Shalott" has often been the subject of many pieces of art, particularly paintings. Discuss why you think artists are so drawn to this poem, and examine some of these artworks, determining different artists' approach to the poem.
2. The obvious setting of this poem is Arthurian England. Discuss what effect this gives the poem and whether the poem would have the same effect if it were set in a different time and place.

## DYLAN THOMAS

## *Do not go gentle into that good night* (1952)

Do not go gentle into that good night,
Old age should burn and rave at close of day;
Rage, rage against the dying of the light.

Though wise men at their end know dark is right,
Because their words had forked no lightning they          5
Do not go gentle into that good night.
Good men, the last wave by, crying how bright
Their frail deeds might have danced in a green bay,
Rage, rage against the dying of the light.

Wild men who caught and sang the sun in flight          10
And learn, too late, they grieved it on its way,
Do not go gentle into that good night.

Grave men, near death, who see with blinding sight
Blind eyes could blaze like meteors and be gay,
Rage, rage against the dying of the light.                                    15

And you, my father, there on the sad height,
Curse, bless, me now with your fierce tears, I pray.
Do not go gentle into that good night.
Rage, rage against the dying of the light.

❋ ❋ ❋

# SOCIETY

# FICTION

**TONI CADE BAMBARA**

## *The Lesson*                                                            (1972)

Back in the days when everyone was old and stupid or young and foolish and me and Sugar were the only ones just right, this lady moved on our block with nappy hair and proper speech and no makeup. And quite naturally we laughed at her, laughed the way we did at the junk man who went about his business like he was some big-time president and his sorry-ass horse his secretary. And we kinda hated her too, hated the way we did the winos who cluttered up our parks and pissed on our handball walls and stank up our hallways and stairs so you couldn't halfway play hide-and-seek without a goddamn gas mask. Miss Moore was her name. The only woman on the block with no first name. And she was black as hell, cept for her feet, which were fish-white and spooky. And she was always planning these boring-ass things for us to do, us being my cousin, mostly, who lived on the block cause we all moved North the same time and to the same apartment then spread out gradual to breathe. And our parents would yank our heads into some kinda shape and crisp up our clothes so we'd be presentable for travel with Miss Moore, who always looked like she was going to church, though she never did. Which is just one of things the grownups talked about when they talked behind her back like a dog. But when she came calling with some sachet she'd sewed up or some gingerbread she'd made or some book, why then they'd all be too embarrassed to turn her down and we'd get handed over all spruced up. She'd been to college and said it was only right that she should take responsibility for the young ones' education, and she not even related by marriage or blood. So they'd go for it. Specially Aunt Gretchen. She was the main gofer in the family. You got some ole dumb shit foolishness you want somebody to go for, you send for Aunt Gretchen. She been screwed into the go-along for so long, it's a blood-deep natural thing with her. Which is how she got saddled with me and Sugar and Junior in the first place while our mothers were in a la-de-da apartment up the block having a good ole time.

So this one day Miss Moore rounds us all up at the mailbox and it's puredee hot and she's knockin herself out about arithmetic. And school suppose to let up in summer I heard, but she don't never let up. And the starch in my pinafore scratching the shit outta me and I'm really hating this nappy-head bitch and her goddamn college degree. I'd much rather go to the pool or to the show where it's cool. So me and Sugar leaning on the mailbox being surly, which is a Miss Moore word. And Flyboy checking out what everybody brought for lunch. And Fat Butt already wasting his peanut-butter-and-jelly sandwich like the pig he is. And Junebug punchin on Q.T.'s arm for potato chips. And Rosie Giraffe shifting from one hip to the other waiting for somebody to step on her foot or ask her if she from Georgia so she can kick ass, preferably Mercedes'. And Miss Moore asking us do we know what money is, like we a bunch of retards. I mean real money, she say, like it's only poker chips or monopoly papers we lay on the grocer. So right away I'm tired of this and say so. And would much rather snatch Sugar and go to the Sunset and terrorize the West Indian kids and take their hair ribbons and their money too. And Miss Moore files that remark away for next week's lesson on brotherhood, I can tell. And finally I say we oughta get to the subway cause it's cooler and besides we might meet some cute boys. Sugar done swiped her mama's lipstick, so we ready.

So we heading down the street and she's boring us silly about what things cost and what our parents make and how much goes for rent and how money ain't divided up right in this country. And then she gets to the part about we all poor and live in the slums, which I don't feature. And I'm ready to speak on that, but she steps out in the street and hails two cabs just like that. Then she hustles half the crew in with her and hands me a five-dollar bill and tells me to calculate 10 percent tip for the driver. And we're off. Me and Sugar and Junebug and Flyboy hangin out the window and hollering to everybody, putting lipstick on each other cause Flyboy a faggot anyway, and making farts with our sweaty armpits. But I'm mostly trying to figure how to spend this money. But they all fascinated with the meter ticking and Junebug starts laying bets as to how much it'll read when Flyboy can't hold his breath no more. Then Sugar lays bets as to how much it'll be when we get there. So I'm stuck. Don't nobody want to go for my plan, which is to jump out at the next light and run off to the first bar-b-que we can find. Then the driver tells us to get the hell out cause we there already. And the meter reads eighty-five cents. And I'm stalling to figure out the tip and Sugar say give him a dime. And I decide he don't need it bad as I do, so later for him. But then he tries to take off with Junebug foot still in the door so we talk about his mama something ferocious. Then we check out that we on Fifth Avenue and everybody dressed up in stockings. One lady in a fur coat, hot as it is. White folks crazy.

"This is the place," Miss Moore say, presenting it to us in the voice she uses at the museum. "Let's look in the windows before we go in."

"Can we steal?" Sugar asks very serious like she's getting the ground rules squared away before she plays. "I beg your pardon," say Miss Moore, and we fall out. So she leads us around the windows of the toy store and me and Sugar screamin, "This is mine, that's mine, I gotta have that, that was made for me, I was born for that," till Big Butt drowns us out.

"Hey, I'm goin to buy that there."

"That there? You don't even know what it is, stupid."

"I do so," he say punchin on Rosie Giraffe. "It's a microscope."

"Whatcha gonna do with a microscope, fool?"

"Look at things."

"Like what, Ronald?" ask Miss Moore. And Big Butt ain't got the first notion. So here go Miss Moore gabbing about the thousands of bacteria in a drop of water and the somethinorother in a speck of blood and the million and one living things in the air around us is invisible to the naked eye. And what she say that for? Junebug go to town on that "naked" and we rolling. Then Miss Moore ask what it cost. So we all jam into the window smudgin it up and the price tag say $300. So then she ask how long'd take for Big Butt and Junebug to save up their allowances. "Too long," I say. "Yeh," adds Sugar, "outgrown it by that time." And Miss Moore say no, you never outgrow learning instruments. "Why, even medical students and interns and," blah, blah, blah. And we ready to choke Big Butt for bringing it up in the first damn place.

"This here costs four hundred eighty dollars," say Rosie Giraffe. So we pile up all over her to see what she pointin out. My eyes tell me it's a chunk of glass cracked with something heavy, and different-color inks dripped into the splits, then the whole thing put into a oven or something. But for $480 it don't make sense.

"That's a paperweight made of semi-precious stones fused together under tremendous pressure," she explains slowly, with her hands doing the mining and all the factory work.

"So what's a paperweight?" asks Rosie Giraffe.

"To weigh paper with, dumbbell," say Flyboy, the wise man from the East.

"Not exactly," say Miss Moore, which is what she say when you warm or way off too. "It's to weigh paper down so it won't scatter and make your desk untidy." So right away me and Sugar curtsy to each other and then to Mercedes who is more the tidy type.

"We don't keep paper on top of the desk in my class," say Junebug, figuring Miss Moore crazy or lyin one.

"At home, then," she say. "Don't you have a calendar and a pencil case and a blotter and a letter-opener on your desk at home where you do your homework?" And she know damn well what our homes look like cause she nosys around in them every chance she gets.

"I don't even have a desk," say Junebug. "Do we?"

"No. And I don't get no homework neither," say Big Butt.

"And I don't even have a home," say Flyboy like he do at school to keep the white folks off his back and sorry for him. Send this poor kid to camp posters, is his specialty.

"I do," says Mercedes. "I have a box of stationery on my desk and a picture of my cat. My godmother bought the stationery and the desk. There's a big rose on each sheet and the envelopes smell like roses."

"Who wants to know about your smelly-ass stationery," say Rosie Giraffe fore I can get my two cents in.

"It's important to have a work area all your own so that . . ."

"Will you look at this sailboat, please," say Flyboy, cuttin her off and pointin to the thing like it was his. So once again we tumble all over each other to gaze at this magnificent thing in the toy store which is just big enough to maybe sail two kittens across the pond if you strap them to the posts tight. We all start reciting the price tag like we in assembly. "Handcrafted sailboat of fiberglass at one thousand one hundred ninety-five dollars."

"Unbelievable," I hear myself say and am really stunned. I read it again for myself just in case the group recitation put me in a trance. Same thing. For some reason this pisses me off. We look at Miss Moore and she lookin at us, waiting for I dunno what.

"Who'd pay all that when you can buy a sailboat set for a quarter at Pop's, a tube of glue for a dime, and a ball of string for eight cents? It must have a motor and a whole lot else besides," I say. "My sailboat cost me about fifty cents."

"But will it take water?" say Mercedes with her smart ass.

"Took mine to Alley Pond Park once," say Flyboy. "String broke, Lost it. Pity."

"Sailed mine in Central Park and it keeled over and sank. Had to ask my father for another dollar."

"And you got the strap," laugh Big Butt. "The jerk didn't even have a string on it. My old man wailed on his behind."

Little Q.T. was staring hard at the sailboat and you could see he wanted it bad. But he too little and somebody'd just take it from him. So what the hell. "This boat for kids, Miss Moore?"

"Parents silly to buy something like that just to get all broke up," say Rosie Giraffe.

"That much money it should last forever," I figure.

"My father'd buy it for me if I wanted it."

"Your father, my ass," say Rosie Giraffe getting a chance to finally push Mercedes.

"Must be rich people shop here," say Q.T.

"You are a very bright boy," say Flyboy. "What was your first clue?" And he rap him on the head with the back of his knuckles, since Q. T. the only one he could get away with. Though Q. T. liable to come up behind you years later and get his licks in when you half expect it.

"What I want to know is," I says to Miss Moore though I never talk to her, I wouldn't give the bitch that satisfaction, "is how much a real boat costs? I figure a thousand'd get you a yacht any day."

"Why don't you check that out," she says, "and report back to the group?" Which really pains my ass. If you gonna mess up a perfectly good swim day least you could do is have some answers. "Let's go in," she say like she got something up her sleeve. Only she don't lead the way. So me and Sugar turn the corner to where the entrance is, but when we get there I kinda hang back. Not that I'm scared, what's there to be afraid of, just a toy store. But I feel funny, shame. But what I got to be shamed about? Got as much right to go in as anybody. But somehow I can't seem to get hold of the door, so I step away for Sugar to lead. But she hangs back too. And I look at her and she looks at me and this is ridiculous. I mean, damn, I have never ever been shy about doing nothing or going nowhere. But then Mercedes steps up and then Rosie Giraffe and Big Butt crowd in behind and shove, and next thing we all stuffed into the doorway with only Mercedes squeezing past us, smoothing out her jumper and walking right down the aisle. Then the rest of us tumble in like a glued-together jigsaw done all wrong. And people lookin at us. And it's like the time me and Sugar crashed into the Catholic church on a dare. But once we got in there and everything so hushed and holy and the candles and the bowin and the handkerchiefs on all the drooping heads, I just couldn't go through with the plan. Which was for me to run up to the altar and do a tap dance while Sugar played the nose flute and messed around in the holy water. And Sugar kept givin me the elbow. Then later teased me so bad I tied her up in the shower and turned it on and locked her in. And she'd be there till this day if Aunt Gretchen hadn't finally figured I was lyin about the boarder takin a shower.

Same thing in the store. We all walkin on tiptoe and hardly touchin the games and puzzles and things. And I watched Miss Moore who is steady watchin us like she waitin for a sign. Like Mama Drewery watches the sky and sniffs the air and takes note of just how much slant is in the bird formation. Then me and Sugar bump smack into each other, so busy gazing at the toys, 'specially the sailboat. But we don't laugh and go into our fat-lady bump-stomach routine. We just stare at that price tag. Then Sugar run a finger over the whole boat. And I'm jealous and want to hit her. Maybe not her, but I sure want to punch somebody in the mouth.

"Watcha bring us here for, Miss Moore?"

"You sound angry, Sylvia. Are you mad about something?" Givin me one of them grins like she tellin a grown-up joke that never turns out to be funny. And she's lookin very closely at me like maybe she plannin to do my portrait from memory. I'm mad, but I won't give her that satisfaction. So I slouch around the store bein very bored and say, "Let's go."

Me and Sugar at the back of the train watchin the tracks whizzin by large then small then gettin gobbled up in the dark. I'm thinkin about this tricky toy I saw in the store. A clown that somersaults on a bar then does chin-ups just cause you yank lightly at his leg. Cost $35. I could see me askin my mother for a $35 birthday clown. "You wanna who that costs what?" she'd say, cocking her head to the side to get a better view of the hole in my head. Thirty-five dollars could buy new bunk beds for Junior and Gretchen's boy. Thirty-five dollars and the whole household could go visit Granddaddy Nelson in the country. Thirty-five dollars would pay for the rent and the piano bill too. Who are these people that spend that much for performing clowns and $1,000 for toy sailboats? What kinda work they do and how they live and how come we ain't in on it? Where we are is who we are, Miss Moore always pointin out. But it don't necessarily have to be that way, she always adds then waits for somebody to say that poor people have to wake up and demand their share of the pie and don't none of us know what kind of pie she talkin about in the first damn place. But she ain't so smart cause I still got her four dollars from the taxi and she sure ain't gettin it. Messin up my day with this shit. Sugar nudges me in my pocket and winks.

Miss Moore lines us up in front of the mailbox where we started from, seem like years ago, and I got a headache for thinkin so hard. And we lean all over each other so we can hold up under the draggy-ass lecture she always finishes us off with at the end before we thank her for borin us to tears. But she just looks at us like she readin tea leaves. Finally she say, "Well, what did you think of F. A. O. Schwartz?"

Rosie Giraffe mumbles, "White folks crazy."

"I'd like to go there again when I get my birthday money," says Mercedes, and we shove her out the pack so she has to lean on the mailbox by herself.

"I'd like a shower. Tiring day," say Flyboy.

Then Sugar surprises me by sayin, "You know, Miss Moore, I don't think all of us here put together eat in a year what that sailboat costs." And Miss Moore lights up like somebody goosed her. "And?" she say, urging Sugar on. Only I'm standin on her foot so she don't continue.

"Imagine for a minute what kind of society it is in which some people can spend on a toy what it would cost to feed a family of six or seven. What do you think?"

"I think," say Sugar pushing me off her feet like she never done before, cause I whip her ass in a minute, "that this is not much of a democracy if you ask me. Equal chance to pursue happiness means an equal crack at the dough, don't it?" Miss Moore is besides herself and I am disgusted with Sugar's treachery. So I stand on her foot one more time to see if she'll shove me. She shuts up, and Miss Moore looks at me, sorrowfully I'm thinkin. And somethin weird is goin on, I can feel it in my chest.

"Anybody else learn anything today?" lookin dead at me. I walk away and Sugar has to run to catch up and don't even seem to notice when I shrug her arm off my shoulder.

"Well, we got four dollars anyway," she says.

"Uh hunh."

"We could go to Hascombs and get half a chocolate layer and then go to the Sunset and still have plenty money for potato chips and ice-cream sodas."

"Uh hunh."

"Race you to Hascombs," she say.

We start down the block and she gets ahead which is O.K. by me cause I'm goin to the West End and then over to the Drive to think this day through. She can run if she want to and even run faster. But ain't nobody gonna beat me at nuthin.

## Study and Discussion Questions

1. What exactly is the lesson Miss Moore is trying to teach? To what extent does the narrator, Sylvia, learn it? What are the sources of her resistance to it?

2. Why does Sylvia feel ashamed entering the toy store? What does this reveal about her?
3. What is the significance of the last sentence of the story?
4. Why does Miss Moore feel the need to teach Sylvia and her friends a lesson now that they would no doubt eventually learn on their own?
5. What does Bambara gain by using Sylvia as a first-person narrator?
6. Who is Miss Moore? What is her role in the neighborhood? Why is she taking the children on these "field trips"?
7. Discuss the interactions between Miss Moore and the children in the toy store. Discuss the interactions between the children while they are in the store.

### Suggestions for Writing

1. What kind of society is it, Miss Moore asks, "in which some people can spend on a toy what it would cost to feed a family of six or seven?" How would you answer?
2. Describe the first time you can remember being aware of social class differences.

### Critical Resources

1. Butler-Evans, Elliot. *Race, Gender, and Desire: Narrative Strategies in the Fiction of Bambara, Morrison and Walker.* Philadelphia: Temple, 1989.
2. Heller, Janet Ruth. "Toni Cade Bambara's Use of African American Vernacular English in 'The Lesson'." *Style* 37.3 (2003): 279–293.
3. Tate, Claudia. "Toni Cade Bambara" Interview. *Black Women Writers at Work.* New York: Continuum, 1983.

❋ ❋ ❋

## WILLIAM FAULKNER

## *A Rose for Emily* (1930)

### I

When Miss Emily Grierson died, our whole town went to her funeral: the men through a sort of respectful affection for a fallen monument, the women mostly out of curiosity to see the inside of her house, which no one save an old man-servant—a combined gardener and cook—had seen in at least ten years.

It was a big, squarish frame house that had once been white, decorated with cupolas and spires and scrolled balconies in the heavily lightsome style of the seventies, set on what had once been our most select street. But garages and cotton gins had encroached and obliterated even the august names of that neighborhood; only Miss Emily's house was left, lifting its stubborn and co-quettish decay above the cotton wagons and the gasoline pumps-an eyesore among eyesores. And now Miss Emily had gone to join the representatives of those august names where they lay in the cedar-bemused cemetery among the ranked and anonymous graves of Union and Confederate soldiers who fell at the battle of Jefferson.

Alive, Miss Emily had been a tradition, a duty, and a care; a sort of heredi-tary obligation upon the town, dating from that day in 1894 when Colonel Sar-toris, the mayor—he who fathered the edict that no Negro woman should appear on the streets without an apron-remitted her taxes, the dispensation dat-ing from the death of her father on into perpetuity. Not that Miss Emily would have accepted charity. Colonel Sartoris invented an involved tale to the effect that Miss Emily's father had loaned money to the town, which the town, as a matter of business, preferred this way of repaying. Only a man of Colonel Sar-toris' generation and thought could have invented it, and only a woman could have believed it.

When the next generation, with its more modern ideas, became mayors and aldermen, this arrangement created some little dissatisfaction. On the first of the year they mailed her a tax notice. February came, and there was no reply. They wrote her a formal letter, asking her to call at the sheriff's office at her convenience. A week later the mayor wrote her himself, offering to call or to send his car for her, and received in reply a note on paper of an archaic shape, in a thin, flowing calligraphy in faded ink, to the effect that she no longer went out at all. The tax notice was also enclosed, without comment.

They called a special meeting of the Board of Aldermen. A deputation waited upon her, knocked at the door through which no visitor had passed since she ceased giving china-painting lessons eight or ten years earlier. They were admitted by the old Negro into a dim hall from which a stairway mounted into still more shadow. It smelled of dust and disuse—a close, dank smell. The Negro led them into the parlor. It was furnished in heavy, leather-covered fur-niture. When the Negro opened the blinds of one window, they could see that the leather was cracked; and when they sat down, a faint dust rose sluggishly about their thighs, spinning with slow motes in the single sun-ray. On a tar-nished gilt easel before the fireplace stood a crayon portrait of Miss Emily's father.

They rose when she entered—a small, fat woman in black, with a thin gold chain descending to her waist and vanishing into her belt, leaning on an ebony cane with a tarnished gold head. Her skeleton was small and spare; perhaps that was why what would have been merely plumpness in another was obesity in her. She looked bloated, like a body long submerged in motionless water, and of that pallid hue. Her eyes, lost in the fatty ridges of her face, looked like two small pieces of coal pressed into a lump of dough as they moved from one face to an-other while the visitors stated their errand.

She did not ask them to sit. She just stood in the door and listened quietly until the spokesman came to a stumbling halt. Then they could hear the invisible watch ticking at the end of the gold chain.

Her voice was dry and cold. "I have no taxes in Jefferson. Colonel Sartoris explained it to me. Perhaps one of you can gain access to the city records and satisfy yourselves."

"But we have. We are the city authorities, Miss Emily. Didn't you get a notice from the sheriff, signed by him?"

"I received a paper, yes," Miss Emily said. "Perhaps he considers himself the sheriff . . . I have no taxes in Jefferson."

"But there is nothing on the books to show that, you see We must go by the—"

"See Colonel Sartoris. I have no taxes in Jefferson."

"But, Miss Emily—"

"See Colonel Sartoris." (Colonel Sartoris had been dead almost ten years.) "I have no taxes in Jefferson. Tobe!" The Negro appeared. "Show these gentlemen out."

## II

So she vanquished them, horse and foot, just as she had vanquished their fathers thirty years before about the smell.

That was two years after her father's death and a short time after her sweetheart—the one we believed would marry her—had deserted her. After her father's death she went out very little; after her sweetheart went away, people hardly saw her at all. A few of the ladies had the temerity to call, but were not received, and the only sign of life about the place was the Negro man—a young man then—going in and out with a market basket.

"Just as if a man—any man—could keep a kitchen properly,"the ladies said; so they were not surprised when the smell developed. It was another link between the gross, teeming world and the high and mighty Griersons.

A neighbor, a woman, complained to the mayor, Judge Stevens, eighty years old.

"But what will you have me do about it, madam?" he said.

"Why, send her word to stop it," the woman said. "Isn't there a law?"

"I'm sure that won't be necessary," Judge Stevens said. "It's probably just a snake or a rat that nigger of hers killed in the yard. I'll speak to him about it."

The next day he received two more complaints, one from a man who came in diffident deprecation. "We really must do something about it, Judge. I'd be the last one in the world to bother Miss Emily, but we've got to do something." That night the Board of Aldermen met—three graybeards and one younger man, a member of the rising generation.

"It's simple enough," he said. "Send her word to have her place cleaned up. Give her a certain time to do it in, and if she don't. .."

"Dammit, sir," Judge Stevens said, "will you accuse a lady to her face of smelling bad?"

So the next night, after midnight, four men crossed Miss Emily's lawn and slunk about the house like burglars, sniffing along the base of the brickwork and at the cellar openings while one of them performed a regular sowing motion with his hand out of a sack slung from his shoulder. They broke open the cellar door and sprinkled lime there, and in all the outbuildings. As they recrossed the lawn, a window that had been dark was lighted and Miss Emily sat in it, the light behind her, and her upright torso motionless as that of an idol. They crept quietly across the lawn and into the shadow of the locusts that lined the street. After a week or two the smell went away.

That was when people had begun to feel really sorry for her. People in our town, remembering how old lady Wyatt, her great-aunt, had gone completely crazy at last, believed that the Griersons held themselves a little too high for what they really were. None of the young men were quite good enough for Miss Emily and such. We had long thought of them as a tableau, Miss Emily a slender figure in white in the background, her father a spraddled silhouette in the foreground, his back to her and clutching a horsewhip, the two of them framed by the back-flung front door. So when she got to be thirty and was still single, we were not pleased exactly, but vindicated; even with insanity in the family she wouldn't have turned down all of her chances if they had really materialized.

When her father died, it got about that the house was all that was left to her; and in a way, people were glad. At last they could pity Miss Emily. Being left alone, and a pauper, she had become humanized. Now she too would know the old thrill and the old despair of a penny more or less.

The day after his death all the ladies prepared to call at the house and offer condolence and aid, as is our custom Miss Emily met them at the door, dressed as usual and with no trace of grief on her face. She told them that her father was not dead. She did that for three days, with the ministers calling on her, and the doctors, trying to persuade her to let them dispose of the body. Just as they were about to resort to law and force, she broke down, and they buried her father quickly.

We did not say she was crazy then. We believed she had to do that. We remembered all the young men her father had driven away, and we knew that with nothing left, she would have to cling to that which had robbed her, as people will.

## III

She was sick for a long time. When we saw her again, her hair was cut short, making her look like a girl, with a vague resemblance to those angels in colored church windows—sort of tragic and serene.

The town had just let the contracts for paving the sidewalks, and in the summer after her father's death they began the work. The construction company came with niggers and mules and machinery, and a foreman named Homer Barron, a Yankee—a big, dark, ready man, with a big voice and eyes lighter than his face. The little boys would follow in groups to hear him cuss the niggers, and the niggers singing in time to the rise and fall of picks. Pretty soon he knew everybody in town. Whenever you heard a lot of laughing anywhere about the square, Homer Barron would be in the center of the group. Presently we began to see him and Miss Emily on Sunday afternoons driving in the yellow-wheeled buggy and the matched team of bays from the livery stable.

At first we were glad that Miss Emily would have an interest, because the ladies all said, "Of course a Grierson would not think seriously of a Northerner, a day laborer." But there were still others, older people, who said that even grief could not cause a real lady to forget *noblesse oblige*—without calling it *noblesse oblige*. They just said, "Poor Emily. Her kinsfolk should come to her." She had some kin in Alabama; but years ago her father had fallen out with them over the estate of old lady Wyatt, the crazy woman, and there was no communication between the two families. They had not even been represented at the funeral.

And as soon as the old people said, "Poor Emily," the whispering began. "Do you suppose it's really so?" they said to one another. "Of course it is. What else could . . ." This behind their hands; rustling of craned silk and satin behind jalousies closed upon the sun of Sunday afternoon as the thin, swift clop-clop-clop of the matched team passed: "Poor Emily."

She carried her head high enough—even when we believed that she was fallen. It was as if she demanded more than ever the recognition of her dignity as the last Grierson; as if it had wanted that touch of earthiness to reaffirm her imperviousness. Like when she bought the rat poison, the arsenic. That was over a year after they had begun to say "Poor Emily," and while the two female cousins were visiting her.

"I want some poison," she said to the druggist. She was over thirty then, still a slight woman, though thinner than usual, with cold, haughty black eyes in a face the flesh of which was strained across the temples and about the eyesockets as you imagine a lighthouse-keeper's face ought to look. "I want some poison," she said.

"Yes, Miss Emily. What kind? For rats and such? I'd recom—"

"I want the best you have. I don't care what kind."

The druggist named several. "They'll kill anything up to an elephant. But what you want is—"

"Arsenic," Miss Emily said. "Is that a good one?"

"Is . . . arsenic? Yes, ma'am. But what you want—"

"I want arsenic."

The druggist looked down at her. She looked back at him, erect, her face like a strained flag. "Why, of course," the druggist said. "If that's what you want. But the law requires you to tell what you are going to use it for."

Miss Emily just stared at him, her head tilted back in order to look him eye for eye, until he looked away and went and got the arsenic and wrapped it up.

The Negro delivery boy brought her the package; the druggist didn't come back. When she opened the package at home there was written on the box, under the skull and bones: "For rats."

## IV

So the next day we all said, "She will kill herself"; and we said it would be the best thing. When she had first begun to be seen with Homer Barron, we had said, "She will marry him." Then we said, "She will persuade him yet," because Homer himself had remarked—he liked men, and it was known that he drank with the younger men in the Elks' Club—that he was not a marrying man. Later we said, "Poor Emily" behind the jalousies as they passed on Sunday afternoon in the glittering buggy, Miss Emily with her head high and Homer Barron with his hat cocked and a cigar in his teeth, reins and whip in a yellow glove.

Then some of the ladies began to say that it was a disgrace to the town and a bad example to the young people. The men did not want to interfere, but at last the ladies forced the Baptist minister—Miss Emily's people were Episcopal—to call upon her. He would never divulge what happened during that interview, but he refused to go back again. The next Sunday they again drove about the streets, and the following day the minister's wife wrote to Miss Emily's relations in Alabama.

So she had blood-kin under her roof again and we sat back to watch developments. At first nothing happened. Then we were sure that they were to be married. We learned that Miss Emily had been to the jeweler's and ordered a man's toilet set in silver, with the letters H. B. on each piece. Two days later we learned that she had bought a complete outfit of men's clothing, including a nightshirt, and we said, "They are married." We were really glad. We were glad because the two female cousins were even more Grierson than Miss Emily had ever been.

So we were not surprised when Homer Barron—the streets had been finished some time since—was gone. We were a little disappointed that there was not a public blowing-off, but we believed that he had gone on to prepare for Miss Emily's coming, or to give her a chance to get rid of the cousins. (By that time it was a cabal, and we were all Miss Emily's allies to help circumvent the cousins.) Sure enough, after another week they departed. And, as we had expected all along, within three days Homer Barron was back in town. A neighbor saw the Negro man admit him at the kitchen door at dusk one evening.

And that was the last we saw of Homer Barron. And of Miss Emily for some time. The Negro man went in and out with the market basket, but the front door remained closed. Now and then we would see her at a window for a moment, as the men did that night when they sprinkled the lime, but for almost six months she did not appear on the streets. Then we knew that this was to be expected too; as if that quality of her father which had thwarted her woman's life so many times had been too virulent and too furious to die.

When we next saw Miss Emily, she had grown fat and her hair was turning gray. During the next few years it grew grayer and grayer until it attained an even pepper-and-salt iron-gray, when it ceased turning. Up to the day of her death at seventy-four it was still that vigorous iron-gray, like the hair of an active man.

From that time on her front door remained closed, save for a period of six or seven years, when she was about forty, during which she gave lessons in china-painting. She fitted up a studio in one of the downstairs rooms, where the daughters and granddaughters of Colonel Sartoris' contemporaries were sent to her with the same regularity and in the same spirit that they were sent to church on Sundays with a twenty-five-cent piece for the collection plate. Meanwhile her taxes had been remitted.

Then the newer generation became the backbone and the spirit of the town, and the painting pupils grew up and fell away and did not send their children to her with boxes of color and tedious brushes and pictures cut from the ladies' magazines. The front door closed upon the last one and remained closed for good. When the town got free postal delivery, Miss Emily alone refused to let them fasten the metal numbers above her door and attach a mailbox to it. She would not listen to them.

Daily, monthly, yearly we watched the Negro grow grayer and more stooped, going in and out with the market basket. Each December we sent her a tax notice, which would be returned by the post office a week later, unclaimed. Now and then we would see her in one of the downstairs windows—she had evidently shut up the top floor of the house—like the carven torso of an idol in a niche, looking or not looking at us, we could never tell which. Thus she passed from generation to generation—dear, inescapable, impervious, tranquil, and perverse.

And so she died. Fell ill in the house filled with dust and shadows, with only a doddering Negro man to wait on her. We did not even know she was sick; we had long since given up trying to get any information from the Negro.

He talked to no one, probably not even to her, for his voice had grown harsh and rusty, as if from disuse.

She died in one of the downstairs rooms, in a heavy walnut bed with a curtain, her gray head propped on a pillow yellow and moldy with age and lack of sunlight.

## V

The Negro met the first of the ladies at the front door and let them in, with their hushed, sibilant voices and their quick, curious glances, and then he disappeared. He walked right through the house and out the back and was not seen again.

The two female cousins came at once. They held the funeral on the second day, with the town coming to look at Miss Emily beneath a mass of bought flowers, with the crayon face of her father musing profoundly above the bier and the ladies sibilant and macabre; and the very old men—some in their brushed

Confederate uniforms—on the porch and the lawn, talking of Miss Emily as if she had been a contemporary of theirs, believing that they had danced with her and courted her perhaps, confusing time with its mathematical progression, as the old do, to whom all the past is not a diminishing road but, instead, a huge meadow which no winter ever quite touches, divided from them now by the narrow bottle-neck of the most recent decade of years.

Already we knew that there was one room in that region above stairs which no one had seen in forty years, and which would have to be forced. They waited until Miss Emily was decently in the ground before they opened it.

The violence of breaking down the door seemed to fill this room with pervading dust. A thin, acrid pall as of the tomb seemed to lie everywhere upon this room decked and furnished as for a bridal: upon the valance curtains of faded rose color, upon the rose-shaded lights, upon the dressing table, upon the delicate array of crystal and the man's toilet things backed with tarnished silver, silver so tarnished that the monogram was obscured. Among them lay a collar and tie, as if they had just been removed, which, lifted, left upon the surface a pale crescent in the dust. Upon a chair hung the suit, carefully folded; beneath it the two mute shoes and the discarded socks.

The man himself lay in the bed.

For a long while we just stood there, looking down at the profound and fleshless grin. The body had apparently once lain in the attitude of an embrace, but now the long sleep that outlasts love, that conquers even the grimace of love, had cuckolded him. What was left of him, rotted beneath what was left of the nightshirt, had become inextricable from the bed in which he lay; and upon him and upon the pillow beside him lay that even coating of the patient and biding dust.

Then we noticed that in the second pillow was the indentation of a head. One of us lifted something from it, and leaning forward, that faint and invisible dust dry and acrid in the nostrils, we saw a long strand of iron-gray hair.

❋ ❋ ❋


## MARY E. WILKINS FREEMAN


# *A Mistaken Charity*                                       (1887)


There were in a green field a little, low, weather-stained cottage, with a foot-path leading to it from the highway several rods distant, and two old women—one with a tin pan and old knife searching for dandelion greens among the short young grass, and the other sitting on the doorstep watching her, or, rather, having the appearance of watching her.

"Air there enough for a mess, Harriét?" asked the old woman on the doorstep. She accented oddly the last syllable of the Harriet, and there was a curious quality in her feeble, cracked old voice. Besides the question denoted by the arrangement of her words and the rising inflection, there was another, broader and subtler, the very essence of all questioning, in the tone of her voice itself; the cracked, quavering notes that she used reached out of themselves, and asked, and groped like fingers in the dark. One would have known by the voice that the old woman was blind.

The old woman on her knees in the grass searching for dandelions did not reply; she evidently had not heard the question. So the old woman on the door-step, after waiting a few minutes with her head turned expectantly, asked again, varying her question slightly, and speaking louder:

"Air there enough for a mess, do ye s'pose, Harriét?"

The old woman in the grass heard this time. She rose slowly and laboriously; the effort of straightening out the rheumatic old muscles was evidently a painful one; then she eyed the greens heaped up in the tin pan, and pressed them down with her hand.

"Wa'al, I don't know, Charlotte," she replied, hoarsely. "There's plenty on 'em here, but I 'ain't got near enough for a mess; they do bile down so when you get 'em in the pot; an' it's all I can do to bend my j'ints enough to dig 'em."

"I'd give consider'ble to help ye, Harriét," said the old woman on the door-step.

But the other did not hear her; she was down on her knees in the grass again, anxiously spying out the dandelions.

So the old woman on the door-step crossed her little shrivelled hands over her calico knees, and sat quite still, with the soft spring wind blowing over her.

The old wooden door-step was sunk low down among the grasses, and the whole house to which it belonged had an air of settling down and mouldering into the grass as into its own grave.

When Harriet Shattuck grew deaf and rheumatic, and had to give up her work as tailoress, and Charlotte Shattuck lost her eyesight, and was unable to do any more sewing for her livelihood, it was a small and trifling charity for the rich man who held a mortgage on the little house in which they had been born and lived all their lives to give them the use of it, rent and interest free. He might as well have taken credit to himself for not charging a squirrel for his tenement in some old decaying tree in his woods.

So ancient was the little habitation, so wavering and mouldering, the hands that had fashioned it had lain still so long in their graves, that it almost seemed to have fallen below its distinctive rank as a house. Rain and snow had filtered through its roof, mosses had grown over it, worms had eaten it, and birds built their nests under its eaves; nature had almost completely overrun and obliterated the work of man, and taken her own to herself again, till the house seemed as much a natural ruin as an old treestump.

The Shattucks had always been poor people and common people; no especial grace and refinement or fine ambition had ever characterized any of them; they had always been poor and coarse and common. The father and his father before him had simply lived in the poor little house, grubbed for their living, and then unquestioningly died. The mother had been of no rarer stamp, and the two daughters were cast in the same mould.

After their parents' death Harriet and Charlotte had lived along in the old place from youth to old age, with the one hope of ability to keep a roof over their heads, covering on their backs, and victuals in their mouths—an all-sufficient one with them.

Neither of them had ever had a lover; they had always seemed to repel rather than attract the opposite sex. It was not merely because they were poor, ordinary, and homely; there were plenty of men in the place who would have matched them well in that respect; the fault lay deeper—in their characters. Harriet, even in her girlhood, had a blunt, defiant manner that almost amounted to surliness, and was well calculated to alarm timid adorers, and Charlotte had always had the reputation of not being any too strong in her mind.

Harriet had gone about from house to house doing tailorwork after the primitive country fashion, and Charlotte had done plain sewing and mending for the neighbors. They had been, in the main, except when pressed by some temporary anxiety about their work or the payment thereof, happy and contented, with that negative kind of happiness and contentment which comes not from gratified ambition, but a lack of ambition itself. All that they cared for they had had in tolerable abundance, for Harriet at least had been swift and capable about her work. The patched, mossy old roof had been kept over their heads, the coarse, hearty food that they loved had been set on their table, and their cheap clothes had been warm and strong.

After Charlotte's eyes failed her, and Harriet had the rheumatic fever, and the little hoard of earnings went to the doctors, times were harder with them, though still it could not be said that they actually suffered.

When they could not pay the interest on the mortgage they were allowed to keep the place interest free; there was as much fitness in a mortgage on the little house, anyway, as there would have been on a rotten old apple-tree; and the people about, who were mostly farmers, and good friendly folk, helped them out with their living. One would donate a barrel of apples from his abundant harvest to the two poor old women, one a barrel of potatoes, another a load of wood for the winter fuel, and many a farmer's wife had bustled up the narrow footpath with a pound of butter, or a dozen fresh eggs, or a nice bit of pork. Besides all this, there was a tiny garden patch behind the house, with a straggling row of currant bushes in it, and one of gooseberries, where Harriet contrived every year to raise a few pumpkins, which were the pride of her life. On the right of the garden were two old apple-trees, a Baldwin and a Porter, both yet in a tolerably good fruit-bearing state.

The delight which the two poor old souls took in their own pumpkins, their apples and currants, was indescribable. It was not merely that they contributed largely towards their living; they were their own, their private share of the great wealth of nature, the little taste set apart for them alone out of her bounty, and worth more to them on that account, though they were not conscious of it, than all the richer fruits which they received from their neighbors' gardens.

This morning the two apple-trees were brave with flowers, the currant bushes looked alive, and the pumpkin seeds were in the ground. Harriet cast complacent glances in their direction from time to time, as she painfully dug her dandelion greens. She was a short, stoutly built old woman, with a large face coarsely wrinkled, with a suspicion of a stubble of beard on the square chin.

When her tin pan was filled to her satisfaction with the sprawling, spidery greens, and she was hobbling stiffly towards her sister on the door-step, she saw another woman standing before her with a basket in her hand.

"Good-morning, Harriet," she said, in a loud, strident voice, as she drew near. "I've been frying some doughnuts, and I brought you over some warm."

"I've been tellin' her it was real good in her," piped Charlotte from the door-step, with an anxious turn of her sightless face towards the sound of her sister's footstep.

Harriet said nothing but a hoarse "Good-mornin', Mis' Simonds." Then she took the basket in her hand, lifted the towel off the top, selected a doughnut, and deliberately tasted it.

"Tough," said she. "I s'posed so. If there is anything I 'spise on this airth it's a tough doughnut."

"Oh, Harriét!" said Charlotte, with a frightened look.

"They air tough," said Harriet, with hoarse defiance, "and if there is anything I 'spise on this airth it's a tough doughnut."

The woman whose benevolence and cookery were being thus ungratefully received only laughed. She was quite fleshy, and had a round, rosy, determined face.

"Well, Harriet," said she, "I am sorry they are tough, but perhaps you had better take them out on a plate, and give me my basket. You may be able to eat two or three of them if they are tough."

"They air tough—turrible tough," said Harriet, stubbornly; but she took the basket into the house and emptied it of its contents nevertheless.

"I suppose your roof leaked as bad as ever in that heavy rain day before yesterday?" said the visitor to Harriet, with an inquiring squint towards the mossy shingles, as she was about to leave with her empty basket.

"It was turrible," replied Harriet, with crusty acquiescence—"turrible. We had to set pails an' pans everywheres, an' move the bed out."

"Mr. Upton ought to fix it."

"There ain't any fix to it; the old ruff ain't fit to nail new shingles on to; the hammerin' would bring the whole thing down on our heads," said Harriet, grimly.

"Well, I don't know as it can be fixed, it's so old. I suppose the wind comes in bad around the windows and doors too?"

"It's like livin' with a piece of paper, or mebbe a sieve, 'twixt you an' the wind an' the rain," quoth Harriet, with a jerk of her head.

"You ought to have a more comfortable home in your old age," said the visitor, thoughtfully.

"Oh, it's well enough," cried Harriet, in quick alarm, and with a complete change of tone; the woman's remark had brought an old dread over her. "The old house'll last as long as Charlotte an' me do. The rain ain't so bad, nuther is the wind; there's room enough for us in the dry places, an' out of the way of the doors an' windows. It's enough sight better than goin' on the town." Her square, defiant old face actually looked pale as she uttered the last words and stared apprehensively at the woman.

"Oh, I did not think of your doing that," she said, hastily and kindly. "We all know how you feel about that, Harriet, and not one of us neighbors will see you and Charlotte go to the poorhouse while we've got a crust of bread to share with you."

Harriet's face brightened. "Thank ye, Mis' Simonds," she said, with reluctant courtesy. "I'm much obleeged to you an' the neighbors. I think mebbe we'll be able to eat some of them doughnuts if they air tough," she added, mollifyingly, as her caller turned down the foot-path.

"My, Harriét," said Charlotte, lifting up a weakly, wondering, peaked old face, "what did you tell her them doughnuts was tough fur?"

"Charlotte, do you want everybody to look down on us, an' think we ain't no account at all, just like any beggars, 'cause they bring us in vittles?" said Harriet, with a grim glance at her sister's meek, unconscious face.

"No, Harriét," she whispered.

"Do you want *to go to the poor-house?*"

"No, Harriét." The poor little old woman on the door-step fairly cowered before her aggressive old sister.

"Then don't hender me agin when I tell folks their doughnuts is tough an' their pertaters is poor. If I don't kinder keep up an' show some sperrit, I sha'n't think nothing of myself, an' other folks won't nuther, and fust thing we know they'll kerry us to the poorhouse. You'd 'a been there before now if it hadn't been for me, Charlotte."

Charlotte looked meekly convinced, and her sister sat down on a chair in the doorway to scrape her dandelions.

"Did you git a good mess, Harriét?" asked Charlotte, in a humble tone.

"Toler'ble."

"They'll be proper relishin' with that piece of pork Mis' Mann brought in yesterday. O Lord, Harriét, it's a chink!"

Harriet sniffed.

Her sister caught with her sensitive ear the little contemptuous sound. "I guess," she said, querulously, and with more pertinacity than she had shown in the matter of the doughnuts, "that if you was in the dark, as I am, Harriét, you wouldn't make fun an' turn up your nose at chinks. If you had seen the light streamin' in all of a sudden through some little hole that you hadn't known of before when you set down on the doorstep this mornin', and the wind with the smell of the apple blows in it came in your face, an' when Mis' Simonds brought them hot doughnuts, an' when I thought of the pork an' greens jest now—O Lord, how it did shine in! An' it does now. If you was me, Harriét, you would know there was chinks."

Tears began starting from the sightless eyes, and streaming pitifully down the pale old cheeks.

Harriet looked at her sister, and her grim face softened.

"Why, Charlotte, hev it that thar *is* chinks if you want to. Who cares?"

"Thar *is* chinks, Harriét."

"Wa'al, thar *is* chinks, then. If I don't hurry, I sha'n't get these greens in in time for dinner."

When the two old women sat down complacently to their meal of pork and dandelion greens in their little kitchen they did not dream how destiny slowly and surely was introducing some new colors into their web of life, even when it was almost completed, and that this was one of the last meals they would eat in their old home for many a day. In about a week from that day they were established in the "Old Ladies' Home" in a neighboring city. It came about in this wise: Mrs. Simonds, the woman who had brought the gift of hot doughnuts, was a smart, energetic person, bent on doing good, and she did a great deal. To be sure, she always did it in her own way. If she chose to give hot doughnuts, she gave hot doughnuts; it made not the slightest difference to her if the recipients of her charity would infinitely have preferred ginger cookies. Still, a great many would like hot doughnuts, and she did unquestionably a great deal of good.

She had a worthy coadjutor in the person of a rich and childless elderly widow in the place. They had fairly entered into a partnership in good works, with about an equal capital on both sides, the widow furnishing the money, and Mrs. Simonds, who had much the better head of the two, furnishing the active schemes of benevolence.

The afternoon after the doughnut episode she had gone to the widow with a new project, and the result was that entrance fees had been paid, and old Harriet and Charlotte made sure of a comfortable home for the rest of their lives. The widow was hand in glove with officers of missionary boards and trustees of charitable institutions. There had been an unusual mortality among the inmates of the "Home" this spring, there were several vacancies, and the matter of the admission of Harriet and Charlotte was very quickly and easily arranged. But the matter which would have seemed the least difficult—inducing the two old women to accept the bounty which Providence, the widow, and Mrs. Simonds were ready to bestow on them—proved the most so. The struggle to persuade them to abandon their tottering old home for a better was a terrible one. The widow had pleaded with mild surprise, and Mrs. Simonds with benevolent determination; the counsel and reverend eloquence of the minister had been called in; and when they yielded at last it was with a sad grace for the recipients of a worthy charity.

It had been hard to convince them that the "Home" was not an almshouse under another name, and their yielding at length to anything short of actual force was only due probably to the plea, which was advanced most eloquently to Harriet, that Charlotte would be so much more comfortable.

The morning they came away, Charlotte cried pitifully, and trembled all over her little shrivelled body. Harriet did not cry. But when her sister had passed out the low, sagging door she turned the key in the lock, then took it out and thrust it slyly into her pocket, shaking her head to herself with an air of fierce determination.

Mrs. Simonds's husband, who was to take them to the depot, said to himself, with disloyal defiance of his wife's active charity, that it was a shame, as he helped the two distressed old souls into his light wagon, and put the poor little box, with their homely clothes in it, in behind.

Mrs. Simonds, the widow, the minister, and the gentleman from the "Home" who was to take charge of them, were all at the depot, their faces beaming with the delight of successful benevolence. But the two poor old women looked like two forlorn prisoners in their midst. It was an impressive illustration of the truth of the saying "that it is more blessed to give than to receive."

Well, Harriet and Charlotte Shattuck went to the "Old Ladies' Home" with reluctance and distress. They stayed two months, and then—they ran away.

The "Home" was comfortable, and in some respects even luxurious; but nothing suited those two unhappy, unreasonable old women.

The fare was of a finer, more delicately served variety than they had been accustomed to; those finely flavored nourishing soups for which the "Home" took great credit to itself failed to please palates used to common, coarser food.

"O Lord, Harriét, when I set down to the table here there ain't no chinks," Charlotte used to say. "If we could hev some cabbage, or some pork an' greens, how the light would stream in!"

Then they had to be more particular about their dress. They had always been tidy enough, but now it had to be something more; the widow, in the kindness of her heart, had made it possible, and the good folks in charge of the "Home," in the kindness of their hearts, tried to carry out the widow's designs.

But nothing could transform these two unpolished old women into two nice old ladies. They did not take kindly to white lace caps and delicate neckerchiefs. They liked their new black cashmere dresses well enough, but they felt as if they broke a commandment when they put them on every afternoon. They had always worn calico with long aprons at home, and they wanted to now; and they wanted to twist up their scanty gray locks into little knots at the back of their heads, and go without caps, just as they always had done.

Charlotte in a dainty white cap was pitiful, but Harriet was both pitiful and comical. They were totally at variance with their surroundings, and they felt it keenly, as people of their stamp always do. No amount of kindness and attention—and they had enough of both—sufficed to reconcile them to their new abode. Charlotte pleaded continually with her sister to go back to their old home.

"O Lord, Harriét," she would exclaim (by the way, Charlotte's "O Lord," which, as she used it, was innocent enough, had been heard with much disfavor in the "Home," and she, not knowing at all why, had been remonstrated with concerning it), "let us go home. I can't stay here no ways in this world. I don't like their vittles, an' I don't like to wear a cap; I want to go home and do different. The currants will be ripe, Harriét. O Lord, thar was almost a chink, thinking about 'em. I want some of 'em; an' the Porter apples will be gettin' ripe, an' we could have some apple-pie. This here ain't good; I want merlasses fur sweeting. Can't we get back no ways, Harriét? It ain't far, an' we could walk, an' they don't lock us in, nor nothin'. I don't want to die here; it ain't so straight up to heaven from here. O Lord, I've felt as if I was slantendicular from heaven ever since I've been here, an' it's been so awful dark. I ain't had any chinks. I want to go home, Harriét."

"We'll go to-morrow mornin'," said Harriet, finally; "we'll pack up our things an' go; we'll put on our old dresses, an' we'll do up the new ones in bundles, an' we'll jest shy out the back way to-morrow mornin'; an' we'll go. I kin find the way, an' I reckon we kin git thar, if it is fourteen mile. Mebbe somebody will give us a lift."

And they went. With a grim humor Harriet hung the new white lace caps with which she and Charlotte had been so pestered, one on each post at the head of the bedstead, so they would meet the eyes of the first person who opened the door. Then they took their bundles, stole slyly out, and were soon on the high-road, hobbling along, holding each other's hands, as jubilant as two children, and chuckling to themselves over their escape, and the probable astonishment there would be in the "Home" over it.

"O Lord, Harriét, what do you s'pose they will say to them caps?" cried Charlotte, with a gleeful cackle.

"I guess they'll see as folks ain't goin' to be made to wear caps agin their will in a free kentry," returned Harriet, with an echoing cackle, as they sped feebly and bravely along.

The "Home" stood on the very outskirts of the city, luckily for them. They would have found it a difficult undertaking to traverse the crowded streets. As it was, a short walk brought them into the free country road—free comparatively, for even here at ten o'clock in the morning there was considerable traveling to and from the city on business or pleasure.

People whom they met on the road did not stare at them as curiously as might have been expected. Harriet held her bristling chin high in air, and hobbled along with an appearance of being well aware of what she was about, that led folks to doubt their own first opinion that there was something unusual about the two old women.

Still their evident feebleness now and then occasioned from one and another more particular scrutiny. When they had been on the road a half-hour or so, a man in a covered wagon drove up behind them. After he had passed them, he poked his head around the front of the vehicle and looked back. Finally he stopped, and waited for them to come up to him.

"Like a ride, ma'am?" said he, looking at once bewildered and compassionate.

"Thankee," said Harriet, "we'd be much obleeged."

After the man had lifted the old women into the wagon, and established them on the back seat, he turned around, as he drove slowly along, and gazed at them curiously.

"Seems to me you look pretty feeble to be walking far," said he. "Where were you going?"

Harriet told him with an air of defiance.

"Why," he exclaimed, "it is fourteen miles out. You could never walk it in the world. Well, I am going within three miles of there, and I can go on a little farther as well as not. But I don't see—Have you been in the city?"

"I have been visitin' my married darter in the city," said Harriet, calmly.

Charlotte started, and swallowed convulsively.

Harriet had never told a deliberate falsehood before in her life, but this seemed to her one of the tremendous exigencies of life which justify a lie. She felt desperate. If she could not contrive to deceive him in some way, the man might turn directly around and carry Charlotte and her back to the "Home" and the white caps.

"I should not have thought your daughter would have let you start for such a walk as that," said the man. "Is this lady your sister? She is blind, isn't she? She does not look fit to walk a mile."

"Yes, she's my sister," replied Harriet, stubbornly: "an' she's blind; an' my darter didn't want us to walk. She felt reel bad about it. But she couldn't help it. She's poor, and her husband's dead, an' she's got four leetle children."

Harriet recounted the hardships of her imaginary daughter with a glibness that was astonishing. Charlotte swallowed again.

"Well," said the man, "I am glad I overtook you, for I don't think you would ever have reached home alive."

About six miles from the city an open buggy passed them swiftly. In it were seated the matron and one of the gentlemen in charge of the "Home." They never thought of looking into the covered wagon—and indeed one can travel in one of those vehicles, so popular in some parts of New England, with as much privacy as he could in his tomb. The two in the buggy were seriously alarmed, and anxious for the safety of the old women, who were chuckling maliciously in the wagon they soon left far behind. Harriet had watched them breathlessly until they disappeared on a curve of the road; then she whispered to Charlotte.

A little after noon the two old women crept slowly up the foot-path across the field to their old home.

"The clover is up to our knees," said Harriet; "an' the sorrel and the whiteweed; an' there's lots of yaller butterflies."

"O Lord, Harriét, thar's a chink, an' I do believe I saw one of them yaller butterflies go past it," cried Charlotte, trembling all over, and nodding her gray head violently.

Harriet stood on the old sunken door-step and fitted the key, which she drew triumphantly from her pocket, in the lock, while Charlotte stood waiting and shaking behind her.

Then they went in. Everything was there just as they had left it. Charlotte sank down on a chair and began to cry. Harriet hurried across to the window that looked out on the garden.

"The currants air ripe," said she; "*an'* them pumpkins hev run all over everything."

"O Lord, Harriét," sobbed Charlotte, "thar is so many chinks that they air all runnin' together!"

### Study and Discussion Questions

1. Look at the paragraphs that describe the Shattuck sisters' house and yard. How does the setting of this story mirror the characters?
2. What are the "chinks" referred to in the story? Why does Charlotte say at the end: "thar is so many chinks that they air all runnin' together"?
3. List the different kinds of charity in the story. Which ones are "mistaken" and which are not?
4. Why are Charlotte and Harriet uncomfortable in the Old Ladies' Home?
5. Describe the relationship between the two sisters.
6. What do you think is the author's attitude toward the Shattuck sisters?
7. Why does Harriet tell Mrs. Simonds that her doughnuts are "turrible tough"?
8. "It is more blessed to give than to receive." Is there any irony in Freeman's use of this maxim?

### Suggestions for Writing

1. This story was published in 1887. What are some of the issues it raises that are still very much with us today?
2. Have you ever been either a recipient or a giver of charity? (Being taken to the movies by a friend when you couldn't afford it and volunteering your time and labor to help someone in need are examples.) Describe the situation and how you felt in it.
3. Define *charity*. Give some examples from your own experience or knowledge. Which of these are "mistaken" and which are not? Why?

### Critical Resources

1. Glasser, Leah Blatt. *In the Closet Hidden: The Life and Work of Mary E. Wilkins Freeman.* Amherst: U of Massachusetts P, 1996.
2. Marchalonis, Shirley, ed. *Critical Essays on Mary Wilkins Freeman.* Boston: G. K. Hall, 1991.
3. Reichardt, Mary. *Mary Wilkins Freeman: A Study of the Short Fiction.* New York: Twayne, 1997.

## SHIRLEY JACKSON

## *The Lottery* (1948)

The morning of June 27th was clear and sunny, with the fresh warmth of a full-summer day; the flowers were blossoming profusely and the grass was richly green. The people of the village began to gather in the square, between the post office and the bank, around ten o'clock; in some towns there were so many people that the lottery took two days and had to be started on June 2th. but in this village, where there were only about three hundred people, the whole lottery took less than two hours, so it could begin at ten o'clock in the morning and still be through in time to allow the villagers to get home for noon dinner.

The children assembled first, of course. School was recently over for the summer, and the feeling of liberty sat uneasily on most of them; they tended to gather together quietly for a while before they broke into boisterous play. and their talk was still of the classroom and the teacher, of books and reprimands. Bobby Martin had already stuffed his pockets full of stones, and the other boys soon followed his example, selecting the smoothest and roundest stones; Bobby and Harry Jones and Dickie Delacroix—the villagers pronounced this name "Dellacroy"—eventually made a great pile of stones in one corner of the square and guarded it against the raids of the other boys. The girls stood aside, talking among themselves, looking over their shoulders at rolled in the dust or clung to the hands of their older brothers or sisters.

Soon the men began to gather. surveying their own children, speaking of planting and rain, tractors and taxes. They stood together, away from the pile of stones in the corner, and their jokes were quiet and they smiled rather than laughed. The women, wearing faded house dresses and sweaters, came shortly after their menfolk. They greeted one another and exchanged bits of gossip as they went to join their husbands. Soon the women, standing by their husbands, began to call to their children, and the children came reluctantly, having to be called four or five times. Bobby Martin ducked under his mother's grasping hand and ran, laughing, back to the pile of stones. His father spoke up sharply, and Bobby came quickly and took his place between his father and his oldest brother.

The lottery was conducted—as were the square dances, the teen club, the Halloween program—by Mr. Summers. who had time and energy to devote to civic activities. He was a round-faced, jovial man and he ran the coal business, and people were sorry for him. because he had no children and his wife was a scold. When he arrived in the square, carrying the black wooden box, there was a murmur of conversation among the villagers, and he waved and called. "Little late today, folks." The postmaster, Mr. Graves, followed him, carrying a three- legged stool, and the stool was put in the center of the square and Mr. Summers set the black box down on it. The villagers kept their distance, leaving a space between themselves and the stool. and when Mr. Summers said, "Some of you fellows want to give me a hand?" there was a hesitation before two men. Mr. Martin and his oldest son, Baxter. came forward to hold the box steady on the stool while Mr. Summers stirred up the papers inside it.

The original paraphernalia for the lottery had been lost long ago, and the black box now resting on the stool had been put into use even before Old Man Warner, the oldest man in town, was born. Mr. Summers spoke frequently to the villagers about making a new box, but no one liked to upset even as much tradition as was represented by the black box. There was a story that the present box had been made with some pieces of the box that had preceded it, the one that had been constructed when the first people settled down to make a village here. Every year, after the lottery, Mr. Summers began talking again about a new box, but every year the subject was allowed to fade off without anything's being done. The black box grew shabbier each year: by now it was no longer completely black but splintered badly along one side to show the original wood color, and in some places faded or stained.

Mr. Martin and his oldest son, Baxter, held the black box securely on the stool until Mr. Summers had stirred the papers thoroughly with his hand. Because so much of the ritual had been forgotten or discarded, Mr. Summers had been successful in having slips of paper substituted for the chips of wood that had been used for generations. Chips of wood, Mr. Summers had argued. had been all very well when the village was tiny, but now that the population was more than three hundred and likely to keep on growing, it was necessary to use something that would fit more easily into he black box. The night before the lottery, Mr. Summers and Mr. Graves made up the slips of paper and put them in the box, and it was then taken to the safe of Mr. Summers' coal company and locked up until Mr. Summers was ready to take it to the square next morning. The rest of the year, the box was put way, sometimes one place, sometimes another; it had spent one year in Mr. Graves's barn and another year underfoot in the post office. and sometimes it was set on a shelf in the Martin grocery and left there.

There was a great deal of fussing to be done before Mr. Summers declared the lottery open. There were the lists to make up—of heads of families. heads of households in each family. members of each household in each family. There was the proper swearing-in of Mr. Summers by the postmaster, as the official of the lottery; at one time, some people remembered, there had been a recital of some sort, performed by the official of the lottery, a perfunctory. tuneless chant that had been rattled off duly each year; some people believed that the official of the lottery used to stand just so when he said or sang it, others believed that he was supposed to walk among the people, but years and years ago this p3rt of the ritual had been allowed to lapse. There had been, also, a ritual salute, which the official of the lottery had had to use in addressing each person who came up to draw from the box, but this also had changed with time, until now it was felt necessary only for the official to speak to each person approaching. Mr. Summers was very good at all this; in his clean white shirt and blue jeans. with one hand resting carelessly on the black box. he seemed very proper and important as he talked interminably to Mr. Graves and the Martins.

Just as Mr. Summers finally left off talking and turned to the assembled villagers, Mrs. Hutchinson came hurriedly along the path to the square, her sweater thrown over her shoulders, and slid into place in the back of the crowd. "Clean forgot what day it was," she said to Mrs. Delacroix, who stood next to her, and they both laughed softly. "Thought my old man was out back stacking wood," Mrs. Hutchinson went on. "and then I looked out the window and the kids was gone, and then I remembered it was the twenty-seventh and came a-running." She dried her hands on her apron, and Mrs. Delacroix said, "You're in time, though. They're still talking away up there."

Mrs. Hutchinson craned her neck to see through the crowd and found her husband and children standing near the front. She tapped Mrs. Delacroix on the arm as a farewell and began to make her way through the crowd. The people separated good-humoredly to let her thought: two or three people said. in voices just loud enough to be heard across the crowd, "Here comes your, Missus, Hutchinson," and "Bill, she made it after all." Mrs. Hutchinson reached her husband, and Mr. Summers, who had been waiting, said cheerfully. "Thought we were going to have to get on without you, Tessie." Mrs. Hutchinson said. grinning, "Wouldn't have me leave m'dishes in the sink, now, would you. Joe?," and soft laughter ran through the crowd as the people stirred back into position after Mrs. Hutchinson's arrival.

"Well, now." Mr. Summers said soberly, "guess we better get started, get this over with, so's we can go back to work. Anybody ain't here?"

"Dunbar." several people said. "Dunbar. Dunbar."

Mr. Summers consulted his list. "Clyde Dunbar." he said. "That's right. He's broke his leg, hasn't he? Who's drawing for him?"

"Me. I guess," a woman said. and Mr. Summers turned to look at her. "Wife draws for her husband." Mr. Summers said. "Don't you have a grown boy to do it for you, Janey?" Although Mr. Summers and everyone else in the village knew the answer perfectly well, it was the business of the official of the lottery to ask such questions formally. Mr. Summers waited with an expression of polite interest while Mrs. Dunbar answered.

"Horace's not but sixteen yet," Mrs. Dunbar said regretfully. "Guess I gotta fill in for the old man this year."

"Right." Sr. Summers said. He made a note on the list he was holding. Then he asked, "Watson boy drawing this year?"

A tall boy in the crowd raised his hand. "Here," he said. "I'm drawing for my mother and me." He blinked his eyes nervously and ducked his head as several voices in the crowd said things like "Good fellow, lack." and "Glad to see your mother's got a man to do it."

"Well," Mr. Summers said, "guess that's everyone. Old Man Warner make it?"

"Here," a voice said. and Mr. Summers nodded.

A sudden hush fell on the crowd as Mr. Summers cleared his throat and looked at the list. "All ready?" he called. "Now, I'll read the names—heads of families first—and the men come up and take a paper out of the box. Keep the paper folded in your hand without looking at it until everyone has had a turn. Everything clear?"

The people had done it so many times that they only half listened to the directions: most of them were quiet. wetting their lips. not looking around. Then Mr. Summers raised one hand high and said, "Adams." A man disengaged himself from the crowd and came forward. "Hi. Steve." Mr. Summers said. and Mr. Adams said. "Hi. Joe." They grinned at one another humorlessly and nervously. Then Mr. Adams reached into the black box and took out a folded paper. He held it firmly by one corner as he turned and went hastily back to his place in the crowd. where he stood a little apart from his family. not looking down at his hand.

"Allen." Mr. Summers said. "Anderson.... Bentham."

"Seems like there's no time at all between lotteries any more." Mrs. Delacroix said to Mrs. Graves in the back row.

"Seems like we got through with the last one only last week."

"Time sure goes fast," Mrs. Graves said.

"Clark.... Delacroix."

"There goes my old man." Mrs. Delacroix said. She held her breath while her husband went forward.

"Dunbar," Mr. Summers said, and Mrs. Dunbar went steadily to the box while one of the women said. "Go on. Janey," and another said, "There she goes."

"We're next." Mrs. Graves said. She watched while Mr. Graves came around from the side of the box, greeted Mr. Summers gravely and selected a slip of paper from the box. By now, all through the crowd there were men holding the small folded papers in their large hand. turning them over and over nervously Mrs. Dunbar and her two sons stood together, Mrs. Dunbar holding the slip of paper.

"Harburt.... Hutchinson."

"Get up there, Bill," Mrs. Hutchinson said. and the people near her laughed.

"Jones."

"They do say," Mr. Adams said to Old Man Warner, who stood next to him, "that over in the north village they're talking of giving up the lottery."

Old Man Warner snorted. "Pack of crazy fools," he said. "Listening to the young folks, nothing's good enough for them. Next thing you know, they'll be wanting to go back to living in caves, nobody work any more, live hat way for a while. Used to be a saying about 'Lottery in June, corn be heavy soon.' First thing you know, we'd all be eating stewed chickweed and acorns. There's always been a lottery," he added petulantly. "Bad enough to see young Joe Summers up there joking with everybody."

"Some places have already quit lotteries." Mrs. Adams said.

"Nothing but trouble in that," Old Man Warner said stoutly. "Pack of young fools."

"Martin." And Bobby Martin watched his father go forward. "Overdyke.... Percy."

"I wish they'd hurry," Mrs. Dunbar said to her older son. "I wish they'd hurry."

"They're almost through," her son said.

"You get ready to run tell Dad," Mrs. Dunbar said.

Mr. Summers called his own name and then stepped forward precisely and selected a slip from the box. Then he called, "Warner."

"Seventy-seventh year I been in the lottery," Old Man Warner said as he went through the crowd. "Seventy-seventh time."

"Watson" The tall boy came awkwardly through the crowd. Someone said, "Don't be nervous, Jack," and Mr. Summers said, "Take your time, son."

"Zanini."

After that, there was a long pause, a breathless pause, until Mr. Summers. holding his slip of paper in the air, said, "All right, fellows." For a minute, no one

moved, and then all the slips of paper were opened. Suddenly, all the women be-
gan to speak at once, saving. "Who is it?," "Who's got it?," "Is it the Dunbars?,"
"Is it the Watsons?" Then the voices began to say, "It's Hutchinson. It's Bill," "Bill
Hutchinson's got it."

"Go tell your father," Mrs. Dunbar said to her older son.

People began to look around to see the Hutchinson. Bill Hutchinson was
standing quiet, staring down at the paper in his hand. Suddenly. Tessie Hutchinson shouted to Mr. Summers. "You didn't give him time enough to take any paper he wanted. I saw you. It wasn't fair!"

"Be a good sport, Tessie." Mrs. Delacroix called, and Mrs. Graves said, "All of
us took the same chance."

"Shut up, Tessie," Bill Hutchinson said.

"Well, everyone," Mr. Summers said, "that was done pretty fast, and now
we've got to be hurrying a little more to get done in time." He consulted his next
list. "Bill," he said, "you draw for the Hutchinson family. You got any other
households in the Hutchinsons?"

"There's Don and Eva," Mrs. Hutchinson yelled. "Make them take their
chance!"

"Daughters draw with their husbands' families, Tessie," Mr. Summers said
gently. "You know that as well as anyone else."

"It wasn't fair," Tessie said.

"I guess not, Joe." Bill Hutchinson said regretfully. "My daughter draws with
her husband's family; that's only fair. And I've got no other family except the
kids."

"Then, as far as drawing for families is concerned, it's you," Mr. Summers said
in explanation, "and as far as drawing for households is concerned, that's you,
too. Right?"

"Right," Bill Hutchinson said.

"How many kids, Bill?" Mr. Summers asked formally.

"Three," Bill Hutchinson said. "There's Bill, Jr., and Nancy, and little Dave.
And Tessie and me."

"All right, then," Mr. Summers said. "Harry, you got their tickets back?"

Mr. Graves nodded and held up the slips of paper. "Put them in the box, then,"
Mr. Summers directed. "Take Bill's and put it in."

"I think we ought to start over," Mrs. Hutchinson said, as quietly as she could.
"I tell you it wasn't fair. You didn't give him time enough to choose. Everybody
saw that."

Mr. Graves had selected the five slips and put them in the box. and he
dropped all the papers but those onto the ground. where the breeze caught them
and lifted them off.

"Listen, everybody," Mrs. Hutchinson was saying to the people around her.

"Ready, Bill?" Mr. Summers asked, and Bill Hutchinson, with one quick
glance around at his wife and children, nodded.

"Remember," Mr. Summers said. "take the slips and keep them folded until
each person has taken one. Harry, you help little Dave." Mr. Graves took the

hand of the little boy, who came willingly with him up to the box. "Take a paper out of the box, Davy." Mr. Summers said. Davy put his hand into the box and laughed. "Take just one paper." Mr. Summers said. "Harry, you hold it for him." Mr. Graves took the child's hand and removed the folded paper from the tight fist and held it while little Dave stood next to him and looked up at him won-deringly.

"Nancy next," Mr. Summers said. Nancy was twelve, and her school friends breathed heavily as she went forward switching her skirt, and took a slip dain-tily from the box "Bill, Jr.," Mr. Summers said, and Billy, his face red and his feet overlarge, near knocked the box over as he got a paper out. "Tessie," Mr. Sum-mers said. She hesitated for a minute, looking around defiantly. and then set her lips and went up to the box. She snatched a paper out and held it behind her.

"Bill," Mr. Summers said, and Bill Hutchinson reached into the box and felt around, bringing his hand out at last with the slip of paper in it.

The crowd was quiet. A girl whispered, "I hope it's not Nancy," and the sound of the whisper reached the edges of the crowd.

"It's not the way it used to be." Old Man Warner said clearly. "People ain't the way they used to be."

"All right," Mr. Summers said. "Open the papers. Harry, you open little Dave's."

Mr. Graves opened the slip of paper and there was a general sigh through the crowd as he held it up and everyone could see that it was blank. Nancy and Bill. Jr.. opened theirs at the same time. and both beamed and laughed. turning around to the crowd and holding their slips of paper above their heads.

"Tessie," Mr. Summers said. There was a pause, and then Mr. Summers looked at Bill Hutchinson, and Bill unfolded his paper and showed it. It was blank.

"It's Tessie," Mr. Summers said, and his voice was hushed. "Show us her pa-per. Bill."

Bill Hutchinson went over to his wife and forced the slip of paper out of her hand. It had a black spot on it, the black spot Mr. Summers had made the night before with the heavy pencil in the coal company office. Bill Hutchinson held it up, and there was a stir in the crowd.

"All right, folks." Mr. Summers said. "Let's finish quickly."

Although the villagers had forgotten the ritual and lost the original black box, they still remembered to use stones. The pile of stones the boys had made ear-lier was ready; there were stones on the ground with the blowing scraps of pa-per that had come out of the box Delacroix selected a stone so large she had to pick it up with both hands and turned to Mrs. Dunbar. "Come on," she said. "Hurry up."

Mrs. Dunbar had small stones in both hands, and she said, gasping for breath, "I can't run at all. You'll have to go ahead and I'll catch up with you."

The children had stones already. And someone gave little Davy Hutchinson few pebbles.

Tessie Hutchinson was in the center of a cleared space by now, and she held her hands out desperately as the villagers moved in on her. "It isn't fair," she said.

A stone hit her on the side of the head. Old Man Warner was saying, "Come on, come on, everyone." Steve Adams was in the front of the crowd of villagers, with Mrs. Graves beside him.

"It isn't fair, it isn't right," Mrs. Hutchinson screamed, and then they were upon her.

## Discussion Questions

1. Were you surprised by the ending of the story? If not, at what point did you know what was going to happen? How does Jackson start to fore-shadow the ending in paragraphs 2 and 3? Conversely, how does Jackson lull us into thinking that this is just an ordinary story with an ordinary town?
2. Where does the story take place? In what way does the setting affect the story? Does it make you more or less likely to anticipate the ending?
3. In what ways are the characters differentiated from one another? Looking back at the story, can you see why Tessie Hutchinson is singled out as the "winner"?
4. What are some examples of irony in this story? For example, why might the title, "The Lottery," or the opening description in paragraph one, be considered ironic?
5. Jackson gives interesting names to a number of her characters. Explain the possible allusions, irony or symbolism of some of these:
   • Delacroix
   • Graves
   • Summers
   • Bentham
   • Hutchinson
   • Warner
   • Martin
7. Take a close look at Jackson's description of the black wooden box (paragraph 5) and of the black spot on the fatal slip of paper (paragraph 72). What do these objects suggest to you? Why is the black box described as "battered"? Are there any other symbols in the story?
8. What do you understand to be the writer's own attitude toward the lottery and the stoning? Exactly what in the story makes her attitude clear to us?
9. This story satirizes a number of social issues, including the reluctance of people to reject outdated traditions, ideas, rules, laws, and practices. What kinds of traditions, practices, laws, etc. might "The Lottery" represent?
10. This story was published in 1948, just after World War II. What other cultural or historical events, attitudes, institutions, or rituals might Jackson be satirizing in this story?

❋ ❋ ❋

# FLANNERY O'CONNOR

## *Revelation* (1965)

The Doctor's waiting room, which was very small, was almost full when the Turpins entered and Mrs. Turpin, who was very large, made it look even smaller by her presence. She stood looming at the head of the magazine table set in the center of it, a living demonstration that the room was inadequate and ridiculous. Her little bright black eyes took in all the patients as she sized up the seating situation. There was one vacant chair and a place on the sofa occupied by a blond child in a dirty blue romper who should have been told to move over and make room for the lady. He was five or six, but Mrs. Turpin saw at once that no one was going to tell him to move over. He was slumped down in the seat, his arms idle at his sides and his eyes idle in his head; his nose ran unchecked.

Mrs. Turpin put a firm hand on Claud's shoulder and said in a voice that included anyone who wanted to listen, "Claud, you sit in that chair there," and gave him a push down into the vacant one. Claud was florid and bald and sturdy, somewhat shorter than Mrs. Turpin, but he sat down as if he were accustomed to doing what she told him to.

Mrs. Turpin remained standing. The only man in the room besides Claud was a lean stringy old fellow with a rusty hand spread out on each knee, whose eyes were closed as if he were asleep or dead or pretending to be so as not to get up and offer her his seat. Her gaze settled agreeably on a well-dressed grey-haired lady whose eyes met hers and whose expression said: if that child belonged to me, he would have some manners and move over-there's plenty of room there for you and him too.

Claud looked up with a sigh and made as if to rise.

"Sit down," Mrs. Turpin said. "You know you're not supposed to stand on that leg. He has an ulcer on his leg," she explained.

Claud lifted his foot onto the magazine table and rolled his trouser leg up to reveal a purple swelling on a plump marble white calf.

"My!" the pleasant lady said. "How did you do that?"

"A cow kicked him," Mrs. Turpin said.

"Goodness!" said the lady.

Claud rolled his trouser leg down.

"Maybe the little boy would move over," the lady suggested, but the child did not stir.

"Somebody will be leaving in a minute," Mrs. Turpin said. She could not understand why a doctor-with as much money as they made charging five dollars a day to just stick their head in the hospital door and look at you-couldn't afford a decent-sized waiting room. This one was hardly bigger than a garage. The table was cluttered with limp-looking magazines and at one end of it there was a big green glass ashtray full of cigarette butts and cotton wads with little blood spots on them. If she had had anything to do with the running of the place, that would have been emptied every so often. There were no chairs against the wall at the head of the room. It had a rectangular-shaped panel in it that permitted a view of the office where the nurse came and went and the secretary listened to the radio. A plastic fern, in a gold pot sat in the opening and trailed its fronds down almost to the floor. The radio was softly playing gospel music.

Just then the inner door opened and a nurse with the highest stack of yellow hair Mrs. Turpin had ever seen put her face in the crack and called for the next patient. The woman sitting beside Claud grasped the two arms of her chair and hoisted herself up; she pulled her dress free from her legs and lumbered through the door where the nurse had disappeared.

Mrs. Turpin eased into the vacant chair, which held her tight as a corset. "I wish I could reduce," she said, and rolled her eyes and gave a comic sigh.

"Oh, you aren't fat," the stylish lady said.

"Ooooo I am too," Mrs. Turpin said. "Claud he eats all he wants to and never weighs over one hundred and seventy-five pounds, but me I just look at something good to eat and I gain some weight," and her stomach and shoulders shook with laughter. "You can eat all you want to, can't YOU, Claud?" she asked, turning to him.

Claud only grinned.

"Well, as long as you have such a good disposition," the stylish lady said, "I don't think it makes a bit of difference what size you are. You just can't beat a good disposition."

Next to her was a fat girl of eighteen or nineteen, scowling into a thick blue book which Mrs. Turpin saw was entitled *Human Development*. The girl raised her head and directed her scowl at Mrs. Turpin as if she did not like her looks. She appeared annoyed that anyone should speak while she tried to read. The poor girl's face was blue with acne and Mrs. Turpin thought how pitiful it was to have a face like that at that age. She gave the girl a friendly smile but the girl only scowled the harder. Mrs. Turpin herself was fat but she had always had good skin, and, though she was forty-seven years old, there was not a wrinkle in her face except around her eyes from laughing too much.

Next to the ugly girl was the child, still in exactly the same position, and next to him was a thin leathery old woman in a cotton print dress. She and Claud had three sacks of chicken feed in their pump house that was in the same print. She had seen from the first that the child belonged with the old woman. She could tell by the way they sat- kind of vacant and white-trashy, as if they would sit there until Doomsday if nobody called and told them to get up. And at right angles but next to the well-dressed pleasant lady was a lank-faced woman who was certainly the child's mother. She had on a yellow sweatshirt and wine-colored slacks, both gritty-looking, and the rims of her lips were stained with snuff. Her dirty yellow hair was tied behind with a little piece of red paper ribbon. Worse than niggers any day, Mrs. Turpin thought.

The gospel hymn playing was, "When I looked up and He looked down," and Mrs. Turpin, who knew it, supplied the last line mentally, "And wona these days I know I'll we-eara crown.

Without appearing to, Mrs. Turpin always noticed people's feet. The well-dressed lady had on red and grey suede shoes to match her dress. Mrs. Turpin had on her good black patent -leather pumps. The ugly girl had on Girl Scout shoes and heavy socks. The old woman had on tennis shoes and the white-trashy mother had on what appeared to be bedroom slippers, black straw with gold braid threaded through them-exactly what you would have expected her to have on.

Sometimes at night when she couldn't go to sleep, Mrs. Turpin would occupy herself with the question of who she would have chosen to be if she couldn't have been herself. If Jesus had said to her before he made her, "There's only two places available for you. You can either be a nigger or white trash," what would she have said? "Please, Jesus, please," she would have said, "Just let me wait un-til there's another place available," and he would have said, "No, you have to go right now", and I have only those two places so make up your mind." She would have wiggled and squirmed and begged and pleaded but it would have been no use and finally she would have said, "All right, make me a nigger then-but that don't mean a trashy one." And he would have made her a near clean respectable Negro woman, herself but black.

Next to the child's mother was a redheaded youngish woman, reading one of the magazines and working a piece of chewing gum, hell for leather, as Claud would say. Mrs. Turpin could not see the woman's feet. She was not white trash, just common. Sometimes Mrs. Turpin occupied herself at night naming the classes of people. On the bottom of the heap were most colored people, not the kind she would have been if she had been one, but most of them; then next to them — not above, just away from — were the white-trash; then above them were the home-owners, and above them the home-and-land owners, to which she and Claud be-longed. Above she and Claud were people with a lot of money and much bigger houses and much more land. But here the complexity of it would begin to bear in on her, for some of the people with a lot of money were common and ought to be below she and Claud and some of the people who had good blood had lost their money and had to rent and then there some colored people who owned their homes and land as well. There was a colored dentist in town who had two red Lin-coln's and a swimming pool and a farm with registered whiteface cattle on it. Usu-ally by the time she had fallen asleep all the classes of people were moiling and roiling around in her head, and she would dream they were all crammed in to-gether in a box car, being ridden off to be put in a gas oven.

"That's a beautiful clock," she said and nodded to her right. It was a big wall clock, the face encased in a brass sunburst.

"Yes, it's very pretty," the stylish lady said agreeably. "And right on the dot too," she added, glancing at her watch.

The ugly girl beside her cast an eye upward at the clock, smirked, then looked directly at Mrs. Turpin and smirked again. Then she returned her eyes to her book. She was obviously the lady's daughter because, although they didn't look anything alike as to disposition, they both had the same shape of face and the same blue eyes. On the lady they sparkled pleasantly but in the girl's scared face they appeared alternately to smolder and to blaze.

What if Jesus had said, "All right, you can be white-trash or a nigger or ugly!"

Mrs. Turpin felt an awful pity for the girl, though she thought it was one thing to be ugly and another to act ugly.

The woman with the snuff-stained lips turned around in her chair and looked up at the clock. Then she turned back and appeared to look a little to the side of Mrs. Turpin. There was a cast in one of her eyes. "You want to know where you can get you one of them there clocks?" she asked in a loud voice.

"No, I already have a nice clock," Mrs. Turpin said. Once somebody like her got a leg in the conversation, she would be all over it.

"You can get you one with green stamps," the woman said. "That's most likely where he got hisn. Save you up enough, you can get you most anythang. I got me some joo'ry."

Ought to have got you a wash rag and some soap, Mrs. Turpin thought.

"I get contour sheets with mine," the pleasant lady said.

The daughter slammed her book shut. She looked straight in front of her, directly through Mrs. Turpin and on through the yellow curtain and the plate glass window which made the wall behind her. The girl's eyes seemed lit all of a sudden with a peculiar light, an unnatural light like night road signs give. Mrs. Turpin turned her head to see if there was anything going on outside that she should see, but she could not see anything. Figures passing cast only a pate shadow through the curtain. There was no reason the girl should single her out for her ugly looks.

"Miss Finley," the nurse said, cracking the door. The gum-chewing woman got up and passed in front of her and Claud and went into the office. She had on red high-heeled shoes.

Directly across the table, the ugly girl's eyes were fixed on Mrs. Turpin as if she had some very special reason for disliking her.

"This is wonderful weather, isn't it?" the girl's mother said.

"It's good weather for cotton if you can get the niggers to pick it," Mrs. Turpin said, "but niggers don't want to pick cotton any more. You can't get the white folks to pick it and now you can't get the niggers because they got to be right up there with the white folks."

"They gonna try anyways," the white-trash woman said, leaning forward.

"Do you have one of those cotton-picking machines?" the pleasant lady asked.

"No," Mrs. Turpin said, "they leave half the cotton in the field. We don't have much cotton anyway. If you want to make it farming now, you have to have a little of everything. We got a couple of acres of cotton and a few hogs and chickens and just enough white-face that Claud can look after them himself."

"One thang I don't want," the white-trash woman said, wiping her mouth with the back of her hand. "Hogs. Nasty stinking things, a-gruntin and a-rootin all over the place."

Mrs. Turpin gave her the merest edge of her attention. "Our hogs are not dirty and they don't stink," she said. "They're cleaner than some children I've seen. Their feet never touch the ground. We have a pig-parlor-that's where you raise them on concrete," she explained to the pleasant lady, "and Claud scoots them down with the hose every afternoon and washes off the floor." Cleaner by far than that child right there, she thought. Poor nasty little thing. He had not moved except to put the thumb of his dirty hand into his mouth.

The woman turned her face away from Mrs. Turpin. "I know I wouldn't scoot down no hog with no hose," she said to the wall.

You wouldn't have no hog to scoot down, Mrs. Turpin said to herself.

"A-gruntin and a-rootin and a-groanin," the woman muttered.

"We got a little of everything," Mrs. Turpin said to the pleasant lady. "It's no use in having more than you can handle yourself with help like it is. We found enough niggers to pick our cotton this year but Claud he has to go after them and take them home' again in the evening. They can't walk that half a mile. No they can't. I tell you," she said and laughed merrily, "I sure am tired of butter'ing up niggers, but you got to love em if you want em to work for you. When they come in the morning, I run out and I say, "How yal this morning?' and when Claud drives them off to the field I just wave to beat the band and they just wave back." And she waved her hand rapidly to illustrate.

"Like you read out of the same book," the lady said, showing she understood perfectly.

"Child, yes," Mrs. Turpin said. "And when they come in from the field, I run out with a bucket of ice water. That's the way it's going to be from now on," she said. "You may as well face it."

"One thang I know," the white-trash woman said. "Two thangs I ain't going to do: love no niggers or scoot down no hog with no hose." And she let out a bark of contempt.

The look that Mrs. Turpin and the pleasant lady exchanged indicated they both understood that you had to have certain things before you could know certain things. But every time Mrs. Turpin exchanged a look with the lady, she was aware that the ugly girl's peculiar eyes were still on her, and she had trouble bringing her attention back to the conversation.

"When you got something," she said, "you got to look after it." And when you ain't got a thing but breath and britches, she added to herself, you can afford to come to town every morning and just sit on the Court House coping and spit.

A grotesque revolving shadow passed across the curtain behind her and was thrown palely on the opposite wall. Then a bicycle clattered down against the outside of the building. The door opened and a colored boy glided in with a tray from the drug store. It had two large red and white paper cups on it with tops on them. He was a tall, very black boy in discolored white pants and a green nylon shirt. He was chewing gum slowly, as if to music. He set the tray down in the office opening next to the fern and stuck his head through to look for the secretary. She was not in there. He rested his arms on the ledge and waited, his narrow bottom stuck out, swaying slowly to the left and right. He raised a hand over his head and scratched the base of his skull.

"You see that button there, boy?" Mrs. Turpin said. "You can punch that and she'll come. She's probably in the back somewhere."

"Is thas right?" the boy said agreeably, as if he had never seen the button before. He leaned to the right and put his finger on it. "She sometime out," he said and twisted around to face his audience, his elbows behind him on the counter. The nurse appeared and he twisted back again. She handed him a dollar and he rooted in his pocket and made the change and counted it out to her. She gave him fifteen cents for a tip and he went out with the empty tray. The heavy door swung to slowly and closed at length with the sound of suction. For a moment no one spoke.

"They ought to send all them niggers back to Africa," the white trash woman said. "That's wher they come from in first place."

"Oh, I couldn't do without my good colored friends," the pleasant lady said.

"There's a heap of things worse than a nigger," Mrs. Turpin agreed. "It's all kinds of them just like it's all kinds of us."

"Yes, and it takes all kinds to make the world go round," the lady said in her musical voice.

As she said it, the raw-complexioned girl snapped her teeth together. Her lower lip turned downwards and inside out, revealing the pale pink inside of her mouth. After a second it rolled back up. It was the ugliest face Mrs. Turpin had ever seen anyone make and for a moment she was certain that the girl had made it at her. She was looking at her as if she had known and disliked her all her life-all of Mrs. Turpin's life, it seemed too, not just all the girl's life. Why, girl, I don't even know you, Mrs. Turpin said silently.

She forced her attention back to the discussion. "It wouldn't be practical to send them back to Africa," she said. "They wouldn't want to go. They got it too good here."

"Wouldn't be what they wanted-if I had anythang to do with it," the woman said.

"It wouldn't be a way in the world you could get all the niggers back over there," Mrs. Turpin said. "They'd be hiding out and lying down and turning sick on you and wailing and hollering and raring and pitching. It wouldn't be a way in the world to get them over there."

"They got over here," the trashy woman said. "Get back like they got over."

"It wasn't so many of them then," Mrs. Turpin explained.

The woman looked at Mrs. Turpin as if here was an idiot indeed but Mrs. Turpin was not bothered by the look, considering where it came from.

"Nooo," she said, "they're going to stay here where they can go to New York and marry white folks and improve their color. That's what they all want to do, every one of them, improve their color."

"You know what comes of that, don't you?" Claud asked.

"No, Claud, what?" Mrs. Turpin said.

Claud's eyes twinkled. "White-faced niggers," he said with never a smile.

Everybody in the office laughed except the white-trash and the ugly girl. The girl gripped the book in her lap with white fingers. The trashy woman looked around her from face to face as if she thought they were all idiots. The old woman in the feed sack dress continued to gaze expressionless across the floor at the high-top shoes of the man opposite her, the one who had been pretending to be asleep when the Turpins came in. He was laughing heartily, his hands still spread out on his knees. The child had fallen to the side and was lying now almost face down in the old woman's lap.

While they recovered from their laughter, the nasal chorus on the radio kept the room from silence.

"You go to blank blank
And I'll go to mine
But we'll all blank along
To-geth-ther,
And all along the blank
We'll help each-other out
Smile-ling in any kind of Weath-ther!"

Mrs. Turpin didn't catch every word but she caught enough to agree with the spirit of the song and it turned her thoughts sober. To help anybody out that needed it was her philosophy of life. She never spared herself when she found somebody in need, whether they were white or black, trash or decent. And of all she had to be thankful for, she was most thankful that this was so. If Jesus had said, "You call be high society and have all the money you want and be thin and svelte-like, but you can't be a good woman with it," she would have had to say, "Well don't make me that then. Make me a good woman and it don't matter what else, how fat or how ugly or how poor!" Her heart rose. He had not made her a nigger or white-trash or ugly! He had made her herself and given her a little of everything. Jesus, thank you! she said. Thank you thank you! Whenever she counted her blessings she felt as buoyant as if she weighed one hundred and twenty five pounds instead of one hundred and eighty.

"What's wrong with your little boy?" the pleasant lady asked the white-trashy woman.

"He has a ulcer," the woman said proudly. "He ain't give me a minute's peace since he was born. Him and her are just alike," she said, nodding at the old woman, who was running her leathery fingers through the child's pale hair. "Look like I can't get nothing down them two but Co' Cola and candy."

That's all you try to get down em, Mrs. Turpin said to herself. Too lazy to light the fire. There was nothing you could tell her about people like them that she didn't know already. And it was not just that they didn't have anything. Because if you gave them everything, in two weeks it would all be broken or filthy or they would have chopped it up for lightwood. She knew all this from her own experience. Help them you must, but help them you couldn't.

All at once the ugly girl turned her lips inside out again. Her eyes were fixed like two drills on Mrs. Turpin. This time there was no mistaking that there was something urgent behind them.

Girl, Mrs. Turpin exclaimed silently, I haven't done a thing to you! The girl might be confusing her with somebody else. There was no need to sit by and let herself be intimidated.

"You must be in college," she said boldly, looking directly at the girl. "I see you reading a book there."

The girl continued to state and pointedly did not answer.

Her mother blushed at this rudeness. "The lady asked you a question, Mary Grace," she said under her breath.

"I have ears," Mary Grace said.

The poor mother blushed again. "Mary Grace goes to Wellesley College," she explained. She twisted one of the buttons on her dress. "In Massachusetts, she added with a grimace. "And in the summer she just keeps right on studying. Just reads all the time, a real book worm. She's done real well at Wellesley; she's taking English and Math and History and Psychology and Social Studies," she rattled on "and I think it's too much. I think she ought to get out and have fun."

The girl looked as if she would like to hurl them all through the plate glass window.

"Way up north," Mrs. Turpin murmured and thought, well, it hasn't done much for her manners.

"I'd almost rather to have him sick," the white-trash woman said, wrenching the attention back to herself. "He's so mean when he ain't. Look like some children just take natural to meanness. It's some gets bad when they get sick but, he was the opposite. Took sick and turned good. He don't give me no trouble now. It's me waitin to see the doctor," she said.

If I was going to send anybody back to Africa, Mrs. Turpin thought, it would be your kind, woman. "Yes, indeed," she said aloud, but looking up at the ceiling, "It's a heap of things worse than a nigger." And dirtier than a hog, she added to herself.

"I think people with bad dispositions are more to be pitied than anyone on earth," the pleasant lady said in a voice that was decidedly thin.

"I thank the Lord he has blessed me with a good one," Mrs. Turpin said. "The day has never dawned that I couldn't find something to laugh at."

"Not since she married me anyways," Claud said with a comical straight face.

Everybody laughed except the girl and the white trash.

Mrs. Turpin's stomach shook. "He's such a caution," she said, "that I can't help but laugh at him."

The girl made a loud ugly noise through her teeth.

Her mother's mouth grew thin and tight. "I think the worst thing in the world," she said, "is an ungrateful person. To have everything and not appreciate it. I know a girl," she said, "who has parents who would give her anything, a little brother who loves her clearly, who is getting a good education, who wears the best clothes, but who can never say a kind word to anyone, who never smiles, who just criticizes and complains all day long."

"Is she too old to paddle?" Claud asked.

The girl's face was almost purple.

"Yes," the lady said, "I'm afraid there's nothing to do but leave her to her folly. Some day she'll wake up and it'll be too late."

"It never hurt anyone to smile," Mrs. Turpin said. "It just makes you feel better all own"

"Of course," the lady said sadly, "but there are just some people you can't tell anything to. They can't take criticism."

"If it's one thing I am," Mrs. Turpin said with feeling, "It's grateful. When I think who all I could have been besides myself and what all I got, a little of everything, and a good disposition besides, I just feel like shouting, 'Thank you, Jesus, for making everything the way it is!' It could have been different!" For one thing, somebody else could have got Claud. At the thought of this, she was flooded with gratitude and a terrible pang of joy ran through her. "Oh thank you, Jesus, Jesus, thank you!" she cried aloud.

The book struck her directly, over her left eye. It struck almost at the same instant that she realized the girl was about to hurl it. Before she could utter a sound, the raw face came crashing across the table toward her, howling. The girl's fingers sank like clamps the soft flesh of her neck. She heard the mother cry out and Claud shout, "Whoa!" There was an instant when she was certain that she was about to be in an earthquake.

All at once her vision narrowed and she saw everything as if it were happening in a small room far away, or as if she were looking at it through the wrong end of a telescope.

Claud's face crumpled and fell out of sight. The nurse ran in, then out, then again. Then the gangling figure of the doctor rushed out of the inner door. Magazines flew this way and that as the table turned over. The girl fell with a thud and Mrs. Turpin's vision suddenly reversed itself and she saw everything large instead of small. The eyes of the white-trashy woman were staring hugely at the floor. There the girl, held down on one side by the nurse and on the other by her mother, was wrenching and turning in their grasp. The doctor was kneeling astride her, trying to hold her arm down. He managed after a second to sink a long needle into it.

Mrs. Turpin felt entirely hollow except for her heart which swung from side to side as if it were agitated in a great empty drum of flesh.

"Somebody that's not busy call for the ambulance," the doctor said in the off-hand voice young doctors adopt for terrible occasions.

Mrs. Turpin could not have moved a finger. The old man who had been sitting next to her skipped nimbly into the office and made the call, for the secretary still seemed to be gone.

"Claud!" Mrs. Turpin called.

He was not in his chair. She knew she must jump up and find him but she felt like someone trying to catch a train in a dream, when everything moves in slow, motion and the faster you try to run the slower you go.

"Here I am," a suffocated voice, very unlike Claud's said.

He was doubled up in the corner on the floor, pale as paper, holding his leg. She wanted to get up and go to him but she could not move. Instead, her gaze was drawn slowly downward to the churning face on the floor, which she could see over the doctor's shoulder.

The girl's eyes stopped rolling and focused on her. They seemed a much lighter blue than before, as if a door that had been tightly closed behind them was now open to admit light and air.

Mrs. Turpin's head cleared and her power of motion returned. She leaned forward until she was looking directly into the fierce brilliant eyes. There was no doubt in her mind that the girl did know her, know her in some intense and personal way, beyond time and place and condition. "What you got to say to me?" she asked hoarsely and held her breath, waiting, as for a revelation.

The girl raised her head. Her gaze locked with Mrs. Turpin's. "Go back to hell where you came from, you old wart hog," she whispered. Her voice was low but clear. Her eyes burned for a moment as if she saw with pleasure that her message had struck its target.

Mrs. Turpin sank back in her chair.

After a moment the girl's eyes closed and she turned her head wearily to the side.

The doctor rose and handed the nurse the empty syringe. He leaned over and put both hands for a moment on the mother's shoulders, which were shaking. She was sitting on the floor, her lips pressed together, holding Mary Grace's hand in her lap. The girl's fingers were gripped like a baby's around her thumb. "Go on to the hospital," he said. "I'll call and make the arrangements."

"Now let's see that neck," he said in a jovial voice to Mrs. Turpin. He began to inspect her neck with his first two fingers. Two little moon-shaped lines like pink fish bones were indented over her windpipe. There was the beginning of an angry red swelling above her eye. His fingers passed over this also.

'Lea' me be," she said thickly and shook him off. "See about Claud. She kicked him."

"I'll see about him in a minute," he said and felt her pulse. He was a thin grey-haired man, given to pleasantries. "Go home and have yourself a vacation the rest of the day," he said and patted her on the shoulder.

Quit your pattin me, Mrs. Turpin growled to herself.

"And put an ice pack over that eye," he said. Then he went and squatted down beside Claud and looked at his leg. After a moment he pulled him up and Claud limped after him into the office.

Until the ambulance came, the only sounds in the room were the tremulous moans of the girl's mother, who continued to sit on the floor. The white-trash woman did not take her eyes off the girl. Mrs. Turpin looked straight ahead at nothing. Presently the ambulance drew up, a long dark shadow, behind the curtain. The attendants came in and set the stretcher down beside the girl and lifted her expertly onto it and carried her out. The nurse helped the mother gather up her things. The shadow of the ambulance moved silently -away and the nurse came back in the office.

"That there girl is going to be a lunatic, ain't she?" the white-trash woman asked the nurse, but the nurse kept on to the back and never answered her.

"Yes, she's going to be a lunatic," the white-trash woman said to the rest of them.

"Po' critter," the old woman murmured. The child's face was still in her lap. His eyes looked idly out over her knees. He had not moved during the disturbance except to draw one leg up under him.

"I thank Gawd," the white-trash woman said fervently, "I ain't a lunatic."

Claud came limping out and the Turpins went home.

As their pick-up truck turned into their own dirt road and made the crest of the hill, Mrs. Turpin gripped the window ledge and looked out suspiciously. The land sloped gracefully down through a field dotted with lavender weeds and at the start of the rise their small yellow frame house, with its little flower beds spread out around it like a fancy apron, sat primly in its accustomed place between two giant hickory trees. She would not have been startled to see a burnt wound between two blackened chimneys.

Neither of them felt like eating so they put on their house clothes and lowered the shade in the bedroom and lay down, Claud with his leg on a pillow and herself with a damp washcloth over her eye. The instant she was flat on her back, the image of a razor-backed hog with warts on its face and horns coming out behind its ears snorted into her head. She moaned, a low quiet moan.

"I am not," she said tearfully, "a wart hog. From hell." But the denial had no force. The girl's eyes and her words, even the tone of her voice, low but clear, directed only to her, brooked no repudiation. She had been singled out for the message, though there was trash in the room to whom it might justly have been applied. The full force of this fact struck her only now. There was a woman there who was neglecting her own child but she had been overlooked. The message had been given to Ruby Turpin, a respectable, hardworking, church-going woman. The tears dried. Her eyes began to burn instead with wrath.

She rose on her elbow and the washcloth fell into her hand. Claud was lying on his back, snoring. She wanted to tell him what the girl had said. At the same time, she did not wish to put the image of herself as a wart hog from hell into his mind.

"Hey, Claud," she muttered and pushed his shoulder.

Claud opened one pale baby blue eye.

She looked into it warily. He did not think about anything.

"Wha, whasit?" he said and closed the eye again.

"Nothing," she said. "Does your leg pain you?"

"Hurts like hell," Claud said

"It'll quit terreckly," she said and lay back down. In a moment Claud was snoring again. For the rest of the afternoon they lay there. Claud slept. She scowled at the ceiling. Occasionally she raised her fist and made a small stabbing motion over her chest as if she was defending her innocence to invisible guests who were like the comforters of Job, reasonable-seeming but wrong.

About five-thirty Claud stirred. "Got to go after those niggers," he sighed, not moving.

She was looking straight up as if there were unintelligible hand writing on the ceiling. The protuberance over her eye had turned a greenish-blue. "Listen here," she said.

"What?"

"Kiss me."

Claud leaned over and kissed her loudly on the mouth. He pinched her side and their hands interlocked. Her expression of ferocious concentration did not change. Claud got up, groaning and growling, and limped off. She continued to study the ceiling.

She did not get up until she heard the pick-up truck coming back with the Negroes. Then she rose and thrust her feet in her brown oxfords, which she did not bother to lace, and stumped out onto the back porch and got her red plastic bucket. She emptied a tray of ice cubes into it and filled it half full of water and went out into the back yard.

Every afternoon after Claud brought the hands in, one of the boys helped him put out hay and the rest waited in the back of the truck until he was ready to take them home. The truck was parked in the shade under one of the hickory trees.

"Hi yawl this evening," Mrs. Turpin asked grimly, appearing with the bucket and the dipper. There were three woman and a boy in the truck. "Us doin nicely," the oldest woman said. "Hi you doin?" and her gaze stuck immediately on the dark lump on Mrs. Turpin's forehead. "You done fell down, ain't you?" she asked in a solicitous voice. The old woman was dark and almost toothless. She had on an old felt hat of Claud's set back on her head. The other two women were younger and lighter and they both had new bright green sun hats. One of them had hers on her head; the other had taken hers off and the boy was grinning beneath it.

Mrs. Turpin set the bucket down on the floor of the truck. "Yawl hep yourselves," she said. She looked around to make sure Claud had gone. "No. I didn't fall down," she said, folding her arms. "It was something worse than that."

"Ain't nothing bad happen to YOU!" the old, woman said. She said it as if they, all knew that Mrs. Turpin was protected in some special way by Divine Providence. "You just had you a little fall."

"We were 'in town at the doctor's office for where the cow kicked Mr. Turpin," Mrs. Turpin said in a flat tone that indicated they could leave off their foolishness. "And there was this girl there. A big fat girl with her face all broke out. I could look at that girl and tell she was peculiar but I couldn't tell how. And me and her mama were just talking and going along and all of a sudden WHAM! She throws this big book she was reading at me and..."

"Naw!" the old woman cried out.

"And then she jumps over the table and commences to choke me."

"Naw!" they all exclaimed, "naw!"

"Hi come she do that?" the old woman asked. "What ail her?"

Mrs. Turpin only glared in front of her.

"Somethin ail her," the old woman said.

"They carried her off in an ambulance," Mrs. Turpin continued, "but before she went she was rolling on the floor and they were trying to hold her down to give her a shot and she said something to me." She paused. "You know what she said to me?"

"What she say," they asked.

"She said," Mrs. Turpin began, and stopped, her face very dark and heavy. The sun was getting whiter and whiter, blanching the sky overhead so that the leaves of the hickory tree were black in the face of it. She could not bring forth the words. "Something real ugly," she muttered.

"She sho shouldn't said nothin ugly, to you," the old woman said. "You so sweet. You the sweetest lady I know."

"She pretty too," the one with the hat on said.

"And stout," the other one said. "I never knowed no sweeter white lady."

"That's the truth befo' Jesus," the old woman said. "Amen! You des as sweet and pretty as you can be."

Mrs. Turpin knew just exactly how much Negro flattery was worth and it added to her rage. "She said," she began again and finished this time with a fierce rush of breath, "that I was an old wart hog from hell."

There was an astounded silence.

"Where she at?" the youngest woman cried in a piercing voice.

"Lemme see her. I'll kill her!"

"I'll kill her with you!" the other one cried.

"She b'long in the sylum" the old woman said emphatically. "YOU the sweetest white lady I know."

"She pretty too," the other two said. "Stout as she can be and sweet. Jesus satisfied with her!"

"Deed he is," the old woman declared.

Idiots! Mrs. Turpin growled to herself. YOU could never say anything intelligent to a nigger. YOU could talk at them but not with them. "Yawl ain't drunk your water," she said shortly. "Leave the bucket in the truck when you're finished with it. I got more to do than just stand around and pass the time of day," and she moved off and into the house.

She stood for a moment in the middle of the kitchen. The dark protuberance over her eye looked like a miniature tornado cloud which might any moment sweep across the horizon of her brow. Her lower lip protruded dangerously. She squared her massive shoulders. Then she marched into the front of the house and out the side door and started down the road to the pig parlor. She had the look of a woman going single-handed, weaponless, into battle.

The sun was a deep yellow now like a harvest moon and was riding westward very fast over the far tree line as if it meant to catch the hogs before she did. The road was rutted and she kicked several good-sized stones out of her path as she strode along. The pig parlor was on a little knoll at the end of a lane that ran off from the side of the barn. It was a square of concrete as large as a small room, with a board fence about four feet high around it. The concrete floor sloped slightly so that the hog wash could drain off into a trench where it was carried to the field for fertilizer. Claud was standing on the outside, on the edge of the concrete, hanging onto the top board, hosing down the floor inside. The hose was connected to the faucet of a water trough nearby.

Mrs. Turpin climbed up beside him and glowered down at the hogs inside. There were seven long-snouted bristly shoats in it-tan with liver-colored spots-and an old sow a few weeks off from farrowing. She was lying on her side grunting. The shoats were running about shaking themselves like idiot children, their little slit pig eyes searching the floor for anything left. She had read that pigs were the most intelligent animal. She doubted it. They were supposed to be smarter than dogs. There had even been a pig astronaut. He had performed his assignment perfectly but died of a heart attack afterwards because they left him in his electric suit, sitting upright throughout his examination when naturally, a hog should be on all fours.

A-gruntin and a-rootin and a-groanin.

"Gimme that hose," she said, yanking it away from Claud. "Go on and carry, them niggers home and then get off that leg."

"You look like you might have swallowed a mad dog," Claud observed, but he got down and limped off. He paid no attention to her humors.

Until he was out of earshot, Mrs. Turpin stood on the side of the pen, holding the hose and pointing the stream of water at the hind quarters of any shoat that looked as if it might try to lie down. When he had had time to get over the hill, she turned her head slightly and her wrathful eyes scanned the path. He was nowhere in sight. She turned back again and seemed to gather herself up. Her shoulders rose and she drew in her breath.

"What do you send me a message like that for?" she said in a low fierce voice, barely above a whisper but with the force of a shout in its concentrated fury. "How am I a hog and me both? How am I saved and from hell too?" Her free fist was knotted and with the other she gripped the hose, blindly pointing the stream of water in and out of the eye of the old sow whose outraged squeal she did not hear.

The pig parlor commanded a view of the back pasture where their twenty beef cows were gathered around the hay-bales Claud and the boy had put out. The freshly cut pasture sloped down to the highway. Across it was their cotton field and beyond that a dark green dusty wood which they owned as well. The sun was behind the wood, very red, looking over the paling of trees like a farmer inspecting his own hogs.

"Why me?" she rumbled. "It's no trash around here, black or white, that I haven't given to. And break my back to the bone every day working. And do for the church."

She appeared to be the right size woman to command the arena before her. "How am I a hog? she demanded. "Exactly how am I like them?" and she jabbed the stream of water at the shoats. "There was plenty of trash there. It didn't have to be me.

"If you like trash better, go get yourself some trash then," she railed. "You could have made me trash. Or a nigger. If trash is what you wanted, why didn't you make me trash?" She shook her fist with the hose in it' and a watery snake appeared momentarily in the air. "I could quit working and take it easy and be filthy," she growled.

"Lounge about the sidewalks all day drinking root beer. Dip snuff and spit in every puddle and have it all over my face. I could be nasty.

"Or you could have made me a nigger. It's too late for me to be a nigger," she said with deep sarcasm, "but I could act like one. Lay down in the middle of the road and stop traffic. Roll on the ground."

In the deepening light everything was taking on a mysterious hue. The pasture was growing a particular glassy green and the streak of the highway had turned lavender. She braced herself for a final assault and this time her voice rolled out over the pasture. "Go on," she yelled, "call me a hog! Call me a hog again. From hell. Call me a wart hog from hell. Put that bottom rail on top. There'll still be a top and bottom!"

A garbled echo returned to her.

A final surge of fury shook her and she roared, "Who do you think you are?"

The color of everything, field and crimson sky, burned for a moment with a transparent intensity. The question carried over the pasture and across the highway and the cotton field and returned to her clearly, like an answer from beyond the wood.

She opened her mouth but no sound came out of it.

A tiny truck, Claud's, appeared on the highway, heading rapidly out of sight. Its gears scraped thinly. It looked like a child's toy. At any moment a bigger truck might smash into it and scatter Claud's and the niggers' brains all over the road.

Mrs. Turpin stood there, her gaze fixed on the highway, all her muscles rigid, until in five or six minutes the truck reappeared, returning. She waited until it had had time to turn into their own road. Then like a monumental statue coming to life, she bent her head slowly and gazed, as if through the very heart of mystery, down into the pig parlor at the hogs. They had settled all in one corner around the old sow who was grunting softly. A red glow suffused them. They appeared to pant with a secret life.

Until the sun slipped finally behind the tree line, Mrs. Turpin remained there with her gaze bent to them as if she were absorbing some abysmal life-giving knowledge. At last she lifted her head. There was only a purple streak in the sky, cutting through a field of crimson and leading, like an extension of the highway, into the descending dusk. She raised her hands from the side of the pen in a gesture hieratic and profound. A visionary light settled in her eyes. She saw the streak as a vast swinging bridge extending upward from the earth through a field of living fire. Upon it a vast horde of souls were tumbling toward heaven. There were whole companies of white trash, clean for the first time in their lives, and bands of black niggers in white robes, and battalions of freaks and lunatics shouting and clapping and leaping like frogs. And bringing up the end of the procession was a tribe of people whom she recognized at once as those who, like herself and Claud, had always had a little of everything and the given wit to use it right. She leaned forward to observe them closer. They were marching behind the others with great dignity, accountable as they had always been for good order and common sense and respectable behavior. They, alone were on key. Yet she could see by their shocked and altered faces even their virtues were being burned away. She lowered hands and gripped the rail of the hog pen, her eyes small but

fixed unblinkingly on what lay ahead. In a moment the vision faded but she remained where she was.

At length she got down and turned off the faucet and in her slow way on the
darkening path to the house. In woods around her the invisible cricket choruses
had struck up, but what she heard were the voices of the souls climbing upward
into the starry field and shouting hallelujah.

❋ ❋ ❋

## FLANNERY O'CONNOR

## *The Turkey* (1947)

His guns glinted sun steel in the ribs of the tree and, half aloud through a
crack in his mouth, he growled, "All right, Mason, this is as far as you go. The
jig's up." The six-shooters in Mason's belt stuck out like waiting rattlers but he
flipped them into the air and, when they fell at his feet, kicked them behind him
like so many dried steer skulls. "You varmit," he muttered, drawing his rope tight
around the captured man's ankles, "this is the last rustlin' you'll do." He took
three steps backward and leveled one gun to his eye. "Okay," he said with cold,
slow precision, "this is...." And then he saw it, just moving slightly through the
bushes farther over, a touch of bronze and a rustle and then, through another
gap in the leaves, the eye, set in red folds that covered the head and hung down
along the neck, trembling slightly. He stood perfectly still and the turkey took
another step, then stopped, with one foot lifted, and listened.

If he only had a gun, if he only had a gun! He could level aim and shoot it
right where it was. In a second, it would slide through the bushes and be up in a
tree before he could tell which direction it had gone in. Without moving his head,
he strained his eyes to the ground to see if there were a stone near, but the
ground looked as if it might just have been swept. The turkey moved again. The
foot that had been poised half way up went down and the wing dropped over it,
spreading so that Ruller could see the long single feathers, pointed at the end.
He wondered if he dived into the bush on top of it.... It moved again and the
wing came up again and it went down.

It's limping, he thought quickly. He moved a little nearer, trying to make his
motion imperceptible. Suddenly its head pierced out of the bush—he was about
ten feet from it—and drew back and them abruptly back into the bush. He began edging nearer with his arms rigid and his fingers ready to clutch. It was lame,
he could tell. It might not to be able to fly. It shot its head out once more and
saw him and shuttled back into the bushes and out again on the other side. Its
motion was half lopsided and the left wing was dragging. He was going to get it.

He was going to get it if he had to chase it out of the country. He crawled through the brush and saw it about twenty feet away, watching him warily, moving its neck up and down. It stooped and tried to spread its wings and stooped again and went a little way to the side and stooped again, trying to make itself go up; but, he could tell, it couldn't fly. He was going to have it. He was going to have it if he had to run it out of the state. He saw himself going in the front door with it slung over his shoulder, and them all screaming, "Look at Ruller with that wild turkey! Ruller! where did you get that wild turkey?"

Oh, he had caught it in the woods; he had thought they might like to have him catch them one.

"You crazy bird," he muttered, "you can't fly. I've already got you." He was walking in a wide circle, trying to get behind it. For a second, he almost thought he could go pick it up. It had dropped down and one foot was sprawled, but when he got near enough to pounce, it shot off in a heavy speed that made him start. He tore after it, straight out in the open for a half acre of dead cotton; then it went under a fence and into some woods again and he had to get on his hands and knees to get under the fence but still keep his eye on the turkey but not tear his shirt; and then dash after it again with his head a little dizzy, but faster to catch up with it. If he lost it in the woods, it would be lost for good; it was going for the bushes on the other side. It would go on out in the road. He was going to have it. He saw it dart through a thicket and he headed for the thicket and when he got there it darted out again and in a second disappeared under a hedge. He went through the hedge fast and heard his shirt rip and felt cool streaks on his arms where they were getting scratched. He stopped a second and looked down at his torn shirt sleeves but the turkey was only a little ahead of him and he could see it go over the edge of the hill and down again into an open space and he darted on. If he came in with the turkey, they wouldn't pay any attention to his shirt. Hane hadn't ever got a turkey. Hane hadn't ever caught anything. He guessed they'd be knocked out when they saw him; he guessed they'd talk about it in bed. That's what they did about him and Hane. Hane didn't know; he never woke up. Ruller woke up every night exactly at the time they started talking. He and Hane slept in one room and their mother and father in the next and the door was left open between and every night Ruller listened. His father would say finally, "How are the boys doing?" and their mother would say, Lord, they were wearing her to a frazzle, Lord, she guessed she shouldn't worry but how could she help worrying about Hane, the way he was now? Hane had always been an unusual boy, she said. She said he would grow up to be an unusual man too; and their father said yes, if he didn't get put in the penitentiary first, and their mother said how could he talk that way? and they argued just like Ruller and Hane and sometimes Ruller couldn't get back to sleep for thinking. He always felt tired when he got through listening but he woke up every night and listened just the same, and whenever they started talking about him, he sat up in bed so he could hear better. Once his father asked why Ruller played by himself so much and his mother said how was she to know? if he wanted to play by himself, she didn't see any reason he shouldn't; and his father said that worried him and she said

well, if that was all he had to worry about, he'd do well to stop; someone told
her, she said, that they had seen Hane at the Ever-Ready; hadn't they told him
he couldn't go there?

His father asked Ruller the next day what he had been doing lately and Ruller
said, "playing by himself," and walked off sort of like he had a limp. He guessed
his father had looked pretty worried. He guessed he'd think it was something
when he came home with the turkey slung over his shoulder. The turkey was
heading out into a road and for a gutter along the side of it. It ran along the gutter and Ruller was gaining on it all the time until he fell over a root sticking up
and spilled the things out of his pockets and had to snatch them up. When he got
up, it was out of sight.

"Bill, you take a posse and go down South Canyon; Joe, you cut around by
the gorge and head him off," he shouted to his men. "I'll follow him this way."
And he dashed off again along the ditch.

The turkey was in the ditch, not thirty feet from him, lying almost on its neck
panting, and he was nearly a yard from it before it darted off again. He chased
it straight until the ditch ended and then it went out in the road and slid under
a hedge on the other side. He had to stop at the hedge and catch his breath and
he could see the turkey on the other side through the leaves, lying on its neck,
its whole body moving up and down with the panting. He could see the tip of its
tongue going up and down in its opened bill. If he could stick his arm through,
he might could get it while it was still too tired to move. He pushed up closer to
the hedge and eased his hand through and then gripped it quickly around the
turkey's tail. There was no movement from the other side. Maybe the turkey had
dropped dead. He put his face close to the leaves to look through. He pushed
the twigs aside with one hand but they would not stay. He let go the turkey and
pulled his other hand through to hold them. Through the hole he had made, he
saw the bird wobbling off drunkenly. He ran back to where the hedge began and
got on the other side. He'd get it yet. It needn't think it was so smart, he muttered.

It zigged across the middle of the field and toward the woods again. It could-
n't go into the woods! He'd never get it! He dashed behind it, keeping his eyes
sharp on it until suddenly something hit his chest and knocked the breath black
out of him. He fell back on the ground and forgot the turkey for the cutting in
his chest. He lay there for a while with things rocking on either side of him. Finally he sat up. He was facing the tree he had run into. He rubbed his hands over
his face and arms and the long scratches began to sting. He would have taken it
in slung over his shoulder and they would have jumped up and yelled, "Good
Lord look at Ruller! Ruller! Where did you get that wild turkey?" and his father
would have said, "Man! That's a bird if I ever saw one!" He kicked a stone away
from his foot. He'd never see the turkey now. He wondered why he had seen it
in the first place if he wasn't going to be able to get it.

It was like somebody had played a dirty trick on him.

All that running for nothing. He sat there looking sullenly at his white ankles
sticking out of his trouser legs and into his shoes. "Nuts," he muttered. He turned

over on his stomach and let his cheek rest right on the ground, dirty or not. He had torn his shirt and scratched his arms and got a knot on his forehead—he could feel it rising just a little, it was going to be a big one all right—all for nothing. The ground was cool to his face, but the grit bruised it and he had to turn over. Oh hell, he thought.

"Oh hell," he said cautiously.

Then in a minute he said just, "Hell."

Then he said it like Hane said it, pulling the e-ull out and trying to get the look in his eye that Hane got. Once Hane said, "God!" and his mother stomped after him and said, "I don't want to hear you say that again. Thou shalt not take the name of the Lord, Thy God, in vain. Do you hear me?" and he guessed that shut Hane up. Ha! He guessed she dressed him off that time.

"God," he said.

He looked studiedly at the ground, making circles in the dust with his finger. "God!" he repeated.

"God dammit," he said softly. He could feel his face getting hot and his chest thumping all of a sudden inside. "God dammit to hell," he said almost inaudibly. He looked over his shoulder but no one was there.

"God dammit to hell, good Lord from Jerusalem," he said. His uncle said "Good Lord from Jerusalem."

"Good Father, good God, sweep the chickens out the yard," he said and began to giggle. His face was very red. He sat up and looked at his white ankles sticking out of his pants legs into his shoes. They looked like they didn't belong to him. He gripped a hand around each ankle and bent his knees up and rested his chin on a knee. "Our Father Who art in heaven, shoot 'em six and roll 'em seven," he said, giggling again. Boy, she'd smack his head in if she could hear him. God dammit, she'd smack his goddam head in. He rolled over in a fit of laughter. God dammit, she'd dress him off and wring his goddam neck like a goddam chicken. The laughing cut his side and he tried to hold it in, but every time he thought of his goddam neck, he shook again. He lay back on the ground, red and weak with laughter, not able not to think of her smacking his goddam head in. He said the words over and over to himself and after a while he stopped laughing. He said them again but the laughing had gone out. He said them again but it wouldn't start back up. All that chasing for nothing, he thought again. He might as well go home. What did he want to be sitting around here for? He felt suddenly like he would if people had been laughing at him. Aw, go to hell, he told them. He got up and kicked his foot sharply into somebody's leg and said, "Take that, sucker," and turned into the woods to take the short trail home.

And as soon as he got in the door, they would holler, "How did you tear your clothes and where did you get that knot on your forehead?" He was going to say he fell in a hole. What difference would it make? Yeah, God, what difference would it make?

He almost stopped. He had never heard himself think that tone before. He wondered should he take the thought back. He guessed it was pretty bad; but heck, it was the way he felt. He couldn't help feeling that way. Heck … hell, it was the way he felt. He guessed he couldn't help that. He walked on a little way, thinking, thinking about it. He wondered suddenly if he were going "bad." That's what Hane had done. Hane played pool and smoked cigarettes and sneaked in at twelve-thirty and boy he thought he was something. "There's nothing you can do about," their grandmother had told their father, "he's at that age." What age? Ruller wondered. I'm eleven, he thought. That's pretty young. Hane hadn't started until he was fifteen. I guess it's worse in me, he thought. He wondered would he fight it. Their grandmother had talked to Hane and told him the only way to conquer the devil was to fight him—if he didn't, he couldn't be her boy any more—Ruller sat down on a stump—and she said she'd give him one more chance, did he want it? and he yelled at her, no! and would she leave him alone? and she told him, well, she loved him even if he didn't love her and he was her boy anyway and so was Ruller. Oh no, I ain't, Ruller thought quickly. Oh no. She's not pinning any of that stuff on me.

Boy, he could shock the pants off her. He could make her teeth fall in her soup. He started giggling. The next time she asked him if he wanted to play a game of parcheesi, he'd say, hell no, goddammit, didn't she know any good games? Get out her goddam cards and he'd show her a few. He rolled over on the ground, choking with laughter. "Let's have some booze, kid," he'd say. "Let's get stinky." Boy, he'd knock her out of her socks! He sat on the ground, red and grinning to himself, bursting every now and then into a fresh spasm of giggles. He remembered the minister had said young men were going to the devil by the dozens this day and age; forsaking gentle ways; walking in the tracks of Satan. They would rue the day, he said. There would be weeping and gnashing of teeth. "Weeping," Ruller muttered. Men didn't weep.

How do you gnash your teeth? he wondered. He grated his jaws together and made an ugly face. He did it several times.

He bet he could steal.

He thought about chasing the turkey for nothing. It was a dirty trick. He bet he could be a jewel thief. They were smart. He bet he could have all Scotland Yard on his tail. Hell.

He got up. God could go around sticking things in your face and making you chase them all afternoon for nothing.

You shouldn't think that way about God, though.

But that was the way he felt. If that was the way he felt, could he help it? He looked around quickly as if someone might be hiding in the bushes; then suddenly he started.

It was rolled over at the edge of a thicket—a pile of ruffled bronze with a red head lying limp along the ground. Ruller started at it, unable to think; then he leaned forward suspiciously. He wasn't going to touch it. Why was it there now for him to take? He wasn't going to touch it. It could just lie there. The picture of himself walking in the room with it slung over his shoulder came back to him. Look at Ruller with that turkey! Lord, look at Ruller! He squatted down beside it and looked without touching it. He wondered what had been wrong with its wing. He lifted it up by the tip and looked under. The feathers were blood-soaked. It had been shot. It must weigh ten pounds, he figured.

Lord, Ruller! It's a huge turkey! He wondered how it would feel slung over his shoulder. Maybe, he considered, he was supposed to take it.

Ruller gets our turkeys for us. Ruller got it in the woods, chased it dead. Yes, he's a very unusual child.

Ruller wondered suddenly if he were an unusual child.

It came down on him in an instant: he was... an... unusual... child.

He reckoned he was more unusual than Hane.

He had to worry more than Hane because he knew more how things were.

Sometimes when he was listening at night, he heard them arguing like they were going to kill each other; and the next day his father would go out early and his mother would have the blue veins out on her forehead and look like she was expecting a snake to jump from the ceiling any minute. He guessed he was one of the most unusual children ever. Maybe that was why the turkey was there. He rubbed his hand along the neck. Maybe it was to keep him from going bad. Maybe God wanted to keep him from that.

Maybe God had knocked it out right there where he'd see it when he got up.

Maybe God was in the bush now, waiting for him to make up his mind. Ruller blushed. He wondered if God could think he was a very unusual child. He must. He found himself suddenly blushing and grinning and he rubbed his hand over his face quick to make himself stop. If You want me to take it, he said, I'll be glad to. Maybe finding the turkey was a sign. Maybe God wanted him to be a preacher. He thought of Bing Crosby and Spencer Tracy. He might found a place for boys to stay who were going bad. He lifted the turkey up—it was heavy all right—and fitted it over his shoulder. He wished he could see how he looked with it slung over like that. It occurred to him that he might as well go home the long way—through town. He had plenty of time. He started off slowly, shifting the turkey until it fit comfortably over his shoulder. He remembered the things he had thought before he found the turkey. They were pretty bad, he guessed.

He guessed God had stopped him before it was too late. He should be very thankful. Thank You, he said.

Come on, boys, he said, we will take this turkey back for our dinner. We certainly are much obliged to You, he said to God. This turkey weighs ten pounds. You were mighty generous.

That's okay, God said. And listen, we ought to have a talk about these boys. They're entirely in your hands, see? I'm leaving the job strictly up to you. I have confidence in you, McFarney.

You can trust me, Ruller said. I'll come through with the goods.

He went into town with the turkey over his shoulder. He wanted to do something for God but he didn't know what he could do. If anybody was playing the accordion on the street today, he'd give them his dime. He only had one dime, but he'd give it to them. Maybe he could think of something better, though. He had been going to keep the dime for something. He might could get another one from his grandmother. How about a goddam dime, kid? He pulled his mouth piously out of the grin. He wasn't going to think that way any more. He couldn't get a dime from her anyway. His mother was going to whip him if he asked his grandmother for money again. Maybe something would turn up that he could do. If God wanted him to do something, He'd turn something up.

He was getting into the business block and through the corner of his eye he noticed people looking at him. There were eight thousand people in Mulrose County and on Saturday every one of them was in Tilford on the business block. They turned as Ruller passed and looked at him. He glanced at himself reflected in a store window, shifted the turkey slightly, and walked quickly ahead. He heard someone call, but he walked on, pretending he was deaf. It was his mother's friend, Alice Gilhard, and if she wanted him, let her catch up with him.

"Ruller!" she cried. "My goodness, where did you get that turkey?" She came up behind him fast and put her hand on his shoulder. "That's some bird," she said. "You must be a good shot."

"I didn't shoot it," Ruller said coldly. "I captured it. I chased it dead."

"Heavens," she said. "You wouldn't capture me one sometime, would you?"

"I might if I ever have time," Ruller said. She thought she was so cute.

Two men came over and whistled at the turkey. They yelled at some other men on the corner to look. Another of his mother's friends stopped and some country boys who had been sitting on the curb got up and tried to see the turkey without showing they were interested. A man with a hunting suit and gun stopped and looked at Ruller and walked around behind him and looked at the turkey.

"How much do you think it weighs?" a lady asked.

"At least ten pounds," Ruller said.

"How long did you chase it?"

"About an hour," Ruller said.

"The goddam imp," the man in the hunting suit muttered.

"That's really amazing," a lady commented.

"About that long," Ruller said.

"You must be very tired."

"No," Ruller said. "I have to go. I'm in a hurry." He worked his face to look as if he were thinking something out and hurried down the street until he was out of their view. He felt warm all over and nice as if something very fine were going to be or had been. He looked back once and saw that the country boys were following him. He hoped they would come up and ask to look at the turkey. God must be wonderful, he felt suddenly. He wanted to do something for God. He hadn't seen anyone playing the accordion, though, or selling pencils and he was past the business block. He might see one before he really got to the streets where people lived at. If he did, he'd give away the dime—even while he knew he couldn't get another one any time soon. He began to wish he would see somebody begging.

Those country kids were still trailing along behind him. He thought he might stop and ask them did they want to see the turkey; but they might just stare at him. They were tenants' children and sometimes tenants' children just stared at you. He might found a home for tenants' children. He thought about going back through town to see if he had passed a beggar without seeing him, but he decided people might think he was showing off with the turkey.

Lord, send me a beggar, he prayed suddenly. Send me one before I get home. He had never thought before of praying on his own, but it was a good idea. God had put the turkey there. He'd send him a beggar. He knew for a fact God would send him one. He was on Hill Street now and there were nothing but houses on Hill Street. It would be strange to find a beggar here. The sidewalks were empty except for a few children and some tricycles. Ruller looked back; the country boys were still following him. He decided to slow down. It might make them catch up with him and it might give a beggar more time to get to him. If one were coming. He wondered if one were coming. If one came, it would mean God had gone out of His way to get one. It would mean God was really interested. He had a sudden fear one wouldn't come; it was a whole fear quick.

One will come, he told himself. God was interested in him because he was a very unusual child. He went on. The streets were deserted now. He guessed one wouldn't come. Maybe God didn't have confidence in—no, God did. Lord, please send me a beggar! he implored. He squinched his face rigid and strained his muscles in a knot and said, "Please! one right now"; and the minute he said it—the minute—Hetty Gilman turned around the corner before him, heading straight to where he was.

He felt almost like he had when he ran into the tree.

She was walking down the street right toward him. It was just like the turkey lying there. It was just as if she had been hiding behind a house until he came by. She was an old woman whom everybody said had more money than anybody in town because she had been begging for twenty years. She sneaked into people's houses and sat until they gave her something. If they didn't, she cursed them. Nevertheless, she was a beggar. Ruller walked faster. He took the dime out of his pocket so it would be ready. His heart was stomping up and down in his chest. He made a noise to see if he could talk. As they neared each other, he stuck out his hand. "Here!" he shouted. "Here!"

She was a tall, long-faced old woman in an antique black cloak. Her face was the color of a dead chicken's skin. When she saw him, she looked as if she suddenly smelled something bad. He darted at her and thrust the dime into her hand and dashed on without looking back.

Slowly his heart calmed and he began to feel full of a new feeling—like being happy and embarrassed at the same time. Maybe, he thought, blushing, he would give all his money to her. He felt as if the ground did not need to be under him any longer. He noticed suddenly that the country boys' feet were shuffling just behind him, and almost without thinking, he turned and asked graciously, "You all wanta see this turkey?"

They stopped where they were and stared at him. One in front spit. Ruller looked down at it quickly. There was real tobacco juice in it! "Wheered you git that turkey?" the spitter asked.

"I found it in the woods," Ruller said. "I chased it dead. See, it's been shot un-der the wing." He took the turkey off his shoulder and held it down where they could see. "I think it was shot twice," he went on excitedly, pulling the wing up.

"Lemme see it here," the spitter said.

Ruller handed him the turkey. "You see down there where the bullet hole is?" he asked. "Well, I think it was shot twice in the same hole, I think it was...." The turkey's head flew in his face as the spitter slung it up in the air and over his own shoulder and turned. The others turned with him and together they saun-tered off in the direction they had come, the turkey sticking stiff out on the spit-ter's back and its head swinging slowly in a circle as he walked away.

They were in the next block before Ruller moved. Finally, he realized that he could not even see them any longer, they were so far away. He turned toward home, almost creeping. He walked four blocks and then suddenly, noticing that it was dark, he began to run. He ran faster and faster, and as he turned up the road to his house, his heart was running as fast as his legs and he was certain that Something Awful was tearing behind him with its arms rigid and its fingers ready to clutch.

❋ ❋ ❋

## TILLIE OLSEN

## *I Stand Here Ironing*                                        (1954)

I stand here ironing, and what you asked me moves tormented back and forth with the iron.

"I wish you would manage the time to come in and talk with me about your daughter. I'm sure you can help me understand her. She's a youngster who needs help and whom I'm deeply interested in helping."

"Who needs help." . . . Even if I came, what good would it do? You think be-cause I am her mother I have a key, or that in some way you could use me as a key? She has lived for nineteen years. There is all that life that has happened out-side of me, beyond me.

And when is there time to remember, to sift, to weigh, to estimate, to total? I will start and there will be an interruption and I will have to gather it all together again. Or I will become engulfed with all I did or did not do, with what should have been and what cannot be helped.

She was a beautiful baby. The first and only one of our five that was beautiful at birth. You do not guess how new and uneasy her tenancy in her now-loveliness. You did not know her all those years she was thought homely, or see her poring over her baby pictures, making me tell her over and over how beautiful she had been—and would be, I would tell her—and was now, to the seeing eye. But the seeing eyes were few or nonexistent. Including mine.

I nursed her. They feel that's important nowadays. I nursed all the children, but with her, with all the fierce rigidity of first motherhood, I did like the books then said. Though her cries battered me to trembling and my breasts ached with swollenness, I waited till the clock decreed.

Why do I put that first? I do not even know if it matters, or if it explains anything.

She was a beautiful baby. She blew shining bubbles of sound. She loved motion, loved light, loved color and music and textures. She would lie on the floor in her blue overalls patting the surface so hard in ecstasy her hands and feet would blur. She was a miracle to me, but when she was eight months old I had to leave her daytimes with the woman downstairs to whom she was no miracle at all, for I worked or looked for work and for Emily's father, who "could no longer endure" (he wrote in his good-bye note) "sharing want with us."

I was nineteen. It was the pre-relief, pre-WPA world of the depression. I would start running as soon as I got off the streetcar, running up the stairs, the place smelling sour, and awake or asleep to startle awake, when she saw me she would break into a clogged weeping that could not be comforted, a weeping I can hear yet.

After a while I found a job hashing at night so I could be with her days, and it was better. But it came to where I had to bring her to his family and leave her.

It took a long time to raise the money for her fare back. Then she got chicken pox and I had to wait longer. When she finally came, I hardly knew her, walking quick and nervous like her father, looking like her father, thin, and dressed in a shoddy red that yellowed her skin and glared at the pockmarks. All the baby loveliness gone.

She was two. Old enough for nursery school they said, and I did not know then what I know now—the fatigue of the long day, and the lacerations of group life in the kinds of nurseries that are only parking places for children.

Except that it would have made no difference if I had known. It was the only place there was. It was the only way we could be together, the only way I could hold a job.

And even without knowing, I knew. I knew the teacher that was evil because all these years it has curdled into my memory, the little boy hunched in the corner, her rasp, "why aren't you outside, because Alvin hits you? that's no reason, go out, scaredy." I knew Emily hated it even if she did not clutch and implore "don't go Mommy" like the other children, mornings.

She always had a reason why we should stay home. Momma, you look sick. Momma, I feel sick. Momma, the teachers aren't there today, they're sick. Momma, we can't go, there was a fire there last night. Momma, it's a holiday today, no school, they told me.

But never a direct protest, never rebellion. I think of our others in their three-, four-year-oldness—the explosions, the tempers, the denunciations, the demands—and I feel suddenly ill. I put the iron down. What in me demanded that goodness in her? And what was the cost, the cost to her of such goodness?

The old man living in the back once said in his gentle way: "You should smile at Emily more when you look at her." What *was* in my face when I looked at her? I loved her. There were all the acts of love.

It was only with the others I remembered what he said, and it was the face of joy, and not of care or tightness or worry I turned to them—too late for Emily. She does not smile easily, let alone almost always as her brothers and sisters do. Her face is closed and sombre, but when she wants, how fluid. You must have seen it in her pantomimes, you spoke of her rare gift for comedy on the stage that rouses a laughter out of the audience so dear they applaud and applaud and do not want to let her go.

Where does it come from, that comedy? There was none of it in her when she came back to me that second time, after I had had to send her away again. She had a new daddy now to learn to love, and I think perhaps it was a better time.

Except when we left her alone nights, telling ourselves she was old enough.

"Can't you go some other time, Mommy, like tomorrow?" she would ask. "Will it be just a little while you'll be gone? Do you promise?"

The time we came back, the front door open, the clock on the floor in the hall. She rigid awake. "It wasn't just a little while. I didn't cry. Three times I called you, just three times, and then I ran downstairs to open the door so you could come faster. The clock talked loud. I threw it away, it scared me what it talked."

She said the clock talked loud again that night I went to the hospital to have Susan. She was delirious with the fever that comes before red measles, but she was fully conscious all the week I was gone and the week after we were home when she could not come near the new baby or me.

She did not get well. She stayed skeleton thin, not wanting to eat, and night after night she had nightmares. She would call for me, and I would rouse from exhaustion to sleepily call back: "You're all right, darling, go to sleep, it's just a dream," and if she still called, in a sterner voice, "now go to sleep, Emily, there's nothing to hurt you." Twice, only twice, when I had to get up for Susan anyhow, I went in to sit with her.

Now when it is too late (as if she would let me hold and comfort her like I do the others) I get up and go to her at once at her moan or restless stirring. "Are you awake, Emily? Can I get you something?" And the answer is always the same: "No, I'm all right, go back to sleep, Mother."

They persuaded me at the clinic to send her away to a convalescent home in the country where "she can have the kind of food and care you can't manage for her, and you'll be free to concentrate on the new baby." They still send children to that place. I see pictures on the society page of sleek young women planning affairs to raise money for it, or dancing at the affairs, or decorating Easter eggs or filling Christmas stockings for the children.

They never have a picture of the children so I do not know if the girls still wear those gigantic red bows and the ravaged looks on the every other Sunday when parents can come to visit "unless otherwise notified"—as we were notified the first six weeks.

Oh it is a handsome place, green lawns and tall trees and fluted flower beds. High up on the balconies of each cottage the children stand, the girls in their red bows and white dresses, the boys in white suits and giant red ties. The parents stand below shrieking up to be heard and the children shriek down to be heard, and between them the invisible wall "Not To Be Contaminated by Parental Germs or Physical Affection."

There was a tiny girl who always stood hand in hand with Emily. Her parents never came. One visit she was gone. "They moved her to Rose Cottage" Emily shouted in explanation. "They don't like you to love anybody here."

She wrote once a week, the labored writing of a seven-year-old. "I am fine. How is the baby. If I write my leter nicly I will have a star. Love." There never was a star. We wrote every other day, letters she could never hold or keep but only hear read—once. "We simply do not have room for children to keep any personal possessions," they patiently explained when we pieced one Sunday's shrieking together to plead how much it would mean to Emily, who loved so to keep things, to be allowed to keep her letters and cards.

Each visit she looked frailer. "She isn't eating," they told us.

(They had runny eggs for breakfast or mush with lumps, Emily said later, I'd hold it in my mouth and not swallow. Nothing ever tasted good, just when they had chicken.)

It took us eight months to get her released home, and only the fact that she gained back so little of her seven lost pounds convinced the social worker.

I used to try to hold and love her after she came back, but her body would stay stiff, and after a while she'd push away. She ate little. Food sickened her, and I think much of life too. Oh she had physical lightness and brightness, twinkling by on skates, bouncing like a ball up and down up and down over the jump rope, skimming over the hill; but these were momentary.

She fretted about her appearance, thin and dark and foreign-looking at a time when every little girl was supposed to look or thought she should look a chubby blonde replica of Shirley Temple. The doorbell sometimes rang for her, but no one seemed to come and play in the house or be a best friend. Maybe because we moved so much.

There was a boy she loved painfully through two school semesters. Months later she told me how she had taken pennies from my purse to buy him candy. "Licorice was his favorite and I brought him some every day, but he still liked Jennifer better'n me. Why, Mommy?" The kind of question for which there is no answer.

School was a worry to her. She was not glib or quick in a world where glibness and quickness were easily confused with ability to learn. To her overworked and exasperated teachers she was an overconscientious "slow learner" who kept trying to catch up and was absent entirely too often.

I let her be absent, though sometimes the illness was imaginary. How different from my now-strictness about attendance with the others. I wasn't working.

We had a new baby, I was home anyhow. Sometimes, after Susan grew old enough, I would keep her home from school, too, to have them all together.

Mostly Emily had asthma, and her breathing, harsh and labored, would fill the house with a curiously tranquil sound. I would bring the two old dresser mirrors and her boxes of collections to her bed. She would select beads and single earrings, bottle tops and shells, dried flowers and pebbles, old postcards and scraps, all sorts of oddments; then she and Susan would play Kingdom, setting up landscapes and furniture, peopling them with action.

Those were the only times of peaceful companionship between her and Susan. I have edged away from it, that poisonous feeling between them, that terrible balancing of hurts and needs I had to do between the two, and did so badly, those earlier years.

Oh there are conflicts between the others too, each one human, needing, demanding, hurting, taking—but only between Emily and Susan, no, Emily toward Susan that corroding resentment. It seems so obvious on the surface, yet it is not obvious. Susan, the second child, Susan, golden- and curly-haired and chubby, quick and articulate and assured, everything in appearance and manner Emily was not; Susan, not able to resist Emily's precious things, losing or sometimes clumsily breaking them; Susan telling jokes and riddles to company for applause while Emily sat silent (to say to me later: that was *my* riddle, Mother, I told it to Susan); Susan, who for all the five years' difference in age was just a year behind Emily in developing physically.

I am glad for that slow physical development that widened the difference between her and her contemporaries, though she suffered over it. She was too vulnerable for that terrible world of youthful competition, of preening and parading, of constant measuring of yourself against every other, of envy, "If I had that copper hair," "If I had that skin. . . ." She tormented herself enough about not looking like the others, there was enough of the unsureness, the having to be conscious of words before you speak, the constant caring—what are they thinking of me? without having it all magnified by the merciless physical drives.

Ronnie is calling. He is wet and I change him. It is rare there is such a cry now. That time of motherhood is almost behind me when the ear is not one's own but must always be racked and listening for the child cry, the child call. We sit for a while and I hold him, looking out over the city spread in charcoal with its soft aisles of light. "*Shoogily,*" he breathes and curls closer. I carry him back to bed, asleep. *Shoogily*. A funny word, a family word, inherited from Emily, invented by her to say: *comfort*.

In this and other ways she leaves her seal, I say aloud. And startle at my saying it. What do I mean? What did I start to gather together, to try and make coherent? I was at the terrible, growing years. War years. I do not remember them well. I was working, there were four smaller ones now, there was not time for her. She had to help be a mother, and housekeeper, and shopper. She had to set her seal. Mornings of crisis and near hysteria trying to get lunches packed, hair combed, coats and shoes found, everyone to school or Child Care on time, the baby ready for transportation. And always the paper scribbled on by a smaller one, the book looked at by Susan then mislaid, the homework not done. Running out to that huge school where she was one, she was lost, she was a drop; suffering over the unpreparedness, stammering and unsure in her classes.

There was so little time left at night after the kids were bedded down. She would struggle over books, always eating (it was in those years she developed her enormous appetite that is legendary in our family) and I would be ironing, or preparing food for the next day, or writing V-mail to Bill, or tending the baby. Sometimes, to make me laugh, or out of her despair, she would imitate happenings or types at school.

I think I said once: "Why don't you do something like this in the school amateur show?" One morning she phoned me at work, hardly understandable through the weeping: "Mother, I did it. I won, I won; they gave me first prize; they clapped and clapped and wouldn't let me go."

Now suddenly she was Somebody, and as imprisoned in her difference as she had been in anonymity.

She began to be asked to perform at other high schools, even in colleges, then at city and statewide affairs. The first one we went to, I only recognized her that first moment when thin, shy, she almost drowned herself into the curtains. Then: Was this Emily? The control, the command, the convulsing and deadly clowning, the spell, then the roaring, stamping audience, unwilling to let this rare and precious laughter out of their lives.

Afterwards: You ought to do something about her with a gift like that—but without money or knowing how, what does one do? We have left it all to her, and the gift has as often eddied inside, clogged and clotted, as been used and growing.

She is coming. She runs up the stairs two at a time with her light graceful step, and I know she is happy tonight. Whatever it was that occasioned your call did not happen today.

"Aren't you ever going to finish the ironing, Mother? Whistler painted his mother in a rocker. I'd have to paint mine standing over an ironing board." This is one of her communicative nights and she tells me everything and nothing as she fixes herself a plate of food out of the icebox.

She is so lovely. Why did you want me to come in at all? Why were you concerned? She will find her way.

She starts up the stairs to bed. "Don't get me up with the rest in the morning." "But I thought you were having midterms." "Oh, those," she comes back in, kisses me, and says quite lightly, "in a couple of years when we'll all be atom-dead they won't matter a bit."

She has said it before. She *believes* it. But because I have been dredging the past, and all that compounds a human being is so heavily and meaningful in me, I cannot endure it tonight.

I will never total it all. I will never come in to say: She was a child seldom smiled at. Her father left me before she was a year old. I had to work her first six years when there was work, or I sent her home and to his relatives. There were years she had care she hated. She was dark and thin and foreign-looking in a world where the prestige went to blondeness and curly hair and dimples, she was slow where glibness was prized. She was a child of anxious, not proud, love. We were poor and could not afford for her the soil of easy growth. I was a young mother, I was a distracted mother. There were the other children pushing up, demanding. Her younger sister seemed all that she was not. There were years she did not want me to touch her. She kept too much in herself, her life was such she had to keep too much in herself. My wisdom came too late. She has much to her and probably little will come of it. She is a child of her age, of depression, of war, of fear.

Let her be. So all that is in her will not bloom—but in how many does it? There is still enough left to live by. Only help her to know—help make it so there is cause for her to know—that she is more than this dress on the ironing board, helpless before the iron.

### Study and Discussion Questions

1. How does ironing function as a symbol in this story?
2. How does the narrator feel about herself as a mother?
3. What regrets does the mother have about Emily's childhood?
4. "And when is there time . . . ," the mother says. How does the paragraph that begins this way anticipate what happens in the story?
5. What forms did the narrator's love for her daughter take?
6. What connections can you make between Emily's gift for comedy and her early life?

### Suggestions for Writing

1. How did economic factors affect the narrator's relationship with her daughter?
2. Who is the narrator's imagined audience, the "you" of the opening sentence? What is the narrator's tone?
3. If Emily were to write an account of these same years, what might she say?

### Critical Resources

1. Coiner, Constance. *Better Red: The Writing and Resistance of Tillie Olsen and Meridel Le Sueur.* New York: Oxford University Press, 1995.
2. Frye, Joanne. *Tillie Olsen: A Study of the Short Fiction.* New York: Twayne, 1995.
3. Nelson, Kay, ed. *The Critical Response to Tillie Olsen.* Westport, CT: Greenwood Press, 1994.
4. Rosenfelt, Deborah. "From the Thirties: Tillie Olsen and the Radical Tradition." *Feminist Studies* 7.3 (1981): 371–406.

❊ ❊ ❊

## HARVEY PEKAR

**(1984)**

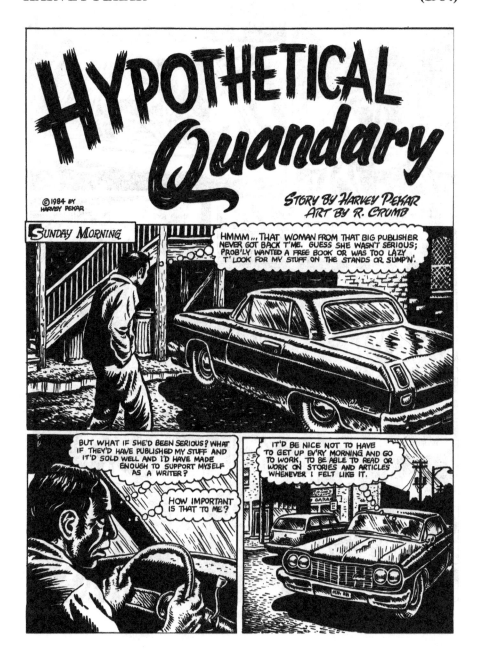

BUT WOULD IT BE AS INTERESTING A LIFE? MAYBE IT'D BE TOO BLAND...

BUT THEN, KNOWIN' MYSELF, I COULD ALWAYS FIND SOMETHING TO GET SHOOK UP OVER AND WRITE ABOUT. LET'S FACE IT, I'M NOT GONNA BECOME A MELLOW MAN OVER NIGHT NO MATTER WHAT HAPPENS!

OH WELL, IT'S ALL HYPOTHETICAL... THAT WOMAN DIDN'T CALL ME BACK...

SNIFF

GAS

SELF-SERVE $1.03

AH, FRESH BREAD!

THE END

## Study and Discussion Questions

1. What is a "hypothetical quandary"? Look up the words in a large dictionary. Give an example of a hypothetical quandary in your own life. What is Pekar's hypothetical quandary in this story?
2. Describe the setting of this story.
3. What literally happens in this story? Give a plot summary.
4. Is the ending of "Hypothetical Quandary" a satisfactory answer to the protagonist's dilemma? Say how or how not. Would it be for you?
5. What do we learn about the main character from the way he is presented visually?
6. In the introduction to the collection *American Splendor: The Life and Times of Harvey Pekar,* from which this piece comes, illustrator R. Crumb writes in 1985, "Pekar has proven once and for all that even the most seemingly dreary and monotonous of lives is filled with poignancy and heroic struggle. . . . What Pekar does is certainly new to the comic book medium. There's never been anything even approaching this kind of stark realism." If you have read other comic books or graphic novels, how were they similar to and different from "Hypothetical Quandary"?
7. Harvey Pekar has worked with several artists in the course of his career creating serious comics about his life and times. Characterize R. Crumb's art work in this particular story.
8. Why include a comic strip such as this in a literature anthology?

## Suggestions for Writing

1. See the 2003 biographical film about Harvey Pekar, *American Splendor* and write about "Hypothetical Quandary" in the context of what you have learned about Pekar's life.
2. Compare/contrast this example of graphic literature with Marjane Satrapi's "The Dowry" from her graphic memoir *Persepolis* (Peace and War). You might discuss the visual style of each and how it is an essential aspect of this narrative medium. Or you could discuss each protagonist's relation to the world he or she lives in. Or choose your own topic.
3. Select one panel or frame in "Hypothetical Quandary" and analyze it— in terms of mood or atmosphere, presentation of character and setting, relation of words to picture, use of black and white, use of space, and any other aspects you find interesting.

## Critical Resources

1. *American Splendor.* Directors Shari Springer Berman and Robert Pulcini. Performers Paul Giamatti, Hope Davis. HBO Films, 2003 (101 minutes).
2. Witek, Joseph. *Comic Books as History: The Narrative Art of Jack Jackson, Art Spiegelman and Harvey Pekar.* Jackson: University Press of Mississippi, 1989.
3. Weiner, Stephen. *Faster Than A Speeding Bullet: The Rise of the Graphic Novel.* New York: NBM Publishers, 2003.

# EDGAR ALLAN POE

## *The Murders in the Rue Morgue*            (1841)

### Part One

Paris! In Paris it was, in the summer of 1840. There I first met that strange and interesting young fellow, August Dupin.

Dupin was the last member of a well-known family, a family which had once been rich and famous; he himself, however, was far from rich. He cared little about money. He had enough to buy the most necessary things of life—and a few books; he did not trouble himself about the rest. Just books. With books he was happy.

We first met when we were both trying to find the same book. As it was a book which few had ever heard of, this chance brought us together in an old bookstore. Later we met again in the same store. Then again in another bookstore. Soon we began to talk.

I was deeply interested in the family history he told me. I was surprised, too, at how much and how widely he had read; more important, the force of his busy mind was like a bright light in my soul. I felt that the friendship of such a man would be for me riches without price. I therefore told him of my feelings toward him, and he agreed to come and live with me. He would have, I thought, the joy of using my many fine books. And I would have the pleasure of having someone with me, for I was not happy alone.

We passed the days reading, writing and talking. But Dupin was a lover of the night, and at night, often with only the light of the stars to show us the way, we walked the streets of Paris, sometimes talking, sometimes quiet, always thinking.

I soon noticed a special reasoning power he had, an unusual reasoning power. Using it gave him great pleasure. He told me once, with a soft and quiet laugh, that most men have windows over their hearts; through these he could see into their souls. Then, he surprised me by telling what he knew about my own soul; and I found that he knew things about me that I had thought only I could possibly know. His manner at these moments was cold and distant. His eyes looked empty and far away, and his voice became high and nervous. At such times it seemed to me that I saw not just Dupin, but two Dupins—one who coldly put things together, and another who just as coldly took them apart.

One night we were walking down one of Paris's long and dirty streets. Both of us were busy with our thoughts. Neither had spoken for perhaps fifteen minutes. It seemed as if we had each forgotten that the other was there, at his side. I soon learned that Dupin had not forgotten me, however. Suddenly he said:

"You're right. He is a very little fellow, that's true, and he would be more successful if he acted in lighter, less serious plays."

"Yes, there can be no doubt of that!" I said.

At first I saw nothing strange in this. Dupin had agreed with me, with my own thoughts. This, of course, seemed to me quite natural. For a few seconds I continued walking, and thinking; but suddenly I realized that Dupin had agreed with something which was only a thought. I had not spoken a single word. I stopped walking and turned to my friend. "Dupin," I said, "Dupin, this is beyond my understanding. How could you know that I was thinking of... " Here I stopped, in order to test him, to learn if he really did know my unspoken thoughts.

"How did I know you were thinking of Chantilly? Why do you stop? You were thinking that Chantilly is too small for the plays in which he acts."

"That is indeed what I was thinking. But, tell me, in Heaven's name, the method—if method there is—by which you have been able to see into my soul in this matter."

"It was the fruit-seller."

"Fruit-seller!? I know no fruit-seller."

"I mean the man who ran into you as we entered this street—it may have been ten or fifteen minutes ago, perhaps less."

"Yes; yes, that's true, I remember now. A fruit-seller, carrying a large basket of apples on his head, almost threw me down. But I don't understand why the fruit-seller should make me think of Chantilly—or, if he did, how you can know that."

"I will explain. Listen closely now:

"Let us follow your thoughts from the fruit-seller to the play-actor, Chantilly. Those thoughts must have gone like this: from the fruit-seller to the cobblestones, from the cobblestones to stereotomy, and from stereotomy to Epicurus, to Orion, and then to Chantilly.

"As we turned into this street the fruit-seller, walking very quickly past us, ran against you and made you step on some cobblestones which had not been put down evenly, and I could see that the stones had hurt your foot. You spoke a few angry words to yourself, and continued walking. But you kept looking down, down at the cobblestones in the street, so I knew you were still thinking of stones.

"Then we came to a small street where they are putting down street stones which they have cut in a new and very special way. Here your face became brighter and I saw your lips move. I could not doubt that you were saying the word stereotomy, the name for this new way of cutting stones. It is a strange word, Isn't it? But you will remember that we read about it in the newspaper only yesterday. I thought that the word stereotomy must make you think of that old Greek writer named Epicurus, who wrote of something he called atoms; he believed that the world and everything in the heavens above are made of these atoms.

"Not long ago you and I were talking about Epicurus and his ideas, his atoms, ideas which Epicurus wrote about more than 2,000 years ago. We were talking about how much those old ideas are like today's ideas about the earth and the stars and the sky. I felt sure that you would look up to the sky. You did look up. Now I was certain that I had been following your thoughts as they had in fact come into your mind. I too looked up, and saw that the group of stars we call Orion is very bright and clear tonight. I knew you would notice this, and think about the name Orion.

"Now follow my thoughts carefully. Only yesterday, in the news-paper, there was an article about the actor Chantilly, an article which was not friendly to Chantilly, not friendly at all. We noticed that the writer of the article had used some words taken from a book we both had read. These words were about Orion. So I knew you would put together the two ideas of Orion and Chantilly. I saw you smile, remembering that article and the hard words in it.

"Then I saw you stand straighter, as tall as you could make yourself. I was sure you were thinking of Chantilly's size, and especially his height. He is small; he is short. And so I spoke, saying that he is indeed a very little fellow, this Chantilly, and he would be more successful if he acted in lighter, less serious plays."

I will not say that I was surprised. I was more than surprised; I was astonished. Dupin was right, as right as he could be. Those were in fact my thoughts, my unspoken thoughts, as my mind moved from one thought to the next. But if I was astonished by this, I would soon be more than astonished.

One morning this strangely interesting man showed me once again his unusual reasoning power. We heard that an old woman had been killed by unknown persons. The killer, or the killers, had cut her head off—and escaped into the night. Who was this killer, this murderer? The police had no answer. They had looked everywhere and found nothing that helped them. They did not know what to do next. And so—they did nothing.

But not Dupin. He knew what to do.

**Part Two**

It was in Paris in the summer of 1840 that I met August Dupin. He was an unusually interesting young man with a busy, forceful mind. This mind could, it seemed, look right through a man's body into his soul, and uncover his deepest thoughts. Sometimes he seemed to be not one, but two people—one who coldly put things together, and another who just as coldly took them apart.

One morning, in the heat of the summer, Dupin showed me once again his special reasoning power. We read in the newspaper about a terrible killing. An old woman and her daughter, living alone in an old house in the Rue Morgue, had been killed in the middle of the night:

*Paris, July 7, 1840. In the early morning today the people in the western part of the city were awakened from their sleep by cries of terror, which came, it seemed, from a house in the street called the Rue Morgue. The only persons living in the house were an old woman, Mrs. L'Espanaye, and her daughter. Several neighbors and a policeman ran toward the house, but by the time they reached it the cries had stopped. When no one answered their calls, they forced the door open.*

*As they rushed in they heard voices, two voices; they seemed to come from above. The group hurried from room to room, but they found nothing until they reached the fourth floor. There they found a door that was firmly closed, locked, with the key inside. Quickly they forced the door open, and they saw spread before them a bloody sickening scene—a scene of horror!*

*The room was in the wildest possible order—broken chairs and tables were lying all around the room. There was only one bed, and from it everything had been taken and thrown into the middle of the floor. There was blood everywhere, on the floor, on the bed, on the walls. A sharp knife covered with blood was lying on the floor. In front of the fireplace there was some long gray hair, also bloody; it seemed to have been pulled from a human head. On the floor were four pieces of gold, an earring, several objects made of silver, and two bags containing a large amount of money in gold. Clothes had been thrown around the room. A box was found under the bed covers. It was open, and held only a few old letters and papers.*

*There was no one there—or so it seemed. Above the fireplace they found the dead body of the daughter; it had been put up into the opening where the smoke escapes to the sky. The body was still warm. There was blood on the face, and on the neck there were dark, deep marks which seemed to have been made by strong fingers. These marks surely show how the daughter was killed.*

*After hunting in every part of the house without finding anything more, the group went outside. Behind the building they found the body of the old woman. Her neck was almost cut through, and when they tried to lift her up, her head fell off.*

The next day the newspaper offered to its readers these new facts:

*The Murders in the Rue Morgue.—Paris, July 8, 1840. The police have talked with many people about the terrible killings in the old house on the Rue Morgue but nothing has been learned to answer the question of who the killers were.*

*Pauline Dubourg, a washwoman, says she has known both of the dead women for more than three years, and has washed their clothes during that period. The old lady and her daughter seemed to love each other dearly. They always paid her well. She did not know where their money came from, she said. She never met anyone in the house. Only the two women lived on the fourth floor.*

*Pierre Moreau, a shopkeeper, says Mrs. L'Espanaye had bought food at his shop for nearly four years. She owned the house and had lived in it for more than six years. People said they had money. He never saw anyone enter the door except the old lady and her daughter, and a doctor eight or ten times, perhaps.*

*Many other persons, neighbors, said the same thing. Almost no one ever went into the house and Mrs. L'Espanaye and her daughter were not often seen.*

*Jules Mignaud, a banker, says that Mrs. L'Espanaye had put money in his bank, beginning eight years before. Three days before her death she took out of the bank a large amount of money, in gold. A man from the bank carried it for her to her house.*

*Isidore Muset, a policeman, says that he was with the group that first entered the house. While he was going up the stairs he heard two voices, one low and soft, and one hard, high, and very strange—the voice of someone who was certainly not French, the voice of a foreigner. Spanish perhaps. It was not a woman's voice. He could not understand what it said. But the low voice, the softer voice, said, in French, "My God!"*

*Alfonso Garcia, who is Spanish and lives on the Rue Morgue, says he entered the house but did not go up the stairs; he is nervous and he was afraid he might be ill. He heard the voices. He believes the high voice was not that of a Frenchman. Perhaps it was English; but he doesn't understand English, so he is not sure.*

*William Bird, another foreigner, an Englishman, says he was one of the persons who entered the house. He has lived in Paris for two years. He heard the voices. The low voice was that of a Frenchman, he was sure, because he heard it say, in French, "My God!" The high voice was very loud. He is sure it was not the voice of an Englishman, nor the voice of a*

*Frenchman. It seemed to be that of an Italian. It might have been a woman's voice. He does not understand Italian.*

*Mr. Alberto Montani, an Italian, was passing the house at the time of the cries. He says that they lasted for about two minutes. They were screams, long and loud, terrible, fearful sounds. Montani, who speaks Spanish but not French, says that he also heard two voices. He thought both voices were French. But he could not understand any of the words spoken.*

*The persons who first entered the house all agree that the door of the room where the daughter's body was found was locked on the inside. When they reached the door everything was quiet. When they forced the door open they saw no one. The windows were closed and firmly locked on the inside. There are no steps that someone could have gone down while they were going up. They say that the openings over the fireplace are too small for anyone to have escaped through them. It took four or five people to pull the daughter's body out of the opening over the fireplace. A careful search was made through the whole house. It was four or five minutes from the time they heard the voices to the moment they forced open the door of the room.*

*Paul Dumas, a doctor, says that he was called to see the bodies soon after they were found. They were in a horrible condition, badly marked and broken. Such results could not have come from a woman's hands, only from those of a very powerful man. The daughter had been killed by strong hands around her neck.*

*The police have learned nothing more than this. A killing as strange as this has never before happened in Paris. The police do not know where to begin to look for the answer.*

When we had finished reading the newspaper's account of the murders neither Dupin nor myself said anything for a while. But I could see in his eyes that cold, empty look which told me that his mind was working busily. When he asked me what I thought of all this, I could only agree with all Paris. I told him I considered it a very difficult problem—a mystery, to which it was not possible to find an answer. No, no, said Dupin.

"No, I think you are wrong. A mystery it is, yes. But there must be an answer. Let us go to the house and see what we can see. There must be an answer. There must!"

**Part Three**

It was in Paris that I met August Dupin. He was an unusually interesting young man with a busy, forceful mind. This mind could, it seemed, look right through a man's body into his deepest soul.

One hot summer morning we read in the newspapers about a terrible killing. The dead persons were an old woman and her unmarried daughter, who lived alone on the fourth floor of an old house on the street called the Rue Morgue. Someone had taken the daughter's neck in his powerful fingers and pressed with fearful strength until her life was gone. Her mother's body was found outside, behind the house, with the head nearly cut off. The knife with which she was killed was found, however, in the room, on the floor.

Several neighbors ran to the house when they heard the women's cries of fear. As they ran up to the fourth floor they heard two other voices. But when they reached the room and broke down the door they found no living person in the room. Like the door, the two windows were firmly closed, locked on the inside. There was no other way that the killer could have got in or out of the room.

The Paris police did not know where to begin to look for the answer. I told Dupin that it seemed to me that it was not possible to learn the answer to the mystery of these killings. No, no, said Dupin.

"No; I think you are wrong. A mystery it is, yes. But there must be an answer. We must not judge what is possible just by what we have read in the newspapers. The Paris police work hard and often get good results; but there is no real method in what they do. When something more than simple hard work is needed, when a little real method is needed, the police fail. Sometimes they stand too near the problem. Often, if a person looks at something very closely he can see a few things more clearly, but the shape of the whole thing escapes him.

"There must be an answer! There must! Let us go to the house and see what we can see. I know the head of the police, and he will allow us to do so. And this will be interesting and give us some pleasure."

I thought it strange that Dupin should believe we would get pleasure out of this. But I said nothing.

It was late in the afternoon when we reached the house on the Rue Morgue. It was easily found for there were still many persons—in fact, a crowd, standing there looking at it. Before going in we walked all around it, and Dupin carefully looked at the neighboring houses as well as this one. I could not understand the reason for such great care.

We came again to the front of the house and went in. We went up the stairs into the room where the daughter's body had been found. Both bodies were there. The police had left the room as they had found it. I saw nothing beyond what the newspaper had told us. Dupin looked with great care at everything, at the bodies, the walls, the fireplace, the windows. Then we went home.

Dupin said nothing. I could see the cold look in his eyes which told me that his mind was working, working busily, quickly. I asked no questions.

Dupin said nothing until the next morning, when he came into my room and asked me suddenly if I had not noticed something especially strange about what we saw at the house on the Rue Morgue. I replied: "Nothing more than we both read in the newspaper."

"Tell me, my friend. How shall we explain the horrible force, the unusual strength used in these murders? And whose were the voices that were heard? No one was found except the dead women; yet there was no way for anyone to escape. And the wild condition of the room; the body which was found head down above the fireplace; the terrible broken appearance of the body of the old lady, with its head cut off; these are all so far from what might be expected that the police are standing still; they don't know where to begin.

"These things are unusual, indeed; but they are not deep mysteries. We should not ask, 'What has happened?' but 'What has happened that has never happened before?' In fact, the very things that the police think cannot possibly be explained are the things which will lead me to the answer. Indeed, I believe they have already led me to the answer."

I was so surprised I could not say a word. Dupin looked quickly at the door. "I am now waiting for a person who will know something about these murders, these wild killings. I do not think he did them himself. But I think he will know the killer. I hope I am right about this. If I am, then I expect to find the whole answer, today. I expect the man here—in this room—at any moment. It is true that he may not come; but he probably will."

"But who is this person? How did you find him?"

"I'll tell you. While we wait for this man we do not know—for I have never met him—while we wait, I will tell you how my thoughts went." Dupin began to talk. But it did not seem that he was trying to explain to me what he had thought. It seemed that he was talking to himself. He looked not at me, but at the wall.

"It has been fully proved that the voices heard by the neighbors were not the voices of the women who were killed. Someone else was in the room. It is therefore certain that the old woman did not first kill her daughter and then kill herself. She would not have been strong enough to put her daughter's body where it was found; and the manner of the old lady's death shows that she could not have caused it herself. A person can kill himself with a knife, yes. But he surely cannot cut his own head almost off, then drop the knife on the floor and jump out the window. It was murder, then, done by some third person—or persons. And the voices heard were the voices of these persons. Let us now think carefully about the things people said about those voices. Did you notice anything especially strange in what was told about them?"

"Well, yes. Everybody agreed that the low voice was the voice of a Frenchman; but they could not agree about the high voice."

"Ah! That was what they said, yes; but that was not what was so strange about what they said. You say you have noticed nothing that makes their stories very different from what might have been expected. Yet there was something. All these persons, as you say, agreed about the low voice; but not about the high hard voice. The strange thing here is that when an Italian, an Englishman, a Spaniard, and a Frenchman tried to tell what the voice was like, each one said it sounded like the voice of a foreigner. How strangely unusual that voice really must have been! Here are four men from four big countries, and not one of them could understand what the voice said; each one gave it a different name.

"Now, I know that there are other countries in the world. You will say that perhaps it was the voice of someone from one of those other lands—Russia, perhaps. But remember, not one of these people heard anything that sounded like a separate word."

Here Dupin turned and looked into my eyes.

"This is what we have learned from the newspaper. I don't know what I have led you to think. But I believe that in this much of the story there are enough facts to lead us in the one and only direction to the right answer. What this answer is, I will not say… not yet. But I want you to keep in mind that this much was enough to tell me what I must look for when we were in that house on the Rue Morgue. And I found it!"

**Part Four**

Murderers had come to the old house on the street called the Rue Morgue! Murderers had come and gone and left behind the dead bodies of an old woman and her daughter. The daughter's body was in the bedroom on the fourth floor. The old woman was lying outside, behind the house, her head almost cut off; but the knife which killed her was up in the bedroom, on the floor. The door and the windows were all firmly closed, locked on the inside; there was no way for anyone to go in or out. Voices had been heard. One voice was speaking in French; the other voice had not spoken even one word that anyone could understand. But there was no one in the room when police arrived.

This much we had learned from the newspapers, my friend Dupin and I. Interested by it, we had gone to look at the house and the bodies. Dupin was now explaining to me what he had learned there.

"That is what we learned from the newspapers. Please remember it; for that much was enough to tell me what I must look for when we were in that house on the Rue Morgue. And I found it!

"Let us now take ourselves again, in our thoughts, to the room where the murders were done. What shall we first look for? The way the murderers escaped. All right. We agree, I am sure, that we do not have to look for anything outside of nature, for anything not having a real form, a body. The killers were not spirits; they were real. They could not go through the walls. Then how did they escape? There is only one way to reason on that subject, and it must lead us to the answer. Let us look, one at a time, at the possible ways to escape. It is clear that the killers were in the room where the daughter was found. From this room they must have escaped. How?

"At first I saw no way out. It had been necessary for the neighbors to break down the door in order to enter the room. There was no other door. The opening above the fireplace is not big enough, near the top, for even a small animal. The murderers therefore must have escaped through one of the windows. This may not seem possible. We must prove that it is possible.

"There are two windows in the room. Both of them, you will remember, are made of two parts; to open the window one must lift up the bottom half. One of these windows is easily seen; the lower part of the other is out of sight behind the big bed. I looked carefully at the first of these windows. It was firmly closed, *fastened,* like the door, on the inside. To keep the window closed, to fasten it, someone had put a strong iron nail into the wood at the side of the window in such a way that the window could not be raised. At least it seemed that the nail held the window closed. The nail was easy to see. There it was. And the people who discovered the killings used their greatest strength and could not raise the window. I, too, tried to raise the window and could not.

"I went to the second window and looked behind the bed at the lower half of the window. There was a nail here, too, which held the window closed. Without moving the bed, I tried to open this window also, and again I could not do so.

"I did not stop looking for an answer, however, because I knew that what did not seem possible must be proved to be possible. The killers—or perhaps I should say, the killer, for I am almost certain there was only one—the killer escaped through one of these windows. Of this I felt certain. After the murderer had left the bedroom he could have closed the window from the outside; but he could not have fastened it again on the inside. Yet anyone could see the nails which held the windows *tightly* closed. This was the fact that stopped the police. How could the murderer put the nail back in its place?"

"Perhaps—perhaps if you pulled out the nail..."

"Yes! That is just what I thought. Two things seemed clear: first, there had to be something wrong with the idea that the nails were holding the windows closed. I didn't know what was wrong. Something was. Second, if it was not the nails which were holding the windows closed, then something else was holding them closed, something hard to see, something hidden.

"I went back to the first window. With great effort I pulled out the nail. Then I again tried to raise the window. It was still firmly closed. This did not surprise me. There had to be a hidden lock, I thought, inside the window. I felt the window carefully with my fingers. Indeed, I found a button which, when I pressed it, opened an inner lock. With almost no effort I raised the window.

"Now I knew that the killer could close the window from outside and the window would lock itself. But there was still the nail. Carefully, I put the nail back into the hole from which I had taken it. Then I pressed the button and tried to raise the window. I could not. The nail also was holding the window closed!"

"Then... then the murderer could not possibly have gone out the window."

"He could not have gone out that window. Therefore, he must have escaped through the other window. The other window was also held closed by a nail. But I knew I must be right. Although no one else had looked carefully at the window behind the bed, I went to it and tried to see whether the two windows were in some way different. The nail in the second window looked the same as the one I had just seen. I moved the bed so that I could look closely. Yes. There was a button here, too. I was so sure I was right that without touching the nail I pressed the button and tried to raise the window. Up it went!

"As the window went up it carried with it the top part of the nail, the head. When I closed the window the head of the nail was again in its place. It looked just as it had looked before. I took the head of the nail in my fingers and it easily came away from the window. I saw that the nail had been broken. But when I put the nail head back in its place, the nail again looked whole.

"What seemed to be not possible we have proved to be possible. The murderer indeed escaped through that window. I could now see, in my mind, what had happened.

"It was a hot summer night. When the murderer first arrived he found that window open, open to let some of the fresh night air come in. Through the open window the murderer went in and came out again. As he came out he closed the window, perhaps with a purpose to do so, perhaps by chance. The special lock inside the window held the window firmly closed. The nail only seemed to be holding it closed. And that which was possible looked not possible."

Dupin had been talking not to me, it seemed, but to himself. His cold eyes seemed to see only what was in his own mind. Now he stopped and looked straight at me. His eyes were now hard and bright. And I understood that using his unusual reasoning power to find the answer to those bloody murders was giving Dupin great pleasure!

At first I could think only of this. Then I said: "Dupin—the windows are on the fourth floor, far above the ground. Even an open window... "

"Yes. That is an interesting question: how did the murderer go from the window down to the ground? Once I was quite certain that the murderer had in fact gone through that window the rest was not so hard to know. And the answer to this question told me still more about who the murderer was!

"When you and I first came to the house on the Rue Morgue we walked around the house. At that time I noted a long, thin metal pole which went from the top of the building to the ground—a *lightning rod,* put there to carry down to the ground a charge of electricity that might come out of the clouds during a bad summer storm. Here, I thought, is a way for someone to go up or down the wall, and then to go in or out the window. He would have to be very strong. Although certain animals could easily go up the pole, not every man could do it—only a man with very special strength and special training. This told me more about what the murderer was like. But I still had the question: who?"

## Part Five

That unusual Frenchman, August Dupin, was still explaining to me how he found the answer to the question of who murdered the two women in the house on the Rue Morgue. We now knew that it was indeed possible for the killer to go in and again out one of the windows and still leave them both firmly closed, locked on the inside. And I agreed with Dupin when he said that only someone with very special strength and training could have gone up the lightning rod on the side of the house and thus entered the window. But who the murderer was, we still did not know.

"Let us look again," said Dupin, "at that room on the fourth floor. Let us now go back, in our minds, to the room we saw yesterday. Consider its appearance. Clothes had been thrown around the room; yet it seemed that none had been taken. The old woman and her daughter almost never left the house. They had little use for many clothes. Those that were found in the room were as good as any they had. If the killer took some, why didn't he take the best—or take all? And why would he take a few clothes and leave all the money? Nearly the whole amount brought from the bank was found, in bags, on the floor.

"I want you therefore to forget the idea in the minds of the police, the idea that a desire for money was what they call the *motive,* the reason for the murders. This idea rose in their minds when they heard how the money was brought to the house three days before the killings. But this is only what we call a *coincidence*—two things happening at the same time, but only by chance and not because of some cause, some cause that brought them together. Coincidences happen to all of us every day of our lives. If the gold was the reason for the murders, the killer must have been quite a *fool* to forget and leave it there.

"No. I don't think the desire for money was the reason for the killings. I think that there was no reason for these killings… except, perhaps, fear.

"Now let us look at the murders themselves. A girl is killed by powerful hands around her neck, then the body is placed in the opening over the fireplace, head down. No murders we usually hear about are like this. There is something here that does not fit our ideas of human actions, even when we think of men of the most terrible kind. Think, also, of the great strength which was necessary to put the body where it was found. The strength of several men was needed to pull it down!

"There are other signs of this fearful strength. In front of the fireplace some gray human hair was lying, thick pieces of it, pulled from the head of the old woman. You saw the hair on the floor yourself, and you saw the blood and skin with it. You know, and I know, that great force is necessary to pull out even twenty or thirty hairs at one time. A much greater force was needed to pull out hundreds of hairs at one time. Also, the head of the old lady was cut almost completely from the body. Why? To kill a woman with a knife it is not necessary to cut her head off!!

"If, now, added to all these things, we add also the condition of the room, we have put together the following ideas: strength more than human; *wildness* less than human; a murder without reason; horror beyond human understanding; and a voice which made no sound that men could understand. What result, then, have you come to? What have I helped you to see?"

A cold feeling went up and down my back as Dupin asked me the question. "A man... someone who has lost his mind," I said. "A *madman*!! A madman!! Only a madman could have done these murders!"

"I think not. In some ways your idea is a good one. But madmen are from one country or another. Their cries may be terrible, but they are made of words, and some of the words can be understood.

"Here! Look! Look at this hair. I took it from the fingers of the old woman. The hair of a madman is not like this. Tell me what you think it is."

"Dupin! This hair is... this hair is not human hair!!"

"I did not say that it is. But, before we decide this matter, look at the picture I had made here on this piece of paper. It is a picture of the marks on the daughter's neck. The doctors said these marks were made by fingers. Let me spread the paper on the table before us. Try to put your fingers, all at the same time, on the picture, so that your hand and its fingers will fit the picture of the marks on the daughter's neck."

"I cannot!"

"No. But perhaps we are not doing this in the right way. The paper is spread out on the table; the human neck is round. Here is a piece of wood about as big as the daughter's neck. Put the paper around it and try again. Go on! Try!"

I tried to put my fingers around the piece of wood, as if it were the girl's neck! But still my hand was not large enough to equal the marks left by the killer. "Dupin! These marks were made by no human hand!"

"No. They were not. I am almost certain that they were made by the hand of an *orangutan,* one of those man-like animals that live in the wild forests. The great size, the strength, the wildness of these animals are well known. Now, Look in this book by Cuvier. Read. Look at the picture."

I did so, and at once I knew that Dupin was right in everything he said. The color of the hair... the size of the hand... the terrible strength... the wildness of the killings... those sounds which were a voice but were not words... everything fit nicely in its place.

No, not everything. "Dupin!" I said. "There were two voices. Whose was the second voice?"

"The second voice! Yes! Remember: we decided that only someone with a very special kind of strength could have gone up the lightning rod, up the side of the house to the window on the fourth floor—perhaps an animal, perhaps a strong man from a **circus,** perhaps a **sailor.** We know now that one of the voices was the voice of an animal, an orangutan. The other was the voice of a man. This voice spoke only two words; they were "My God!" spoken in French.

"Upon those two words I have placed my hopes of finding a full answer to this horrible question. The words were an expression of horror. This means that a Frenchman knew about these murders. It is possible—indeed it is *probable*—that the Frenchman himself did not help the orangutan to kill. Perhaps the animal escaped from him, and he followed it to the house on the Rue Morgue. He could not have caught it again. It must still be free somewhere in Paris.

"I will not continue with these guesses—for I cannot call them more than that. If I am right, and if the Frenchman did not himself help with the killings, I expect him to come here. Read this. I paid to have this put in the newspaper."

I took the newspaper and read the following:

*CAUGHT—Early in the morning of the seventh of this month: a very large orangutan. The owner, who is known to be a sailor, may have the animal again if he can prove it is his.*

"But, Dupin. How can you know that the man is a sailor?"

"I do not know it. I am not sure of it. I think the man is a sailor. A sailor could go up that pole on the side of the house. Sailors travel to strange, *faraway* places where such things as orangutans can be got. If I am right...

"Think for a moment! The sailor will say to himself: 'The animal is valuable. Why shouldn't I go and get it? The police do not know the animal killed two women. And clearly somebody knows I am in Paris. If I do not go to get the animal, they will ask why. I don't want anyone to start asking questions about the animal. So I will go and get the orangutan and keep it where no one will see it, until this trouble has passed.' This, I believe, is how the sailor will think. But listen! I hear a man's step on the stairs."

Dupin had left the front door of the house open, and the visitor entered without using the bell. He came several steps up the stairs, then stopped. We heard him go down again. Dupin was moving toward the door when we again heard the stranger coming up. He did not turn back a second time, but came straight to the door of our room.

In a strong, warm, friendly voice, Dupin said:

"Come in, my friend! Come in!"

Slowly the door opened, and in came—a sailor!

**Part Six**

My friend dupin was now certain that the murders in the Rue Morgue had been done by a wild animal of the *jungle,* the manlike animal known as an orangutan. The animal had escaped from its owner, he thought; and the owner was probably a sailor. He had put a notice in the newspaper that the man who owned the orangutan could have it again if he came to our house to get it. Now, as the owner came to our door, we were both wondering if that man would, as Dupin guessed, be a sailor.

Yes. The man who entered was indeed a sailor. He was a large man, and strong. He carried a big, heavy piece of wood, but no gun. He said to us, in French: "Good evening."

"Sit down, my friend. I suppose you have come to ask about the orangutan. A very fine animal. I have no doubt that it is a very valuable animal. How old do you think it may be?"

"I have no way of guessing how old it is, but it can't be more than four or five years old. Have you got it here?"

"No, no. We have no place for it here. You can get it in the morning. Of course you can prove it is yours?"

"Yes. Yes, I can."

"I wish I could keep it."

"I would like to have it. I… of course I will pay you for finding and keeping the animal. Anything… anything within reason."

"Well… That is very fair, indeed. Let me think. What shall I ask for? I know! Let this be my pay. Tell me everything you know about the murders in the Rue Morgue."

As quietly as he had spoken Dupin walked to the door, locked it, and put the key in his coat. At the same time he took a gun out of his coat and placed it on the table.

The sailor's face had become red. He jumped to his feet and reached for his stick of wood, but in the next moment he fell back into his chair, *trembling*. His face become quite white, bloodless. He spoke not a word. His eyes were closed.

"My friend, you must not be afraid. We are not going to hurt you. I know very well that you yourself are not the killer. But it is true that you know something about him—or about it. From what I have already said, you must know that I have ways of learning about the matter—ways you could never have dreamed of.

"Now, I know that you yourself have done nothing wrong. You didn't even take any of the money. You have no reason to be afraid to talk and to tell the truth. It is a matter of honor for you to tell all you know. And you know who the killer is."

"So help me God! I... I'll tell you all I know about this, all I know—but I don't expect you to believe one half of what I say—not one half. Still, I didn't kill anyone, and I'll tell the whole story if I die for it. It was that animal! The orangutan!...

"About a year ago our ship *sailed* to the Far East, to the island of Borneo. I had never before seen Borneo. The forest, the jungle, was thick with trees and other plants, and hot and wet and dark. But we went—a friend and I—we went into that forest—for pleasure. There we saw this orangutan, a big animal. But we were two, and we caught it. We took it with us on the ship. Soon, however, my friend died, and the animal was mine. But it was very strong and caused a lot of trouble.

"In the end I brought it back to Paris with me. I kept it in my house, in my own house, carefully locked up, so the neighbors could not know about it. The animal had cut one foot badly while on the ship. I thought... I thought that as soon as it got well I would sell it. I was certain it was of great value. And it was so much trouble to keep! I wanted to sell it, soon.

"The night of the murders, very late, I came home and found the animal in my bedroom. It had got free, I don't know how. It held a knife in its hands, and was playing with it. I was afraid. I didn't know what to do. When it saw me it jumped up, ran out of the room and down the stairs. There it found an open window and jumped into the street. I followed, never far behind, although I had no hope of catching it again. The animal, with the knife still in its hand, stopped often to look back at me. But before I could come near enough to even try to catch it, the animal always started to run again. It seemed to be playing with me.

"It was nearly morning, but the streets were still dark, and quiet. We passed the back of a house in the Rue Morgue. The animal looked up and saw a light in the open window of a room high above. It was the only lighted window in sight. The animal saw the metal pole, went up it easily and quickly, and jumped into the room. All this didn't take a minute.

"I didn't know what to do. I didn't know what I could do. I followed the animal. I too went up the pole. As I am a sailor it was easy for me. But the open window was far from the pole and I was afraid to try to jump. I could see into the room, however, through the other window, which was closed.

"The two women were sitting there, with their backs to the windows. Who can guess why they were not sleeping at that hour of the night? A box was in the middle of the floor. The papers which had been in the box were lying around on the floor. The women seemed to be studying some of these. They did not see the animal, which was just standing there, watching, the knife still in one hand. But the old woman heard it and turned her head and saw the animal there, knife in hand, and then... then I heard the first of those terrible cries.

"When the animal heard the old woman's cry it caught her by the hair and slowly moved the knife before her face. The daughter, filled with terror, fell to the floor and remained there without moving, her eyes closed. The old woman continued to cry for help, screaming with fear. I think the animal now was as afraid as the old woman was. With terrible force it pulled out a handful of hair. And when the woman, covered with blood, tried to run from it, the animal caught her again by the hair and with one move of its arm it nearly cut her head from her body. Throwing down the body, the animal turned and saw that the daughter was moving, watching it with horror. With fire in its eyes it rushed to the girl, put its powerful fingers around her neck, and pressed them firmly there until she died.

"When the girl stopped moving, the animal dropped her body to the floor and looked up. It saw my face in the window. It began to run around the room, quickly, without purpose. It jumped up and down, breaking the chairs, pulling the bed to pieces. Suddenly it stopped and took the body of the daughter and, as if to hide it, with terrible strength it put the body up above the fireplace, where it was found. It threw the old woman out the window.

"All this time I was hanging from the pole, filled with horror. It seemed I had lost the power to move. But when I saw the animal coming toward the window with the old woman's body, my horror became fear. I went quickly down—I almost fell down the pole, and I ran. I didn't look back. I ran! Oh, my God! My God!"

The Chief of the police was not happy that the answer to the mystery of the killings had been found by someone who was not a policeman. He said that people should keep to their own business. "Let him talk," said Dupin.

"Let him talk. He'll feel better for it. And he's a good fellow. But he makes things less simple than they really are. Still, people call him *skillful,* and even wise. I think they say this because of the way he explains, carefully, fully, something which is not here, or there, or anywhere; and says, 'Not possible!' about something which is there before his eyes."

❋ ❋ ❋

# JOHN UPDIKE

## *A & P* (1962)

In walks these three girls in nothing but bathing suits. I'm in the third check-out slot, with my back to the door, so I don't see them until they're over by the bread. The one that caught my eye first was the one in the plaid green two-piece. She was a chunky kid, with a good tan and a sweet broad soft-looking can with those two crescents of white just under it, where the sun never seems to hit, at the top of the backs of her legs. I stood there with my hand on a box of HiHo crackers trying to remember if I rang it up or not. I ring it up again and the customer starts giving me hell. She's one of these cash-register-watchers, a witch about fifty with rouge on her cheekbones and no eyebrows, and I know it made her day to trip me up. She'd been watching cash registers for fifty years and probably never seen a mistake before.

By the time I got her feathers smoothed and her goodies into a bag—she gives me a little snort in passing, if she'd been born at the right time they would have burned her over in Salem—by the time I get her on her way the girls had circled around the bread and were coming back, without a pushcart, back my way along the counters, in the aisle between the checkouts and the Special bins. They didn't even have shoes on. There was this chunky one, with the two-piece—it was bright green and the seams on the bra were still sharp and her belly was still pretty pale so I guessed she just got it (the suit)—there was this one, with one of those chubby berry-faces, the lips all bunched together under her nose, this one, and a tall one, with black hair that hadn't quite frizzed right, and one of these sunburns right across under the eyes, and a chin that was too long—you know, the kind of girl other girls think is very "striking" and "at-tractive" but never quite makes it, as they very well know, which is why they like her so much—and then the third one, that wasn't quite so tall. She was the queen. She kind of led them, the other two peeking around and making their shoulders round. She didn't look around, not this queen, she just walked straight on slowly, on these long white primadonna legs. She came down a little hard on her heels, as if she didn't walk in her bare feet that much, putting down her heels and then letting the weight move along to her toes as if she was testing the floor with every step, putting a little deliberate extra action into it. You never know for sure how girls' minds work (do you really think it's a mind in there or just a little buzz like a bee in a glass jar?) but you got the idea she had talked the other two into coming in here with her, and now she was showing them how to do it, walk slow and hold yourself straight.

She had on a kind of dirty-pink—beige maybe, I don't know—bathing suit with a little nubble all over it and, what got me, the straps were down. They were off her shoulders looped loose around the cool tops of her arms, and I guess as a result the suit had slipped a little on her, so all around the top of the cloth there was this shining rim. If it hadn't been there you wouldn't have known there could have been anything whiter than those shoulders. With the straps pushed off, there was nothing between the top of the suit and the top of her head except just *her*, this clean bare plane of the top of her chest down from the shoulder bones like a dented sheet of metal tilted in the light. I mean, it was more than pretty.

She had sort of oaky hair that the sun and salt had bleached, done up in a bun that was unravelling, and a kind of prim face. Walking into the A & P with your straps down, I suppose it's the only kind of face you *can* have. She held her head so high her neck, coming up out of those white shoulders, looked kind of stretched, but I didn't mind. The longer her neck was, the more of her there was.

She must have felt in the corner of her eye me and over my shoulder Stokesie in the second slot watching, but she didn't tip. Not this queen. She kept her eyes moving across the racks, and stopped, and turned so slow it made my stomach rub the inside of my apron, and buzzed to the other two, who kind of huddled against her for relief, and then they all three of them went up the cat-and-dog-food-breakfast-cereal-macaroni-rice-raisins-seasonings-spreads-spaghetti-soft-drinks-crackers-and-cookies aisle. From the third slot I look straight up this aisle to the meat counter, and I watched them all the way. The fat one with the tan sort of fumbled with the cookies, but on second thought she put the package back. The sheep pushing their carts down the aisle—the girls were walking against the usual traffic (not that we have one-way signs or anything)—were pretty hilarious. You could see them, when Queenie's white shoulders dawned on them, kind of jerk, or hop, or hiccup, but their eyes snapped back to their own baskets and on they pushed. I bet you could set off dynamite in an A & P and the people would by and large keep reaching and checking oatmeal off their lists and muttering "Let me see, there was a third thing, began with A, as-paragus, no, ah, yes, applesauce!" or whatever it is they do mutter. But there was no doubt, this jiggled them. A few houseslaves in pin curlers even looked around after pushing their carts past to make sure what they had seen was correct.

You know, it's one thing to have a girl in a bathing suit down on the beach, where what with the glare nobody can look at each other much anyway, and an-other thing in the cool of the A & P, under the fluorescent lights, against all those stacked packages, with her feet paddling along naked over our checkerboard green-and-cream rubber-tile floor.

"Oh Daddy," Stokesie said beside me. "I feel so faint."

"Darling," I said. "Hold me tight." Stokesie's married, with two babies chalked up on his fuselage already, but as far as I can tell that's the only difference. He's twenty-two, and I was nineteen this April.

"Is it done?" he asks, the responsible married man finding his voice. I forgot to say he thinks he's going to be manager some sunny day, maybe in 1990 when it's called the Great Alexandrov and Petrooshki Tea Company or something.

What he meant was, our town is five miles from a beach, with a big summer colony out on the point, but we're right in the middle of town, and the women generally put on a shirt or shorts or something before they get out of the car into the street. And anyway these are usually women with six children and varicose veins mapping their legs and nobody, including them, could care less. As I say, we're right in the middle of town, and if you stand at our front doors you can see two banks and the Congregational church and the newspaper store and three real-estate offices and about twenty-seven old freeloaders tearing up Central Street because the sewer broke again. It's not as if we're on the Cape; we're north of Boston and there's people in this town haven't seen the ocean for twenty years.

The girls had reached the meat counter and were asking McMahon something. He pointed, they pointed, and they shuffled out of sight behind a pyramid of Diet Delight peaches. All that was left for us to see was old McMahon patting his mouth and looking after them sizing up their joints. Poor kids, I began to feel sorry for them, they couldn't help it.

Now here comes the sad part of the story, at least my family says it's sad, but I don't think it's so sad myself. The store's pretty empty, it being Thursday afternoon, so there was nothing much to do except lean on the register and wait for the girls to show up again. The whole store was like a pinball machine and I didn't know which tunnel they'd come out of. After a while they come around out of the far aisle, around the light bulbs, records at discount of the Caribbean Six or Tony Martin Sings or some such gunk you wonder they waste the wax on, sixpacks of candy bars, and plastic toys done up in cellophane that fall apart when a kid looks at them anyway. Around they come, Queenie still leading the way, and holding a little gray jar in her hands. Slots Three through Seven are unmanned and I could see her wondering between Stokes and me, but Stokesie with his usual luck draws an old party in baggy gray pants who stumbles up with four giant cans of pineapple juice (what do these bums *do* with all that pineapple juice? I've often asked myself) so the girls come to me. Queenie puts down the jar and I take it into my fingers icy cold. Kingfish Fancy Herring Snacks in Pure Sour Cream: 49¢. Now her hands are empty, not a ring or a bracelet, bare as God made them, and I wonder where the money's coming from. Still with that prim look she lifts a folded dollar bill out of the hollow at the center of her nubbled pink top. The jar went heavy in my hand. Really, I thought that was so cute.

Then everybody's luck begins to run out. Lengel comes in from haggling with a truck full of cabbages on the lot and is about to scuttle into that door marked MANAGER behind which he hides all day when the girls touch his eye. Lengel's pretty dreary, teaches Sunday school and the rest, but he doesn't miss that much. He comes over and says, "Girls, this isn't the beach."

Queenie blushes, though maybe it's just a brush of sunburn I was noticing for the first time, now that she was so close. "My mother asked me to pick up a jar of herring snacks." Her voice kind of startled me, the way voices do when you see the people first, coming out so flat and dumb yet kind of tony, too, the way it ticked over "pick up" and "snacks." All of a sudden I slid right down her voice into her living room. Her father and the other men were standing around in ice-cream coats and bow ties and the women were in sandals picking up herring snacks on toothpicks off a big glass plate and they were all holding drinks the color of water with olives and sprigs of mint in them. When my parents have somebody over they get lemonade and if it's a real racy affair Schlitz in tall glasses with "They'll Do It Every Time" cartoons stencilled on.

"That's all right," Lengel said. "But this isn't the beach." His repeating this struck me as funny, as if it had just occurred to him, and he had been thinking all these years the A & P was a great big dune and he was the head lifeguard. He didn't like my smiling—as I say he doesn't miss much—but he concentrates on giving the girls that sad Sunday-school-superintendent stare.

Queenie's blush is no sunburn now, and the plump one in plaid, that I liked better from the back—a really sweet can—pipes up. "We weren't doing any shopping. We just came in for the one thing."

"That makes no difference," Lengel tells her, and I could see from the way his eyes went that he hadn't noticed she was wearing a two-piece before. "We want you decently dressed when you come in here."

"We *are* decent," Queenie says suddenly, her lower lip pushing, getting sore now that she remembers her place, a place from which the crowd that runs the A & P must look pretty crummy. Fancy Herring Snacks flashed in her very blue eyes.

"Girls, I don't want to argue with you. After this come in here with your shoulders covered. It's our policy." He turns his back. That's policy for you. Policy is what the kingpins want. What the others want is juvenile delinquency.

All this while, the customers had been showing up with their carts but, you know, sheep, seeing a scene, they had all bunched up on Stokesie, who shook open a paper bag as gently as peeling a peach, not wanting to miss a word. I could feel in the silence everybody getting nervous, most of all Lengel, who asks me, "Sammy, have you rung up their purchase?"

I thought and said "No" but it wasn't about that I was thinking. I go through the punches, 4, 9, GROC, TOT—it's more complicated than you think, and after you do it often enough, it begins to make a little song, that you hear words to, in my case "Hello *(bing)* there, you *(gung)* happy *pee*-pul *(splat)!*"—the *splat* being the drawer flying out. I uncrease the bill, tenderly as you may imagine, it just having come from between the two smoothest scoops of vanilla I had ever known there were, and pass a half and a penny into her narrow pink palm, and nestle the herrings in a bag and twist its neck and hand it over, all the time thinking.

The girls, and who'd blame them, are in a hurry to get out, so I say "I quit" to Lengel quick enough for them to hear, hoping they'll stop and watch me, their unsuspected hero. They keep right on going, into the electric eye; the door flies open and they flicker across the lot to their car, Queenie and Plaid and Big Tall Goony-Goony (not that as raw material she was so bad), leaving me with Lengel and a kink in his eyebrow.

"Did you say something, Sammy?"

"I said I quit."

"I thought you did."

"You didn't have to embarrass them."

"It was they who were embarrassing us."

I started to say something that came out "Fiddle-de-doo." It's a saying of my grandmother's, and I know she would have been pleased.

"I don't think you know what you're saying," Lengel said.

"I know you don't," I said. "But I do." I pull the bow at the back of my apron and start shrugging it off my shoulders. A couple customers that had been heading for my slot begin to knock against each other, like scared pigs in a chute.

Lengel sighs and begins to look very patient and old and gray. He's been a friend of my parents for years. "Sammy, you don't want to do this to your Mom and Dad," he tells me. It's true, I don't. But it seems to me that once you begin a gesture it's fatal not to go through with it. I fold the apron, "Sammy" stitched in red on the pocket, and put it on the counter, and drop the bow tie on top of it. The bow tie is theirs, if you've ever wondered. "You'll feel this for the rest of your life," Lengel says, and I know that's true, too, but remembering how he made that pretty girl blush makes me so scrunchy inside I punch the No Sale tab and the machine whirs "pee-pul" and the drawer splats out. One advantage to this scene taking place in summer, I can follow this up with a clean exit, there's no fumbling around getting your coat and galoshes, I just saunter into the electric eye in my white shirt that my mother ironed the night before, and the door heaves itself open, and outside the sunshine is skating around on the asphalt.

I look around for my girls, but they're gone, of course. There wasn't anybody but some young married screaming with her children about some candy they didn't get by the door of a powder-blue Falcon station wagon. Looking back in the big windows, over the bags of peat moss and aluminum lawn furniture stacked on the pavement, I could see Lengel in my place in the slot, checking the sheep through. His face was dark gray and his back stiff, as if he'd just had an injection of iron, and my stomach kind of fell as I felt how hard the world was going to be to me hereafter.

## Study and Discussion Questions

1. What does the story gain from being narrated by Sammy rather than, say, by Stokesie, or even by an omniscient narrator?
2. Characterize Sammy's attitude toward "girls" and toward women. Does the way he views Queenie change?
3. What evidence is there of a difference in social class between Sammy and the three young women? Does this difference in any way help explain his quitting?
4. Aside from his desire to impress Queenie and her friends, why *does* Sammy quit? Explain the significance of his last words in the story: "I felt how hard the world was going to be to me hereafter."

## Suggestions for Writing

1. Briefly retell of the story from Queenie's point of view.
2. "A & P" was published in 1962 and, presumably, takes place around then, before the women's liberation movement that began in the late 1960s. What, if anything, would likely be different if the story took place today?

**Critical Resources**

1. De Bellis, Jack. *The John Updike Encyclopedia*. Westport, CT: Green-wood, 2000.
2. Dessner, Lawrence Jay. "Irony and Innocence in John Updike's 'A & P.'" *Studies in Short Fiction* 25.3 (1988): 315–17.
3. Saldivar, Toni. "The Art of John Updike's 'A & P.'" *Studies in Short Fiction* 34.2 (1997): 215–25.
4. Updike, John. *Self Conscious: Memoirs*. New York: Knopf, 1989.

## KURT VONNEGUT, JR.

## *Harrison Bergeron*                                    (1962)

The year was 2081, and everybody was finally equal. They weren't only equal before God and the law. They were equal every which way. Nobody was smarter than anybody else. Nobody was better looking than anybody else. Nobody was stronger or quicker than anybody else. All this equality was due to the 211th, 212th, and 213th Amendments to the Constitution, and to the unceasing vigilance of agents of the United States Handicapper General.

Some things about living still weren't quite right, though. April for instance, still drove people crazy by not being springtime. And it was in that clammy month that the H-G men took George and Hazel Bergeron's fourteen-year-old son, Harrison, away.

It was tragic, all right, but George and Hazel couldn't think about it very hard. Hazel had a perfectly average intelligence, which meant she couldn't think about anything except in short bursts. And George, while his intelligence was way above normal, had a little mental handicap radio in his ear. He was required by law to wear it at all times. It was tuned to a government transmitter. Every twenty seconds or so, the transmitter would send out some sharp noise to keep people like George from taking unfair advantage of their brains.

George and Hazel were watching television. There were tears on Hazel's cheeks, but she'd forgotten for the moment what they were about.

On the television screen were ballerinas.

A buzzer sounded in George's head. His thoughts fled in panic, like bandits from a burglar alarm.

"That was a real pretty dance, that dance they just did," said Hazel.

"Huh" said George.

"That dance-it was nice," said Hazel.

"Yup," said George. He tried to think a little about the ballerinas. They weren't really very good-no better than anybody else would have been, anyway. They were burdened with sashweights and bags of birdshot, and their faces were masked, so that no one, seeing a free and graceful gesture or a pretty face, would feel like something the cat drug in. George was toying with the vague notion that maybe dancers shouldn't be handicapped. But he didn't get very far with it before another noise in his ear radio scattered his thoughts.

George winced. So did two out of the eight ballerinas.

Hazel saw him wince. Having no mental handicap herself, she had to ask George what the latest sound had been.

"Sounded like somebody hitting a milk bottle with a ball peen hammer," said George.

"I'd think it would be real interesting, hearing all the different sounds," said Hazel a little envious. "All the things they think up."

"Um," said George.

"Only, if I was Handicapper General, you know what I would do?" said Hazel. Hazel, as a matter of fact, bore a strong resemblance to the Handicapper General, a woman named Diana Moon Glampers. "If I was Diana Moon Glampers," said Hazel, "I'd have chimes on Sunday-just chimes. Kind of in honor of religion."

"I could think, if it was just chimes," said George.

"Well-maybe make 'em real loud," said Hazel. "I think I'd make a good Handicapper General."

"Good as anybody else," said George.

"Who knows better than I do what normal is?" said Hazel.

"Right," said George. He began to think glimmeringly about his abnormal son who was now in jail, about Harrison, but a twenty-one-gun salute in his head stopped that.

"Boy!" said Hazel, "that was a doozy, wasn't it?"

It was such a doozy that George was white and trembling, and tears stood on the rims of his red eyes. Two of of the eight ballerinas had collapsed to the studio floor, were holding their temples.

"All of a sudden you look so tired," said Hazel. "Why don't you stretch out on the sofa, so's you can rest your handicap bag on the pillows, honeybunch." She was referring to the forty-seven pounds of birdshot in a canvas bag, which was padlocked around George's neck. "Go on and rest the bag for a little while," she said. "I don't care if you're not equal to me for a while."

George weighed the bag with his hands. "I don't mind it," he said. "I don't notice it any more. It's just a part of me."

"You been so tired lately-kind of wore out," said Hazel. "If there was just some way we could make a little hole in the bottom of the bag, and just take out a few of them lead balls. Just a few."

"Two years in prison and two thousand dollars fine for every ball I took out," said George. "I don't call that a bargain."

"If you could just take a few out when you came home from work," said Hazel. "I mean-you don't compete with anybody around here. You just sit around."

"If I tried to get away with it," said George, "then other people'd get away with it-and pretty soon we'd be right back to the dark ages again, with everybody competing against everybody else. You wouldn't like that, would you?"

"I'd hate it," said Hazel.

"There you are," said George. The minute people start cheating on laws, what do you think happens to society?"

If Hazel hadn't been able to come up with an answer to this question, George couldn't have supplied one. A siren was going off in his head.

"Reckon it'd fall all apart," said Hazel.

"What would?" said George blankly.

"Society," said Hazel uncertainly. "Wasn't that what you just said?"

"Who knows?" said George.

The television program was suddenly interrupted for a news bulletin. It wasn't clear at first as to what the bulletin was about, since the announcer, like all announcers, had a serious speech impediment. For about half a minute, and in a state of high excitement, the announcer tried to say, "Ladies and Gentlemen."

He finally gave up, handed the bulletin to a ballerina to read.

"That's all right-" Hazel said of the announcer, "he tried. That's the big thing. He tried to do the best he could with what God gave him. He should get a nice raise for trying so hard."

"Ladies and Gentlemen," said the ballerina, reading the bulletin. She must have been extraordinarily beautiful, because the mask she wore was hideous. And it was easy to see that she was the strongest and most graceful of all the dancers, for her handicap bags were as big as those worn by two-hundred pound men.

And she had to apologize at once for her voice, which was a very unfair voice for a woman to use. Her voice was a warm, luminous, timeless melody. "Excuse me-" she said, and she began again, making her voice absolutely uncompetitive.

"Harrison Bergeron, age fourteen," she said in a grackle squawk, "has just escaped from jail, where he was held on suspicion of plotting to overthrow the government. He is a genius and an athlete, is under-handicapped, and should be regarded as extremely dangerous."

A police photograph of Harrison Bergeron was flashed on the screen-upside down, then sideways, upside down again, then right side up. The picture showed the full length of Harrison against a background calibrated in feet and inches. He was exactly seven feet tall.

The rest of Harrison's appearance was Halloween and hardware. Nobody had ever born heavier handicaps. He had outgrown hindrances faster than the H-G men could think them up. Instead of a little ear radio for a mental handicap, he wore a tremendous pair of earphones, and spectacles with thick wavy lenses. The spectacles were intended to make him not only half blind, but to give him whanging headaches besides.

Scrap metal was hung all over him. Ordinarily, there was a certain symmetry, a military neatness to the handicaps issued to strong people, but Harrison looked like a walking junkyard. In the race of life, Harrison carried three hundred pounds.

And to offset his good looks, the H-G men required that he wear at all times a red rubber ball for a nose, keep his eyebrows shaved off, and cover his even white teeth with black caps at snaggle-tooth random.

"If you see this boy," said the ballerina, "do not - I repeat, do not - try to reason with him."

There was the shriek of a door being torn from its hinges.

Screams and barking cries of consternation came from the television set. The photograph of Harrison Bergeron on the screen jumped again and again, as though dancing to the tune of an earthquake.

George Bergeron correctly identified the earthquake, and well he might have - for many was the time his own home had danced to the same crashing tune. "My God-" said George, "that must be Harrison!"

The realization was blasted from his mind instantly by the sound of an automobile collision in his head.

When George could open his eyes again, the photograph of Harrison was gone. A living, breathing Harrison filled the screen.

Clanking, clownish, and huge, Harrison stood - in the center of the studio. The knob of the uprooted studio door was still in his hand. Ballerinas, technicians, musicians, and announcers cowered on their knees before him, expecting to die.

"I am the Emperor!" cried Harrison. "Do you hear? I am the Emperor! Everybody must do what I say at once!" He stamped his foot and the studio shook.

"Even as I stand here" he bellowed, "crippled, hobbled, sickened - I am a greater ruler than any man who ever lived! Now watch me become what I can become!"

Harrison tore the straps of his handicap harness like wet tissue paper, tore straps guaranteed to support five thousand pounds.

Harrison's scrap-iron handicaps crashed to the floor.

Harrison thrust his thumbs under the bar of the padlock that secured his head harness. The bar snapped like celery. Harrison smashed his headphones and spectacles against the wall.

He flung away his rubber-ball nose, revealed a man that would have awed Thor, the god of thunder.

"I shall now select my Empress!" he said, looking down on the cowering people. "Let the first woman who dares rise to her feet claim her mate and her throne!"

A moment passed, and then a ballerina arose, swaying like a willow.

Harrison plucked the mental handicap from her ear, snapped off her physical handicaps with marvelous delicacy. Last of all he removed her mask.

She was blindingly beautiful.

"Now-" said Harrison, taking her hand, "shall we show the people the meaning of the word dance? Music!" he commanded.

The musicians scrambled back into their chairs, and Harrison stripped them of their handicaps, too. "Play your best," he told them, "and I'll make you barons and dukes and earls."

The music began. It was normal at first-cheap, silly, false. But Harrison snatched two musicians from their chairs, waved them like batons as he sang the music as he wanted it played. He slammed them back into their chairs.

The music began again and was much improved.

Harrison and his Empress merely listened to the music for a while-listened gravely, as though synchronizing their heartbeats with it.

They shifted their weights to their toes.

Harrison placed his big hands on the girls tiny waist, letting her sense the weightlessness that would soon be hers.

And then, in an explosion of joy and grace, into the air they sprang!

Not only were the laws of the land abandoned, but the law of gravity and the laws of motion as well.

They reeled, whirled, swiveled, flounced, capered, gamboled, and spun.

They leaped like deer on the moon.

The studio ceiling was thirty feet high, but each leap brought the dancers nearer to it.

It became their obvious intention to kiss the ceiling. They kissed it.

And then, neutraling gravity with love and pure will, they remained suspended in air inches below the ceiling, and they kissed each other for a long, long time.

It was then that Diana Moon Glampers, the Handicapper General, came into the studio with a double-barreled ten-gauge shotgun. She fired twice, and the Emperor and the Empress were dead before they hit the floor.

Diana Moon Glampers loaded the gun again. She aimed it at the musicians and told them they had ten seconds to get their handicaps back on.

It was then that the Bergerons' television tube burned out.

Hazel turned to comment about the blackout to George. But George had gone out into the kitchen for a can of beer.

George came back in with the beer, paused while a handicap signal shook him up. And then he sat down again. "You been crying" he said to Hazel.

"Yup," she said.

"What about?" he said.

"I forget," she said. "Something real sad on television."

"What was it?" he said.

"It's all kind of mixed up in my mind," said Hazel.

"Forget sad things," said George.

"I always do," said Hazel.

"That's my girl," said George. He winced. There was the sound of a rivetting gun in his head.

"Gee - I could tell that one was a doozy," said Hazel.

"You can say that again," said George.

"Gee-" said Hazel, "I could tell that one was a doozy."

❀ ❀ ❀

# ALICE WALKER

## *Everyday Use*                                              (1973)

*for your grandmama*

I will wait for her in the yard that Maggie and I made so clean and wavy yesterday afternoon. A yard like this is more comfortable than most people know. It is not just a yard. It is like an extended living room. When the hard clay is swept clean as a floor and the fine sand around the edges lined with tiny, irregular grooves, anyone can come and sit and look up into the elm tree and wait for the breezes that never come inside the house.

Maggie will be nervous until after her sister goes: she will stand hopelessly in corners, homely and ashamed of the burn scars down her arms and legs, eying her sister with a mixture of envy and awe. She thinks her sister has held life always in the palm of one hand, that "no" is a word the world never learned to say to her.

You've no doubt seen those TV shows where the child who has "made it" is confronted, as a surprise, by her own mother and father, tottering in weakly from backstage. (A pleasant surprise, of course: What would they do if parent and child came on the show only to curse out and insult each other?) On TV mother and child embrace and smile into each other's faces. Sometimes the mother and father weep, the child wraps them in her arms and leans across the table to tell how she would not have made it without their help. I have seen these programs.

Sometimes I dream a dream in which Dee and I are suddenly brought together on a TV program of this sort. Out of a dark and soft-seated limousine I am ushered into a bright room filled with many people. There I meet a smiling, gray, sporty man like Johnny Carson who shakes my hand and tells me what a fine girl I have. Then we are on the stage and Dee is embracing me with tears in her eyes. She pins on my dress a large orchid, even though she has told me once that she thinks orchids are tacky flowers.

In real life I am a large, big-boned woman with rough, man-working hands. In the winter I wear flannel nightgowns to bed and overalls during the day. I can kill and clean a hog as mercilessly as a man. My fat keeps me hot in zero weather. I can work outside all day, breaking ice to get water for washing; I can eat pork liver cooked over the open fire minutes after it comes steaming from the hog. One winter I knocked a bull calf straight in the brain between the eyes with a sledge hammer and had the meat hung up to chill before nightfall. But of course all this does not show on television. I am the way my daughter would want me to be: a hundred pounds lighter, my skin like an uncooked barley pancake. My hair glistens in the hot bright lights. Johnny Carson has much to do to keep up with my quick and witty tongue.

But that is a mistake. I know even before I wake up. Who ever knew a Johnson with a quick tongue? Who can even imagine me looking a strange white man in the eye? It seems to me I have talked to them always with one foot raised in flight, with my head turned in whichever way is farthest from them. Dee, though. She would always look anyone in the eye. Hesitation was no part of her nature.

"How do I look, Mama?" Maggie says, showing just enough of her thin body enveloped in pink skirt and red blouse for me to know she's there, almost hidden by the door.

"Come out into the yard," I say.

Have you ever seen a lame animal, perhaps a dog run over by some careless person rich enough to own a car, sidle up to someone who is ignorant enough to be kind to him? That is the way my Maggie walks. She has been like this, chin on chest, eyes on ground, feet in shuffle, ever since the fire that burned the other house to the ground.

Dee is lighter than Maggie, with nicer hair and a fuller figure. She's a woman now, though sometimes I forget. How long ago was it that the other house burned? Ten, twelve years? Sometimes I can still hear the flames and feel Maggie's arms sticking to me, her hair smoking and her dress falling off her in little black papery flakes. Her eyes seemed stretched open, blazed open by the flames reflected in them. And Dee. I see her standing off under the sweet gum tree she used to dig gum out of; a look of concentration on her face as she watched the last dingy gray board of the house fall in toward the red-hot brick chimney. Why don't you do a dance around the ashes? I'd wanted to ask her. She had hated the house that much.

I used to think she hated Maggie, too. But that was before we raised the money, the church and me, to send her to Augusta to school. She used to read to us without pity; forcing words, lies, other folks' habits, whole lives upon us two, sitting trapped and ignorant underneath her voice. She washed us in a river of make-believe, burned us with a lot of knowledge we didn't necessarily need to know. Pressed us to her with the serious way she read, to shove us away at just the moment, like dimwits, we seemed about to understand.

Dee wanted nice things. A yellow organdy dress to wear to her graduation from high school; black pumps to match a green suit she'd made from an old suit somebody gave me. She was determined to stare down any disaster in her efforts. Her eyelids would not flicker for minutes at a time. Often I fought off the temptation to shake her. At sixteen she had a style of her own: and knew what style was.

I never had an education myself. After second grade the school was closed down. Don't ask me why: in 1927 colored asked fewer questions than they do now. Sometimes Maggie reads to me. She stumbles along good-naturedly but can't see well. She knows she is not bright. Like good looks and money, quickness passed her by. She will marry John Thomas (who has mossy teeth in an earnest face) and then I'll be free to sit here and I guess just sing church songs to myself. Although I never was a good singer. Never could carry a tune. I was always better at a man's job. I used to love to milk till I was hooked in the side in '49. Cows are soothing and slow and don't bother you, unless you try to milk them the wrong way.

I have deliberately turned my back on the house. It is three rooms, just like the one that burned, except the roof is tin; they don't make shingle roofs any more. There are no real windows, just some holes cut in the sides, like the portholes in a ship, but not round and not square, with rawhide holding the shutters up on the outside. This house is in a pasture, too, like the other one. No doubt when Dee sees it she will want to tear it down. She wrote me once that no matter where we "choose" to live, she will manage to come see us. But she will never bring her friends. Maggie and I thought about this and Maggie asked me, "Mama, when did Dee ever *have* any friends?"

She had a few. Furtive boys in pink shirts hanging about on washday after school. Nervous girls who never laughed. Impressed with her they worshiped the well-turned phrase, the cute shape, the scalding humor that erupted like bubbles in lye. She read to them.

When she was courting Jimmy T she didn't have much time to pay to us, but turned all her faultfinding power on him. He *flew* to marry a cheap city girl from a family of ignorant flashy people. She hardly had time to recompose herself.

When she comes I will meet—but there they are!

Maggie attempts to make a dash for the house; in her shuffling way, but I stay her with my hand. "Come back here," I say. And she stops and tries to dig a well in the sand with her toe.

It is hard to see them clearly through the strong sun. But even the first glimpse of leg out of the car tells me it is Dee. Her feet were always neat-looking, as if God himself had shaped them with a certain style. From the other side of the car comes a short, stocky man. Hair is all over his head a foot long and hanging from his chin like a kinky mule tail. I hear Maggie suck in her breath. "Uhnnnh," is what it sounds like. Like when you see the wriggling end of a snake just in front of your foot on the road. "Uhnnnh."

Dee next. A dress down to the ground, in this hot weather. A dress so loud it hurts my eyes. There are yellows and oranges enough to throw back the light of the sun. I feel my whole face warming from the heat waves it throws out. Earrings gold, too, and hanging down to her shoulders. Bracelets dangling and making noises when she moves her arm up to shake the folds of the dress out of her armpits. The dress is loose and flows, and as she walks closer, I like it. I hear Maggie go "Uhnnnh" again. It is her sister's hair. It stands straight up like the wool on a sheep. It is black as night and around the edges are two long pigtails that rope about like small lizards disappearing behind her ears.

"Wa-su-zo-Tean-o!"[1] she says, coming on in that gilding way the dress makes her move. The short stocky fellow with the hair to his navel is all grinning and he follows up with "Asalamalakim,[2] my mother and sister!" He moves to hug Maggie but she falls back, right up against the back of my chair. I feel her trembling there and when I look up I see the perspiration falling off her chin.

"Don't get up," says Dee. Since I am stout it takes something of a push. You can see me trying to move a second or two before I make it. She turns, showing white heels through her sandals, and goes back to the car. Out she peeks next with a Polaroid. She stoops down quickly and lines up picture after picture of me sitting there in front of the house with Maggie cowering behind me. She never takes a shot without making sure the house is included. When a cow comes nibbling around the edge of the yard she snaps it and me and Maggie *and* the house. Then she puts the Polaroid in the back seat of the car, and comes up and kisses me on the forehead.

Meanwhile Asalamalakim is going through motions with Maggie's hand. Maggie's hand is as limp as a fish, and probably as cold, despite the sweat, and she keeps trying to pull it back. It looks like Asalamalakim wants to shake hands but wants to do it fancy. Or maybe he don't know how people shake hands. Anyhow, he soon gives up on Maggie.

"Well," I say. "Dee."

"No, Mama," she says. "Not 'Dee,' Wangero Leewanika Kemanjo!"

"What happened to 'Dee'?" I wanted to know.

"She's dead," Wangero said. "I couldn't bear it any longer, being named after the people who oppress me."

"You know as well as me you was named after your aunt Dicie," I said. Dicie is my sister. She named Dee. We called her "Big Dee" after Dee was born.

"But who was *she* named after?" asked Wangero.

"I guess after Grandma Dee," I said.

"And who was she named after?" asked Wangero.

"Her mother," I said, and saw Wangero was getting tired. "That's about as far back as I can trace it," I said. Though, in fact, I probably could have carried it back beyond the Civil War through the branches.

"Well," said Asalamalakim, "there you are."

"Uhnnnh," I heard Maggie say.

"There I was not," I said, "before 'Dicie' cropped up in our family, so why should I try to trace it that far back?"

He just stood there grinning, looking down on me like somebody inspecting a Model A car. Every once in a while he and Wangero sent eye signals over my head.

"How do you pronounce this name?" I asked.

"You don't have to call me by it if you don't want to," said Wangero.

---

[1] Swahili greeting.
[2] Arabic greeting.

"Why shouldn't I?" I asked. "If that's what you want us to call you, we'll call you."

"I know it might sound awkward at first," said Wangero.

"I'll get used to it," I said. "Ream it out again."

Well, soon we got the name out of the way. Asalamalakim had a name twice as long and three times as hard. After I tripped over it two or three times he told me to just call him Hakim-a-barber. I wanted to ask him was he a barber, but I didn't really think he was, so I didn't ask.

"You must belong to those beef-cattle peoples down the road," I said. They said "Asalamalakim" when they met you, too, but they didn't shake hands. Always too busy: feeding the cattle, fixing the fences, putting up salt-lick shelters, throwing down hay. When the white folks poisoned some of the herd the men stayed up all night with rifles in their hands. I walked a mile and a half just to see the sight.

Hakim-a-barber said, "I accept some of their doctrines, but farming and raising cattle is not my style." (They didn't tell me, and I didn't ask, whether Wangero (Dee) had really gone and married him.)

We sat down to eat and right away he said he didn't eat collards and pork was unclean. Wangero, though, went on through the chitlins and corn bread, the greens and everything else. She talked a blue streak over the sweet potatoes. Everything delighted her. Even the fact that we still used the benches her daddy made for the table when we couldn't afford to buy chairs.

"Oh, Mama!" she cried. Then turned to Hakim-a-barber. "I never knew how lovely these benches are. You can feel the rump prints," she said, running her hands underneath her and along the bench. Then she gave a sigh and her hand closed over Grandma Dee's butter dish. "That's it!" she said. "I knew there was something I wanted to ask you if I could have." She jumped up from the table and went over in the corner where the churn stood, the milk in it clabber by now. She looked at the churn and looked at it.

"This churn top is what I need," she said. "Didn't Uncle Buddy whittle it out of a tree you all used to have?"

"Yes," I said.

"Uh huh," she said happily. "And I want the dasher, too."

"Uncle Buddy whittle that, too?" asked the barber.

Dee (Wangero) looked up at me.

"Aunt Dee's first husband whittled the dash," said Maggie so low you almost couldn't hear her. "His name was Henry, but they called him Stash."

"Maggie's brain is like an elephant's," Wangero said, laughing. "I can use the churn top as a centerpiece for the alcove table," she said, sliding a plate over the churn, "and I'll think of something artistic to do with the dasher."

When she finished wrapping the dasher the handle stuck out. I took it for a moment in my hands. You didn't even have to look close to see where hands pushing the dasher up and down to make butter had left a kind of sink in the wood. In fact, there were a lot of small sinks; you could see where thumbs and fingers had sunk into the wood. It was beautiful light yellow wood, from a tree that grew in the yard where Big Dee and Stash had lived.

After dinner Dee (Wangero) went to the trunk at the foot of my bed, and started rifling through it. Maggie hung back in the kitchen over the dishpan. Out came Wangero with two quilts. They had been pieced by Grandma Dee and then Big Dee and me had hung them on the quilt frames on the front porch and quilted them. One was in the Lone Star pattern. The other was Walk Around the Mountain. In both of them were scraps of dresses Grandma Dee had worn fifty and more years ago. Bits and pieces of Grandpa Jarrell's Paisley shirts. And one teeny faded blue piece, about the size of a penny matchbox, that was from Great Grandpa Ezra's uniform that he wore in the Civil War.

"Mama," Wangero said sweet as a bird. "Can I have these old quilts?"

I heard something fall in the kitchen, and a minute later the kitchen door slammed.

"Why don't you take one or two of the others?" I asked. "These old things was just done by me and Big Dee from some tops your grandma pieced before she died."

"No," said Wangero. "I don't want those. They are stitched around the borders by machine."

"That'll make them last better," I said.

"That's not the point," said Wangero. "These are all pieces of dresses Grandma used to wear. She did all this stitching by hand. Imagine!" She held the quilts securely in her arms, stroking them.

"Some of the pieces, like those lavender ones, come from old clothes her mother handed down to her," I said, moving up to touch the quilts. Dee (Wangero) moved back just enough so that I couldn't reach the quilts. They already belonged to her.

"Imagine!" she breathed again, clutching them closely to her bosom.

"The truth is," I said, "I promised to give them quilts to Maggie, for when she marries John Thomas."

She gasped like a bee had stung her.

"Maggie can't appreciate these quilts!" she said. "She'd probably be backward enough to put them to everyday use."

"I reckon she would," I said. "God knows I been saving 'em for long enough with nobody using 'em. I hope she will!" I didn't want to bring up how I had offered Dee (Wangero) a quilt when she went away to college. Then she had told me they were old-fashioned, out of style.

"But they're *priceless!*" she was saying now, furiously; for she has a temper. "Maggie would put them on the bed and in five years they'd be in rags. Less than that!"

"She can always make some more," I said. "Maggie knows how to quilt."

Dee (Wangero) looked at me with hatred. "You just will not understand. The point is these quilts, *these* quilts!"

"Well," I said, stumped. "What would *you* do with them?"

"Hang them," she said. As if that was the only thing you *could* do with quilts.

Maggie by now was standing in the door. I could almost hear the sound her feet made as they scraped over each other.

"She can have them, Mama," she said, like somebody used to never winning anything, or having anything reserved for her. "I can 'member Grandma Dee without the quilts."

I looked at her hard. She had filled her bottom lip with checkerberry snuff and it gave her face a kind of dopey, hangdog look. It was Grandma Dee and Big Dee who taught her how to quilt herself. She stood there with her scarred hands hidden in the folds of her skirt. She looked at her sister with something like fear but she wasn't mad at her. This was Maggie's portion. This was the way she knew God to work.

When I looked at her like that something hit me in the top of my head and ran down to the soles of my feet. Just like when I'm in church and the spirit of God touches me and I get happy and shout. I did something I never had done before: hugged Maggie to me, then dragged her on into the room, snatched the quilts out of Miss Wangero's hands and dumped them into Maggie's lap. Maggie just sat there on my bed with her mouth open.

"Take one or two of the others," I said to Dee.

But she turned without a word and went out to Hakim-a-barber.

"You just don't understand," she said, as Maggie and I came out to the car.

"What don't I understand?" I wanted to know.

"Your heritage," she said. And then she turned to Maggie, kissed her, and said, "You ought to try to make something of yourself, too, Maggie. It's really a new day for us. But from the way you and Mama still live you'd never know it."

She put on some sunglasses that hid everything above the tip of her nose and her chin.

Maggie smiled; maybe at the sunglasses. But a real smile, not scared. After we watched the car dust settle I asked Maggie to bring me a dip of snuff. And then the two of us sat there just enjoying, until it was time to go in the house and go to bed.

### Study and Discussion Questions

1. Who is the first-person narrator of this story?
2. Why do you think the mother describes herself in terms of the work she does? What are the differences between the real mother and the TV version she sometimes dreams?
3. What are we told about Dee before we ever meet her?
4. What does the house-burning incident tell us about the three characters and their relation to each other?
5. What does the title of the story refer to?
6. How has Dee changed, according to her mother? What have social class and class mobility to do with this?
7. Why does Dee take pictures of the house and want the churn top and the quilts?
8. What does Dee plan to do with the quilts? What will Maggie do with them?

## Suggestions for Writing

1. Contrast Maggie and Dee.
2. Do you have any sympathy for Dee? If so, on what grounds? If not, why not?
3. Discuss the importance in this story of education, what it is, and what one does with it.
4. What is the wealth this family possesses? How do Maggie, Dee, and the mother each see that wealth and themselves in relation to it?
5. What does "Everyday Use" suggest about one's relation to one's past, heritage, and tradition?
6. Discuss the importance of names in the story.
7. Write about an experience you've had going home, either from your own perspective or from the point of view of another family member.

## Critical Resources

1. *Alice Walker.* Lannan Foundation (documentary), 1989 (60 minutes). See <http://www.lannan.org/lf/lit/search_detail/alice-walker/> for more information.
2. Christian, Barbara, ed. *Everyday Use: Alice Walker.* New Brunswick, NJ: Rutgers University Press, 1994.
3. Gates, Henry Louis, ed. *Alice Walker: Critical Perspectives Past and Present.* New York: Amistad, 1993.
4. Lauret, Maria. *Alice Walker.* New York: St. Martin's, 2000.

# H.G. WELLS

# *The Door in the Wall*        (1911)

## I

One confidential evening, not three months ago, Lionel Wallace told me this story of the Door in the Wall. And at the time I thought that so far as he was concerned it was a true story.

He told it me with such a direct simplicity of conviction that I could not do otherwise than believe in him. But in the morning, in my own flat, I woke to a different atmosphere, and as I lay in bed and recalled the things he had told me, stripped of the glamour of his earnest slow voice, denuded of the focussed shaded table light, the shadowy atmosphere that wrapped about him and the pleasant bright things, the dessert and glasses and napery of the dinner we had shared, making them for the time a bright little world quite cut off from every-day realities, I saw it all as frankly incredible. "He was mystifying!" I said, and then: "How well he did it!. . . . . It isn't quite the thing I should have expected him, of all people, to do well."

Afterwards, as I sat up in bed and sipped my morning tea, I found myself trying to account for the flavour of reality that perplexed me in his impossible reminiscences, by supposing they did in some way suggest, present, convey—I hardly know which word to use—experiences it was otherwise impossible to tell.

Well, I don't resort to that explanation now. I have got over my intervening doubts. I believe now, as I believed at the moment of telling, that Wallace did to the very best of his ability strip the truth of his secret for me. But whether he himself saw, or only thought he saw, whether he himself was the possessor of an inestimable privilege, or the victim of a fantastic dream, I cannot pretend to guess. Even the facts of his death, which ended my doubts forever, throw no light on that. That much the reader must judge for himself.

I forget now what chance comment or criticism of mine moved so reticent a man to confide in me. He was, I think, defending himself against an imputation of slackness and unreliability I had made in relation to a great public movement in which he had disappointed me. But he plunged suddenly. "I have" he said, "a preoccupation—"

"I know," he went on, after a pause that he devoted to the study of his cigar ash, "I have been negligent. The fact is—it isn't a case of ghosts or apparitions—but—it's an odd thing to tell of, Redmond—I am haunted. I am haunted by something—that rather takes the light out of things, that fills me with longings . . . . ."

He paused, checked by that English shyness that so often overcomes us when we would speak of moving or grave or beautiful things. "You were at Saint Athelstan's all through," he said, and for a moment that seemed to me quite ir-relevant. "Well"—and he paused. Then very haltingly at first, but afterwards more easily, he began to tell of the thing that was hidden in his life, the haunt-ing memory of a beauty and a happiness that filled his heart with insatiable longings that made all the interests and spectacle of worldly life seem dull and tedious and vain to him.

Now that I have the clue to it, the thing seems written visibly in his face. I have a photograph in which that look of detachment has been caught and intensified. It reminds me of what a woman once said of him—a woman who had loved him greatly. "Suddenly," she said, "the interest goes out of him. He forgets you. He doesn't care a rap for you—under his very nose . . . . ."

Yet the interest was not always out of him, and when he was holding his at-tention to a thing Wallace could contrive to be an extremely successful man. His career, indeed, is set with successes. He left me behind him long ago; he soared up over my head, and cut a figure in the world that I couldn't cut—anyhow. He was still a year short of forty, and they say now that he would have been in of-fice and very probably in the new Cabinet if he had lived. At school he always beat me without effort—as it were by nature. We were at school together at Saint

Athelstan's College in West Kensington for almost all our school time. He came into the school as my co-equal, but he left far above me, in a blaze of scholarships and brilliant performance. Yet I think I made a fair average running. And it was at school I heard first of the Door in the Wall—that I was to hear of a second time only a month before his death.

To him at least the Door in the Wall was a real door leading through a real wall to immortal realities. Of that I am now quite assured.

And it came into his life early, when he was a little fellow between five and six. I remember how, as he sat making his confession to me with a slow gravity, he reasoned and reckoned the date of it. "There was," he said, "a crimson Virginia creeper in it—all one bright uniform crimson in a clear amber sunshine against a white wall. That came into the impression somehow, though I don't clearly remember how, and there were horse-chestnut leaves upon the clean pavement outside the green door. They were blotched yellow and green, you know, not brown nor dirty, so that they must have been new fallen. I take it that means October. I look out for horse-chestnut leaves every year, and I ought to know.

"If I'm right in that, I was about five years and four months old."

He was, he said, rather a precocious little boy—he learned to talk at an abnormally early age, and he was so sane and "old-fashioned," as people say, that he was permitted an amount of initiative that most children scarcely attain by seven or eight. His mother died when he was born, and he was under the less vigilant and authoritative care of a nursery governess. His father was a stern, preoccupied lawyer, who gave him little attention, and expected great things of him. For all his brightness he found life a little grey and dull I think. And one day he wandered.

He could not recall the particular neglect that enabled him to get away, nor the course he took among the West Kensington roads. All that had faded among the incurable blurs of memory. But the white wall and the green door stood out quite distinctly.

As his memory of that remote childish experience ran, he did at the very first sight of that door experience a peculiar emotion, an attraction, a desire to get to the door and open it and walk in. And at the same time he had the clearest conviction that either it was unwise or it was wrong of him—he could not tell which—to yield to this attraction. He insisted upon it as a curious thing that he knew from the very beginning—unless memory has played him the queerest trick—that the door was unfastened, and that he could go in as he chose.

I seem to see the figure of that little boy, drawn and repelled. And it was very clear in his mind, too, though why it should be so was never explained, that his father would be very angry if he went through that door.

Wallace described all these moments of hesitation to me with the utmost particularity. He went right past the door, and then, with his hands in his pockets, and making an infantile attempt to whistle, strolled right along beyond the end of the wall. There he recalls a number of mean, dirty shops, and particularly that of a plumber and decorator, with a dusty disorder of earthenware pipes, sheet lead ball taps, pattern books of wall paper, and tins of enamel. He stood pretending to examine these things, and coveting, passionately desiring the green door.

Then, he said, he had a gust of emotion. He made a run for it, lest hesitation should grip him again, he went plump with outstretched hand through the green door and let it slam behind him. And so, in a trice, he came into the garden that has haunted all his life.

It was very difficult for Wallace to give me his full sense of that garden into which he came.

There was something in the very air of it that exhilarated, that gave one a sense of lightness and good happening and well being; there was something in the sight of it that made all its colour clean and perfect and subtly luminous. In the instant of coming into it one was exquisitely glad—as only in rare moments and when one is young and joyful one can be glad in this world. And everything was beautiful there . . . . .

Wallace mused before he went on telling me. "You see," he said, with the doubtful inflection of a man who pauses at incredible things, "there were two great panthers there . . . Yes, spotted panthers. And I was not afraid. There was a long wide path with marble-edged flower borders on either side, and these two huge velvety beasts were playing there with a ball. One looked up and came towards me, a little curious as it seemed. It came right up to me, rubbed its soft round ear very gently against the small hand I held out and purred. It was, I tell you, an enchanted garden. I know. And the size? Oh! it stretched far and wide, this way and that. I believe there were hills far away. Heaven knows where West Kensington had suddenly got to. And somehow it was just like coming home.

"You know, in the very moment the door swung to behind me, I forgot the road with its fallen chestnut leaves, its cabs and tradesmen's carts, I forgot the sort of gravitational pull back to the discipline and obedience of home, I forgot all hesitations and fear, forgot discretion, forgot all the intimate realities of this life. I became in a moment a very glad and wonder-happy little boy—in another world. It was a world with a different quality, a warmer, more penetrating and mellower light, with a faint clear gladness in its air, and wisps of sun-touched cloud in the blueness of its sky. And before me ran this long wide path, invitingly, with weedless beds on either side, rich with untended flowers, and these two great panthers. I put my little hands fearlessly on their soft fur, and caressed their round ears and the sensitive corners under their ears, and played with them, and it was as though they welcomed me home. There was a keen sense of homecoming in my mind, and when presently a tall, fair girl appeared in the pathway and came to meet me, smiling, and said 'Well?' to me, and lifted me, and kissed me, and put me down, and led me by the hand, there was no amazement, but only an impression of delightful rightness, of being reminded of happy things that had in some strange way been overlooked. There were broad steps, I remember, that came into view between spikes of delphinium, and up these we went to a great avenue between very old and shady dark trees. All down this avenue, you know, between the red chapped stems, were marble seats of honour and statuary, and very tame and friendly white doves . . . . .

"And along this avenue my girl-friend led me, looking down—I recall the pleasant lines, the finely-modelled chin of her sweet kind face—asking me questions in a soft, agreeable voice, and telling me things, pleasant things I know, though what they were I was never able to recall . . . And presently a little Capuchin monkey, very clean, with a fur of ruddy brown and kindly hazel eyes, came down a tree to us and ran beside me, looking up at me and grinning, and presently leapt to my shoulder. So we went on our way in great happiness . . . ."

He paused.

"Go on," I said.

"I remember little things. We passed an old man musing among laurels, I remember, and a place gay with paroquets, and came through a broad shaded colonnade to a spacious cool palace, full of pleasant fountains, full of beautiful things, full of the quality and promise of heart's desire. And there were many things and many people, some that still seem to stand out clearly and some that are a little vague, but all these people were beautiful and kind. In some way—I don't know how—it was conveyed to me that they all were kind to me, glad to have me there, and filling me with gladness by their gestures, by the touch of their hands, by the welcome and love in their eyes. Yes—"

He mused for awhile. "Playmates I found there. That was very much to me, because I was a lonely little boy. They played delightful games in a grass-covered court where there was a sun-dial set about with flowers. And as one played one loved . . . .

"But—it's odd—there's a gap in my memory. I don't remember the games we played. I never remembered. Afterwards, as a child, I spent long hours trying, even with tears, to recall the form of that happiness. I wanted to play it all over again—in my nursery—by myself. No! All I remember is the happiness and two dear playfellows who were most with me . . . . Then presently came a sombre dark woman, with a grave, pale face and dreamy eyes, a sombre woman wearing a soft long robe of pale purple, who carried a book and beckoned and took me aside with her into a gallery above a hall—though my playmates were loth to have me go, and ceased their game and stood watching as I was carried away. 'Come back to us!' they cried. 'Come back to us soon!' I looked up at her face, but she heeded them not at all. Her face was very gentle and grave. She took me to a seat in the gallery, and I stood beside her, ready to look at her book as she opened it upon her knee. The pages fell open. She pointed, and I looked, marvelling, for in the living pages of that book I saw myself; it was a story about myself, and in it were all the things that had happened to me since ever I was born . . . .

"It was wonderful to me, because the pages of that book were not pictures, you understand, but realities."

Wallace paused gravely—looked at me doubtfully.

"Go on," I said. "I understand."

"They were realities—yes, they must have been; people moved and things came and went in them; my dear mother, whom I had near forgotten; then my father, stern and upright, the servants, the nursery, all the familiar things of home. Then the front door and the busy streets, with traffic to and fro: I looked and marvelled, and looked half doubtfully again into the woman's face and turned the pages over, skipping this and that, to see more of this book, and more, and so at last I came to myself hovering and hesitating outside the green door in the long white wall, and felt again the conflict and the fear.

"'And next?' I cried, and would have turned on, but the cool hand of the grave woman delayed me.

"'Next?' I insisted, and struggled gently with her hand, pulling up her fingers with all my childish strength, and as she yielded and the page came over she bent down upon me like a shadow and kissed my brow.

"But the page did not show the enchanted garden, nor the panthers, nor the girl who had led me by the hand, nor the playfellows who had been so loth to let me go. It showed a long grey street in West Kensington, on that chill hour of afternoon before the lamps are lit, and I was there, a wretched little figure, weeping aloud, for all that I could do to restrain myself, and I was weeping because I could not return to my dear play-fellows who had called after me, 'Come back to us! Come back to us soon!' I was there. This was no page in a book, but harsh reality; that enchanted place and the restraining hand of the grave mother at whose knee I stood had gone—whither have they gone?"

He halted again, and remained for a time, staring into the fire.

"Oh! the wretchedness of that return!" he murmured.

"Well?" I said after a minute or so.

"Poor little wretch I was—brought back to this grey world again! As I realised the fulness of what had happened to me, I gave way to quite ungovernable grief. And the shame and humiliation of that public weeping and my disgraceful home-coming remain with me still. I see again the benevolent-looking old gentleman in gold spectacles who stopped and spoke to me—prodding me first with his umbrella. 'Poor little chap,' said he; 'and are you lost then?'—and me a London boy of five and more! And he must needs bring in a kindly young policeman and make a crowd of me, and so march me home. Sobbing, conspicuous and frightened, I came from the enchanted garden to the steps of my father's house.

"That is as well as I can remember my vision of that garden—the garden that haunts me still. Of course, I can convey nothing of that indescribable quality of translucent unreality, that difference from the common things of experience that hung about it all; but that—that is what happened. If it was a dream, I am sure it was a day-time and altogether extraordinary dream . . . . . . H'm!—naturally there followed a terrible questioning, by my aunt, my father, the nurse, the governess—everyone . . . . . .

"I tried to tell them, and my father gave me my first thrashing for telling lies. When afterwards I tried to tell my aunt, she punished me again for my wicked persistence. Then, as I said, everyone was forbidden to listen to me, to hear a word about it. Even my fairy tale books were taken away from me for a time—

because I was 'too imaginative.' Eh? Yes, they did that! My father belonged to the old school . . . . . And my story was driven back upon myself. I whispered it to my pillow—my pillow that was often damp and salt to my whispering lips with childish tears. And I added always to my official and less fervent prayers this one heartfelt request: 'Please God I may dream of the garden. Oh! take me back to my garden! Take me back to my garden!'

"I dreamt often of the garden. I may have added to it, I may have changed it; I do not know . . . . . All this you understand is an attempt to reconstruct from fragmentary memories a very early experience. Between that and the other consecutive memories of my boyhood there is a gulf. A time came when it seemed impossible I should ever speak of that wonder glimpse again."

I asked an obvious question.

"No," he said. "I don't remember that I ever attempted to find my way back to the garden in those early years. This seems odd to me now, but I think that very probably a closer watch was kept on my movements after this misadventure to prevent my going astray. No, it wasn't until you knew me that I tried for the garden again. And I believe there was a period—incredible as it seems now—when I forgot the garden altogether—when I was about eight or nine it may have been. Do you remember me as a kid at Saint Athelstan's?"

"Rather!"

"I didn't show any signs did I in those days of having a secret dream?"

## II

He looked up with a sudden smile.

"Did you ever play North-West Passage with me? . . . . . No, of course you didn't come my way!"

"It was the sort of game," he went on, "that every imaginative child plays all day. The idea was the discovery of a North-West Passage to school. The way to school was plain enough; the game consisted in finding some way that wasn't plain, starting off ten minutes early in some almost hopeless direction, and working one's way round through unaccustomed streets to my goal. And one day I got entangled among some rather low-class streets on the other side of Campden Hill, and I began to think that for once the game would be against me and that I should get to school late. I tried rather desperately a street that seemed a _cul de sac_, and found a passage at the end. I hurried through that with renewed hope. 'I shall do it yet,' I said, and passed a row of frowsy little shops that were inexplicably familiar to me, and behold! there was my long white wall and the green door that led to the enchanted garden!

"The thing whacked upon me suddenly. Then, after all, that garden, that wonderful garden, wasn't a dream!" . . . .

He paused.

"I suppose my second experience with the green door marks the world of difference there is between the busy life of a schoolboy and the infinite leisure of a child. Anyhow, this second time I didn't for a moment think of going in straight away. You see ... For one thing my mind was full of the idea of getting to school in time—set on not breaking my record for punctuality. I must surely have felt _some_ little desire at least to try the door—yes, I must have felt that ..... But I seem to remember the attraction of the door mainly as another obstacle to my overmastering determination to get to school. I was immediately interested by this discovery I had made, of course—I went on with my mind full of it—but I went on. It didn't check me. I ran past tugging out my watch, found I had ten minutes still to spare, and then I was going downhill into familiar surroundings. I got to school, breathless, it is true, and wet with perspiration, but in time. I can remember hanging up my coat and hat ... Went right by it and left it behind me. Odd, eh?"

He looked at me thoughtfully. "Of course, I didn't know then that it wouldn't always be there. School boys have limited imaginations. I suppose I thought it was an awfully jolly thing to have it there, to know my way back to it, but there was the school tugging at me. I expect I was a good deal distraught and inattentive that morning, recalling what I could of the beautiful strange people I should presently see again. Oddly enough I had no doubt in my mind that they would be glad to see me ... Yes, I must have thought of the garden that morning just as a jolly sort of place to which one might resort in the interludes of a strenuous scholastic career.

"I didn't go that day at all. The next day was a half holiday, and that may have weighed with me. Perhaps, too, my state of inattention brought down impositions upon me and docked the margin of time necessary for the detour. I don't know. What I do know is that in the meantime the enchanted garden was so much upon my mind that I could not keep it to myself.

"I told—What was his name?—a ferrety-looking youngster we used to call Squiff."

"Young Hopkins," said I.

"Hopkins it was. I did not like telling him, I had a feeling that in some way it was against the rules to tell him, but I did. He was walking part of the way home with me; he was talkative, and if we had not talked about the enchanted garden we should have talked of something else, and it was intolerable to me to think about any other subject. So I blabbed.

"Well, he told my secret. The next day in the play interval I found myself surrounded by half a dozen bigger boys, half teasing and wholly curious to hear more of the enchanted garden. There was that big Fawcett—you remember him?—and Carnaby and Morley Reynolds. You weren't there by any chance? No, I think I should have remembered if you were .....

"A boy is a creature of odd feelings. I was, I really believe, in spite of my secret self-disgust, a little flattered to have the attention of these big fellows. I remember particularly a moment of pleasure caused by the praise of Crawshaw—you remember Crawshaw major, the son of Crawshaw the composer?—who said it was the best lie he had ever heard. But at the same time there was a really painful undertow of shame at telling what I felt was indeed a sacred secret. That beast Fawcett made a joke about the girl in green—."

Wallace's voice sank with the keen memory of that shame. "I pretended not to hear," he said. "Well, then Carnaby suddenly called me a young liar and disputed with me when I said the thing was true. I said I knew where to find the green door, could lead them all there in ten minutes. Carnaby became outrageously virtuous, and said I'd have to—and bear out my words or suffer. Did you ever have Carnaby twist your arm? Then perhaps you'll understand how it went with me. I swore my story was true. There was nobody in the school then to save a chap from Carnaby though Crawshaw put in a word or so. Carnaby had got his game. I grew excited and red-eared, and a little frightened, I behaved altogether like a silly little chap, and the outcome of it all was that instead of starting alone for my enchanted garden, I led the way presently—cheeks flushed, ears hot, eyes smarting, and my soul one burning misery and shame—for a party of six mocking, curious and threatening school-fellows.

"We never found the white wall and the green door . . ."

"You mean?—"

"I mean I couldn't find it. I would have found it if I could.

"And afterwards when I could go alone I couldn't find it. I never found it. I seem now to have been always looking for it through my school-boy days, but I've never come upon it again."

"Did the fellows—make it disagreeable?"

"Beastly . . . . . Carnaby held a council over me for wanton lying. I remember how I sneaked home and upstairs to hide the marks of my blubbering. But when I cried myself to sleep at last it wasn't for Carnaby, but for the garden, for the beautiful afternoon I had hoped for, for the sweet friendly women and the waiting playfellows and the game I had hoped to learn again, that beautiful forgotten game . . . . .

"I believed firmly that if I had not told— . . . . . I had bad times after that—crying at night and wool-gathering by day. For two terms I slackened and had bad reports. Do you remember? Of course you would! It was _you_—your beating me in mathematics that brought me back to the grind again."

## III

For a time my friend stared silently into the red heart of the fire. Then he said: "I never saw it again until I was seventeen.

"It leapt upon me for the third time—as I was driving to Paddington on my way to Oxford and a scholarship. I had just one momentary glimpse. I was leaning over the apron of my hansom smoking a cigarette, and no doubt thinking myself no end of a man of the world, and suddenly there was the door, the wall, the dear sense of unforgettable and still attainable things.

"We clattered by—I too taken by surprise to stop my cab until we were well past and round a corner. Then I had a queer moment, a double and divergent movement of my will: I tapped the little door in the roof of the cab, and brought my arm down to pull out my watch. 'Yes, sir!' said the cabman, smartly. 'Er—

well—it's nothing,' I cried. '_My_ mistake! We haven't much time! Go on!' and he went on . . .

"I got my scholarship. And the night after I was told of that I sat over my fire in my little upper room, my study, in my father's house, with his praise—his rare praise—and his sound counsels ringing in my ears, and I smoked my favourite pipe—the formidable bulldog of adolescence—and thought of that door in the long white wall. 'If I had stopped,' I thought, 'I should have missed my scholarship, I should have missed Oxford—muddled all the fine career before me! I begin to see things better!' I fell musing deeply, but I did not doubt then this career of mine was a thing that merited sacrifice.

"Those dear friends and that clear atmosphere seemed very sweet to me, very fine, but remote. My grip was fixing now upon the world. I saw another door opening—the door of my career."

He stared again into the fire. Its red lights picked out a stubborn strength in his face for just one flickering moment, and then it vanished again.

"Well", he said and sighed, "I have served that career. I have done—much work, much hard work. But I have dreamt of the enchanted garden a thousand dreams, and seen its door, or at least glimpsed its door, four times since then. Yes—four times. For a while this world was so bright and interesting, seemed so full of meaning and opportunity that the half-effaced charm of the garden was by comparison gentle and remote. Who wants to pat panthers on the way to dinner with pretty women and distinguished men? I came down to London from Oxford, a man of bold promise that I have done something to redeem. Something—and yet there have been disappointments . . . . .

"Twice I have been in love—I will not dwell on that—but once, as I went to someone who, I know, doubted whether I dared to come, I took a short cut at a venture through an unfrequented road near Earl's Court, and so happened on a white wall and a familiar green door. 'Odd!' said I to myself, 'but I thought this place was on Campden Hill. It's the place I never could find somehow—like counting Stonehenge—the place of that queer day dream of mine.' And I went by it intent upon my purpose. It had no appeal to me that afternoon.

"I had just a moment's impulse to try the door, three steps aside were needed at the most—though I was sure enough in my heart that it would open to me—and then I thought that doing so might delay me on the way to that appointment in which I thought my honour was involved. Afterwards I was sorry for my punctuality—I might at least have peeped in I thought, and waved a hand to those panthers, but I knew enough by this time not to seek again belatedly that which is not found by seeking. Yes, that time made me very sorry . . . . .

"Years of hard work after that and never a sight of the door. It's only recently it has come back to me. With it there has come a sense as though some thin tarnish had spread itself over my world. I began to think of it as a sorrowful and bitter thing that I should never see that door again. Perhaps I was suffering a little from overwork—perhaps it was what I've heard spoken of as the feeling of forty. I don't know. But certainly the keen brightness that makes effort easy has gone out of things recently, and that just at a time with all these new political developments—when I ought to be working. Odd, isn't it? But I do begin to find life toilsome, its rewards, as I come near them, cheap. I began a little while ago to want the garden quite badly. Yes—and I've seen it three times."

"The garden?"

"No—the door! And I haven't gone in!"

He leaned over the table to me, with an enormous sorrow in his voice as he spoke. "Thrice I have had my chance—_thrice!_ If ever that door offers itself to me again, I swore, I will go in out of this dust and heat, out of this dry glitter of vanity, out of these toilsome futilities. I will go and never return. This time I will stay . . . . . I swore it and when the time came—I didn't go.

"Three times in one year have I passed that door and failed to enter. Three times in the last year.

"The first time was on the night of the snatch division on the Tenants' Redemption Bill, on which the Government was saved by a majority of three. You remember? No one on our side—perhaps very few on the opposite side—expected the end that night. Then the debate collapsed like eggshells. I and Hotchkiss were dining with his cousin at Brentford, we were both unpaired, and we were called up by telephone, and set off at once in his cousin's motor. We got in barely in time, and on the way we passed my wall and door—livid in the moonlight, blotched with hot yellow as the glare of our lamps lit it, but unmistakable. 'My God!' cried I. 'What?' said Hotchkiss. 'Nothing!' I answered, and the moment passed.

"'I've made a great sacrifice,' I told the whip as I got in. 'They all have,' he said, and hurried by.

"I do not see how I could have done otherwise then. And the next occasion was as I rushed to my father's bedside to bid that stern old man farewell. Then, too, the claims of life were imperative. But the third time was different; it happened a week ago. It fills me with hot remorse to recall it. I was with Gurker and Ralphs—it's no secret now you know that I've had my talk with Gurker. We had been dining at Frobisher's, and the talk had become intimate between us. The question of my place in the reconstructed ministry lay always just over the boundary of the discussion. Yes—yes. That's all settled. It needn't be talked about yet, but there's no reason to keep a secret from you . . . . . Yes—thanks! thanks! But let me tell you my story.

"Then, on that night things were very much in the air. My position was a very delicate one. I was keenly anxious to get some definite word from Gurker, but was hampered by Ralphs' presence. I was using the best power of my brain to keep that light and careless talk not too obviously directed to the point that concerns me. I had to. Ralphs' behaviour since has more than justified my caution. . . . . Ralphs, I knew, would leave us beyond the Kensington High Street, and then I could surprise Gurker by a sudden frankness. One has sometimes to resort to these little devices. . . . . And then it was that in the margin of my field of vision I became aware once more of the white wall, the green door before us down the road.

"We passed it talking. I passed it. I can still see the shadow of Gurker's marked profile, his opera hat tilted forward over his prominent nose, the many folds of his neck wrap going before my shadow and Ralphs' as we sauntered past.

"I passed within twenty inches of the door. 'If I say good-night to them, and go in,' I asked myself, 'what will happen?' And I was all a-tingle for that word with Gurker.

"I could not answer that question in the tangle of my other problems. 'They will think me mad,' I thought. 'And suppose I vanish now!—Amazing disappearance of a prominent politician!' That weighed with me. A thousand inconceivably petty worldlinesses weighed with me in that crisis."

Then he turned on me with a sorrowful smile, and, speaking slowly; "Here I am!" he said.

"Here I am!" he repeated, "and my chance has gone from me. Three times in one year the door has been offered me—the door that goes into peace, into delight, into a beauty beyond dreaming, a kindness no man on earth can know. And I have rejected it, Redmond, and it has gone—"

"How do you know?"

"I know. I know. I am left now to work it out, to stick to the tasks that held me so strongly when my moments came. You say, I have success—this vulgar, tawdry, irksome, envied thing. I have it." He had a walnut in his big hand. "If that was my success," he said, and crushed it, and held it out for me to see.

"Let me tell you something, Redmond. This loss is destroying me. For two months, for ten weeks nearly now, I have done no work at all, except the most necessary and urgent duties. My soul is full of inappeasable regrets. At nights—when it is less likely I shall be recognised—I go out. I wander. Yes. I wonder what people would think of that if they knew. A Cabinet Minister, the responsible head of that most vital of all departments, wandering alone—grieving—sometimes near audibly lamenting—for a door, for a garden!"

## IV

I can see now his rather pallid face, and the unfamiliar sombre fire that had come into his eyes. I see him very vividly to-night. I sit recalling his words, his tones, and last evening's _Westminster Gazette_ still lies on my sofa, containing the notice of his death. At lunch to-day the club was busy with him and the strange riddle of his fate.

They found his body very early yesterday morning in a deep excavation near East Kensington Station. It is one of two shafts that have been made in connection with an extension of the railway southward. It is protected from the intrusion of the public by a hoarding upon the high road, in which a small doorway has been cut for the convenience of some of the workmen who live in that direction. The doorway was left unfastened through a misunderstanding between two gangers, and through it he made his way . . . . .

My mind is darkened with questions and riddles.

It would seem he walked all the way from the House that night—he has frequently walked home during the past Session—and so it is I figure his dark form coming along the late and empty streets, wrapped up, intent. And then did the pale electric lights near the station cheat the rough planking into a semblance of white? Did that fatal unfastened door awaken some memory?

Was there, after all, ever any green door in the wall at all?

I do not know. I have told his story as he told it to me. There are times when I believe that Wallace was no more than the victim of the coincidence between a rare but not unprecedented type of hallucination and a careless trap, but that indeed is not my profoundest belief. You may think me superstitious if you will, and foolish; but, indeed, I am more than half convinced that he had in truth, an abnormal gift, and a sense, something—I know not what—that in the guise of wall and door offered him an outlet, a secret and peculiar passage of escape into another and altogether more beautiful world. At any rate, you will say, it betrayed him in the end. But did it betray him? There you touch the inmost mystery of these dreamers, these men of vision and the imagination. We see our world fair and common, the hoarding and the pit. By our daylight standard he walked out of security into darkness, danger and death. But did he see like that?

## EUDORA WELTY

### *A Worn Path*                                                         (1941)

It was December—a bright frozen day in the early morning. Far out in the country there was an old Negro woman with her head tied red rag, coming along a path through the pinewoods. Her name was Phoenix Jackson. She was very old and small and she walked slowly in the dark pine shadows, moving a little from side to side in her steps, with the balanced heaviness and lightness of a pendulum in a grand-father clock. She carried a thin, small cane made from an umbrella, and with this she kept tapping the frozen earth in front of her. This made a grave and persistent noise in the still air, that seemed meditative like the chirping of a solitary little bird.

She wore a dark striped dress reaching down to her shoe tops, and an equally long apron of bleached sugar sacks, with a full pocket: all neat and tidy, but every time she took a step she might have fallen over her shoelaces, which dragged from her unlaced shoes. She looked straight ahead. Her eyes were blue with age. Her skin had a pattern all its own of numberless branching wrinkles and as though a whole little tree stood in the middle of her forehead, but a golden color ran underneath, and the two knobs of her cheeks were illumined by a yellow burning under the dark. Under the red rag her hair came down on her neck in the frailest of ringlets, still black, and with an odor like copper.

Now and then there was a quivering in the thicket. Old Phoenix said, "Out of my way, all you foxes, owls, beetles, jack rabbits, coons and wild animals!... Keep out from under these feet, little bob-whites.... Keep the big wild hogs out of my path. Don't let none of those come running my direction. I got a long way." Under her small black-freckled hand her cane, limber as a buggy whip, would switch at the brush as if to rouse up any hiding things.

On she went. The woods were deep and still. The sun made the pine needles almost too bright to look at, up where the wind rocked. The cones dropped as light as feathers. Down in the hollow was the mourning dove—it was not too late for him.

The path ran up a hill. "Seem like there is chains about my feet, time I get this far," she said, in the voice of argument old people keep to use with themselves. "Something always take a hold of me on this hill— pleads I should stay."

After she got to the top she turned and gave a full, severe look behind her where she had come. "Up through pines," she said at length. "Now down through oaks."

Her eyes opened their widest, and she started down gently. But before she got to the bottom of the hill a bush caught her dress.

Her fingers were busy and intent, but her skirts were full and long, so that before she could pull them free in one place they were caught in another. It was not possible to allow the dress to tear. "I in the thorny bush," she said. "Thorns, you doing your appointed work. Never want to let folks pass, no sir. Old eyes thought you was a pretty little green bush."

Finally, trembling all over, she stood free, and after a moment dared to stoop for her cane.

"Sun so high!" she cried, leaning back and looking, while the thick tears went over her eyes. "The time getting all gone here."

At the foot of this hill was a place where a log was laid across the creek.

"Now comes the trial," said Phoenix.

Putting her right foot out, she mounted the log and shut her eyes. Lifting her skirt, leveling her cane fiercely before her, like a festival figure in some parade, she began to march across. Then she opened her eyes and she was safe on the other side.

"I wasn't as old as I thought," she said.

But she sat down to rest. She spread her skirts on the bank around her and folded her hands over her knees. Up above her was a tree in a pearly cloud of mistletoe. She did not dare to close her eyes, and when a little boy brought her a plate with a slice of marble-cake on it she spoke to him. "That would be acceptable," she said. But when she went to take it there was just her own hand in the air.

So she left that tree, and had to go through a barbed-wire fence. There she had to creep and crawl, spreading her knees and stretching her fingers like a baby trying to climb the steps. But she talked loudly to herself: she could not let her dress be torn now, so late in the day, and she could not pay for having her arm or her leg sawed off if she got caught fast where she was.

At last she was safe through the fence and risen up out in the clearing. Big dead trees, like black men with one arm, were standing in the purple stalks of the withered cotton field. There sat a buzzard.

"Who you watching?"

In the furrow she made her way along.

"Glad this not the season for bulls," she said, looking sideways, "and the good Lord made his snakes to curl up and sleep in the winter. A pleasure I don't see no two-headed snake coming around that tree, where it come once. It took a while to get by him, back in the summer."

She passed through the old cotton and went into a field of dead corn. It whispered and shook and was taller than her head. "Through the maze now," she said, for there was no path.

Then there was something tall, black, and skinny there, moving before her.

At first she took it for a man. It could have been a man dancing in the field. But she stood still and listened, and it did not make a sound. It was as silent as a ghost.

"Ghost," she said sharply, "who be you the ghost of? For I have heard of nary death close by."

But there was no answer—only the ragged dancing in the wind.

She shut her eyes, reached out her hand, and touched a sleeve. She found a coat and inside that an emptiness, cold as ice.

"You scarecrow," she said. Her face lighted. "I ought to be shut up for good," she said with laughter. "My senses is gone. I too old. I the oldest people I ever know. Dance, old scarecrow," she said, "while I dancing with you."

She kicked her foot over the furrow, and with mouth drawn down, shook her head once or twice in a little strutting way. Some husks blew down and whirled in streamers about her skirts.

Then she went on, parting her way from side to side with the cane, through the whispering field. At last she came to the end, to a wagon track where the silver grass blew between the red ruts. The quail were walking around like pullets, seeming all dainty and unseen.

"Walk pretty," she said. "This the easy place. This the easy going."

She followed the track, swaying through the quiet bare fields, through the little strings of trees silver in their dead leaves, past cabins silver from weather, with the doors and windows boarded shut, all like old women under a spell sitting there. "I walking in their sleep," she said, nodding her head vigorously.

In a ravine she went where a spring was silently flowing through a hollow log. Old Phoenix bent and drank. "Sweet-gum makes the water sweet," she said, and drank more. "Nobody know who made this well, for it was here when I was born."

The track crossed a swampy part where the moss hung as white as lace from every limb. "Sleep on, alligators, and blow your bubbles." Then the track went into the road.

Deep, deep the road went down between the high green-colored banks. Overhead the live-oaks met, and it was as dark as a cave.

A black dog with a lolling tongue came up out of the weeds by the ditch. She was meditating, and not ready, and when he came at her she only hit him a little with her cane. Over she went in the ditch, like a little puff of milkweed.

Down there, her senses drifted away. A dream visited her, and she reached her hand up, but nothing reached down and gave her a pull. So she lay there and presently went to talking. "Old woman," she said to herself, "that black dog come up out of the weeds to stall you off, and now there he sitting on his fine tail, smiling at you."

A white man finally came along and found her—a hunter, a young man, with his dog on a chain.

"Well, Granny!" he laughed. "What are you doing there?"

"Lying on my back like a June-bug waiting to be fumed over, mister," she said, reaching up her hand.

He lifted her up, gave her a swing in the air, and set her down. "Anything broken, Granny?"

"No sir, them old dead weeds is springy enough," said Phoenix, when she had got her breath. "I thank you for your trouble."

"Where do you live, Granny?" he asked, while the two dogs were growling at each other.

"Away back yonder, sir, behind the ridge. You can't even see it from here."

"On your way home?"

"No sir, I going to town."

"Why, that's too far! That's as far as I walk when I come out myself, and I get something for my trouble." He patted the stuffed bag he carried, and there hung down a little closed claw. It was one of the bob-whites, with its beak hooked bitterly to show it was dead. "Now you go on home, Granny!"

"I bound to go to town, mister," said Phoenix. "The time come around."

He gave another laugh, filling the whole landscape. "I know you old colored people! Wouldn't miss going to town to see Santa Claus!"

But something held old Phoenix very still. The deep lines in her face went into a fierce and different radiation. Without warning, she had seen with her own eyes a flashing nickel fall out of the man's pocket onto the ground.

"How old are you, Granny?" he was saying.

"There is no telling, mister," she said, "no telling."

Then she gave a little cry and clapped her hands and said, "Git on away from here, dog! Look! Look at that dog!" She laughed as if in admiration. "He ain't scared of nobody. He a big black dog." She whispered, "Sic him!"

"Watch me get rid of that cur," said the man. "Sic him, Pete! Sic him!"

Phoenix heard the dogs fighting, and heard the man running and throwing sticks. She even heard a gunshot. But she was slowly bending forward by that time, further and further forward, the lids stretched down over her eyes, as if she were doing this in her sleep. Her chin was lowered almost to her knees. The yellow palm of her hand came out from the fold of her apron. Her fingers slid down and along the ground under the piece of money with the grace and care they would have in lifting an egg from under a setting hen. Then she slowly straightened up, she stood erect, and the nickel was in her apron pocket. A bird flew by. Her lips moved. "God watching me the whole time. I come to stealing."

The man came back, and his own dog panted about them. "Well, I scared him off that time," he said, and then he laughed and lifted his gun and pointed it at Phoenix.

She stood straight and faced him.

"Doesn't the gun scare you?" he said, still pointing it.

"No, sir, I seen plenty go off closer by, in my day, and for less than what I done," she said, holding utterly still.

He smiled, and shouldered the gun. "Well, Granny," he said, "you must be a hundred years old, and scared of nothing. I'd give you a dime if I had any money with me. But you take my advice and stay home, and nothing will happen to you."

"I bound to go on my way, mister," said Phoenix. She inclined her head in the red rag. Then they went in different directions, but she could hear the gun shooting again and again over the hill.

She walked on. The shadows hung from the oak trees to the road like curtains. Then she smelled wood-smoke, and smelled the river, and she saw a steeple and the cabins on their steep steps. Dozens of little black children whirled around her. There ahead was Natchez shining. Bells were ringing. She walked on.

In the paved city it was Christmas time. There were red and green electric lights strung and crisscrossed everywhere, and all turned on in the daytime. Old Phoenix would have been lost if she had not distrusted her eyesight and depended on her feet to know where to take her.

She paused quietly on the sidewalk where people were passing by. A lady came along in the crowd, carrying an armful of red-, green- and silver-wrapped presents; she gave off perfume like the red roses in hot summer, and Phoenix stopped her.

"Please, missy, will you lace up my shoe?" She held up her foot.

"What do you want, Grandma?"

"See my shoe," said Phoenix. "Do all right for out in the country, but wouldn't look right to go in a big building." "Stand still then, Grandma," said the lady. She put her packages down on the sidewalk beside her and laced and tied both shoes tightly.

"Can't lace 'em with a cane," said Phoenix. "Thank you, missy. I doesn't mind asking a nice lady to tie up my shoe, when I gets out on the street."

Moving slowly and from side to side, she went into the big building, and into a tower of steps, where she walked up and around and around until her feet knew to stop.

She entered a door, and there she saw nailed up on the wall the document that had been stamped with the gold seal and framed in the gold frame, which matched the dream that was hung up in her head.

"Here I be," she said. There was a fixed and ceremonial stiffness over her body.

"A charity case, I suppose," said an attendant who sat at the desk before her.

But Phoenix only looked above her head. There was sweat on her face, the wrinkles in her skin shone like a bright net.

"Speak up, Grandma," the woman said. "What's your name? We must have your history, you know. Have you been here before? What seems to be the trouble with you?"

Old Phoenix only gave a twitch to her face as if a fly were bothering her.

"Are you deaf?" cried the attendant.

But then the nurse came in.

"Oh, that's just old Aunt Phoenix," she said. "She doesn't come for herself— she has a little grandson. She makes these trips just as regular as clockwork. She lives away back off the Old Natchez Trace." She bent down. "Well, Aunt Phoenix, why don't you just take a seat? We won't keep you standing after your long trip." She pointed.

The old woman sat down, bolt upright in the chair.

"Now, how is the boy?" asked the nurse.

Old Phoenix did not speak.

"I said, how is the boy?"

But Phoenix only waited and stared straight ahead, her face very solemn and withdrawn into rigidity.

"Is his throat any better?" asked the nurse. "Aunt Phoenix, don't you hear me? Is your grandson's throat any better since the last time you came for the medicine?"

With her hands on her knees, the old woman waited, silent, erect and motionless, just as if she were in armor.

"You mustn't take up our time this way, Aunt Phoenix," the nurse said. "Tell us quickly about your grandson, and get it over. He isn't dead, is he?'

At last there came a flicker and then a flame of comprehension across her face, and she spoke.

"My grandson. It was my memory had left me. There I sat and forgot why I made my long trip."

"Forgot?" The nurse frowned. "After you came so far?"

Then Phoenix was like an old woman begging a dignified forgiveness for waking up frightened in the night. "I never did go to school, I was too old at the Surrender," she said in a soft voice. "I'm an old woman without an education. It was my memory fail me. My little grandson, he is just the same, and I forgot it in the coming."

"Throat never heals, does it?" said the nurse, speaking in a loud, sure voice to old Phoenix. By now she had a card with something written on it, a little list. "Yes. Swallowed lye. When was it?—January—two, three years ago—"

Phoenix spoke unasked now. "No, missy, he not dead, he just the same. Every little while his throat begin to close up again, and he not able to swallow. He not get his breath. He not able to help himself. So the time come around, and I go on another trip for the soothing medicine."

"All right. The doctor said as long as you came to get it, you could have it," said the nurse. "But it's an obstinate case."

"My little grandson, he sit up there in the house all wrapped up, waiting by himself," Phoenix went on. "We is the only two left in the world. He suffer and it don't seem to put him back at all. He got a sweet look. He going to last. He wear a little patch quilt and peep out holding his mouth open like a little bird. I remembers so plain now. I not going to forget him again, no, the whole enduring time. I could tell him from all the others in creation."

"All right." The nurse was trying to hush her now. She brought her a bottle of medicine. "Charity," she said, making a check mark in a book.

Old Phoenix held the bottle close to her eyes, and then carefully put it into her pocket.

"I thank you," she said.

"It's Christmas time, Grandma," said the attendant. "Could I give you a few pennies out of my purse?"

"Five pennies is a nickel," said Phoenix stiffly.

"Here's a nickel," said the attendant.

Phoenix rose carefully and held out her hand. She received the nickel and then fished the other nickel out of her pocket and laid it beside the new one. She stared at her palm closely, with her head on one side.

Then she gave a tap with her cane on the floor.

"This is what come to me to do," she said. "I going to the store and buy my child a little windmill they sells, made out of paper. He going to find it hard to believe there such a thing in the world. I'll march myself back where he waiting, holding it straight up in this hand."

She lifted her free hand, gave a little nod, turned around, and walked out of the doctor's office. Then her slow step began on the stairs, going down.

❋ ❋ ❋

# Poetry

## WILLIAM BLAKE

### *The Garden of Love* (1794)

I went to the Garden of Love,
And saw what I never had seen:
A Chapel was built in the midst,
Where I used to play on the green.

And the gates of this Chapel were shut,                                   5
And "Thou shalt not" writ over the door;
So I turn'd to the Garden of Love
That so many sweet flowers bore;

And I saw it was filled with graves,
And tomb-stones where flowers should be;                                  10
And Priests in black gowns were walking their rounds,
And binding with briars my joys & desires.

### Study and Discussion Questions

1. What contrast runs through the poem?
2. What does "Thou shalt not" allude to?
3. Why a *garden* of love?
4. Why are the gates of the chapel shut?
5. Discuss the importance of the rhythm and internal rhymes of the last two
   lines.

### Suggestion for Writing

1. What is the poem saying about organized religion? What do you think of
   what it is saying?

### Critical Resources

1. Adams, Hazard, ed. *Critical Essays on William Blake.* Boston: G. K.
   Hall, 1991.
2. Behrendt, Stephen. *Reading William Blake.* New York: St. Martin's,
   1992.

3. Bentley, G. E. *The Stranger from Paradise: a biography of William Blake.* New Haven, CT: Yale UP, 2001.
4. Robertson, Graham W. *The Life of William Blake by Alexander Gilchrist.* Mineola, NY: Dover, 1997.

❋ ❋ ❋

## GWENDOLYN BROOKS

## *Bronzeville*[1] *Woman in a Red Hat* (1960)

*hires out to Mrs. Miles*

### I

They had never had one in the house before.
      The strangeness of it all. Like unleashing
A lion, really. Poised
To pounce. A puma. A panther. A black
Bear.           5
There it stood in the door,
Under a red hat that was rash, but refreshing—
In a tasteless way, of course—across the dull dare,
The semi-assault of that extraordinary blackness.
The slackness           10
Of that light pink mouth told little. The eyes told of heavy care . . .
But that was neither here nor there,
And nothing to a wage-paying mistress as should
Be getting her due whether life had been good
For her slave, or bad.           15
There it stood
in the door. They had never had
One in the house before.

But the Irishwoman had left!
A message had come.           20
Something about a murder at home.
A daughter's husband—"berserk," that was the phrase:
The dear man had "gone berserk"

---

[1]African American neighborhood in Chicago.

And short work—
With a hammer—had been made                                    25
Of this daughter and her nights and days.
The Irishwoman (underpaid,
Mrs. Miles remembered with smiles),
Who was a perfect jewel, a red-faced trump,
A good old sort, a baker                                       30
Of rum cake, a maker
Of Mustard, would never return.
Mrs. Miles had begged the bewitched woman
To finish, at least, the biscuit blending,
To tarry till the curry was done,                             35
To show some concern
For the burning soup, to attend to the tending
Of the tossed salad. "Inhuman,"
Pasty Houlihan had called Mrs. Miles.
"Inhuman." And "a fool."                                       40
And "a cool
One."

The Alert Agency had leafed through its files—
On short notice could offer
Only this dusky duffer                                         45
That now made its way to her kitchen and sat on her kitchen stool.


    **II**


Her creamy child kissed by the black maid! square on the mouth!
World yelled, world writhed, world turned to light and rolled
Into her kitchen, nearly knocked her down.

Quotations, of course, from baby books were great              50
Ready armor; (but her animal distress
Wore, too and under, a subtler metal dress,
Inheritance of approximately hate).
Say baby shrieked to see his finger bleed,
Wished human humoring—there was a kind                         55
Of unintimate love, a love more of the mind
To order the nebulousness of that need.
—This was the way to put it, this the relief.
This sprayed a honey upon marvelous grime.
This told it possible to postpone the reef.                    60
Fashioned a huggable darling out of crime.

Made monster personable in personal sight
By cracking mirrors down the personal night.

Disgust crawled through her as she chased the theme.
She, quite supposing purity despoiled,                                    65
Committed to sourness, disordered, soiled,
Went in to pry the ordure from the cream.
Cooing, "Come." (Come out of the cannibal wilderness,
Dirt, dark, into the sun and bloomful air.
Return to freshness of your right world, wear                            70
Sweetness again. Be done with beast, duress.)

Child with continuing cling issued his No in final fire,
        Kissed back the colored maid,
        Not wise enough to freeze or be afraid.
        Conscious of kindness, easy creature bond.             75
        Love had been handy and rapid to respond.

Heat at the hairline, heat between the bowels,
Examining seeming coarse unnatural scene,
She saw all things except herself serene:
Child, big black woman, pretty kitchen towels.                           80

## Study and Discussion Questions

1. Who is the speaker of this poem?
2. How is the Bronzeville woman described in part I? What is she compared to?
3. Why does Mrs. Miles refer to her as "it"?
4. What does the stanza about her previous domestic worker, the Irish woman, tell us about Mrs. Miles?
5. What is the crisis described in part II? Why is it a crisis for Mrs. Miles?

## Suggestions for Writing

1. Gwendolyn Brooks, who is black, has created a white upper-middle-class persona, Mrs. Miles, through whose eyes we see the black woman who comes to work for her. How does this situation create intentional irony in the poem?
2. Are there any places where human sympathy and identification begin to break through the wall of Mrs. Miles's racism? What does she do when that happens?
3. What does Mrs. Miles's racism consist of? Give examples.

### Critical Resources

1. Mootry, Maria and Gary Smith, eds. *A Life Distilled: Gwendolyn Brooks, Her Poetry and Fiction.* Urbana: University of Illinois Press, 1987.
2. Smith, Gary. "Gwendolyn Brooks's A Street in Bronzeville, the Harlem Renaissance and the Mythologies of Black Women." *Melus* 10.3 (1983): 33–46.
3. Upton, Lee. "Language in a Red Hat." *Field: Contemporary Poetry and Poetics* 61 (1999): 48–54.

❊ ❊ ❊

## BRUCE COHEN

## *Smuggled Candy*                                                      (2012)

Can we all just agree the price of movie snacks is wacky?
Even the tax-math is illusively compounded when they ring you up.

As a responsible parent you have no choice you must
Advise your children to smuggle snowcaps under their hoodies.

The ushers know the scan but haven't yet resorted to cavity                5
Searches. For the price of popcorn you should insist on real butter!

For just an extra penny you get triple the soda so how can you turn
That down? See, I'm junk-food drunk on my soapbox & they haven't

Even torn my stub. Good thing they've amputated my legs so I'll fit
Comfortably in my row. I know there's more important stuff,                10

But shouldn't we only endure commercials & previews if the movie's free?
Right is right. The government has its secret formulas; they factor

You'll cheat by X percentage on your taxes, lie about your "charitable"
Contributions. It's all figured in. Nobody really gets away with anything;

They just want you to think you do. Grocers absorb & assume              15
A certain percentage for spoilage, shoplifters, theft by employees,

Crooked delivery men. Built in losses. It's all a little game.
Even the age for mature audiences. 14 is really what they want

So they set the bar at 17 knowing Americans lie & cheat by three years.
Kids too short for the dangerous rides at Amusement Parks stand            20

On their tippy-toes & the carnival attendants wink & welcome them on.
We are even born with built in losses, parents' deaths, the whole

Broken heart thing, opportunities squandered, money flying out the
Windows of speeding cars or shoved in g-strings, & the utter emptiness

In the street as you walk homelessly towards home & see a desperate        25
     couple floating
Out of an Edward Hopper painting, leaving a diner digesting & neither
     revealing.

## PAUL LAURENCE DUNBAR

## *We Wear the Mask*                                                       (1896)

We wear the mask that grins and lies,
It hides our cheeks and shades our eyes,—
This debt we pay to human guile;
With torn and bleeding hearts we smile,
And mouth with myriad subtleties.                                           5

Why should the world be overwise,
In counting all our tears and sighs?
Nay, let them only see us, while
     We wear the mask.

We smile, but, O great Christ, our cries                                    10
To thee from tortured souls arise.
We sing, but oh the clay is vile
Beneath our feet, and long the mile;
But let the world dream otherwise,
     We wear the mask!                                                      15

## JUDY GRAHN

### *Ella, in a square apron, along Highway 80*  (1969)

She's a copperheaded waitress,
tired and sharp-worded, she hides
her bad brown tooth behind a wicked
smile, and flicks her ass
out of habit, to fend off the pass                                     5
that passes for affection.
She keeps her mind the way men
keep a knife—keen to strip the game
down to her size. She has a thin spine,
swallows her eggs cold, and tells lies.                               10
She slaps a wet rag at the truck drivers
if they should complain. She understands
the necessity for pain, turns away
the smaller tips, out of pride, and
keeps a flask under the counter. Once,                               15
she shot a lover who misused her child.
Before she got out of jail, the courts had pounced
and given the child away. Like some isolated lake,
her flat blue eyes take care of their own stark
bottoms. Her hands are nervous, curled, ready                        20
to scrape.
The common woman is as common
as a rattlesnake.

### Study and Discussion Questions

1. Describe Ella's character. What kind of person is she? What outside forces
   have helped shape who she is?
2. Would you call Ella a survivor? What are the means she uses to survive,
   psychologically and spiritually as well as physically?
3. The last line of this poem is "The common woman is as common/as a rattlesnake." How is Ella like a rattlesnake? List words and phrases in the
   poem that contribute to the rattlesnake image.
4. Grahn said in her preface to *The Common Woman Poems,* of which "Ella,
   in a square apron, along Highway 80" is the second in the sequence, that
   one of her goals in writing these poems was to change the stereotypes of
   the work that women do. How has your sense of the person who brings
   your coffee changed now that you've read Grahn's poem?

5. Read the poem out loud. Locate and list some of the sound patterns in the poem. These may include end rhyme, internal rhyme, off rhyme, consonance, assonance. (See "How Poetry Works" for explanations of these terms.)

### Suggestions for Writing

1. "Ella, in a square apron, along Highway 80" is the second in a sequence of seven poems Judy Grahn wrote about women and their lives. She called this sequence *The Common Woman Poems.* Freewrite for five or ten minutes on the word *common,* writing down all the meanings and associations of "common" that come to mind and any words you can think of that are related to the word "common." In what ways is Ella a "common woman"? How is Grahn redefining the concept of "common"?
2. Write a poetic portrait of a woman or man: (a) about their relation to their work and (b) using a controlling metaphor or image as Grahn does in "Ella . . ." with the rattlesnake image.

### Critical Resources

1. Carruthers, Mary S. "The Re-Vision of the Muse: Adrienne Rich, Audre Lorde, Judy Grahn, Olga Broumas." *The Hudson Review,* Summer 1983, 36:2.
2. Felstiner, John. "Judy Grahn." *Women Writers of the West-Coast: Speaking of Their Lives and Careers.* Santa Barbara: Capra Press, 1983.
3. Ostriker, Alicia. *Stealing the Language: The Emergence of Women's Poetry in America.* Boston: Beacon Press, 1986.
4. Whitehead, Kim. *The Feminist Poetry Movement.* Jackson: University Press of Mississippi, 1996.

# LANGSTON HUGHES

## *Ballad of the Landlord* (1951)

Landlord, landlord,
My roof has sprung a leak.
Don't you 'member I told you about it
Way last week?

Landlord, landlord,                                                5
These steps is broken down.

When you come up yourself
It's a wonder you don't fall down.

Ten Bucks you say I owe you?
Ten Bucks you say is due?                                           10
Well, that's Ten Bucks more'n I'll pay you
Till you fix this house up new.

What? You gonna get eviction orders?
You gonna cut off my heat?
You gonna take my furniture and                                     15
Throw it in the street?

Um-huh! You talking high and mighty.
Talk on—till you get through.
You ain't gonna be able to say a word
If I land my fist on you.                                           20

*Police! Police!*
*Come and get this man!*
*He's trying to ruin the government*
*And overturn the land!*

Copper's whistle!                                                   25
Patrol bell!
Arrest.

Precinct Station.
Iron cell.
Headlines in press:                                                 30

MAN THREATENS LANDLORD

•

• •

TENANT HELD NO BAIL

•

• •

JUDGE GIVES NEGRO 90 DAYS IN COUNTY JAIL

### Study and Discussion Questions

1. Who is speaking in the first five stanzas? Who is speaking in stanza six?
2. Describe what is happening in the last 10 lines of the poem.
3. Why does Hughes call this poem a "ballad"? Look up the word, consider its form and themes, and discuss how this might be a ballad.

4. What happens in the opening five stanzas? What we hear is a monologue, yet we get the sense of a drama. How does Hughes accomplish this?
5. Make an outline of the events described in the poem from the opening stanza to the final line. How do events escalate?
6. What do race and social class have to do with the dynamics and the outcome of this ballad/story?

### Suggestions for Writing

1. Compare/contrast "Ballad of the Landlord" with one of the other Langston Hughes poems included in *Literature and Society.*
2. Write a ballad poem of your own about trying to ask for something reasonable from someone higher in the power structure than yourself (a teacher, a boss, a parent, a landlord) and what might happen.

### Critical Resources

1. Alston, Francis. "Harlem: A Major Motif in the Poetry of Langston Hughes from the 1920's to the 1950's." *MAWA Review* 10.2 (1995): 77–85.
2. Gates, Henry Louis and K. A. Appiah, eds. *Langston Hughes: Critical Perspectives Past and Present.* New York: Amistad, 1993.
3. Hughes, Langston. "The Negro Artist and the Racial Mountain," in *Langston Hughes,* James C. Hall, ed. New York: Harcourt Brace, 1998.
4. Jarroway, David R. "Montage of an Otherness Deferred: Dreaming Subjectivity in Langston Hughes." *American Literature* 68.4 (December 1996): 819–41.
5. Tracy, Steven C. *A Historical Guide to Langston Hughes.* New York: Oxford University Press, 2004.

## LANGSTON HUGHES

## *A Dream Deferred* (1951)

What happens to a dream deferred?

> Does it dry up
> like a raisin in the sun?
> Or fester like a sore—
> And then run?
> Does it stink like rotten meat?　　　　　5
> Or crust and sugar over—
> like a syrupy sweet?

Maybe it just sags
like a heavy load.

*Or does it explode?*                                              10

## LANGSTON HUGHES

### *The Negro Speaks of Rivers*                                   (1921)

I've known rivers:
I've known rivers ancient as the world and older than the
  flow of human blood in human veins.

My soul has grown deep like the rivers.

I bathed in the Euphrates when dawns were young.                   5
I built my hut near the Congo and it lulled me to sleep.
I looked upon the Nile and raised the pyramids above it.
I heard the singing of the Mississippi when Abe Lincoln
  went down to New Orleans, and I've seen its muddy
  bosom turn all golden in the sunset.                            10

I've known rivers:
Ancient, dusky rivers.

My soul has grown deep like the rivers.

## LANGSTON HUGHES

### *In Time Of Silver Rain*                                       (1947)

In time of silver rain
The earth puts forth new life again,
Green grasses grow

And flowers lift their heads,
And over all the plain                                              5
The wonder spreads

    Of Life,
    Of Life,
    Of life!

In time of silver rain                                             10
The butterflies lift silken wings
To catch a rainbow cry,
And trees put forth new leaves to sing
In joy beneath the sky
As down the roadway                                               15
Passing boys and girls
Go singing, too,

    In time of silver rain When spring
    And life
    Are new.                                                  20

## CLAUDE MCKAY

### *If We Must Die*                                              (1922)

If we must die, let it not be like hogs
Hunted and penned in an inglorious spot,
While round us bark the mad and hungry dogs,
Making their mock at our accursed lot.
If we must die, O let us nobly die,                                5
So that our precious blood may not be shed
In vain; then even the monsters we defy
Shall be constrained to honor us though dead!
O kinsmen! we must meet the common foe!
Though far outnumbered let us show us brave,                      10
And for their thousand blows deal one deathblow!
What though before us lies the open grave?
Like men we'll face the murderous, cowardly pack,
Pressed to the wall, dying, but fighting back!

## DUDLEY RANDALL

### *Ballad of Birmingham* (1968)

*(On the bombing of a church in Birmingham, Alabama, 1963)*

"Mother dear, may I go downtown
Instead of out to play,
And march the streets of Birmingham
In a Freedom March today?"

"No, baby, no, you may not go,                                   5
For the dogs are fierce and wild,
And clubs and hoses, guns and jails
Aren't good for a little child."

"But, mother, I won't be alone.
Other children will go with me,                                 10
And march the streets of Birmingham
To make our country free."

"No, baby, no, you may not go,
For I fear those guns will fire.
But you may go to church instead                                15
And sing in the children's choir."

She has combed and brushed her night-dark hair,
And bathed rose petal sweet,
And drawn white gloves on her small brown hands,
And white shoes on her feet.                                    20

The mother smiled to know her child
Was in the sacred place,
But that smile was the last smile
To come upon her face.

For when she heard the explosion,                               25
Her eyes grew wet and wild.
She raced through the streets of Birmingham
Calling for her child.

She clawed through bits of glass and brick,
Then lifted out a shoe.                                         30
"O, here's the shoe my baby wore,
But, baby, where are you?"

❀ ❀ ❀

# CARL SANDBURG

## *Chicago*                                                                    (1916)

Hog Butcher for the World,
Tool Maker, Stacker of Wheat,
Player with Railroads and the Nation's Freight Handler;
Stormy, husky, brawling,
City of the Big Shoulders:                                                        5
They tell me you are wicked and I believe them, for I have seen your
    painted women under the gas lamps luring the farm boys.
And they tell me you are crooked and I answer: Yes, it is true I have
    seen the gunman kill and go free to kill again.
And they tell me you are brutal and my reply is: On the faces of          10
    women and children I have seen the marks of wanton hunger.
And having answered so I turn once more to those who sneer at this
    my city, and I give them back the sneer and say to them:
Come and show me another city with lifted head singing so proud
    to be alive and coarse and strong and cunning.                         15
Flinging magnetic curses amid the toil of piling job on job, here is a tall
    bold slugger set vivid against the little soft cities;
Fierce as a dog with tongue lapping for action, cunning as a savage
    pitted against the wilderness,
        Bareheaded,                                                     20
        Shoveling,
        Wrecking,
        Planning,
        Building, breaking, rebuilding,
Under the smoke, dust all over his mouth, laughing with white teeth,       25
Under the terrible burden of destiny laughing as a young man laughs,
Laughing even as an ignorant fighter laughs who has never lost a battle,
Bragging and laughing that under his wrist is the pulse,
    and under his ribs the heart of the people,
            Laughing!                                                 30
Laughing the stormy, husky, brawling laughter of Youth, half-naked,
    sweating, proud to be Hog Butcher, Tool Maker, Stacker of Wheat,
    Player with Railroads and Freight Handler to the Nation.

### Study and Discussion Questions

1. What criticisms of the city does the speaker accept? What is it about the
   city that the speaker celebrates nonetheless?
2. How does the style of the poem match the speaker's feelings about Chicago?

3. What do the way the city is personified and the dismissal of "the soft little cities" tell us about the speaker's values?

### Suggestions for Writing

1. What do the treatment of the city's problems and the way physical labor is portrayed in the poem suggest about the social class of the
   speaker?
2. Write a poem or an image-filled prose piece about the city or town you
   live in. Like "Chicago," it might be a poem of praise. If you don't like
   where you live, you might consider writing a parody of Sandburg's style.

### Critical Resources

1. Callahan, North. *Carl Sandburg: His Life and Works.* University Park, PA:
   Pennsylvania State University Press, 1987.
2. Niven, Penelope. *Carl Sandburg: A Biography.* New York: Charles Scrib-
   ner's & Sons, 1991.
3. Salwak, Dale. *Carl Sandburg: A Reference Guide.* Boston: G. K. Hall, 1988.
4. Van Wienen, Mark. "Taming the Socialist: Carl Sandburg's *Chicago Poems*
   and Its Critics." *American Literature* 63.1 (1991): 89–103.

# WILLIAM STAFFORD

## *Traveling through the Dark*                                (1962)

Traveling through the dark I found a deer
dead on the edge of the Wilson River road.
It is usually best to roll them into the canyon:
that road is narrow; to swerve might make more dead.

By glow of the tail-light I stumbled back of the car       5
and stood by the heap, a doe, a recent killing;
she had stiffened already, almost cold.
I dragged her off; she was large in the belly.

My fingers touching her side brought me the reason—
her side was warm; her fawn lay there waiting,             10
alive, still, never to be born.
Beside that mountain road I hesitated.

The car aimed ahead its lowered parking lights;
under the hood purred the steady engine.

I stood in the glare of the warm exhaust turning red; 15
around our group I could hear the wilderness listen.

I thought hard for us all—my only swerving—,
then pushed her over the edge into the river.

# JONATHAN SWIFT

## *Description of the Morning* (1709)

Now hardly here and there a hackney-coach
Appearing, showed the ruddy morn's approach.
Now Betty from her master's bed had flown,
And softly stole to discompose her own;
The slip-shod 'prentice from his master's door 5
Had pared the dirt and sprinkled round the floor.
Now Moll had whirled her mop with dext'rous airs,
Prepared to scrub the entry and the stairs.
The youth with broomy stumps began to trace
The kennel-edge, where wheels had worn the place.[1] 10
The small-coal man was heard with cadence deep,
Till drowned in shriller notes of chimney-sweep:
Duns at his lordship's gate began to meet;
And brickdust Moll had screamed through half the street.
The turnkey now his flock returning sees, 15
Duly let out a-nights to steal for fees:[2]
The watchful bailiffs take their silent stands,
And schoolboys lag with satchels in their hands.

### Study and Discussion Questions

1. Spell out what each person described is doing and why.
2. What is the speaker's attitude toward what is described?
3. What comment is the poem making on differences in social class?
4. What is the significance of the juxtaposition in the last two lines?
5. What is the rhyme scheme of this poem?
6. How does the use of couplets as a structure for Swift's description of a morning work with the content or meaning of the poem? How does what he does with the couplets change as the poem goes on?

---

[1]The youth is scavenging in the gutter.
[2]To pay their jailer.

### Suggestions for Writing

1. There is a long tradition of poems describing the morning's beauty in *pastoral* terms, picturing glorious fields, idle shepherds, and so on. What relation does "A Description of the Morning" have to such poems?
2. Try capturing Swift's tone in a poem or a paragraph describing the morning at a place you are familiar with. Use whatever genre (prose or poetry) and whatever form within the genre (e.g., if poetry, line length, rhyme or not) are appropriate to the place you are describing and your feelings about it.

### Critical Resources

1. Fox, Christopher, ed. *The Cambridge Companion to Jonathan Swift.* New York: Cambridge University Press, 2003.
2. Manlove, C. N. "Swift's Structures: A Description of the Morning and Some Others." *Studies in English Literature 1500–1900* 29.3 (1989): 463–72.
3. Rawson, Claude. *Jonathan Swift: A Collection of Critical Essays.* Englewood Cliffs, NJ: Prentice Hall, 1995.
4. Vieth, David. *Essential Articles for the Study of Jonathan Swift's Poetry.* Hamden: Archon Books, 1984.

❁ ❁ ❁

## JAMES WRIGHT

### *Autumn Begins in Martins Ferry, Ohio*     (1963)

In the Shreve High football stadium,
I think of Polacks nursing long beers in Tiltonsville,

And gray faces of Negroes in the blast furnace at Benwood,
And the ruptured night watchman of Wheeling Steel,
Dreaming of heroes.                                                                    5

All the proud fathers are ashamed to go home.
Their women cluck like starved pullets,
Dying for love.

Therefore,
Their sons grow suicidally beautiful                                          10
At the beginning of October,
And gallop terribly against each other's bodies.

# ADDITIONAL READINGS: SELECTIONS FROM MSU CREATIVE WRITING FACULTY

## FICTION

### BECKY HAGENSTON

Becky Hagenston's second book of stories, *Strange Weather*, won the Spokane Prize for Short Fiction. Her first collection, *A Gram of Mars*, received the Mary McCarthy Prize. Her fiction has appeared in *The Southern Review, Crazyhorse, The Gettysburg Review, Mid-American Review, Shenandoah,* and many other journals. Hagenston's story "The Upside-Down World" was recently selected for the prestigious collection titled *The O. Henry Prize Stories 2015.* Currently an Associate Professor of English at Mississippi State University, Hagenston earned her M.A. from New Mexico State University and her M.F.A. from the University of Arizona. "Vines" and "Anthony" appear in *Strange Weather*, published in 2010 by Press 53. "Scavengers" was published in 2012 in the *Indiana Review,* volume 34, number 2.

## *Vines*

Their house sat on the beach, behind three palm trees, in a shade that came and went with the winds. Ronald flew an airplane and his wife Haley, who grew tomatoes, could look up and see the shadow of his plane flying over her garden. It wasn't easy growing a tomato garden right on the beach, but she had read a lot of books and taken some gardening classes at the community college, so she knew what she was doing. She used a very rare and special dirt that she made herself, and the winds blew enough that the palm trees provided just the right amount of shade.

Every day, Ronald got in his plane and scoured the seas for anyone who might be drowning, or for ships that were in trouble. It wasn't a job he got paid for—he had enough money from his late father's baked bean emporium—but it was one he took very seriously. Just last month, a cruise ship full of chefs sank, and if Ronald hadn't been flying his plane right then, they all would have drowned. The ocean was strewn with herbs and vegetables and chefs, bobbing frantically and screaming, waving spatulas and corkscrews. Ronald called the Coast Guard on his radio and flew around in circles until they arrived in boats to scoop up the chefs.

When he told his wife what he'd done, she insisted he invite the chefs over for dinner. They used up every last tomato on her vines, for their sauces and soups. They baked bread and made hors d'oeuvres with cheese sauces and tiny fish, and clapped each other on their backs and stuck their fingers in the pots while they cooked.

For the occasion, Ronald drove across the beach to the liquor store and bought wine, and Haley pulled out the folding chairs, and they all sat late into the night, talking—some of the chefs could speak English—and enjoying the food, most of which was tomato-based. Later, inside the house, Haley and Ronald made love, while the chefs slept on the beach, rolled in blankets. The next morning the chefs got in their van and drove away, tooting their horn, leaving behind their dirty pots and pans, and a garden full of empty vines.

Haley and Ronald met four years ago, in a dating class. Ronald was there because even though he was rich, he wasn't very attractive–he was ugly—and women dumped him after he'd bought them presents. They told him he didn't have enough personality to make up for his ugliness, so he was hoping this class would help him have more personality, at least on dates. At least on a first date.

Haley was there because even though she was very beautiful, she had a terrible, terrible secret: for three days every year, everything she touched turned to dirt. This had, of course, created problems in all of her relationships; as a child she had ruined her mother's necklaces, her father's shoes, her sister's prom dress. She'd been trying it on, six years old, and it turned to dirt right on her, crumbling away and leaving her standing naked in front of the mirror. Her sister had threatened to throw her out the window, then screamed nonstop until their mother took her to J.C. Penny for another, even more expensive, dress. It was kept locked in the armoire, along with the other things Haley was not allowed to touch. The one thing that didn't turn to dirt at her touch was human flesh. But only *human* flesh; she'd reduced five cats and two dogs to mulch by the time she was two.

For three days every year, Haley's mother and father kept her home from school, put her in a tent in the backyard where she couldn't do any damage. In the winter, they set up a heater for her. In the summer, she was instructed to play in the dirt that was already there, and when she was finished they used it on their garden.

There was, unfortunately, never any way of predicting when the three dirt days would happen.

When she was sixteen, she let a neighbor boy take her to McDonald's, and was just getting over her nervousness when her Big Mac crumbled into soil. The boy tried to ignore it—he was very polite—but she was afraid to touch his car so she walked home, and he thought that was rude.

She hadn't been on a date since, and she was twenty-five years old. She hoped to learn some skills in this class about how to meet men she could communicate with, men who would accept her for who she was and not think her rude when she refused to touch their cars.

In the first class, the instructor paired up the students and made them interview each other. She ended up with the ugliest man she'd ever seen, who told her he wanted to meet a woman who saw him for who he was on the inside; she told him about her Terrible Secret, and he took hold of her hands and kissed them. They didn't go to any of the other classes. They got married and moved to the beach, and Ronald bought an airplane with his late father's fortune, and Haley grew tomatoes, and for a while everything was perfect.

Two months after the chefs left, Haley realized she was pregnant. When she told her husband, they cried for happiness and for despair, because what if their baby had to suffer as they'd suffered? What if she turned her crib to dirt, what if no one liked her, what if she grew up ugly and afraid? Then they vowed that they would never keep her outside in a tent, and they would tell her she was beautiful even if she was not, even if it meant hiding mirrors from her.

But then the baby was born, a girl, and she *was* beautiful. They named her Stacy. A year passed, and she grew hair and teeth and learned how to say words, and nothing turned to dirt in her grasp. And better still, nothing turned to dirt in Haley's grasp, either. She thought maybe, somehow, she might have missed those three days, but the next year again nothing happened, and then the next, until she realized she was cured.

Stacy loved tomatoes; she'd crawl around outside in the summer and eat them off the vine. And when she was older, Haley told her the story of the chefs who came to their house the night she was conceived, and how they made tomato soup and tomato sauce and tomato and cheese dips, and fish with tomatoes. Stacy wanted to hear that story over and over. She listened rapt, her face and mouth covered with seeds and juice, her eyes as wild as the bobbing, soupy sea.

As the years went by, Ronald continued to fly his plane, and the beach became more and more crowded with tourists, some of whom came from far away to buy Haley's sauces. Stacy went to school, and when she was 18 she told her parents she wanted to move to Paris and become a chef.

Ronald and Haley were not happy. "Can't you go to the community college?" Haley asked her, knowing she was asking the impossible. Because Stacy needed to know more than Haley or the noncredit cooking classes could teach her, she needed to use spices Haley had never heard of, oils from exotic lands, leaves from trees that grew far away. She needed to learn about puddings and cakes, things that went beyond tomatoes, things tomatoes had no use for.

So she went. Her parents stood on the beach and watched the sliver of her jumbo jet vanish over the water, and five days later they got a post card of the Eiffel Tower.

Condos were going up all over the beach, and sometimes camera crews filmed tv shows there. Haley and Ronald were asked to sell their house, and they said no, so a construction crew cut down their palm trees instead, and built a

Sno-Cone stand and parking lot. Next to that was a kiosk where you could get your picture made into a keychain.

When Stacy left, the tomatoes didn't grow as well, and when the palm trees came down they didn't grow at all. Haley bought Miracle Grow, but that didn't work. And even though they were rich, they felt starved, and even though they were together, they felt alone. Stacy called rarely, and her voice was sounding different, foreign and staticky and annoyed. She told her parents she couldn't see them anymore because they made her feel strange and unwell, and why couldn't they be like other parents? Why couldn't they go out to movies with friends? Why didn't they move to New York or someplace exciting?

Sometimes she sent them canned tomatoes, but they weren't the same, and they weren't enough.

There was something wrong with Haley. She felt old and tired and sad. Ronald asked, "What can I get you?" but she couldn't think of anything she wanted except her daughter and tomatoes, and since Stacy would not come home, Ronald flew over the countryside looking for the best tomatoes he could find. He'd bring them to her in her bed, on a golden plate. She'd take one weary bite and then shake her head and fall back against her pillows. But Ronald had noticed something: when he flew his plane across their garden, the tomatoes grew a little. He told this to Haley, and she struggled out of bed with a look on her face that made him want to weep.

"Would you?" she asked, and he would.

He flew and he flew, and because he loved her so much, cruise ships sank and children floated out to sea in their blow-up rafts. And finally Haley couldn't remember his face at all, and it was as if all she'd ever loved was the angel-shaped shadow that cast itself across her garden, and made it grow.

## Anthony

The ghost had gotten inside her daughter like a tapeworm and refused to come out. How had it happened? Was it something Cindy ate? Something in the water? The water in Boardtown, Alabama was bad, everybody knew it; Nia usually bought bottled water at Wal-Mart but this week she'd been cheap, she'd been lazy, she hadn't wanted to haul all those bottles to the car. And now a ghost inhabited her child and wouldn't be budged.

Her husband Jake blamed it on Nia; *he* would never let something like this happen to their child; he would have beat the crap out of that ghost before it could get near his daughter. Nia didn't argue with him. She had been planning to leave him for months. He had a temper and she was almost positive he was screwing the waitress at Longshots, the bar where they'd met seven years ago and where he spent more and more of his time, sometimes not coming home until three-thirty in the morning. The bar closed at two, so what the hell was he doing until three-thirty? Not that she cared.

"It's because you don't make her take a bath every day," he said. "It's because you feed her macaroni and cheese from a box. That shit is horrible for a kid."

"How the hell do you know what I feed her? Since when are you around for any meals anyway?" Sometimes she argued with him just because she wanted to see how close he would get to hitting her. He'd done it once and she'd threatened to take Cindy and leave if he ever did it again, and now when he clenched his fists and got up in her face, she stared right back at him and said, "I dare you," and watched him use every ounce of his strength not to bash her in the nose. She wanted to laugh every time, because she was leaving him anyway.

It must have happened on Tuesday night, when—yes, she *had* forgotten to give Cindy a bath after her dinner of mac and cheese from a box. Nia had been on the computer finishing up her homework for Accounting 101, a ridiculously easy course taught by a man who looked like he was twelve. Still, it was hard to keep up when you had a child and a full-time job at Blockbuster. She wanted more for herself, and just when she thought she was getting somewhere— didn't it figure—something like this had to happen.

The kindergarten teacher, Miss Missy, had been the one to take Cindy to the nurse's office on Wednesday morning. Miss Missy had seen many things in her life: she'd seen a crop dusting plane fall out of the sky above the cotton fields behind her house; she'd woken up in the middle of the night to see her baby sister in the arms of a Skunk Ape (startled by Missy's cries, it had dropped the baby back in the crib and fled out the window); she'd seen the spirit of her lynched grandfather swinging from a tree.

So when tiny, blonde Cindy Morgan's stomach shouted, "Time to party!" in the voice of a young black male, Miss Missy kept her wits. The children were just down for their naps, and Miss Missy was in the process of cleaning up the Nilla wafer crumbs and milk cartons from snack time. She detested Nilla wafers, but the children loved them. Those, and Fig Newtons. Her own childhood in Tuscaloosa had been filled with chitlins—which stunk halfway down the street— and pork barbeque. She and her sister munched happily on fried pig snouts ("*Snoots*," her Mawmaw called them) after school, watching The *Munsters* and *Gilligan's Island* until their mother came home from work.

"Time to party!" said Cindy Morgan's belly, and the other children turned on their mats and yawned, and Cindy sat up and said, in her own baby-voice, "Miss Missy, I feel funny."

Miss Missy walked briskly across the room, knelt, and felt Cindy's forehead.

"I ain't sick, I'm dead," said the voice from Cindy's stomach. Or maybe it was more the solar plexis. It was hard to be sure.

Nurse would know.

Nurse felt dread when she saw Miss Missy marching Cindy Morgan into her office. She had noticed the girl earlier that month, being dropped off twenty minutes late in a rusty orange El Camino by a woman in a too-short skirt and too-high heels. Mothers like this were usually bad news; they usually had boyfriends with tattoos and motorcycles, boyfriends who didn't like little children. Or liked them too much.

*Please, no bruises*, Nurse prayed silently, and looked Miss Missy in the eye, as if daring her to say what Nurse least wanted to hear.

"Cindy here is having stomach . . . . difficulties," said Miss Missy. She put her hands on Cindy's shoulders and said, "Sweetheart, Nurse will take care of you, okay?"

"Okay," said Cindy Morgan, and then Miss Missy spun on a heel—Nurse admired Miss Missy's ability to wear heels—and was gone.

Nurse leaned down and looked into Cindy's pale blue eyes. "Does your tummy hurt?" she asked, smiling, relieved that her worst fears had not come to pass. Two weeks ago, she had lifted up Timmy Maxwell's Pooh Bear shirt to discover cigarette burns around his nipples. A woman from Social Services had arrived to lead a sobbing Timmy out to a big white car. Nurse hadn't seen him since.

She led Cindy into an examination room and helped the girl up to the paper-covered table. "Can you tell me where it hurts?"

"I feel like dancin'," said the voice of a young black man. Then he laughed, a joyful sound that made Nurse almost laugh, too.

Cindy frowned. "He wants to dance," she said. "But I don't."

"Well, now, let's just take a look." Nurse lifted up Cindy's pink Care Bears shirt and placed her stethoscope on her white stomach.

"It's cold," Cindy said, and then giggled.

"Breathe deeply," said Nurse. "That's a good girl. Will you lie down for me, sweetheart?"

Cindy lay her head back on the paper pillow and closed her eyes. Nurse touched around her belly button very gently, trying to locate the source of the strange male voice. She had never encountered anything like this before, had never read about it in nursing school or on any of the nursing blogs she looked at every evening while she ate a Lean Cuisine in front of her computer.

"Hello?" said Nurse. "Is anybody there?"

"*I'm* here," said the young male voice. "I'm here and I'm ready to party. Hell yeah!" He laughed again, and Nurse couldn't help smiling. Then he said, gently, "You're a damn good nurse," and Nurse felt herself blushing and had to turn away and clear her throat.

Nia was at work that Wednesday afternoon, scanning in new DVDs of some violent Mexican movie she couldn't pronounce, when she got the phone call from the nurse's office. Then she had to bribe Sherry to cover for her by offering to work the weekend shift. Sherry was a sorority girl and she worked at Blockbuster because, as the poorest girl in the sorority, she needed the money but only if she could work a job that wouldn't make her seem like too much of a loser. Before Blockbuster, she had worked at McDonalds, which was humiliating, absolutely mortifying, all that grease, all those miserable single mothers she had to work with! She lasted one day because at the start of her second shift, Tad from Psi Upsilon came in and ordered hashbrowns and then said, "Fuck, Sherry. What are you doing here?" and Sherry took off her paper cap and yelled, "I quit!" right there. She'd hoped Tad might be so impressed by this that he'd ask her out, but he'd just laughed and asked for ketchup.

Blockbuster was better because a) there was no grease and b) she could watch movies all day long and c) sometimes she could get Nia to take over the weekend shift for her, so she could go out with her friends, cruise the bars—there weren't many—and meet up with boys, though not Tad, because he'd date-raped this girl Racine and everybody knew it, even though she refused to go to campus police.

Nia always had a frazzled look about her, and her hair looked like it had been bleached too many times. Sometimes Sherry wished she could give Nia a make-over.

When Nia got Cindy home, she took her temperature (normal, just as the nurse had said) and tucked her into bed and brought her some chicken noodle soup.

"It's probably just a virus, sweetheart," she told Cindy, and she heard the young man sigh heavily and mutter something.

"Did you want to speak up?" Nia demanded, and the young man said, "No, ma'am," very politely. "Do you want to leave, then?" she said, and he didn't answer.

When Jake got home, Nia took him into the living room and explained, quietly, what the nurse had told her: Cindy had the ghost of a young black man living in her stomach, and he didn't seem dangerous, but they ought to keep an eye on her.

That's when Jake accused her of not feeding or bathing Cindy properly, and that's when Nia dared him to smack her.

Jake could be a good father when he put his mind to it, and he picked Cindy up from her bed and kissed her on the cheek and said, "What's this about feeling bad?"

"I'm okay now," she said.

"Who are you?" Jake demanded of Cindy's stomach. "What do you want from us?"

"Don't yell at him," said Nia. "His name is Anthony." She'd actually had a pleasant, though brief, conversation with the young man. He'd died in a car accident, but he wouldn't talk much about that except to say that people should wear their seatbelts.

"Anthony?" shouted Jake. "Make thyself known!"

"For God's sake, Jake," said Nia. "He's not a Shakespearan actor. He's just a teenaged boy."

"Can I have the television in my room?" Cindy wanted to know, and Anthony said, "Say please," and Cindy said, "Please?"

"Show some respect," Anthony said, and then didn't say anything else for the rest of the night, although he chuckled occasionally during the *Happy Days* reruns.

That night, Miss Missy told her new boyfriend Hank about Cindy Morgan.

"It must be so hard on the family," she said. "But people learn to live with things, you find ways to get by."

Hank, who taught third grade, thought Miss Missy (he just called her Missy) was the most graceful, beautiful, intelligent woman he had ever met. He loved the little gap in her teeth and he loved that she wore such sexy clothes to work, those tight pencil skirts and high heels. No jumpers and sneakers for her, like the other kindergarten teachers wore.

They had only been dating for two months but he was ready to ask her to marry him; he could picture their children playing in the swingset at his mother's house, could imagine calling, "Henry! Deanne! Time for dinner!"

Now was not the time to propose, however; Missy looked vexed. She paced the floor in her bare feet. She sat down on the sofa and put her head in her hands. The polish on her toenails was pink and the polish on her fingernails was silver. He felt his breath catch, and tried to focus.

Hank had never heard of this particular situation, but he admired Missy's ability to try to get to the bottom of things. "I think they'll be fine," he told her, and she leaned against him and closed her eyes. And even though he had transparencies to make and dioramas to grade, he stroked her head and said "There, there," until she was snoring.

Nurse was at home, eating a Lean Cuisine in front of her computer and Googling "child ghosts", which did not produce the result she was looking for. "Stomach ghost" she tried, and then "haunted stomach" but again, the results proved fruitless. Then she found herself tempted to type in the dating website that had gotten her here in the first place, living alone in a podunk Alabama town, so she turned the computer off. She told herself she wasn't that lonely, and if she was she should just go to sleep and not think about it.

Cindy's pediatrician said, "I can't vaccinate her for this, but I don't think she's in any danger."

"She's not," said Anthony.

"They're getting along pretty well," said Nia. "I hear them talking late at night sometimes."

"How long has this been going on?" the pediatrician asked, suddenly suspicious.

"Only about . . . less than a week?" Nia said. She was lying. It had been three weeks since Anthony made his appearance, but she told herself it wasn't as if Cindy was *ill*. Besides, Cindy hated the doctor. But the school Nurse was scaring Nia with stories of parasites and poltergeists and wanted Cindy to take antibiotics, so Nia thought she'd better get a second opinion.

And Cindy and Anthony *were* getting along; that part was true. Last night Nia had hovered outside Cindy's door—Cindy liked to keep it closed now, even though she used to be afraid of the dark—and heard Cindy giggling, and then Anthony laughing, and then Cindy talking, Anthony replying. More giggling from both of them. What on earth did they have to say to one another, a six-year-old and a dead fifteen-year-old? Nia was tempted to hide a tape recorder under Cindy's bed, but she wasn't entirely sure how to rig it so it wouldn't click loudly when it shut off.

"How's your husband handling this?" the pediatrician asked, in low tones.

Nia rolled her eyes. "Fine," she said.

The truth was, Jake had been mad because Anthony was black. He wanted a white ghost. He wanted, specifically, Marilyn Monroe. "Or James Dean!" he'd said. "How cool would that be?"

What could you do with a man like that?

"You feel all right, don't you, Cindy-girl?" said the pediatrician, producing a green lollipop from his coat, and Cindy said, "Yes, sir, I feel fine. Thank you for asking."

"Well, now!" laughed the pediatrician. "Aren't you polite."

Nia felt stung. It was Anthony who'd taught her that.

He still sometimes said "hell" and wistfully said he wanted to party, but only when Cindy was taking a nap or preoccupied with cartoons.

"What kind of party do you want, Anthony?" Nia asked once, when they were watching tv together on the sofa. (Cindy had fallen asleep during *Dateline*; Anthony enjoyed it, as he enjoyed most of the programs Nia watched.) All she could get out of him was a sigh. He did that a lot, and it made her sad for him. It made him seem older than his years.

Jake thought Anthony was a riot. At first, yes, he was pissed off, and not because he was a racist, either. He just figured that if his daughter was going to have a ghost in her stomach, it ought to be someone . . . . well, famous. Someone interesting. He wanted the tv news crews to come over and interview him, and interview the famous person, and maybe film the two of them together—Jake and James Dean—chatting about cars or something.

But Anthony was a cool little dude, and he cracked Jake up. One evening, when Nia was at her accounting class and Cindy was napping on the sofa (Cindy napped a lot lately), he had said, "You know how to make a hormone?"

"A what?" said Jake.

"Don't pay her."

When Jake stopped laughing he said, "Do you—did you play any sports when you were alive? Basketball, maybe?"

"Nah," said Anthony. "I had to take care of my little brothers after school, help out my mother and shit."

"What about your dad?"

"What about him?" Anthony said bitterly.

Anthony needed a father figure, someone to talk about guy stuff with, someone to guide him in the ways of women.

"You can talk to me," Jake said. "I'm here for you."

"'Preciate it," Anthony said.

One night, when Cindy was sound asleep, Nia tiptoed into her daughter's bedroom and whispered, "Anthony? Are you awake?"

"I'm awake," he said. "Don't need no sleep. Just lyin' here, collectin' my thoughts."

She pulled a chair next to the bed, stroked Cindy on her pale forehead. "I'm just wondering how long you were planning on staying? Not that it isn't nice having you."

"Nice bein' here!" he cried. "I mean it. I like you people. You all right."

Nia felt relieved, then remembered why she was there. "I was just thinking," she said, "that there might be something you want, or need . . . something to, I don't know, help you go toward the light? Somehow?"

He didn't say anything.

"Don't you have parents wondering where you are? I know that if I were dead and Cindy was also dead, and I didn't get to see her, I'd worry."

"Dunno," he said, and gave one of his sad little sighs.

Then, because she had spent lunch hour crying in the Blockbuster bathroom, and because she was failing her accounting class, and because here was this sad boy lost and far from home, she broke down and wept. "I'm sorry," she sniffled, "I'm sorry if it's my fault."

"It ain't," Anthony said gently. "Shit just happens."

"I'm thinking I should leave Jake," she admitted, and cried a little harder.

"Aw, man, that sucks," Anthony said. "Whaddya gonna do that for anyways?"

"He's a terrible husband," she said. "He's never home, and I know he's screwing some slut he met at Longshots! Sorry," she added, and blushed. Sometimes it was hard to remember that Anthony was barely more than a child himself.

"Seems like he's home all the time," Anthony said, and Nia realized it was true. Just last night, she had come home from class to find Jake, Cindy and Anthony playing Candyland on the kitchen table. "Where's the babysitter?" she had demanded, and Jake said, "I sent her home," and moved his marker toward Gumdrop Mountain.

And two nights ago, Jake had offered to help cook dinner.

"Because I'm such a terrible cook, is that right?" she'd snapped, and he'd kissed her on the cheek and said no, he just wanted to help out.

"I only married him because I was pregnant," she whispered. Anthony didn't say anything, and so after a moment she gave Cindy's tummy a pat and tiptoed from the room.

Miss Missy enjoyed having Anthony in the classroom. He was never disruptive, and the other students listened to him. If anyone got too rambunctious—if Gino pulled Caroline's hair, or Dana hit Rachel—Anthony would say, "Have some respect!" and they would stop.

You expected ghosts to be trouble, but Anthony was a joy, and this is what she wrote on his progress report. But it concerned her that he wasn't getting the kind of education he needed. *Anthony could go very far*, she wrote, *if he had the opportunity*.

On Cindy's report, she wrote: *Needs to speak up more in class*. Then, because she liked the girl, she added: *Cindy is a sweet child, and she knows most of her numbers*.

At the parent-teacher conference, she suggested to Cindy's parents that Anthony needed a tutor. Just because he was dead and stuck inside a six-year-old's body didn't mean he should be denied a good education. Everyone had things to overcome.

"We're all," she said, "differerently-abled, in our own way."

"We'll look into it," Cindy's father said. "We only want the best for him."

"You're good parents," Miss Missy said. "Anthony is lucky he found you."

Their usual babysitter was busy, so when Jake asked Nia on a date ("Remember dates?" he asked), they had to scramble to find someone else. Nia immediately thought of Sherry.

"He doesn't need a babysitter," Jake had insisted.

"No, but she does," said Nia.

Really, thank God she was the responsible parent around here. Thank God at least one of them was watching out for their daughter.

"Will you be nice to the babysitter?" Nia asked Cindy, and Cindy yawned and said, "Okay," in a tiny voice.

"That's my girl," Nia said.

Sherry was surprised by how neat Nia's house was; she'd been expecting something much dumpier and red-necky—maybe a Confederate flag and a beat-up pickup truck in the driveway—but it wasn't bad at all, certainly no trashier than some of the fraternity houses she'd been to. There were candles and potpourri in the living room and framed pictures of Cindy as a baby, Nia holding her and smiling at the camera, looking almost beautiful. Most surprising of all, Nia's husband was a hottie. How did someone like her end up with someone like him?

Nia had led Sherry through the house (she caught a glimpse of the master bedroom, of the neatly made bed and the big pillows), ending up in the kitchen and saying, "Here's all the emergency numbers, poison control, you know the drill. I'll have my cell phone with me. Help yourself to the Hot Pockets in the freezer. Cindy already had her dinner."

"Is there anybody else I should call if I can't get through? Cindy's grandparents or something?" Sherry didn't care about Cindy's grandparents, she was just nosy.

"Grandparents are dead," Nia said, and then frowned as if something had just occurred to her. "Actually, there is someone you could contact." That's when she told Sherry about Anthony. "He's been quiet the past few hours, but he'll probably be around later on. He likes to watch Dateline. He's really good with kids, and he's smarter than you'd think for someone so young. I just didn't feel comfortable leaving her alone, you know? Because they do share the same body, so if she fell down or something, there's nothing he could really do."

Sherry nodded. "Gotcha," she said. She couldn't wait to call up Tad—he wasn't her boyfriend, exactly, but he had started hanging around the store lately, and a couple of times they made out in the back room. She gave him DVDs from the sale rack—who was going to notice if they were gone anyway? But she didn't think that was the only reason he liked her. He told her Racine made up the date-rape stuff, and she believed him because it was exactly the sort of thing Racine would do.

Cindy was lying on the floor, coloring in a My Pretty Pony coloring book. Sherry sat down next to her. She was terrible with kids, but she needed the money, so what could she do? "Hey there," she said, in a fake-sounding voice. "Whatcha got there?"

"My Pretty Pony," Cindy said. "Do you want to color with me?"

The girl looked pale and her eyes were bleary.

"Um, not really," Sherry said. She'd read somewhere that it was important to be honest with kids. Was that in her Marriage and the Family class? She'd pretty much snoozed through that one. That class was full of brainless debutantes who wanted to be married by the time they were twenty.

"Okay," Cindy sighed, and went back to listlessly running a blue crayon over the page.

With Cindy occupied, Sherry made herself comfortable on the sofa and took out her cell phone.

"Who you callin?" It startled her, that voice coming out of Cindy's stomach.

"Tad," she said, and the voice laughed as if that was the funniest thing in the world.

"Tad! Tad ain't a name. *Tad. Oh, Tad.*" He was imitating a British voice now. "I *say* now Tad, tally ho and all that."

"Cut that out. You don't even know him. He's in a fraternity and he's really cute and really cool."

"Yeah, he sounds like a real—" he lowered his voice. "A real dick weed, you know?"

"You don't know shit," she said. Then something occurred to her. "Do you? I mean, can you see what he's doing right now?"

"Jackin' off," he said. "But he sure ain't thinking of you."

Sherry didn't buy it. "You're just being a jerk."

Cindy gave a loud sigh and put her head down on her coloring book.

"That's right sweetie," said Sherry. "You take a nap now."

Sherry told Anthony about Tad, about how he came to the store and she gave him DVDs and how they kissed in the back room, and how he didn't date rape Racine after all.

"He's using you," Anthony said. "That is typical male behavior, is what that is. He ever take you on a date?"

"No," she said. "But so what?"

"You know so what," he said. "You can do better."

"I can?" said Sherry. She felt herself getting weepy. It was true, everything Anthony was saying. "I want him to like me!" she wailed. "I want him."

"Why?"

"Because," she said, and started crying again. Finally she managed to whisper, "Because he doesn't want me."

They talked and talked, and Anthony told her jokes, and she forgot all about the Hot Pockets and watching tv and she even forgot about calling Tad. When she heard the keys jingling in the lock a little before midnight, she quickly scooped up snoring Cindy and tucked her into bed. When Nia peeked her head in, Sherry was stroking Cindy's cheek and saying, "You're such a sweetheart, such a sweetheart."

Sometimes Nurse poked her head into Miss Missy's classroom and said, "Can I please speak to Cindy?" She felt it was important to keep close tabs on the girl, make sure she was doing all right.

Also, she enjoyed talking to Anthony. She even found herself telling him about Rick, the man she'd met online, the man she had moved to Alabama for and who had broken her heart. She'd met him in a chat room for certain personality types, and after chatting for a few months he bought a plane ticket to Boston. Nurse was 42 and Rick was 36, and—she didn't tell Anthony this part—the sex as the best she'd ever had. Her ex-husband Denny had been clumsy. Two months later she'd quit her job at Boston General and moved to Alabama for love. Or, more accurately, for sex—again, she didn't tell Anthony this, only that "I really thought I'd found my soul mate, the man I'd spend the rest of my life with."

But after supporting him for six months—paying his rent, buying dog food for his ridiculous Doberman—she'd had enough. Soon, she would make her way back east, but she had used up all her savings and she had to get her head on straight, "so here I am," she said, "and I have to tell myself I'm doing some good with my life, that I'm making some kind of difference, orthewise I'll go nuts." Then she told him—because he was such a good listener—about the poverty and the abuse and the kids who came to her office twice a week for baths because they had no hot water at home. It almost broke her heart, she was almost ready to give up, and then—

"And then?" said Anthony.

"And then you came along," she said, and patted Cindy on the knee.

Miss Missy found Cindy hiding in the coat cubby, crying and pounding on her stomach.

"Cindy sweetheart, what is it?"

Cindy continued pummeling her stomach with her tiny fists. "I hate you!" she sobbed. "Go home."

Miss Missy took her by the hand and led her down the hall to the Nurse, who gave Cindy a red lollipop and told her she shouldn't hit people.

"Yes, ma'am," Cindy said weakly.

"I'm sure you didn't mean to hurt Anthony's feelings."

"Yes, ma'am," Cindy whispered.

The pediatrician said, "She'll eat when she's hungry."

"But it's been two whole days," Nia said. "Her teacher says she won't even drink her milk during snack time."

"You feeling all right, Cindy-girl?" said the pediatrician.

"She's fine," said Anthony.

"You're looking out for her, young man, aren't you?" said the pediatrician. "Keep it up. Maybe you-all should take her out for a cheeseburger. You feel like a cheeseburger, Cindy?"

Cindy shrugged.

"She doesn't have a fever," the pediatrician said. "But if she's feeling poorly, let her stay home from school a couple of days."

The tutor came for three hours in the morning and taught Anthony history, English, and math. Since Cindy couldn't stay awake long enough to read, the tutor read the text books out loud to Anthony and then asked him questions. The Socratic Method. The tutor was a twenty-nine-year-old named Mark who was majoring in Special Education and needed the money to pay tuition. Last year he'd tutored a blind girl, but she was kind of a bitch—he hated to admit it, but it was true—and so it was a pleasure to have a tutee as enthusiastic and intelligent as Anthony. He was lazy at times—but what fifteen-year-old wasn't?

Mark read him "A Good Man is Hard to Find" and Anthony laughed at the beginning, at the grandmother and the cat and the bratty kids, and then he got quiet and then he started saying, "Oh no way, man. No way." After Mark finished Anthony said, "I didn't see that coming. Man. That was a damn good story. What else you got?"

Sometimes Mark stayed for four hours instead of three, but he told Nia not to worry about paying him for the extra hour.

"Anthony honey," said Nia, spooning chicken noodle soup into Cindy's mouth. "You have to go." It broke her heart to say it.

"Got nowhere *to* go," he said. "I like you people."

"Well, Cindy's feeling bad and I hate to say it, but I think it's because of you."

"Maybe she has the flu," said Anthony, sulkily. "Ain't my fault if she has the flu."

"It *might* be the flu," Nia allowed. "But I don't think so."

Anthony didn't answer. He didn't say anything the rest of the day, or the next, or the day after that. Cindy got out of bed and lay on the floor in her nightgown, coloring.

One evening at dinner, Jake said, "Anthony, you want to watch *Die Hard* with me?" No response. "God damn it," said Jake. "I'm going out for a little while."

Alone in the house with Cindy, Nia felt a depth of emptiness she hadn't felt in months. When Cindy crawled into her lap with a Berenstein Bears book, Nia said, "Not now honey, Mommy's tired." Then, feeling guilty, she said, "Oh, okay." But she couldn't muster up much enthusiasm.

It wasn't that she was upset that Jake had left, that he had probably gone to Longshots to meet up with the waitress. She felt relieved. She had realized, over the past few months, with Jake always around—always wanting to spend time with her, always after her in bed—that not only did she not love him, she never could. His hands were rough; he had a dumb sense of humor. *He's a good man,* she told herself; *he's a good father.*

She had married him because she couldn't think of a better alternative. It was hard being a single mother; her own mother had raised her and they had nearly starved, had slept in the car for two weeks, had shoplifted milk and hot dogs.

She and Jake had hardly even known each other; they had slept together more than dated; she was missing her ex when he came along. She'd had too much too drink.

She used to tell herself that she could fall in love with him, if he'd give her the chance. But she couldn't. She never would.

Miss Missy noticed that Cindy Morgan was losing her blank, haunted look. Her eyes were no longer lined with black circles. She was drinking her milk, and she played patty cake.

But the class was in shambles.

Without Anthony in the classroom, Dana hit Rachel and Gregory pushed Benjamin off the swings and Wendall gave Marty a black eye. Veronica cried in the corner during story time and kicked anyone who got near her.

"Children need role models," Miss Missy said to Hank.

"Our children will be happy," he said, and Miss Missy was so surprised she couldn't think of a response.

Nurse treated the children's cuts and took their temperatures, and she called Social Services when a third grader named Reggie showed up in her office with welts on his back.

Sometimes she stayed awake until three a.m., emailing men and telling them she was thinner, blonder, and happier than she actually was. Sometimes she told them she would meet them, but she never did.

Jake started staying out until three-thirty every night, and when he got home he passed out on the sofa. One early morning Nia thought she heard him crying in his sleep, and she wished there was something she could do. But there wasn't.

She missed Anthony. She knew he was there—where else could he go?—but he refused to speak. Sometimes she could swear she heard him sniffling, just a little. It broke her heart.

And then one night when she was tucking Cindy in, Anthony said, "I missed talking to ya'll."

Nia was so happy she picked Cindy out of bed and kissed her on the stomach, which made her daughter shriek and kick and wail.

"Don't do that again," Nia said. "Do you promise?"

"I promise," said Anthony, but he had to say it twice, so Nia could hear him over Cindy's sobs.

It was Miss Missy who told Nurse that Cindy Morgan was no longer enrolled in school, that Cindy's mother had moved away, taking the child and leaving the father behind. He had come home from work and found them gone.

"That's too bad," said Nurse. She looked like she was about to cry. "I'll miss them."

"Yes," said Miss Missy. She was mulling over Hank's proposal and had been distracted for the past few days; there was so much risk involved, this tying of oneself to another. Things could get complicated.

Nurse was staring sullenly at the floor. Miss Missy thought of giving her a hug, of telling her everything would be fine. She wanted to reassure Nurse that she would find love someday, that she had to have faith that everything would work out for the best. She wanted to ask Nurse if she thought she was doing the right thing, marrying Hank, because things could go so wrong so fast, and you never knew what you were in for.

"They might be back," Nurse said, in a hoarse whisper. "They might."

"They might," said Miss Missy. She gave Nurse an awkward pat on the arm, then headed back to her classroom to dole out the Nilla wafers.

## Scavengers

On the game show, Margaret veered from the script and did not say, "Yes, I'm married to my wonderful husband, Donny." In response to the exuberant host's note-carded question—"And it says here you've been married for eight years?"—Margaret looked straight at the camera and said, "No, Chip, you're mistaken." Then, unable to stop herself, she practically shouted, "Everything I win is all mine!"

Then they were on to the next contestant, married for thirteen years to his beautiful wife Barbara, and the next, a chubby red-headed girl who collected insects and had come "all the way from Kansas City." By the time the show aired a week later, Margaret couldn't bear to watch herself lose to the insect girl, and even worse, she had decided not to leave Donny after all.

Back home in Mississippi, he was a dental hygienist, and he hadn't gone with her to the taping because he had to hose out the mouths of root canal patients. "Why not just go ahead and be a dentist?" she had asked him on their first date, and he said, "You go ahead and be a dentist." Not that she could make fun of him now, because he had a job and she didn't.

"Everything I win is all mine," Donny called from the living room, where he was watching the program even though she told him not to. "That's funny."

*The game show, the game show, the game show!* She lay in bed after Donny had gone to work and tried to will herself back there, back to California and the studio lot and the palm trees, the green room and the make-up people and the studio audience who had seemed to genuinely care so much about her. When she asked for a D and there was no D on the board, a loud *Awww* echoed around her, and she felt cradled in support and goodwill. Maybe that's what church was supposed to be like, but at church she'd always felt itchy and only read the bulletin to find typos. Our Lard in Heaven, Here my Prayer! That was the best one.

On the phone to her mother in Memphis, she said, "They were so nice backstage, after I lost. Chip shook my hand, and his assistant Julianna gave me a hug."

"What was that about not being married?" her mother said.

"I was joking. We're encouraged to joke."

"Oh," said her mother, who watched nothing but infomercials.

"If we're funny, we might get invited back." No one had told her this, but it sounded plausible. "Or maybe some talent scout will watch and think, Oh, I need this person in my reality show."

"Who needs a reality show?" her mother said. "Real life is real enough."

"True," said Margaret. "It's plenty real all right."

Would it hurt or help her chances if there were children? She set up the camera in her living room, in front of the open window that revealed the springtime lawn of the front yard. The magnolia tree hid the trashy house across the street, with the rusty swing set and dilapidated picnic table in the yard. Margaret and Donny had been meaning to move for five years now but hadn't gotten around to it.

If she wanted to be on that show where they swapped wives, she would need children. It was called *Wife Swap*, but really it was about putting the Redneck Woman in a household full of little liberal Poindexters, and the Professor Wife in a trailer filled with shotgun-carrying hillbilly children. That didn't seem fun to Margaret. She didn't know if she could survive in the wild or eat bugs, but maybe she could. *Would you rather live with a bunch of hillbilly children or eat bugs?* she Twittered. She liked Twittering; she liked having followers. There were over 500 of them now, and she didn't know who any of them were. After she lost on the game show, she Twittered, *O the agony of defeat*, which wasn't clever but it expressed how she felt, and GrlPwr3 wrote, *You rock n dont forget it!!!!!!* Many of her followers did not spell correctly, but she didn't let it bother her much.

*BUGZ DEFIANTLY* Twittered MelDel, and no one wrote back for a while so Margaret decided she might as well make a tape for a program where the winner gets to work for Donald Trump. She knew she had no chance of winning, but she could be a spitfire and say outrageous things, and sometimes that was more important than winning.

When she had told Donny about her video audition idea, he said, "Or you could apply for jobs."

"I will, I will," she said. They lived in a university town in Mississippi, and if you weren't a dental hygienist, like Donny, you had to work at the university. Which Margaret had, until a month ago.

It wasn't such a great job anyway, administrative assistant for an engineering professor. The professor was a woman, and she was always talking about her kids and how smart they were. When Margaret said, "You should go on *Wife Swap*," the woman looked alarmed and then asked Margaret to fax some documents to Austin. Margaret had lost her job because she spent too much time on her computer filling out applications for game shows, Twittering, checking to see if anyone had Friended her, and trying to figure out who was ignoring her.

She was wondering if she should change her clothes for the video—it was eighty degrees, but she looked better in a turtleneck—when the doorbell rang. A college-aged girl in a pink sorority sweatshirt stood on the front steps smiling at her. She had a thick blonde ponytail and her teeth looked like she'd never needed a root canal. "Hiya," she drawled. "My name is Delores, and this is going to sound weird, but I'm on a scavenger hunt, and I'm wondering if you have a pair of red mittens I can borrow."

"Red mittens," said Margaret. She saw the girl giving the camera a curious glance. "I'm making a tape. Wait here."

She had to dig all the way in the back of the storage closet, behind Donny's old climbing boots and camouflage jacket, from when he used to hunt. There were no mittens in the Winter Clothes box, because it never got cold enough in central Mississippi for mittens. They were in the Stuff box, sent to her by her mother last Christmas with a note saying, "Just some of your little things I didn't have the heart to throw out. Cute!!"

Enclosed were Margaret's third grade composition book, a photo of her dressed as a cat for Halloween, her ballet shoes, and a pair of tiny red mittens. She pulled a black turtleneck out of the Winter Clothes box, too, might as well.

"I hope they weren't supposed to be grown-up mittens," Margaret told Delores.

"These are perfect," she said, beaming. "Thank you so much. I really want to win this thing."

"Losing is no fun," Margaret agreed.

Donny came home smelling of mint and rubber gloves. "You're not gonna leave me," he said to her. "Because you love me too much." He smacked her ass. He was right, of course. If only he would just give in about the babies. She was thirty-eight years old.

"If you're not going to man up and get the job done, then I'll find someone who will," she told him. She had heard a wife say this on a talk show, and the husband had burst into tears and promised to man up.

But Donny held her chin in his hands and said, "It's your hormones talking. Give it another couple of years."

"But I can't help it! It's a biological imperative!" She sniffled.

"So is death," he said, and kissed her.

The next afternoon, Delores was back, but she didn't return the mittens. "It turns out," she said, "this scavenger hunt is kind of an ongoing thing. I didn't wake you, did I?"

Margaret had put a bathrobe over her bathing suit before answering the door. "No, of course not," she said. "I was just making a tape where I'm supposed to be at the beach." She had been standing on a yellow seat cushion, wondering if it would look like a surfboard from the right angle. There was a show called *Beach Hut* that filmed in Malibu, and all she had to do was prove she was fun in the sun.

The girl was wearing the same pink sweatshirt. Margaret noticed now that the letters were too faded to read, not that she knew anything about sororities anyway. "So, what I need now is a postcard from a European country. Would you happen to have one of those?" She arched her eyebrow at Margaret the way investigators did on TV when they were tricking the criminal into confessing.

"Right," said Margaret. "I wish."

Delores seemed pleased with this response for some reason. "Excellent!" she said. "A cork from a bottle of Spanish wine?"

"A can of Budweiser is more like it," Margaret said, and then cleared her throat because she had already had two tallboys today, and it was barely four o'-clock. She thought it might make her seem fun on her audition tape.

"Okay, well what about a white cupcake-shaped ceramic music box that says 'You're Very Special' across it in pink script and plays 'Edelweiss.' "

Margaret felt her heart lurch a little. "Oh my," she said. "I have one of those."

It was in a box up in the crawl space. "I appreciate you going to all this trouble!" Delores called from below while Margaret pawed carefully through the pink fiberglass. Why oh why had she and Donny not gotten rid of all this junk? There was even a box of *National Geographics*.

Margaret handed down a battered Thom McCann shoebox. "This is sort of where old Christmas presents go to die," she said, as she made her way down the ladder.

On the living room carpet, they pulled out the contents of the box: a Hallmark ornament of a cat on a Christmas tree, a pair of shiny fake-gold candlesticks, and the music box. "My mother gave this to me when I was way too old for it," Margaret said. "What thirty-year-old woman wants a music box?"

"It's pretty," said Delores, holding it as if it might break. Margaret thought of saying, "Just keep it!" but then what if her mother came to visit and wondered where it was? She was always threatening to visit.

"This is some scavenger hunt," Margaret said.

"I worry that we're drifting apart," Margaret told Donny. "So drift more towards me."

"I'm not doing Facebook," he said. "And you need real friends."

She pretended not to hear him. "We could try out for a reality show together," she suggested, and when he didn't say anything she said, "I just want some of the finer things in life, that's all I want. We're not going to get them with good old-fashioned hard work, so why not be on TV?"

"What fine things do you want?"

"Trips to Europe. Spanish wine. I want dresses that come from a store that doesn't have the word *mart* in its name."

"This is all because you're mad about the babies," Donny said. "When we got married, you didn't want babies, and in another couple of years you'll come back to your senses. We just need to stick it out until then. We have fun together, just you and me."

"We go out for tacos on Fridays," she said, and he said, "See?"

She had no idea who it was babbling on the other end of the phone, but eventually she figured out it was the insect girl from the game show—or Amanda, as she was apparently called. "I was thinking about you," said Amanda. "I'm in town. Can you see me?"

They had exchanged phone numbers and fake hugs in the green room after the show, but Margaret hadn't expected they would actually keep in touch.

"I thought you lived all the way in Kansas City," she said.

"I do, but I'm staying at the Comfort Suites. I need to see you!" She sounded a little crazy. Margaret was almost finished recording a tape expressing her desire to live in a house full of ranting lunatics, serving as the "calm voice of reason, or if that's not fun enough, to encourage my housemates to do incredibly stupid things."

"Sure," she said to Amanda.

Amanda's hair was flatter and greasier than it was on the game show, but she looked just as happy as she had after solving the puzzle and winning twenty-five grand. "I had a fight with my boyfriend, but he's going to marry me because now I'm rich." She smiled; apparently, this didn't bother her. "But he said I had to get rid of some of my very prized possessions. And I thought of you! I don't know why, you were just nice. And I don't have a ton of friends."

Margaret sat on the edge of the king-sized bed and bounced a little in anticipation. "That's very kind of you," she said. "I'm sure I couldn't take anything valuable," she added, because of course she knew she could.

Amanda was standing next to a cloth-draped object beside the ice bucket, grinning like she had when the confetti fell from the ceiling at the TV studio. She pulled the cloth off to reveal what looked like a shoebox-sized clear plastic aquarium. Only instead of fish, there was dirt. And more dirt. And two oblong creatures moving around in the dirt.

"Good God," said Margaret. "I saw someone eat those on a reality show once." She was on her knees, staring.

"They're scarabs," Amanda said. "They're beautiful and sacred."

"Oh, they are!" cried Margaret. They seemed to glow, their brown bodies shining like jewels, their wings a glimmering, iridescent gold.

"There's some cow poo in there," Amanda said. "Just so you know."

"They're dung beetles," said Donny. "They spend their days rolling up balls of shit. But that's cool. At least they're keeping busy, being productive members of society." He gave her a look that suggested she could learn a thing or two from the dung beetles.

"They're scarabs," she said. "Egyptians worshipped them because they roll the sun across the sky."

"I can see that," said Donny.

She took a picture of the two beetles in their cage and posted them on Facebook. The reactions were immature: *Ick, Gross,* and the like. "They are beautiful and sacred!" she wrote. "Maybe you can't tell so much from the pix, but trust me." Sometimes instead of making videos or Twittering, she would just stare at them as they rolled their big balls of dung; she liked to carry their cage from room to room with her. She read about them online and found herself hoping that they would lay eggs (or that at least one of them would) and that she would have a whole cage full of glimmering creatures and smooth round balls. Sometimes instead of going to bed, she would stay in the living room (Donny didn't want them in the bedroom) and put them on the top of the TV and stare at them. They had little faces, and she was almost sure the black glittering eyes were smiling at her.

One Friday afternoon, Donny said he needed to get away, clear his head. "To the cabin," he said, but there wasn't really a cabin, just a rundown shack out in the Alabama woods where his family used to stay during hunting season. "You could come with me," he offered, but they both knew she wouldn't. He had taken her there once, and when Donny said, "I can skin a squirrel, you want to watch?" she had threatened to leave. There was no cell phone reception or even dial-up out there. Not even dial-up! Before he left, Donny said, "Good luck with your audition tapes. I'll be back on Sunday night." Then he sighed and left without kissing her goodbye.

"I know you're probably surprised to see me yet again," said Delores. "But I need something else, if you don't mind."

"What if I do mind?" Margaret said. "Just kidding." Although she really wasn't. She had asked some of her Facebook friends if they'd heard of any "on-going scavenger hunts" and several people—including her old boss, the engineering professor—wrote to tell her it was clearly a scam, and to expect to be robbed.

Delores frowned. "I need a stuffed white bunny wearing a homemade gingham apron. Also, a blue hot water bottle, and a soft white towel that was never used. Check the top of Donny's closet—his mother sent you those for Christmas and you forgot about them. Dig around while you're in there and grab me a Gnome diary, but rip out the first three pages because you wrote in them when you were fourteen."

It wasn't as if Margaret *decided* to get these things, or even knew where to find them—but suddenly she was moving through the house, rooting through drawers and closets—the towel and the old diary right where Delores said they would be.

*Please don't take the scarabs*, she thought, as she handed over everything. Just not the scarabs. *I love those damn bugs*, she realized, and tried not to cry at how pathetic she was.

"And go ahead and email me those videos of yourself," Delores said, "while you're at it."

"Is this a robbery?" Margaret asked at last, when she'd hit *send* and put the pile of objects at Delores' sandaled, red-toenailed feet.

"Does a robber give you presents?" Delores said, and produced a box from seemingly nowhere. "For your trouble," she said. "I shoplifted it for you." And she handed Margaret a pregnancy test.

Donny had gone out to the wilderness to get away from her, and now she couldn't even call to tell him the good news! Or was it good? It was news. At first she thought: *It's a miracle*, and then she realized that she'd been so obsessed with audition tapes and scarabs that she hadn't taken her pills in almost a month.

Before she left, Delores had asked for something to carry her things in.

"*My* things," Margaret corrected, tossing everything into a Wal-Mart bag. "I don't think this is a scavenger hunt at all!"

"These aren't for me," said Delores. "They're for my baby. The mittens and blanket and hot water bottle are to keep her warm when I take her to the north, the music box is so she'll know how much I love her, the bunny is to keep her laughing, and the diary is so she can get out her feelings on paper when she's going through those awkward teenaged years. The towel is just because every-one needs a towel. The videos are so if she ever finds out about you, I can show them to her and she can realize how much better off she is with me, because you're a lunatic. I'll come back tomorrow for that box of scrapbooking stuff you bought at Wal-Mart last year and never got around to using. I think I'll like to scrapbook." She smiled. "When she grows up, she's going to send me postcards from Europe and drink expensive Spanish wine, and marry a minor prince. You'll probably see her in fashion magazines."

"She'll have the finer things in life," Margaret said miserably. "But why do you want *my* baby?"

"Ask your mother if she remembers an old sorority sister named Delores who wanted to come to her baby shower and she said no, you're just a dumb mooch, and then I said, 'I curse your baby girl, and I will take her firstborn as my own.' Ask her if she remembers *that*."

"Oh, her," said Margaret's mother. "Delores was always eating our food and never replacing it. Did you see her? How does she look?"

"It turns out she's a never-aging sorority girl scavenger-fairy," Margaret said. "She looks good."

"Well, what on earth did she want?"

Margaret stared at the two pink lines on the pregnancy test. "Just to say hi," she said to her mother, who evidently didn't have the best memory in the world.

As a child, Margaret had held her parents' dinner guests hostage with her ren-dition of "The Good Ship Lollipop," because she had seen Cindy Brady do it. But otherwise, she had been content with her parents' attention, then her boyfriends', then Donny's. She hadn't realized she craved another, tinier audi-ence until mid-way through her thirty-seventh year, when she woke up one morning sobbing and not knowing why. Only gradually as the day went on—the typing of memos, the answering of phone calls, the lonely lunch at her desk—did she understand what was wrong with her, what she wanted. *Is it unreason-able to want this?* she had Twittered, and pretty much everyone said she wasn't. *You go get what you want, gurl*, said someone called RacyLacy.

When Margaret had asked Delores, "How on earth did you even find me?" Delores laughed and said, "Credit check, Google, YouTube, Facebook, Twitter. I couldn't have not-found you if I'd tried."

Food, trees, shelter, water, fire. What more could a growing child need? It was worth a shot anyway.

She took the lid off the plastic cage and tipped it over, telling the scarabs, "The world is full of shit. Go and enjoy." Then she got in her car and headed up the street to refuel for possibly the very last time. Who needed a car in the wilder-ness? She wondered what would happen when Delores came back and found no one home—the front door wide open and a note taped to it: *Take everything!* Maybe other scavengers would already be there, carting out the computer, video recorder, the big screen TV, the credit cards, the iPhones—staring bewildered at the open box of funny-smelling dirt on the floor. By then the scarabs would already be safely away, rolling, rolling, rolling the sun across the world while the humans filled their arms with all they could hold.

❁ ❁ ❁

## MICHAEL KARDOS

Michael Kardos is the author of the story collection *One Last Good Time*. He received a degree in music from Princeton University, an M.F.A. in fiction from Ohio State University, and a Ph.D. in English from the University of Missouri. His short stories have appeared in *The Southern Review, Crazyhorse, Prairie Schooner,* and many other magazines and anthologies, and were cited as Notable Stories in the 2009 and 2010 editions of *Best American Short Stories.* He has also had two novels published that have garnered much praise and acclaim: The *Three-Day Affair* (2012), which was listed as Esquire's Best Book of the Year, and *Before He Finds Her* (2015); in addition, he has published *The Art and Craft of Fiction: A Writer's Guide* (2012). He co-directs the creative writing program at Mississippi State University. "Lures of Last Resort" and "Population 204" appear in *One Last Good Time*, published in 2011 by Press 53. "America, Etc." appears in *One Teen Story*, volume 3, issue 4, published in 2014 by One Story, Inc.

## *Lures of Last Resort*

One July morning, three men came walking up to my dad and me while we fished off the public pier. This was back in my hometown, in Breakneck Beach, home of the Breakneck Beach Sea Devils and Rex's Italian Sausages. The particular rod I was fishing with, and the reel, too, I'd gotten that spring for doing nothing more than turning a year older. I had just dropped my line into the water when I saw the three men coming our way. They weren't fishermen. Their work pants were ironed smooth, and as they got close I could smell aftershave. Their faces didn't have the wrinkles you get from squinting into the sun. Didn't carry fishing rods either, these men. One of them held an expensive-looking camera. Another carried a small plastic box. The third man didn't carry anything; he just smiled dumbly.

"Take a look at this, gentlemen," the man carrying the box said to us. His voice sounded deep and resonant like the disc jockeys that my folks listened to on the radio. *Fat Billy spinning the oldies. Big Joey bringin' it to you.* This man wasn't big, though, just tall. And skinny like me. He unclasped the box. "You gentlemen won't believe what you see."

I wasn't any gentleman. What ten-year-old is? And the green plastic box, and those feathery lures that looked like little peacocks—I'd seen them before. They were Reel Catch lures, manufactured right here in Breakneck Beach, and my dad used to sell them. Until a month earlier, Dad had sold all sorts of Reel Catch gear to tackle shops and sporting-goods stores. He had spent his days driving up and down the Jersey Shore drumming up orders for reels and fillet knives and those portable toilets for boats with no johns. And lures, too, same as these.

"You'll catch your supper in no time flat," the man said. His v-neck shirt said Reel Catch in one corner and had a stitched-on logo that looked like the lures in the box.

Since mid-June we'd been fishing that pier, my dad and I, every sticky morning from sunrise to ten a.m. I'd wake to the sound of my bedroom door squeaking open. "Up and at 'em," my dad would say, then leave me in the dark to pull on some clothes while he went to the kitchen for coffee, which always smelled good even though, like beer, it was off-limits.

That summer you could have caught fish just by asking nicely. Flukes and snappers. Flounders. Bluefish. Didn't matter to me what we caught; I didn't eat fish, and Dad was allergic. (Mom would eat anything we put on her plate and pretend to like it.) At the end of the fishing pier, my dad would fillet our day's catch and separate the fillets into baggies, and when we came home we'd strut around the apartment complex like a couple of heroes, ringing doorbells and giving everybody free fish that'd stink up their apartments in about a minute. What we didn't give away my dad would put in the freezer, till the freezer had nothing but fish in it and my mother would say things like "We have enough fish, don't we?" or "Maybe tomorrow you two ought to take a rest." But we never did.

The man holding the box said, "These lures're made special like that, colorful, to attract—"

"I know exactly what they're meant to do," my dad said. "Who the hell do you think I am? Son, why don't you tell these men who I am."

So I told them. "My dad is Lee Gernipoethy."

The men looked at one another and then back at my dad. "Well, Jesus, we didn't . . . we were sent out here on a little promotional stint. That's all. Giving away some lures. We didn't know. . . ."

You say our last name like Gunnipuddy, and it's a name people don't forget. Especially when you're a big man like my dad, six-two and broad like the linebacker he'd been till senior year, when he quit high school for reasons that, though he never said so outright, had a lot to do with my being born. These men obviously had started working for Reel Catch after my dad got fired, because they hadn't recognized him. Though by now the name Gernipoethy must have already been legend. Dad had been chewed out for some minor infraction, the story goes, when he lifted his manager's desk right up in the air—and this wasn't some small desk, either—and threw it through the window. It fell two stories to the parking lot below. Then Dad spent the night in jail.

It's a story I learned years later, when I was fifteen. By then my mother had already been remarried a while. To Rodney. One night, Rodney got home from his job as customer service manager at the water company and found me in the parking lot setting free a daddy-longleg I'd caught in the bathroom sink. I'd scooped it up in my cupped hands and run outside with it tickling my palms. After I let it go, Rodney and I went inside, and Rodney got a bottle of Budweiser from the refrigerator and then told me the story of my dad's night in jail. Rodney liked to tell stories, and I didn't like the way he told this one—his eyes gleaming, hands in motion, voice animated, pausing every so often to take long swallows from his beer. It was exactly the way he told my mom and me the outrageous and sad excuses customers had for not paying their water bill. *But that's Lee*, he concluded. *That's old Lee for you. A real character, that one.*

Except he wasn't a character—he was my dad, even if I hadn't seen him in a few years—and I sat there at the kitchen table wondering what Rodney's point was in telling me a story that made my dad look foolish, till Rodney slapped me on the shoulder and said, as if we were old chums, *But you know something? You don't have one bit of your old man's mean streak in you.*

He went to the refrigerator again, I remember, and came back with two more bottles of Budweiser. *I'm going to give you a beer tonight, son*, he said, and I punched that man in the eye as hard as I could. In thirty minutes a brown shopping bag full of my clothes sat next to me on the curb where you wait for Greyhound busses to take you away to new places. Mom was still out, working the four-to-midnight shift at the Breakneck Beach Diner, and I knew she'd be heartbroken. But I went anyway. When you make up your mind to move on, you move on. And so that's what I did.

Back when I was ten, though, I didn't know the details of Dad's job or how he lost it. I knew that suddenly he had time for fishing, and that he expected me to come along. But once our lines were in the water, he had this way of forgetting I was even there, of looking off at the horizon for long periods, not answering my questions about why clouds went pink at sunrise, or whether fish felt pain when they bit the hook, or whether a tidal wave would demolish this whole town. *Dad?* I would say, trying to draw him back to me. Nothing. *Dad!* My dad was obviously involved in some heavy thinking. All the same, I'd have preferred that he answer my questions.

"Give my son some lures, then, if that's what you're here to do." Dad sure was paying attention now, watching the men hard. The man holding the box of lures handed me three of them. "Is that all you're planning to give my kid? Kid's a good fisherman, needs plenty of lures."

"It's okay, Dad," I said. "Three's enough." But my dad wasn't listening. He had taken a small step closer to the man with the lures, and the men were glancing down at the fishing knife that hung free in Dad's belt. They were taking that knife seriously. Dad spat off to the side, looked again at the man holding the lures, and raised his eyebrows as if waiting for an answer.

The man handed me the entire box. Must've been thirty lures in there, all peacock-looking and ready for action.

"Thanks," I said, taking the box.

"No thanks necessary, son," my dad said. "That's his job, giving out fishing tackle. Don't know what that other man's job is"—he nodded to the dumb-looking one—"I never heard of it taking two men to hand out lures. Big waste of money, you ask me."

"We're on the same sales team," the man said, the man who barely reached my dad's chin.

"Sales team!" My dad ran a hand through his hair. "Fellows are teammates? Like in baseball?" He shook his head in disbelief. "Salesmen have what're called territories," he explained to me. "If they start working in pairs, then they've got to start splitting commissions." He waited for them to dispute what he'd said, but they didn't. "And *that* man"—he nodded to the photographer—"it's that man's job to take pictures of the people who've gotten the lures. Action photos, preferably. Isn't that right? For next year's catalogue?"

The photographer said, "Or the local paper. Or both."

"Well, then," my dad said to me, "let's catch some fish." He pulled the knife from his belt, cut off the lure he'd been using, and dropped it into the little bucket where we kept our tackle. Then he removed one of the Reel Catch lures from its plastic package and tied it on. He did the same with my line, too, then tucked the knife back through his belt. This all took a few minutes. Some other fishermen were on the pier that morning, but I had all the giveaways. So the three men waited.

The fishing pier wasn't two blocks from the firehouse, and as Dad was slowly tying on the Reel Catch lures—deliberately slowly, I'm sure, because I'd seen him tie on lures before in two seconds—the firehouse started blaring its siren. Loudest thing you ever heard. Happened almost every day, far more often than there could be fires. I yelled from deep within my throat: "I love you Carla Van Sickle I love you Carla Van Sickle I love you Carla Van Sickle!" Over and over I yelled it, for maybe thirty seconds. What I knew was, as long as you matched your yelling to the pitch of the siren, nobody could hear you. It could be your own secret. Carla was the third-smartest and second-prettiest girl in my class, and I loved her with a wholeness that I had never loved anybody with before or probably ever would again. She was skinny, with eyes the color of a first-place ribbon and a voice like smooth paint. She wore cutoffs that her mom trimmed for her, and little white strands of denim were always draping down her legs. I walked into walls for her, literally missed doors on purpose, because when I did, she laughed, and her laugh was worth an army of bruises.

By the time the siren died down again, Dad had the Reel Catch lures on. I set down the plastic box at my feet and we both cast our lines into the water. Fluke, we were going for, so we stood there jiggling our rods, waiting for the fish to bite.

"Get yourself ready," Dad said to the photographer.

"Are we going to be in the newspaper?" I asked my dad, and the end of my rod bent over. I yanked the rod upward, and the reel made a metallic buzzing sound, an exhilarating sound, the sound of a big fish. Everything that had been said or thought only seconds before was now miles in the past.

"Dad!" My rod bent like crazy. "I got one!"

The three men came closer. The photographer raised his camera. I imagined Dad and me in the paper, the sports section, and we were smiling big newsprint teeth, and there was a caption that made us seem tough and outdoorsy. I could smell fish blood.

But my dad shook his head. "Nah—he's only caught the ground. Look." He took the rod from my hands and held it steady. The whirring stopped and the rod straightened. He yanked the rod again—more whirring. "See? It's just the ground."

The men exhaled. The photographer lowered his camera.

My dad pulled the knife from his belt and cut the line. "That's one Reel Catch lure we won't be seeing again."

Once the Reel Catch reps saw we weren't catching any fish with their tackle, they and the photographer started muttering to one another about having to get back to the showroom. Yet they waited, and at first Dad appeared to pay no notice, just kept jerking his fishing rod up and down. Finally, without turning toward them, he said, "I don't think you men are going to get what you're after today." Without another word, the men nodded and slunk away.

As soon as they were gone, Dad reeled in his line. "There's a reason I don't use these lures, son. See that hook?" He laid the Reel Catch lure on his palm. "Hook's too big for that lure. The design's all wrong."

I reeled in my line, and we rigged up our old lures again. Dad put the Reel Catch lures back into the plastic box and closed the clasp. "Those are lures of last resort," he said. "If I was stranded on a deserted island with no food, I'd rather try clubbing fish over the head than catching them with a Reel Catch lure."

I laughed, and cast my line into the water. Dad told me that it's more important for lures to reflect light off the sun than it is for them to look like actual fish. Better off using tin foil than some fancy colorful lure.

"I'd rather jump into the water and grab them myself," I said, "than catch them with a Reel Catch lure."

My dad cast his own line into the water. "I'd rather call them on the phone, invite them to dinner, than catch them with a Reel Catch lure."

"I'd rather shoot them with a gun," I said, looking up at my dad, "than catch them with a Reel Catch lure."

"Guns are dangerous," my dad said. "You keep away from guns."

We stood there for a while, not talking, just fishing, until my dad spat over the end of the pier, sized me up, and said, "Biggest animal on Earth's the blue whale, not some dinosaur." Then he said, "Whales eat a lot of plankton. Tons and tons of it."

My dad had been doing some heavy thinking on the pier, but now he was done with thinking. Now he was looking at me, telling me that love made you do crazy things, but that sometimes crazy things were called for. Saying that I'm likely to grow to his height if I eat and sleep enough. That the tide rises just over six feet during a full moon. He was answering every question I'd ever asked, and others I'd forgotten or never asked in the first place.

He said that fighting never got you anywhere, and that only lazy people fished past noon. That tidal waves didn't ever hit this coast. But yes, in theory the town would flood.

He didn't speak quickly, yet there was urgency in his voice as if what he was telling me was vitally important. I know now he believed he was talking with me, father to son, for the last time, and so he was making up for all the lost moments, and the lost moments to come. I have no idea what he had planned, specifically, beyond getting in his car and driving in some predetermined direction, but my hunch is that his destination was beside the point. After leaving Breakneck Beach myself at fifteen, I picked up and moved every year or two, and not once did the destination matter at all. It's more a feeling that if you stay, your bones will crush. Your gut will bleed. You'll behave in a way you can't live with.

A dull knife is more dangerous than a sharp one, he said. In lake fishing, you're better off along the shoreline than in the middle of the lake. He said that every mass has gravity—it's why the Earth revolves around the sun, and why the moon revolves around the Earth. An albacore fights like a fish twice its size. "Albacore's the best thing you'll ever catch," he said, and I imagined what a battle that must be.

"Do you know why the beach erodes?" my dad asked.

I said that I didn't.

So he told me. And then he told me some more.

The next morning at eight-thirty, I got out of bed and found Mom at the kitchen table staring at the wall, a half-eaten English muffin on her plate. The radio was on, the volume low, probably so that it wouldn't wake me. I was almost next to her before she seemed to notice me.

"Where's Dad?" I asked.

Mom pursed her lips, stood, and went to the refrigerator. "Which jelly do you want?" She opened the refrigerator door. "Strawberry?"

"Where is he?" I sat down in one of the kitchen chairs. But she didn't answer me. She'd begun moving things around in the refrigerator, slamming down jars on the shelves, rearranging everything. I started to feel seasick. "Mom?" I tried to sound calm, although I could feel my neck beating and the spit in my mouth going dry. "What's going on? Where is he?"

"*Where is he, where is he* . . ." She slammed the refrigerator door and spun to glare at me. I must have shrunk away, because then her face softened and she came over to the table. She stood over me for a few seconds, just looking. "Listen to me. Just be quiet and listen." She sat next to me at the table. Mom still had long hair then, and some strands had fallen over her face, but she didn't seem to notice. She was watching me closely. "You're ten years old and I'm not going to lie to you. You think your father's a great man, don't you? Your hero, probably. He isn't perfect, you know." She picked up her English muffin, examined it, and put it back in her plate.

I asked her for the millionth time, Where *was* he?

"How the hell should I know?" Mom scrunched up her face like she might sneeze, but she didn't. She stayed frozen that way while the clock over the stove clicked a few times. Then she said, "Sorry. Okay? I'm sorry. I'm just telling you how it is. He leaves sometimes, but he always comes home. The last time, you were too young for me to explain what was going on. You probably don't even remember."

But suddenly I did remember. Sort of. Actually, all I remembered was the seasick feeling, as if the apartment building were rolling in waves, same as I was feeling now. "How many times has he left?" I asked.

"Several times," she said. "But not for a few years."

"Where does he go?"

"That depends. It all depends."

"Why does he leave?" I asked. We were both calming down, now. We were just talking. I was asking questions, and my mother was answering them.

"Your father would say for love. He loves me, so he leaves. He loves me, so he returns. Love, love, love. So finally I said to him . . ." She shook her head. "Well, never mind what I said to him. But don't worry. He'll be back. I'm not going to lie to you. Your father's left, but he's coming back. He'll be back."

Either Dad's departures had lost their weight, or else Mom needed to act as if they had, because she spent the day doing ordinary things. Sweeping. Studying for a class she was taking in stenography. Humming along to the radio. Making me snacks: a plate of bologna and cheese, crackers, slices of carrots.

I couldn't eat. For two days I sat on the rug in the living room with one hand on the telephone, convincing myself that I could feel it preparing to ring. Convinced that if one hand *weren't* on the phone, then it wouldn't ring and it would be my fault.

"Go outside," my mother told me. "I'll let you know if anybody calls."

On the third day, I woke up early without even meaning to, before sunup, and decided to be a man. I got my fishing rod and tackle from behind the washing machine, and without waking Mom I went outside and walked the five blocks to the fishing pier. I didn't want to use the regular lures. They were my dad's, and I didn't want any help from him or his lures. And so I rigged up one of my own—the Reel Catch lures—but all morning long I didn't get a single hit. Dad had been right about one thing: these lures were no good.

A few of the usual fishermen were out, all grown men, everyone standing at a polite distance from one another and looking off to the horizon. Closest to me, a thin, silver-haired man wearing overalls and dirty sneakers uncapped a thermos and poured himself a steaming drink into the lid. He met my gaze while taking a sip and then saluted me with the lid. We were just two men, fishing. I laid down my rod and went over to him.

"Is that coffee?"

When he said that it was, I asked him for a sip. The man creased his forehead at me, he tilted his head, but then he offered the thermos lid and said to be careful, it's hot. I hadn't ever drunk coffee before, and it tasted as bitter as I imagined tar must, but I swallowed a big mouthful anyway, burning my throat some, said thank you, and went for my rod again.

The morning was cooler than usual, the ocean calm, and watching the horizon myself I started making plans. I would quit school and find a job earning money for Mom and me. I imagined starting my own newspaper where I would sell advertising space to companies like Reel Catch. I was ten, but I swear I thought of that idea and several others as well. I would become famous for having a successful newspaper and being so young. I decided to start my newspaper that afternoon, walking door-to-door in the apartment building and selling subscriptions.

When I got home, drunk from my own ideas, both my parents were sitting at the kitchen table, their pinkies interlocked. Mom's eyes were red, but she was smiling and seemed content. Proud almost, as if she'd won a bet with herself. Dad's hair was mussed, he was unshaven, but other than that it could have been any other summer morning.

"Son," my dad said, and nodded as if we were both men who understood something important.

But I understood nothing. Seeing him, all I knew was that I wouldn't get to prove myself after all. There would be no newspaper, no fame, because my dad had failed at something as easy as walking out on us. And feeling disappointed in him made me feel shameful for feeling disappointed, and that, you can imagine, led me to feeling angry, furious, for having been made to feel shame over how I was feeling, which isn't exactly something that a person had any control over. Not at ten. Not when we're talking about a person's dad leaving and then coming home again. I glared at him.

"Well?" he said, his eyes clear and wide and inviting. "Were they biting?"

For a moment I'd forgotten I was carrying a fishing rod. "Like crazy," I said, and went to put away the gear and pretend that he had never even come home. I made it as far as the doorway when my dad must have decided it wasn't time yet to be written off by his own damn son.

"What kind of fish did you catch?"

"Bluefish," I said. "Big ones. And an albacore." I turned around to face him. He was sitting back in his chair, his arms folded, his gaze on me. "Yeah, I did. And you were right about albacore, it really . . ."—and then I realized too late that he had drawn me into the lie so that he could catch me in it and watch me thrash around.

## *Population 204*

No customers were in the Wawa food mart when the thunderclap hit and the lights went out. At one a.m. there were just the three of us—me in the stockroom tagging cans, Jillian on the register, and Phillip behind the hoagie counter. I felt my way out of the stockroom and looked around the store. The emergency lights had come on and were casting long, weird shadows. And while normally the place is filled with buzzing and humming from the refrigeration unit, the cash register, the air-conditioning—now, nothing. Just the rain hitting the roof overhead and the pavement outside. Jillian and Phillip were looking at me for advice or maybe reassurance. I wasn't used to being looked at for those things. I wasn't even their boss. But after the manager and the assistant manager, I was next in the chain of command. So I told them, "Maybe it'll come back on real quick."

It didn't. We listened to the rain and waited. The rain got heavier, then heavier still. A few people went by on the sidewalk, hunched into themselves underneath their raincoats and umbrellas. Usually this time of night our customers were quiet, middle-aged guys like myself looking for milk and TV dinners. Or they're teenagers with the munchies. Business was slow even on clear nights, let alone a stormy one. I told Jillian and Phillip that they could go home if they wanted. It was summer in New Jersey, and without the air-conditioning the store was already getting stuffy. Customers weren't going to come in here with all the lights off, and the register wouldn't work even if they did. Phillip said thanks, but no thanks. He'd punched in already and needed the money. Standing around like this was easy work.

"You feel the same way, Jillian?" I asked.

She sniffled. "I could use the money."

"You crying?" I asked. She'd been very quiet since she got here. I mean she'd always been quiet, but tonight she was being extra quiet.

She sniffled again. "No, Joe, I'm all right." But I went to aisle three and got a box of tissues anyway.

"You should tell us what's the matter," Phillip said. "Tell us all about it." He came over and sat on Jillian's counter, on the conveyer belt that had stopped moving. I punched my thumb through the top of the tissue box to open it and handed it to Jillian. She pulled out a few tissues, set the box next to her at the register, and dried her eyes as one of the emergency lights back by the fruit flickered a few times and went out.

"So go ahead," Phillip said. "Spill your guts." Phillip studied communications at Jersey Central College, and customers seemed to like talking with him while he made their hoagies. He was very outgoing for a guy with so many pimples on his face. Jillian, on the other hand, kept to herself, rarely saying more to the customers than *Enjoy your day*, or more to Phillip than *Good morning* or *Is there cheese on this hoagie?* So Phillip must have been hoping that with the lights off and him sitting so close, Jillian might open up a little.

"I received a letter today," she said. "My grandmother fell and broke her hip."

"Well, that's too bad," I said. "She an old lady, your grandmother?"

"Eighty-three."

"That's too bad for her—when you break your hip at that age, isn't much chance you're going to walk again." I wasn't saying it to be mean, just stating a fact of life.

"How'd she fall?" Phillip asked. "Stairs?"

"She fell off a tightrope," Jillian said. Phillip looked at me, but I didn't know what to say to that.

Jillian came out from behind the register and opened up a beach chair with porpoises on it that we sold for $9.99. She set the box of tissues on the floor next to her and sighed. "When you drive to my hometown, there's a sign at the border saying Population 204." Phillip was looking at her skeptically. So was I. I'd never heard of a town that small. "This is in Missouri," she said. "A pretty little town in the Ozark Mountains."

So here was her life story, I thought. Unlike Phillip, I wasn't so determined to get quiet people to start talking. I figured that not talking was their right. I felt like not talking myself sometimes, and while Phillip wasn't a bad kid, I had no special urge to communicate with him. Sure, I was lonely, I could have told him. Hadn't seen a naked woman outside of a magazine for four years, not since Lilah's speech got muddy and her memories went haywire and the population of my apartment decreased by one. I could have told him about that. But I wasn't going to.

Jillian must have felt different from me, though, because here came her life story, just for the asking—even if the part about her grandmother walking a tightrope at eighty-three made no sense at all. And when she went on to say that everybody in her little town in the Ozarks was training to be circus performers, I knew she was pulling our leg. What I didn't know was why. I sat on the floor near the two of them, put my arms around my knees, and listened to Jillian talk about the town's children learning to guess people's weight and juggle flaming torches and ride unicycles and paint their faces. "And my best friend growing up," she said, "was a lion named Grouchy."

That old lion was a regular piece of work from the sound of it, rolling around on its back so that you'd scratch its belly and always on the lookout for apple butter. But that wasn't all. This town of hers had a tightrope—the one that led to her grandmother's busted hip—tied between an old sugar maple tree and the schoolhouse. Every day at lunchtime the children in town had to walk the length of the rope before heading home to eat their sandwiches.

"Sounds pretty difficult," I said.

"It wasn't so hard," she said. "Though some days we'd be blindfolded. Other days, we'd have to walk backwards. Anyone fell and the whole class had to start again." Each spring, she explained, the town put on a festival for all the neighboring towns, two whole weeks of circus acts, and part of it was showing off all of the children's new skills.

I wasn't too comfortable sitting on the ground, but I wasn't about to move. This was by far the most I'd heard out of Jillian since she'd applied for the job two years earlier.

"The problem," she said, "was that the town's population was 204. Like the sign said. You've seen signs like that, haven't you? When you drive into a town?"

"I've seen it," I said. "Never a town that small, though."

"Well, in Missouri, towns can get even smaller than that. But my town had 204, like the sign said. Whenever someone died, somebody new was needed in town so that the population would stay at 204. After a funeral, there'd be festive celebrations in the days that followed, so that people would go home and make love, and soon enough there would be a new child—"

When I laughed, Jillian narrowed her eyes as if I'd done something I shouldn't have, and I *felt* ashamed. Then her eyes widened again. "But sometimes a child would be born without someone having passed away first. Those times, people didn't like so much. It meant someone had to die."

"So that the population would stay at 204," I said soberly.

She nodded.

Men coming into the Wawa were always fascinated by Jillian. They'd linger at the register and say things too goofy to say in front of their girlfriends or wives. She wasn't pretty in the usual way—her teeth were crooked, for one, and her arms were thick, and her neck had moles on it—but she had grayish blue eyes that watched you more closely than most eyes did. I would sometimes get to thinking about Jillian when I was at home alone. I didn't run into many women in the course of a day. And of the three women who worked at this Wawa, Jillian was the prettiest. I hadn't ever taken much of a liking to her personally. Not that I didn't like her. I just never felt one way or the other. But that was before I knew she would sit here with the power out and spin tales like this one, touching her throat absently with the bony fingers of her left hand, and clenching her jaw a little when recalling a detail like the brassy *oom-pah* of her mother's tuba-playing.

"Guess my weight," I said to her. "Guess it right now." Not that I even knew my own weight. Probably 230, maybe more. I'd been eating junk for a long time.

"That isn't my skill," she said. "And anyway, I'm telling a story. I'm just about to get to the important part."

But her story got interrupted by two boys, high-school age, knocking on the glass door of the Wawa. They both wore baseball caps and smirks. They looked exactly like every boy I'd ever seen in my entire life. One of them leaned his head in. "You open or what?" Water dripped from the brim of his cap onto the floor.

"Look like we're open?" I didn't get up.

"We're dying for some Wa-dogs, man. Come on, we're starving."

Stoned, too. At night, kids coming in here were always drunk or stoned. I knew they didn't mean it as a personal insult, but I couldn't help thinking of it that way. As if we were people you couldn't come and visit sober.

"We're closed," I said.

After the kids had left, I said to Jillian and Phillip that we ought to eat some hotdogs. Over by the hoagie counter was a machine that rotated the dogs and kept them warm. But with the power off, they were just going to get cold. "What do you say?"

"Lay one on me, big guy," Phillip said. "Jillian?"

"I'm a little hungry," she said.

"Go on with your story," I said, but Jillian waited until I had gone behind the hoagie counter and gotten our dogs. I put mustard and kraut on them and carried them back. Then I went to the refrigerated section and got us each a soda. Jillian handed Phillip and me each a few tissues for napkins.

When I sat down again, we each took a bite of our hotdogs. I liked the idea of this, us all eating together. It felt like something we ought to be doing. Jillian chewed politely and then swallowed. She wiped her mouth with a tissue and explained that whenever there was a birth, one of the town's elders usually would volunteer to keep the town's population steady, but not always. "It could get thorny," she said. One day, the town needed someone to step forward and nobody would, until her favorite schoolteacher said, *I'll do it.* This teacher wasn't old; the only gray in her hair came from worrying about her students.

In a state of despair, early the next morning—and without telling anyone—Jillian did something nobody in her town had ever done: she went away, vowing never to return. All of her money bought her a used car that she drove east, farther and farther, until there were no more states to cross, no more towns. Just a studio apartment and a job as a cashier. She cut her hair short, and colored it brown, and changed her name, because she didn't want any reminders of the life she had left behind.

And after a few years, sometimes entire days went by without her thinking about life back in the Ozarks.

"But now your grandmother is ill," I said.

"Not just ill," she said. "*Old* and ill. And I just keep thinking about that sign."

"Population 204."

"That's right," she said. "So if I'm ever going to see her again—"

"Now wait just a minute," Phillip said. "How'd you find out about your grandmother's injury if nobody knows where you are?"

"My mother knows where I am," she said.

Phillip was missing the point, though, and I wanted to set him right. So what if Jillian was pulling our leg? Who cared, for that matter, why she was doing it? She was taking herself seriously, and so should we.

"Well, I sure am sorry about your situation," I said, and gave Phillip the hard look I gave him whenever he left the deli station a mess. "You must love your grandmother a lot."

"I do."

Phillip sighed. "Do you think . . . you'll go back there, to your circus town?" He glanced at me, and I nodded.

"I'm not sure," she said. "I'm thinking I might."

Jillian took a long draw from her soda. Phillip had already finished his, and asked Jillian for a sip. I felt like I should say something vague and uplifting. But how could I know what to say when I didn't know if her grandmother really was ill, or what sort of town she was raised in, or even if she'd ever been to Missouri? She didn't have a trace of an accent. I didn't even know if her real name was Jillian or not. I didn't know *what* to believe, or if Jillian knew for herself. But I'd have been grateful if the Wawa's lights never came on again. Later, when the sun rose and I was home again, I knew that I'd lie in bed and think about the three of us sitting together in the dark with our hotdogs and sodas. I could almost believe that we were beside a campfire, old friends telling stories from deep inside our hearts.

"I think that'd be the right thing, Jillian," I told her. "It's important to be with your family when they're sick." And before I could stop myself, I was telling them about Lilah. I didn't get emotional. I didn't need to borrow any of Jillian's tissues. But I told them things. How Lilah was exactly my height but wore heels so she'd look taller. How after she lost her sense of smell, she always overdid the perfume. I talked about headaches and seizures. I told the story of how, on one of the last good days, our car had skidded on black ice and nearly gone off a drawbridge, and how for the couple of seconds we were sliding toward the edge

I had felt relieved because at least we'd go out together. And when the car had come to a stop up against the guardrail, and we knew we were alive and safe for the moment, I had felt a different sort of relief—a lot like what I was feeling right now, here in the Wawa. With the two of them. Which was probably more than I needed to say. Jillian touched her throat, and Phillip nodded, then wiped his sweaty forehead with his palm. It was getting very warm.

The rain was still hitting the roof, the sky still rumbling, and I had no reason to think the lights were coming on anytime soon. I coughed into my closed fist and suggested that we put all the fruit into shopping carts and wheel them back to the storeroom where there was a refrigerator that even without power would keep things cold for several hours.

"Right, chief," Phillip said, and hopped off the conveyer belt. He extended a hand to Jillian, helping her out of the chair.

The three of us went to the rear aisle, where the fruit was. Jillian started picking over the apples in the dark, lifting one, turning it over in her hand, setting it back down. Before long she had four small apples in her right hand and three in her left.

She threw them high in the air.

## America, Etc.

My dad, the drone pilot, is losing to me again at Missile Command. He's only on level three and is already desperate with the joystick, jerking it around and repeatedly stabbing the fire button like it's Morse Code for *I'll be dead in three seconds.* "The smart bombs are too smart!" he says, and winks. But the game we're playing is thirty years old, and, trust me, the bombs aren't that smart. And anyway, why is he winking? Maybe if he kept both eyes open, he'd successfully defend more cities.

Mom's in bed. The baby, Avery, is in her crib being quiet for now. I should probably be in bed, too, since I have basketball in the morning, but while I was brushing my teeth, Dad found me in the bathroom and asked how my thumbs were feeling.

"They're feeling restless," I said.

"Then let's have at it," he said.

That's our routine. So I spat into the sink and followed him downstairs.

"Hands down, this is the best part of my day," he said as the cartridge loaded up and he went to work on the stack of Keebler cookies on the coffee table in front of us.

I shut off the halogen lamp to make the game look better, and when I returned to the couch, half the cookies were gone. Good thing I'd eaten a few after supper—Dad eats cookies like a Hoover. Especially after a rough day at the office. That's what he calls it. *I'm off to the office; I'm home from the office*—a joke, because he's a pilot, not an accountant. But it's also true that he works in an office. I've seen it from the outside, and it looks like every other brown building on the base. You'd never guess that pilots are in there making actual planes rise and turn and bomb targets halfway around the world. *Your father has a stressful job*, Mom tells me sometimes when Dad complains about having "a rough day at the office" or when he acts sad or too happy for no reason. *Duh*, I always feel like saying to her. *Like, duh*—though before tonight, Dad would never tell me what exactly made the rough days rough. Not that it ever stopped me from asking. But whenever I did, his answer was always a glance over at Mom, who'd intercept: *Jeremy, your father deserves some peace at home.*

Mom is pretty much our translator, especially at the table. Dad talks, Mom translates, I pipe in, Mom translates some more, until eventually I'm excused to the living room to play Nintendo DS. We've got supper conversation pretty much down to a system, mostly thanks to Mom—not surprising, considering that she's an actual translator. Her specialty is Italian novels being published in America, but I think she probably works harder at the kitchen table with us.

So I was kind of shocked when tonight Dad looked right at me over our plates of food and said, "We hit a dog."

"*Reid.*" My mother shot my father a glance—his response was a shrug—and then she got up to refill water glasses.

"Oh," I said. "Huh?"

"One of our Hellfire missiles was about to hit its target when a dog came around the corner."

"Oh." I felt like I ought to say more, now that we had this open channel of communication. Maybe I should console him. But how? And also—why? Because when you're fighting in an actual war like he is against terrorists who would kill every last one of us if they had the chance—even me, even Avery—a dead dog might be sad, but it isn't tragic. It just isn't. "What kind of dog was it?" I asked.

My father looked at me long enough to make it clear I'd messed up somehow, and our open channel closed again. "The kind that barks, Jeremy."

I ate a few more sweet potato fries, nodding and pretending that I hadn't just been shamed.

"Can I be excused now?" I asked.

Yes, I could.

Me, the brown loveseat, my Nintendo DS, and four Keebler chocolate chip cookies stacked on a napkin. That's pretty much bliss, and I get to do it every single night. We live in a house. When I was younger, we lived in an apartment on the base, where Dad worked as a historian. That was his major in college—history. Mom's, too. That was how they met and fell in love. When Mom got pregnant with Avery, Dad changed jobs within the Air Force and trained to become a pilot for remotely powered aircraft. Apparently, it didn't matter that he'd never flown planes before or that the one flight I remember us all taking, to Florida, my dad was more interested in watching *Six Days, Seven Nights* than in the view outside or the hum of the engine. A few dozen hours up in a Cessna, and *voilà*—pilot. Soon after, we moved into a house with four bedrooms and a backyard with two oak trees that are the perfect distance apart for holding up the hammock we're going to get in the spring.

Mom and Dad's voices from the kitchen faded into the background as I went to work on the DS. I was getting near the end of Pokémon *Diamond and Pearl*, the best Pokémon game yet. If I played until bedtime, I could probably win. But after only a few minutes, I noticed my mind wandering. I had what felt like an itch inside my forehead that I couldn't scratch. I kept thinking about how maybe the rough days Dad mentioned from time to time weren't actually all that rough—not when you compared them to what Ted Wolff's dad must be dealing with. Ted's dad is a marine in Afghanistan. *His boots are on the ground*, Ted likes to remind me and everyone. This is his dad's third tour of duty, and Ted hasn't seen him in eleven months. I'll admit it: Sometimes I'm jealous. Every day, Ted wonders if he and his mom will receive tragic news. They still live on the base, surrounded by people who worry about them. When people pray for our troops, it's Ted's dad, not mine, they're praying for.

Mornings on the school bus, Ted tells me about his nightmares, grisly scenes straight out of a first-person shooter. Sometimes I think he makes them up to shock me, but other times I'm not so sure. His schoolwork is suffering. That's the word his teachers use and therefore he uses—"suffering"—as if Ted's notebooks and quizzes are connected to tubes and life-support systems. And he's gotten into trouble at recess for fighting—suspended twice this year. What would I get suspended for? What would I be acting out against? My dad brings home Chick-fil-A on Mondays, when Mom has ice-skating. Weekends, he makes Western omelets. He coaches my basketball team.

My dad's boots? They're on the front hall mat beside the purple lunch cooler that he brags about finding on mega-sale at Costco. On field trip days, he lets me borrow the cooler. It really does keep the hot stuff hot and the cold stuff cold.

Okay, I decide. Maybe killing a dog could be tragic. I like dogs. In two years, when I'm fifteen and my sister isn't a baby anymore, we're going to *get* a dog. And if that dog were ever to escape and run into a car's path—yeah. That would be a rough day for me, and for the driver, too, unless he was totally heartless. A dead dog in Afghanistan is just as dead as a dead dog in New Jersey. That's something else that I've been thinking about—how it isn't the dog's fault that its owner is a terrorist. I mean, that doesn't make the dog a terrorist. It just makes it an unlucky dog—for having a terrorist for an owner, and for stepping into the path of a Hellfire missile.

I had those deep thoughts while playing the DS, and I'm still having them now as my Dad loses his cities one by one. He's wincing, his face too serious for Atari, and I consider letting him win. But I'm already too far ahead for that. And from the look of things, he won't be completing this level, anyway. It's just as well. He wouldn't want me throwing the game. He's more interested in playing fair and trying hard than in winning or losing. It's the coach in him. The coach that doesn't win many games.

"I'm in big trouble, boy," he says. "These lines are coming at me too fast!"

I almost correct him—they're *missiles*, not lines—but don't, because he's right. They don't look anything like missiles. The fact is, no one should be stuck playing an Atari 2600. But Dad was saying before Christmas how he wasn't allowed to play video games as a kid, and so Mom won him a console off eBay. She didn't know she should've bid on a Nintendo—that Atari was even before *his* time. Not only are the graphics amazingly bad, but the joystick only has one button. One!

But here's the thing: Missile Command is all right. It's actually creepier than anything on the Xbox or PlayStation. When you lose and the aliens have flattened all your cities, the words THE END appear on the screen in huge letters. Not *game over*, but THE END. Those words mean business. It almost feels like it could actually be the end of the world, until you remember that the game is from 1980 and that the world is still here.

My dad grunts as his remaining cities get squashed. But he's a helluva sport and waits around for me to clear level after level. I get into some sort of crazy zone and it's my best game ever. Dad is kicked back on the sofa, arms behind his head. He's actually smiling, as if the most amazing thing he's seen in his whole life is me, his son, calmly defending our pixelated planet.

"What's it like," I ask him the next afternoon on our way to the game, "flying the planes and dropping bombs and stuff?" I've never thought to ask before. Does a dentist's son ask his dad what it's like to drill a tooth? But yesterday in homeroom Ted Wolff was telling other kids that my dad wasn't a real pilot, and I told Ted he was crazy, because what else do you call someone who flies planes and bombs people? And as I said it, it occurred to me that, whoa—he bombs people.

"Ain't a pilot if he can't get blown apart," Ted said.

"That only makes him smart," I said, emphasizing that last word and immediately regretting it. I didn't mean to imply that his old man was dumb for having his boots on the ground, but that's how it sounded. If I were anybody else, Ted would've murdered me on the spot. Instead, he only got a hurt look and told me to screw off, which I immediately did. We were best friends back when our families both lived on the base. It isn't a very large base, and few kids at school come from military families and know what it's like having to prove yourself to a whole new set of kids every time your family is transferred. So it's good to stick together, look out for one another in case there's any trouble.

Mom says that Ted *is* trouble—and I guess she's right if "trouble" is Italian for really, really good at basketball. Thankfully, we aren't playing the Jaguars today. We're up against the Tigers. We're the Pumas. There are eight teams in the league, and six of them are cats.

Dad drives slowly through the school parking lot, as if he didn't hear my question. I don't even know why I felt compelled to ask it, except that Ted's accusation is still sitting in my stomach like bad tacos. I think I know why he said it, too: Yesterday, six marines died when their helicopter crashed in the Helmand province. That's where his father is. He wasn't hurt, but still—the man is creeping through hostile territory seven thousand miles away. I can't imagine my own father being there in the thick of combat. Where would he keep his fountain pens? But even if I could imagine my dad in Afghanistan, I know I wouldn't want him there, not if the other choice is staying here, staying safe.

My dad stops the car for some kid who's dribbling his basketball and not looking where he's going. Then he starts driving again. "Jeremy, I don't—" He shakes his head and starts again. "Ninety-nine percent of what I do is nothing." He goes on to say that he and his copilot watch the monitors as the remotely piloted aircraft makes passes over the enemy. "We observe," he says. "We take photographs and report on what we see. To tell you the truth, it's pretty boring most of the time. We almost never engage the enemy."

"Yeah, but when you do. What's that like?"

"What's it like?" Anger has crept into his voice. "What do you *think* it's like?" This is what happens when our translator has to take Avery to Kindermusik.

Dad pulls the car into the nearest parking space. It's the same school I go to Monday through Friday but less dreary without the teachers. All around us, excited kids are rushing ahead of their parents toward the gym. Half these kids will lose today. I don't think my father meant for me to answer his question, but I really want to know and don't see myself bringing up the subject again anytime soon. "I don't know what it's like," I tell him. "That's why I'm asking."

We're parked, but the engine is still idling. "I have a duty," he says, looking ahead at the windshield even though the only thing to see is the tinted windshield of the SUV facing us. His voice sounds different—deeper than normal, flatter, almost as if he's directing his words to someone other than me. "I execute the duty."

He shuts off the engine and yanks up the parking break.

The middle-school gym has two basketball courts, which means four teams play simultaneously. With all the kids yelling and the coaches yelling and the parents yelling, it's complete mayhem, and above all that yelling is the sound of sneakers squeaking on the polished wooden floor. And four simultaneous games means a lot of refs blowing whistles, especially when the refs are high-school JV and varsity players who love reminding us how well they know the rules.

Our games aren't long—six-minute quarters. Halfway into the second quarter we're down by ten and pretty confident it's only going to get worse. I'm sitting on the bench, already thinking about our game next week against the 0-7 Bobcats, when I see Ted standing by the water fountain wearing jeans and a hoodie, even though his team is playing right now on the other court. I nod in his direction and he catches my eye and nods back, takes one hand out of the hoodie, and motions for me to go over there.

I can't. I'm on the bench during a game. This should be obvious, so I shrug at him and stay where I am. But at halftime he's still there and motions me over again, so I tell my dad that I need to talk to Ted a second.

"The game's still on," my dad says. "We can't all be—"

"I know, but it's really important." And maybe because Ted is trouble but I'm not, my dad says okay, but to make it quick. Everyone else mills around the bench, drinking paper cups of Gatorade.

The water fountain where Ted is standing hasn't worked in years. One hand is stuffed deep into his pocket, and the fingers of his other hand are flicking the side of the metal fountain.

"You guys are getting killed," he says.

"Very perceptive," I say. "How come you aren't playing?"

"My mom won't let me," he says.

"Why not?"

"Punishment. I'm failing everything."

"But she let you come and watch?"

"She made me tell Mr. Meltzer in person." He shrugs. "Kind of embarrassing, but I guess it's fair. Anyway, I want to ask you a question."

"Okay."

"Do you think you can help me pass my classes?"

"You mean cheat?"

He laughs out loud. "No, you idiot—I mean, will you tutor me?"

"Oh." I'm not the best student, but I'm not even close to the worst. I feel a flash of pride that he's chosen me—even if his mom made him—especially after what I said yesterday. "What subject?"

"Read my lips: *I'm failing everything*. Take your pick." He leans against the water fountain and crosses one sneakered foot casually in front of the other.

Ted is more than half a year older than I am. He's a head taller, has the beginnings of a moustache, and has already had girlfriends and dumped them. I get the sense that he doesn't mind being here, causing other to look at him in his street clothes and wonder.

"We can start with history. That's my best subject." Ever since I was a kid, I seemed to know more about Ronald Reagan and Mikhail Gorbachev than I ever knew about Elmo and Thomas the Train.

"History." He turns the word around in his mouth as if it's a food he's never tasted before. "Yeah, okay."

Over by the bench, my team huddles with my dad, who is tapping his clipboard and revealing the secret to our amazing second-half turnaround.

"Listen," I say to Ted. "I'm sorry about yesterday. I know it must suck having your dad away for so long."

He shakes his head. "Forget it—my dad's an asshole. Trust me, everything's a lot better when he's overseas."

"For real?"

"Of course."

His confession makes me uncomfortable—it's too candid, too honest—and the only thing I can think to do is reveal something in return. "Well, my dad practically cried at dinner last night over bombing a dog."

Ted squints a little. "He did?"

"I mean, there were no actual tears, but—"

"No, I mean the dog. He said he did that?"

"Yeah, but it was an accident."

"I'm talking about his words—he said he killed a dog?"

"Um, that's what I just said."

Ted shakes his head. "Oh, man, that's no good."

"What do you mean?"

He waits a second, then leans in and lowers his voice. "That's *code*, man. Your dad killed a kid." He sucks in his breath, lets it out. "When they kill a kid, they call it a dog."

"Screw off," I tell him.

"I'm sorry, Jeremy, but they do."

"You don't know what the hell you're talking about."

"It's common knowledge on the base."

The base. It's true, you hear things on the base—in the commissary, the laundromat, the exchange—that you don't hear anywhere else. "Why would they call it that?"

The look he gives me makes me feel like he's twice my age. "Think about it, man. You blow the arms and legs off a kid, you'd better start thinking of it as a dog in a hurry."

My dad, in his ironed khakis and button-down white shirt, is still on his haunches, motivating the team. In a couple of minutes the refs will blow their whistles and the second half will start. My dad will call out which five of us will take the floor, not that it matters. He'll give us all equal time. He catches my gaze and flashes a smile so quick and knowing, it seems to say, *Take your time with Ted. He's in trouble and needs your help.* But when I turn back to Ted to say forget it, find another damn tutor, he's already on his way out of the gym.

My vision gets swimmy. My skin feels like it isn't my skin. Two years ago, when we were still living on the base, I caught my mother smoking a cigarette behind the apartment, and it was as if my universe had twisted inside-out. All I was ever told about smoking—at school, at home—was that it killed you, and here she was killing herself. She swore she wasn't a smoker, that it was only occasional, a rare lapse, swore it up and down, but the secret she'd been keeping from me (for years? my whole life?) felt as heavy as a meteor and all I could think was, *You aren't you. You're somebody else.* It took me months to get past it, or maybe I still haven't gotten past it.

But this. Does my father really kill children? Is that his job? Was it even an accident? What if it had been me living in Afghanistan? Would he have bombed me? Would he have done it sadly? Gladly? Would he have lied about it afterward, said I was a dog? I have no idea who my father is and no idea what to do: leave the building and go after Ted? Go someplace else? Go where? I'm trying to figure out what the hell I should be doing right now with these useless hands and this skin that isn't mine when I hear a harsh whistle—not a ref's whistle but the piercing, three-fingered hoot of all coaches. "Jeremy!" my father shouts. "Shake a leg, will you?"

So I shake a leg and let myself be coached into a season-high eight points. Despite the other team's insurmountable lead, I play so hard on both ends of the floor that when the game ends and I throw up in the bathroom, it's possible that it was from giving it my all.

I say as little as possible on the drive home and suffer through a supper of my mother asking for a play-by-play of the game and my dad asking what it was that Ted wanted, then the two of them being so proud of me for agreeing to become Ted's tutor. When I'm finally excused, I go upstairs and cry in my bedroom, a kid into his pillow. I stay there, pretending to rest, pretending to read, then really reading, then playing the DS. Eventually my father comes by my room, as I know he will, and asks how my thumbs are feeling.

I tell him not tonight. I tell him I'm tired.

"You played well today," he says.

"Thanks," I say. "Dad?"

He's standing in the doorway looking worn out, as if he was the one running the court earlier.

"What kind of dog was it?" I ask.

He takes a moment before asking, "Is this a for-real question?"

"Yeah," I say.

He looks at me some more. "It was mid-sized, Jeremy. Brown. Short-haired." It's darker in the hall than in my bedroom, and I can't tell if his eyes are focused on me or above my head, looking at something that isn't there. "Probably some kind of hound, if I had to guess," he says, and I can't help picturing a boy about my size. "Big ears," he says, and that boy's ears are poking out from his head, same as mine do, a boy with a new haircut. He takes a breath. "Well, good-night, son."

Maybe I say good-night; maybe I don't. He walks away, down the hall toward his bedroom, leaving me to picture the animal he described in so much detail that it brings me no comfort, no assurance.

*You're so full of crap*, I say under my breath—to my father, to Ted—way too softly for anyone to hear. But what if they aren't? It would mean that my mother isn't the only translator in the family, that my father takes what he sees on his monitor and turns it into something that he can live with, if not understand. It isn't fair play. It makes all play unfair.

When he shuts the door I pick up the DS and kill time until everyone else goes to sleep. It takes a while. The moment the crack under my parents' door goes dark, Avery starts crying in the nursery, and so my mother gets up and heads off to feed and hold her until she burps.

Then she comes into my room. "Are you still awake?"

I had the covers pulled up over my head so she wouldn't see the light coming from the game. "How'd you know?"

"All the clicking. You have strong thumbs."

It occurs to me that I need to start sleeping with my bedroom door shut. "I just want to win the game. I'm really close." The truth is, I finished it this morning before soccer. I'm just breezing through the early levels again to pass the time.

"You can win tomorrow," she says.

"Can I ask you something?"

"You just did." An automatic response—we do that all the time. But then my mattress shifts as she sits on the edge of my bed, and I ask her if Dad likes being a pilot.

"The truth? We don't talk about it much." She's practically whispering. Even I can tell the difference between not wanting to wake anybody and not wanting anyone to hear.

"I thought you guys tell each other everything."

"Yeah, well. Communicating is what a historian does," she says. "Your father flies planes now."

When she first came into the room, I considered asking her about the dog—what it means or might mean. I wanted answers. I wanted company. I wanted my mother to tell me that there's nothing to panic about. But the way she's talking—it isn't like her. Nothing's like anybody. So I ask if I can keep playing the DS a while longer, so that she'll be able to keep telling herself that my greatest concern is Pokémon.

"Five more minutes." Then she says *buona notte* and kisses the top of my head, which makes me feel like I'm half my age, but then again that's what I was going for, and I retract, turtle-like, back under the covers.

After my mother goes back to bed, I wait until the house has been quiet for some time, and then I sneak downstairs, where I stare at the TV screen and, with the lights off and the volume low, begin to defend my cities. I want to feel whatever it is my father feels, and I imagine that the missiles raining down on me are real ICBMs and MIRVs. The cities I'm defending are real, too: New York, Philadelphia, Chicago. Then I take it further, imagining that each city is actually an entire country: Australia, England, America, etc. Every human soul, and I'm responsible for them all.

Yet the more real I try to make it, the worse my score. So the next game, I remind myself that I'm shooting at slanty lines. That I'm defending blobs of pixels. I'm playing a simple game, a game for kids, created long before an on-screen explosion meant anything more than it was your buddy's turn. And almost at once, my breathing eases, my thumbs and wrists relax. I'm seriously locked in—with the game, with my father—and I stay on the loveseat, postponing THE END late into the night, through another level, and another level, and another.

❋ ❋ ❋

# Poetry

**RICHARD LYONS**

Richard Lyons graduated from the University of Massachusetts Amherst, from the University of Arizona with an M.F.A. in Creative Writing (1979), and from the University of Houston with a Ph.D. in English and Creative Writing (1991). He taught at the University of Maryland, then at Rhodes College. He currently teaches in the English Department at Mississippi State University. His collections of poetry are *These Modern Nights* (U of Missouri P), *Hours of the Cardinal* (U of S. Carolina P), and *Fleur Carnivore* (The Word Works in Washington, D.C.). His work has appeared in *The Nation, Poetry, The New Republic, The Paris Review,* and *The North American Review.* He is a 1988 Devins Award winner for *These Modern Nights,* a recipient of a 1992 Lavan Award from the Academy of American Poets, and a 2005 Washington prizewinner for *Fleur Carnivore.* "Symmetry" was first published in *Hours of the Cardinal* in 2000 (U of S. Carolina P), and "Neither Road Taken" was first published in *Fleur Carnivore* in 2006 (Word Works).

## *Symmetry*

I remember erecting a screened-in porch
for a house I lived in, the staple gun
all afternoon like a giant mosquito

whirring above a sleeper's ear.
One month later, to the day, I found a hummingbird, dead,          5
and I thought *be careful*

as I turned it over with a long yellow pencil.

It was terrifyingly symmetrical, each wing an inch,
its torso, even its needle nose compass an inch.

Its neck an iridescent emerald.          10
Its underside a burnt sandalwood ash
coming off a bit with the pencil.

## *Neither Road Taken*

A bright car pulled up where I was walking,
the driver leaning over. I didn't hear his questions,

my arms gesticulated some configuration of streets.

It was winter & ice hung in the branches like a thousand lost
sewing needles descending through the fabric of the afternoon.                    5

It was spring & everything was imminence.
It was summer & the clouds swiftly passed over our heated element.

I told the man I was born beneath the wooden trestle of a train,
that loud noises captured my attention,

not the lefts & rights of destination.                                            10

Bearing the white needlepoint of a scar at the base of my neck,
I told him the road to the right was covered in hyacinth,

the one to the left dropped down along the aqueduct to hell.
Choose the oldest, I said to him, choose the oldest.

## CATHERINE PIERCE

Catherine Pierce is the author of *Famous Last Words* (Saturnalia, 2008) and *The
Girls of Peculiar* (Saturnalia, 2012). Her poems have appeared in *Slate, Boston
Review, Ploughshares, The Best American Poetry 2011,* and elsewhere. She earned
her B.A. from Susquehanna University, her M.F.A. from the Ohio State University, and her Ph.D. from the University of Missouri. She co-directs the creative
writing program at Mississippi State University. "Love Poem to Fear," "Why You
Love the Annoyances in Your Dreams," "In Which I Imagine Myself Into a
Slasher Flick," and "'Well gentlemen, you are about to see a baked Appel.'" appear in *Famous Last Words,* and "Dear Atom Bomb," "For This You Have No
Reason," and "The Guidance Counselor" appear in *The Girls of Peculiar*. Pierce
has another collection of poetry forthcoming in 2015.

## *Love Poem to Fear*

Around you, my body is a wire
pulled taut, my jaw a bear-trap
waiting. You have such wicked timing—

arriving just before I drop
into sleep, or worse, when                                                        5
the one I'm trying to love

is close enough to see me
waver. Then it's questions
and concern, and I feel only

your fingers on my lips, your teeth           10
against my neck, your smooth-
as-cyanide voice spinning

all your false promises.
Sometimes you vanish
for days. Then, I sleep           15

till morning, wake against
a shadowless body to clear sky,
green grass, perfect eggs

for breakfast. Those days
I almost forget you. But you're           20
no gentleman—no warning

and you're back, all bombast
and mystery. Everything
yours for the taking.


## Why You Love the Annoyances in Your Dreams


You can't get your basketball shoes laced.
When you do, the game is nearly over
and you've just realized you're late

for a Spanish final. When you reach
the classroom, you remember you dropped           5
Spanish three months ago. You rush back

to the game, which is just wrapping up. Then
you're at a conference, but the conference
is in Schenectady and it's March. Also,

the hotel bathroom is covered in cat fur.           10
Gross, you say. You can't find
the number for your friend's room

and when you do he is that kid
from sixth grade who stole your copy
of *The Hobbit* and called you troll boy.                    15

He wears a business suit and is marginally
successful. He busts you about old times
and on your way out you stub your toe.

In dreams, these annoyances are epic.
Your stomach twists; your teeth grind. And          20
you love them for this. Even in sleep, you know

that once you drop like a rock into waking,
everything will shift. In your daytime world,
when your car stalls on I-70, or you miss

the big deadline, or the cat runs out of food          25
during the county's biggest snowstorm
since '94, even as you pound your steering wheel,

even then, you'll know all too well
that these are your life's small highlights.
You're just biding time until the tragedies.          30

Soon, your wife will take the day off,
make the bed with perfect hospital
corners, and vanish for Cabo.

You'll feel a lump in some never-before-
considered spot. Your mother will fall          35
and shatter her hip and your sister

will call you, frantic and frightened, but
you'll be across the country
at a conference in Schenectady, New York,

with no one to shake you awake and say,          40
what a bummer of a night for you, but
it's morning now, wake up, it's morning.


## In Which I Imagine Myself Into a Slasher Flick

The Jennies get it first.
The Trishes. The Ambers.

Never my silhouette through
shower steam. Never my red
mouth in close-up. I've got
straight As and no boyfriend.
I've got Friday nights
and sleeping neighbor children.
But worry. Because I've got
an unadorned name. Sharp
vision by moonlight.
My father's rusted hatchet
and a jetliner scream.

5

10

## *"Well, gentlemen, you are about to see a baked Appel."*

—last words of gangster George Appel, before being put to death by
electric chair

Each time his girl visited, lips pressed
like stained tulips, cheeks pinched
into heat for the man behind the glass,
she left shaking her head, scuffing
her Sunday shoes against the pavement.

5

Why did she believe this time
might be different? That this morning
he might remember her breasts beneath
the winter coat, the nub of her earlobe
in his teeth? All he watched for now

10

was the expression of her mouth.
*What about this*, he'd say. *What's cooking?*
Or *How about you fry up something good?*
Then he'd grin and say *I'm on fire!*
*Electric, even.* At first, the girl wept,

15

chewed her nails—he was hysterical,
surely raped and maddened in that cell.
But each imagined rimshot carried her
further from her wedding,
her sand-white dress, solid hands

20

around her waist. She tried,
she told her mother. She brought
caramels, pinups, photographs of herself
naked, and he would say *I got a good one*
*today. What do you call a fruit in a chair?*                           25

*What do you get when you cross . . .*
She threatened to stop coming. But
each time he would beg, his face drooping
like a wet stocking. When the day came,
the girl was there, eyes swollen, hands nervous.                        30

She heard the words, then silence broken
only by his choked laugh, the laugh
broken by the current. In bed that night
she would not tell him how the orderlies
wheeled the gurney in. How,                                              35

when they strapped him on, no one
made a sound. She would tell him instead
about the guards doubling over, the priest bowing
into his grin. The whole gray room vibrating
with the aftershock of his wit.                                         40

## Dear Atom Bomb

I confess—you were my high school obsession.
You bloomed inside my chest until I howled. You shook me
with your booming zillion wattage. You were bigger
than rock and roll. I lost days to you, the way you expanded

to become more than even yourself. In Science class                     5
movies, you puffed men like microwaved marshmallows,
raked blood from their insides, and always I could feel
your heat like a massive cloak around my shoulders.

You embarrassed me. You were too depraved for dignity,
not caring whose eyes you melted, whose innards oozed;                   10
you balled up control in your God-huge palms
and tossed it into the stratosphere. Oh, Atom Bomb,

I miss you. These days my mind is no incandescent
blur but a narrow infrared beam spotlighting
bounded fears: cancer in a single throat; a shock                       15
of blood on the clean sheets; a careless turn from

the grocery store lot into the pickup with the pit bull
in the bed. Oh, Atom Bomb, come back. Take me away
from the twitch in my leg, the cracking lead paint,
the lurking salmonella. Sweep me up in your blinding          20

white certainty. Make me sure once again that
I'll live till the world's brilliant end.


## For This You Have No Reason


In Sacramento, a Virgin Mary has begun spilling
blood from its stone eyes. Articles offer theories:

a prank, a rusting mineral. *There is no explanation*,
I say over and over, my heart tensed like a fist. Once,

at Chez la Mer, I watched a magician turn silver coins          5
into yellow fin tuna while diners oohed. When the room

shuddered with calls for the big reveal, I ducked
outside, humming to cover the sound of the secret.

Here are facts: the dog gone for a decade makes
its way to Arizona and finds its family still pining,          10

now joy-struck. The wooden Christ in St. Stephen's
Cathedral grows hair, and is groomed every year

before Easter. A friend's father saw three UFOs
zoom into a lit triangle, then shoot to far

corners of the lake-dark sky. He was not a man          15
who lied. For years I found playing cards facedown

on sidewalks, and each was the jack of hearts—
absurd, but I swear this is true. *Here*, each face said,

*for this you have no reason*. Each new finding shores up
something always close to collapse inside my ribs.          20

Let these strangenesses be like the impossible lizard's
tail: gone forever, because how could it be otherwise,

and then reappearing, iridescent and blood-warmed,
because how could it be otherwise?

## *The Guidance Counselor to the Girl*

The test suggests an aptitude for solitary work.
Have you considered a career as a computer

programmer? Flower arranger? Planetarium
operator? No? What about zebrawood cultivation?

Minor-league mascotry? Those heads muffle        5
all voices, even your own. Column A indicates

a proclivity for nature. You may have more luck
as a bobcat than a sea turtle, a muskrat than a bobcat.

What do you mean, why? We just discussed
your inclination toward solitude! Here's the list        10

of promising careers. Muskrat we'll cross out.
Blue spruce on a half-acre? Nest-fleeing cardinal?

Maybe? Let's mark it. Throw-pillow by the fire?
Asphalt-dinged Route 40 road sign? Lost gold

stud in the sand? Anything? We'll keep going.        15
Abandoned Chevy in near-mint condition? One stone

in the Grand Canyon at sunset? No, I agree, too much
responsibility. How about this—the iron clapper

in a wind chime. Well, I don't know, my dear—
I imagine you'd have to create the wind yourself.        20

# BIOGRAPHIES

## SHERMAN ALEXIE (b. 1966)

Sherman Alexie was born on the Spokane Indian Reservation in the state of Washington. Learning to read by the age of three, Alexie excelled at the BIA (Bureau of Indian Affairs) reservation school, but decided to attend Reardon High School, 32 miles from the reservation because he thought he would receive a stronger education there. Alexie, "[t]he only Indian . . . except for the school mascot" (shermanalexie.com), graduated with honors. After receiving his B.A. in American Studies, Alexie was granted a National Endowment for the Arts Poetry Fellowship in 1992. Whether in poetry, prose or drama, Alexie has sought to bring the realities of modern reservation life to the public. His work is laden with dark humor—a humor full of irony that is both critical of the dominant culture and hopeful of a better future for all Native Americans. Alexie has also gained notoriety as a slam poet and screenplay writer. His writings include the poetry collections *The Business of Fancydancing* (1991), *I Would Steal Horses* (1993), and *The Man Who Loves Salmon* (1998); the short story collection *The Lone Ranger and Tonto Fistfight in Heaven* (1993); the novels *Reservation Blues* (1995) and *Indian Killer* (1996); and the screenplays *Smoke Signals* (1998) and *The Business of Fancydancing* (2003). His latest work is the collection of short stories *Ten Little Indians* (2003). "Jesus Christ's Half-Brother Is Alive and Well on the Spokane Indian Reservation" appears in *The Lone Ranger and Tonto Fistfight in Heaven*.

## JULIA ALVAREZ (b. 1950)

Julia Alvarez was born in the United States but lived in the Dominican Republic until she was ten years old. Her father was a member of the resistance movement against the Dominican dictator, Trujillo, and her family fled the country for New York City in 1960. Thrust into an unfamiliar culture, Alvarez retreated from her classmates' unfriendliness through writing literature. She focuses on the struggles and intersections of Latino and American cultures from her own experiences as a Latina and from her research into recent Dominican history and culture. After receiving her B.A. from Middlebury College and M.A. in creative writing from Syracuse University, she taught creative writing at Middlebury for ten years. She now holds a writer-in-residence post there. An author of novels, essays, short stories, and poetry, her most famous works are *In the Time of the Butterflies*, which tells the story of the founders of the Dominican resistance movement, and *How the Garcia Girls Lost Their Accents*, which explores the difficulty of straddling two cultures when a Latino family relocates to the United States. "How I Learned to Sweep" is a poem that reflects on domestic impressions of war and how much it affects the lives of those who only hear about it.

## MARGARET ATWOOD (b. 1939)

Margaret Atwood was born in Ottawa, Canada, and spent her early childhood in the rugged wilderness of northern Quebec until her family moved to Toronto in 1946. While attending the University of Toronto, Atwood took classes with the literary critic and scholar Northrop Frye and was introduced to the thought of Carl Jung and archetypal theory—ideas that would later have an impact on her writing. In 1962, she obtained her M.A. from Radcliffe College and continued on to do Ph.D. work at Harvard. The political ferment of the 1960s, and especially the rise of feminism (and her own active role in the movement), set the backdrop for her early poetry and fiction. In 1969, she published her first novel, *The Edible Woman*—a book that explores representations of women and female identity in a patriarchal society—themes that surface again and again in Atwood's work. While feminist concerns are at the base of Atwood's writing, it is her literary technique and experimentation that force readers to reassess the social implications of power. Through satire and the use of dystopian settings, Atwood "creates unease" in the reader, thus (ideally) instigating awareness. Selected works include the poetry collections *Double Persephone* (1961), *Power Politics* (1973), *True Stories* (1981), and *The Journals of Susanna Moodie* (1997); the short story collections *Wilderness Tips* (1991), *Good Bones and Simple Murders* (1992); and the novels *Surfacing* (1972), *The Handmaid's Tale* (1985), *The Robber Bride* (1993), *Alias Grace* (1996), *The Blind Assassin* (2000), and *Oryx and Crack* (2003). In her poem "At first I was given centuries," Atwood moves through a history seen by women who, for centuries, have endured the loss of their lovers to war.

## JAMES BALDWIN (1924–1987)

Son of a Harlem preacher, Baldwin himself began preaching at age 14; this experience and his early religious training would have an enduring effect on his writing style. Throughout the 1950s and 1960s, Baldwin was a voice for civil rights, speaking and writing in protest of racial hatred. In both his essays and novels, he seeks to understand the social and psychological effects of racism and the role of love in combating such forces. He is perhaps best known for his nonfiction essays, collected in *Notes of a Native Son* (1955), *Nobody Knows My Name* (1961), and *The Fire Next Time* (1963), and for his fiction *Go Tell It On The Mountain* (1953), a coming-of-age story about a young black man in Harlem; *Giovanni's* Room (1956), a novel about gay life in Paris; and *Going to Meet the Man* (1965), a collection of short stories. He has also won acclaim as a dramatist, with *The Amen Corner* (1955) and *Blues for Mister Charlie* (1964). "Sonny's Blues," published in 1957, is demonstrative of the emotional, lyrical prose found in much of Baldwin's work.

## TONI CADE BAMBARA (1939–1995)

Toni Cade Bambara was born in New York City. In 1959, she obtained her B.A. in Theater Arts at Queens College and her M.A. from City College of the City University of New York in 1964. During this time, and throughout the 1960s,

Bambara worked persistently as a social activist in Harlem and Brooklyn and published a few short stories in magazines. Her experiences as a "cultural worker" (a phrase she often used) inevitably found their way into her stories—stories with radical plots, lively street dialogue, and resilient characters: "I work to celebrate, to applaud the tradition of struggle in our community, to bring together all those characters, just ordinary folks on the block who've been waiting in the wings, characters we thought we had to ignore because they weren't pimp-flashy or hustler-slick . . ." (*Notable Black American Women*, 2002). The publication of *The Black Woman: An Anthology* (1970), edited by Bambara, was one of the first anthologies specifically about the black female experience. In 1972, with Toni Morrison as her editor, Bambara published her first collection of short stories, *Gorilla My Love*. In addition to her writing, Bambara was also active in the theater and wrote several screenplays. Her other works include *Tales and Stories for Black Folks* (1971, editor and contributor); the short story collection *The Sea Birds Are Still Alive* (1977); and the novels *The Salt Eaters* (1980), *If Blessing Comes* (1987), and *These Bones Are Not My Child* (1999). "The Lesson" first appeared in *Gorilla My Love*.

## DONALD BARTHELME (1931–1989)

Donald Barthelme was born in Philadelphia but grew up in Houston, Texas. As a college student at the University of Houston, Barthelme was active as an editor and reporter for the school newspaper. After serving in the army for a couple of years, Barthelme returned to Houston and began writing in a variety of contexts, as well as taking a job as the director of the Contemporary Arts Museum. In 1962, he moved to New York and began writing short stories for *The New Yorker* magazine. His work was instantly recognized for its radical, unconventional uses of language—intentional misspellings, ambiguous meanings, and unusual form. Indeed, one of Barthelme's goals was to draw attention to the complexities of language while at the same maintaining the semblance of a narrative structure that supported his satirical critique of modern life. Yet his work tends to defy easy categorization into one set genre. Like Franz Kafka, Barthelme works in the world of the absurd and bizarre. Selected works include the short story collections *Unspeakable Practices, Unnatural Acts* (1968), *City Life* (1970), *Sadness* (1972), *Guilty Pleasures* (1974), and *Sixty Stories* (1981); and the novels *Snow White* (1967), *The Dead Father* (1975), *Paradise* (1986), and *The King* (1990, published posthumously). "Report" was first published in *Unspeakable Practices, Unnatural Acts*.

## AMBROSE BIERCE (1842– circa1914)

Born in rural Meigs County, Ohio, Ambrose Bierce grew up working on the family farm. Despite not having any formal education, his father's library exposed him to a wide range of books. At 19, he joined the Union Army at the beginning of the Civil War and served four years. The experience of war would make a deep imprint on his view of the world. When the war ended, Bierce went to San Francisco and began to forge his reputation as "The Wickedest Man in San Francisco"—a title earned for his scathing and often misanthropic satires of people and human nature. His fiction carries a similar tone, cynical and full of dark humor. Following in the American gothic tradition of Edgar Allen Poe, Bierce's stories hover between reality and the supernatural where characters are faced with morbid twists of fate, vengeful ghosts, and irrationality. In 1913 he went to Mexico to cover the Mexican Civil War and disappeared; his death remains a mystery. Selected works include *Tales of Soldiers and Civilians* (1891), *Can Such Things Be?* (1893), *Fantastic Fables* (1899), and *The Cynic's Word Book* (1906), later retitled *The Devils Dictionary* (1911). "An Occurrence at Owl Creek Bridge," first published in *Tales of Soldiers and Civilians*, is one of Bierce's most famous stories.

## ELIZABETH BISHOP (1911–1979)

Elizabeth Bishop was born in Worcester, Massachusetts. Her father died while she was still an infant, and, when Elizabeth was five, her mother was hospitalized for mental illness, leaving her to be raised by her grandparents and other relatives. She studied at Vassar College (1930–1934), where she developed a friendship with poet Marianne Moore, who encouraged her to pursue poetry instead of medicine. The two became life-long friends. After graduating, Bishop led a transient, traveling life, living in New York City, France, and Key West, and eventually settled in Brazil, though she spent her last few years in Boston. Her experiences traveling and living as an exile would become central themes in her poetry. During her life, Bishop composed only 101 poems. Despite this relatively small number, her work was recognized by her contemporaries (like her good friend Robert Lowell) as some of the most evocative, crafted verse in American poetry, and in 1956 she was awarded the Pulitzer Prize for her collection *North and South—A Cold Spring*. Known for her astute observation and subtle irony, Bishop's poetry often details human relationships and human interaction with the natural world in a language noted for its rhythm and meter. Other poetry collections include *Questions of Travel* (1965), *The Complete Poems* (1969), and *Geography III* (1976). "One Art," published in *Geography III*, is written in the form of a villanelle, composed of five tercets and a final quatrain.

## WILLIAM BLAKE (1757–1827)

William Blake was born in London to a middle class family, but his bent toward seeing the world in terms of visions quickly appeared. Blake saw more than the dirty world of a big city; rather he saw angels and other spiritual beings as he walked through life. He considered the world he lived in to be corrupted by its lack of imagination, and he set about creating his own Golden Age of art and poetry. Showing great artistic talent early in life, by age ten he began drawing in school and later became an engraver and design artist. He did not earn great sums as an artist because his work was strange in an era that loved landscapes and careful representations of classic events such as Bible stories and historic battles. Blake's art illustrated more that could not be seen than that which could be seen.

He married his wife, Catherine, in 1782. She was devoted to him though the story goes that she nearly fainted when she first saw him due to his fiery eyes and passionate presence. From that early era came his first collection of poetry, *Poetical Sketches* (1783). When his younger brother Robert died, Blake's sense of connection to the spiritual world was strengthened. He wrote the *Songs of Experience* (1789) during this time of elation and spiritual growth, and these poems express his sense of the heavenly and spiritual. This bliss, however, was short-lived as Blake first followed and then rejected the Swedish theologian, Emanuel Swendenborg. Blake rejected Swendenborg's ideas about predestination, and wrote *The Marriage of Heaven and Hell* (1790–1793) as an attack on any such doctrine.

Blake then became connected with the champions of the French Revolution, including William Godwin, Tom Paine, and the Romantic poets, William Wordsworth, Samuel Coleridge, Robert Southey, and William Hazlitt. His protest against those who interfere with the rights of their fellow humans expressed itself in the most famous of his collections, *Songs of Experience* (1798–1794), and in *The French Revolution, America*, and the *Visions of the Daughters of Albion*. The last poem attacks marriage, which Blake disapproved of while he continued to be a faithful and devoted husband. The *Book of Thel* (1783) followed, a tale of a soul that refuses to be born into this wicked world. His mythology was elaborated and illustrated in *The Book* of *Urizen, The Song of Los, The Book of Ahania*, and *The Book of Los*.

From 1800 to 1803, the Blakes lived in a small town called Felpham, supported by a patron and poet friend named William Hayley, but Blake and Hayley differed in the nature of the poetry the two wrote, Hayley's being simple and sentimental, Blake's being mystical and complex. While at Felpham, Blake finished *The Four Zoas* and *Milton*; upon returning to London, he wrote the third of his "prophetic" works, *Jerusalem*. After that he spent many years in poverty, even painting dishes for Wedgwood, but was finally rediscovered in 1818 by a younger generation of painters, John Linnell, Samuel Palmer, John Varley, and George Richmond. He began to illustrate Dante and the book of Job, but these remained unfinished at the time of his death in 1827.

## RAY BRADBURY (1920–2012)

Born in Waukegan, Illinois, Ray Bradbury grew up reading the "pulp" fiction of his era and began writing at an early age. During high school, his family moved to Los Angeles, where he further worked on his writing, publishing his first story in 1938 at the age of 18. He would begin his reputation as an author writing science fiction and fantasy stories for the same pulp magazines he read growing up. The publication of *The Martian Chronicles* in 1950 brought him new literary fame. While he is usually thought of as a science fiction writer, Bradbury's work cannot be classified into one genre. Often allegorical in nature, much of Bradbury's work serves as a warning to humanity about the ills and moral deprivations that may come from technological advance. He has published novels, essays, poetry, screenplays, and plays, including the novels *Fahrenheit 451* (1953, which was made into a film), *Dandelion Wine* (1957), and *Something Wicked This Way Comes* (1962); and the story collections *The Illustrated Man* (1951) and *I Sing The Body Electric* (1969). His most recent work is *One For the Road: A New Story Collection* (2002). "August 2026: There Will Come Soft Rains" is a story from *The Martian Chronicles*.

## GWENDOLYN BROOKS (1917–2000)

Gwendolyn Brooks grew up in Chicago. She began writing poetry at an early age, publishing her first poem at age thirteen. After receiving her BA in English from Wilson Junior College in 1936, Brooks worked for the NAACP Youth Council. During this time, Brooks was greatly influenced by poet Langston Hughes and other writers from the Harlem Renaissance who encouraged her to study the modernist poetry of Eliot and Pound. As is evident in much of her early work, Brooks combines the technical skill and form of modernist poetry with the imagery and rhythms of African American life and language. In 1950, she became the first African American to win the Pulitzer Prize for her poetry collection *Annie Allen* (1950). In 1967, Brook's visit to Fisk University was a transformative moment for her as a poet and African American. Impressed by the energy of young black poets like Leroi Jones, Brooks' penchant for formal structures (she was a master of the sonnet) and themes loosened. While her devotion to the African American experience remained, her poetry increasingly became more political, more contentious, as she became aware of her role as a black feminist in the Civil Rights Movement. In 1985, she was appointed poetry consultant to the Library of Congress (Poet Laureate). She has written several poetry collections, including *A Street in Bronzeville* (1945), *Annie Allen* (1950), *The Bean Eaters* (1960), *In the Mecca* (1968), *Beckonings* (1975), *Black Love* (1982), and *In Montgomery* (2001, posthumously); the novel *Maud Martha* (1953); and the autobiography *Report from Part One* (1972). "Bronzeville Woman in a Red Hat" appeared in Brooks's collection *The Bean Eaters*.

## OLGA BROUMAS (b. 1949)

Olga Broumas was born in Greece and moved to the United States at age ten. She obtained her B.A. in architecture from the University of Pennsylvania and her M.F.A. at the University of Oregon, where she helped found the women's studies program. Although English is Broumas's second language, her poetic skill won her the Yale Younger Poets Award in 1977 for *Beginning with O—* a mixed collection of poems on female relationships and love, erotic desire, and myth. While many of these themes surface again and again in her poetry, what makes them uniquely Broumas's is the compact syntax and rhythmic quality of her verse. Other poetry collections include *Soie Sauvage* (1980), *Pastoral Jazz*

(1983), *Perpetua* (1989), and *All of the Above* (1991); four works with classical scholar T. Begley (including *Sappho's Gymnasium*, [1994] and *Rave: Poems, 1975–1999* [1999]). She has also translated the work of Greek poet Odysseus Elytis. Broumas's propensity for feminist revision of myth appears in the poem "Cinderella," first published in *Beginning with O*.

## ROBERT BROWNING (1812–1889)

Robert Browning was born to a wealthy banker whose library became the playground for the eager young scholar. Browning's schooling consisted of a few years at Peckham and some lectures at London University in 1830. Otherwise he was educated by private tutors and by himself, reading his father's vast collection of books. His father had his son's first small volume of verses privately printed as *Incondita*, while Browning was still a child. Browning's first real publication was *Pauline* in 1833. Shortly after the publication of this poem, he left on the first of his many travels to Europe. While in Italy, he wrote *Paracelsus*, a poem about a sorcerer's experiences and motivations. This poem was published in 1835. His next two works did not enhance his reputation, a play called *Strafford* that closed after five nights and a dense poem *Sordello* (1840) that was so learned and complex that it gave Browning the reputation of being unintelligible to the reading public. In 1846 he met, fell in love with, and married the much more successful poet Elizabeth Barrett. They moved to Florence and had one son. They lived in Florence until her death in 1861. There he wrote *Christmas Eve and Easter Day* (1850) and *Men and Women* (1855). Browning had begun the writing that would build the reputation which he now holds. He was not much appreciated by the Victorians, who admired sentiment and feeling, while his poetry took a tactile view of the human psyche, often letting his speakers reveal damaging information about themselves while apparently boasting or reporting events. He is considered one of the great psychological poets.

After Barrett Browning's death, he moved to London where he withdrew for a short time but then began to travel and give presentations widely. He published *Dramatis Personae* (1864) and *The Ring and the Book* four years later. The latter is one of the longest and most complex poems in English. It deals with a trial for a murder of a young woman, but the real content of the poem includes dramatic monologues of everyone involved in the crime. Each speaker has seen and experienced something different, making the poem a testimony to modern psychological research into the unreliability of eyewitnesses. The poem never resolves the truth of the murder, for there is not truth, only the many perspectives of those involved, truly a postmodern perspective on reality. After completing this poem Browning began to write mysterious and grotesque poems and also began to translate Greek tragedies, but none of these was successful. At the end of his life he moved to Venice to live, dying at his son's palazzo. He is buried in poet's corner in Westminster Abbey. He remains one of the brilliant thinkers and philosophers of his era, as well as a great poet.

## RAYMOND CARVER (1938–1988)

Raymond Carver grew up in a working class family in Yakima, Washington. At nineteen, he married Maryann Burk and by age twenty was the father of two. Struggling to support a family of four, he worked in a sawmill and at various part time jobs while attending Yakima Community College. With a growing interest in writing, Carver moved his family to Paradise, California, so he could attend Chico State College where he took creative writing classes taught by an early mentor, novelist John Gardner. In 1963, he earned a bachelor's degree and left California for the Iowa Writers Workshop. In 1976, Carver's first short story collection *Will You Please Be Quiet, Please?* was published, followed in 1981 by *What We Talk about When We Talk about Love* and *Where I'm Calling From* in 1988. He received much acclaim for his fiction, including a National Endowment for the Arts award and a Guggenheim fellowship.

## KATE CHOPIN (1851–1904)

Katherine O'Flaherty was born in St. Louis to an Irish immigrant father and a French Creole mother, experiencing a childhood of wealth and privilege. During her early years, she was influenced heavily by a number of strong women; after her father's death in 1855, Chopin was reared by her mother, grandmother, and great-grandmother. Although her upbringing was conventional according to genteel Southern standards, she exhibited an independent spirit at an early age. At nineteen, she wed a Louisiana businessman, Oscar Chopin, to whom she was happily married for twelve years before his untimely death. A young widow with six children, Chopin returned to St. Louis and began writing. Her first stories were published in 1889, followed by a novel, *At Fault*, in 1890. Chopin gained national attention with the 1894 publication of *Bayou Folk*, a collection of stories that featured settings and characters culled from her years in Louisiana among French Creoles. In 1897, a second collection, *A Night in Acadie*, was widely acclaimed; however, readers and critics turned against Chopin in 1899 when her novel *The Awakening* was published. Exploring the sexual and social rebellion of protagonist Edna Pontellier, a young wife and mother, the novel challenged existing moral standards and shocked the public. Chopin was accused of fostering immoral behavior with her uncritical depiction of Edna, who chooses suicide rather than succumb to the rigid requirements of marriage and motherhood. Reception of the novel was so harsh that Chopin's publisher cancelled publication of her next volume of short stories, *A Voice and a Vocation*, in 1899.

## BRUCE COHEN

Bruce Cohen was born in the Bronx, New York. His poems and non-fiction essays have appeared in over one hundred literary periodicals, such as *AGNI, The Georgia Review, The Harvard Review, Ploughshares, Poetry, Prairie Schooner & The Southern Review*, and have been featured on *Poetry Daily & Verse Daily*. He has published two acclaimed volumes of poetry: *Disloyal Yo-Yo* (Dream Horse

Press), which was awarded the 2007 Orphic Poetry Prize, and *Swerve* (Black Lawrence Press). *Placebo Junkies Conspiring with the Half-Asleep* (Black Lawrence Press) was published in 2012, and his new book *No Soap, Radio!* is scheduled to appear in 2015. He was recently awarded the Green Rose Prize for *Imminent Disappearances, Impossible Numbers & Panoramic X-Rays*, which will be published in 2016. He earned both a B.A. and M.F.A from the University of Arizona. The recipient of an individual artist grant from the Connecticut Commission on Culture & Tourism, Cohen directed, developed, and implemented nationally recognized academic enhancement programs at the University of Arizona, the University of California at Berkeley, and the University of Connecticut. He joined the creative writing faculty at the University of Connecticut in 2012 and lives in Coventry, Connecticut, with his wife and three sons.

## EMILY DICKINSON (1830–1886)

Emily Dickinson was born in Amherst, Massachusetts, in 1830. Raised in an intellectual and religious environment, Dickinson's exposure to both literature and Calvinism would play central roles in her poetry. While the common assumption has been that Dickinson made few attempts to publish her poetry in her lifetime, it is clear now, by evidence of the hundreds of letters she wrote, that she made an earnest effort to be recognized, submitting poetry quite often throughout the 1850s and 1860s. It was after these decades of rejection that Dickinson assumed the reclusive lifestyle she is now famous for. At the time of her death in 1886, Dickinson had written over 1500 poems, the majority of them found bundled in her dresser drawer. Due to her sister Lavinia's dedication and work, Dickinson's first volume of poems (titled *Poems*) was published in 1890. Even at this time, publishers were reluctant to publish Dickinson's verse, claiming it was unorthodox and amateur, but the public thought differently. *Poems* was an instant success and went through 16 editions in the next eight years. As is the case with many artists, Dickinson was an innovator ahead of her time. Her radical verse, eschewing traditional forms and meter, experimented with what was later called "slant" and internal rhymes—rhymes that did not necessarily fall at the end of a line, but were often embedded within lines. Moreover, her uneven line breaks, abrupt dashes, and terse, lyrical metaphors were techniques that would not be accepted as valid poetic forms until the Imagist Movement of the early twentieth-century. Dickinson was a constant revisionist, reworking and polishing her poems and their meanings. Thus, when you read a Dickinson poem, you are presented with rich allegories, irony, and symbolism packed tightly in precise language. The 770-page *The Complete Poems of Emily Dickinson*, edited by Thomas Johnson, was published in 1970.

## JOHN DONNE (1572–1631)

John Donne was born in London into a prominent Roman Catholic family. Because of his religion, he was prevented from taking a degree at Oxford; he became an Anglican convert soon after. He participated in naval expeditions and upon return to England studied law and was appointed secretary to Sir Thomas Egerton, but his secret marriage to Egerton's niece cost him his position and led to brief imprisonment. Donne struggled to earn a living for a number of years, but eventually found a patron to support his writing. In 1615, he was ordained an Anglican priest and his sermons became immensely popular. Only after his death did he gain a reputation as the leading "metaphysical" poet. His *Poems* were published by his son in 1633.

## PAUL LAURENCE DUNBAR (1872–1906)

The son of former slaves, Paul Laurence Dunbar became one of the first African-American writers to achieve national prominence. As a high school student in Dayton, Ohio, Dunbar saw several of his poems published in the *Dayton Herald*; pervasive race discrimination, however, prevented him from obtaining a job in journalism after graduation, despite having been voted as class poet and president of his graduating class. His first collection of poems, *Oak and Ivy*, appeared in 1893 when Dunbar was only twenty-one years old. Working as an elevator operator at the time, Dunbar enlisted the help of friends Wilbur and Orville Wright to publish the volume privately. His reputation was enhanced by the recognition of prominent orator Frederick Douglass, who hired Dunbar to work in the Haitian Pavilion at the World Columbian Exposition in Chicago in 1893. In 1896, Dunbar's second collection, *Majors and Minors*, was published; his first two collections were later published as a single volume titled *Lyrics of Lowly Life*. In 1898, after a reading tour of England, Dunbar married fellow African-American poet Alice Ruth Moore and published another collection, *Lyrics from the Hearthside*. By this time, however, his health was failing badly. He had suffered from tuberculosis for some time, and in the ensuing years, he fought several bouts of pneumonia and other related illnesses. Dunbar's illness placed a strain on the marriage, and in 1902, he and his wife separated. He continued writing, publishing a highly acclaimed volume of poetry, *Lyrics of Love and Laughter*, the following year. This collection, appearing after several poorly reviewed novels, revived the poet's reputation, but not his health. An increasing dependence on alcohol exacerbated his condition, and Dunbar died in 1906 at the age of thirty-three.

## T. S. ELIOT (1888–1965)

Thomas Stearns Eliot was born in St. Louis into a well-to-do family with roots in New England. At a young age, Eliot was encouraged to write poetry by his mother. He received both his B.A. and M.A. at Harvard and spent time studying at Oxford and at the Sorbonne in Paris. Eliot is considered a key figure in modernist poetry and criticism. His major work, *The Waste Land* (1922), is considered one of the most important poems of the twentieth century, influencing and influenced by both the symbolist and imagist schools of poetry that sought to create layers of meaning through simplified language and concrete images. Eliot's other major volumes of poetry are *Prufrock and Other Observations* (1917) and *Four Quartets* (1943). Eliot's early, influential critical essays are collected in *The Sacred Wood* (1920), and he wrote several verse plays, including *Murder in the Cathedral* (1935) and *The Cocktail Party* (1949). He received the Nobel Prize for literature in 1948. "The Love Song of J. Alfred Prufrock" is an example of Eliot's early style and the beginnings of modernist poetry.

## LOUISE ERDRICH  (b. 1954)

Louise Erdrich grew up in Wahpeton, North Dakota. Her father, a German immigrant, and her mother, an Ojibwa Indian, passed down to her a rich tradition of story telling. She would eventually obtain her B.A. at Dartmouth and her M.A. in writing from John Hopkins. In 1981, she married another writer, Mike Dorris. During the next decade, the two collaborated on several publications, working together and providing feedback for each other. For a short time they published under their pen name "Milou North." When her poem "Indian Boarding School" won the 1983 Pushcart Prize, the public began to notice her work—both poetry and prose. Although she has written more prose in her career, her two volumes of poetry, *Jacklight* (1984) and *Baptism of Desire* (1989), have been highly acclaimed. In these two volumes, Erdrich uses her imaginative story-telling abilities to write multifaceted poetry—wandering deftly through themes of family, love, history, Native American mythologizing, and the tension between Ojibwa reservation life and white America. These same story-telling techniques can be found in her prose. Among her novels are *The Beet Queen* (1986), *Tracks* (1988), *A Link With the River* (1989), *The Crown of Columbus* (1991), *The Antelope Wife* (1998), and her latest work *Four Souls* (2004). "The Red Convertible" is one of fourteen stories that comprise her first novel, *Love Medicine* (1984).

## WILLIAM FAULKNER  (1897–1962)

William Faulkner grew up in Oxford, Mississippi. His ancestors included a great-grandfather who was a famous Civil War colonel and popular novelist. Little interested in high school, Faulkner dropped out and, because he was too short for the U.S. Army, enlisted in the Canadian Royal Air Force. He studied briefly at the University of Mississippi, held odd jobs in New York City, and in 1924 published a volume of poetry. He then turned to fiction and published the novel *Soldier's Pay* in 1926. *Sartoris* (1929) was the first of his many novels set in the fictional Yoknapatawpha County in Mississippi and *The Sound and the Fury* (1929) and *As I Lay Dying* (1930) followed soon after. One distinguishing aspect of much of Faulkner's work is his use of the literary device called "stream of consciousness," where the author attempts to describe the continuous flow of thought as it passes through a character's mind. Among Faulkner's major novels are *Sanctuary* (1931), *Light in August* (1932), *Absalom, Absalom!* (1936), and the three novels that comprise the Snopes Trilogy: *The Hamlet* (1940), *The Town* (1957), and *The Mansion* (1959). He received the Nobel Prize for literature in 1950.

## ROBERT FRANCIS (1901–1987)

Robert Francis was born in Upland, Pennsylvania, and attended Harvard University. After graduating in 1923, he moved into a small house in Amherst, Massachusetts, that he named "Fort Juniper," later inspiring editors at the University of Massachusetts Press to name their poetry award the Juniper Prize. One of his poetic mentors was Robert Frost; indeed, Francis's first volume of poems, *Stand with Me Here* (1936), displays a poetic voice that is reminiscent of Frost's nature poems. Although Francis published very little during the 1940s–1950s, his reputation as a poet was revived in 1960 with the publication of *The Orb Weaver*; his autobiography, *The Trouble with Francis*, was published in 1971 and details his struggle with neglect. He was sixty-seven when *Satirical Rogue* was published in 1968. He lived another nineteen years, long enough to see his collected poems in print and to produce a final slender volume, *Late Fire, Late Snow*. Francis served as Phi Beta Kappa poet at both Tufts and Harvard. A world traveler, he often journeyed to Europe, at one time teaching at the American University in Beirut, Lebanon. Francis's poems are widely varied in form and subject, though a kind tone permeates much of his work. His first collection of poetry, *Stand with Me Here* (1936), was followed by nine other volumes, including *The Orb Weaver* (Wesleyan University Press). His complete poetic texts can be found in *Collected Poems: 1936-1976* (1976). Prolific in many genres, Francis also produced a novel, *We Fly Away* (1948), and essays. In 1939, Francis won the Shelley Memorial Award, in 1957, he received the Rome Prize of the American Academy of Arts and Letters, and in 1984, he received the award for distinguished poetic achievement from the Academy of American Poets. Francis died July 13, 1987.

## MARY E. WILKINS FREEMAN (1852–1930)

Mary Eleanor Wilkins was born and lived much of her life in Randolph, Massachusetts. After high school, she spent a year at Mount Holyoke Female Seminary and soon began earning a living writing. She married Dr. Charles Freeman in 1902, when she was almost fifty, and moved with him to New Jersey, but their marriage fell apart due to his growing alcoholism. Freeman was widely read during her lifetime, but her work fell into obscurity after her death. Although she wrote children's books, poetry, novels, and plays, it is her short fiction that brought a revaluation of her work in the 1980s. Working within a realist mode, Freeman was a protofeminist voice from the nineteenth century—questioning the sentimental fiction of her day as well as the limited roles available to women. Her most well-known story collections are *A Humble Romance* (1887) and *A New England Nun* (1891). "A Mistaken Charity" looks at the struggle of two aging women and their desire to be independent.

## ROBERT FROST (1874–1963)

The son of a journalist who died when Robert Frost was only eleven, the now well-known poet lived with his mother in Lawrence, Massachusetts, where he worked at many jobs while finishing high school, where he was co-valedictorian of his class. While in school, he wrote for the *Lawrence High School Bulletin*. He married his co-valedictorian, Elinor White, and began his college career. Frost attended Dartmouth and Harvard, but dropped out of both shortly before the deaths of his three-year-old son and his mother. In search of financial stability, Frost bought a farm in Derry, New Hampshire, where he and Elinor had four more children while he wrote poetry and taught at the Pinkerton Academy. His first book, *A Boy's Will* appeared in 1913. Frost then sold the farm and moved his family to London where he met Ezra Pound who viewed Frost as a follower and composer of "Imagist" poems—poems of vivid pictoral language and minimal sentiment. However, Frost developed his own theory of the sound of poetry, that is, catching the word as it is heard and spoken. His *North of Boston* (1914) poems characterize his particular view of the purpose and practice of poetry. These poems use dramatic monologues to capture the realities of human life and words.

Frost returned to the United States in 1915 and bought another farm in New Hampshire, but this time he was not dependent on farm income and minimal teaching. While in Europe, Frost had become friends with powerful editors and publishers, including Ellery Sedgwick, editor of the *Atlantic Monthly*, and Henry Holt of the *New Republic*. He also became friends with the powerful poet and critic Louis Untermeyer. Frost taught at Amherst College and published his third book, *Mountain Interval* (1916). His fourth book, *New Hampshire*, won the Pulitzer Prize, followed by *West-Running Brook* in 1928, and *Collected Poems* in 1930, which won a second Pulitzer. Frost refused to join the political literary movements of the thirties but chose to write another personal and individual book, *A Further Range* (1936), which the critics attacked for lack of social relevance. In spite of its critics, the book also won a Pulitzer. In the late thirties, he suffered the deaths of two children and his wife, and he collapsed for a time. By 1942, however, he completed *A Witness Tree*, winner of yet another Pulitzer. This book was followed by *The Steeple Bush* in 1947 and *In the Clearing* in 1962. Frost spoke to the nation by reading "The Gift Outright" at President Kennedy's inauguration in 1961. He died two years later, a poet whose characters questioned their own comfortable assumptions about the world. With many well-wrought poems that demonstrate effective revisions of years of working and reworking, Frost was, above all, a craftsman.

## CRISTINA GARCÍA (b. 1958)

Born in Havana in 1958, during the Cuban Revolution, Cristina García was taken to the United States by her parents at the age of two. García grew up in Brooklyn and would receive her B.A. in political science from Barnard College in 1979, followed by a degree in Latin American Studies from John Hopkins in 1981. After spending several years as a reporter and researcher for *Time* magazine, García resigned her position to write fiction full time. In 1993 she published her first novel, *Dreaming in Cuban*, which became a finalist for the National Book Award and established her as a respected contemporary novelist. *Dreaming in Cuban* was followed by *The Aguero Sisters* (1997) and *Monkey Hunting* (2003). These generational epics explore Cuban American identity (with a focus on the feminine) and are characterized by dramatic shifts from realism to magical realism. García's poetic prose style eloquently shows the connections between history and character. "Inés in the Kitchen," one of her few short stories, was first published in *Little Havana Blues: A Cuban-American Literature Anthology* (1996).

## DAGOBERTO GILB (b. 1950)

Dagoberto Gilb is the son of a Mexican mother and a Germanic father. His parents divorced when he was very young, leaving him to be raised by his mother alone. He attended several community colleges, eventually earning a B.A. and an M.A. in Religious Studies from the University of California at Santa Barbara. After graduating in 1976, he worked in construction for several years, all the while continuing to write. However, he did not publish until the early 1980s. He writes candidly about Chicano culture in the American Southwest, depicting Mexican-American culture from an authentic perspective. He has won the PEN/Faulkner Award and a Guggenheim fellowship for his work, of which his most famous are *The Last Known Residence of Mickey Acuna* and *The Magic of Blood,* a collection of short stories that includes "Love in L.A." The story chronicles the unexpected results of a car crash in Los Angeles. He also has several writings that have been adapted into films and documentaries. Gilb currently lives in Austin, Texas, where *Writ Writer* debuted at the SXSW Film Festival in 2008.

## CHARLOTTE PERKINS GILMAN (1860–1935)

Soon after Charlotte Perkins Gilman's birth in Hartford, Connecticut, her father abandoned his wife and two children, leaving them in poverty. In need, Gilman's mother sought the help of relatives, in particular, Harriet Beecher Stowe and her sisters, all prominent writers and feminists during the era. In such an environment, Gilman developed a strong and independent sense of her self-worth as a woman. Early on in her career she worked as a teacher and a commercial artist. After becoming deeply depressed after the birth of her first child, a famous neurologist ordered complete bed rest, which made matters worse. Eventually, Gilman left her husband, moved to California, and began writing and speaking on economics and feminism. She edited *The Forerunner*, a feminist journal, from 1909 until 1916. Among Gilman's writings are *Women and Economics* (1898); *Herland* (1915), a utopian novel; and *The Living of Charlotte*

*Perkins Gilman* (1935), her autobiography. The short story "The Yellow Wallpaper," considered one of Gilman's finest works, was written out of her encounter with the late-nineteenth-century medical profession's misdiagnosis of women's physiology and psychology.

## JUDY GRAHN (b. 1940)

Judy Grahn grew up in New Mexico and has worked as a waitress, typist, sandwich maker, and meat wrapper. She has also taught in women's writing programs in New York and Berkeley, and she cofounded the Gay and Lesbian Studies Program at the New College of California in San Francisco. Grahn was a cofounder of the Women's Press Collective in 1970 in northern California. Her writings include *The Work of a Common Woman* (1978) and *The Queen of Wands* (1982), poetry; *Another Mother Tongue: Gay Words, Gay Worlds* (1984) and *Blood and Bread and Roses* (1986), nonfiction; *Mundane's World* (1988) a novel; and *Really Reading Gertrude Stein* (1989). She has also edited two volumes of *True to Life Adventure Stories* (1978, 1980). Grahn has consistently brought a working-class perspective into feminist poetry. "Ella, in a square apron, along Highway 80" is one of seven portraits of working-class women in the sequence, *The Common Woman Poems* (1969).

## NATHANIEL HAWTHORNE (1804–1864)

Nathaniel Hawthorne was born into an established Puritan family in Salem, Massachusetts. After graduating from Bowdoin College in 1825, Hawthorne aspired to literary fame and returned to Salem to begin writing stories. For the next decade, he irregularly sold his work to literary magazines. Finally, in 1837, Hawthorne published his first collection of short stories (then called "romances") *Twice-Told Tales*, which would bring him the literary acknowledgment he was seeking, but not the income necessary to support his new family. To supplement his income, Hawthorne was forced to take on other work, serving as a customs inspector in Boston for a few years, then as the American consul to Liverpool, appointed by his close friend President Franklin Pierce. Throughout these years, he continued to write, crafting short stories and novels that probed the individual's struggle with conscience and the weight of Puritan guilt. In a lush prose style, and with the frequent use of allegory, his works tend to move in and out of ambiguity, creating multiple levels of meaning. His other works include *Mosses from an Old Manse* (1846), *The Scarlet Letter* (1850), *The House of the Seven Gables* (1851), *The Blithedale Romance* (1852), and *The Marble Faun* (1860). "Young Goodman Brown," first published in *Mosses from an Old Manse*, is a prime example of the gothic and Puritan influences in Hawthorne's writing and "has provoked perhaps more discussion than any other short story in American fiction" (*Nathaniel Hawthorne*, Introduction, 1979).

## ROBERT HAYDEN (1913–1980)

Placed in a foster home as an infant, Robert Hayden grew up in a Detroit ghetto ironically called "Paradise Valley" by its residents. He attended Wayne State University for a short time but left in 1936 to work for the Federal Writer's Project, researching African American history and folklore that had been neglected by conventional history books. This experience with alternative historical narratives would have a profound impact on his poetry. In 1941, he entered Michigan University and studied under the poet W. H Auden, honing the technical aspects of his writing. In 1946, Hayden began teaching at Fisk University and would remain there for the next 23 years. Although he published his first poetry collection, *Heart-Shape in the Dust* in 1940, it was not until *Selected Poems* (1966) that Hayden was recognized as a skilled poet with his own poetic vision. In 1976, he was appointed as Consultant in Poetry to the Library of Congress (later retitled Poet Laureate). His other works include *Figure of Time: Poems* (1955), *A Ballad of Remembrance* (1962), *Words of Mourning Time* (1970), *The Night-Blooming Cereus* (1972), and *Angel of Ascent* (1975). "Those Winter Sundays," first published in *Selected Poems*, takes on the appearance of a loose sonnet, exploring the hard realizations of childhood.

## ERNEST HEMINGWAY (1899–1961)

Ernest Hemingway was born in Oak Park, Illinois. As a boy he went on frequent hunting and fishing trips in northern Michigan with his father, a doctor. He boxed and played football in high school and, after graduating, worked as a newspaper reporter. Near the end of World War I, Hemingway was a volunteer ambulance driver and then a soldier in Italy, where he was wounded. He spent much of the 1920s in Paris and the 1930s in Key West, Florida. He was an active supporter of the Republican Revolutionary Cause in the Spanish Civil War and worked as a war correspondent during World War II. His writings include the novels *The Sun Also Rises* (1926), *A Farewell to Arms* (1929), and *The Old Man and The Sea* (1952); the collections *In Our Time* (1925) and *The Fifth Column and the First Forty-Nine Stories* (1938); and the memoir *A Moveable Feast* (1964, posthumously).

## LANGSTON HUGHES (1902–1967)

Langston Hughes was born in Joplin, Missouri, and raised primarily by his maternal grandmother in Lawrence, Kansas. He entered Columbia University in 1920, but left a year later, working odd jobs and traveling throughout Europe and Africa. During this time Hughes would publish his first poems and novels and establish himself as a central figure in the literary and artistic movement known as the Harlem Renaissance. Influenced by such writers as W.E.B. Dubois and the poet Walt Whitman, Hughes' work often expresses subtle political meaning in a style influenced by the rhythms of African American music (the blues) and language. Intentionally eschewing traditional poetic form, his poetry aspired to reach ordinary people, both black and white, by writing in an accessible way that spoke to and acknowledged their experiences. For this he became known as a "the bard of Harlem." His works include the poetry collections *The Weary Blues* (1926), *Fine Clothes to the Jew* (1927), *The Dream Keeper and Other Poems* (1932), *Freedom's Plow* (1943), *Fields of Wonder* (1947), *Montage of a Dream Deferred* (1951), *Ask Your Mama: Twelve Moods for Jazz* (1961), and *The Panther and the Lash* (1967); the novels *Not Without Laughter* (1930) and *Tambourines of Glory* (1958); the short story collections *The Ways of White Folks* (1934), *Simple Speaks His Mind* (1950), *Simple Takes a Wife* (1953), and *Something in Common and Other Stories* (1963); and the autobiography *I Wonder as I Wander* (1956).

## SHIRLEY JACKSON (1916–1965)

Shirley Jackson was born in San Francisco, the first child of an affluent and conservative family. In 1933, Jackson's family moved to Rochester, New York. After attending the University of Rochester from 1934 to 1936, she withdrew from school and spent a year at home, writing a thousand words a day. In 1937, she entered Syracuse University, where she edited the campus humor magazine, won second prize in a poetry contest, and founded the literary magazine *Spectre*. She married the magazine's managing editor, Stanley Edgar Hyman, immediately after her graduation in 1940. The couple moved to New York City, where Jackson held a variety of jobs while continuing to write. In 1941, her experience selling books at Macy's formed the basis for "My Life with R. H. Macy," published in *The New Republic*. This success was followed by the birth of her first child and the publication of many stories in *The New Yorker*. Her reputation as a writer of short fiction grew, and in 1944 "Come Dance with Me in Ireland" was the first of her four stories chosen for *Best American Short Stories*. Jackson's family continued to grow, and her body of writing continued to expand after she moved to North Bennington, Vermont. She had three more children and published short stories, novels, family chronicles, a one-act play, a children's book, and a nonfictional account of witchcraft in Salem. Her works were made into plays, films, and television shows. Her short story "The Lottery" has been translated into a short play, a television drama, a radio show, an opera, and a ballet. The family chronicles *Life Among the Savages* (1953) and *Raising Demons* (1957) were best-sellers, and Jackson's popular success was matched by critical acclaim for her short fiction and novels alike. These latter include *The Road Through the Wall* (1948), *Hangsaman* (1951), *The Bird's Nest* (1954), and *The Sundial* (1958), along with her last two novels, *The Haunting of Hill House* (1959) and *We Have Always Lived in the Castle* (1962). She died of heart failure on August 8, 1965.

## GHASSAN KANAFANI (1936–1972)

Ghassan Kanafani was born in Acre, a city in North Palestine; Ghassan Fayiz Kanafani was a Palestinian journalist, political activist, short story writer, and novelist. The 1948 Arab-Israeli War forced Kanafani and his family into exile in Lebanon and then Syria. Over his lifetime, he lived and worked in Kuwait and Beruit. In 1952, while exiled in Damascus, Kanafani completed his secondary education and received a United Nations Relief and Works Agency for Palestine Refugees (UNRWA) teaching certificate. This same year, while teaching in UNRWA schools in refugee camps, he enrolled in the Department of Arabic Literature at the University of Damascus. However, because of his political affiliations with the Movement of Arab Nationalists, he was expelled from the university and exiled to Kuwait. In 1960, he relocated to Beirut, and in 1962, his first novel, *Men in the Sun*, was published. He continued to publish his novellas, among which were *All that's Left of You* (1966), *Umm Sa'd* (1969), and *Return to Haifa* (1970). His affiliation with the Palestine Liberation Movement, the Popular Front for the Liberation of Palestine (PFLP), and the Arab Nationalist movement formed his most important contributions to society. He believed a social revolution in the Arab world and national unity would solve the problem that Palestine faced. He attributed his passion for politics to his work as a novelist, asserting that politics and novelists are indivisible. Over his lifetime, Ghassan published eighteen books and hundreds of articles on culture, politics, and the Palestinian people's struggles. His writing has been translated into over seventeen languages and published worldwide. On July 8, 1972, Ghassan Kanafani was assassinated by a car bomb in Beirut.

## BRIGIT PEGEEN KELLY (b. 1951)

Brigit Pegeen Kelly is a contemporary American poet who was born in Palo Alto, California. She published her first collection of poems, *To The Place of Trumpets*, in 1987, after which *Song* (1995) followed. She has earned various awards, such as the Discovery/the Nation Award, the Yale Younger Poets Prize, a Whiting Writers Award, and fellowships from the Guggenheim Foundation, the National Endowment for the Arts, and the Academy of American Poets. In 2005, she was a finalist for the Pulitzer Prize in poetry for *The Orchard* (2004). In addition to being an established poet, she also taught at the University of California-Irvine, Warren Wilson College, and Purdue University, and has participated at writers' conferences in the United States and Ireland. She is currently a professor of English at the University of Illinois in Urbana-Champaign.

## JAMAICA KINCAID (b. 1950)

Elaine Potter Richardson (Kincaid's original name) was born in St. John's, Antigua, in the Caribbean. The only daughter in a family of four children, Richardson left Antigua for the United States in 1966 at the age of 17 and entered the New School for Social Research in New York City to study photography and began to write. In 1973, Richardson changed her name to Jamaica Kincaid so she could write anonymously and in 1976 landed a job as a staff writer at *The New Yorker*, a job she held until 1995. While at *The New Yorker*, Kincaid published a collection of short stories, *At the Bottom of the River* (1983), as well as the novels *Annie John* (1985) and *Lucy* (1990), and *A Small Place* (1988)—a book-length essay on the British legacy in Antigua after independence in 1981. Since 1995, Kincaid's works include *Autobiography of My Mother* (1996), *My Brother* (1997), *My Favorite Plant* (1988), and *My Garden Book* (1999). She currently teaches and lives in Bennington, Vermont. "Girl" is an early example of a recurring theme in Kincaid's work: the complex relationship between mothers and daughters.

## GALWAY KINNELL (1927–2014)

Galway Kinnell was born in Rhode Island and earned degrees from Princeton University and the University of Rochester. After serving in the United States Navy, Kinnell traveled to Europe on a Fulbright fellowship. He received the Pulitzer Prize for poetry and the National Book Award. After working for the Congress of Racial Equality, Kinnell pursued an academic career, retiring from New York University in 2011. Kinnell published several volumes of poetry, most notably *What Kingdom It Was* (1960), *Body Rags* (1968), *The Book of Nightmares* (1971), *Mortal Acts, Mortal Words* (1980), *When One Had Lived a Long Time Alone* (1990), and *New Selected Poems* (2000). He was poet laureate for the state of Vermont from 1989 to 1993.

## YUSEF KOMUNYAKAA (b. 1941)

Born James William Brown in Louisiana, Yusef Komunyakaa graduated from high school in 1965 and enlisted in the United States Army; he served in Vietnam and was awarded the Bronze Star. It was in the service that he began to write as editor of the military newspaper. After leaving the army, he enrolled at the University of Colorado and graduated in 1975. It was in Colorado that Komunyakaa began to write poetry in earnest. He went on to graduate study at Colorado State University and the University of California at Irvine. In 1988, he published *Dien Cai Dau*, followed by *Magic City* in 1992. He won the 1994 Pulitzer Prize for *Neon Vernacular*, followed by the William Faulkner Prize from the University of Rennes in France and the Levinson Prize from *Poetry Magazine*. *Thieves of Paradise* (1998) and *Talking Dirty to the Gods* (2000) further established him as an important and unique voice in American poetry. He was elected chancellor of the Academy of American Poets in 1999. That year, he co-edited two volumes of poetry, titled *The Jazz Poetry Anthology*.

## RICHARD LOVELACE (1618–1657)

Richard Lovelace was born to a socially prominent family in England; he attended Oxford University for two years but left school in order to fight on behalf of King Charles I. He served in the First and Second Scottish expeditions, both of which were dismal failures. He was later imprisoned twice for advancing the Royalist cause. While in prison the first time, he wrote his famous poem "To Althea, from Prison." Once released, he went abroad and fought with the French against Spain; he was wounded in a 1646 battle at Dunkirk. Once Lovelace returned to England, which was then under rule of the Lord Protector Oliver Cromwell, he was imprisoned for the second time in 1648. During this confinement, he prepared his volume of poems, *Lucasta: Episodes, Odes, Sonnets, Songs, Etc.* (1649). Both "To Althea, from Prison" as well as the famed song "To Lucasta: On Going to the Wars" appeared in this collection. After 1649, little is known of Lovelace. Once released from prison, he continued to struggle on behalf of the king and died in penury. Following Lovelace's death in 1658, his brother Dudley published his remaining poems in the collection *Lucasta: Postume Poems* (1660).

## KATHERINE MANSFIELD (1888–1923)

Katherine Mansfield Beauchamp was born in Wellington, New Zealand. Mansfield displayed her talents as a writer at a young age, and in 1903, she was sent to Queen's College, London, to complete her education. She edited the college literary magazine and participated in musical activities. Her return to New Zealand was short, for she persuaded her father to support her financially while she endeavored to succeed as a writer in London. There she was married briefly, had financial difficulties, traveled with an opera company, and quickly damaged her fragile health. While in Germany recuperating, she wrote and published her first stories under the title of *In a German Pension* (1911). She also wrote articles for *The Westminster Gazette* to supplement her income. In 1918, Mansfield met and married the critic John Middleton Murry. They co-edited a journal called *Rhythm*, where several of her stories first appeared. These were later collected in *Something Childish and Other Stories* in 1924. Mansfield and Murry made their home in Buckinghamshire, but in early 1914 Mansfield again fell ill and traveled to the Continent to improve her health. Her brother, Leslie Beauchamp, was killed in action in World War I, further contributing to her distress but spurring on her creative impulses and productiveness. She wrote *Prelude* (1918) in France and then contributed to D. H. Lawrence's journal *Signature* under the pen name of Matilda Berry. In 1918, Mansfield was diagnosed with tuberculosis. Despite her declining health, she published *Bliss and Other Stories* in 1920 and wrote reviews for her husband's journal, *Athenaeum*, most of which were published after her death in 1930 as *Novels and Novelists*. In 1920, she went to Switzerland where she wrote a collection of short of stories, *The Garden Party and Other Stories* (1922). These received critical acclaim, but her career was to go no further, for her health was rapidly failing. She traveled to Paris and its environs to study with the Russian mystic Gurdjieff, one of the many spiritual thinkers working and writing in Europe at the time. After her death, her husband published the rest of her works in *The Dove's Nest and Other Stories* (1923), *Journal* (1927), *Letters* (1928), *Selected Stories* (1929), *Poems* (1930), and *Scrapbook* (1939).

## ANDREW MARVELL (1621–1678)

Andrew Marvell was born in England, in the region of Yorkshire, the son of a reverend. He began his studies at Trinity College in Cambridge at the age of twelve but eventually abandoned his formal studies after his father died in a drowning accident. By sixteen he had already published two poems, one written in Latin and the other in Greek, in a Cambridge anthology. While still in his twenties, he traveled throughout Europe, learning French, Spanish, Italian, and Dutch in the process. He worked as a tutor and was for a time the secretary to poet John Milton. In 1660, he was elected to Parliament under Oliver Cromwell during a period of much political upheaval in England. An astute politician and pamphleteer, Marvell was a severe critic of the English parliament and court system. He wrote poems and satires, many of them related to the political topics of the period. Some of his best-known poems include "Upon Appleton House," the *Mower* series, and "The Garden." No collection of Marvell's poetry was published until three years after his sudden death of a fever; although a few individual poems appeared during his lifetime, his more famous poems were published posthumously. Marvell is remembered for his sharp political satire and his poetic lyricism. He wrote in the neoclassical tradition, a period in which writers sought to imitate the lessons from the classical period, a time of aesthetic discipline and perfection. "To His Coy Mistress" is perhaps his best-known poem, a carpe diem lyric, a poem that explores how time acts upon physical beauty and sexual desire.

## BRENDAN MATHEWS

Brendan Mathews is an author and faculty member at Bard College, Simon's Rock in Annandale-On-Hudson, New York. He earned a B.A. from the University of North Carolina at Chapel Hill and an M.F.A. from the University of Virginia, and he was the recipient of a Fulbright Scholarship. His short stories have been published in *The Southern Review* and *The Manchester Review*, and he was a finalist for the Flannery O'Connor Short Fiction Prize in 2011. His short stories "My Last Attempt to Explain to You What Happened with the Lion Tamer" and "This is Not a Love Story" appeared in *The Best American Short Stories*, 2010 and 2014, respectively.

## CLAUDE MCKAY (1889–1948)

Claude McKay was born Festus Claudius McKay in Jamaica, the youngest of eleven children in an affluent farming family; McKay was sent as a young child to live with his oldest brother, a school teacher, in the hopes that he would receive the best education possible. An avid reader as a child, McKay began writing poetry at age ten. After a period spent as an apprentice to a cabinet and carriage maker, McKay joined the constabulary forces. By the time McKay immigrated to the United States, he had published two significant volumes of poetry, *Songs of Jamaica* (1912) and *Constab Ballads* (1912), each of which explored the poeticism of the Caribbean dialect. McKay came to the United States in 1912 to study agriculture at Tuskegee Institute in Alabama, intending to return to the family farm; instead, while in Alabama, McKay had his first encounters with the violence of American racism, which laid the foundation for much of his later writing. He moved to New York, where he became increasingly involved in both the burgeoning literary scene and radical political movements. During this period, McKay published frequently in *The Liberator*, a socialist journal for which he later became an editor; many of McKay's poems from this era show evidence of his identification with the experiences of African Americans, especially "If We Must Die," "The White House," and "The Lynching," three sonnets of protest against racist violence. He published two more volumes of poetry, *Spring in New Hampshire* (1920) and *Harlem Shadows* (1922), which firmly established McKay among the leading voices of the Harlem Renaissance. McKay published three novels, *Home to Harlem* (1928), *Banjo* (1929), and *Banana Bottom* (1933), as well as *Gingertown* (1932), a collection of short stories. In the later years of his life, McKay distanced himself from the American Communist Party due to issues of Stalinist censorship, which he felt repressed issues of race from socialist discourse. McKay became a naturalized U.S. citizen in 1940 and was baptized a Roman Catholic in 1944 before he died in Chicago in 1948.

## PETER MEINKE (b. 1932)

Peter Meinke was born in Flatbush, New York, and graduated from Hamilton College in 1955. After two years in the Army, mostly in Würzburg, Germany, he married artist Jeanne Clark in 1957. He received his M.A. in literature in 1961 from the University of Michigan, then spent the next five years teaching at Hamline University while earning his Ph.D. in English literature at the University of Minnesota. In 1966, Meinke moved to St. Petersburg, Florida, to teach at Florida Presbyterian College, now Eckerd College. His poems gained national attention in the 1960s when many of them appeared in *The New Republic*. In addition to publishing two children's books and several chapbooks (a small collection of poetry that often centers on a specific theme), he has a long association with the Pitt Poetry Series with the publication of *The Night Train & the Golden Bird* in 1976; his eighth and most recent collection with them is *Lucky Bones* (2014). Along with his poems, book reviews, and travel articles, he wrote several short stories. His first collection of short stories, *The Piano Tuner*, received the 1986 Flannery O'Connor Award for Short Fiction. For the last several years, he has written a biweekly column, *The Poet's Notebook* — illustrated by Jeanne — for St. Petersburg's alterntive newspaper, *Creative Loafing*. On May 14th, 2009, Peter Meinke was appointed the first ever Poet Laureate of St. Petersburg, Florida.

## EDNA ST. VINCENT MILLAY (1892–1950)

Raised in Camden, Maine, Millay published her first poem at the age of fourteen. Under the guidance of a dedicated mother, Millay underwent an intensive study program of music and literature, always encouraged to be strong-willed and independent. Her poem "Renascence," published in *Lyric Year* in 1912, was met with critical praise and helped secure a scholarship for Millay at Vasser College. After graduating, she moved to New York's Greenwich Village—a "bohemian" community of actors, painters and writers—and began to write poetry and plays. In 1923, she became the first woman to win the Pulitzer Prize for poetry for her collection *The Ballad of the Harp-Weaver* (1923). Although Millay was an active and popular poet during the modernist movement of the first half of the twentieth century, her conservative and formal techniques (she is best known for her sonnets) set her apart from the free-verse developments of the era. While her form remained traditional, her content did not. Like the work of the Greek poet Sappho, many of Millay's precise and lyric poems explore the physical and mental aspects of female sexuality and sexual autonomy. Select works from her 15 volumes of poetry, several plays, essays, and short fiction include the poetry works *Renascence and Other Poems* (1912), *A Few Figs from Thistles: Poems and Sonnets* (1921), *Fatal Interview* (1931), *Wine from These Grapes* (1934), *Make Bright the Arrows* (1940), and the drama collection *Three Plays* (1926). In "An Ancient Gesture," Millay's distinct lyricism enhances the poem's subtle play of meanings.

## TONI MORRISON (b. 1931)

Born in Lorain, Ohio, Toni Morrison received a B.A. in English from Howard University and her M.A. in English at Cornell. Yet it was her early life experiences in Ohio that would become a cornerstone of her writing: "No matter what I write, I begin there . . . Ohio offers an escape from the stereotyped black settings. It is neither plantation or ghetto" (*Black Women Writers at Work*, 1986). From such a vantage point, Morrison has sought to offer a more complicated version of the African American experience—one infused with myth and folklore, race and identity. After teaching for a few years, Morrison accepted a position as a book editor at Random House in New York in 1964. In 1969, Morrison published her first book, *The Bluest Eye*, at the age of 38. She spent the next 25 years at Random House, helping raise public awareness of other black writers as well as publishing her own work: *Sula* (1973); *Song of Solomon* (1977); *Tar Baby* (1981); *Beloved* (1987), which won the Pulitzer Prize for Fiction; *Jazz* (1992); *Paradise* (1998); and her most recent novel, *Love* (2003). In addition to her novels Morrison has written and edited several critical works, including *Playing in the Dark: Whiteness and the Literary Imagination* (1992), and coauthored several children's books with her son Slade Morrison. In 1993, Morrison became the first African American to win the Nobel Prize for literature.

## ALICE MUNRO (b. 1930)

Alice Laidlaw was born in Wingham, Ontario, and grew up in a rural area that provided the setting for much of her fiction. Living on a fox farm some distance from town, young Alice discovered that writing gave her the confidence to cope during her teenage years. She won a scholarship to the University of Western Ontario, where she studied for two years before leaving school and marrying James Munro. The couple settled in Victoria, where they ran a bookshop and raised three daughters. During this time, Munro embarked on a successful writing career, contributing stories to such magazines as *The New Yorker*, *The Atlantic Monthly*, and *The Paris Review*. She often attributes her facility with short fiction to the hectic life she led while her children were young. Munro served as writer-in-residence at her alma mater in 1972 and at the University of British Columbia and the University of Queensland in 1980. Munro's early collection of short stories, *Dance of the Happy Shades* (1968), won the Governor General's Award, as did her later collections *Who Do You Think You Are?* (1978) and *The Progress of Love* (1986). Other awards include the W.H. Smith Award for *Open Secrets* (1994) and the Giller Award for *The Love of a Good Woman* (1998). She was awarded the Man Booker International Prize in 2009 and the Nobel Prize for Literature in 2013. Munro was also the first Canadian recipient of the U.S. PEN-Malamud Award for Excellence in Short Fiction. Her most recent original collections are *Hateship, Friendship, Courtship, Loveship, Marriage* (2001) and *Runaway: Stories* (2004). Her work focuses on the lives of ordinary people who attempt to connect with their pasts by returning home and retelling the stories of their lives.

## LEWIS NORDAN (1939–2012)

Mississippian Lewis Nordan was born in Forest and grew up in Itta Bena, dedicating much of his writing to exploring the strange beauty of his home state. He earned his B.A. at Millsaps College, his M.A. from Mississippi State University, and his Ph.D. from Auburn University, then went on to teach at the University of Pittsburgh. In 1983, he published his first collection of short stories, *Welcome to the Arrow-Catcher Fair*. His fiction is often noted for incorporating elements of magical realism and for finding comedy in tragic moments. Of his four novels, three collections of short stories, and a memoir, his most notable work is the novel *Wolf Whistle*, which deals with the murder of Emmett Till, a fourteen-year-old African American who was murdered in the Mississippi Delta in 1955. Like many of his works, "The All-Girl Football Team" is set in Arrow Catcher, MS, a town loosely based on Itta Bena.

## JOYCE CAROL OATES (b. 1938)

Joyce Carol Oates was born in Lockport, New York, and spent much of her time growing up on her grandparents' farm. She began writing at an extremely early age, completing her first novel at fifteen; the publisher she submitted it to, however, felt that it was too dark for young adult readers. Oates attended Syracuse University, from which she graduated in 1960, and received a master's degree from University of Wisconsin in 1961. She married that same year, and she and her husband, Raymond Joseph Smith, moved to Detroit, where Oates taught at the University of Detroit from 1961-1967. She was a member of the faculty of the University of Windsor, in Ontario, Canada, from 1967 to 1978, and became a writer-in-residence at Princeton University in 1978, where she remains today as the Roger S. Berlind Distinguished Professor in the Humanities. Oates has won a plethora of prizes, including three O. Henry Awards, the Rosenthal Award of the National Institute of Arts and Letters, the National Book Award, the O. Henry Special Award for Continuing Achievement (twice), the Elmer Holmed Bobst Award for Lifetime Achievement in Fiction, and the Bram Stoker Lifetime Achievement Award for horror fiction. Oates has a wide range of literary interests and styles; she is equally successful at domestic novels and at horror fiction, at crime stories and at the gothic romance. Much of her writing bears a thread of subterranean, and at times overt, violence. Among her many novels are *them* (1969), *Because It Is Bitter, and Because It Is My Heart* (1990), *Black Water* (1992), *Foxfire* (1993), *We Were the Mulvaneys* (1996), and *Blonde* (2000).

## TIM O'BRIEN (b. 1946)

Tim O'Brien was born in Austin, Minnesota. After high school, he entered Macalester College in St. Paul to study political science. He graduated in 1968 summa cum laude. Any intentions of studying further, however, were dashed after being drafted into the army to fight in Vietnam. The traumatic experience of Vietnam had a deep impact on his life, and, after returning to the United States, he turned to writing as a way to cope with the insanity of war. In 1973, while studying at Harvard, O'Brien published *If I Die in a Combat Zone, Box Me Up and Ship Me Home*, a memoir of his experience in Vietnam—a work that compelled American culture to rethink the human costs of war and established him as the writerly conscience of Vietnam. In a terse, compact prose style (he is often compared to Ernest Hemingway in both theme and technique), O'Brien often disrupts standard narrative sequence by rearranging linear plot schemes through the blurring of reality and imagination. Within this mode, his protagonists grapple with false and romantic notions of courage, integrity, wisdom, and fear. While Vietnam serves as the backdrop for many of his works, O'Brien has explored other themes in more recent books yet still maintains a commitment to the human desire to find understanding in a chaotic world. Selected works include *Northern Lights* (1975), *The Nuclear Age* (1985), *The Things They Carried* (1990), *Tomcat in Love* (1998), and *July, July* (2002). He has won numerous literary awards, including the National Book Award for *Going After Cacciato* (1978) and the James Fenimore Cooper Prize for Best Historical Fiction for *In the Lake of the Woods* (1994). In 2013, he received the Pritzker Military Library Literature Award.

## FLANNERY O'CONNOR (1925–1964)

Flannery O'Connor was born an only child in Savannah, Georgia, and moved with her parents to a farm near Milledgeville, Georgia, at age twelve. Her father died of lupus, a disease of the immune system, when O'Connor was fifteen, and she succumbed to the same disease at age thirty-nine. An intellectual in a rural environment, she quickly began to see the world as sometimes annoying, but often amusing. O'Connor graduated from Georgia State College of Women in 1945, where she was a cartoonist for the student newspaper. Many of her stories depict characters in cartoonish ways, a whimsical, and sometimes slightly cruel, way of seeing humanity. O'Connor went on to the University of Iowa, where she received her Masters of Fine Arts in 1947 and published her first short story, "The Geranium," in *Accent* (1946). She went on to an artist's residency at Yaddo in Saratoga Springs, New York, where she developed the professional friendships that were to sustain her throughout her artistic life. Though she returned to the family farm permanently due to her health, she continued to correspond with her artistic colleagues. Her correspondence was collected and published in 1979 as *Letters of Flannery O'Connor: The Habit of Being*. O'Connor wrote constantly throughout her short life, producing two novels and numerous short stories that have amused readers for decades. Her novels, *Wise Blood* (1952) and *The Violent Bear It Away* (1960), present a world where grotesque characters search for meaning, almost without awareness of their own searches. The critical reaction to O'Connor's short stories, collected in *A Good Man is Hard to Find* (1955) and *Everything That Rises Must Converge* (1965), has been consistently positive throughout the years. Two important aspects of O'Connor – her southern roots and her devout Catholicism – are present in all her works as characters search for grace and forgiveness.

## TILLIE OLSEN (circa 1913–2007)

Tillie Lerner was born in Omaha, Nebraska, the daughter of social activist Jewish-Russian immigrants. During the Great Depression she had to quit high school to work; she also began work as a labor activist and writer. She joined the Communist Party at the age of seventeen and was arrested and jailed for her part in several Depression-era strikes. She then married Jack Olsen and raised four children while continuing to work as a waitress and secretary, writing little until the 1950s. Those twenty years of raising children and making ends meet served as the foundation of much of her writing. Although Olsen did not publish much in her lifetime, she gained acclaim for the emotional intensity of her prose and her ability to make apparent the heroic in common people. As the title of her book *Silences* (1978) suggests, Olsen's work, steeped in issues of class, race, and gender, seeks to give an authentic voice to the silent and stifled worlds of the oppressed. Her other works include the short story collection *Tell Me a Riddle* (1961) and the novel *Yonnondio* (1974). In "I Stand Here Ironing," first published in *Tell Me a Riddle*, Olsen shifts narration from present to past as a mother takes inventory of her daughter's life and her own role as a working-class parent.

## WILFRED OWEN (1893–1918)

Wilfred Owen was born in Oswestry, England, and raised in a strict Calvinist home. His interest in poetry began at an early age, in particular the poetry of John Keats. Hoping to enroll at the University of London, Owen was unable to secure a scholarship that would have enabled him to pay the tuition. In 1913, he left to teach English in France, returning two years later to enlist in the British Army at the height of World War I. After many months fighting on the Western Front, Owen suffered shell shock and was hospitalized. It was during this convalescence that Owen met Siegfried Sassoon, another injured soldier and poet who encouraged and worked with Owen on his poetry. At the time, Owen had already published a few poems, but Sassoon's influence impelled Owen to develop the innovative poetry he would become known for. His brutal depictions of the realities of war helped to dismantle the era's popular and romanticized versions of valor and heroism. Owen's verse stood as the voice of the silent and unknown soldier. He was killed at the front in 1918, a week before the Armistice that ended World War I.

## OCTAVIO PAZ (1914–1998)

Octavio Paz was born in Mexico City at the center of a strong tradition of twentieth century Latin American literature. While Paz's work is firmly rooted in Mexican culture and history, it also blurs lines between genres, traditions, and critical categories. As the first Mexican writer to win the Nobel Prize in Literature (1990), Paz represents the significance of a Latin American literary tradition. As such, his work is often read in terms of its presentation of Mexican art, culture, and even politics. While attending the National Autonomous University, Paz published his first collection of poetry, *Sylvan Moon* in 1933. The 1930s and 1940s, for Paz, marked a time of exploration and discovery. Travels to Spain, France, and the United States informed his sense of politics and aesthetics and became the foundation for his works during that period and throughout his career. Paz's critical reception is represented by prestigious international praise: the Guggenheim fellowship (1944); Grand Prix International de Poesie (1963); Jerusalem Prize, Critics Prize and National Prize for Letters (1977); Grand Aigle d'Or (1979); T.S. Eliot Award for Creative Writing (1987); Tocqueville Prize (1989); Nobel Prize for Literature (1990). Paz was appointed ambassador to India in 1962 but resigned in 1968 after the massacres in Mexico. He went on to become a visiting professor of Spanish-American Literature at the University of Texas at Austin and the University of Pittsburgh (1968-70) and a professor at Cambridge University (1970-71) and Harvard University (1971-71, 1973-80). In 1995, Paz published his last book, *In Light of India*, representing, in part, a final development in his work but also a return to origins. His death in 1998 marked the end of an era: a twentieth century Latin American literature that is well grounded in a cultural tradition and is open to (and animated by) experimentation.

## HARVEY PEKAR (1939–2010)

Harvey Pekar was born in Cleveland, Ohio, and lived there all his life. The town itself has been the setting for Pekar's autobiographical *American Splendor*—a literary comic-book series based on his life as a file clerk at a Veteran's Administration hospital. Pekar self-published the comic annually from 1976 to the early 1990s, employing various illustrators (Robert Crumb, Sue Cavey, Frank Stack, and Joe Zabel, among others) to do the drawings. In 1987, it won the American Book Award. A few years later, the comic's popularity caught the attention of Dark Horse Comics, who took over publication. Pekar calls himself a "working-class intellectual," and *American Splendor* focuses on Pekar's introspective and heroic search for meaning amidst the complexity of a modern working-class life. In addition to *American Splendor*, Pekar has written as a music critic and is currently a freelance writer for a radio station in Cleveland. His other works include *Our Cancer Year* (1994)—a graphic novel about his fight with cancer, and most recently, his book-length graphic autobiography, *The Quitter* (2005).

## EDGAR ALLAN POE (1809–1849)

The son of traveling actors, Edgar Allan Poe was probably abandoned by his father shortly after his birth. In any case, his father died in 1810, and his mother continued to act, moving frequently with her children until 1811, when she, too, died, leaving Poe and his siblings destitute. Poe was adopted by the family of John and Frances Allan, and at his baptism assumed his benefactor's name. Despite this early gesture of connectedness, Poe's relationship with the Allans was fractious, especially after Poe began attending the University of Virginia in 1836. Here, Poe was known both for his writing and also for his gambling and drinking. His repeated, abusive pleas for money caused John Allan to cut him off periodically. After one such incident, Poe left the university and joined the army. During his service, he published his first book of poetry, *Tamerlane and Other Poems* (1827). His second, *Al Aaraaf*, was published in 1829. In 1830, through Allan's influence, Poe was awarded an appointment to West Point, but he was soon expelled. Among cadets the legend still circulates that he forced this himself by showing up naked for morning formation, but it is more likely that drinking and gambling lay at the heart of the matter. In any event, this disgrace seems to have been fortuitous because at this time Poe began to devote himself to writing, publishing several stories and winning a fiction contest in 1832.

In 1833, he became editor of the *Southern Literary Messenger*, one of several important literary posts he would fill in his life. In 1839, he became editor of *Burton's Gentleman's Magazine*; in 1840 editor of Graham's; and in 1845 editor of the *Broadway Journal*. He published a great deal of his own poetry and fiction in these journals, as well as numerous reviews (many of them quite strident), and in this way had a significant impact on literary trends and tastes. However, despite the fact that he continued to be awarded editorial positions, the same kind of behavior that resulted in his dismissal from West Point—drinking, gambling, and a disinclination to bow to authority—led him regularly into conflict with his employers. And although he published his work regularly, he was never far from poverty. He also had a tendency to pick literary fights and was most famously dismissive of the New England transcendentalists. Some speculate that this kind of controversy may have been a ploy to sell magazines.

Although his writing career was relatively brief and his habits were self-destructive, Poe managed to amass an impressive canon before his death in 1849. In addition to such works as "Ligeia"(1838); "The Fall of the House of Usher" (1839); *Tales of the Grotesque and Arabesque* (1840); and the popular "The Raven" (1844); Poe is credited with the invention of the detective story. His character C. Auguste Dupin from "The Murders in the Rue Morgue"; "The Mystery of Marie Roget"; and "The Purloined Letter" served as type for Sherlock Holmes and countless other detectives. In these and other stories, Poe demonstrates an obsession with the dark side of human psychology. Many of his tales explore a concept he labeled "the spirit of perverseness . . . the unfathomable longing of the soul to vex itself." This phenomenon can be seen in stories such as "The Black Cat" and "The Tell-Tale Heart," in which seemingly rational characters are drawn to commit ghastly crimes for reasons they cannot explain. While his last years were clouded by the death of his wife from tuberculosis in 1846, he seemed on the road to recovery when, in 1849, he stopped in Baltimore on his way to Philadelphia and was found on the street four days later, unconscious and near death. The exact cause of his death on October 7 remains a mystery.

—David L. G. Arnold, *University of Wisconsin, Stevens Point*

## DUDLEY RANDALL (1914–2000)

Dudley Randall was born in Washington, D.C., the son of a minister and a teacher, and moved to Detroit at the age of six. He had a varied career as a worker in a foundry, poet, translator, publisher, editor, and founder of Broadside Press in 1965, which he operated out of his home. He served in the military during WWII. He earned a B.A. from Wayne State University, earned an M.A. from the University of Michigan, and later studied briefly at the University of Ghana. Randall published his first poem in the *Detroit Free Press* when he was thirteen. Moreover, Randall's sizable efforts as a publisher and editor were designed to promote and support black writers. Broadside Press was inspired by key events from the Civil Rights movement, such as the bombing of the Sixteenth Street Baptist Church in Birmingham, Alabama, in 1963. The tragedy of that event, in which four young girls were killed, was captured in what is perhaps Randall's most famous poem, "Ballad of Birmingham." This poem and others were published as "broadsides," and the tradition of broadsides goes back to the sixteenth century; typically, as ballads, they were used to call attention to culturally important events. Randall's first book of poetry, titled *Poem Counterpoem*, appeared in 1966. He co-edited *For Malcolm: Poems on the Life and Death of Malcolm X*. He won several awards in his lifetime, including a National Endowment for the Arts fellowship in 1981.

## RON RASH (b. 1953)

Ron Rash is a poet and prose writer who grew up in both South Carolina and western North Carolina, the latter having been the home of his ancestors since the mid-1700s. More than 100 of his poems and short stories have appeared in magazines and journals, and he has published four poetry collections, six short story collections, and five novels. He has twice been a finalist for the PEN/Faulkner Award (*Chemistry and Other Stories* and *Serena*), and he won the Frank O'Connor International Short Story Award for his collection *Burning Bright*. His novel *The Cove* is a *New York Times* bestselling novel, and he has also twice been a recipient of the O. Henry Prize. Rash's works primarily cover the lives of folks within southern Appalachia, and his most recent publication, *Something Rich and Strange*, comprises thirty-four of his best short stories that critic Alan Cheuse calls "searingly beautiful." Rash combines the mundane and the natural world with the supernatural with lyrical ease, creating horrifyingly beautiful portraits of everyday life in Appalachia. Rash is the Parris Distinguished Professor in Appalachian Cultural Studies at Western Carolina University.

## ADRIENNE RICH (1929–2012)

Born in Baltimore, Maryland, Adrienne Rich grew up in an intellectual and artistic environment—her mother was a musician, her father a professor at Johns Hopkins University. Her poetic ability was first recognized by W. H. Auden when he selected *A Change of World* for the Yale Younger Poets Award in 1951 while Rich was attending Radcliffe College. Rich married two years later and had three children. The experience of motherhood had a large impact on her perception of women in society (a topic she explored in *Of Woman Born: Motherhood as Experience and Institution*, 1976). While family responsibilities slowed her artistic output, amidst the arrival of the 1960s, the Vietnam War, and the rise of feminism, Rich's work moved from its early formal structure to a more radical and political style, experimenting with line length, unorthodox spacing, dialogue, and longer sequencing. By the end of the 1960s, and into the 1970s, Rich produced some of her best-known work (poetry as well as essays)—writing that centers on acts of "transformation." For Rich, change is inevitable, but change and transformation are not synonymous: ". . . if the imagination is to transcend and transform experience, it has to question, to challenge, to conceive of alternatives, perhaps to the very life you are living at that moment" (from her essay, "When We Dead Awaken: Writing as Re-Vision"). This process often centered on questions of sexuality and what Rich saw as a patriarchal culture that has degraded the value of women. Throughout her career, Rich asserted the need for writers to participate actively in both the private and public well-being of a culture. Her other works include the poetry collections *Snapshots of a Daughter-in-Law: Poems 1954–1962* (1963), *Leaflets: Poems* (1969), The Will to Change: Poems, 1968–1970 (1971), *Diving into the Wreck: Poems, 1971–1972* (1973), *Twenty-One Love Poems* (1977), *The Fact of a Doorframe: Poems Selected and New, 1950–1984* (1984), *Dark Fields of the Republic, 1991–1995* (1995); and the essay collections *On Lies, Secrets, and Silence: Selected Prose, 1966–1978* (1979) and *What is Found There: Notebooks on Poetry and Politics* (1993).

## THEODORE ROETHKE (1908–1963)

Theodore Roethke is credited as being a strong influence on the tradition of confessional poetry that includes poets such as Sylvia Plath, Anne Sexton, Robert Lowell, and John Berryman. His life was complicated by bouts of depression and mania that caused turmoil within his life both socially and professionally. Roethke was born in Saginaw, Michigan, to German immigrant parents. His father, Otto Roethke, owned a commercial greenhouse where Roethke spent much time as a child. This environment became a pervasive influence in Roethke's writing, as did the strained relationship with his over-bearing, stern father. His first collection of poems was titled *Open House* (1941). In 1945, he suffered a major bout of depression for which he received shock treatments, but by 1947 he was teaching at the University of Washington and the next year published *The Lost Son and Other Poems*. In 1957, Roethke published *Words for the Wind*; that year he won the Bollingen Prize and the National Book Award. While in Europe, he published *The Waking: Poems 1933-1953* (1953), which received the Pulitzer Prize. After another mental breakdown and admission into a Seattle sanitarium (1959), he completed his last work, *The Far Field* (1962). His work remains popular today, but it is Roethke's metaphoric sense of the relation between the psyche and the physical landscape that makes him engaging as a poet.

## CHRISTINA ROSSETTI (1830–1894)

Christina Georgina Rossetti was born in London on December 5, 1830, to Gabriele Rossetti, an Italian poet and political exile, and Frances Rossetti nee Polidori, the sister of the famous doctor and friend of Lord Byron, John William Polidori. She was raised among brilliant artists and poets amidst high society, and she and her siblings Dante, William, and Maria all became successful writers. Her father was a Roman Catholic, but Rossetti was raised by her mother in the Church of England. She began writing poetry at the age of twelve, mostly in the style of her favorite poets, John Keats, Sir Walter Scott, and Ann Radcliffe, and was first published at the age of eighteen. She was involved, along with her brothers, in the Pre-Raphaelite artistic movement, and was for a time engaged to James Collinson, a member of the Pre-Raphaelite Brotherhood, breaking off the engagement due to his reversion to Catholicism. Her most famous collection, *Goblin Market and Other Poems*, was published in 1862. This garnered her acclaim among the most influential poets of the time, and following the death of Elizabeth Barrett Browning the previous year, Rossetti was recognized as the most prominent female poet of the English language. Most of Rossetti's poetry engages in the tradition of the Romantic poets and often focuses on religious and feminist themes. She passed away in 1894 from breast cancer, only a few weeks after her 64th birthday. Her published collections of poetry include *Goblin Market and Other Poems* (1862), *The Prince's Progress and Other Poems* (1866), *Sing-Song: A Nursery Rhyme Book* (1872), *A Pageant and Other Poems* (1881), *Verses* (1893), and *New Poems* (1895).

## CARL SANDBURG (1878–1967)

Born to Swedish immigrants in Galesburg, Illinois, Sandburg's imagistic poetry celebrated the vibrant and continuous flow of Midwestern America. Sandburg left school at thirteen to work odd jobs and to travel (sometimes in freight trains), experiencing first hand working-class life. He served as a war correspondent during the Spanish-American War and afterward enrolled in college in Galesburg, but left to continue his travels. Although he never obtained his degree, it was at college that Sandburg began to write poetry. In addition to his vagabond lifestyle, Sandburg's participation in socialist politics in Milwaukee (1908–1914) and his subsequent job as a private secretary for the town's socialist mayor helped shape his humanistic view of the world. In 1916, he published his first book of poetry, *Chicago Poems*, establishing himself as an important figure in the literary scene of the Chicago Renaissance. Sandburg's rhythmic free verse is often compared to Walt Whitman's (whom he read in college), characterized by the colloquial patterns of everyday speech and a profound belief in the essential goodness of the common American. His *Complete Poems* was awarded the Pulitzer Prize for poetry in 1950. Other poetic works include *Cornhuskers* (1918), *Smoke and Steel* (1920), and *The People, Yes* (1936). Sandburg also won a Pulitzer for his six-volume biography of Abraham Lincoln, a work that took 15 years to complete. "Chicago" was first published in *Chicago Poems*.

## WILLIAM SHAKESPEARE (1564–1616)

Born in Stratford-on-Avon in England, William Shakespeare attended the free grammar school there, married Anne Hathaway when he was eighteen, and soon after went to live in London. Once there, Shakespeare began working as an actor and playwright, his first plays being presented in 1589. As a member of the acting company Lord Chamberlain's Men, Shakespeare established himself as the most popular playwright in London. Eventually, the company had the resources to build The Globe Theater and, with Shakespeare as the principal playwright, established themselves as the leading troupe in London. While Shakespeare is considered the most important dramatist in the English language, his sonnets, published in 1609, have acquired renown based on their own literary merit, patterned after the traditional Petrarchan sonnet and arranged as a dialogue between the poet and two central figures (a "friend" and the "Dark Lady").

## KARL SHAPIRO (1913–2000)

Carl Shapiro was raised in a middle-class Jewish family in Baltimore, Maryland. He attended the University of Maryland for a short time, but left after feeling alienated by the largely Anglo-Saxon student body and by the German Jewish students who seemed to look down upon his Russian-Jewish ancestry. This experience prompted him to change his first name to the German "Karl." His self-published *Poems* won him a scholarship to Johns Hopkins University in 1937. In 1941, his studies were cut short after being drafted to fight in World War II. The war would be the inspiration for his Pulitzer Prize–winning *V-Letter and Other Poems* (1944). Shapiro's work spans five decades, and, while it shows considerable variation throughout this time, the satirical and imagistic nature of his verse has remained consistent—moving between formal and free-verse structures, with one eye on the local and the other on society at large. He taught at a number of universities and was editor of *Poetry* magazine. His other publications include *Essays on Rime* (1945), *Poems of a Jew* (1958), *The Bourgeois Poet* (1964), *Adult Bookstore* (1976), and *New and Selected Poems, 1940–1986* (1987). "Buick" was published in *Poems: 1940–1953* (1953).

## PATRICIA SMITH (b. 1955)

Born on the West Side of Chicago, Patricia Smith would go to sleep at night listening to her father, a factory worker, read stories from the local newspaper. After graduating from high school, Smith entered Southern Illinois University in hopes of studying journalism, but soon left and took a job as a typist at the *Chicago Daily News*. Over time, Smith began writing entertainment reviews for the paper and in 1978 was hired at the *Chicago Sun-Times* as an entertainment writer. Smith would eventually become the first African American woman to write a weekly column at the *Boston Globe*. During these years as a journalist, Smith was also busy writing and performing poetry in both Chicago's and Boston's rising "slam" scene, of which she would become one of its central figures, winning the National Poetry Slam four times. Slam poetry has since taken hold throughout the country as one of our most vibrant and contemporary poetic forms. Smith has published three books of poetry: *Life According to Motown* (1991), *Big Towns, Big Talk* (1992), and *Close to Death* (1993). After her falling out with the *Boston Globe*, Smith coauthored with novelist Charles Johnson *Africans in America: America's Journey Through Slavery* (1998). Smith's live performance of "Undertaker" (dir. Angelica Brisk, Tied to the Tracks Films) was the subject of an award-winning short film on slam poetry.

## WILLIAM STAFFORD (1914-1993)

William Stafford was born in Hutchison, Kansas, and as a child learned an appreciation for nature from his father. A child of the Great Depression, Stafford worked to help his family survive by taking jobs as an itinerant farmer and skilled laborer. He graduated from high school in 1933, graduated from the University of Kansas in 1937, and began graduate studies in 1940 until he was drafted into the military during World War II. A registered pacifist, Stafford chose to perform his national service in labor camps for conscientious objectors; he served by fighting fires, building trails, and conserving soils in the western United States. Following the war, he finished his graduate work and published *Down in My Heart* (1948), detailing his experiences during the war and his belief in the principle of conscientious objection. He accepted a teaching position at Lewis and Clark College in Portland, Oregon, where he remained until his retirement in 1980. Stafford published his first collection of poems, *West of Your City*, in his mid-forties. *Traveling through the Dark* received the National Book Award in 1963.

## JONATHAN SWIFT (1667–1745)

Jonathon Swift was born in Dublin, Ireland, and educated at Trinity College there. Throughout a very active and political life, Swift held a variety of positions—secretary for essayist and diplomat Sir Williams Temple; vicar; political pamphleteer; journalist; and Dean of St. Patrick's Cathedral in Dublin. By 1720, he had become a passionate critic of British imperial exploitation of Ireland, writing caustic satire on behalf of Irish national interests. Swift is best known for his prose writings, including *Battle of the Books* (1704), *The Tale of a Tub* (1704), *Gulliver's Travels* (1726), and *A Modest Proposal* (1729). "A Description of the Morning," written in rhymed couplets, was first published in the Tory journal *The Tattler*.

## ALFRED, LORD TENNYSON (1809–1892)

Alfred Tennyson's life spanned most of the years of Queen Victoria's reign. He was born in a Lincolnshire rectory into a talented and literate family, the fourth child and one of eight sons and four daughters. All the children were brought up as intellectuals. Tennyson's publication of poetry included the works of his two brothers, Frederick and Charles (*Poems by Two Brothers*, 1827). Tennyson looked the part of a poet, tall and slender with an elegant head, and he was quickly adopted by the artistic circle at school. At Trinity College, Cambridge, he became a member of the poets' club, The Apostles, where he met Arthur Henry Hallam, whose early death was to shape both Tennyson's temperament and his poetry. Before that event, however, Tennyson won the Chancellor's prize for a poem titled "Timbuctoo" and saw his first volume of poetry published in 1830, *Poems, Chiefly Lyrical*. His second volume appeared in 1832. In 1833, Hallam, by then engaged to Tennyson's sister, Emily, died in Vienna. Tennyson began his poem on faith and doubt, *In Memoriam*, that was eventually to make him famous. He worked on the poem for seventeen years. At the same time, he worked on *Idylls of the King*, a long work retelling the tales of King Arthur from Malory but molded into the Victorian mindset. In 1842, he published Poems, which included *Ulysses* and *Morte D'Arthur*. In 1847, his popular satire on women's place in the world, *Princess*, appeared. These were difficult times for Tennyson, despite the success of the latest poems. Then, in 1850, he married Emily Sellwood and finally published *In Memoriam*. That year he was chosen to succeed Wordsworth as Poet Laureate. A long formal poem, *Ode on the Death of the Duke of Wellington* (1852) preceded *Maud* (1855), a romantic tale of love and death, followed by *Enoch Arden* and *Northern Farmer* (1964). He dedicated a new edition of *Idylls* to the memory of Queen Victoria's beloved husband

Prince Albert, who had died in 1861, and became a great favorite of the queen. In 1884, he became Lord Tennyson and published *Becket*, a successful drama. In his last years, he wrote apace, publishing *Tiresias and Other Poems* in 1885, *Locksley Hall Sixty Years After* in 1886, *Demeter and Other Poems* in 1889, and *The Death of Oenone* in 1892, published just after his death. Assessments of Tennyson's work was, in turn, criticized and then praised in the past century. During most of the twentieth century, he was thought to be too ornate for most readers, but in time his poetic talent and his ability to bring sound and light to life were honored. Those who love a talented wordsmith and those who love a mythic vision of ancient England love Tennyson.

## DYLAN THOMAS (1914–1953)

Dylan Thomas was born in the town of Swansea, Wales; he attended Swansea Grammar School, dropped out of school at sixteen, and became a reporter for *The South Wales Daily Post*. By the age of twenty, he published his first book of poems, drawing high praise. He then published several more books of poems and prose, made radio broadcasts for the BBC, and by 1950, embarked on the first of his legendary reading tours of the United States. Always productive, Thomas published *In Country Sleep, and Other Poems* and his *Collected Poems* in 1952. In 1954, he published the memoir of his Welsh childhood, *A Child's Christmas in Wales* and a radio play, *Under Milk Wood*, which also recalls memories of the coastal town where he was raised. Thomas was, as another poet described him, "the maddest of the word-mad poets." A popular image of a poet is, perhaps, as a hard-drinking, womanizing, rabblerousing, egotistic, irresponsible, and ultimately tragic figure, and no poet more conformed to this image than Thomas did. Consistent with the Romantic, self-destructive image he cast, Thomas died at thirty-nine after a heavy bout of drinking at the renowned White Horse Tavern in New York City.

## JOHN UPDIKE ( 1932–2009)

John Updike was born in Shilington, Pennsylvania. He graduated from Harvard in 1954 and then moved to Oxford, England, to study art for a year. He later returned to the United States to work for the *New Yorker* magazine, which began publishing his work. Updike eventually settled in Ipswich, Massachusetts. Updike's subjects are the values and problems of middle-class America. In this fiction, Updike seeks to problematize this seemingly mundane world, addressing such themes as family, religion, morality, sports, and the dynamics of intimate relationships. His novels include *Rabbit, Run* (1960), *Couples* (1968), *Rabbit Redux* (1971), *Rabbit Is Rich* (1981), *The Witches of Eastwick* (1984), *Roger's Version* (1986), *Rabbit at Rest* (1990), *In the Beauty of the Lilies* (1996), and *Gertrude and Claudius* (2000). In "A & P," first published in *Pigeon Feathers and Other Stories* (1962), Updike's rare use of humor adds to the ambiguity of the story's meaning.

## KURT VONNEGUT, JR. (1922–2007)

Kurt Vonnegut, Jr. was born in Indianapolis, Indiana; his father was a well-to-do architect, but during the Depression, he had virtually no work, and the family lived in reduced circumstances. Vonnegut attended Cornell University as a biochemistry major, spending two years there before enlisting in the Army in 1943. He was captured during the Battle of the Bulge in December 1944 and held as a prisoner of war; he witnessed and survived the firebombing of Dresden, Germany, in February 1945. Following his military service, Vonnegut attended the University of Chicago as a graduate student in anthropology, then wrote for the City News Bureau of Chicago before taking a job as the public relations writer for General Electric. In 1951, having successfully published a number of short stories, Vonnegut left G.E. to write full time. His early novels, including *Player Piano* (1952) and *The Sirens of Titan* (1959), led many critics to classify him as a science-fiction writer, but his relationship to the genre is more complex than such a classification would seem. His work draws readily on the tropes, settings, and imagery of science fiction while adding in a dark, satiric humor, and a clear critique of contemporary techno culture. His best-selling novel *Slaughterhouse-Five* appeared in 1969. Many other books have followed, including a collection of essays titled *A Man Without a Country* (2005). "Harrison Bergeron," published in 1961 in *The Magazine of Fantasy and Science Fiction*, was included in Vonnegut's 1968 short story collection *Welcome to the Monkey House*; it was also adapted as a television film in 1995 and twice as a short film, once in 2006 and again in 2009 when it was renamed *2081*.

## ALICE WALKER (b. 1944)

Alice Walker was born in Eatonton, Georgia. Her parents were sharecroppers who managed to raise eight children (Walker was the youngest) on minimal wages. At the age of eight, Walker's brother accidentally shot her in the eye with a BB gun, blinding her right eye. Due to the accident, Walker withdrew and became very shy. It was during this time that she began to develop an acute ability to observe people and to write. In 1961, she was awarded a scholarship to Spelman College. After graduating, she moved to Mississippi and became active in the Civil Rights movement. In 1967, she published her first essay, "The Civil Rights Movement: What Good Was It?" and her professional career as a writer began. While her reputation as a writer grew through the 1970s with the publication of the short story collection *In Love and Trouble* (1973) and the novel *Meridian* (1976), it was her novel *The Color Purple* (1983), winner of the Pulitzer Prize, that signaled Walker's recognition by a broader audience. Influenced by Zora Neale Hurston and Jean Toomer, Walker's work is imbued with the concept of the "womanist"—a phrase she penned as an alternative to "feminist." And indeed, Walker is best known for her powerful depictions of black women who persevere despite brutal oppression from men and society.

## ROBERT WALLACE (1932–1999)

Robert Wallace was born in Springfield, Missouri; influenced by Ogden Nash and Richard Armour, he began writing poems at age ten and was published in *The Rotarian* magazine at age sixteen. He graduated *summa cum laude* from Harvard in 1953, where he formed a life-long friendship with fellow student John Updike. His poems were then appearing in *Christian Science Monitor* and *The Lyric*. He traveled to England as a Fulbright scholar and Woodrow Wilson fellow, enrolling in St. Catharine's College, Cambridge, where he earned a second Bachelor of Arts degree in English. His first collection, *This Various World and Other Poems*, was published in 1957. Wallace taught at Bryn Mawr College, Sweet Briar College, and Vassar College before he joined the faculty of Case Western Reserve University in Cleveland, Ohio, in 1965. His second book, *Views from a Ferris Wheel*, appeared that same year, followed by *Ungainly Thing* (1968), for which he received the Cleveland Arts Prize. *Swimmer in the Rain* (1979) was published next, after which *Girlfriends and Wives* (1984) and *The Common Summer: New and Selected Poems* (1989) followed. While teaching and writing, he launched Bits Press in 1974. Devoted to the short poem, Bits Press began by publishing a magazine, *Bits*, from 1975 to 1980, but quickly branched out to publish chapbooks. Robert Wallace died in April 1999 at the age of 67 while working on his text *Writing Poems*.

## BRUCE WEIGL (b. 1949)

Born in Lorain, Ohio, Bruce Weigl is an English professor, poet, and translator. He served in the Vietnam War, an experience that strongly influenced his work. In addition to publishing more than a dozen collections of poetry, several of which address the horrors of war, he has translated poems written by captured Vietnamese and Viet Cong soldiers. Additionally, he founded a student veterans support group and an online journal, *North Coast Review*. He has won numerous literary awards, including first place honor form the American Academy of Poets, the Pushcart Prize, and the Lannan Literary Award; he was nominated twice for a Pulitzer Prize, once in 1988 for *Song of Napalm* and again in 2013 for *The Abundance of Nothing*.

## H.G. WELLS (1866–1946)

Known as the father of science fiction, Herbert George Wells was an English novelist, historian, and journalist. He began reading at age five, and he attended Morley's School in Bromley, though much of his knowledge and education came from his own avid reading. During college, he published a short story about time travel called "The Chronic Argonauts" that foreshadowed his future literary success. In addition to his fiction, Wells wrote many essays, articles and nonfiction books. He served as a book reviewer for *The Saturday Review of Literature* for several years, during which time he promoted the careers of James

Joyce and Joseph Conrad. In 1901, Wells published *Anticipations*, a non-fiction collection of predictions that has proved to be remarkably accurate. Wells forecasted the rise of major cities and suburbs, economic globalization, and aspects of future military conflicts. He was an outspoken socialist who worked for the betterment of mankind by exposing the suffering of the underprivileged through his writings. His more famous novels include *The Invisible Man, The War of the Worlds* and *The Time Machine. The War of the Worlds* was later adapted for a radio broadcast in 1938 and caused widespread panic in the United States. He had four children and was married twice; he was first married to his cousin Isabel Mary Wells, and his second marriage to Amy Catherine Robbins was an open marriage. Wells remained productive until the very end of his life, but his attitude seemed to darken in his final days. Among his last works was 1945's "Mind at the End of Its Tether," a pessimistic essay in which Wells contemplates the end of humanity. Some critics speculated that Wells's declining health shaped this prediction of a future without hope. He died on August 13, 1946, in London. At the time of his death, Wells was remembered as an author, historian, and champion of certain social and political ideals. So many of his predictions for the future came true in the ensuing years that he is sometimes called "the Father of Futurism," but today is best known as "the Father of Science Fiction."

## EUDORA WELTY (1909-2001)

Eudora Welty was born in Jackson, Mississippi, the eldest child and only daughter in her family. She was educated at the Mississippi State College for Women (now Mississippi University for Women), the University of Wisconsin, and Columbia University Graduate School of Business. After completing her education, Welty wrote about Jackson society for the *Commercial Appeal*, a Memphis, Tennessee, newspaper. She also conducted interviews, took photographs, and collected stories for the Works Progress Administration during the 1930s; *One Time, One Place* (1971) and *Photographs* (1989) are published collections of her Depression era photographs. The literary magazine *Southern Review* published several of her stories in the 1930s, and her first collection, *A Curtain of Green*, appeared in 1941. This book was followed by a novella, *The Robber Bridegroom* (1942) and another collection *The Wide Net* (1943). She continued with *Delta Wedding* (1946), *The Ponder Heart* (1954), and *The Optimist's Daughter* (1972, winner of the Pulitzer Prize for fiction in 1973), and during this time she won two O. Henry Short Story Prizes, one for "A Worn Path" and one for "The Wide Net." Her essays and book reviews appeared in a number of periodicals, and she lectured across the country until shortly before her death. In 1980, Welty was awarded the National Medal of Arts and the Presidential Medal of Freedom, and in 2000 she was inducted into the National Women's Hall of Fame. Her family home in Jackson, Mississippi, where she lived most of her life, is a National Historic Landmark and open to the public as a museum.

## WALT WHITMAN (1819–1892)

Walt Whitman was born in West Hills, New York. At an early age, his family moved to Brooklyn, where he attended grammar school until, at the age of 12, he was apprenticed to a printer to help meet the financial needs of his family. This early experience in the world of printing inevitably exposed the young Whitman to journalism and to a life of writing and publishing. In 1855, Whitman anonymously published *Leaves of Grass*, a book of poetry that he continued to revise, expand, and republish throughout his life. At the time, Whitman's effusive free verse radically challenged traditional notions of democracy, race, and religion. In like manner, his explicit treatment of sexuality, both heterosexual and homosexual, also engendered controversy, prompting several areas of the country to ban the book on grounds of obscenity. As Whitman evolved as a poet, so did later versions of *Leaves of Grass*, most notably the poems he wrote as a volunteer nurse during the Civil War that demonstrate a turn toward a more simplified, realist verse. Often referred to as the father of modern American poetry, Whitman's pioneering break from conventional poetic forms and themes has inspired generations of subsequent writers. His prose works include *Democratic Vistas* (1871).

## WILLIAM CARLOS WILLIAMS (1883–1963)

Born of an English father and a Puerto Rican mother, William Carlos Williams grew up in Rutherford, New Jersey. Although his father introduced him to Shakespeare and Dante, the young Williams was more interested in math and science. While a medical student at the University of Pennsylvania, Williams began reading the poetry of John Keats and Walt Whitman; however, it was his friendship with Ezra Pound and other Imagist poets that helped him break from traditional, structured poetry and move toward a more precise, compact verse that sought to render images as they are perceived by the poet. With the publication of Eliot's "Wasteland" in 1922, Williams began to dislike the shape contemporary poetry was taking. In contrast to the angst of modernism, he was more concerned with creating a distinctively American poetry—a poetry that was intimately connected to locale. As a doctor in a small town (Paterson, New Jersey), he was privy to a side of ordinary life not traditionally seen as poetic. The real, human experience of his patients and townspeople were what Williams believed poetry should communicate. Although not widely known during his lifetime, Williams's work has had a considerable influence on American poetry. The more than 20 volumes of poetry he wrote during his lifetime have been gathered in the two-volume *The Collected Poems of William Carlos Williams* (1986), edited by A. Walton Litz and Christopher MacGowan. He was also a prolific writer of nonfiction essays and fiction (novels and short stories). For a complete bibliography, see the *Guide to the Poetry of William Carlos Williams* (1995). "To a Poor Old Woman" was published in *The Earlier Poems* (1951).

## JAMES WRIGHT (1927–1980)

James Wright was born into poverty and grew up during the Great Depression in Martins Ferry, Ohio, where his father was employed in a glass factory and his mother worked in a laundry. As the family struggled financially, Wright found solace in his grandmother, Elizabeth Lyons, who supported his interest in poetry. By age eleven, Wright was crafting highly formal poems in the styles of James Whitcomb Riley and Lord Byron. After high school, he served in the Army in Japan. Although his parents' education never progressed beyond eighth grade, Wright graduated cum laude and Phi Beta Kappa from Kenyon College, then traveled to Austria on a Fulbright Fellowship, where he studied the works of Theodor Storm and Georg Trakl at the University of Vienna. He later earned his M.A. and Ph.D. at the University of Washington where he worked with poets Theodore Roethke, Stanley Kunitz, and Richard Hugo. After winning the prestigious Yale Younger Poets Award in 1957, Wright left to teach at the University of Minnesota, at which time he began to publish extensively. His childhood experiences with human suffering and poverty have a strong presence in his work, which often addresses social and political issues. Wright was elected a fellow of the Academy of American Poets in 1971, and the following year his *Collected Poems* received the Pulitzer Prize in poetry.